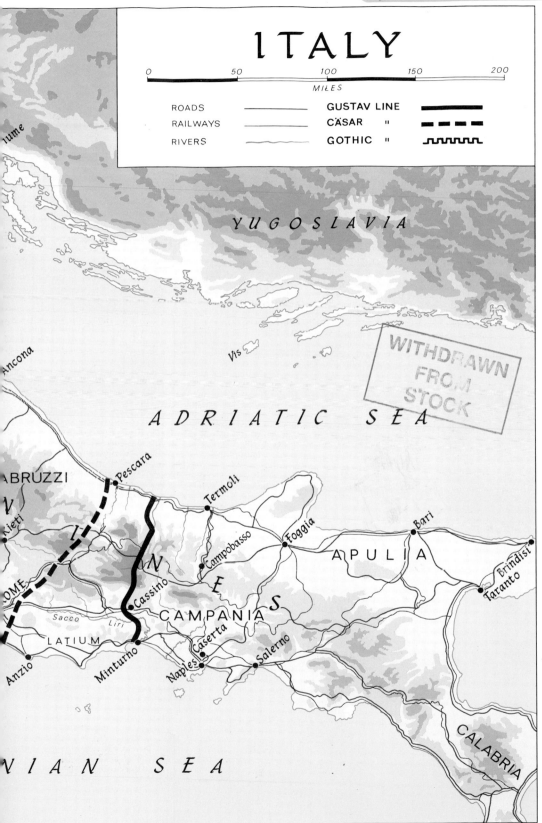

ITALY

| 0 | 50 | 100 | 150 | 200 |

MILES

ROADS	———	**GUSTAV LINE**	
RAILWAYS	———	**CÄSAR** "	
RIVERS	———	**GOTHIC** "	

YUGOSLAVIA

Vis

ADRIATIC SEA

Ancona

ABRUZZI

Pescara

Termoli

Nieti

Campobasso

Foggia

Bari

APULIA

ROME

Cassino

Brindisi

Taranto

Sacco   Liri

CAMPANIA

LATIUM

Caserta

Salerno

Anzio

Minturno

Naples

CALABRIA

NIAN   SEA

HISTORY OF
THE SECOND WORLD WAR
UNITED KINGDOM MILITARY SERIES

Edited by Sir James Butler

The authors of the Military Histories have been given full access to official documents. They and the editor are alone responsible for the statements made and the views expressed.

THE
MEDITERRANEAN
AND
MIDDLE EAST

VOLUME VI
Victory in the Mediterranean

PART II
June to October 1944

BY

GENERAL SIR WILLIAM JACKSON, G.B.E., K.C.B., M.C.

WITH

GROUP CAPTAIN T. P. GLEAVE, C.B.E., F.R.Hist.S.

LONDON
HER MAJESTY'S STATIONERY OFFICE

HMSO publications are available from:

HMSO Publications Centre
(Mail and telephone orders only)
PO Box 276, London, SW8 5DT
Telephone orders 01-622 3316
General enquiries 01-211 5656
(queuing system in operation for both numbers)

HMSO Bookshops
49 High Holborn, London, WC1V 6HB   01-211 5656 (Counter service only)
258 Broad Street, Birmingham, B1 2HE   021-643 3740
Southey House, 33 Wine Street, Bristol, BS1 2BQ   (0272) 24306/24307
9-21 Princess Street, Manchester, M60 8AS   061-834 7201
80 Chichester Street, Belfast, BT1 4JY   (0232) 238451
13a Castle Street, Edinburgh, EH2 3AR   031-225 6333

HMSO's Accredited Agents
(see Yellow Pages)

And through good booksellers

ISBN 0 11 630946 6
Printed for Her Majesty's Stationery Office
by Hobbs the Printers of Southampton
(1974/86) Dd739464 C11 1/87 G443

CONTENTS

PART II

CHAPTER XV. FRUSTRATION IN ITALY: (OCTOBER 1944)

CONTENTS

MAPS AND DIAGRAMS

CABINET OFFICE

The Mediterranean and Middle East Vol. VI Part I

ISBN 0 11 630936 9

CORRECTIONS

page 14   H.Q. 4th U.S. Corps (*Lieutenant-General* Willis D. Crittenberger)

page 116

Bridge	*Div Sector*	*Date and time of completion*	*Built by*
Amazon Class 30		13th May 5 a.m.	7th, 59th, 225th and 578th (Corps Tps) Field Companies R.E.
Congo Class 30		14th May 8.30 a.m.	7th and 586th (Army Tps) Field Companies R.E.
Blackwater Class 40			59th Field Company R.E.

* Amendments taken from T. M. J. Riordan: *A History of the 7th Field Company R.E.* (York 1984) p. 140–58.

page 389 para 1 line 5:   *Special* Boat Squadron

page 408   Note: the *Special* Boat Squadron (later named the *Special* Boat Service)

OCTOBER 1986   *LONDON*   HER MAJESTY'S STATIONERY OFFICE

INTRODUCTION

THIS is Part II of the sixth and last volume of the British
official history of the Mediterranean and Middle East Campaigns in the Second World War. In Part I, published in
1984, the main theme was the highly successful 'Diadem' offensive
launched by General Alexander on 11th May 1944, which ended
with the fall of Rome on 4th June. It covered the final battle for
Cassino, the break out from Anzio, the breaching of the Hitler
Line and the battles for Rome itself.

Now in Part II we deal with the pursuit of Army Group C to
the Gothic Line, the breaching of that line, and the subsequent
and much less successful autumn battles fought by the Allied
Armies in Italy to break into the Po valley. We review the problems
which a second winter in the Italian hills presented to Allied
Commanders, including the worrying question of morale, and we
end with Alexander's decision, made in late October, to limit his
objectives to the seizure of Bologna and Ravenna, or the next best
winter positions to the south. British policy for Italy during the
summer and autumn of 1944 was however influenced by developments elsewhere in the Mediterranean. We therefore look at the
planning and execution of the landings in southern France, as well
as at the situation in Yugoslavia and the reasons for sending a
British force into Greece.

In Part III we continue the story of British involvement in
Balkan affairs, but our main theme will be the Allied Armies in
Italy. Halted in late winter in order to rest, retrain and re-equip
for the great Spring offensive of 1945, they accomplished the near
destruction of Army Group C south of the Po and advanced
northwards to Trieste and into Austria.

As we explained in the introduction to Part I, our original team
of four was sadly depleted by the deaths of the Editor and the
Naval and Army historians. For Parts II and III General Sir
William Jackson became Editor and assumed the role of Army
historian as well. Captain F. C. Flynn R.N., the Naval Historian,
left only in draft the naval sections for the landings in southern
France. We are very grateful to Mr. J. D. Brown of the Ministry
of Defence Naval Historical Branch for scrutinizing the final texts
of the naval coverage.

The loss of so many of the original members of the team throws
a greatly increased burden of responsibility upon the shoulders of
Miss Diana F. Butler and Mrs. N. B. Taylor who have continued
their able and meticulous research work on the Allied and German

sides respectively. Without their willing and conscientious efforts it would not have been possible to complete Volume VI. Mrs. Taylor has compiled the very detailed index for Part II and has helped to revise the text in so doing.

In our interpretation of events we have used the procedures and sources of evidence defined in the Introduction to Volume V. Our Intelligence material, as in the previous volume, has been studied at field level as it influenced the commanders in their decision making. For a fuller study of the Intelligence aspects of the Campaign the reader is referred to Professor F. H. Hinsley's *British Intelligence in the Second World War*, Volume III.

There has been a change in the style of the maps in Parts II and III. For reasons of cost there has been some reduction in the use of colour and the methods of showing relief have also been simplified. Mr. A. E. Kelleway of the Cabinet Office Mapping Section designed the maps for Part II but, due to his retirement, much of the drawing was carried out by draughtsmen of the Graphic Design Unit.

We are particularly indebted to Colonel W. M. Cunningham, Field-Marshal Alexander's Military Assistant, who allowed us access to the diaries that he kept for the years 1944–1945, and to quote from them. We also wish to record our appreciation of the help given to us by the Hon. C. M. Woodhouse on Greece, by Sir William Deakin on Yugoslavia, and by Sir David Hunt, who drafted Field-Marshal Alexander's despatches.

On the Allied side we are grateful for the support and help we have received from the Historical Branches of the three Service Departments of the Ministry of Defence, from the Keepers of records and documents in the Cabinet Office, and from the staffs of the Public Record Office and the Imperial War Museum. We are also indebted to the Official Historians of Canada, New Zealand, South Africa, France and the United States of America whose works we have used extensively, as our references show.

In the field of German records, we have had generous help from the National Archive and Records Service, Washington, from the Canadian Directorate of History, Ottawa, and from the *Militärarchiv* of the *Bundesarchiv* in Freiburg. We also wish to thank all those former members of the *Wehrmacht* who served in Italy, for the information they have provided through correspondence.

W.G.F.J.
T.P.G.

CHAPTER IX

THE PURSUIT TO LAKE
TRASIMENO
(5th June to 2nd July 1944)

(i)

The week of the 4th to 10th June 1944 marked the beginning of the end of the Second World War. Rome fell on the 4th; Normandy was invaded on the 6th; and on the 10th the Russians launched an attack in Finland which was to precede their great summer offensive in Belo–Russia. Many strategic uncertainties were removed by these events, but just as many new dilemmas were created for the strategic policy makers and senior commanders on both sides.

In the Allied camp the arguments about 'Anvil' versus a continuing offensive in Italy, described in Chapter VI, Part I of this Volume, were brought to the fore by General Alexander's capture of Rome and partial destruction of Field-Marshal Kesselring's Army Group C.[1] Two telegrams were sent from the Mediterranean to the British Chiefs of Staff: one from General Wilson and the other from General Alexander, both on 7th June.

In the first telegram General Wilson announced that, in view of the success of the spring offensive, he was now definitely ready to carry out amphibious landings in southern France (Operation 'Anvil') with a target date of 15th August.*[2] In reaching his decision Wilson strove to act with absolute impartiality, but the differences in strategic views between Washington and Whitehall were still reflected in Allied Force Headquarters (guided by the opinions of its largely American staff) and the British staffed H.Q. Allied Armies in Italy.[3] Alexander was made well aware of the priority given to 'Anvil', when Wilson spelt out the time-table of with-

---

* The principal Army commanders in the Mediterranean were:
   Supreme Allied Commander, Mediterranean Theatre: General Sir Henry Maitland Wilson.
   Deputy Supreme Allied Commander, Mediterranean Theatre: Lieutenant-General Jacob L. Devers, U.S. Army:
   C.-in-C. Allied Armies in Italy: General the Hon. Sir Harold Alexander.

I

drawals from A.A.I. in his directive of 22nd May.[4] Again, on
7th June Wilson sent a goading reminder, which ran:

> 'Each day's delay in release of one U.S. Corps Headquarters
> from A.A.I. delays the planning and launching of an amphibious
> operation covered in my . . . [reference to 'Anvil']. This will
> have to be Truscott's 6th Corps as it was with this understanding
> that the [U.S.] War Department agreed to leave Truscott in
> this theatre. Consider you can now release the Corps Head-
> quarters by 10th June. . . .'[5]

Alexander replied to Wilson on 8th June agreeing to release 6th
U.S. Corps on 11th June and adding the rider:

> 'I most seriously hope however that this demand does not mean
> that a final decision has been taken to remove from my command
> for other operations formations mentioned in your . . . [signal
> of 22nd May listing "Anvil" units.]'[6]

The second telegram sent from the Mediterranean was from
Alexander to the C.I.G.S. on 7th June (and repeated to Wilson)
giving his appreciation for operations north of Rome. His clearly
expressed views can be taken as the starting point for the second
half of the Italian campaign:

> 'My object is to complete the destruction of the German armed
> forces in Italy and in the process to force the enemy to draw to
> the maximum on his reserves whereby I shall be rendering the
> greatest assistance to the Western invasion . . . I have now two
> highly organised and skilful Armies capable of carrying out
> large scale attacks and mobile operations in the closest co-
> operation. Morale is irresistibly high . . . Neither the Apennines
> nor even the Alps should prove a serious obstacle to their
> enthusiasm and skill.'*[7]

Alexander, although 'seriously perturbed at the probability' that
his successful operations were 'going to be hamstrung again' by
the removal of troops for other operations, was determined to
continue his own operations in a style which would prove his case.[8]
He aimed to hustle Kesselring out of the Gothic Line† in the
Northern Appenines during the latter half of August, and to
position his forces to strike westwards into France or north-
eastwards across the River Po towards Austria before the autumn
weather could slow down military activity. So hopeful was he of
achieving these timings, provided his armies, his administrative
resources and the support of M.A.T.A.F. were not eroded, that
he agreed to postpone a plan, which was being developed, for the

---

* The appreciation is fully covered in Part I of this Volume (H.M.S.O. 1984) p. 312-4.

† The position was re-named by the Germans in April 1944. The Allies still tended to
refer to the 'Pisa-Rimini line'. See Part I of this Volume (H.M.S.O. 1984) p. 57n.

destruction of all the bridges over the Po by air action.[9] Instead he and his staff began to consider ways of seizing these bridges intact by airborne assault so that their demolition by the Germans would not impede his armies' advance across the Po valley. The key to success would lie in his ability to prevent the Germans stabilizing their front north of Rome in country which was little less defensible than southern Italy had been the year before, when his advance from Salerno had been brought to a halt for the winter in front of the Bernhardt Line.

Before considering the German reactions to the fall of Rome a recapitulation of the Allied orders of battle and a brief description of the topography of central Italy may be helpful to the reader. Alexander's Allied Armies in Italy consisted of the American 5th Army under General Mark W. Clark, the British 8th Army under General Sir Oliver Leese, and the British 5th Corps under Lieutenant-General C. W. Allfrey operating east of the Apennines on the Adriatic coast directly under H.Q. A.A.I.'s orders. The River Tiber, which runs almost north-south as it approaches Rome, formed the natural boundary between 5th and 8th Armies and was made inclusive to 8th Army. 5th Army had four corps under command and 8th Army had three. Logistic considerations limited the number of troops deployed in each Army's advance.

See Map 1

The topography north of Rome was not as harsh as the rocky hill and mountain country through which 'Diadem' had been fought. It was no less hilly but far more cultivated and much richer in every way: deeper and more fertile soil, better and more numerous roads, larger and more prosperous towns and villages, and more resources of every kind, from vineyards and intensively cultivated fields to industrial complexes. Militarily the countryside still favoured the defender: observation from the hills was just as good and obstacles in the valleys formed by rivers, streams and irrigation channels were even more effective because they did not dry out in summer. Furthermore the weather was less certain, heavy rain occurring at intervals throughout the summer, which, coupled with the deeper topsoil, made deployment off the roads and tracks less practicable. There was, however, more cover for the attacker and in bad weather troops could find shelter more easily. There was little difference in the stoutness of village and farm construction, but the defender could find more buildings on the tops of hills and ridges which could be quickly fortified and defended by relatively few troops.

'All roads lead to Rome'; to the Allies in 1944 they fanned outwards from Rome towards the north, leading to the major cities in the Arno valley and thence over the Northern Apennines to the plains of Lombardy. A staff planner looking at a map of central Italy and knowing he had four corps to deploy west of the main Apennine range would note two things: first, that four corps' axes of advance could be found running up the peninsula west of the Apennines; and secondly that room for military manoeuvre increased north of Rome as the coastline and the Apennine backbone of Italy diverged until they reached their widest point of divergence between Perugia and the Isle of Elba, and then closed in again to the relatively narrow zone between Florence and Pisa. To the north of this line lay the challenging barrier of the Northern Apennines along which ran the Gothic line.

The four axes of advance started from Rome on the four ancient Roman roads: the Via Aurelia (Route 1) along the west coast, the Via Cassia (Route 2) through the extinct volcano region between the west coast and the Tiber valley, the Via Flaminia (Route 3) and the Via Salaria (Route 4).[10] Routes 1 and 2 ran direct to Leghorn and Florence respectively, but Routes 3 and 4 became less useful north of Orte and Rieti as they veered too far east and made their way over the Apennine watershed. Route 3 was replaced by a general network of roads which passed Lake Trasimeno to the west and converged on Arezzo. Route 4 was similarly replaced by roads running due north which converged on Perugia and then entered the narrow Upper Tiber valley to reach Sansepolcro. Thus the four general corps axes were:

> West Coast (Route 1): Rome–Civitavecchia–Leghorn–Pisa.
> Via Cassia (Route 2): Rome–Viterbo–Siena—Florence.
> West of Lake Trasimeno: Rome–Orte–Orvieto–Arezzo.
> East of Lake Trasimeno: Rome–Rieti–Terni–Foligno–Perugia–Sansepolcro.

On 5th June the outline Allied order of battle (excluding 5th Corps which was under command H.Q. A.A.I. on the Adriatic coast) was:

5th ARMY (Commander: Lieutenant-General Mark W. Clark)[11]

> 2nd U.S. Corps (Major-General Geoffrey T. Keyes)
> > 3rd U.S. Division (Major-General John O'Daniel)*
> > 85th U.S. Division (Major-General John M. Coulter)
> > 88th U.S. Division (Major-General John E. Sloan)
> 6th U.S. Corps (Major-General Lucian K. Truscott)
> > 1st U.S. Armoured Division (Major-General Ernest N. Harmon)

---

* On 5th June 3rd U.S. Division was transferred to Army command to act as garrison troops for Rome.

34th U.S. Division (Major-General Charles W. Ryder)
36th U.S. Division (Major-General Fred L. Walker)
45th U.S. Division (Major-General William W. Eagles)
1st British Division (acting commander Brigadier C. F. Loewen)
5th British Division (Major-General P. G. S. Gregson-Ellis)

French Expeditionary Corps (General A. Juin)
1st French Infantry Division (Major-General D. Brosset)
2nd Moroccan Infantry Division (Major-General A. W. Dody)
3rd Algerian Infantry Division (Major-General de Goislard de Monsabert)
4th Moroccan Mountain Division (Brigadier-General F. Sevez)
Moroccan Goums (Brigadier-General A. Guillaume)

Army Reserve
H.Q. 4th U.S. Corps (Major-General Willis D. Crittenberger)

8th ARMY (Commander: General Sir Oliver Leese)[12]
10th Corps (Lieutenant-General Sir Richard McCreery)
2nd New Zealand Division (Lieutenant-General Sir Bernard Freyberg V.C.)
8th Indian Division (Major-General D. Russell)
10th Indian Division (Major-General D. W. Reid)*
1st Canadian Armoured Brigade (less regiment)
2nd Army Group R.A.

13th Corps (Lieutenant-General S. C. Kirkman)
6th Armoured Division (Major-General V. Evelegh)
4th Division (Major-General A. D. Ward)
78th Division (Major-General C. F. Keightley)
9th Armoured Brigade
6th South African Armoured Division (Major-General W. H. E. Poole)
25th Tank Brigade
6th Army Group R.A.

Army Reserve
1st Canadian Corps (Lieutenant-General E. L. M. Burns)
5th Canadian Armoured Division (Major-General B. M. Hoffmeister)
1st Canadian Division (Major-General C. Vokes)
1st Canadian Army Group R.C.A.

1st Armoured Division (Major-General A. Galloway):
2nd Armoured Brigade concentrating at Altamura (in the Heel of Italy)
12th A.A. Brigade

---

* Not complete in Corps area until 7th June.

Kesselring's immediate problem was the reverse of Alexander's: how to retain stability in the face of Allied superiority on the ground and in the air. The defensive strength of the Italian terrain, Hitler's willingness to make good his losses and the stamina of the German soldier were his main assets. *AOK 14* had scrambled back over the Tiber west of Rome in disordered rout with its commander, General von Mackensen, sacked and his replacement, General Joachim Lemelsen, just taking over. To make matters worse *AOK 14's* sector was more open, better roaded and less easily defended than *AOK 10's* east of the Tiber, where von Vietinghoff had the twin advantages of operating in the hills and mountains of Italy's Apennine backbone and of the tactical cohesion of his army which had developed an effective withdrawal rhythm since its defeat in the battles of the Gustav and Hitler Lines in the latter half of May.

The outline order of battle of Kesselring's Army Group C on 5th June was:

ARMY GROUP C (Commander and C.-in-C. Southwest: Field-Marshal Albert Kesselring)

AOK 14 (Commander: General Joachim Lemelsen)*

   1st Parachute Corps (General Alfred Schlemm)
      3rd Panzer Grenadier Division (Lieutenant-General Fritz-Hubert Gräser)
      4th Parachute Division (Major-General Heinrich Trettner)
      362nd Infantry Division (Lieutenant-General Heinrich Greiner)
      65th Infantry Division (Major-General Helmuth Pfeifer)

   En route from Northern Italy, earmarked for AOK 14
      162nd (Turkoman) Infantry Division (Major-General Ralph von Heygendorff)
      356th Infantry Division (Lieutenant-General Karl Faulenbach)
      20th *Luftwaffe* Field Division (Major-General Erich Fröhnhofer)

AOK 10 (Commander: Colonel-General Heinrich-Gottfried von Vietinghoff)

   51st Mountain Corps (General Valentin Feuerstein)
      5th Mountain Division (Major-General Max Schrank)
      114th Jäger Division (Major-General Alexander Bourquin)
      44th Infantry Division (Lieutenant-General Bruno Ortner)

   76th Panzer Corps (General Traugott Herr)
      15th Panzer Grenadier Division (Major-General Eberhard Rodt)
      Hermann Göring Panzer Division (Major-General Benno Schmalz)

---

* From 7th June replacing Colonel-General Eberhard von Mackensen.

334th Infantry Division (Major-General Hellmuth Böhlke)

14th Panzer Corps (General Fridolin von Senger und Etterlin)*
    1st Parachute Division (Lieutenant-General Richard Heidrich)
    305th Infantry Division (Lieutenant-General Friedrich-Wilhelm Hauck)
    94th Infantry Division (Major-General Bernhard Steinmetz)
    26th Panzer Division (Major-General Smilo von Lüttwitz)
    29th Panzer Grenadier Division (Lieutenant-General Walter Fries)
    90th Panzer Grenadier Division (Major-General Ernst-Günther Baade)

Group Hoppe
    278th Infantry Division (Lieutenant-General Harry Hoppe)
    71st Infantry Division (Lieutenant-General Wilhelm Raapke)

ARMEEABTEILUNG VON ZANGEN (General Gustav von Zangen)

75th Corps (General Anton Dostler)
    16th SS Panzer Grenadier Division (Lieutenant-General Max Simon)
    19th *Luftwaffe* Field Division (Lieutenant-General Bässler)
    42nd Jäger Division (Major-General Walter Jost)

Corps Witthöft (General Joachim Witthöft, Commander Venetian Coast)
    188th Reserve Mountain Division (Lieutenant-General Hans von Hösslin)
    715th Infantry Division (Major-General Hans-Georg Hildebrand)

    Fortress Brigade 135 (Colonel Almers)
    Commandant Elba (Major-General Richard Gall)

On 5th June the German High Command was uncertain whether the Allies would opt to concentrate on the pursuit of *AOK 14*, or would wheel eastwards to cut deep into the flank of *AOK 10* which would be withdrawing more slowly through the more defensible foothills of the Apennines, impeded both by the paucity of suitable withdrawal routes and by the attacks of the Allied Air Forces.[13] Two urgent corrective measures were needed before any thought could be given to longer term policy. First, a rallying line had to be designated on which some semblance of order could be restored and co-ordination between the two armies re-established. The line chosen, code-named Dora, ran from just south of Orbetello on the west coast then along the southern edge of Lake Bolsena to Terni and Rieti, and thence to Aquila where it merged with the Cäsar Line as it crossed the Apennines to the Adriatic.[14] Kesselring's

---

* On 8th June H.Q. 14th Panzer Corps, with 26th Panzer, 29th and 90th Panzer Grenadier Divisions, was placed under command of *AOK 14*. 1st Parachute Division, 305th and 94th Infantry Divisions were absorbed into 76th Panzer Corps by 12th June.

directive of 4th June envisaged a withdrawal by both armies, covered by strong rear-guards, via four intermediate phase lines to the Dora/Cäsar Line. At the same time he informed *OKW* that he would stand on a number of lines north of Dora to win time for strengthening and consolidating the Gothic Line. The first delaying line to be reconnoitred north of Dora would be Line E from Talamone on the west coast through Radicofani, Norcia and Mt Vettore to S. Benedetto on the Adriatic.

The second corrective measure was reinforcement of *AOK 14*. The Tiber's north/south course as it nears Rome formed the natural boundary between the two German armies. Schlemm's 1st Parachute Corps with the remnants of 3rd Panzer Grenadier, 4th Parachute, and 65th and 362nd Infantry Divisions, had withdrawn over the Tiber either through Rome or to the west of the city, whereas Herr's 76th Panzer Corps had fallen back east of the Tiber and had been placed under *AOK 10's* command for ease of co-ordination. This left *AOK 14* with only four badly mauled and exhausted divisions to oppose Clark's 5th Army as it emerged through Rome and started its pursuit northwards on Route 1 along the coast to the port of Civitavecchia and on Route 2 towards Lake Bracciano and the group of German airfields around Viterbo. There were three fresh divisions moving down from northern Italy (162nd (Turkoman), 356th Infantry and 20th Luftwaffe Field Divisions).[15] Kesselring decided to give all three to Lemelsen, but they were not mobile divisions of the type needed to check the American advance in open country, nor had they much battle experience. It soon became apparent that unless *AOK 14* was reinforced with better troops its hopes of regaining its balance on the Dora Line would not be realised.

Between 6th and 8th June Kesselring issued orders for the transfer from *AOK 10* first of 26th Panzer Division, and then of 29th and 90th Panzer Grenadier Divisions, at the same time warning Lemelsen that early arrival could not be expected. This caveat was timely, for the cross-country journey of all three formations was seriously delayed by Allied air attacks, the problems of crossing the Tiber, and the failure of south-bound fuel convoys to catch up with units whose prescribed routes differed in each case.*[16] As von Vietinghoff had intended to concentrate his veteran

---

* For example, 26th Panzer Division was ordered to cross the Tiber at Orte where the river was thought to be fordable—a significant point because all bridges north of Rome had been destroyed, either by Allied air action or by premature demolition by German engineers. Advance elements of 90th Panzer Grenadier Division were reported to be approaching Orvieto by the evening of 8th June, but due to fuel problems 29th Panzer Grenadier Division, ordered to proceed to Lemelsen's western wing via Perugia and Siena, was still well south of Perugia on the 11th.[17]

mobile formations for protection of his own western flank, and on 6th June had withdrawn Headquarters 14th Panzer Corps from the line for their command, he was much displeased to learn on 8th June that this Headquarters must also move to *AOK 14*. Pleas and protests were unavailing, however, for as von Senger was told on the 12th, the only hope for the restoration of a firm front on the Army Group's right wing lay in the presence there of an experienced and vigorous Corps command.

At strategic level, in the aftermath of the fall of Rome, Kesselring was of the view that, after his forces had rallied in the Dora Line, a subsequent gradual withdrawal to the Gothic Line in the Northern Apennines must be considered.[18] Hitler, on the other hand, demanded the defence of Italy as far south as possible. Apart from his psychological inability to surrender territory, he had, at this point, sound military reasons for such a policy. First, as we have shown in Part I Chapter VI of this Volume, there was continuing uncertainty about the Allies' strategic aims in the Mediterranean. The 'African Group' of Allied divisions, thought to be concentrated ready for a descent on southern France when 'Overlord' was launched, had not been used. The most sensitive alternative target for these divisions from the German point of view was the Balkans. Moreover, *OKW* had its eye on another mythical group of Allied divisions in and around the Italian 'Heel' ports which had been dubbed the 'Slav Concentration', because it was believed to be centred upon the non-existent 3rd Polish Corps with the equally fictitious 2nd Polish Armoured and 4th Polish Infantry Divisions from Egypt. The further south Kesselring managed to stabilize his front in Italy, the more he would cramp any Allied trans-Adriatic operations. Hitler believed the Italian front represented the forward defence (*Vorwerk*) of the Balkans, the natural resources of which in such materials as chrome and bauxite were indispensable to the German war economy.[19]

Hitler's second reason was simply to keep the Allies, particularly their air forces, as far away from the Reich as possible. And his third and most important military reason was his personal distrust of the defensive strength of the Gothic Line. We will be discussing the details of this Line in the next chapter. Suffice it to say here that Hitler was well aware that work upon it had been fitful and inadequate and it fell far short of German fortress standards. He declared on 5th June that the Gothic Line was quite unsuited to long-term defence as its fortification had barely begun. He could also have pointed out that its frontage was no shorter than a line running from Ancona on the east coast via Lake Trasimeno to Grosseto on the west coast. In due course this line was to be called the Albert Line upon which Hitler was to demand a major stand.

The strength of Kesselring's case for a slow but continuous withdrawal into the Gothic Line lay in his twin needs to trade space for time in order to rest, reinforce, re-equip and reorganise his battered and battle weary divisions; and to reduce his vulnerability to amphibious landings behind his front. There was, however, one factor in Kesselring's disagreement with Hitler which could be assessed more objectively than the others. *OKW* decided to send General Walter Warlimont, Deputy Chief of its Operations Branch, to make a personal tour of the Gothic Line to provide 'a basis for further decisions'.[20] Warlimont's tour lasted from 7th to 12th June, so this is an appropriate moment to look at the tactical events immediately following the fall of Rome before turning back to the substantive orders issued by the opposing Commanders-in-Chief, at the end of the first week of Kesselring's retreat, for the future development of the campaign.

(ii)

As the Mediterranean Allied Tactical Air Force played a major role in the pursuit of Army Group C after the fall of Rome we will first outline the direct air support given to 5th and 8th Armies and then describe the land operations.*

On 6th June at midnight A.O.C. D.A.F. resumed responsibility for supporting 8th Army.[22] This he had temporarily relinquished (other than for 5th Corps) during Operation 'Diadem', as the Allied spring offensive was called, when U.S. XII T.A.C. took over responsibility for air support in the whole area west of the Apennines to ensure optimum use of the available resources. Now, C.G. U.S. XII T.A.C. confined himself to the support of 5th Army within its boundary and A.O.C. D.A.F extended his area of responsibility to cover the whole of 8th Army.

Tactical air operations in direct air support of the armies during this period were more affected by the state of Kesselring's troops and by the weather than by the future 'Anvil' decision. Four phases can be discerned in the pattern of tactical operations.[23] Between dawn 5th and dawn 20th June the rear routes of *AOK 14* and the transfer of von Senger's 14th Panzer Corps from *AOK 10* to the west coast provided a harvest of opportunity targets which U.S. XII T.A.C and D.A.F. could enjoy garnering without risk

---

* Because 'Direct Air Support' is that given within the battle area it would be helpful if we defined the northern limits of the battle area. On 5th June these can be represented by a line running east to west from Citta S. Angelo (north-west of Pescara)–Carsoli–Civita Castellana–northern shore of Lake Bracciano–Cerveteri (shown on Map 3 of Part I of this Volume). By 17th July the northern limits formed a line running east to west from Senigallia–Cagli–S. Angelo in Vado–Florence–Pistoia–Torre di Lago.[21]

of endangering the advance of Allied troops.[24] Between dawn 20th June and dawn 3rd July, when the Germans managed to regain some stability on the Albert Line, targets became fewer and more dependent upon the demands of the forward troops. In fact, in this Second Phase, the average daily bomb tonnage dropped in the battle area was 37 as compared with 179 during the First Phase.[25] As will be described in Chapter X the pattern changed again between dawn 3rd July and dawn 17th July when the Germans developed their own methodical withdrawal rhythm as they fell back to the River Arno. This rhythm was reflected in new Army/Air Co-operation methods developed by the Allies. And finally, the Fourth Phase between dawn 17th July and dawn 6th August was different again, consisting of the direct air support of 8th Army in the battles of Ancona and Florence as will also be described in Chapter X. The distribution of sorties flown and bombloads dropped in each of the four tactical phases as compared with the efforts north of the battle area in Italy and beyond Italy are given in Table III at the end of Chapter X.

The return to normal control of tactical air operations meant that D.A.F. required more squadrons to meet its enlarged commitment.[26] Some of the R.A.F. formations on loan to U.S. XII T.A.C. were returned to D.A.F., namely Nos. 239 and 244 Wings (fighters) and Nos. 40 (S.A.A.F.) and 208 Tac.R Squadrons, and the U.S. 79th Fighter Group was lent to D.A.F. This left two light bombers, one night-fighter, one Tac.R and a wing of four fighter squadrons belonging to D.A.F. still under the operational control of U.S. XII T.A.C. There were, also, two fighter wings belonging to D.A.F. in Corsica under the operational control of U.S. 87th Fighter Wing which itself was directly responsible to H.Q. M.A.T.A.F. although part of U.S. XII T.A.C.*

For army air support control, a detachment of No. 2/5 A.A.S.C. was sent by Advanced H.Q. D.A.F. to No. 1 Mobile Operations Room Unit 'B' on the east coast to support 5th Corps†, so that once again D.A.F. was in full control of all air support activities on the British sectors of the front. On 17th June when the Polish Corps relieved 5th Corps it was supported by a Polish A.A.S.C.

---

* By 24th May further loans of squadrons to U.S. XII T.A.C. had reduced D.A.F. to four fighter, one Tac.R, one Strat.R, half a photographic reconnaissance, five light bomber and one medium day bomber squadrons—a total of 12½. By the second week of June after the return of some of the squadrons on loan to U.S. XII T.A.C., the strength of D.A.F. had risen to 17 fighter (including U.S. 79th Fighter Group), three Tac.R, one Strat.R, half a photographic reconnaissance, five light bomber and one medium day bomber squadrons—a total of 27½. These figures include No. 13 (Hellenic) Squadron (light bomber) which joined No. 3 (S.A.A.F.) Wing from the Middle East on or about 24th May.

† On 28th May No. 1 M.O.R.U. had been split into two units No. 1 M.O.R.U. 'A' and No. 1 M.O.R.U. 'B'. No. 1 M.O.R.U. 'A' was employed as an operational centre in Central Italy and No. 1 M.O.R.U. 'B' as a Forward Fighter Control on the east coast.

The areas of responsibility of the various subordinate air formations of M.A.T.A.F. for attacks on the enemy's Lines of Communication were redefined in a Directive issued by C.G. M.A.T.A.F. on 15th June. With effect from midnight on that date these redefined areas were to be, from west to east:—

U.S. XII T.A.C. (U.S. 87th Fighter Wing)
   Sea communications on west coast of Italy from 20 miles north of bombline to Genoa (exclusive).
   Road and rail communications north of the line Cecina–Poggibonsi–Arezzo–Fabriano–Fano (all inclusive).

U.S. XII T.A.C. (other than U.S. 87th Fighter Wing)
   All communications within the area 20 miles north of bombline in own Army area.
   Rail communications north of bombline up to the line Cecina–Poggibonsi–Arezzo–Fabriano–Fano (exclusive).

Desert Air Force
   All road communications within the area 20 miles north of bombline in own Army area.
   Sea communications on east coast of Italy from bombline to Ancona (inclusive).
   Any day bomber effort available after meeting direct support requirements was to be directed against land and sea communications in general area Rimini–Fabriano–Ancona. This effort was to be regarded as supplementary to attacks made by other subordinate air formations of M.A.T.A.F.

In the area 20 miles north of the bombline and south of the general line Pisa–Florence–Fano enemy movement was to be attacked regardless of Army areas by U.S. XII T.A.C. (including U.S. 87th Fighter Wing) and the Desert Air Force, who were to keep each other informed daily of their intentions. The medium day bombers of M.A.T.A.F. (U.S. 42nd and 57th Medium Bombardment Wings) were to continue their attacks on the enemy's L. of C. in the general area north of the line Pisa–Arezzo–Fano, supplementing those by the fighter-bombers in this same area. For night bombing C.G. U.S. XII T.A.C. was given operational control of the night-flying Bostons and Baltimores of No. 232 Wing R.A.F. for employment against L. of C. targets in direct support of 5th and 8th Armies, A.O.C. D.A.F. passing to C.G. U.S. XII T.A.C. any specific requirements as were necessary.

To return to 5th and 8th Armies, there was no relaxation for the victors after the capture of Rome since both Clark and Leese were well aware that Alexander gave higher priority to the destruction of the German armies than to the seizure of the Italian Capital. He had outlined his policy for the pursuit before 'Diadem'

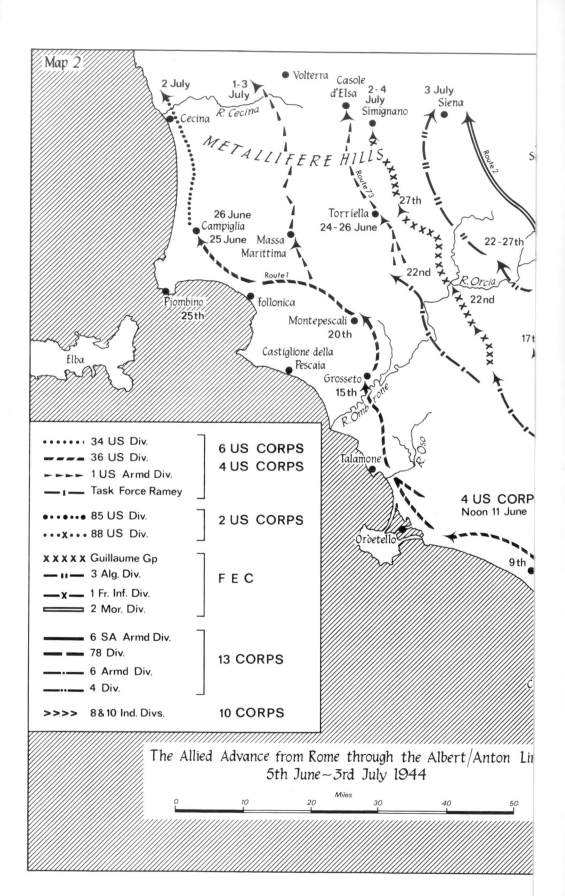

Map 2

2 July

1-3 July

Volterra

Casole d'Elsa

2-4 July Simignano

3 July Siena

Cecina

R. Cecina

METALLIFERE HILLS

Route 2

S

Route 73

27th

26 June Campiglia

Torriella 24-26 June

25 June Massa Marittima

22-27th

Route 1

22nd

R. Orcia

22nd

Piombino 25th

Follonica

Montepescali 20th

17t

Elba

Castiglione della Pescaia

Grosseto 15th

R. Ombrone

R. Oso

Talamone

4 US CORP
Noon 11 June

	34 US Div.	6 US CORPS
	36 US Div.	4 US CORPS
	1 US Armd Div.	
	Task Force Ramey	

Orbetello

9th

| | 85 US Div. | 2 US CORPS |
| | 88 US Div. | |

x x x x x Guillaume Gp

—ıı— 3 Alg. Div.   F E C

—x— 1 Fr. Inf. Div.

═══ 2 Mor. Div.

	6 SA Armd Div.	13 CORPS
	78 Div.	
	6 Armd Div.	
	4 Div.	

>>>> 8 & 10 Ind. Divs.   10 CORPS

The Allied Advance from Rome through the Albert/Anton Li
5th June~3rd July 1944

Miles

0   10   20   30   40   50

started in his Operation Order No. 1, in which paragraph 6, *Tasks of Armies,* had directed 8th Army to 'Pursue the enemy on the general axis Terni-Perugia'; 5th Army to 'Pursue the enemy north of Rome and capture the Viterbo airfields and the port of Civitavecchia'; and 5th Corps to pursue him vigorously should he attempt to withdraw (up the Adriatic coast).[27] 5th Army's task was rather easier because its sector consisted of more open rolling country than 8th Army's Tiber valley which, though not as difficult as the Liri valley, offered the German rear-guards ample opportunities for delaying actions, especially east of the river.[28]

The start of 5th Army's pursuit was initially constrained by two factors.[29] There was dense traffic congestion in the Rome area caused by the bottlenecks over the Tiber bridges, which the Germans had fortunately left intact; and Clark had to deploy his troops in pursuit in such a way that he could release 6th U.S. Corps and the French Expeditionary Corps to 7th Army, which was beginning to concentrate for amphibious training around Naples for the 'Anvil' assault on southern France.* He needed to release 2nd U.S. Corps as well for rest and refit in preparation for the assault on the Gothic Line if one proved to be necessary. The relief of formations tended to compound the traffic difficulties, which were a continuing feature of the Italian campaign throughout the summer.

8th Army's problems were of a different nature. The roads it was bound to use had first been attacked by the Allied Air Forces when they had tried to disrupt *AOK 10's* withdrawal east of Rome during the latter phases of 'Diadem'. Any bridges and even culverts, which were still intact, were subsequently blown up and diversions around them mined by *AOK 10's* engineers as its rear-guards withdrew. 8th Army's pursuit became a never-ending story of leading troops held up by relatively minor demolitions covered by one or two tanks or S.P. guns, which took time to locate and destroy before the British Sappers could clear a way through. The most precious weapons in 8th Army's armoury at this time were the humble bulldozer and the Sappers' simple mine probe, which was often used instead of the electronic mine detector because the latter frequently broke down and did not locate the deeper buried mines. One arm, however, lay almost unused. There were in Italy no less than three Indian Divisions: 4th, 8th and 10th, all of which had experience in and were adept at hill and mountain warfare.

---

* Hitler forbade the demolition of bridges in Rome much to the annoyance of the German Commanders in the field who were struggling to break contact with the enemy.[30] There was an element of propaganda in Hitler's order, which was intended to mark the contrast between the Allied bombing of Monte Cassino Abbey and his acceptance of Rome as an 'Open City'. The controversy over the treatment of Italian antiquities was to recur as the Allies approached Siena and Florence.

General Leese seemed to have been almost unaware of their potential. In a letter to the A.C.I.G.S. (Ops) in the War Office written on 8th June he stressed the importance of mountain troops and said he was training 4th Indian Division 'on a temporary mountain basis.'[31] It is hard to believe that the victors of Keren and Wadi Akarit needed much additional training before taking part in a pursuit in which their ability to move rapidly through hill country would have been invaluable.

See Map 2

In describing the tactical events during the pursuit we will normally work from west to east, looking at the actions of 5th Army's corps first and then those of 8th Army.

In the 5th Army sector Clark advanced on 5th June with two corps abreast, using Routes 1 and 2 as their centre lines. Clark, according to the official U.S. Historian, chose to use 6th U.S. Corps and 2nd U.S. Corps initially, although the men were very tired after their heavy fighting, because he was due to release the former for 'Anvil' and the latter was due for rest and refit.[32] He wished to get the most out of both of them before they had to be withdrawn. This may have been so but he was also aware that Alexander wished him to retain as many fresh troops in reserve as possible for the probable assault on the Gothic Line.

Truscott's 6th U.S. Corps thrust north-west from Rome with 34th U.S. Division on the coast road (Route 1), heading for Civitavecchia, and 36th U.S. Division inland, using a good secondary road leading to Viterbo on the western side of Lake Bracciano.[33] Both divisions were led by a Combat Command of 1st U.S. Armoured Division. Keyes' 2nd U.S. Corps with 85th and 88th U.S. Divisions advanced astride Route 2, heading for Viterbo as well but on the eastern side of Lake Bracciano. Keyes was allowed to keep Task Force Howze of 1st U.S. Armoured Division for tank support. Both American Corps advanced on as wide a front as possible, using small armoured columns during daylight on every available road and track and handing over to their infantry, embussed in trucks, to carry on the pursuit through the night. Each day fresh units were used in leap-frog fashion to maintain momentum. Divisions were restricted to essential fighting vehicles only, to reduce traffic congestion and to ease supply problems. German resistance was scattered and unco-ordinated, their rearguards breaking contact whenever possible. The port of Civitavecchia was taken early on 7th June with minimal resistance, and by the end of 9th June when *AOK 14* fell back to the Dora line, 5th Army's front ran from Montalto di Castro, on the coast 65 miles north-west of Rome, through Tuscania to Viterbo with reconnaissance troops, across the inter-Army boundary, occupying Orte in the 8th Army sector.

At this point, A.F.H.Q. pressure for release of troops for 'Anvil' made Clark regroup to release H.Q. 6th U.S. Corps. He also took the opportunity to withdraw H.Q. 2nd U.S. Corps as well. H.Q. 6th U.S. Corps was relieved by Crittenberger's H.Q. 4th U.S. Corps, and H.Q. 2nd U.S. Corps handed over to a specially constituted Pursuit Corps under Lieutenant-General E. R. M. de Larminat from the F.E.C.*

8th Army's advance against *AOK 10's* unbroken front was to be much slower.[35] Two of its Corps, 13th and 10th, advanced abreast with 1st Canadian Corps held in reserve. 13th Corps was directed up the Tiber valley towards the Terni and Rieti area with 6th South African Armoured Division on Route 3 west of the Tiber alongside 2nd U.S. Corps, 6th British Armoured Division on Route 4 east of the river, and 4th Division, supported by 25th Tank Brigade, moving by minor roads on its eastern flank. 10th Corps' 8th Indian and 2nd New Zealand Divisions continued their advance through the Central Apennines as they had done since the beginning of 'Diadem'; and over on the Adriatic coast 5th Corps, directly under control of H.Q. A.A.I., watched for signs of a German withdrawal, with 4th and 10th Indian Divisions under command.[36] 10th Indian Division was relieved early in June by the newly assembled Italian Corps of Liberation (*C.I.L.* Major-General U. Utili) so that it could be used to reinforce 10th Corps.†

---

* In this regrouping:
  6th *U.S. Corps* left for Naples to join 7th U.S. Army and was followed by divisions on a timed programme for 'Anvil':
  45th U.S. Division on 22nd June
  3rd U.S. Division (from garrisoning Rome) on 24th June
  36th U.S. Division on 27th June

  2nd *U.S. Corps* was withdrawn for rest with:
  1st U.S. Armoured Division around Bracciano
  34th U.S. Division near Tarquinia
  85th U.S. Division)
  88th U.S. Division)   south of Rome

  French Pursuit Corps consisted of:
  1st French Infantry Division
  3rd Algerian Infantry Division

  The 2nd Moroccan Infantry Division and 4th Moroccan Mountain Division were in F.E.C. reserve; and 1st and 5th British Divisions left 6th U.S. Corps, the former for rest and refit and the latter for transfer to the Middle East.[34]

  † Although officially formed in April 1944 it was only early in June that the *C.I.L.* (*Corpo Italiano di Liberazione*) was assembled together in 5th Corps' sector.[37] The force did not assume its final order until 20th June when it consisted of the 'Nembo' Group, and 1st and 2nd Brigade Groups; in all 13 battalions together with two field regiments and one medium battery of Italian artillery and service troops. At this period the *C.I.L.* was not well equipped and had barely sufficient vehicles to lift one battalion. Readers wishing to know more are advised to consult the Italian Official Histories.

In 13th Corps' sector 6th South African Division was hampered in the earliest stage of its advance by having to debouch from the Rome bottleneck in the wake of 2nd U.S. Corps.[38]* Traffic congestion was at its height, but, with the willing co-operation of the Americans, 11th South African Armoured Brigade was clear of the city early on 6th June and after an advance of thirty miles reached Civita Castellana, where it captured a German casualty clearing station, with 573 German wounded, that evening. Pushing forward the next day its patrols found that the bridges over the Tiber both to Narni and to Orte had been destroyed. On 8th June, in accordance with Alexander's orders issued the day before, they swung their axis of advance towards Orvieto, keeping to the west side of the Tiber valley.[39]

East of the Tiber the advance of 6th British Armoured Division was opposed by strong German rear-guards from the Hermann Göring Panzer and 15th Panzer Grenadier Divisions, which had orders to protect at all costs the Rieti–Terni road along which much of 51st Mountain Corps were withdrawing from Avezzano.[40]† There was a stiff battle round the hilltop village of Monterotondo, involving both 26th Armoured Brigade and 61st Brigade, which was not cleared till 7th June; Passo Corese on Route 4 was held until the evening of the 8th. Meanwhile further to the east 4th Division, with 10th Brigade leading, began its advance across the hills west of the Tivoli–Palombara road on the night 5th/6th June and made slow progress against rear-guards from 15th Panzer Grenadier and 1st Parachute Divisions during 7th and 8th June.[41] By the evening of 9th June 10th Brigade had reached Route 4 near Monte Libretti.

See Map 1

During the period 5th–9th June 8th Indian Division, leading 10th Corps in the pursuit, advanced steadily and without serious

---

* *6th South African Armoured Division* (Major-General W. H. Evered Poole) consisted of 11th S.A. Armoured Brigade, 12th S.A. Motorised Brigade, and 24th Guards Brigade (5th Grenadier Guards, 3rd Coldstream Guards, 1st Scots Guards).
For outline Order of Battle see Part I of this Volume (H.M.S.O. 1984) p.256n.

† Outline Order of Battle of *6th Armoured Division* (Major-General V. Evelegh) as on 8th June 1944:
    26th Armoured Brigade
        16th/5th Lancers, 17th/21st Lancers, 2nd Lothians and Border Horse
    1st Guards Brigade
        3rd Grenadier Guards, 2nd Coldstream Guards, 3rd Welsh Guards
    61st Infantry Brigade
        2nd, 7th and 10th Rifle Brigade (Motorised)
    Reconnaissance: 1st Derbyshire Yeomanry
        R.H.A. 12th Regiment (S.P.)
        R.A. 152nd Field Regiment; 72nd A/Tk Regiment; 51st L.A.A. Regiment
        R.E. 8th, 625th, 627th Field Squadrons; 144th Field Park Squadron

resistance to Subiaco which it reached during the afternoon of the 6th and Arsoli, on the Rome–Pescara highway (Route 5), by the evening of the 9th.[42]* The New Zealand Division, which had been halted by strong enemy resistance at Balsorano (Route 82) on 3rd June, now found the German 44th Infantry Division (part of 51st Mountain Corps) pulling out in a hurry in face of the threat to their withdrawal route through Rieti.[43] The New Zealanders entered Balsorano on 6th June and advanced from there, without regaining contact with the enemy, though hampered by demolitions, to Avezzano which they found clear on 9th June.[44]

On the Adriatic coast the German withdrawal started on 6th June, but was not detected by 5th Corps until 7th/8th June.[45] 4th Indian Division started up the coast making for Pescara, impeded only by demolition and mines,[46] while further inland, the *C.I.L.* found the strong German positions at Orsogna, which had defied 8th Army all the previous winter, abandoned. 5th Corps reached and occupied Pescara and Chieti on 10th June but was directed by H.Q. A.A.I. not to press its advance, to save bridging equipment. This was fortunate from the German point of view because 51st Mountain Corps was so short of towing vehicles for its artillery that is was compelled at times to use oxen and was harried more by Italian Partisan attacks than by 5th Corps' advance.[47]

After the first five days of the pursuit the pattern was beginning to emerge to which the German commanders were fully alive and acutely sensitive. *AOK 10's* western flank was becoming more and more exposed by 5th Army's success in driving back *AOK 14* quicker than 8th Army could prise *AOK 10* out of its stronger delaying positions. This situation was pointed out in both H.Q. A.A.I. and 8th Army Intelligence summaries, but there was no

---

* Outline Order of Battle of *8th Indian Division* (Major-General D. Russell)

  17th Indian Infantry Brigade
    1st Royal Fusiliers, 1st/12th Frontier Force Regiment, 1st/5th Gurkha Rifles F.F.

  19th Indian Infantry Brigade
    1st Argyll and Sutherland Highlanders, 3rd/8th Punjab Regiment, 6th/13th Frontier Force Rifles

  21st Indian Infantry Brigade
    5th Queen's Own Royal West Kent Regiment, 1st/5th Mahratta Light Infantry, 3rd/15th Punjab Regiment
    I.A.C. 6th Duke of Connaught's Own Lancers
    M.G. M.G. Battalion 5th Mahratta Light Infantry
    R.A. and I.A. 3rd, 52nd, 53rd Field Regiments R.A.; 5th Mahratta A/Tk Regiment I.A.; 26th L.A.A. Regiment R.A.
    I.E. 7th, 66th, 69th Field Companies, 47th Field Park Company, Bengal Sappers and Miners.

concerted attempt by the Allies to exploit the situation.[48] 5th Army's regrouping on 10th June is symptomatic of this blindness to the possibility of forcing *AOK 14* back so fast that *AOK 10* could be attacked from the west and driven into the Central Apennines for its destruction by air action. Withdrawal of 6th U.S. Corps for 'Anvil' and the resting of 2nd U.S. Corps for a probable assault on the Gothic Line, dominated Allied affairs, whereas protection of *AOK 10's* western flank became a continuous worry to the German operational staffs. To be fair to Alexander, he was not entirely to blame. Wilson's A.F.H.Q. was constantly pressing him to release troops for 'Anvil' or such other amphibious operations as the Combined Chiefs of Staff might order after the fall of Rome. Explaining the situation to Clark, who had protested strenuously about these premature withdrawals, Alexander showed that he treated his advance to the Gothic Line as a mechanical process of keeping the Germans on the run, the aim of which was to bring them to a decisive battle on the Gothic Line and not south of it as the Combined Chiefs of Staff envisaged in their signal to A.F. H.Q. on 14th June:

> 'The destruction of the German armed forces in Italy, south of the Pisa-Rimini Line must be completed. There should be no withdrawal from the battle of any Allied forces that are necessary for this purpose.'[49]

Alexander's explanatory signal to Clark on 16th June read:

> '1.   I fully realise that the withdrawal of divisions as ordered by AFHQ from your command at this stage must create considerable difficulties for you. At the same time we should lay ourselves open to a very serious charge of impeding the overall war effort if we continued to press for the retention of formations which in my opinion we cannot fully employ during the present phase of operations. [Logistic limitations restricted the number of divisions which could be employed in the pursuit].
> 2.   When we have captured Florence and Leghorn and have driven the enemy back to the Rimini–Pisa Line we shall I consider be in a strong position to press for the return of all the divisions you are now being asked to release to enable us to complete the destruction of the enemy's armed forces in Italy by another all out offensive.'[50]

It was one of the weaknesses of British Army command and staff training that so much emphasis was placed on the foresight needed to be ready for the major setpiece offensive like 'Diadem' that shorter term opportunities of decisive action in the mobile phases of a campaign were often lost. This was seen on a number of occasions in the fighting in the Western Desert in which the Germans showed themselves superior in seizing tactical opportunities whereas the British excelled in the planned offensive. There is no evidence in contemporary documents that any thought was given in June 1944 to enveloping *AOK 10's* western flank. Leese, in his unpublished memoirs, does mention a gap appearing in the German front 'towards Orvieto'.[51] He explains that delay in issuing orders and some lack of co-operation on Clark's part prevented its exploitation, but that is all. He shows no appreciation of the possibilities which so concerned the German commanders. The pursuit north of Rome was just another 'Partridge drive' as Montgomery unkindly described Alexander's final offensive to take Tunis in 1943.[52]

(iii)

See Map 1

Neither opposing Commander-in-Chief issued substantive orders for the developing of the campaign until several days after the pursuit began. Alexander was the first to do so. His order is dated 7th June 1944 but could not start to affect the action of his Armies for several days. It is worth quoting his directive in full as it highlights the emphasis Alexander placed upon seizing appropriate springboards for an attack on the Gothic Line rather than destroying Kesselring's forces to the south of it as the Combined Chiefs of Staff envisaged:

'1. The enemy has been greatly weakened by the fighting since 11 May and is now thoroughly disorganised. He is certainly in no position at present to launch a serious counter-attack. He will continue to suffer seriously during his retreat from attacks by our Air Forces and advancing columns.

2. To take full advantage of this situation Eighth Army will advance with all possible speed direct on the general area Florence–Bibbiena–Arezzo and Fifth Army on the general area Pisa–Lucca–Pistoia. Armies will maintain general contact with their inner flanks but will not wait on each other's advance. Enemy resistance will be by-passed wherever possible in order to reach the above vital areas quickly. Eighth Army will be responsible for any protection that may be necessary on its right flank.

3. To save transportation resources and bridging material 5 Corps will not follow up the enemy on their front. If the advance of Eighth Army fails to force the enemy to abandon Ancona, Polish Corps will be moved forward later on Eighth Army's eastern axis to take Ancona from the west.

4. Commander-in-Chief authorises Army Commanders to take extreme risks to secure the vital strategic areas mentioned in paragraph 2 above before the enemy can reorganise or be reinforced'.[53]

Kesselring issued his directive two days later on 9th June. Its introductory paragraph reflected the High Command's preoccupation, starting:

'The retention of as much Italian territory as possible is of decisive importance to the conduct of the war in the Mediterranean, particularly in relation to the opportunities open to the enemy for jumping off into the Balkans from Italy'.[54]

He went on to affirm that the Dora Line would be defended for as long as the tactical situation allowed.[55] Badly mauled divisions could, however, be sent back to garrison the Gothic Line forthwith, as could supply troops, field replacement battalions etc. which were not urgently needed at the front. A co-ordinated and phased withdrawal from the Dora Line would be carried out via a series of intermediate phase lines not more than 9 miles apart which could only be abandoned with Army Group approval. Retreat from the next delaying line north of Dora, which ran east and west of Lake Trasimeno, would signal the evacuation of Elba. On its taking up all northern Italy, south of the River Po, would become an operational zone with *AOK 14* and *AOK 10* responsible for the western and eastern sector respectively, their boundary being the line Pontassieve (just east of Florence) to Ferrara in the Po valley north of Bologna. The two armies were to plan their occupation of the Gothic Line on the assumption that *AOK 14* would deploy three corps headquarters and eleven divisions of which two would be motorised and in reserve, and *AOK 10* would control four corps headquarters and fourteen divisions of which three would be motorised and in reserve. *AOK 10* would also be responsible for the Venetian and Adriatic coastal regions. When these Armies reached the Gothic Line, the Rear Army Command known as *Armeeabteilung von Zangen*, which had earlier supervised its construction, would revert to corps status as 87th Corps.

Kesselring's directive ended by stating that the Allied advance must be impeded by a more intense scale of demolition. Anything of conceivable military value, including ports, bridges, tunnels, power-stations and so forth, were to be destroyed, and 'every last engineer' must be employed on demolition work. They were no longer to be used as infantry. In subsequent signals to *OKW* on 9th and 10th June Kesselring reiterated that it was 'his fixed intention' to defend Italy at maximum distance from the Apennines; but that he had a 'second absolute obligation' not to let his armies be destroyed before they reached the Gothic Line.[56]

Kesselring's second obligation was not accepted, for the first had become suspect when Warlimont reported from Italy on 8th June that in Kesselring's view it might become necessary, 'in the most unfavourable circumstances', to pull back to the Gothic Line within three weeks. In his own post-war account, Jodl's deputy was ready to argue on his return on 12th June that these defences had a natural strength in the centre and were well advanced in the west, albeit weak in the Adriatic sectors.[57] It appears that Hitler would not listen, and contemporary sources show that he had, in fact, already decreed on 9th June that Kesselring must 'hold south of the Apennines'—and far enough south to preclude any need for the evacuation of Elba. As this small island was not reckoned by his naval advisers to be of major significance either for the Germans or for the Allies, it was probably in order to anchor Kesselring's front as far south as possible that Hitler decided to treat it as another Crimea. When the Gothic Line was next discussed in conference on 13th June, Jodl so summarised his deputy's findings as to stress the risk of an armoured break through into the Po valley. His recommendation that Army Group C be again ordered to go over to defence south of the Apennines was at once accepted and Hitler signed the directive which was despatched to Kesselring on the following day.

Before the fall of Rome, the Field-Marshal had received few orders bearing Hitler's own signature, so there was an ominous hint of loss of confidence in the heading 'Führer to *OB Südwest*'.[58] The text opened by pointing out that the Apennine range was the last obstacle which could prevent the Allies breaking into the Po valley, but it would take many months of intense work before the Gothic Line could offer adequate security. Army Group C must accordingly fight to gain time, preferably on the line Orbetello–Spoleto–River Tronto, but, if this was not practicable, on the line Piombino–Lake Trasimeno–Portocivitanova. Elba must be held and Kesselring must disabuse all his officers and men of the idea that a fortified defence system existed in the Apennines. The directive ended with an abrupt instruction that Kesselring report his intentions and proposed distribution of forces. Hitler also decreed that the title 'Gothic Line' was too pretentious and should be changed to 'Green Line' to avoid creating false impressions in the minds of both German and Allied troops. We will, however, continue to use Gothic because this was the main description of the German defence in the Northern Apennines used by the Allies and we will refer to Green I and Green II as components of that line.

Faced with this ultimatum (or 'very clear orders' as Kesselring described it when talking to von Vietinghoff) *OB Südwest* had few options left.[59] The Allies had already overrun parts of the Dora Line, and so he could only inform his two Army Commanders on 14th June that delaying tactics were to cease when their troops reached the line running east and west through Lake Trasimeno, now known as the 'Albert Line', and upon which the Allies were to be brought to a 'conclusive' halt. Divisional reconnaissance officers were to select positions which would be economical to man and which were as tank-proof as possible. All available engineer and construction units were to be concentrated upon building obstacles and clearing fields of fire, and to procure Italian labour Armies were authorised to 'exercise compulsion' over civilian men and women between 15 and 50 years of age.[60]

The early trace for the Albert Line ran from Castiglione della Pescaia on the west coast via Grosseto to Magione (east of Lake Trasimeno) and across the Central Apennines to Mt. Conero, just south of Ancona on the Adriatic. On 16th June the Armies were further instructed to reconnoitre a number of lay-back positions in rear of Albert to block likely Allied thrust lines. In view of *AOK 14's* consistent failure to check the American advance up the west coast, priority was given to a reserve position on this wing 12 miles north of the Albert Line, which was code-named Anton and which was to run from Follonica, just south of Piombino, to merge into Albert at the River Orcia.

Neither Lemelsen nor von Vietinghoff wished to go over to defence in positions which were both unprepared and uncomfortably close to major Allied objectives. They continually pressed Kesselring for freedom of action, but as this was as constantly denied him by the High Command, the Field-Marshal's position in mid-June was far from happy. On the 16th he went so far as to request a personal interview with the Führer, to 'justify his previous conduct of operations and to discuss further possibilities'. He was informed that as Hitler was conferring with von Rundstedt and Rommel in France, his visit, though 'much desired', must be postponed for a few days. It did not take place until 3rd July. By then the Battle of Lake Trasimeno was over and the Albert/Anton Line had been lost.

(iv)

See Maps 1 and 2

We left events on the battlefield at the end of 10th June when the first onrush after the fall of Rome had been slowed by regrouping on both the Allied and German sides. The American 6th and 2nd U.S. Corps were being relieved by 4th U.S. Corps and the 'Pursuit Corps' of the F.E.C., so that 6th U.S. Corps could start its preparations for 'Anvil' and 2nd U.S. Corps could be rested and re-equipped in the Alban Hills. Some regrouping of 8th Army was also necessary.[61] The Tiber river became the boundary between 13th and 10th Corps with the latter now taking command of all troops east of the river.*

On the German side *AOK 10* was retreating slowly and methodically towards the Dora Line, which it planned to reach on 12th June. On this date von Senger and H.Q. 14th Panzer Corps took command of *AOK 14's* coastal sector, where Dora was manned only by 20th Luftwaffe Field Division, 162nd (Turkoman) Infantry Division, and some remnants of 65th Infantry Division.[63] The third arrival from northern Italy, 356th Infantry Division, was fighting on the right wing of 1st Parachute Corps, and although von Senger was promised 90th Panzer Grenadier Division none of the mobile formations had as yet reached *AOK 14*. Its efforts to hold Dora were accordingly shortlived, and there was hardly a pause in Fifth Army's advance as 4th U.S. Corps and the F.E.C. took over. Between the coast and Lake Bolsena 20th Luftwaffe Field and 162nd (Turkoman) Divisions were soon thrown back by 4th U.S. Corps, using 36th U.S. Division reinforced with an extra regimental combat team from 91st U.S. Division (recently arrived from North Africa).[64] These troops took Orbetello on 12th June, and having reached the Ombrone river two days later were patrolling into Grosseto by the 15th. 162nd (Turkoman) Division was now crumbling, and to add to Lemelsen's troubles Italian Partisans were extremely active in this battle area. Allied columns were guided through the hills, while German telephone lines were cut and liaison officers ambushed as they travelled between formations. The Partisans also demolished bridges and blocked roads and on 13th June, when he learnt that it was impossible for this reason to bring supplies down to Grosseto from Siena, Lemelsen asked and obtained authority from Army Group C to shoot up to ten Italians of military age for every German soldier killed, or for proven acts of military sabotage.†

---

* After regrouping the outline 8th Army order of battle became:

13th Corps:	6th South African Armoured Division (left)
(Left)	78th Division with 9th Armoured Brigade under command (right)
	In reserve: 4th Division
	1st Canadian Armoured Brigade
10th Corps:	6th Armoured Division (left)
(Right)	8th Indian Division (right)
	In reserve: 10th Indian Division
	7th Armoured Brigade
	25th Army Tank Brigade
	Kings Dragoon Guards (armoured cars)
	12th Lancers (armoured cars)

2nd New Zealand Division in the Avezzano area passed from 10th Corps to 8th Army reserve.[62]

† This 'reprisal ratio' of 10 to 1 had been ordered by Hitler in March 1944, when 32 members of a German police battalion were killed as they were marching through Rome. For the subsequent murder of 320 Italian civilians Kesselring, von Mackensen and Maelzer (the then Military Governor of Rome) were tried and convicted by Allied military courts in 1946/47.[65]

Nevertheless, von Senger's assumption of command was soon reflected in the increasing resistance which the troops of 4th U.S. Corps began to feel as they fought their way over the Ombrone river and into the hills north of Grosseto which constituted the western end of the Albert Line. From 14th June, 19th Luftwaffe Field Division began to relieve the unreliable 162nd (Turkoman) Division and 90th Panzer Grenadier Division moved piecemeal into the line of 14th Panzer Corps.[66] von Senger also received some detachments of tanks and assault guns, plus the engineer battalions of 42nd Jäger Division and 16th SS Panzer Grenadier Division. All of the latter formation was placed under Lemelsen's command on 18th June, as part of 75th Corps which was then entrusted with coastal defence from Marina di Carrara (north of the Arno) down to Follonica.[67] Crittenberger, commanding 4th U.S. Corps, decided that a Corps assault would be needed to compel another German withdrawal.[68] He timed his assault for 18th June.

The F.E.C. thrust on the right of 5th Army's front was made astride Route 2 on the axis Acquapendente–Siena–Poggibonsi. [69] The 3rd Algerian Infantry Division advanced west of Lake Bolsena, while 1st French Infantry Division used Route 2 east of the lake. The French advance was generally opposed by Schlemm's 1st Parachute Corps, the divisions of which, though exhausted, were of a higher calibre than those on the coast. They had been reinforced by 26th Panzer Division from *AOK 10* and were later given 29th Panzer Grenadier Division as well. These reinforcements did not initially prevent de Larminat's Pursuit Corps making rapid progress northwards. His two divisions joined hands around the northern shores of Lake Bolsena on 14th June and went on to seize Acquapendente on the same day. The front gradually widened as the Italian coast-line turns west and so an extra French group under Brigadier-General A. Guillaume, drawn from 4th Moroccan Mountain Division and the 1st Group of Tabors, was brought into the line between 4th U.S. Corps and the Pursuit Corps. The French troops like the Americans began to experience increasing resistance as 1st Parachute Corps tried to obey *OB Südwest's* orders to stand on the Albert Line. By 18th June the F.E.C. was about ten miles short of the Orcia river, a tributary of the Ombrone, along which 4th U.S. Corps was about to launch a co-ordinated Corps assault.

8th Army's advance was exhilarating and yet frustrating. Each day the leading troops went off to an encouraging start until they met the first German demolition of the day.[70] They were never sure whether it was an uncovered obstacle, designed solely to slow their advance; whether it was covered by a rear-guard which would fight for a few hours and then withdraw; or whether it was the first obstacle in a defensive line which the Germans intended to hold for some days. Whichever it was, some degree of deployment was necessary to find a way round and to cover the Sappers while they cleared the mines around the demolished bridge and either bulldozed a diversion through the stream-bed or built a Bailey bridge on or near the road. All this took time and caused a steady flow of casualties amongst the leading brigades, both from mines and from harassing artillery fire brought down by the artillery O.P. parties of the German rear-guards. The speed of advance was dictated by the skill and determination of the opposing Sappers and the opportunities for demolition and mining afforded by the terrain in each sector. And there was another factor which played a random but nonetheless decisive part in 8th Army's affairs: rain. In spite of brilliant summer weather with stifling heat and billowing dust for two thirds of the time, sudden storms and longer periods of rain occurred which were so heavy that they turned Sapper built diversions into impassable quagmires and prevented the supply vehicles from reaching the forward troops with essential fuel, ammunition and food. An extract from a study of the War Diary of 26th Armoured Brigade, leading 6th Armoured Division during its advance through Marsciano to Perugia on 17th and 18th June, paints the picture:[71]

> 'The move of 26th Armoured Brigade to the west bank of the Tiber was delayed because of difficulties in completing the bridge . . . warning of the delay was given by 8th Field Squadron R.E. at 0400 hrs and the bridge was not finished until 1100 hrs. The K.D.G. [Divisional reconnaissance regiment] then led the advance . . . Soon afterwards, at the first sign of opposition, the armour was ordered through. 17th/21st Lancers divided, the right hand squadron taking the minor road which runs along the Tiber valley, and the left hand squadron the better, metalled road leading to S. Valentino. The left squadron had to work round an enemy post at Cerquito and then had trouble with mines. "Considerable" shell fire on the approaches to S. Valentino gave warning that they were approaching the new enemy defence line, as did the casualties to the unsuspecting reserve squadron, travelling in the centre across country, which had a complete troop of tanks knocked out and the crew of another gunned down as they dismounted (total casualties for the day 6 killed and 6 wounded). At 1900 hrs the Brigade called for "all available artillery support" on S. Valentino but no more progress was to be made that day. 17th/21st Lancers withdrew slightly to harbour at 2130 hrs; an advance . . . of some 13 miles.

During the afternoon it had started raining heavily. The ground became slippery and boggy so quickly that 2nd Lothians could not get through to Cerquito. The ford over the Nestor became almost impassable and it was approaching midnight before 2nd Rifle Brigade, on their way forward to screen the leading armour, could report that the village was clear of the enemy.

The storm raged long into the night, causing great difficulty with communication. "Normal administrative traffic which goes on before midnight on the Brigade Command Net took until 0500 hrs the next morning to pass." Diversions round blown bridges and road craters were rapidly churned up and unfortunate supply echelons journeyed most of the night; those of 2nd Lothians reached their tanks at 0330 hrs, those of 17th/21st Lancers were only at Marsciano at dawn, which caused the Regiment to halt for refuelling the following afternoon.'

This description is a microcosm of a day in the life of any of the British, South African or Canadian armoured brigades during 8th Army's advance towards Lake Trasimeno.

13th Corps, west of the Tiber, continued its drive on Orvieto during 10th June with 6th South African Armoured Division in the lead, working through the hill country astride the secondary road from Viterbo via Bagnoregio to Orvieto and 78th Division, supported by 9th Armoured Brigade, moving up on their right on the western bank of the Tiber.[72] The South Africans ran into the rear-guards of Schlemm's 1st Parachute Corps, formed mainly by 356th Infantry Division, holding the line of the railway running due east from Montefiasconi at the southern end of Lake Bolsena to the Tiber valley. 11th South African Armoured Brigade had a successful day overrunning these positions, inflicting some 300 casualties on the Germans and capturing 20 anti-tank guns. The following day 24th Guards Brigade passed through 11th South African Armoured Brigade but were halted by a strong defensive position south of Bagnoregio.[73] After testing out the defences during the 12th June it was found necessary to mount a divisional attack to break through. This attack went in on 13th June and met stubborn resistance from 1st Parachute Corps, which was under orders from Kesselring to maintain contact with *AOK 10* south-east of Orvieto, and also to find forces for defence of the town.[74] Orvieto had, by then, lost much of its importance to the Germans as a centre of communication because 14th Panzer Corps' divisions had already scrambled through this bottleneck in their lateral move to reinforce *AOK 14*. However as 13th June wore on the pressure of the F.E.C. and 13th Corps became so severe that Kesselring was forced to sanction the withdrawal of 1st Parachute Corps to a line running east and west of Acquapendente, abandoning Orvieto.

The withdrawal was followed up on 14th June by the South Africans, who entered the town ahead of 78th Divison, which was still clearing the Tiber valley.[75] As the motorised divisions of *AOK 10* were already over the Tiber the loss of Orvieto was not a disaster for the Germans, but Kesselring's two Armies were failing to keep in step and relations between their staffs were very strained.*

For the next three days 13th Corps pressed northwards astride Route 71 with the South Africans advancing through the hills on the western side towards Allerona and then Chiusi, while 78th Division worked up the highway heading for Citta della Pieve.[77] Well pleased with his troops' progress, on 16th June General Leese gave directions for their future advance: 13th Corps was to move west of Lake Trasimeno, 10th Corps to the east, both converging on Arezzo (*Map 1*).[78] 10th Corps was then to make for Bibbiena and Pontassieve. If Arezzo was strongly held, he intended that 13th Corps should by-pass it to the west and drive direct on Florence. 'My object' he wrote, 'is to face up to the Apennine position north of Florence, with 13th Corps, at the earliest opportunity.' Leese was too optimistic. The tempo of the advance slowed as it was doing on the American and French fronts in the face of German attempts to implement Hitler's order to stand on the Albert Line. The weather also broke on 17th June, continuing foul with heavy rain until 21st June and making operations difficult as the tracks broke up and the fields turned to mud.[79]

On the night 16th/17th June 78th Division failed in its attack on Citta della Pieve.[80] When the strength of the German opposition became clear the Division tried to by-pass it in a wide right hook. After hard fighting in pouring rain the paratroopers of 1st Parachute Division were cleared out of Citta della Pieve during 18th June. Better progress was made during 19th June, but by evening the Division was brought to a halt by determined opposition on the Sanfatucchio ridge and in villages around the south-western end of Lake Trasimeno astride Route 71. The following day the South Africans met similar opposition advancing from Cetona towards Chiusi, which is an ancient walled town commanding the country west of Lake Trasimeno and blocking the secondary road to Arezzo via Sinalunga.[81] They found Chiusi and the surrounding area was

---

* At *AOK 14*, Lemelsen and his Chief of Staff Hauser resented having to accommodate their tactics to those of *AOK 10*, which they considered less hard-pressed, and their sense of grievance was enhanced by Hitler's order to stand on the Albert Line, stigmatised as being quite unrealistic where their Army was concerned. von Vietinghoff and his Chief of Staff Wentzell (who on 11th June bracingly reminded Hauser that he had been given *AOK 10's* 'best corps command, best divisions and best G.H.Q. artillery') were for their part constantly critical of *AOK 14* for falling back too soon and thus endangering their own withdrawal.[76]

held by far more than the usual rear-guards. 13th Corps seemed to be up against a fully organised position anchored on Chiusi in the west and Lake Trasimeno in the east.

13th Corps had been aware that it was approaching the Albert Line but had not expected to be opposed so far south.[82] The Corps Intelligence summaries suggested that the forward defended localities would not be much south of Castiglione half-way up the western side of Lake Trasimeno. It was not until 21st June that it was realised that the forward German positions ran from the south-western corner of Lake Trasimeno through Sanfatucchio and Chiusi.[83] This was confirmed by a German map captured by 78th Division.[84] Kirkman, like Crittenberger, decided a Corps operation would be needed to compel the German withdrawal from the Albert Line.[85]

While 13th Corps had been fighting its way forward to Orvieto and then Trasimeno, 10th Corps was advancing on Terni, through which units of 51st Mountain Corps were withdrawing from Avezzano.[86] The available roads ran through mountainous country susceptible to rear-guard action and offering great opportunities for demolitions. It took 10th Corps five days to cover the 30 miles between Passo Corese, from which 6th Armoured Division (now under Corps command) began the advance on 9th June, and Terni, which was eventually reached on 13th June.

Since it appeared to General McCreery that opposition would be heavy north of Cantalupo but that the eastern Tiber valley might be 'very thinly held' he directed 6th Armoured Division towards Todi and Perugia and 8th Indian Division, moving on the right flank, towards Terni.[87] Thereafter the Indians would advance across minor roads to Foligno on Route 3.[88]

Greatly delayed by demolitions, which involved the bridging of a number of quite considerable streams and rivers, and by mortar and artillery fire on the bridging parties, 6th Armoured Division entered Narni about midday on 13th June.[89] Some tanks of 6th Armoured Division's 2nd Lothians made a swift dash for Terni but arrived just too late to prevent the enemy demolition party blowing the bridge over the River Nera. 8th Indian Division meanwhile had been advancing up the indifferent mountain road through Cantalupo and, although unopposed by enemy, had been having even greater difficulty overcoming the comprehensive demolitions left by *AOK 10*. 21st Indian Brigade, leading the Division, entered Terni on the 14th.

Anticipating that the Germans would probably pull back quickly towards Perugia, General McCreery allotted the King's Dragoon Guards and the 12th Lancers, both armoured car regiments, to the 6th Armoured and 8th Indian Divisions respectively, to carry out wide reconnaissance and to precede the movement of the main formations.[90] Todi was occupied by 6th Armoured Division on 15th June but enemy rear-guards blocked the advance a few miles north of the town, whereupon it was decided to bridge the Tiber south of Todi and press the advance up the west bank of the river where the country was not so suitable for German defensive tactics.[91]

The bridge over the Tiber was not completed until early on 17th June. 6th Armoured Division, now led by the King's Dragoon Guards, crossed the Nestore river east of Marsciano where it was again held up. 8th Indian Division made better progress. Led by 19th Indian Brigade, with 142nd Royal Tank Regiment under command, Foligno was secured on 16th June and Bastia, just west of Assisi, was reached the following day.[92] Perugia was now threatened from both flanks and 10th Corps issued orders for its capture.[93] 6th Armoured Division was to advance on the town from the south and south-west and, after clearing it, was to strike north-west on Highway 75 around the north-eastern shores of Lake Trasimeno. 8th Indian Division was to seal off the exits from Perugia east of the Tiber and to advance northwards up the Tiber valley towards Umbertide.

In the event, 76th Panzer Corps did not put up much of a fight for Perugia itself, and rear-guards abandoned the city during the night of 19th/20th June, when 6th Armoured Division approached it from the south-west.[94] 6th Armoured's 61st Brigade made a rapid advance during the same night and captured Pt 652 overlooking Highway 75 which it held despite persistent counter-attacks, but on its right 1st Guards Brigade failed to gain Pt 648.[95] With a gradual withdrawal into the main Albert Line anticipated by von Vietinghoff on 21st June, 15th Panzer Grenadier and 305th Infantry Divisions were at this time putting up a vigorous defence north-east and north-west of Perugia.

East of the main Apennine range the German withdrawal had been carried out as fast as their paucity of transport and fuel would allow, (*Map 1*). After taking Pescara on 10th June, 5th Corps followed up on the coast as far as the Saline river and, inland, occupied Aquila on 13th June.[96] In accordance with the original instructions of A.A.I., 5th Corps' advance was stopped and on 17th June command of the sector was handed over to 2nd Polish Corps (Lieutenant-General W. Anders).* General Anders was directed to press ahead with all speed to seize the important port of Ancona, while 5th Corps was in turn withdrawn into Army Group reserve in anticipation of the assault on the Gothic Line.†[98]

The Polish advance was very rapid and followed much the same pattern as that of the other Allied corps, though less strenuously opposed by 51st Mountain Corps which was intent on breaking contact wherever possible.[100] On 20th June the Poles seized a small bridgehead over the Chienti river, some 60 miles from their Start Line on the Saline. Next day the German 278th Infantry Division counter-attacked and re-established its line on the Chienti which was its outpost position some 20 miles south of the Albert Line. Anders appreciated that a Corps attack would be needed to force the German defences and obtained Alexander's permission to build up supplies and ammunition for an assault on about 4th July.[101]

Thus the battle of the Albert Line seemed destined to open with a succession of independent Allied corps assaults, starting with 4th U.S. Corps in the west on 18th June; then 8th Army's two corps in the centre; and finally the Poles on the eastern flank early in July. The F.E.C. as it approached the Albert Line, became involved in a series of reliefs for 'Anvil': that of 1st French Infantry Division began on 20th/21st June and 3rd Algerian Infantry Division was to follow early in July.[102] As a result, we are told, much of the former *élan* of their units vanished.‡

Quite unexpectedly the pattern of Corps assaults on the Albert Line was upset on 17th June by the German reaction to French landings on the island of Elba, called Operation 'Brassard'. The Allies had intended to invade Elba with 9th French Colonial

---

* 2nd Polish Corps outline order of battle was:[97]
   3rd Carpathian Division
   5th Kresowa Division
   2nd Polish Armoured Brigade
   Army Group Polish Artillery
   C.I.L. (Corpo Italiano di Liberazione)
   318th Polish Fighter Reconnaissance Squadron
British troops: 7th Hussars, two medium regiments of artillery, engineers and service troops.

† When 5th Corps handed over to 2nd Polish Corps on 17th June it moved to the Campobasso area and took over the temporary command of the following formations, remaining in Army Group reserve:[99]
   1st Division
   1st Armoured Division
   4th Indian Division
   10th Indian Division
   7th Armoured Brigade.

‡ It was on 16th June that General Juin first expressed concern for the effect on morale engendered by rumours of withdrawal from Italy. Colonel P. Le Goyet: *La Participation Française à la Campagne d'Italie* (Ministère des Armées, Paris 1969) pp.164–5.

Division, any time after 25th May, as part of the 'Diadem' offensive when its impact on the main battle for Rome could have been considerable.[103] The operation had to be postponed until mid-June due to French training difficulties.[104] There were mixed motives for its resuscitation.[105] H.Q. A.A.I. considered that the postponement had taken away much of the operation's value; greater importance was attached to the early capture of Piombino for supply purposes. A.A.I., therefore, asked A.F.H.Q. on 7th June whether the Elba assault force could be employed subsequently to seize and hold the port until 5th Army could reach it. Five days later H.Q. A.A.I. had second thoughts and asked for the assault force to be placed under 5th Army's command for an amphibious left-hook in tactical co-operation with 4th U.S. Corps' advance.[106] If 9th French Colonial Division, which was to provide the bulk of the troops, could not be spared, then H.Q. A.A.I. hoped that at least the assault shipping could be transferred to 5th Army to help loosen up the German defences of the Albert Line along the Ombrone river. Neither request was granted. A.F.H.Q. made it clear on 13th June that the French troops were needed for 'Anvil', as was the shipping, and must be withdrawn from Elba as soon as possible after the island had been secured.[107] In any case French troops could not be used without the consent of the French High Command and this was unlikely to be forthcoming as the division would be needed in France. General Wilson, writing to General de Lattre de Tassigny on 16th June, did not share A.A.I.'s doubts.[108] He had always felt that the operation might be of vital importance to the battle for Italy, and this was proving to be the case as 5th Army's advance had been checked on a line almost due east of Elba, just as he had personally anticipated.

Fighting on Elba was short but severe.[109] 9th French Colonial Division lost 400 killed and 600 wounded. Hitler ordered the evacuation of the island too late, and in consequence 1,200 German and 600 Italian troops were taken prisoners. 'Brassard' was a costly and unnecessary operation. The Elba garrison could have been ignored and allowed to rot. Nevertheless this apparently minor Allied success, which had been mounted almost as an afterthought, fortuitously contributed to a major change in German tactical policy which reduced the importance of the Albert Line.

(v)

The effect of the fall of Elba on the German High Command was largely psychological. It reawakened and reinforced German fears of Allied landings behind *AOK 14's* western flank near

Leghorn and along the Ligurian coast, and it enabled Kesselring to claim that a 'new situation' had arisen since Hitler had ordered the defence of the Albert Line.[110] In a report to *OKW* on 18th June he pointed to the heavy pressure on 14th Panzer Corps, the new threat to its coastal flank represented by the impending loss of Elba, and the progress made by 8th Army since 16th June, which led him to admit 'concern' for the Albert Line though he would do everything in his power to ensure its defence.[111] Nevertheless it was his duty to report that the stamina of his troops had been weakened by six weeks' exposure to non-stop air attacks, and that the problems of road and rail transport, intensified as they were by the activities of Italian Partisans and the wear and tear on M.T. by a journey of 125 miles to the main railheads, had reached 'almost unmanageable proportions'. The report ended on a note which Kesselring had not used since he had fallen out of favour with Hitler for his 'pro-Italian' inclinations in the summer of 1943. He affirmed that he was convinced of the necessity to defend Italy as far south of the Apennines as possible, and he was 'doubly bound' thereto by the Führer's orders, but he needed to be sure that he had his master's confidence.

Also on 18th June Kesselring sent the High Command a separate appreciation of the options open to the Allies in which he discussed their immediate tactical opportunities and longer term repercussions on his chances of defending northern Italy successfully.[112] Tactically, the Allies could use their troops on Elba to land on the coast north or south of Piombino where they would have the support of strong Partisan bands operating in this region. Such landings would be accompanied by heavy air attacks to block the coastal roads, imperilling 14th Panzer Corps' withdrawal. Strategically, the capture of Elba might be the stepping-stone for landings near Leghorn, aimed at cutting his Lines of Communication and thus destroying Army Group C. In his view it was significant that Elba was being occupied by French troops from Corsica where the Allies had enough troops and landing craft for a large scale landing at Leghorn without calling on reserves in North Africa.

Hitler seems to have been sufficiently impressed with these forebodings to sanction the retraction of *AOK 14's* coastal wing, although he insisted on no retreat without necessity. Kesselring therefore raised no objection when, on 20th June, Lemelsen sought permission for 14th Panzer Corps to take up the Anton reserve position in the coastal sector, and for the bulk of 1st Parachute Corps to move into the main Albert Line.[113] The pulling back of *AOK 14's* right wing was rendered inevitable by tactical pressures and by the loss of Elba, but it created a further imbalance between the two German Armies which might have been their undoing, had the senior Allied commanders been less concerned with their arguments over 'Anvil'. Although Lemelsen reminded his Corps on 20th June of the Führer's orders to stand in Albert, Schlemm and von Senger had already, on 16th June, been informed that at some later period it would 'probably be necessary' to withdraw to the Gothic Line. Only the Corps Commanders and their immediate staffs were to be privy to the requisite planning, but whatever the degree of secrecy these orders indicated that *AOK 14* looked to the Gothic Line as a haven. In contrast, von Vietinghoff was confident that *AOK 10* could hold Albert for some time, and backed this view on 18th June by issuing instructions to comb out the rear areas, and to bring forward as much transport and fighting equipment as possible. In conversation with Lemelsen on 21st June he described his Army's general situation as 'quite tolerable', and reckoned that it would withdraw gradually into Albert except in the area of Chiusi, which on Kesselring's orders was to be defended as a 'fortress'.[114] Lemelsen retorted that his Army was already in Albert and was hard pressed by the Americans and the French, the latter being 'the trickiest of all our opponents'. It is not therefore surprising that the German front remained dangerously echeloned back, with *AOK 10's* front becoming progressively more exposed by *AOK 14's* inability to stand for any length of time. Nor is it surprising that Lemelsen and Hauser were frequently at odds with Kesselring and his staff, whose relations with *AOK 10* were much closer, born as they were of nine months of experience shared since the Allies first landed in Italy.

In brief then, Army Group C faced its first set-piece battle since the fall of Rome in an unbalanced and uncertain mood. Between 18th–30th June *AOK 14* tried but failed to get a firm grip on its sectors of the Anton/Albert Line, while *AOK 10's* operations around Lake Trasimeno would show that on this front the Germans underestimated the natural strength of the Italian countryside south of the Northern Apennines, the defensive skill of their own soldiers, and the problems which the Allies were facing in trying to bring their material superiority to bear in an effective way.

At A.F.H.Q. and H.Q. A.A.I. command and staff effort was concentrated upon the Anglo–American debate over 'Anvil' described in Chapter VI Part I of this Volume. On 17th June Alexander conferred with Wilson prior to the latter's meeting with General Marshall's team on 19th June. Alexander was sufficiently encouraged to go on advocating his plan to drive on Austria, while at the same time he realised that he would only win his case by intensive lobbying of Churchill and the British War Cabinet through political as well as military channels. On 21st June Mr.

Harold Macmillan, Resident Minister at A.F.H.Q., accompanied by General Gammell, Wilson's Chief of Staff, arrived in London by air to present Alexander's case.[115] Meanwhile the withdrawal of troops from A.A.I. for 'Anvil' continued, weakening 5th Army at a time when its opponents in *AOK 14* were only too willing to give away if pressed hard and continuously.

In the First Phase of tactical air operations, between 5th–20th June, of the estimated 4,085 sorties flown and 2,685 tons of bombs dropped in the battle area 2,604 or so sorties were flown and some 1,945 tons of bombs dropped on M.T. on roads and on the roads themselves.[116] The greatest contribution was made by the medium day bombers of M.A.T.A.F.; the fighter-bombers of U.S. XII T.A.C. and D.A.F. (in equal shares) were a close second. It was during the first five days that the greatest havoc was caused among the enemy's M.T. In the period 5th–9th June 1,366 M.T. and horse-drawn vehicles, eight tanks and four armoured vehicles were claimed destroyed, and 1,253 M.T. and horse-drawn vehicles and four tanks damaged.

Railway targets were next in importance, but the effort against them was understandably small, being about 734 sorties during which 399.1 tons of bombs were dropped, nearly all by the fighter-bombers of M.A.T.A.F. with those of U.S. XII T.A.C. playing the greater part.[117] Of the remainder of the effort within the battle area, ammunition and other dumps received 116 tons and guns 124·4 tons of bombs or thereabouts, again from the fighter-bombers, which also contributed in a small way to attacks on towns in which the light day and night bombers of U.S. XII T.A.C. and D.A.F. did most of the work.

On 8th Army's front, despite the speed of the advance, there were several demands from Army formations for immediate assistance. On 5th June, for example, Rover David, operating solely on 6th South African Armoured Division's axis, directed aircraft on to some 8.8-cm. guns holding up the leading brigade.* The air attack was completely successful, enabling the brigade to push on again. From 7th June onwards 8th Army was supported exclusively by D.A.F. and on this day a call from 8th Indian Division and one from 6th Armoured Division were answered.†

On 8th June calls came from 26th Armoured Brigade, 19th Indian Brigade and 6th Armoured Division, all of which were

---

* Rover David is explained in Part I of this Volume (H.M.S.O. 1984) p. 205.

† *AOK 10's* report for the 7th stated that because the bridge at Narni and the roads at Terni had been so badly damaged by air attack, it was impossible to predict when 14th Panzer Corps' move would be complete.

answered, the targets being infantry, support weapons, a defended locality, guns and 100 parked M.T. From the 9th onwards, because of high aircraft casualties from flak, strafing attacks were forbidden which resulted in reduced claims of M.T. destroyed and damaged. Three calls for assistance were answered on the 9th, one mission being briefed by Rover David, and exceptionally good results were reported in each case. The bad weather then began to affect flying over the battle area, but on the 12th three calls for assistance were answered, the targets being tanks, M.T. and guns. On the 14th, too, and despite bad weather, Rover David directed three missions in support of 6th South African Armoured Division, and did so again on the 15th on which day a call from 1st Guards Brigade was also answered.[118] On the 16th no enemy movement was seen on 8th Army's front until 8 p.m. when three concentrations of 100 vehicles each were found by armed reconnaissance aircraft heading back to base. With little petrol left in their tanks they were unable to attack on a large scale but did enough to claim a considerable number of vehicles destroyed and damaged. During the remaining three days of this First Phase on 8th Army's front very bad weather, followed by waterlogging of the airfields, drastically reduced flying, the fighter-bombers, for example, being grounded completely on the 18th and 19th. The Germans exploited the opportunity to move by day.

(vi)

See Map 2

We left 5th Army at the point when 4th U.S. Corps was about to launch a co-ordinated attack to hustle von Senger's 14th Panzer Corps out of the Albert position on the higher ground beyond the Ombrone river north and north-east of Grosseto.[119] The assault started on 18th June and after two days hard fighting von Senger was authorised to withdraw his weakened divisions back to the Anton Line.[120] Route 1 along the coast became the responsibility of 75th Corps with 16th SS Panzer Grenadier and 19th *Luftwaffe* Division as its principal components.

As the coastline turned westwards again towards Piombino, widening 4th U.S. Corps front once more, Crittenberger brought 1st U.S. Armoured Division back into the line on the inland flank of 36th U.S. Division.[121] He directed the latter to concentrate its advance in a north-westerly direction astride Route 1, while 1st U.S. Armoured Division headed due north on the minor roads through the Metallifere Hills towards Volterra. Crittenberger chose to use his infantry division on the coast and armoured division in the hills to save time in regrouping and because he hoped to outflank the main German positions blocking the coast road by using his armour in this way.[122] 1st U.S. Armoured Division was to experience the same type of frustration that 6th South African and 6th British Armoured Divisions suffered south of Lake Trasimeno.[123] Crittenberger did however stress to both divisional commanders that they were to help each other along by hooking over the inter-divisional boundary when it was profitable to do so.

Despite reinforcement by the veteran 3rd Panzer Grenadier Division from 1st Parachute Corps, between 21st–24th June the rear-guards of 14th Panzer Corps were pushed back so fast that von Senger was unable to stabilise his front on the Anton Line.[124] With Kesselring's sanction, his Corps withdrew during the night of 24th/25th June into a layback position which covered Campiglia and Massa Marittima, abandoning Piombino and Follonica to the Americans. Further transfers from 1st Parachute Corps were authorised, which included that of 26th Panzer Division, but this did not prevent penetration of von Senger's new line which quickly crumbled.

Piombino was entered by U.S. Engineer units on 25th June and was soon opened to Allied supply ships.[125] 36th U.S. Division was relieved by 34th U.S. Division in the coastal sector next day, the former being withdrawn for 'Anvil'. The American regrouping was done so smoothly that 4th U.S. Corps' pressure did not relax and the German rear-guards were tumbled back as fast as ever. This was no reflection upon the dogged determination of the German soldier who had always to be routed out of his delaying positions.[126] His tanks and S.P. guns were the backbone of his defence, and it was the primary task of his infantry to cover these hard-hitting equipments. Tank commanders chose the delaying positions and, however junior they might be, they could order senior infantry commanders to cover the withdrawal of their valuable machines. There were just too few Germans to hold the numbers of men and weight of material available to the Americans who could usually find a way round or blast a way through any position the Germans took up. In these circumstances it was not unreasonable of Lemelsen to demand on 26th June that Kesselring should try to persuade Hitler to give up limited withdrawals in favour of a large scale retreat which would allow the consolidation of the shortest line across Italy instead of the echeloned formation into which Hitler's policy of no voluntary withdrawals had forced the Army Group.[127]

Perturbed by the frailty of *AOK 14's* right wing and the growing risk of an Allied break through to the Arno via Volterra, Kesselring had already on 25th June asked *OKW* for authority to pull Lemelsen's line back to the Cecina river.[128] He was informed on the 26th that in the Führer's view a line which was further back was no better than a line further forward, unless the rear position was strongly fortified. At present, no such line existed and time for its creation could only be gained by giving battle; the casualties inflicted on the enemy would serve to slow up his advance and at the same time free the Germans from the demoralising influence of perpetual retreats. There was to be no voluntary abandonment of territory. Kesselring was then reminded that his Army Group had received 10,000 reinforcements in May, and would receive 15,000 in June. Taking into account the flow of equipment replacements supplied to the Italian Theatre, the performance of *OB Südwest's* formations should, in the Führer's view, soon show a substantial improvement. Although there was no suggestion, as far as is known, that Kesselring should be replaced, he was prepared to admit that his relations with the Führer were at a low ebb. Speaking to von Vietinghoff on the telephone on 24th June about a withdrawal proposed by *AOK 10* he said:

> 'I will not deny that I have similar thoughts . . . but you know the distrust I am facing and if you want to be my successor you have only to let this leak out . . .'[129]

At least Hitler did not demand on 26th June, as he had on the 13th, that Army Group C stand for defence of named positions. Given unimpeachable reasons for withdrawal by 4th U.S. Corps and by the F.E.C. Kesselring accordingly authorised a new main line ('Lilo') behind the Cecina river for *AOK 14* on 28th June.[130] Taking up Lilo was preceded by numerous local withdrawals, as the Americans drove 14th Panzer Corps out of Campiglia and Massa Marittima, and von Senger lost ground as well on his left wing. Despite German demolitions and some counter-attacks, 4th U.S. Corps continued to advance steadily northwards and was approaching the Cecina river by 29th June. By 2nd July it was over the river and was probing the German defences of Lilo, preparatory to a further advance on Leghorn, Pisa and the River Arno.

This was not the only Allied thrust to worry Lemelsen. On 22nd June the F.E.C. began to attack the positions held by Schlemm's 1st Parachute Corps on the Orcia river sector of the Albert Line.[131] 3rd Algerian and 2nd Moroccan Infantry Divisions made little headway before the 25th, but that day they threw the German rear-guards back across the Orcia and struck vigorously towards Route 2, leading to Siena. The brunt of a hard fight was borne by 29th Panzer Grenadier Division, and as the exhausted 90th Panzer Grenadier Division could not hold the thrusts of 1st U.S.

Armoured Division the right wing of 1st Parachute Corps had to be withdrawn. With Lemelsen clamouring for the straightening of his Army's front, on 28th June Kesselring extended *AOK 10's* front westwards to Montepulciano and authorised the withdrawal of 1st Parachute Corps to Lilo which on Schlemm's front skirted south of Volterra and south of Siena to Montepulciano.[132] In the same directive he stated that from 5th July *AOK 10* and *AOK 14* would be responsible for their respective sectors of the Gothic Line. Kesselring was clearly beginning to plan ahead. But there could be no change in tactics without Hitler's approval, and while 14th Panzer Corps scrambled into its sectors of the Lilo Line 1st Parachute Corps was forced back to Siena.

The city of Siena was lucky. Neither side wished any damage to be done to its historic buildings and monuments. On 29th June Kesselring instructed Lemelsen to avoid fighting in the city.[133] He was to prevent a French thrust through it by heavy mining of the outskirts. By this time 1st Parachute Corps' strength was too low to hold the city anyway and it was evacuated during the night 2nd/3rd July. General de Gaulle, as leader of the Free French, had also promised Pope Pius XII that the French would spare the city.[134] Juin, therefore, manoeuvred to outflank it. On 3rd July the Algerians entered an undamaged Siena.

See Map 1

We left 8th Army with 13th Corps driving 76th Panzer Corps' rear-guards into the Albert Line west of Lake Trasimeno and 10th Corps doing the same east of the lake, having taken Perugia on 20th June. The advance on Chiusi had shown that the Chiusi–Sinalunga road could not, by itself, support the weight of traffic of 13th Corps.[135] On 18th June Leese therefore amended his orders. 10th Corps was deprived of Route 71 and ordered to advance up the Tiber valley north of Perugia, capture Sansepolcro and strike at Arezzo from the east. 13th Corps was given both roads and was to advance on Arezzo from the south, using the Chiana valley, which, though wider and flatter than the Tiber valley, was cut up by streams and irrigation ditches. Unfortunately the axes of the two Corps were separated initially by the waters of Lake Trasimeno, and subsequently by the mountain watershed which separates the two valleys. There would be no firm contact until Arezzo was taken and thereafter the axes of the two corps would diverge again either side of the high Pratomagno massif, as they followed the road leading to Florence through the Middle Arno

valley and the road to Bibbiena in the Upper Arno valley.* There
would be little opportunity for mutual support between 8th Army's
two corps.

The order of battle of 8th Army at the beginning of the Battle
of Lake Trasimeno was:[136]

10th Corps (Right)

6th Armoured Division	26th Armoured Brigade
(Left)	1st Guards Brigade
	61st Infantry Brigade
8th Indian Division (Right)	17th Indian Infantry Brigade
	19th Indian Infantry Brigade
	21st Indian Infantry Brigade
3rd Hussars	attached from 9th Armoured Brigade

13th Corps (Left)

6th South African	11th S.A. Armoured Brigade
Armoured Division (Left)	12th S.A. Motorised Brigade
	24th Guards Brigade
78th Division (Right)	11th Infantry Brigade
	36th Infantry Brigade
	38th (Irish) Infantry Brigade
	9th Armoured Brigade (less 3rd Hussars)
	11th Canadian Armoured Regiment

In 13th Corps Reserve

4th Division	10th Infantry Brigade
	12th Infantry Brigade
	28th Infantry Brigade
	1st Canadian Armoured Brigade (less 11th Canadian Armoured Regiment)

A further regrouping would become necessary at the end of June
when 78th Division was due to leave the Italian Theatre for a
prolonged rest and refit in the Middle East.

See Map 3

The country ahead of 13th Corps as it pushed back 76th Panzer
Corps' rear-guards between Chiusi and Lake Trasimeno consisted

---

* The course of the Arno should be noted. From Pisa to Florence it is called the Lower
Arno; from Florence south-eastwards to its great bend just north of Arezzo it is the Middle
Arno; and from Arezzo north to its source in the Apennines above Bibbiena it is the Upper
Arno.

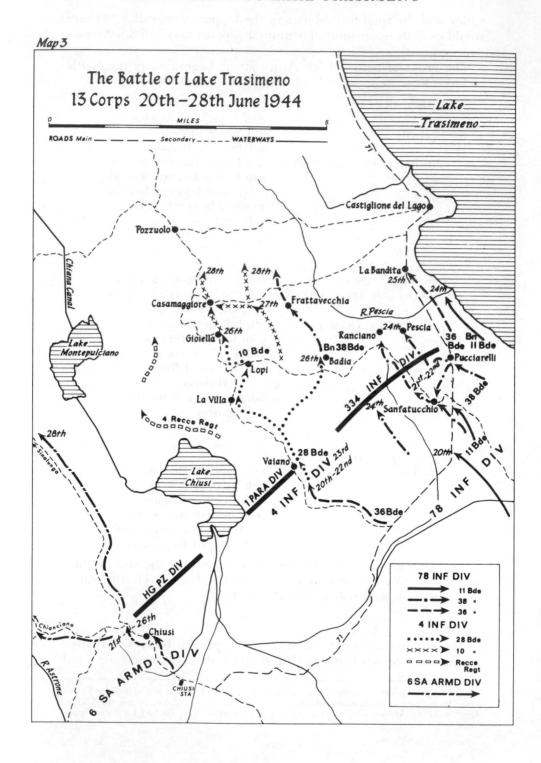

Map 3

The Battle of Lake Trasimeno
13 Corps 20th – 28th June 1944

of a belt of rolling hills with ridges running east and west to a depth of some fifteen miles.[137]

The area was highly cultivated with fields of growing crops and vineyards which gave cover to the defender and obstructed the attacker. Numerous small villages and farms provided useful defended localities with good observation because most of them were on the ridges. The roads, apart from Route 71, were little more than lightly built farm tracks which threaded their way between farms and villages. In the valley bottoms streams and irrigation channels tended to be tank obstacles and the bridges and culverts over them easy demolition targets. Each mile was so like another that map reading was difficult, making fighting confused and confusing. It was ideal country for defence in depth and could only be penetrated by steady crumbling actions, designed to gnaw a way through the German defences.

The Trasimene Line, as it was known to the British, was anchored in the east to the south-west corner of Lake Trasimeno and in the west to the high ground upon which Chiusi stood. The Chiusi ridge constituted a very strong natural defensive position which rose sharply from the lower ground south and east of the town. The steepness of the slopes and the absence of usable roads, together with the small but awkward obstacle of the Astrone river, made it difficult to outflank the Chiusi position from the west. The German defensive line between the Lake and Chiusi was based on a series of dug-in localities on the high ground astride the Pescia river, which had been artificially improved to make it an effective anti-tank obstacle. The main defence line incorporated the villages of Frattavecchia, Casamaggiore and Gioiella and extended to the northern shore of Lake Montepulciano due north of Chiusi. Forward of this main line was a further series of well prepared battle outposts which included the hamlets of Pescia, Ranciano, Badia and Lopi; and further south still there was the covering position along the ridge between Sanfatucchio and Vaiano, extending to the eastern shore of Lake Chuisi, which 78th Division had come up against on 19th June.

The whole position was thus in considerable depth, secure on both flanks and adequately dug in to assist protracted defence. It was backed by a high proportion of anti-tank guns, mortars and *nebelwerfer*, sited well forward to obtain maximum range, and by a powerful artillery. But as the South African historians aptly point out: 'the great difficulty about the Trasimene Line was that nobody knew where it was supposed to be—not even the Germans!'[138]

Three German divisions and part of a fourth held the sector west of the lake. 334th Infantry Division occupied the covering position from the lake shore through Sanfatucchio to excluding

Vaiano.[139] The 1st Parachute Division, seriously depleted by casualties, was positioned between Vaiano and Lake Chiusi. West and south of this lake, holding the town of Chiusi and the ridge on which it stands, was the Hermann Göring Panzer Division, with 356th Infantry Division of *AOK 14's* 1st Parachute Corps on its right flank astride the Sarteano-Chianciano road.

When General Kirkman, commanding 13th Corps, decided on 21st June that a Corps attack would be necessary to break through the Trasimene defences,[140] he arranged to bring forward 4th Division from reserve to strengthen the assault and deployed it south of Vaiano, with orders to take over from the left hand brigade of 78th Division on the night 22nd/23rd June. He instructed all three divisions (78th, 4th and 6th South African Armoured) to continue their advance, 78th Division on Route 71, 4th Division by the Vaiano-Gioiella road, and 6th South African Division by the Chiusi-Sinalunga road running north on the west side of the Chiana Canal. He envisaged 4th Division taking over the whole of the eastern sector of the front from 78th Division if the battle was still being fought when the latter had to be withdrawn at the end of June.*

---

* Outline Order of Battle of 4th Division (Major-General A. D. Ward)
  10th Infantry Brigade
      2nd Bedfordshire and Hertfordshire Regiment, 1st/6th East Surrey Regiment, 2nd Duke of Cornwall's Light Infantry
  12th Infantry Brigade
      2nd Royal Fusiliers, 6th Black Watch, 1st Royal West Kents
  28th Infantry Brigade
      2nd Kings's Liverpool Regiment, 2nd Somerset Light Infantry, 2nd/4th Hampshire Regiment
  R.A.C. 4th Reconnaissance Regiment
  R.A. 22nd, 30th, 77th Field Regiments; 14th A/Tk Regiment; 91st L.A.A. Regiment
  R.E. 7th, 59th, 225th Field Companies; 18th Field Park Company
  M.G. 2nd Northumberland Fusiliers

  Additional troops

  1st Canadian Armoured Brigade
      11th, 12th and 14th Canadian Armoured Regiments

  Outline Order of Battle of 78th Division (Major-General C. F. Keightley)
  11th Infantry Brigade
      2nd Lancashire Fusiliers, 1st East Surrey Regiment, 5th Northamptonshire Regiment
  36th Infantry Brigade
      5th Buffs, 6th Royal West Kent Regiment, 8th Argyll and Sutherland Highlanders
  38th Infantry Brigade
      6th Royal Inniskilling Fusiliers, 1st Royal Irish Fusiliers, 2nd London Irish Rifles
  R.A.C. 56th Reconnaissance Regiment
  R.A. 17th, 132nd, 138th Field Regiments; 64th A/Tk Regiment; 49th L.A.A. Regiment
  R.E. 214th, 237th, 256th Field Companies; 281st Field Park Company
  M.G. 1st Kensington Regiment

  Additional troops

  9th Armoured Brigade
      3rd Hussars, Royal Wiltshire Yeomanry, Warwickshire Yeomanry
      1st Regiment R.H.A.

While 4th Division deployed in the centre during 21st and 22nd June, 78th Division continued to probe the enemy defences round Sanfatucchio.[141] 334th Infantry Division resisted stubbornly, counter-attacking any gains and bringing down heavy defensive fire with artillery and *nebelwerfer*. 11th Brigade of 78th Division led the attacks on the Sanfatucchio ridge.[142] The 2nd Lancashire Fusiliers succeeded by dawn on the 21st in securing a foothold in the southern fringe of Sanfatucchio village. The 2nd London Irish Rifles (38th Brigade) supported by a regiment of tanks from 1st Canadian Armoured Brigade reinforced the attack during the morning and the village was cleared by noon after close hand to hand fighting.[143] The Germans counter-attacked violently, but without success, throughout the following night. Further to the east 6th Inniskillings, also supported by Canadian tanks, secured the hamlet of Pucciarelli during the 21st and the next morning attacked westwards down the ridge against enemy still holding on around Sanfatucchio. This breached the German outpost line but they continued to counter-attack without success and with heavy loss.

At the western end of the Corps' front the Imperial Light Horse from 11th South African Armoured Brigade failed to gain an entry into Chiusi town at their first attempt due to strong opposition from the Hermann Göring Panzer Division.[144] The Brigade then staged an attack on the town during the night 21st/22nd June, 1st City of Capetown Highlanders advancing from Chiusi railway station with an armoured regiment operating on each flank. One company of the Capetown Highlanders broke through into Chiusi but was violently counter-attacked and could not be reinforced. After a gallant resistance the company was overrun during the morning of the 22nd. The South Africans succeeded, however, in closing up to and blocking the western road exit from Chiusi towards Chianciano. Further west 24th Guards Brigade made slow progress much hampered by indifferent tracks which were rendered almost impassable by the heavy rain.[145] By 23rd June the Brigade was still two miles south of the Astrone river line but was about to enter Sarteano on 8th Army's extreme western flank.

During 22nd and 23rd June 78th Division consolidated its gains round Sanfatucchio.[146] *AOK 10* reckoned that the British were licking their wounds as casualties had been heavy on both sides. 334th Infantry Division was singled out for its staunchness, its reconnaissance battalion and its 754th Grenadier Regiment having lost a third and a half of their fighting strength respectively. At dawn on 24th June 78th Division attacked again, 38th Brigade aiming to secure the hamlets of Pescia and Ranciano and the line of the Pescia river.[147] 36th Brigade was held ready to move across the river and advance to the line of the lateral road running from Castiglione del Lago to Casamaggiore. On 78th Division's left 28th Brigade (4th Division) advanced on Vaiano.[148]

The Royal Irish Fusiliers secured Pescia hamlet by 10 a.m. and Ranciano by 4 p.m. and with the Inniskillings and 5th North-amptons in line on their right reached the Pescia river during the evening.[149] The Pescia was found to be impassable for wheels or tracks without bridging but 5th Buffs moved over unsupported and established a bridgehead.[150] The engineers worked all night in a heavy thunderstorm to repair a demolished bridge carrying Route 71 over the river and had it ready for use by 5 a.m. on the 25th. Unfortunately the tanks of the Wiltshire Yeomanry, earmarked to support the further advance north of the Pescia, had bogged down in the muddy ground and did not cross until 9.30 a.m. by which time the Royal West Kents and 8th Argylls of 36th Brigade had reached La Bandita where they had been checked for want of armoured support. This advance brought 36th Brigade to within sight of its objective, the Castiglione del Lago–Casamaggiore lateral road, and also up against the main German defensive position. Here the battered troops of 334th Infantry Division were reinforced by a battalion from 1st Parachute Division and one from 15th Panzer Grenadier Division, the latter formation being earmarked on 25th June to move round from the eastern side of Lake Trasimeno to bolster the defence.[151]

78th Division's western flank was now somewhat exposed and it was decided to halt and consolidate until 4th Division had fought its way forward on the left and could bring added pressure to bear.[152] 28th Brigade, leading 4th Division, had had a hard fight to clear Vaiano where the much depleted but still tenacious 1st Parachute Division was fighting with its usual stubborness.[153] Threatened by the advance of 78th Division across the Pescia river, the Germans withdrew on 25th June from Vaiano and fell back towards their main line of resistance on the Casamaggiore-Fratta-vecchia ridge. 28th Brigade moved forward on a two battalion front, 2nd/4th Hampshires on the left making for Gioiella and the Somerset Light Infantry on the right for Badia, to establish contact with the left wing of 78th Division. There was a stiff fight for Gioiella, eventually taken by 2nd King's, who came up to support the Hampshires after dark on 26th June. Badia fell to the Somersets the same day. Meanwhile further to the west 4th Reconnaissance Regiment was probing round the north shore of Lake Chiusi, threatening the German withdrawal routes from Chiusi itself.[154] This persuaded the Hermann Göring Panzer Division that the time had come to give up the town which was evacuated during the night 25th/26th.[155] The South Africans entered it the following morning. Demolished bridges and cratered roads rendered any swift pursuit northwards by the South African Armoured Brigade impracticable. One armoured regiment was despatched to follow up along the Sinalunga road while the rest of the brigade attacked west along the north bank of the Astrone river to help 24th Guards Brigade, which was still held up by this obstacle.[156]

During the 27th, 10th Brigade of 4th Division, supported by a regiment of Canadian armour, passed through 28th Brigade and concentrated near Lopi in readiness to assault the ridge between Casamaggiore and Frattavecchia the following day.[157] Assisted by 2nd Lancashire Fusiliers from 78th Division on their right, 10th Brigade, with 2nd Duke of Cornwall's Light Infantry and 2nd Bedfords, cleared the ridge, the village of Casamaggiore falling to 1st/6th East Surreys in the late evening of 28th June. Further right the Lancashire Fusiliers entered Frattavecchia and dug in north of the Casamaggiore road the same night.[158] The main German line of resistance had been breached.

13th Corps' success was bought at high cost. In the last two weeks of June, for instance, 11th Brigade had suffered 257 casualties and 38th Brigade 621.[159] In the latter 6th Inniskillings had to be disbanded after 78th Division's withdrawal from the line and the survivors were sent to 2nd Inniskillings. 1st Royal Irish Fusiliers ended the battle under the command of its Adjutant as it had no field officers left.

West of Lake Chiusi 6th South African Armoured Division was on the move again.[160] After crossing the Astrone river 24th Guards Brigade reached Chianciano and 11th South African Armoured Brigade pushed past Lake Montepulciano on 29th June. Later the same day Montepulciano town was entered by the Scots Guards, two days after the F.E.C. had taken S. Quirico on Route 2 (*Map 2*).[161] When the French entered Siena on 3rd July, 13th Corps had nosed its way up the Chiana valley and was moving through Cortona, 15 miles south of Arezzo.[162]

13th Corps' success in forcing its way through the Albert Line west of Lake Trasimeno cannot be ascribed entirely to its own efforts. As we have seen *AOK 14* was in dire straits in the last few days of June and had been forced back to the Cecina river by 4th U.S. Corps and to the gates of Siena by the French. It was with the greatest reluctance that *AOK 10* conformed. Herr, commanding 76th Panzer Corps, told von Vietinghoff on the afternoon of 28th June that as his divisions fighting west of Lake Trasimeno seemed still to have control of the battle he was extremely unwilling to 'leave the lake'.[163] He appreciated, however, that this was inevitable if the dangerous situation on the inter-Army boundary was not to be exacerbated. On the evening of 29th June von Vietinghoff told Kesselring he was 'rather sad to have to go back'. *OB Südwest* assured him that he was too, but as things were not going well 'over there' (on *AOK 14's* front) *AOK 10* must watch its flanks. Thus at the end of the battle of Lake Trasimeno, *AOK 10* was more inclined to ascribe its withdrawal to the problems of *AOK 14* than to any breach made in its sector of the Albert Line by 13th Corps, although it acknowledged that the casualties of formations such as 334th Infantry Division were heavy.[164]

See Maps 1 and 2

10th Corps' operations east of Lake Trasimeno were in a relatively low key. General McCreery's intention, subsequent to the capture of Perugia, was to strike north up the Tiber valley with 8th Indian Division making for Sansepolcro.[165] Having first established a firm base astride Route 75 6th Armoured Division had the dual role of exploiting north-west from Perugia to cut Route 71 at the north-western corner of Lake Trasimeno and of advancing north to secure the high ground of Mt Tezio (Pt 961) to protect the left flank of 8th Indian Division. 12th Lancers were to range over the roads running east from the Tiber valley as a reconnaissance and protective screen. Neither division could undertake these tasks for long. H.Q. 8th Army had already decided that at the end of June 6th Armoured Division was to relieve the hard worked 78th Division in 13th Corps and that 10th Indian Division should relieve 8th Indian Division, which also needed rest and refit after nearly nine months of continuous fighting.[166]

8th Indian Division attacked on the east side of the Tiber valley with some success on 26th June, catching 114th Jäger Division off balance and inflicting severe losses on one of its regiments.[167] von Vietinghoff expressed his displeasure to General Feuerstein, commanding 51st Mountain Corps, telling him that it was impermissible for a German Division to be 'overrun by Indians'. 114th Jäger Division must be inculcated with the toughness of its colleagues west of Lake Trasimeno. To be fair to the Jäger Division there was no break through and it did stop the Indian advance by counter-attack. 6th Armoured Division was less successful as it lacked enough infantry for what was virtually mountain warfare. It reached but did not take Magione on the lake shore before it was withdrawn from the line.

When 10th Indian Division moved up from Army Reserve and took over 10th Corps' front, elements of 8th Indian Division remained behind to protect its eastern flank at Foligno, and 9th

Armoured Brigade arrived to provide tank support.* The relief of 6th Armoured and 8th Indian Divisions was carried out between 28th June and 1st July.[168]

10th Indian Division started its advance on 30th June, just as the Germans were readjusting their front at the end of the battle of Lake Trasimeno.[170] Eight miles were gained up the Tiber valley by 2nd July. A short stand was made on the Mt Acuto–Mt Corona (Pt 920–Pt 693) ridge south of Umbertide and west of the Tiber, which a brigade attack had to be launched to clear on the night of the 2nd/3rd. Umbertide itself was entered without opposition on 5th July and on the following day 10th Indian Division met stubborn resistance from German positions along the line of the Nestore river and south of the Montone–Carpini lateral road, on which 51st Mountain Corps clearly intended to stand.

On the Adriatic coast the Polish Corps was placed under command of 8th Army on 29th June and continued to make preparations for its assault on Ancona which Anders now hoped to launch on 13th July.[171] This date was subsequently further postponed until 17th July and, therefore belongs to the story of the next phase of Alexander's advance from Rome to the Gothic Line. Both Allied and German strategic policies were to suffer transformation before the Poles eventually attacked.

During this Second Phase of tactical air support, 20th June–3rd July, the air effort within the battle area dropped steeply. Just under half of the estimated 892 bomber and fighter-bomber sorties flown were devoted to M.T. and the balance was shared between artillery (166 tons or so), railways (some 66 tons) and miscellaneous targets like headquarters and troops caught in the open.[172]

---

* *Outine Order of Battle of 10th Indian Division* (Major-General D. Reid)
  10th Indian Infantry Brigade
    1st Durham Light Infantry, 4/10th Baluch Regiment, 2nd/4th Gurkha Rifles
  20th Indian Infantry Brigade
    8th Manchester Regiment, 3rd/5th Mahratta Light Infantry, 2nd/3rd Gurkha Rifles
  25th Indian Infantry Brigade
    1st Kings Own Royal Regiment, 3rd/1st Punjab Regiment, 3rd/18th Royal Garhwal Rifles
  Reconnaissance: Skinner's Horse
    M.G. 1st Royal Northumberland Fusiliers
    R.A. 68th, 97th, 154th Field Regiments, 13th A/Tk Regiment
    I.E. 5th, 10th, 61st Field Companies, 41st Field Park Company, 'A' Indian Bridging Section

Unfortunately the weather was not favourable to direct air support during 8th Army's attack on the Trasimene Line. On 8th Army's front, when on the 21st there was some improvement, five calls for assistance were answered. The weather worsened during the next two days, and only two calls were answered on the 22nd and three on the 23rd, when a further two calls for assistance had to be refused. On the 24th it was possible for Rover David, operating on the axis of the leading division to use the Cabrank* seven times aided by an Observation Post at Panicale. Targets included guns, enemy headquarters and strongly defended localities. The results were reported as 'good'. On the 25th the Desert Air Force airfields were waterlogged until early afternoon. Thereafter seven calls for assistance from army formations were answered, Rover David helping in directing two of them. On the 26th, two regimental headquarters of the Hermann Göring Panzer Division were claimed well hit by Kittyhawk fighter-bombers of No. 239 Wing R.A.F. The weather on 8th Army's front on the 27th seems to have been much better than elsewhere, and six calls for assistance were answered. In the late evening Rover David operated three Cabrank missions. Next day, the 28th, the chief interest for the fighter-bombers of D.A.F. centred on the Rimini–Forli railway line well north of the battle area. These operations are described later, but within the battle area that day four calls for assistance were answered and Rover David directed attacks on to five targets consisting of strongpoints and an Observation Post in a tower. The Rimini–Forli railway line still claimed pride of place for the fighter-bombers on the 29th, but within the battle area four calls for assistance were answered. On the 30th tactical reconnaissance aircraft reported a target of 50 M.T. and another of 20 M.T., and as a result of attacks on them, and other M.T. elsewhere, 33 were claimed destroyed and 25 damaged. Six calls for assistance were also answered. This day proved a tragic one for Rover David's crew. A delayed action bomb wounded two officers, and four other ranks were missing believed killed.[173] Nevertheless, by the end of June the policy of having a mobile Rover David had proved itself. On occasions when 13th Corps was temporarily held up, Rover David came into action quickly and effectively. On the first day of July some of the Desert Air Force fighter-bombers reverted to attacks on rolling stock, but within the battle area five calls for assistance were answered, the targets being mostly guns, and some tanks. On 2nd July, the last day of this Second Phase, some of the fighter-bombers and fighters occupied themselves with armed reconnaissance of roads and railways within

---

* For an explanation of the Cabrank method see Part I of this Volume *op. cit.* p. 68n.

the battle area, claiming seven M.T. destroyed and 33 damaged, as well as five railway trucks and one locomotive destroyed.*

The effects of the Allies' dominance of the air on the movements of German troops and supplies have been noted. On 27th June, when reporting to *OKW* on the state of Army Group C, Kesselring mentioned that this factor was having a depressing effect on his divisions.[175]

---

* To appreciate the importance accorded each type of target attacked in Italy, the approximate number of sorties flown against and bombloads dropped on each type of target during the period 5th June–17th July are given in Table I at the end of this chapter.[174]

AIR FORCE	Railway targets	N	TOTALS
M.A.S.A.F. H.B. (Day)	1,664 (3,739.1)	5.8)	2,816 (6,216.0)
M.A.S.A.F. H.B. (Night)	57 (164.8)	7.4)	96 (265.6)[1]
M.A.S.A.F. M.B. (Night)	270 (501.4)	48.7)	443 (816.9)[2]
M.A.T.A.F. M.B. (Day)	3,794 (6,429.6)	1,306.5)	5,613 (9,194.5)
M.A.T.A.F. M.B. (Night)		21.4)	21 (28.7)
M.A.C.A.F. M.B. (Night)	3 (5.1)		6 (10.1)
M.A.T.A.F. L.B. (Day) 202.6	582 (467.1)		1,157 (905.3)
M.A.T.A.F. L.B. (Night)	85 (55.0)	35 .6)	626 (415.9)
M.A.T.A.F. F.B. (Day)	5,049 (2,202.6)	2,593.1)	8,566 (3,708.1)
M.A.S.A.F. F.B. (Day)	56 (22.2)		69 (25.5)
M.A.C.A.F. F.B. (Day)	94 (20.8)	21.7)	182 (39.1)
M.A.C.A.F. F.B. (Night)	21 (4.7)		25 (5.6)
TOTALS	11,675 (13,612.4)	4,345.2)	19,620 (21,631.3)
M.A.S.A.F. H.B. (Night)			5 (13.4)
M.A.S.A.F. M.B. (Night)			73 (146.8)[3]
M.A.T.A.F. M.B. (Day)	40 (69.4)	59.6)	720 (1,241.0)
M.A.T.A.F. L.B. (Day)	12 (10.7)	150.5)	492 (379.0)
M.A.T.A.F. L.B. (Night)	21 (20.1)	204.5)	459 (325.0)
M.A.T.A.F. F.B. (Day)	902 (430.2)	3,606.7)	6,635 (2,735.6)
TOTALS	975 (530.4)	4,711.3)	8,384 (4,840.8)
GRAND TOTALS	12,650 (14,142.8)	9,066.5)	28,004 (26.472.1)

NOTES [1] Excludes a total of 36 flare dropping sorties
[2] Excludes a total of 4 flare dropping sorties
[3] Excludes a total of 14 flare dropping sorties

CHAPTER X

THE APPROACH TO THE
GOTHIC LINE
(3rd July to 4th August 1944)

(i)

JULY 1944 was a disappointing month for the Allies and conversely provided some, though not many, crumbs of encouragement for the Germans. The operations of Montgomery's 21st Army Group were not progressing as fast as expected. Apart from von Rundstedt's and Rommel's success in containing the Allies' Normandy bridgehead, a great channel storm of unseasonable intensity had raged from 19th to 22nd June and had seriously delayed the Allied build up, bringing with it fears of stalemate in Normandy.[1] The storm was perhaps the last straw in the 'Anvil' debate. In any event on 23rd June General Eisenhower cabled to the Combined Chiefs of Staff, recommending:

'A. That "Anvil" be launched not later than August 30th and preferably by August 15th, either on the scale desired by General Wilson assuming that the resources can be made available, or with lesser acceptable resources.

B. That if "Anvil" can *not* be launched by August 30th with sufficient strength all French divisions plus one or two American divisions previously allocated for "Anvil" be made available for "Overlord" as soon as shipping and port capacity permit their transportation and maintenance . . .'[2]

On 2nd July the Combined Chiefs of Staff made known their decision in favour of 'Anvil' to General Wilson, as a result of which he issued a new directive to Alexander on 5th July:[3]

'1. . . . As from receipt of this telegram overriding priority for all resources in the Mediterranean Theatre as between Operation 'Anvil' and the battle in Italy is given to Operation 'Anvil' to the extent necessary to complete a build up of 10 divisions in the South of France.

2. . . . For your guidance it is not planned to remove from your command for this purpose more than three U.S. divisions

and four French divisions together with their necessary Corps, Army and Service troops. Further it is proposed to allocate to your command 92nd U.S. (Coloured) Infantry Division and a Brazilian Infantry Division . . .

3. Your task will continue to be the destruction of the German forces in Italy. To this end:

(a) You will advance through the Apennines and seize the line of the River Po to secure the area Ravenna–Bologna– Modena to the coast covering Leghorn. Should the situation permit you should also bear in mind the importance of denying to the enemy the important road centre of Piacenza.

(b) Thereafter you will advance north of the Po and secure the line Venice–Padua–Verona–Brescia. It is appreciated that these manoeuvres, coupled with the advance of "Anvil" formations up the Rhone Valley, will almost certainly result in the clearance of North-West Italy of all German formations without the necessity of undertaking an offensive in that direction.

6. Air C.-in-C. has been requested to afford you maximum air support consistent with the overriding priority given to "Anvil" '.

See Map 4

Alexander and his Army Commanders, although acutely disappointed by this decision, were not taken by surprise. They had been planning for two possible courses of action. On 19th June Lieutenant-General Harding, Alexander's Chief of Staff, had circulated a detailed appreciation and plan (*C.G.S. Appreciation No. 3*) for breaching the Gothic Line with 5th and 8th Armies attacking side by side between Route 64–Bologna and Route 67–lateral to Faenza.[4] This plan was discussed at Advanced H.Q. A.A.I. on 23rd June during a conference attended by all the principal Army and Air Force Commanders and their Chiefs of Staff.[5] Afterwards both Army Commanders set in hand detailed planning for the final approach to the Gothic Line, regrouping their corps in such a way as to avoid any delay in mounting a full scale assault if one were to be needed. Meanwhile Harding and Major-General Sir Brian Robertson, Alexander's Chief Administrative Officer, had been working on an alternative appreciation (*C.G.S. Appreciation No. 4*) of what could be done if 'Anvil' denuded A.A.I. of 6th U.S. Corps, the F.E.C. and large numbers of important American logistic units such as bulk petroleum installation and pipeline construction battalions, and railway troops.[6] Based on their work, Alexander had written to Wilson on 25th June recommending that he should 'continue the campaign into North-Eastern Italy and

Southern Germany', while every effort was made to 'comb the Mediterranean, Iraq and Persia, India and the U.K. for land and air forces to provide the necessary means'. He added, 'I cannot believe that with the immense Allied resources we cannot find the comparatively small increase in air forces required?'.[7] He felt the same about logistic units, and he made a special plea to be allowed to keep 2nd Parachute Brigade to secure crossings over the River Po as soon as he was through the Gothic defences.

On 1st July Alexander learnt that 'Anvil' was likely to go against him in a signal sent by the C.I.G.S., Field-Marshal Sir Alan Brooke, who went on to suggest that he should return home to discuss further plans.[8] By 2nd July Harding had finalised Appreciation No. 4.[9] In it he estimated that the Germans had 12 to 14 equivalent divisions* in Italy and a further 6 to 7 available in Germany and south-eastern Europe which might be used as reinforcements. Against these 18 to 21 German divisions A.A.I. could muster 18 divisions: 14 infantry and 4 armoured. There were also 7 independent armoured brigades, but he pointed out that these were 'supporting formations in this type of terrain' and could not therefore be 'lumped together and assessed as equivalent divisions for tactical purposes, any more than corps and army artillery'. He envisaged a three phase advance for each of which at least 18 divisions would be needed:

> '*First Phase*: penetration of the Rimini–Pisa line, followed by exploitation to secure bridgeheads over the Po.
> *Second Phase*: advance across the Adige to the general line Padua–Vicenza–Verona and exploit to the line of the Piave.
> *Third Phase*: force the crossing of the Piave and exploit to secure the Ljubljana Gap'.

In Harding's view, Alexander would need to rest and refit one third of his force at any one time to keep the offensive rolling; 'consequently six additional divisions' were needed, 'and to maintain a proper balance between infantry and armour these six formations should be infantry divisions'. He suggested they should be found by retaining 78th Division in Italy and dispatching 52nd Division from the United Kingdom, 6th Indian Division from the Persian and Iraq Command, divisions from India which could not be employed in Burma during the monsoon period and U.S. divisions from America which could not be accepted in France.

From the administrative point of view a great deal would depend upon the pace of the advance. The best would be a rapid advance in each phase, thus reducing the degree of destruction executed by the Germans, followed by a distinct pause for the build up of

---

* Calculations based on the estimated effective strength of German formations in Italy.

administrative resources at the end of each phase. 'A slogging advance, without any pause, from the Apennines to the Ljubljana Gap' would be administratively impracticable.

Appreciation No. 4 ended with an assessment of the courses open to both sides and concluded:

> 'The Italian offensive can continue to a limited extent with the forces that remain, but it will soon die out if A.A.I. cannot be reinforced.
> The strategical advantages of continuing it to the logical conclusion of securing the Ljubljana Gap, preparatory to an invasion of southern Germany, are so great that supreme efforts should be made to find the means to enable that to be done'.

Alexander's acceptance of these conclusions set two complementary and concurrent processes in motion: first, the search for additional divisions; and secondly, detailed planning at all levels for the First Phase of the advance towards the Ljubljana Gap, namely breaching the Gothic Line. The search for more troops was to go on for the rest of the Italian campaign as Eisenhower's operations in north-west Europe, the primary theatre, absorbed more and more of the Allies' resources. In this struggle to keep the Italian Theatre alive, Alexander took most of the initiatives. After hearing of the attempt on Hitler's life on 20th July, he cabled to the C.I.G.S.[10]

> 'In view of good news from Germany, what about altering your decision over the two divisions from PAIC [Persia and Iraq Command] and Mideast?'

Brooke's reply was discouraging:

> 'Not clear how news from Germany strengthens your case for these divisions. If it meant an early end to the European war you would surely require less not more troops. In any case political and internal security requirements in Mideast and Persia would not be altered'.[11]

At Staff level, H.Q. A.A.I.'s pressure for reinforcements was well supported by A.F.H.Q.* Concern for the internal security situation in the Middle East made it less easy for the War Office to be as helpful. On 4th July the Middle Eastern branch of the Military Operations' Directorate (M.O.4) noted:[12]

> 'While the internal security situation in the Middle East gives rise to no immediate alarm, it cannot be stated to be satisfactory.
>   In Syria and the Lebanon relations between the French and the Levantine Governments are not good. Difficulties have

---

* The Theatre's efforts to provide reinforcements from within its own resources are described in Part I of this Volume (H.M.S.O. 1984) pp.447–50.

arisen over the transfer of powers to the Native Governments who have stated that if the French continue in their policy of deliberate procrastination, they will obtain their legitimate demands if necessary by force.

In Egypt the recent political crisis did not end in agreement between King Farouk and Nahas Pasha [the Prime Minister] and the latter has warned HMR Cairo that the King is only biding his time and will seize any opportunity when we are embarrassed to precipitate a further crisis.

In Palestine the situation is at all times fraught with potential danger and a considerable garrison is permanently necessary. The collapse of Germany may bring the crisis to a head. Similarly the Jews may take advantage of the absence of British formations from the Middle East to forward more overtly their extremist designs'.

On 14th July the War Office decided that the Middle East garrison could be reduced by one infantry division and one brigade.[13] 78th Division was still to rest and refit there but would be available on call to Alexander without relief. 43rd Gurkha Lorried Infantry Brigade was also released to A.A.I. but with the caveat that the Commander-in-Chief India doubted his ability to keep the brigade reinforced due to shortage of Gurkhali speaking British officers. 52nd Division was not released from the U.K. nor was 6th Indian Division from P.A.I.C.[14]* The U.S. Chiefs of Staff would not provide more than 92nd U.S. Infantry Division and the U.S. equipped Brazilian Division, only one brigade of each of which had arrived in the Mediterranean by late July. Neither division would be completed for some months. A.A.I. was, however, successful in obtaining 3rd Greek Mountain Brigade from the Middle East and a newly formed 66th Brigade (composed of two infantry battalions from Gibraltar and its third previously earmarked for disbandment) to feed the reinforcement pool.[16]

Alexander made three other suggestions of a longer term nature which could help to provide him with more troops in the autumn. He suggested that equipment should be provided to raise three divisions of Italian troops; that a Jewish Brigade, the formation of which was being actively considered, should be employed in Italy; and that in order to raise two more Polish Brigades the necessary British equipment and additional Polish troops, raised from German Army prisoners taken in France, should be sent to Italy; 11,000 such troops, he understood, had been promised to Anders by General Sosnkowski (the Polish Commander-in-Chief).[17]

---

* 52nd Division was first in action in October 1944 during operations to clear the Scheldt estuary.[15]

It was not until mid-August that the Americans would agree that Lend-Lease equipment could be used to equip the Italians.[18] We will be describing the formation of the Jewish Brigade in Part III Chapter XIX when we are considering the build up for the final offensive. The argument about the Poles was no less protracted and went on until October. In the words of the War Office:

> 'The overriding difficulty is not a question of availability of men, but the state of utter confusion which exists amongst the senior Polish officers concerned as to whether troops should be allowed to go to Italy. Three or four conflicting views on this subject have been expressed by General Sosnkowski and others'.[19]

By the end of September agreement had been reached to send 2,200 Polish reinforcements from the United Kingdom, 7,000 ex-German Army Polish prisoners from southern France, and 10,000 Polish civilian volunteers, also from southern France, to build up 2nd Polish Corps in Italy.[20] Some 5,500 Polish reinforcements had reached Italy by mid-October.[21]

Alexander received one welcome windfall. After 'Diadem' most commanders in Italy had concluded that the standard armoured division of one armoured and one infantry brigade was too light in infantry for the difficult Italian terrain. General Burns, commanding 1st Canadian Corps, drew the attention of the Canadian Military Headquarters to the need for a second infantry brigade for 5th Canadian Armoured Division.[22] Alexander supported Burns, but the C.I.G.S. ruled against any 'diversions from Overlord'. Nevertheless, Burns was allowed to raise 12th Canadian Infantry Brigade in July and August from Canadian resources in Italy.

In the end Alexander's persistence produced almost the equivalent of the six extra divisions which Harding estimated would be needed to continue the Italian campaign. The Middle East provided one infantry division and three brigades (43rd Gurkha Lorried Infantry Brigade, a Greek Brigade and a Jewish Brigade). The Mediterranean garrisons produced 66th Brigade, and the Canadians 12th Infantry Brigade. The three Italian divisions eventually resulted in five operational Italian battle groups; and the Polish reinforcements created the extra infantry brigades for the two existing Polish divisions, thus supplying them with a third brigade which they had lacked so far. All these troops except the Jewish Brigade, the Italians and the Poles would be available by the end of August.[23]

Before considering the problems of breaching the Gothic Line, we must look briefly at the development of German policy for its defence.

(ii)

On the German side there were, at last, some grounds for optimism. The worst had not happened. *AOK 14* had not collapsed entirely, and the Allies had not tried a second Valmontone style thrust across *AOK 10's* Lines of Communications. Hitler's demand for defensive rather than delaying tactics south of the Apennines had been carried out successfully though at some considerable cost. *

Before setting out for his delayed interview with Hitler, Kesselring sent *OKW* on 1st July a summary of the policy which he would be proposing to the Führer, and rehearsed his arguments with von Vietinghoff and Lemelsen at his headquarters near Pistoia.[25] He started by emphasising the costly nature of the step-by-step defensive tactics imposed upon him since the fall of Rome in terms of men and equipment losses. Since further losses on the present scale could place the retention of the Gothic Line at risk, he proposed to revert to delaying tactics as his armies fell back to a new line north of the Arno, called 'Heinrich' on which they would stand until the Gothic Line was fully consolidated. He told his Army Commanders that Heinrich (which was to run along the north bank of the Arno from the river's mouth to just short of Florence, then round the north of the city before turning south-east along the Pratomagno massif to Subbiano on the Upper Arno, and thence to Senigallia on the Adriatic coast) was to be held for some four to six weeks. (*See Map* 1.) As the Adriatic half of the Gothic Line was as yet weakly fortified, additional reserve lines were to be reconnoitred in front of and from behind the main line on *AOK 10's* central and eastern sectors. No date was given for the occupation of Heinrich, but the memorandum for the conference listed numerous intermediate withdrawal lines, the first of which was christened Georg and covered Volterra and Arezzo. When Kesselring left for the Führer's headquarters on 3rd July his Armies were preparing to parry four Allied thrusts: towards Volterra and Poggibonsi; towards Arezzo; up the Tiber valley to Citta di Castello; and along the Adriatic coast to Ancona.

Kesselring was more successful in re-establishing his rapport with Hitler than he dared hope. From the account of their meeting,

---

* On the evidence of the field records, which in the case of *AOK 14* did not extend to monthly breakdowns, this Army lost about 42,500 men from all causes during the three months April–June, as against 37,000 lost by *AOK 10* in the same period.[24] At *OKW*, the total losses of Army Group C were put at just over 80,000 for the period 11th May–5th July, and at 39,000 for the month of July. The latter figure denotes an average daily loss of 1,260, and supports the constant complaints of Lemelsen and von Vietinghoff about the drain on their Armies imposed by the slow fighting withdrawal from the Albert to the Gothic Lines.

which is contained in Jodl's fragmentary War Diary and in that of the German Naval Staff, it appears that mutual confidence was restored, and with it a measure of freedom of action for *OB Südwest*.[26] The Gothic Line was no longer taboo, and, although the Führer continued to insist that every inch of central Italy must be contested, he made the point that Italy was only 'one part' of the Mediterranean Theatre. Any abandonment of territory on the Adriatic wing would bring the Allies closer to the Balkans and to Istria which would be at risk if they reached and penetrated the Apennine defences. Kesselring was reminded of the need to buy time for the production of the new weapons of which so much was expected, and was told that it was the duty of the soldiers on every front to 'fight, defend and hold'. Nevertheless, the subsequent directive to *OB Südwest,* signed by Jodl on 5th July, offered loopholes. Army Group C was still to stand as far south as possible, while at the same time protecting the Ligurian and Adriatic coasts and the Istrian Peninsula from outflanking landings. Time was still needed to strengthen the Gothic Line, 'the last bulwark in front of the plains of Upper Italy', from which the Allies must be kept 'at a distance' by stubborn resistance in order to deny them the important ports of Leghorn and Ancona, and to disrupt their plans for an assault on the western Balkans, for which strong forces would probably be assembled when they reached the Gothic Line. Tactical flexibility was authorised indirectly in that defence south of the Apennines need only be offered in 'suitable terrain', and *OB Südwest* was empowered to permit retreat to the next line of resistance when all available reserves had been exhausted and an Allied break through seemed inevitable. Rear-guards, however, must always be left to give battle between lines of resistance. As regards reinforcements, no fresh formations, other than two Italian divisions trained in Germany for Graziani's command (3rd Infantry and 4th Alpini), could be sent to Italy 'for the time being'.[27]* *OB Südwest's* present divisions were to be kept up to strength and mobile by the allocation of replacement battalions, heavy weapons and, above all, towing vehicles.[28]† It was up to *OB Südwest* to

---

* By early July 1944 four Italian divisions had been raised and were training in Germany for eventual service with Army Group C. In the traumatic circumstances of their meeting on 20th July, Mussolini won Hitler's consent to the early return to Italy of 3rd Marine Infantry Division San Marco and 4th Mountain Division Monte Rosa. By 25th July it had been agreed that these formations, with the German 34th Infantry and 42nd Jäger Divisions from 87th Corps, would form a new Army of Liguria to be commanded by Marshal Rodolfo Graziani, with a German Chief of Staff in the person of General Nagel, C.O.S. 87th Corps.

† Sceptically received in Italy, this assurance presumably constituted Jodl's response to a report from Kesselring of 30th June, which stressed that his Army Group's lack of towing equipment had led to the loss of numerous guns and vehicles which could otherwise have been salvaged.

continue resting and refitting his divisions in rotation on a short-term *ad hoc* basis, preferably in defensive positions close behind the front. Kesselring was also authorised to disband units which had proved unreliable in battle, and to amalgamate those for which reinforcements were not at present available. Supply and Signal units thereby released should be sent back to the Reich for use elsewhere. The directive ended by reiterating that everything possible must be done to consolidate the defences of the Gothic Line and a deep outpost zone in front of it (*Vorfeld*) in which all roads and buildings were to be demolished and 'lavishly' mined.

In response to this directive Kesselring reported to *OKW* on 8th July that he proposed to hold his present front as long as possible before retiring to the Heinrich Line which he would defend.[29] He was satisfied that he could cover the Ligurian coast, which he had decided Graziani's Italian divisions should watch, and the Rimini-Ravenna strip of the Adriatic coast, but he was anxious about Istria for which he could only improvise makeshift arrangements. His full restoration to Hitler's confidence was shown by a marked reduction in meddling directives from *OKW* from this time onwards, and the award of diamonds to his Knight's Cross, which he received on his next visit to Hitler on 19th July, the day before von Stauffenberg's assassination attempt.[30] The *Putsch* of 20th July was to cost many German officers their lives and their commands, but Kesselring's loyalty to his Führer was not in doubt and there were no upheavals on this score within the Italian Theatre.

In accordance with Kesselring's directive of 28th June, *AOK 10* and *AOK 14* became responsible for their respective sectors of the Gothic Line on 5th July.[31] They took over the existing plans from von Zangen's headquarters, which then reverted to Corps status, and overall supervision was given to Kesselring's Chief Engineer, General Hildemann. The two Army Commanders and their staffs tackled their new task very differently. Lemelsen was pre-occupied with the battle for Florence, which we shall describe later, and throughout July showed little interest in the fortifications of *AOK 14*'s sector of the Gothic Line. It was not until 1st August, after three changes in the 'special staff' appointed to handle work on this sector, that it was inspected by a senior staff officer in the person of the Army Chief of Staff, Major-General Hauser. On his return, Hauser reported that the defences 'in no way conformed with requirements', but the measures taken thereafter for their improvement were still less vigorous than those already set in train by *AOK 10*. von Vietinghoff's attitudes and actions reflected German anxiety for the Adriatic sectors of the line which had a sound strategic basis. On the assumption that the Allies could tell from air surveillance how ill-prepared these sectors were, von

Vietinghoff had predicted as early as 16th June that to further their main strategic aim of a break through into the Po valley the Allies would switch their effort to the eastern wing rather than continue with their laborious operations west of the Apennines. A practical result of this concern was that on 23rd June von Vietinghoff secured the services of the Engineer General Bessell, whose experience of field fortifications in Italy went back to the preparation of the Bernhardt Line in 1943, and who, with his own 'special staff', would supervise work on *AOK 10's* sector of the Gothic Line throughout the preparatory period of July and August. That Bessell would find much to do was evident from a report forwarded to Kesselring on 28th June, which set out the findings of a mid-month inspection by a team of officers from the Alpine Training School, Mittenwald. They complained that the line was without depth, lacked emplacements for heavy weapons, and was little more than a chain of light machine gun posts. Fields of fire had not been cleared, anti-tank obstacles were rudimentary and the 'main line' ran across forward slopes. The apparent failure of von Zangen's staffs to appreciate the need to avoid such positions, upon which the Allies always concentrated their artillery fire, was roundly condemned and after von Vietinghoff had himself inspected the line on 12th July he told Kesselring that he had seen things which made him wonder 'if in fact they had been done by soldiers'. Defence systems are, however, invariably criticised by their inheritors, and von Zangen's period of supervision had been continually beset by labour shortages and by Partisan sabotage. These problems were eased by Corps Commanders taking over their sectors on 10th July, and by the close supervision by Bessell and interest of von Vietinghoff, who reinspected the work as did Wentzell, his Chief of Staff, at the end of the month.[32]

There remained the need for greater depth, which was acknowledged by Kesselring when he authorised on 3rd July the reconnaissance of a second line, north of the original, on which the Armies were to start work as soon as they could find the necessary resources of men and material.[33] The approximate trace of the original line, which became known as Green I, and the new line, Green II, are shown on *Map 8*. On the central and eastern sectors with which we will be most concerned, Green I ran along the north bank of the River Foglia from Pesaro on the Adriatic coast to north of Badia Tedalda in the Apennines, above Pieve S. Stefano at the source of the Tiber, and then along the Apennine range to the Futa Pass above Florence on Route 65 to Bologna. It continued to follow the southern peaks of the Apennines until it dropped down to the west coast at Marina di Carrara just south of Spezia. The final trace of Green II started at Riccione on the Adriatic,

skirted the Republic of San Marino to the south, and then ran along the northern slopes of the main Apennine ridge roughly about 12 miles behind Green I.* The *Vorfeld* or covering position was defined on *AOK 10's* front as running from Fano on the Adriatic coast along the hills on the north bank of the Metauro river to Fossombrone, thence across the Apennines to the hills overlooking Sansepolcro, Bibbiena and Pontassieve.

Thus by early July the Gothic Line had a firm place in German planning. Whether adequate fortifications would result depended on how much time would be allowed by the Allies. When considering the merits of Alexander's plan for breaching the Gothic Line, which we discuss in the next chapter, his opponents' need for more time should be borne in mind.

We should also note that at the end of July Hitler began to turn his attention to the foothills of the Alps, in rear of the zone of command of Army Group C. On 27th July he decreed that a line known as *Voralpen*, which on the map ran from the south-eastern corner of Switzerland across the Julian Alps to Monfalcone, was to be prepared for defence, as were additional lines running along the Adige and Piave rivers and across the Istrian plateau.[34] (*End paper* i) These territories lay within the zones of Alpine Foreland and Adriatic Coastland, which were administered by Gauleiters Hofer and Rainer as 'Commissars', and to the vexation of the military it was to them that Hitler gave responsibility for fortification of the Alpine complex.

(iii)

See Map 4

The first major change of policy on the Allied side stemming from the final decision to mount 'Anvil', was the resuscitation of Operation 'Mallory', the destruction of the Po bridges by air action, under the new code name of 'Mallory Major'. Alexander appreciated that, although he still hoped to force a passage through the Gothic Line, he would not have sufficient strength to exploit across the Po without a pause. He decided, therefore, to pin his hopes on being able to bring Kesselring to battle between the Apennines and the Po, driving him back against a bridgeless river.[35] German supply would suffer as well from the loss of the Po bridges. General Clark, who was consulted on 11th July, concurred,

---

* 12 miles behind Green I is a fair generalisation for Green II's alignment on *AOK 10's* front. We do not know the final course of Green II on *AOK 14's* front but can assume it was a similar distance in the rear.

adding the further reason that although 5th Army would try to capture a Class 70 bridge intact over the Po it was unlikely to succeed.[36] It was preferable to destroy all the bridges by air action to create an interdiction line in the Germans' rear.

On the same day Major-General Cannon, Commander M.A.T.A.F., issued his directive for the destruction of all the road and railway bridges, including pontoon bridges, over the Po river.[37]* Initially the medium day bombers were to destroy all rail and road bridges from Piacenza in the west to the Po estuary in the east, and also the combined rail/road bridge over the Trebbia river near Piacenza. The more westerly bridges were to be the responsibility of the Marauders and the remainder would be attacked by the Mitchells. Rail and combined rail/road bridges were to have first priority, road bridges second and pontoon bridges third. Fighter-bombers were to be used to supplement the attacks of the medium day bombers by preventing the Germans repairing damaged bridges and by destroying reserve pontoons stored near existing bridges. The initial allocation of 22 priority targets, west to east, was as follows:

Maurauders (U.S. 42nd Medium Bombardment Wing)
Combined rail/road bridge over the Trebbia river near *Piacenza*
Rail and road bridges at *Piacenza*
Pontoon bridge at *S. Nazzaro*
Combined double-decker rail/road bridge at *Cremona.*
Rail and pontoon bridges at *Casalmaggiore*
Pontoon bridge near *Viadana*
Pontoon bridge near *Guastalla*

Mitchells (U.S. 57th Medium Bombardment Wing)
Rail and pontoon bridges at *Borgoforte*
Pontoon bridge at *S. Nicolo*
Pontoon bridge north of *S. Benedetto*
Combined rail/road bridge at *Ostiglia*
Pontoon bridge at *Sermide*
Pontoon bridge near *Ficarolo*
Rail and road bridges at *Pontelagoscuro*
Pontoon bridge at *Polesella*
Rail and road bridges near *Corbola*
Road bridge at *Taglio*

The dates of the attacks, and the efforts expended in terms of sorties and bombloads on each of these targets, are shown in Tables IV to VI at the end of this chapter. They include concurrent attacks on railway targets north and south of the Po. The locations

---

* This new directive replaced one Cannon had issued on 17th June for Operation 'Mallory', which had lapsed when Alexander decided to establish a bridgehead over the Po river and exploit northwards. The title was changed to 'Mallory Major'.

of all the targets attacked during Operation 'Mallory Major' whether across the Po river, or north or south of it, are shown on *Map 4*.

Operation 'Mallory Major' was an outstanding success. It showed that the main German north-south supply routes could be interdicted where they crossed the Po river. Conversely it also demonstrated that the German south-north retreat routes over the Po river could likewise be cut, as, indeed, they were to be later. The operation was far from straightforward. The main rail route south from the Brenner Pass split into two at Verona and crossed the Po river at Borgoforte and Ostiglia, and the main rail route from the east (Ljubljana-Padua-Bologna) crossed the Po river at Pontelagoscuro (Ferrara). It looked as if these three bridges were the nodal points in the German rail supply system, but the prolific number of diversions available in Italy north of the Po meant that every rail bridge crossing the river had to be put out of action if complete rail interdiction was to be achieved. The construction of some of the bridges also presented problems. Between Turin and the Po estuary all the bridges other than the pontoon variety, were permanently constructed in heavy steel lattice girder, masonry or concrete. None was of the suspension type found in southern France which were comparatively easy to destroy. The strength of the Po bridges was a major challenge to the Mitchells and Marauders of M.A.T.A.F., but the bombers were helped by one important feature of the bridges. Their length varied from 1,000 to 3,700 feet and many had unusually long spans of up to 250 feet. It was believed that, if a span could be blown out of one of these massively constructed bridges, it would never be repaired during the war, and this proved to be the case. The pontoon bridges were, of course, easy to destroy, not only by direct hits but also by near misses which swamped the pontoons or severed the anchor cables. On the other hand they could be repaired or replaced almost as quickly.

Operation 'Mallory Major' took place during 12th–27th July. In the first four days the medium bombers of M.A.T.A.F. concentrated, although not exclusively, on 21 bridges over the Po river (counting combined rail/road bridges as single bridges) from Piacenza to the Po estuary and on the combined rail/road bridge over the Trebbia river near Piacenza, bringing the total to 22 primary targets. 840 sorties were flown and 1,261 tons of bombs dropped. The combined side-by-side rail/road bridge at Ostiglia received the greatest bombload (171.4 tons), next came the rail bridge at Pontelagoscuro (149 tons) and close behind were the combined double-decker rail/road bridge at Cremona (145.9 tons) and the rail bridge at Piacenza (144.3 tons). On the 12th and 13th

July eleven bridges were thought to be impassable, including the pontoon bridge at S. Nazzaro, which was completely destroyed; three other bridges were thought to be half-destroyed; and the rest to have sustained lesser damage. By the 15th, 12 bridges were seen to be completely destroyed or had gaps torn in them of over 500 feet in length; six other bridges were at least cut; and the rest blocked or sufficiently damaged to stop traffic with the exception of the combined rail/road bridge at Ostiglia. After the 15th it was claimed that no north-south rail traffic could cross the Po until 'Mallory Major' was over.

Damage assessments by H.Q. M.A.T.A.F. were based mainly on photographic reconnaissance by the aircraft of M.A.P.R.W. (Mediterranean Allied Photographic Reconnaissance Wing), whose pilots' untiring efforts kept M.A.T.A.F. H.Q. informed daily of the progress of 'Mallory Major'. It is interesting to compare M.A.T.A.F.'s claims based on photographic reconnaissance with information derived from the German Army records, and from Kesselring's daily reports to *OKW*. That for 13th July stated that all the Po bridges from Piacenza to Pontelagoscuro had been hit, and that six rail and two road bridges were expected to be out of action for a considerable time. Other reports confirmed that the road bridge at Piacenza had suffered heavy damage, and that the road bridge at Ficarolo was closed to all but light traffic. The combined rail/road bridge at Cremona and the bridges at Casalmaggiore were also named as targets, and on the 14th Kesselring added to the list the delta bridges at Polesella, Corbola and Taglio, and stated that the road element of the rail/road bridge at Ostiglia was now open. However, after its third pounding the rail bridge over the Po at Piacenza had been completely destroyed. The loss of the bridge, together with the destruction and damage suffered by the other Po bridges, meant that the road element of the combined rail/road bridge at Ostiglia was the only bridge still usable between Ostiglia and the Po estuary. More details of the destruction and damage wrought by M.A.T.A.F.'s Mitchells and Marauders came from *AOK 10* on the 15th. One of the bridges at Casalmaggiore and the pontoon bridge near Ficarolo had been destroyed. Half of the rail bridge at Pontelagoscuro was in the river, and the repair of the road bridge was doubtful because of a shortage of engineers and materials. Additionally the pontoon bridges at Polesella and Sermide, the rail and road bridges at Corbola and the road bridge at Taglio were all badly damaged and out of action. *AOK 10* also confirmed that no bridge over the Po east of Ostiglia was usable. On the 14th Kesselring appealed to *OKW* for fighter reinforcements to meet the threat of an Allied air offensive which, he reckoned, aimed to destroy his main Lines of

Communication. His pleas seem to have gone unanswered, because the G.A.F. fighter force in Italy continued to decline.

In the follow up operations, which began on 16th July, the medium day bombers attacked three bridges over the Po west of Piacenza: the rail bridge at Casale Monferrato, the combined rail/road bridge at Torreberetti and the combined double-decker rail/road bridge at Bressana. Later others were included so that on the 27th the rail bridge at Moncalieri on the western reach of the Po river was attacked, and the rail bridge at Chivasso received its fourth attack. Of those attacked on the 16th, the rail bridge at Casale Monferrato was bombed twice more and the combined rail/road bridge at Torreberetti once more. Three arches of the combined double-decker rail/road bridge at Bressana were claimed destroyed with 65.2 tons of bombs, leaving a 600 foot gap in the structure, and the combined rail/road bridge at Torreberetti was claimed blocked by direct hits. After the rail bridge at Casale Monferrato had succumbed to 74.9 tons of bombs dropped on 16th and 17th July, all south-bound rail traffic from Milan was claimed halted.*

Because some of the damage to the more solidly constructed Po bridges could be repaired quite quickly, it was decided to renew attacks on some of those bombed in the initial stages of the operation before the Germans could move heavy flak for their protection. Some of the bridges were particularly tough, like the rail bridge over the Po at Piacenza which was a combination of two single-track bridges on separate piers. The road bridge over the Trebbia at Piacenza had been claimed almost completely destroyed, but on the 16th the rail bridge, though blocked, had defied the fourth attempt to cut it. On the 19th, 118.3 tons of bombs were dropped on it, followed by another 30.8 tons next day, which completed its destruction. The combined rail/road bridge at Ostiglia was equally tough. Despite six previous attacks it remained partially usable until the 26th, when one span was blown out of the rail section and another out of the road section by 88.2 tons of bombs in two attacks. The rail bridge at Borgoforte took seven attacks before a span was blown out on the 27th during three assaults in which 122.3 tons of bombs were dropped.

These repetitive attacks overwhelmed, temporarily at any rate, the repair facilities at the Germans' disposal. It is hardly surprising that by 23rd July, when all permanent bridges over the Po river from Cremona to Ostiglia were reported cut, no appreciable effort had been made to repair them. By the 27th all bridges over the

---

* Single road bridges over the Po river west of Piacenza were not included in 'Mallory Major'.

Po east of Torreberetti were believed impassable and others to the west damaged. The medium day bombers of M.A.T.A.F. had flown 1,496 sorties and dropped 2,366.7 tons of bombs between 12th and 27th July on targets from the rail bridge at Moncalieri on the western reach to the road bridge at Taglio, which is the last bridge before the Po flows into the Adriatic Sea.

So far we have dealt only with the bridges over the Po. The operation also covered almost the entire Po valley system of bridges and important bridges in the Ligurian mountain valleys. A total of another 70 bridges of all kinds were attacked, at 61 different places. The attacks on rail bridges and viaducts north of the Po began on 15th July and were directed against eight targets on which 385 tons of bombs were dropped in 218 sorties by the end of 'Mallory Major'. The rail bridge at Bozzolo, which was on the single-track lateral line nearest the Po river, was claimed destroyed, and the railway viaduct at Desenzano del Garda (1,640 feet long) which was on the double-track lateral further north was cut, thus stopping eastwards and westwards traffic on both laterals. The rail bridges at Mantua, on the single-track lateral, received the greatest attention amounting to 118.7 tons of bombs.

The bridges attacked south of the Po are best divided into two areas: those east of the Alessandria–Ronco Scrivia–Genoa railway line on the north-south supply routes and those west of and on that railway line which served the north-western routes from France into Italy. The attacks on the eastern group absorbed 273 sorties and 437.7 tons of bombs, which were dropped on 13 rail bridges and viaducts, two combined rail/road bridges and two road bridges. Successes claimed were the destruction of the combined rail/road bridge over the Trebbia river near Piacenza, and of the combined rail/road bridge at Sassuolo on the loopline between Reggio and Modena. The attacks on the western group were made on rail bridges and viaducts on the north-south Ligurian valley routes: Turin–Borgo S. Dalmazzo–Ventimiglia; Turin–Fossano–Savona; Turin–Asti–Savona;   Turin–Alessandria–Ovada–Genoa;   and Alessandria–Ronco Scrivia–Genoa. The important laterals and the Ligurian coastal line to Genoa were also attacked. Altogether 485 sorties were flown and 847.7 tons of bombs dropped on at least 17 rail bridges and viaducts and on two combined rail/road bridges. These attacks were not only in support of 'Mallory Major' but were also designed to sever rail communications to and from Genoa in preparation for Operation 'Anvil' in August.

Taking 'Mallory Major' as a whole, the total effort expended by M.A.T.A.F.'s medium day bombers amounted to 2,472 sorties, during which 4,037.7 tons of bombs were dropped from 12th to 27th July.

The plan for the fighter-bombers to attack reserve pontoons for bridges did not materialise for lack of suitable targets. Although rolling stock and M.T. remained the prime fare of the fighter-bombers whenever the opportunity presented itself, their greatest contribution to Operation 'Mallory Major' was supplementing the interdiction already achieved by the medium day bombers and maintaining it by interfering with German repair. In the first few days of July the fighter-bombers of U.S. XII T.A.C. had already moved their activities northwards with the object of cutting the Genoa–Pisa railway line, and of isolating Bologna from the north. When 'Major Mallory' began they switched their main effort to the Po valley. As it proved useless to pit them against bridges of massive construction which defied the medium day bombers, they took on bridges north of the Po which were not so solidly built.

To interfere with repair work in the Po valley network generally their system was to crater the tracks at each end of a bridge, making it more difficult to bring up repair materials, while at the same time increasing the distance for trans-shipment of supplies across the gap. This had an accumulative effect because it forced the Germans to use minor alternative routes and M.T., the latter increasingly in daylight, thus providing more fighter-bomber targets.

Railway tracks between rail bridges north and south of the river were also attacked. For example, on 16th July the main railway line running south-east from Milan was cut in four places south of Piacenza, and the Casalmaggiore–Parma railway line in eleven places. The approach to the combined rail/road bridge at Ostiglia was blocked from the south, and the railway line between Borgoforte and Mantua cut in several places. This process continued throughout 'Mallory Major' over a wide area, principally through the efforts of the fighter-bombers of U.S. XII T.A.C. based in Corsica. Their attacks were against such a variety of targets in so many locations that it is impossible to say where and when their support for 'Mallory Major' began and ended, but it was substantial.

German fighter opposition was largely ineffectual. On 12th July 20–22 Me. 109s attempted to interfere with the attacks by Mitchells on the bridges at Pontelagoscuro, near Ferrara, and one German aircraft was probably destroyed. Two days later about 20 Me. 109s and F.W. 190s attempted to interfere with the attacks by Mitchells on the bridges at Corbola and this time two of the German aircraft were probably destroyed. Another example took place on the 19th when Mitchells on their way to attack the combined rail/road bridge at Sassuolo met about 10 enemy fighters over Corregio, again without undue interference. Fortunately flak too was not as great as had been expected, only being serious in the Ferrara, Verona and Ostiglia areas.

Though the magnitude of the repair work facing the Germans at the height of 'Mallory Major' appeared to be temporarily overwhelming, they remained undeterred and used great ingenuity to offset the effects of the damage. By 15th July two ferry crossings had been established, and by the end of the month 19 ferries were in operation for night traffic. Cable-ways were slung across the Po river at Piacenza, Cremona, Borgoforte and Ostiglia. Pontoon bridges were repaired or replaced and others established at new sites. Railway ferries were brought into use at Ostiglia and later at Piacenza and Pontelagoscuro and pipelines for liquid fuel were installed in some places. An interesting observation was made by General Karl Koerner, on the staff of the German Chief of Transportation at *OKH,* to the effect that if the Allies had attacked the Brenner Pass and the Po river bridges in 1943 as steadily as they had done in mid-1944 'German resistance in Italy would have collapsed'. General Koerner's post-war observation tends to justify the school of thought that the peculiar lay out of the Italian railway system lent itself more readily to interdiction than to the attacks on marshalling-yards which had been the basis of Operation 'Strangle' during the previous winter. Further evidence of the effects of 'Mallory Major' will emerge as the story of the approach to the Gothic Line unfolds.

(iv)

See Map 8

Ways of forcing a passage through the Gothic Line had been in all the Allied commanders' minds since Harding wrote his initial Appreciation No. 1 in February.*

Their thoughts were focussed more directly on the problem by his Appreciation No. 2, which was distributed to senior commanders on 25th March, and set the pattern of their ideas in a distinct and important mould; so important that it is worth quoting verbatim one of his significant conclusions:[38]

> '*BREAKING INTO THE PO VALLEY*
> An advance along the west coast beyond the distance necessary to secure Leghorn would have little if any effect and it is not considered. There appear to be two possible ways of breaking into the valley of the Po. One by way of the east coast *which would cross the grain of the country* [author's italics]. The other in a

---

* *Mediterranean and Middle East,* Volume V, p. 832.

series of columns attacking across the Apennines by parallel
main and subsidiary roads that run from Sansepolcro, Bibbiena,
Pontassieve and Florence to Rimini, Cesena, Forli and Faenza.
These routes are difficult, follow the grain of the country and
offer the only possibility of anything approaching an advance
on a broad front. Such an operation would entail a concentration
of troops in the centre, and priority for the development of the
central line of communications over both coastal routes. If
adopted as the general plan it becomes of great importance to
concentrate on the early capture of the Florence–Arezzo area
as a base for operations, and Ancona becomes of secondary
importance'.

The next step in A.A.I. thinking came with Harding's Appreciation No. 3 which, as already mentioned, was discussed at
Alexander's conference on 23rd June.[39] His views were now even
more firmly set upon an attack on the centre of the Gothic Line.

'The terrain on the west flank is very difficult and poorly roaded,
and an attack on the east coast would have to be made across
the grain of the country.
   Consideration of these facts leads very definitely to the conclusion that any large scale attack should be planned to effect
penetration in the centre; that the front of the original attack
should be between the roads Pontassieve–Faenza and Pistoia–
Bologna; and that the penetration should be followed by the
most rapid advance possible, first of all to secure control of the
Rimini–Modena lateral road between Imola and Modena, and
then bridge sites over the Po north of Ferrara at Ostiglia and
south of Mantua.
   A study of the topography north of the Apennines shows that
to cut off the enemy forces holding the eastern part of his front
rapid exploitation to secure Ferrara and the area east of it will
be essential, while the early capture of Mantua and Parma is
necessary to secure the left flank'.

Tactical planning at H.Q. 8th Army was to come to exactly the
same conclusion, supporting it with evidence from a detailed
interpretation of air photographs of the Gothic Line taken throughout its development.[40] In an appreciation which first appeared in
draft on 25th June 8th Army Staff suggested that there were three
possible areas for assault: A, along the eastern flank; B, on the
Florence–Bologna axis; and C, between the other two. In assessing
the pros and cons of A, they said:[41]

   'Advantages
      —Avoids fighting in mountainous country.
      —Large forces can be concentrated and maintained from
         Ancona.
      —Whole area is well served with minor roads.

Disadvantages
—It drives the enemy straight back on his line of withdrawal.
—Minimum exploitation possible.
—We put ourselves against the grain of the country and will have to cross numerous rivers, which is playing into the hands of a withdrawing enemy.
—It involves swinging the Army's administrative tail back to the other side of the Apennines, with consequent loss of time.'

Their assessment of Course B brought in the additional arguments that the defences north of Florence were incomplete and could be outflanked, and the Apennines were lowest and the mountain belt narrowest here, but these advantages were offset by it being the obvious course. They discarded C because the Apennines were highest, widest and most poorly roaded in this sector, and they concluded firmly:

'Course B appears the best'.

So certain did the planning staffs feel as to the soundness of their judgement that a deception plan called 'Ottrington' was initiated on 3rd July:[42]

'(a) To simulate an increase of forces on the Adriatic, with fresh formations ready to pass through Polcorps and assault the Gothic Line.

(b) To simulate an assault force in the Naples–Salerno area preparing to make a landing in the Gulf of Genoa.

(c) To persuade the enemy that these two assaults will take place simultaneously on D + 7, D being D day for 8th Army's attack on the Gothic Line'.

When Alexander visited London at the beginning of July he addressed the War Cabinet on the results of 'Diadem' and about his future plans.[43] He could at present use only nine of the 19 divisions available to him due to supply difficulties but once these were overcome he hoped to assault the centre of the German line. He believed it was essential to keep one senior American commander in Italy, and he won the Prime Minister's continued support for operations directed towards the Ljubljana Gap.

When Alexander returned to Italy he found that the only difficult problem to be settled was the part 5th Army could and should take in the assault on the Gothic Line in its weakened state, after its 'Anvil' troops had been withdrawn. Having little official information about 5th Army's supply situation, Alexander wrote to Clark on 19th July to forewarn him of his thinking and to seek an estimate of his capabilities.[44] He stated his intention to attack in the centre and suggested that 5th Army should force the Arno east of Pontedera, aiming to seize Lucca and Pistoia as a base for its operations against the Gothic Line. He also suggested that Clark should risk holding the line of the Arno west of Pontedera with little more than an observation line, backed up by mobile reserves to conserve resources, because he would very much like 5th Army to take part in the main assault alongside 8th Army. He proposed to visit Clark on 20th July to settle the matter. At their meeting Clark rightly pointed out that his troops needed a couple of weeks' rest before tackling the Arno.[45] He had arranged for 34th U.S. Division to be relieved by Task Force 45, an *ad hoc* grouping of anti-aircraft units made redundant by the virtual disappearance of the German Air Force. Their training as infantry was hurried, some units having as little as two days before taking over on the Arno, where their training was continued on the job. Nevertheless, the insertion of Task Force 45 into the line would enable the infantry of 5th Army to be relieved in rotation before starting operations to seize Lucca and Pistoia. After the meeting Harding was able to issue A.A.I.'s directive for the assault on the Gothic Line with the agreement, or so it was thought, of both Army Commanders.*[46] The operative paragraph of the directive dated 26th July ran:

'The C.-in-C.'s general plan is:—

(a) To penetrate the centre of the Gothic Line roughly between Dicomano and Pistoia.

(b) To thrust forward over the Apennines to secure the general line Imola–Bologna–Modena.

(c) To complete the destruction of the enemy forces south of the Po by rapid exploitation across the Po valley.

(d) To secure a bridgehead over the Po north of Ferrara, and if possible at Ostiglia as well'.

The stage was being set for the Allied Armies' assault on the German positions in the Northern Apennines. When it could be mounted would depend on how quickly the Germans could be driven back. Every day lost by the Allies was a day won by the Germans for further preparation of their defences: more mines laid, more positions dug, more bunkers constructed and more reserves of ammunition and supplies ferried over the Po and dumped behind their positions.

---

* We discuss at the start of Chapter XI when and why General Leese revised his opinions on the plan of attack.

(v)

See Map 5

We left the field armies at the beginning of July with 5th Army over the Cecina and up against *AOK 14's* Lilo Line, covering Volterra; and 8th Army having forced its way past Lake Trasimeno. By 4th July *AOK 10's* 76th Panzer Corps was installed for defence of the Georg Line, which ran south of Montevarchi in the Middle Arno valley—road junction south of Arezzo—southeast to Montone overlooking the Tiber valley.[47] Near Gualdo Tadino, where Route 76 crosses the main Apennine ridge, Georg merged into the existing Albert Line, to which the left wing of 51st Mountain Corps had withdrawn on 30th June. The coastal sector north of the Musone river was held by 278th Infantry Division, whose efforts to hold back the Poles gained in significance when Hitler decreed on 4th July that the important port of Ancona must be denied to the Allies for as long as possible. As we have seen, Jodl's directive of 5th July named Ancona and Leghorn as main Allied objectives, requiring 'stubborn resistance' from *AOK 10* and *AOK 14* respectively.

On 5th Army's front, Clark was regrouping to relieve 1st U.S. Armoured Division, due for an extensive refit, with 88th U.S. Division; and 91st U.S. Division was on its way to the front where it would re-absorb its two advanced Regimental Combat Teams which had already been in operation with 34th and 36th U.S. Divisions respectively.[48] 4th U.S. Corps' plan for its thrust to the Arno was to use its heavily reinforced 34th U.S. Division to advance on Pisa by sending the bulk of the division along hill roads to the east of Leghorn, an outflanking move which would threaten the enemy garrison's route of withdrawal. 88th U.S. Division would use the road along the Era valley, aiming for the Arno in the vicinity of Pontedera, to be followed later by 91st U.S. Division. The F.E.C. was to continue its thrust towards Poggibonsi up Route 2 until its sector was taken over by 8th Army on 22nd July and it withdrew to train and embark for 'Anvil'.

34th U.S. Division's advance began on 3rd July and progressed slowly against very effective opposition by 16th SS Panzer Grenadier and 26th Panzer Divisions. It took until 9th July to clear the hill features east of the great chemical works at Rosignano. It took a further ten days to break out of the hills and converge on Leghorn which was entered on 19th July. The abandonment of this city, *'point d'honneur* though it might be', was mooted by Hauser in conversation with Wentzell of *AOK 10* on 15th July, and at higher levels of command it was a measure of Kesselring's new found freedom of action that *OKW* did not protest at the withdrawals

which began that night on the front of *AOK 14*.[49] By 19th July 14th
Panzer Corps was back to the Heinrich Line north of the Arno.
The rear-guards of 16th SS Panzer Grenadier Division, which
suffered heavy casualties fighting in Leghorn, left the city on this
date, and with the rest of 75th Corps were installed in Heinrich
by 20th July. German demolition teams had effectively blocked the
port of Leghorn with sunken block-ships, thoroughly mined the
harbour and destroyed its installations. It took many weeks to
restore Leghorn's usefulness as a port, its capacity rising slowly to
meet the needs of both 5th and 8th Armies. Meanwhile, 34th U.S.
Division pushed on northwards against 75th Corps' rear-guards
and entered the suburbs of Pisa on the south bank of the Arno on
23rd July.

In the centre and left of 4th U.S. Corps' advance, 91st U.S.
Division came into the line to the west of 88th U.S. Division on
12th July.[50] A steady methodical advance brought both divisions
up to the Arno by nightfall on 25th July. The F.E.C. on 4th U.S.
Corps' eastern flank had to fight hard to break through to Poggibonsi which they took on 14th July. Thereafter 14th Panzer Corps
remained under pressure south and south-east of Pontedera, and
by 17th July 90th Panzer Grenadier Division was so weakened by
casualties that a break through seemed imminent and von Senger
was permitted by Kesselring to withdraw.[51] When the units of 8th
Army took over the French front it was steeply echeloned back
south-eastwards, with 4th Moroccan Mountain Division well ahead
of 2nd Moroccan Infantry Division.[52] The French line ran from
S. Stefano to Castelfiorentino on the River Elsa, then along its
course for six miles to Certaldo and ended at S. Donato north-
east of Poggibonsi. Although Kesselring had abandoned Leghorn,
he was still intent on holding Florence.

Described by Jodl as the 'jewel of Europe', Florence had been
given the status of an open city by the Germans in the winter of
1943.[53] By June 1944 attitudes about Florence were ambivalent, for
on 20th June Kesselring's Chief Engineer was instructed by the
Army Group Chief of Staff to investigate the technical possibilities
of blowing up the Arno bridges within the city. Strictest secrecy
was to surround the preparations for their demolition at short
notice, and in less covert orders all of *OB Südwest's* commands
were reminded on this date that no members of the *Wehrmacht*
could enter or remain in Florence without authorisation.[54] At the
headquarters of *AOK 14*, the demands of war were mooted in
orders issued by Lemelsen on 14th July, which stated that while
Florence was still an open city 'for the time being', it would be
occupied and defended by German troops if the military situation
so required.[55] The prospect of a stand by 1st Parachute Corps in a

bridgehead south of the Arno had already been rated unfavourably by Schlemm on 5th July, and after the further depletion of this Corps Hauser also doubted that it could defend such a bulge, commenting on 18th July that it was 'no use having a Great Wall of China, if we have no Chinese to defend it'. But Hitler was the arbiter, and during his meeting with Kesselring on 19th July the Führer gave firm instructions, as he informed Mussolini the next day, that 1st Parachute Corps must hold a line five to eight miles south of Florence for as long as possible. At the same time, he announced that in order to save its art treasures the city itself would not be defended, and despite a reminder from Kesselring about the 'lesson of Rome' he would not countenance the demolition of any of the bridges spanning the Arno within the city.

The battle for Florence, for which the stage was being set, was, in the eyes of 8th Army, part of the process of facing up to the centre of the Gothic Line, and was preceded by the battle for Arezzo which lasted from 5th to 16th July. The Staff of *AOK 10* and *AOK 14* viewed the whole operation as one great battle for Florence with the fighting around Arezzo as part of the phased withdrawal from Georg to Heinrich. The opposing British and German Army Commanders held divergent views on the main threat. General Leese was anxious to avoid fighting in the mountain country of the Pratomagno massif, where 10th Corps was having 'a lot of sticky fighting . . . partly due to the country and partly due to the fact that both divisions [4th and 10th Indian] were new to mountain warfare'![56] He was, therefore, putting his main effort behind 13th Corps' advance into the Chianti mountains between the Pesa river and the Middle Arno. von Vietinghoff, however, was more concerned for 10th Corps' thrust towards Bibbiena and the Polish drive towards Ancona, because he reckoned in mid-July that 1st Canadian Corps might be sent into action in the Tiber valley, or alternatively used to relieve the Polish Corps which would threaten *AOK 10's* thinly-held eastern flank.[57]

8th Army was still hampered by supply problems, which so dominated operations at this stage of the British advance to the Gothic Line that they need a brief reference here, although the development of the Lines of Communication has been looked at in more detail in Part I Chapter VIII Section (iv) and illustrated on *Map 19*.[58] General Robertson pointed out at a conference of Army Commanders on 23rd June that the number of formations which could be deployed against the German defences in the Apennines would depend mainly on the speed with which rail communications could be repaired and railheads moved forward. The proposed withdrawal of American railway construction units for the 'Anvil' operation would seriously affect progress. On 28th

June, when 13th Corps had finally broken through the Trasimene Line, the forward troops of 8th Army were some 200 miles north of their nearest railhead, while those of 5th Army were 90 miles from the port of Civitavecchia whence they were being supplied by road.[59] To add to 8th Army's difficulties two major bottlenecks had existed on its L. of C. until very recently. One was the bridge over the Tiber at Civita Castellana, which could only take single line traffic till as late as 22nd June (*Map 1*). The other was at Narni where solid medieval gateways and a one way street, over a quarter of a mile long, seriously hampered traffic flow. This was not corrected until 26th June when a bypass came into use. By the end of June the logistic traffic flow was just beginning to improve. It was the intention to open railheads at Civita Castellana (2,500 tons per day) and at the nearby Gallese Teverina (1,000 tons per day) for 8th Army early in July, and roadheads were being planned at Narni and Arezzo.[60]

The curse of traffic congestion on the roads still dogged the operational and administrative staffs. 13th Corps made a particular effort to grapple with the problem by issuing on 23rd–24th July special regulations to control the density and flow of traffic, based on its Liri valley experience.[61] Some of the rules were: every vehicle, whether in convoy or not, was to travel 'at best speed', subject to safety limits; no overtaking of 15-cwt or 3-tonners on the move, except by staff cars and jeeps, was allowed; no unit or detachment was to move without an authorised timing; and divisions were limited to 30 vehicles per hour, including their maintenance traffic which was to be spread evenly throughout the day. Traffic Posts were to impound any vehicles exceeding these limits or transgressing the regulations. Unfortunately the Corps was to repeat its Liri valley mistake of trying to deploy more divisions in the line than the paucity of roads and restricted nature of the country would allow.

Of necessity future administrative planning influenced Leese's current operations.[62] It was assumed, in Army Planning Notes issued on 24th June, that not more than six or, if a set-piece co-ordinated attack were required, seven divisions could be employed in an advance north of Florence, but these it was thought would be sufficient if the attack were mounted quickly. Leese thus had to decide almost immediately how to apportion them between his two British Corps, operating on independent axes, so that he would be properly poised for his assault on the Gothic Line when he reached the Arno. As his axis of assault was to be Route 65, the Florence–Bologna highway, Arezzo, with its excellent road and rail communications, was earmarked as his administrative base and Florence as his operational springboard. The capture of

Bibbiena, the third of his original objectives, became of secondary importance because Intelligence showed the Germans were likely to deny the Bibbiena-Pontassieve lateral road.

The grouping on which Leese decided for the advance on Florence was:[63]

13th Corps
4th Division
6th Armoured Division
6th South African Armoured
    Division
1st Canadian Armoured Brigade
6th A.G.R.A.

10th Corps
4th Indian Division
10th Indian Division
9th Armoured Brigade
2nd A.G.R.A.

Army Reserve
1st Canadian Corps
2nd New Zealand Division
8th Indian Division
25th Tank Brigade.

13th Corps moved forward from Cortona on 4th July with its three divisions abreast, heading for Arezzo, which lies in a flat plain but is surrounded on three sides by mountains. Some five miles short of the city the broad fertile Chiana valley, which was 13th Corps' approach route, ends in a ridge of hills between it and the Middle Arno valley. Two main roads lead into Arezzo from the head of the Chiana valley through a narrow natural defile in the north-east corner: Route 73 from Siena and Route 71 from Lake Trasimeno. The whole of the Chiana valley, and in particular Route 71, is dominated from the east by a mass of steep, crumpled hills, topped by Mt Lignano.

6th Armoured Division on the right advanced up Route 71 led by 1st Derbyshire Yeomanry (armoured reconnaissance regiment), which was sharply checked on 5th July when it tried to cross Route 73 at the head of the valley.[64] The rest of the Division came under artillery fire directed from Observation Posts on Mt Lignano. 4th Division, in the centre, crossed Route 73 on a broad front, but was checked as well in the hills around Civitella di Chiana. And 6th South African Armoured Division, advancing on the left in two columns through Rapolano and Palazzuolo, experienced the same check on the north side of Route 73. 13th Corps was up to 76th Panzer Corps' sector of the Georg Line.

The full strength of 76th Panzer Corps' positions was not immediately apparent during 5th and 6th July.[65] The leading brigades of 13th Corps continued to probe forward in the expectation that the German line would begin to crumble under continued pressure without the need to mount a full scale attack.

Nevertheless, the Commander of 6th Armoured Division, Major-General Evelegh, decided he must clear the Mt Lignano feature before his division could make any progress up Route 71 into the Middle Arno valley.[66] An attempt to secure this dominating ground by the leading battalion of 61st Brigade was made during the night 5th/6th July. 10th Rifle Brigade, given this task, was not strong enough to gain the heights. The fighting on the hill mass continued throughout 6th and 7th July until eventually the whole of 61st Brigade had been committed. In spite of its efforts 15th Panzer Grenadier Division still held the crests and the Brigade consolidated its positions along the lower slopes during the night 7th/8th July.

In the centre the commander of 4th Division, Major-General Ward, brought up his reserve brigade and launched a converging attack against Civitella di Chiana.[67] There was heavy fighting to clear the ridge east of the town and some gains were made north-east of it, but they could not be consolidated and Civitella remained in the hands of 334th Infantry Division. Attacks west of the town were equally unsuccessful, bringing about a stalemate across the divisional front.

On 13th Corps' left flank the 6th South African Armoured Division came to a standstill as well, with its two infantry brigades stretched over a front of more than ten miles and the armoured brigade drawn back into reserve because of the difficult tank going. A full Corps operation appeared the only way in which to restart the German withdrawal.[68] Strong German gun lines north of Route 73 with excellent flanking observation from the Mt Lignano hills and the closeness of the country convinced General Kirkman that the task required more infantry. It was equally evident that 6th Armoured Division could not tackle the whole of the Lignano feature alone. The freshest infantry were in 4th Indian Division, but they had just been committed to 10th Corps' advance up the Tiber valley, east of Arezzo. Short of recommitting 8th Indian Division, which was already on its way back to rest and refit, the only suitable formation available was 2nd N.Z. Division, which was being held in reserve for the Gothic Line assault. After some hesitation, the New Zealanders were placed under command of 13th Corps on 7th July, but it would be several days before they could arrive and start operations in the hills. In the meantime, it was necessary to protect the eastern flank of 13th Corps until 10th Corps drew level. Leese instructed 10th Corps to release part of the recently reinforced 9th Armoured Brigade to undertake this task.[69] The new force took over operations on Mt Lignano from 8th to 13th July to allow 61st Brigade to prepare for the forthcoming assault on the Arezzo position.[70] Kirkman's plan was for 6th Armoured Division to open its main thrust up the Chiana valley and along the lower western slopes of Mt Lignano while the New Zealanders secured the tops of those features which overlooked 6th Armoured Division's axis.[71] 4th Division and 6th South African Armoured Division would demonstrate on their respective fronts and exploit any German withdrawals. While the New Zealanders were assembling Kirkman ordered artillery bombardments and requested air attacks on the German gun positions to cover the lull.* There were four days of reduced ground activity between 9th and 12th July punctuated by minor enemy counter-attacks against 4th Division positions.

In the air during 10th–14th July direct air support was considerable, amounting to 264 sorties, during which 125 tons of bombs were dropped. To give some examples, on the 10th when three calls were answered, the fighter-bombers from D.A.F. joined with the British artillery in and around Arezzo.[72] There was low cloud in the morning, and airfields were waterlogged, but in the afternoon 35 Kittyhawks and Mustangs from D.A.F. dropped 18.5 tons on guns and enemy positions in and around Arezzo and well to the west of the town. Next day, the 11th, the effort against the guns rose sharply. Against 12 gun targets 95 Kittyhawks and Mustangs from D.A.F. dropped 38.6 tons of bombs south-west of Arezzo and 15 Baltimores added another 11.7 tons. Five calls for assistance were also answered. There was a pre-arranged anti-gun programme on the 12th resulting in 86 Kittyhawks and Mustangs from D.A.F. attacking guns south-west, west and north-west of Arezzo with 42.3 tons of bombs, and Spitfires bombed guns well to the west of the town. These attacks successfully reduced the enemy shelling. Seven other calls for assistance were answered, two of them against targets only 800 yards from our own forward troops and indicated by coloured artillery smoke. Both attacks were described by the Army as 'outstandingly successful'. On the 13th five calls were answered and next day seven when the targets included strongly defended localities and headquarters. Also on the 14th there was another pre-arranged anti-gun programme in which 33 Mustangs from D.A.F. dropped 13.3 tons of bombs on guns north of Arezzo.

The battle of Arezzo proved to be an anti-climax after all these preparations.[73] 6th Armoured Division began its assault at 1 a.m. on 15th July in the midst of a thunder-storm with 1st Guards Brigade attacking along the lower slopes of Mt Lignano, its three battalions in depth. Simultaneously 6th New Zealand Brigade attacked and captured the crest from 15th Panzer Grenadier Division. The only serious trouble came from the difficulty of scram-

---

* A total of four field, five medium and one heavy regiments from 6th A.G.R.A. and 6th Armoured Division, plus two field regiments from 4th Division and two heavy A.A. Regiments of 12th A.A. Brigade were engaged in these bombardments.

bling up the steep hillsides and from shell fire, some of which was probably from supporting artillery. The precipitous nature of the country made accurate artillery support difficult. Throughout 15th July the enemy gave ground unwillingly and slowly, fighting hard from the reverse slopes of Mt Lignano. 3rd Grenadier Guards secured their objectives in the early morning and 2nd Coldstream Guards passed through and continued to make encouraging progress. The Germans counter-attacked strongly and the fighting continued all the afternoon. The New Zealanders were held by continued enemy opposition north of Mt Lignano, which probably came from the Hermann Göring Panzer Division and 305th Infantry Division.[74] During the night the German artillery began a heavy telltale bombardment which the Allies had begun to recognise as the first sign of another German withdrawal. Contact was broken during the night, and next morning 26th Armoured Brigade was able to push rapidly towards the Arno river crossings, 16th/5th Lancers entering Arezzo at 9.15 a.m. on the 16th. During the rest of the day the armoured regiments and 10th Rifle Brigade drove forward along the roads to the west and north-west. 2nd Lothians advanced with great speed to Quarata, overrunning a number of anti-tank guns which tried to stop them, and capturing the bridge over the Arno before it could be demolished. By the evening of the 16th their tanks were across the river and moving north-west on the eastern side of the Arno valley skirting the Pratomagno massif. 16th/5th Lancers and 10th Rifle Brigade had not been so lucky. Advancing west along Route 69 towards Montevarchi on the west bank of the Arno, they were stopped when the Germans blew the bridge over the Chiana canal just as the riflemen were approaching it.[75]

General Leese was delighted with Kirkman's success, commenting 'Kirkie laid on a first-rate plan . . . It was an excellent battle, well planned and well executed'.[76] The higher commanders of *AOK 10* were not dismayed by 13th Corps' success, as it gave impetus to withdrawal plans which had their origin in other earlier factors. On 11th July von Vietinghoff learnt that on orders from *OKW* he must release the Hermann Göring Panzer Division for service on the Eastern front.[77] This formation's tendency to appeal to its patron whenever it felt imposed upon had not endeared it to its colleagues, but it was much stronger than its proposed replacement, 715th Infantry Division, which was to be moved from coast-watching around Ravenna and which had perforce to be given a narrower sector in the line. As *OKW's* order coincided with a proposed retraction of *AOK 14's* left wing, von Vietinghoff warned Kesselring on 13th July that if the two Armies were to keep contact 76th Panzer Corps might have to pull back its centre. The observed build up of 13th Corps lent force to this argument, and although Mt Lignano was acknowledged to be the corner-stone of *AOK 10's* defence south of Arezzo, after its loss the Army Chief of Staff, Wentzell, told Hauser that there would be no counter-attack, as this would only 'cause unnecessary casualties'. With Kesselring's concurrence, and with the need to maintain contact with *AOK 14,* while simultaneously extracting the Hermann Göring Panzer Division forming a useful face-saver, von Vietinghoff authorised 76th Panzer Corps to begin a fighting withdrawal towards the Heinrich Line on the afternoon of 15th July. In its first delaying position, known as 'Irmgard', the junction with Schlemm's 1st Parachute Corps was to be at Gaiole on the southern edge of the Chianti hills, and with 51st Mountain Corps at Ranco, on Route 73 due east of Arezzo. Herr's disengagement was successful and *AOK 10's* Daily Report for 16th July claimed that he had withdrawn just in time to forestall a major Allied offensive—which he had![78]

Meanwhile McCreery's 10th Corps was developing its operations methodically in the mountain country astride the Tiber.[79] On 8th July 4th Indian Division, with 10th Indian Brigade under command, took over the western side of the valley, to allow 10th Indian Division to concentrate on clearing the mountains on the eastern side.* Feuerstein's 51st Mountain Corps was holding Citta di Castello with 44th Infantry and 114th Jäger Divisions west and east of the Tiber respectively, and 305th Infantry Division of 76th Panzer Corps was holding the near-trackless mountain country between 10th and 13th Corps around Mt Favalto through which operations had to be conducted on foot, supported by mules.[82]

4th Indian Division started its advance from the line of the Nestore river south-east of Mt Favalto (3,552 feet) on 10th July.[83] By hard climbing, skilful mountain tactics and some severe fighting it took Mt Favalto on 13th July, thus threatening Arezzo from the east. This success led 8th Army to direct 10th Corps to help 13th

---

* *Outline Order of Battle of 4th Indian Division* (Major-General A. W. W. Holworthy)[80]
  5th Indian Infantry Brigade
  1st/4th Essex Regiment; 3rd/10th Baluch Regiment; 1st/9th Gurkha Rifles.
  7th Indian Infantry Brigade
  1st Royal Sussex Regiment; 2nd Royal Battalion 11th Sikh Regiment; 1st/2nd Gurkha Rifles.
  11th Indian Infantry Brigade
  2nd Cameron Highlanders; 3rd Royal Battalion 12th Frontier Force Regiment; 2nd/7th Gurkha Rifles.
  I.A.C. Central India Horse.
  R.A. 1st, 11th, 31st Field Regiments; 149th Anti-Tank Regiment; 57th L.A.A. Regiment; Divisional Counter-Mortar Battery.
  I.E. 4th, 12th, 21st Field Companies S. & M.; 11th Field Park Company S. & M.; 5th Bridging Platoon S. & M.
  M.G. 6th Rajputana Rifles.
Initially the Division had only two brigades forward; 11th Indian Infantry Brigade moved up when the supply situation allowed and came under command on 19th July.[81]

Corps by seizing the high ground north of Route 73.[84] 4th Indian Division demonstrated its prowess in mountain warfare by not only working its way forward to cut Route 73 east of Arezzo and securing a foothold on the steep Alpe di Poti (3,199 feet) on the north side of the road, but also clearing the mountains overlooking Citta di Castello from the west.*

10th Indian Division cleared the eastern side of the valley, working across equally rough country of scrub covered ridges and deep ravines.[86] Attacking usually by night, they fought a series of hand to hand encounters, during one of which Naik Yashwant Ghadge of 3rd/5th Mahrattas won a posthumous V.C.† By 17th July they too were overlooking Citta di Castello from the east. To protect 10th Corps' eastern flank and maintain contact with the Poles an armoured car force of the Household Cavalry Regiment and 12th Lancers moved along Route 3, where they were held up by German rear-guards at Scheggia (*Map 1*).[87]

See Map 6

Over on the Adriatic coast Anders' 2nd Polish Corps was making ready to attack Ancona. Preparations began on 10th July, and D.A.F. joined in on the 15th by concentrating 24 Marauder medium and 48 Baltimore light bombers on guns in the Iesi area.[88] Next day more of these bombers struck at guns south of Ancona while an even greater force, of 39 Marauders and 48 Baltimores, started fires and bombed roads south of Ancona where fighter-bombers also attacked a dump. General Leese had intended Anders to attack on 15th July but he delayed the Polish operation two days for two reasons: first, to avoid splitting the available air support between the battles for Arezzo and Ancona;[89] and secondly to give the Italian *C.I.L.* more time to reach its assembly area on the Polish Corps' left flank.

On 17th July the battle of Ancona started with the Polish Corps breaking out from its bridgehead over the Musone river. Anders' plan was to develop his main thrust north of Osimo and Montoro in order to break through 278th Infantry Divisions's front well to the west of the city and then to encircle its garrison.[90] He envisaged a rapid thrust with his tanks once the enemy crust was broken and exploitation to cut Route 16, the Via Adriatica, west of Ancona

---

* To supply the Division from the Nestore river to Route 73 the Divisional and Corps Engineers constructed a jeep track through the Mt Favalto area which rose 1,150 feet with a gradient of one in ten. The track became known as 'Jacob's Ladder'.[85]

† After the death of the Company Commander, Yashwant Ghadge, the only active survivor of his section, rushed and captured a machine gun post, wielding the butt of his Tommy gun as a weapon when the magazine had been exhausted.

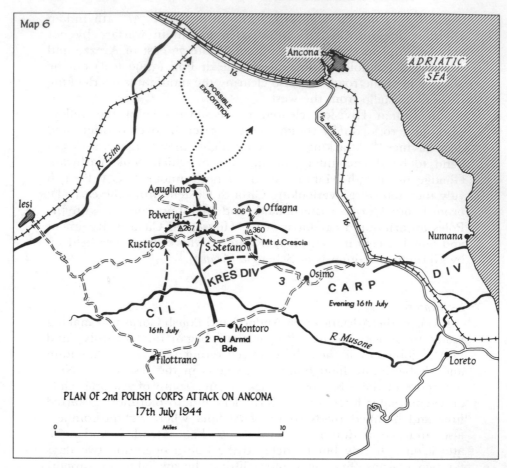

PLAN OF 2nd POLISH CORPS ATTACK ON ANCONA
17th July 1944

before 278th Infantry Division had time to escape. 5th Kresowa
Division was to secure the high ground between Mt della Crescia
and S. Stefano, subsequently advancing to seize Offagna. 2nd
Polish Armoured Brigade, reinforced by one reconnaissance regiment and one infantry battalion, was to attack on the left of the
Kresowa Division, directed on Polverigi, and was to operate from
there against the enemy's artillery and rear areas, exploiting north
and north-east through Agugliano. 3rd Carpathian Division was
to operate in a holding role on the coastal flank, advancing
northwards against Ancona as opportunity offered. And on the
extreme left flank the Italian *C.I.L.* was to secure Rustico with
one brigade and protect the left flank of the Corps by moving up
the Filottrano–Iesi road axis.

5th Wilenska Brigade spearheaded the attack of the Kresowa
Division and after heavy fighting throughout the 17th secured its

first objective in the Mt della Crescia–San Stefano area. The same day 2nd Polish Armoured Brigade cleared Polverigi and Augugliano.* These successes broke the main enemy defence system north of the Musone river and opened the way for exploitation to the coast north-west of Ancona. In support of their attacks D.A.F. was out in considerable strength; 96 medium and light bombers and 215 fighter-bombers attacked a variety of targets guarding Ancona, guns receiving the greatest attention.[92]

Momentarily von Vietinghoff's attention had been diverted from the Adriatic sector by 10th Corps' progress towards Citta di Castello, which he had identified as 8th Army's most dangerous thrust, and by a breakdown in communications with the east coast caused by the move of *AOK 10* Headquarters on 17th July to a new location 7 miles east of Bologna.[93] That day the Army Commander put it to Kesselring that Ancona had little strategic value as the Allies had ample land and air bases in Foggia, Taranto and Brindisi for operations in the Balkans; therefore the port should be abandoned to enable *AOK 10* to shorten its front. Kesselring, who had just been on an inspection tour of the Gothic Line, dismissed the suggestion on the grounds that there was 'so much to be done in rear'. As the Poles had already opened their attack when this conversation took place the chance of saving 278th Infantry Division by a voluntary withdrawal was missed, although it is worth recording that early on 17th July von Vietinghoff reckoned that the main battles of the day would be fought east and west of the Tiber. He was soon to be disillusioned. 51st Mountain Corps' Morning Report for 18th July made it clear that if 278th Infantry Division did not withdraw at once, its escape routes would be cut. At about 11 a.m. it started to pull back to the River Esino, some miles west of Ancona, and managed to get most of its units away but with heavy and unnecessary loss. Its claim that it had frustrated the Polish intention of cutting it off rang hollow as its three regiments had been reduced to a fighting strength of 150, 190 and 230 respectively.† Anders' men entered the city during the afternoon of 18th July. In their support the D.A.F. had flown 696 sorties and dropped 535 tons of bombs in the four days, 15th–18th July.[95]

---

* On 19th July Lieutenant-General Hans Röttiger, who in June had replaced Westphal as Kesselring's Chief of Staff, learnt from Wentzell that the Poles had recently used some 200 tanks in a massed assault on a narrow front with strong air support. This was so different from 8th Army's usual infantry battalion/tank squadron tactics that Wentzell called for greater efforts to improve the anti-tank defences of the Gothic Line.[91]

† An 8th Army Intelligence Summary shows that between 16th and 21st July the Poles took 827 prisoners of whom 601 came from 278th Infantry Division, which brought the total taken from the Division in recent fighting to 1,490.[94]

Ancona was a great prize. It provided the Allies with a large port on the Adriatic second only in size to Bari, and it was to prove an invaluable base for further operations in northern Italy.

(vi)

It is time to see what had been happening in the air as the Germans fell back on the Heinrich Line. The main characteristics of this Third Phase, dawn 3rd to dawn 17th July, was the rise in sorties flown and bombloads dropped in the battle area to a level almost comparable to the halcyon days of the First Phase, immediately after the fall of Rome, and described in Chapter IX. An estimated total of 3,407 sorties was flown within the battle area and some 1,670 tons of bombs dropped.[96] Of these totals, about 1,720 sorties (663 tons) were flown against M.T. and roads. M.A.T.A.F.'s fighter-bombers made the greatest contribution. Against guns D.A.F.'s fighter-bombers delivered most of the 587 tons of bombs.* Of the remaining targets bombed, 134 tons of bombs were dropped on ammunition and fuel dumps. Understandably there were few attacks on railway targets and even fewer on towns, troops and miscellaneous targets. The most significant changes came from the introduction of the 'Dixie' system. After Kesselring had won some freedom of action from Hitler he adopted in early July, as we have seen, the technique of a slow fighting withdrawal in which the main bodies of his divisions fell back through a series of closely spaced delaying lines, while their rear-guards pulled back, even more slowly, using still more closely spaced positions. It gradually became apparent to 8th Army and D.A.F. staffs that the German habit of fighting rear-guard actions by day and withdrawing to a new line of defence each night meant that the Allied troops were frequently unable to make contact until late afternoon because of the extensive German demolitions. On those occasions when contact could be made early in the day, the Germans were usually forced to withdraw before dark and then

---

* The areas of responsibility of the various subordinate air formations of M.A.T.A.F. for attacks on the enemy's L. of C. were redefined on 2nd July, to be effective next day, as follows (*See Map 4*):-

U.S. XII T.A.C. (other than U.S. 87th Fighter Wing)
    All land and sea communications within the area bounded on the east by the Florence–Prato–Bologna–Ferrara railway line and on the north by the Po river and on the west by the Pavia–Genoa railway line.
U.S. XII T.A.C. (U.S. 87th Fighter Wing)
    All land and sea communications within U.S. XII T.A.C.'s area but north of the line Spezia–Bologna.
D.A.F.
    All land and sea communications within the area east of but exclusive of the Florence–Prato–Bologna–Ferrara railway line and south of the Po river.

targets became available for the fighter-bombers. The new system, called 'Dixie', was introduced to make the best use of the few hours of daylight left. When enemy targets appeared a Corps was to call for Dixie, which would normally be available from 7 to 8.30 p.m. During this period a tactical reconnaissance aircraft, in V.H.F. contact with Rover David and the fighter-bombers in the Cabrank, was to be over the forward area for the entire time and more tactical reconnaissance aircraft were to be made available if necessary. The tactical reconnaissance task was to find suitable targets for the fighter-bombers and report them to Rover David, the controller when in doubt referring them to the leading brigade. Responsibility for the order to attack remained with Rover David. It was for the tactical reconnaissance aircraft pilot, or pilots, to confirm that targets found by ground troops were suitable for air attack. Throughout the Dixie period fighter-bomber aircraft were to be kept in the Cabrank in successive formations of six. The Cabrank was refilled every 15 minutes.

On 8th Army's front on 3rd July two calls for assistance from army formations were answered—one to deal with a concentration of M.T. and the other with some heavy guns. The same day No. 24 (S.A.A.F.) Squadron, re-equipped with Marauder II medium day bomber aircraft, rejoined No. 3 (S.A.A.F) Wing in D.A.F. after a spell in the Middle East. During the night of the 3rd/4th three Bostons and seven Baltimores from D.A.F. dropped 7.6 tons of bombs on troops south-west and west of Arezzo, an area which was to receive increasing attention from D.A.F. until the capture of Arezzo on 16th July. On 4th July, in bad weather conditions, armed reconnaissances were flown in the battle area, and a call from the Polish Corps to attack mortar positions was successfully complied with. Next day, the 5th, heavy cloud restricted flying but six calls for assistance were answered, five against guns and one against a concentration of infantry, M.T. and guns resulting in 65 Kittyhawks and Mustangs from D.A.F. attacking these targets with 32.2 tons of bombs, mostly south-west of Arezzo. On the 6th the number of calls for assistance rose to seven. The first Dixie operations took place on the 7th. In a total of five such operations the fighter-bombers had to attack alternative targets in three of them, but in the last two tactical reconnaissance aircraft found 20 M.T. and tanks dispersed around a building and more of them on a road. The attacks were described as 'very successful'. Seven other calls for assistance were answered that day which included the guns north and east of Arezzo on which 56 Kittyhawks from D.A.F. dropped 29.8 tons of bombs. On the 8th the number of calls rose to nine, mostly against guns, and on those in and west of the Arezzo area 36 Kittyhawks and Mustangs from D.A.F.

dropped 12.5 tons of bombs. Next day the pattern was similar with 29 Kittyhawks and Mustangs dropping 14.3 tons on the guns south-west and north of Arezzo. We have already discussed the air support given to 13th Corps in its drive on Arezzo during 10th–14th July.

On 15th July the fighter-bombers of D.A.F. were fully extended in support of 8th Army. In assistance to 13th Corps in its attack on Arezzo 90 Kittyhawks and Mustangs bombed roads in the area with 45.6 tons of bombs while another 89 (44.8 tons) bombed guns in the Arezzo-Sansepolcro area, and some Spitfire fighter-bombers attacked roads north of Arezzo. During the Army's attack on Arezzo, and in supporting the New Zealand Division on the right flank, the locations of some of the targets D.A.F. was asked to bomb were again only 800 yards ahead of the forward troops marked with coloured smoke. The Army was well pleased with the results. Also on the 15th, pre-D day support was given to the Polish Corps for its attack on Ancona, Marauders and Baltimores bombing guns at Iesi as already described. That same evening three Dixie operations were laid on between 7 and 8 p.m. In two of them alternative targets had to be attacked, but in the third a small concentration of M.T. which had been spotted by tactical reconnaissance was effectively bombed.

The last day in this Third Phase, 16th July, was another busy one for the fighter-bombers of D.A.F. Nearly half of the 259 sorties flown were in direct support of 13th Corps or closely associated with its operations. Calls for assistance by 13th Corps included an enemy strongpoint at Chiani, directly west of Arezzo, which was bombed by 16 Mustangs with 8.2 tons and various gun positions were attacked by about 50 Kittyhawks and Mustangs dropping about 30 tons of bombs. A staging area at Agazzi, on the south-west outskirts of Arezzo, was bombed by 19 Kittyhawks with 11.4 tons, and roads to the north-west and north (Route 71) by a force of Mustangs and Spitfires. As already described, a large force of Marauders and Baltimores supported the Polish Corps in its attack on Ancona. On the evening of the 16th there were no less than 14 Dixie operations amounting to 84 sorties. Targets included two concentrations of M.T., a suspected enemy headquarters, a small concentration of tanks, several groups of guns and half-track vehicles.

(vii)

On the German side the loss of Ancona was quickly followed by rumours, reported on 19th July and possibly emanating from

A.A.I.'s deception plan 'Ottrington', that 2nd Polish Corps was about to be relieved by a British formation. As it was also suspected that 1st Canadian Corps might appear on the Adriatic coast, when Kesselring returned from Hitler's Headquarters on 19th July he authorised von Vietinghoff to extract 1st Parachute Division and to move it to Cattolica, as a long stop for 51st Mountain Corps.[97] At the same time Lemelsen was instructed to extract 90th Panzer Grenadier Division to form an Army Group reserve, to be located north of Florence while it refitted. These measures to create mobile reserves behind the front reflected views held at *OKW* where, as we have seen in Chapter VI Part I of this Volume, it was thought in mid-July that the Allies might turn their whole strategic attention to Italy. On the 22nd Kesselring told his Army Commanders that if this were to be the case, both his seaboards would be threatened. To guard the rear Adriatic sector, a Corps command under General Witthöft was assigned 98th Infantry Division, transferred from the Balkans on orders from *OKW* and originally destined for Istria, plus 162nd (Turkoman) Division and the cadres of the decimated 94th Infantry Division.[98] Concern for the Adriatic sector was also evident in the decision, taken on 28th July but not implemented until 8th August, that on reaching the Gothic Line Herr's 76th Panzer Corps would change places with Feuerstein's 51st Mountain Corps. The latter would thus move into the high country north-east of Florence, and Herr would defend the coast and control operations in the open and flatter country. There is no direct evidence that anything but logical military thinking lay behind this proposal, but like all good deception plans 'Ottrington' probably reinforced ideas which were already there. We have shown in Chapter VI how fears for a landing in Genoa were also fostered by deception. For this eventuality Kesselring decreed on 31st July that the nascent Army of Liguria would be reinforced by 26th Panzer Division from *AOK 14*. 90th Panzer Grenadier Division, now stationed between Parma and Modena, was to be ready to move to either coast if invasion threatened, as were 15th Panzer Grenadier Division and reinforcing arms from *AOK 10*. Though relatively modest in scale, these precautions testify to strategic uncertainties which persisted well into August.

See Map 5

With the fall of Leghorn, Arezzo and Ancona all attention turned to the battle for Florence which was waged between Kirkman's 13th Corps, and Schlemm's 1st Parachute Corps and the western wing of Herr's 76th Panzer Corps. Since the fall of Arezzo 13th Corps' front had been widened to include the F.E.C.'s sector in which

8th Indian Division had been re-committed after a very short rest and refit.[99] Kirkman's plan was to develop two strong armoured thrusts towards Florence, using his two armoured divisions with 4th Division acting as a link between them. 6th Armoured Division was to advance along the east bank of the Middle Arno which was far from attractive armoured country. There were only about four miles between the river, which was to form the Division's left boundary with 4th Division, and the Pratomagno massif which dominated the whole valley. 6th Armoured Division's War Diary complains:[100]

> 'The valley itself was by no means flat, closely wooded in parts and criss-crossed by small ravines. Not for the first time it could be said of the Division's allotted sector for advance—this is no country for an Armoured Division! . . . The prospect of a slow and arduous advance seemed inescapable'.

6th South African Armoured Division's axis was to be Radda-Greve on the western side of the Chianti Mountains, which are a range of steep, thickly wooded hills stretching north-west through Mt Maione (Pt 812) towards Florence.[101] 4th Division was to clear from the eastern side of the Chianti Mountains to the Middle Arno. 8th Indian Division would cover the Corps' left flank. If the Germans resisted the Corps' advances strongly, General Kirkman intended to strengthen his thrust by bringing in 2nd New Zealand Division to help 6th British Armoured Division; otherwise the New Zealanders would be held in Corps reserve.

AOK *14* fought its part of the battle on a series of map lines which led back to the position south of Florence which 1st Parachute Corps was informed on 20th July that it must defend for 'some time'.[102] This was the 'Paula' Line, running from Montelupo at the junction of the Pesa and Arno rivers four miles east of Empoli, across to Mt Scalari (Pt 787) and on to Figline on the Middle Arno. With 29th Panzer Grenadier, 4th Parachute and 356th Infantry Divisions under his command, on 17th July Schlemm was about to take up an intermediate line covering Castelfiorentino, Tavernelle, and the western ridges of the Chianti Mountains. On this date Mt Maione (Pt 812) became the prescribed contact point with AOK *10's* 76th Panzer Corps, which was holding a delaying line from south of Montevarchi along the Arno north of Arezzo to the Alpe di Poti.

6th Armoured Division, led by 26th Armoured Brigade, started to thrust north-west from Arezzo on 17th July making for Castiglion Fibocchi.[103] 4th Division advanced north across the hills towards Montevarchi which it approached on the 18th. Both divisions, however, had come up against 76th Panzer Corps' Irmgard position, which was strongly held. Failing to gain Castiglion Fibocchi,

6th British Armoured Division sent some tanks across the Middle Arno at Laterina but could make no progress on the west bank either. 4th Division was stopped by the newly arrived 715th Infantry Division holding the high ground north-west of Montevarchi. 6th Armoured Division's fears were being confirmed.

6th South African Armoured Division fared rather better.[104] It had advanced on a two brigade front during 16th July on the axis of the Castel di Brolio-Radda road, 12th Motor Brigade astride the road and 24th Guards Brigade protecting its right flank along the western slopes of the Chianti Mountains. The Guards made good progress on 17th July and Radda was entered that night, when 1st Parachute Corps withdrew northwards because of 5th Army's pressure on 14th Panzer Corps. The South African advance was then directed to securing the main features in the Chianti range: Mt Maione (Pt 812) and Mt S. Michele (Pt 892) both over 2,000 feet high. 24th Guards Brigade took the former by a surprise night march on 18th/19th July and went on, ably supported by the tanks of the Pretoria Regiment, over the forested hills to take S. Michele on 20th July. 12th Motor Brigade advanced over equally rough country on the left to Mt Querciabella (Pt 845). The Division had captured the highest points in the Chianti Mountains from which the ground sloped steadily down to the Arno valley and Florence. The loss of these dominating peaks by 715th Infantry Division forced 76th Panzer Corps to withdraw to its next delaying position covering S. Giovanni.

General Kirkman appreciated that some hard fighting lay ahead of his Corps before it could reach the Lower Arno and his main objective, Florence. He had become disenchanted with the Middle Arno valley. Besides being unsuitable for an armoured thrust, it was being tenaciously defended by 76th Panzer Corps, although the newly arrived and inexperienced 715th Infantry Division was making a poor showing in the Chianti Mountains.[105] Kirkman therefore decided on 20th July to concentrate his effort on 6th South African Armoured Division's front, stating his intention as follows:[106]

> '13 Corps will make a powerful thrust to seize the crossings over R. Arno at and west of Florence.'

To do this he decided to bring 2nd New Zealand Division out of reserve and into the line between the South Africans and 8th Indian Division as part of the relief of the F.E.C. It was to thrust northwards on the axis S. Casciano on Route 2 to the Lower Arno crossings at Signa, five miles west of Florence. 6th South African Armoured Division was to continue its advance up the road axis Radda-Greve-Impruneta with 4th Division on its right. On the flanks of this two pronged thrust 6th Armoured Division, in the

Middle Arno valley, and 8th Indian Division, in the Elsa river valley, were to push forward as opportunity offered.

This revision necessitated some changes in the F.E.C. relief plan. On 21st July the New Zealand Division moved a brigade forward ready to pass through the right flank of the F.E.C. while 8th Indian Division moved up north of Poggibonsi through the F.E.C. centre and left. A large proportion of 13th Corps artillery, which now included both 1st and 6th A.G.R.A., was decentralised to manage a front which was forty miles wide.[107] Two medium regiments and one S.P. gun regiment were placed under command of 2nd New Zealand Division, one medium regiment under 6th South African Division, and one medium regiment under 4th Division. To 8th Indian Division was given one S.P. gun regiment and to 6th Armoured Division one regiment of field artillery. 1st and 6th A.G.R.A. retained between them two heavy and two medium regiments.

6th South African Division continued its advance from Mt S. Michele (Point 892) during 21st July against stiffening resistance. Using its two infantry brigades forward, the division pressed on towards the Mt Fili (Pt 554) high ground just south-west of Greve. The approaches were heavily mined and a number of the tanks were lost. Nevertheless most of the high ground was secured on 22nd July except Mt Fili itself. A further attack with full divisional artillery support was put in on the morning of 23rd July. This was successful but 1st Parachute Corps continued to counter-attack throughout the day before withdrawing during the night 23rd/24th July. 11th South African Armoured Brigade passed through and thrust towards Mercatale the next day, against strong rear-guards of 356th Infantry Division supported by Tiger tanks. At dusk on 26th July the Brigade entered Mercatale. It was then checked on the River Greve by units of 4th Parachute Division fighting on the right of 356th Infantry Division.

Meanwhile the New Zealand Division on the left of the South Africans began to make its presence felt.[108] Stubbornly opposed by 4th Parachute Division, which was well supported by artillery and mortars and, on occasion, by Tiger tanks, the division advanced on Tavernelle on Route 2 which was in New Zealand hands by 23rd July. Continuing their advance on the 24th the Division reached the vicinity of Fabbrica, to which the Germans were clinging stubbornly. However, outflanked by the advance of the South African Division on Mercatale, the paratroopers withdrew during the night 24th/25th to a new delaying position which in their sector covered S. Casciano on Route 2.

On 13th Corps' eastern flank the advance of 6th Armoured Division lagged behind the rest of the Corps, as its axis was dominated by the slopes of the Pratamagno massif.[109]* 4th Division, which was attempting to clear the west bank of the Arno, entered S. Giovanni on 23rd July, but 76th Panzer Corps was not much perturbed by this and 4th Division found it difficult to develop its subsequent operations against Figline. On 13th Corps' western flank, the progress of 8th Indian Division's advance north of Castelfiorentino met little oposition before 25th July, when it was halted by 29th Panzer Grenadier Division of 1st Parachute Corps, holding positions between Montespertoli and Cambiano in the Elsa valley. On the 26th Kesselring commended to *OKW* the powers of resistance and discipline shown by Schlemm's divisions in the blistering July heat, against an enemy with overwhelming superiority in artillery and air support. *AOK 14* confirmed that the morale of 1st Parachute Corps had been raised by its defensive successes, but stressed that numbers were seriously depleted by casualties and heat exhaustion. Schlemm was authorised to retire into the Paula Line during the night of 26th/27th July, and to help him fulfil the order that this was to be held for several days, the flanking 14th Panzer Corps took over a part of his sector. Lemelsen reckoned that the battle for Florence had now opened in earnest, and its progress was closely followed by Kesselring who believed that 8th Army attached 'much more than average significance' to the capture of the city.†

The South Africans, New Zealanders and Indians followed up Schlemm's withdrawal and by the evening of the 28th were in contact with the Paula Line over most of the front.[112] 4th Division was given the unenviable task of clearing the high, trackless area of the Scalari massif which gave excellent observation over the south-eastern approaches to Florence. Advancing from Dudda on the southern side of the feature on 27th July, its 12th Brigade established itself on the southern slopes, but 28th Brigade was held up. Next day neither brigade was successful and so 12th Brigade's reserve battalion was brought forward with orders to pass through and clear the summit. 6th Black Watch attacked on 29th July and after fierce fighting succeeded in reaching the summit and

---

* On 24th July Major-General G.W.R. Templer assumed command of 6th Armoured Division, replacing General Evelegh, who was to take up the appointment of A.C.I.G.S. Unfortunately Templer was seriously wounded as the result of a mine explosion on 5th August.[110]

† During the morning of 26th July 13th Corps was visited by H.M. King George VI, who drove through the areas held by 6th Armoured Division, 4th Division, 6th South African Armoured Division and 8th Indian Division. At 4th Division and 8th Indian Division investiture parades were held for the award of the Victoria Cross. Kesselring attributed heavy fighting on 28th July to the visit of the King, who had, Kesselring claimed, 'pointed to Florence and asked for its capture'. This image of George VI emulating his ancestors' military command in the field gave colour to Kesselring's belief that Florence was needed by the British as a 'prestige success' to offset the Americans' capture of Rome.[111]

consolidating its hold on Mt Scalari during the night 29th/30th July. As Mt Scalari lay on the boundary between 1st Parachute Corps of *AOK 14* and 76th Panzer Corps of *AOK 10*, its loss caused considerable German confusion. It also breached an outcrop of the Heinrich Line known as Heinrich 1, into which Herr had pulled back on his right wing during the night of 26th/27th July. His further local withdrawal on the 29th enabled 6th Armoured Division to make some useful ground along the east bank of the Middle Arno.

During the same two days, 28th and 29th July, the New Zealand Division (which crossed the Pesa river without opposition on 27th July) attempted to clear the higher ground north of Cerbaia and S. Casciano, but these positions were outposts of the Paula Line and were stubbornly defended.[113] By now, Kirkman had decided he must mount a fresh Corps' attack for which the South African and New Zealand Divisions would be best placed to undertake the final thrust to break through the Paula Line and reach Florence.[114] 4th Division on the right and 8th Indian Division on the left would protect the flanks of his main thrust, with 6th Armoured Division advancing as opportunity offered.

Kirkman issued his orders for the attack late on 29th July (*see Map 7*). 2nd New Zealand Division was to carry out the main assault with its final objectives the dominating heights of Poggio al Pino and La Poggiona on the far side of the Pesa river. To give the assault more punch 8th Indian Division was to take over the western third of the New Zealand sector. The New Zealand Division's attack was to be supported by a heavy artillery programme in which the artillery of 6th South African and 8th Indian Divisions as well as 1st A.G.R.A. were to take part, the latter being responsible for co-ordinating counter-battery fire. Altogether one heavy regiment, the greater part of two medium regiments, two heavy anti-aircraft batteries and two field regiments were to be employed, in addition to the four field regiments which were already under the command of the New Zealand Division. On the New Zealand Division's right 6th South African Armoured Division was to neutralise the enemy occupying the high ground west of Impruneta and prepare to take over the clearance of Route 2 into Florence. The three divisions, Indian, New Zealand and South African, were in effect executing a half right wheel along the line of the Pesa to converge on Florence from the south-west.

2nd New Zealand Division regrouped during the night 29th/30th July and 8th Indian Division moved up to the Pesa river on their left.[115] The New Zealanders were now on a three brigade front: 5th N.Z. Brigade facing Faltignano; 4th N.Z. Armoured Brigade opposite La Romola and 6th N.Z. Brigade in S. Michele. 5th

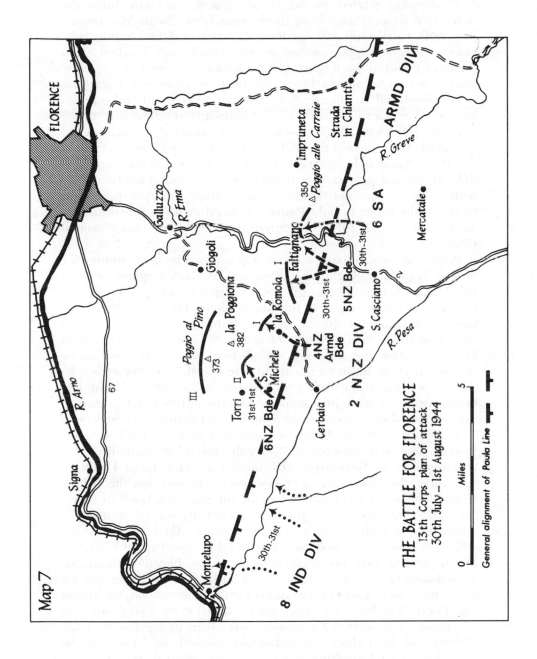

Map 7

FLORENCE

R. Arno

Signa

67

Saltuzzo

R. Ema

Giogoli

Poggio al Pino

△ 373

△ 382 la Poggiona

Torri

31st-1st

III

II

I

S. Michele

6NZ Bde

la Romola

4NZ Armd Bde

I

Cerbaia

R. Pesa

2 N Z DIV

30th-31st

5NZ Bde

S. Casciano

faltignano

30th-31st

Impruneta

350
△ Poggio alle Carraie

Strada in Chianti

R. Greve

6 S A ARMD DIV

Mercatale

Montelupo

30th-31st

8 IND DIV

THE BATTLE FOR FLORENCE
13th Corps plan of attack
30th July – 1st August 1944

0   Miles   5

General alignment of Paula Line

N.Z. Brigade started its attack at 10 p.m. on 30th July, the Armoured Brigade assaulting three hours later. By midday on 31st July both Faltignano and La Romola were in Allied hands. The heavy artillery support given to the attack had resulted in a temporary ammunition shortage and Kirkman agreed to a 24-hour pause in the assault to bring up fresh supplies. 1st Parachute Corps also faced an ammunition shortage, as reduced fuel supplies hampered replacement of the large amounts recently shot off.[116] On 28th July, when high casualties were reported, Lemelsen had informed Army Group that Schlemm could only continue to hold the Paula Line if he were allocated fresh troop reserves, which *AOK 14* did not possess. An alternative retraction of his boundary with *AOK 10* was sanctioned by Kesselring on 29th July, and although the order to hold Paula remained in force Schlemm was authorised on 30th July to reconnoitre a fallback position closer to Florence.

Within the city, a tough attitude was adopted by the Commander of 10th Parachute Regiment, appointed its Commandant on 23rd July. Influenced perhaps by the experiences of 4th Parachute Division in Rome, on 29th July this Colonel Fuchs told the Swiss Consul that it must not be supposed that the Germans 'would expose themselves to military defeat for the sake of the beauties of Florence', and his adjutant added that they would withdraw through it from south to north 'in one breath'. At higher levels, the excuse for a hardening of policies came when Alexander, broadcasting on 28th July, appealed to the citizens of Florence to inform the Allies where German mines and demolitions had been laid, and to clear the streets of barricades and obstacles. Leaflets to this effect were dropped on the 30th, and when their discovery was reported to Kesselring, *OB Südwest* at once asked Hitler to reconsider the 'open' status of Florence, claiming that the British clearly had no intention of 'honouring international law'. In reply, the Führer directed on 31st July that Kesselring was to conduct his operations in such a way as to demonstrate that it was only the Allies who failed to respect the 'irreplaceable treasures' of Florence. He stipulated that no bridges were to be blown without his permission. Nonetheless, *AOK 14* was authorised by Kesselring on this same date to make preparations for their demolition, excluding the Ponte Vecchio. The subsequent decision to carry out this operation, code-named *Feuerzauber*, was taken in the name of *OB Südwest* and the Führer was not again invoked, but there can be little doubt that Kesselring acted under his covert direction.

On the Allied side Alexander had no intention of fighting in Florence.[117] Kirkman gave conditional orders to his divisions for by-passing the city on 28th July. He foresaw two possibilities:

' . . . If the enemy does not destroy the bridges and thus carries out his declared policy to treat Florence as an open town, it is desirable that as far as possible Divs should cross by the most easterly and westerly bridges and pass through the outskirts of the town, so as to give the enemy as little excuse as possible for shelling the place . . .

In the event of all bridges being destroyed, including those in Florence, and Florence itself being held, it is my intention that 4 Brit Div and 2 NZ Div should attempt to secure a crossing outside Florence within their div bdys, 6 SA Armd Div probably confining itself to containing the enemy holding Florence'.

During 31st July and 1st August D.A.F. harried the German positions in front of the New Zealand Division, flying about 100 fighter-bombers sorties on each of the two days.[118] The attack was resumed at 11 p.m. on 1st August, the New Zealand Division assaulting with its three brigades simultaneously.[119] Both 4th New Zealand Armoured Brigade on the right and 6th New Zealand Brigade on the left made significant progress and by dawn on 2nd August La Poggiona and Poggio al Pino were under close attack. At 6 p.m. that day 22nd New Zealand Motor Battalion (4th New Zealand Armoured Brigade) supported by a heavy artillery bombardment finally cleared the enemy off La Poggiona. 1st Parachute Corps, which had pulled out of the Paula Line during the night of 31st July/1st August, reported on the 2nd that the artillery battering had caused high casualties and that in some of its battalions the companies could muster only 10–15 men. With Army Group's sanction, Schlemm accordingly withdrew that night into a bridgehead position on the line of the Ema river, and on the following night the bulk of his troops crossed the Arno. On the right of the New Zealand Division, 11th South African Armoured Brigade had cleared Poggio alle Carraie during the evening of 2nd August, and at the same time elements from this brigade and from 24th Guards Brigade, moving up from Strada in Chianti, converged on Impruneta which the Germans abandoned during the night.

Throughout 3rd August strong columns from the New Zealand, South African and 4th British Divisions fought their way towards Florence, 5th New Zealand Brigade making for Giogoli and the South Africans for Galluzzo.[120] German rear-guards made a brief stand at Galluzzo before withdrawing completely during the night 3rd/4th August, allowing the New Zealand and South African advanced guards to move cautiously through the southern outskirts of Florence. By dawn on 4th August they had reached the Arno. They found all the bridges destroyed except the Ponte Vecchio, which was too narrow and weak to take military traffic and had been blocked at either end by the demolition and mining of nearby buildings. By the end of 5th August the whole south bank of the Arno between Florence and Montelupo was in Allied hands, 8th Indian Division having moved up to the river between Signa and Montelupo. *AOK 14's* records show that Kesselring's Chief of Staff authorised the activation of *Feuerzauber* at 6 p.m. on 3rd August.[121] In *OKW's* War Diary, it was explained that the 'original orders' for the Arno bridges had been rescinded because the Allies were themselves shelling them, and because it was necessary to prevent the enemy from crossing to the north bank of the Arno as swiftly and easily as he had crossed the Tiber in Rome.[122] *OKW's* diarist added that the 'cultural value' of the Ponte Vecchio exempted it from destruction, and it may be that this bridge, described by Churchill as 'venerable but inadequate', was spared as a gambit for propaganda. In any event, it is ironical that the treasures of Florence suffered more from the floods of 1966 than from either the Germans or the Allies in 1944.

See Map 5

While the battle for Florence was being fought to a conclusion 10th Corps continued its difficult advance north on 8th Army's third objective, Bibbiena. The town lies in a narrow plain some eighteen miles north of Arezzo at the head of the valley of the Upper Arno and is flanked on the east by a roadless massif called the Alpe di Catenaia (4,641 feet) and on the west by the longer and higher massif of the Pratomagno (5,224 feet). With the fall of Arezzo there was a change in the inter-Corps boundary, 10th Corps being given Arezzo and Route 71, which runs due north to Bibbiena in the valley of the Upper Arno.[123] This allowed it to deploy 4th Indian Division in the Upper Arno valley, leaving 10th Indian Division to advance astride the Tiber valley on Sansepolcro and thence north-westwards across the Alpe di Catenaia, to turn the German defences of Bibbiena from the east.

During the five days needed for regrouping, 17th–21st July, only minor operations took place: 25th Indian Brigade of 10th Indian Division carried out an assault against Citta di Castello at dawn on 21st July.[124] Two troops of Sherman tanks from 3rd Hussars (in support of the Brigade) crossed the Soara river by a ford a mile east of its confluence with the Tiber and climbed the very steep ascent to the ridge beyond, where the infantry of 51st Mountain Corps' 114th Jäger Division lacked anti-tank weapons because they were relying on the ground being impassable to tanks. They panicked and broke. Two 3rd Hussar squadrons and 1st Kings Own Regiment swiftly followed up the leading tanks and secured the crest. 741st Jäger Regiment lost 90 dead—30 corpses were found in one small area—and 30 prisoners.[125] von Vietinghoff reluctantly agreed that the Jäger Division could abandon Citta di Castello and withdraw a few miles to the north of the town.

On the Alpe di Poti, 7th Indian Brigade of 4th Indian Division continued to increase its foothold on the southern part of the massif, helped by the newly arrived 11th Indian Brigade which operated against the western slopes.[126]

McCreery's immediate objective for 10th Corps after regrouping was the lateral road due north of Arezzo, running from Route 71 along the Chiassa stream to Anghiari, west of the Tiber valley, which would bring the Corps up to the southern face of the Alpe di Catenaia.[127] East of the Tiber he hoped to reach S. Giustino (south-east of Sansepolcro) which he expected would be firmly held to block Route 73 over the Apennines.

The advance, which started again on 22nd July, was arduous as in all mountain fighting.[128] 51st Mountain Corps did not give ground easily as it was instructed by von Vietinghoff on the same day that the Allies must be held at bay in the Sansepolcro valley as long as possible. The two Indian divisions were ideally suited to their tasks which involved hard climbing and close quarters fighting in that sparsely roaded country. 10th Indian's advance from Citta di Castello east of the Tiber was fairly rapid until it neared S. Giustino where it was checked. West of the Tiber the fighting was harder, and many counter-attacks were staged by 44th Infantry Division. Only on 28th July was this Division driven off the high ground south-east of Anghiari, causing Kesselring to authorise 51st Mountain Corps to pull back to Campalla-S. Giustino. The speed of 4th Indian Division's advance was limited by the need to build jeep tracks through the mountains to bring forward supplies. It was not until 26th July that it could develop its attack to clear the Alpe di Poti, but by 29th July it too was on its sector of the Corps' objective. Both divisions were then given a few days' rest to carry out reliefs and build up supplies before pressing north again towards Bibbiena.

See Map 1

On the Adriatic coast the fall of Ancona marked a change in the role of 2nd Polish Corps which became responsible for acting out the 'Ottrington' deception plan. Anders' aim became to draw German attention away from the proposed Florence-Bologna axis of attack and towards the ostensibly concealed preparations for a major offensive to breach the Gothic Line in its Adriatic sector and so enter the Po valley via Rimini.[129] The Corps also needed to absorb some 4,000 reinforcements to make good the losses, particularly in infantry, which it had suffered during its attacks on Mt Cassino and its subsequent advance up the Adriatic coast.* At the same time it needed to switch its maintenance from the distant Ortona railhead to the port of Ancona.

In conformity with his new deception role, Anders prepared to continue pressure with an advance to the Misa river, some ten miles further north of the Esino. He used two battle groups, one from each division, operating under Corps' control. The advance began on 20th July but was soon checked on the high ground just south of the Misa by 278th Infantry Division of 51st Mountain Corps, which withdrew behind the river on 25th July.[130] Anders then moved up the main bodies of his two Polish divisions, which re-absorbed their battle groups, and started extensive patrolling until the night 3rd/4th August when the Germans carried out a further voluntary withdrawal.[131] This brought 278th Infantry Division into a new defensive position between the Misa and Cesano rivers. 2nd Polish Corps, with the *C.I.L.* protecting its inland flank, followed up and secured Senigallia on the coast and the higher ground between the two rivers.

AOK 10 had not been unduly alarmed by these operations, but the effects of 'Ottrington' were nonetheless reflected in a general situation report which preceded the daily entries in its War Diary for August 1944. This observed that the pattern of 8th Army's reconnaissance and artillery activity, together with shipping movements in Ancona and the rumoured presence of Canadian troops on 51st Mountain Corps' left wing, pointed to a strike up the Adriatic coast. 1st Parachute Division was accordingly redeploying in and forward of the Adriatic sector of the Gothic Line, and to guard against landings the Army was endeavouring to reinforce and improve its coastal defences in the vulnerable sector north of Rimini.

(viii)

During the last and final of the four air phases of the pursuit from Rome to the Arno (dawn 17th July to dawn 6th August) preparations for 'Anvil' affected the control of tactical air operations, but nevertheless a high degree of continuity of support for the Allied armies on the mainland was maintained. By 18th July the move of all the units of U.S. XII T.A.C. to Corsica had been completed, including that of No. 324 Wing R.A.F. which brought the number

---

* Most of these reinforcements were found by internal re-organisation, by reducing the strength of artillery and Service Corps units.

of R.A.F. fighter wings in Corsica up to three.[132] M.A.T.A.F.'s Mitchell medium bombers were already in Corsica and its Marauders in Sardinia.

H.Q. M.A.T.A.F. moved to Corsica and began to function there on 19th July. Major-General Cannon continued to be responsible for the control of the two U.S.A.F. medium bomber wings of U.S. XII T.A.C. in Corsica and of D.A.F. on the mainland. Cannon left his Deputy, Air Vice-Marshal D'Albiac, together with a small staff on the mainland to form a subsidiary headquarters to be known as H.Q. Tactical Air Force (Italy), of which D'Albiac was appointed the A.O.C. His responsibilities were: to represent Cannon on the mainland; to act as adviser to the C.-in-C. A.A.I.; and to vet requests from A.O.C. D.A.F. for additional air support, passing on those requests of which he approved to H.Q. M.A.T.A.F. in Corsica for action.

Air Vice-Marshal Dickson, A.O.C. D.A.F., worked to a general directive from Cannon which included the responsibility for providing air support for both 5th and 8th Armies as from 5 a.m. on 20th July. Dickson kept his Advanced H.Q. D.A.F. alongside H.Q. 8th Army and, initially, the existing Mobile Operations Room Unit (No. 1 M.O.R.U. 'B') on the east coast of Italy continued to control the defensive fighters in that area and at the same time acted as a link between D.A.F. and the Polish Corps. To assist in the control of air support for 5th Army Dickson created a branch of his headquarters known as 'Ops A', composed of one officer from D.A.F. and two on loan from U.S. XII T.A.C., located alongside H.Q. 5th Army to act as Dickson's representative there. Requests for air support were discussed by 5th Army with 'Ops A', which in turn passed them to H.Q. D.A.F., where arrangements were made to meet them according to the resources available and 8th Army's requirements. To control the defensive fighters on the west coast of Italy Dickson decided on 21st July to move No. 1 M.O.R.U. 'B' to the west coast, No. 287 Wing R.A.F. (from M.A.C.A.F.) taking over the same day, acting temporarily until No. 1 M.O.R.U. 'A' could replace it on the east coast on 18th September. Dickson kept the bulk of his fighters and fighter-bombers centrally located and under his control so that the main effort could be directed to either Army front.

During this period Dickson was reinforced with No. 454 (R.A.A.F.) Squadron with Baltimores from the Middle East and No. 87 Squadron with Spitfires from Mediterranean Allied Coastal Air Force, raising his total strength to 29½ squadrons with which to support both 5th and 8th Armies.* Five more squadrons (one

---

* D.A.F.'s Order of Battle on 2nd August is given at the end of this Chapter at Table I.

medium and one light bomber and three fighter) as well as the
services of a U.S.A.A.F. photographic reconnaissance squadron
were promised as added reinforcements. H.Q. M.A.T.A.F. also
agreed that from 21st July No. 225 Tac. R. Squadron, which had
moved to Corsica for Operation 'Anvil', could assist No. 285 Wing
R.A.F. (which controlled all the reconnaissance squadrons) by
continuing to provide tactical reconnaissance for 5th Army on the
mainland until required for 'Anvil'. No. 225 Squadron would leave
some of its aircraft with No. 285 Wing until then.

We will be examining the preliminary air operations in support
of 'Anvil' in Chapter XII and so will confine ourselves here to
operations in Italy. Within the battle area the division of
M.A.T.A.F.'s effort between 5th and 8th Army naturally reflected
the level of activity of the two armies. 5th Army was approaching
the River Arno and had started to prepare for its part in the
assault on the Gothic Line. 8th Army had still to capture Ancona
and Florence. The estimated totals of sorties flown in support of
each Allied army and the corresponding tonnages of bombs dropped during this Fourth Phase, dawn 17th July to dawn 6th August,
but excluding 440 sorties flown and 261 tons of bombs dropped in
support of the Polish Corps on 17th and 18th July in their attack
on Ancona, were:[133]

Air formation	5th Army battle area		8th Army battle area	
	Sorties	Tons of bombs	Sorties	Tons of bombs
M.A.T.A.F. (M.B.)	48	46.0	—	—
U.S. XII T.A.F.				
(L.B. and F.B.)	214	99.0	79	46.8
D.A.F. (L.B. and F.B.)	291	156.6	2,020	1,015.7
	553	301.6	2,099	1,062.5

During the first week of the Fourth Phase, though the Polish
Corps was heavily supported in its attack on Ancona during 17th
and 18th July, 5th Army was given the lion's share of direct air
support for the rest of the week. Thereafter 5th Army received
minimal support while 8th Army fought its battles for Florence.
The averages of the direct air support effort are interesting: 5th
Army received a daily average of 60 sorties and 33 tons of bombs
from 17th to 23rd July during the fighting around Leghorn, and
thereafter had to be satisfied with an average of 10 sorties and five
tons of bombs per day. On four days in this Fourth Phase (30th–31st
July, and 4th–5th August) during 8th Army's battles for Florence
5th Army received none at all. During the whole three weeks of
the Fourth Phase 8th Army averaged 105 sorties and 53 tons of

bombs per day, but from 30th July to 4th August during the closing stages of the operations south of Florence it received an average of 121 sorties and 61 tons of bombs a day. The largest number of sorties were flown on 3rd August when the figure reached 160, and the heaviest load of bombs used was on 2nd August when 86 tons were dropped.

It would be tedious to describe every day in this period of hard fighting while both armies were closing up to the River Arno, so we have chosen two days (27th and 28th July) when the sorties flown in support of 8th Army were about average, and the crescendo day of 3rd August when the 160 sorties were flown, to give examples of days in the life of the Desert Air Force in this Fourth Phase.[134]

On 27th July the Germans were falling back to their Paula Line south of Florence (*Maps 1 and 7*) and on 29th July Kirkman decided that another Corps' attack would be needed to break through to Florence. The sorties flown on 27th July and the approximate effort against the various types of targets was as follows. About 40 Kittyhawk fighter-bombers attacked guns seven miles S.S.W., eight miles north and eight miles south-east of Florence with well over 20 tons of bombs, and another ten Kittyhawks attacked a fuel dump four and a half miles north-west of Florence. Twenty-five or so Spitfire fighter-bombers attacked guns with about six tons of bombs two and a half to four miles south of the city, a few others bombed an ammunition dump eight miles north-west of it and a further seven or so attacked railway tracks serving Florence. That night the Desert Air Force Bostons and its Baltimores flew 22 sorties and dropped over 16 tons of bombs on centres of communications, and on roads and rail tracks serving Florence.

On the 28th 13th Corps was in contact with Paula, and direct air support that day was almost entirely concentrated within an arc around Florence stretching from east through south to W.S.W. some four to 15 miles from the city. Targets requested for attack by 8th Army included guns and defended localities, and the German 1st Parachute Division's Headquarters.* The total direct air support effort that day in 8th Army's battle area and the approximate effort against the various types of targets was as follows. Attacks on guns were made by some 20 Spitfires with a total of about four and a half tons of bombs against positions $10\frac{1}{2}$–13 miles south-east of Florence. Otherwise with the exception of about 28 Spitfires, Kittyhawks and Mustangs which were given

---

* Information was receivced that the G.O.C. of 1st Parachute Division was dining his Corps Commander at 'a large house' 11–13 miles east of Florence.[135] Fifteen minutes after the dinner was due to start, 18 Allied fighter-bombers attacked the headquarters 'with good results'.

M.T. and roads feeding Florence as targets, the rest of the Desert Air Force fighter-bomber effort was spent on an enemy headquarters 11–13 miles east of Florence and troops south-west of Impruneta. That night only seven of D.A.F.'s light bombers operated. On 3rd August its Spitfires, Kittyhawks and Mustangs flew in great strength in support of 8th Army. About 111 sorties were devoted to the advance on Florence. Guns defending the city and positioned at virtually all points of the compass, from the outskirts of the city to a depth in some cases beyond 12 miles and in one instance 18 miles west of Florence, absorbed something like 79 sorties and 26 tons of bombs. Other guns north-west of Arezzo, south and south-east of Pistoia and particularly south-west of Senigallia on the east coast received 17 or more tons of bombs in over 30 sorties. Next in terms of attention paid were M.T. and roads leading to Florence, with the remainder of the effort spent on trenches near and barracks within the city and an ammunition dump south-west of Senigallia.[136]

That night, the 3rd/4th, two Baltimores and one Boston from D.A.F. dropped two tons of bombs on troops in woods in the battle area. Ju. 87s were active again in the Arezzo area and the Beaufighters claimed one shot down. German records show that one 'night ground attack' aircraft failed to return to base.[137]

Behind the smooth, clockwork functioning of Army/Air Co-operation, which had reached a state of development between the Allied armies and tactical air forces that became the pattern for every other theatre of war, were those oft-forgotten yet vital administrative services and by no means least the work carried out by the airfield construction units.[138] In the Desert Air Force area No. 69 Airfield Construction Group was responsible for the rehabilitation and construction of airfields along the Adriatic coast and No. 15 A.C.G. west of the Apennines. The U.S. XII T.A.C.'s requirements were met by the U.S. 815th Engineer Aviation Battalion and the British No. 3 A.C.G. The rapid advance of the Allied armies threw a great strain on these groups. During the first five weeks after the fall of Rome the Desert Air Force groups completed 15 airfields and those of U.S. XII T.A.C. another 12 airfields, the last being at Cecina which was only captured on 2nd July and was open for operations by the 12th.

Before describing the air operations carried out by Mediterranean Allied Air Forces north of the battle area in Italy, and beyond Italy, we will briefly examine the final preparations by both sides for the proposed Allied assault on the centre of the Gothic Line.

(ix)

See Map 1

The final preparations for the assault on the Gothic Line were being made at the end of July as the last German troops fell back over the Arno into their Heinrich positions. Leese's plan, issued in the form of planning notes to Corps Commanders on 28th July, envisaged the use of both 13th and 10th Corps in the main assault in the Florence sector with 1st Canadian Corps filling the central mountain sector between his striking force and 2nd Polish Corps on the Adriatic coast. 5th Corps would be in Army Reserve.[139]

Regrouping for the assault began on 30th July with a series of side-stepping moves designed to concentrate 13th and 10th Corps in their assembly areas either side of Florence and to bring the Canadian Corps, with 10th Indian Division under command, into the central Apennine sector.[140] A number of *ad hoc* forces were formed to help in these moves but neither their composition nor the regrouping moves need concern us because, as we will be describing in the next chapter, the whole plan was changed at the last moment.

In 5th Army a similar regrouping was in progress on the Lower Arno.[141] 4th U.S. Corps held the coastal half of the front with Task Force 45 (*ad hoc* groups of anti-aircraft regiments) and Task Force Ramey (a battle group from 1st U.S. Armoured Division) on the river and the balance of 1st U.S. Armoured Division in reserve at Cecina. 2nd U.S. Corps, which came forward on 25th July and was intended to be 5th Army's assault force, had 91st U.S. Division on the river, 85th U.S. Division in Corps reserve and 88th U.S. Division out of the line, resting and refitting at Volterra. 34th U.S. Division was under 5th Army control, resting at Rosignano.

On the German side, there was relief that *AOK 14* was safely back across the Arno and no longer under pressure in the coastal sector. The defence of Florence had been a respectable performance and had raised morale. *AOK 10* had accomplished its gradual withdrawal into Heinrich, and was becoming more confident about its Adriatic sector of the Gothic Line. On 26th July von Vietinghoff told Kesselring that the development of Green I was showing solid progress.[142] Bessell reported that Panther turrets were being installed, and that anti-tank defences were well in hand. He estimated that a fortnight's more work was needed. 'We shall have that time' Kesselring commented. On 2nd August Kesselring announced that he was very impressed with the defences which 278th and 71st Infantry Divisions had prepared on the Adriatic coast, which he felt was the most vulnerable of his two flanks. von Vietinghoff was less euphoric and his Chief of Staff, Wentzell, bluntly assessed the *AOK 10* sectors as passing muster in the west, lacking depth in the centre, and still inadequate in the east. The ample statistics, which still exist, suggest that preparation of bunkers and weapon positions was well advanced but the vital anti-tank defences were behind schedule. Two lines of figures illustrate the point. They are taken from a table supplied by Bessell on 6th August and relate to 51st Mountain Corps' sector, which covered the Adriatic coast prior to its take-over on 8th August by 76th Panzer Corps.

Shelters: 972 completed; 838 under construction; 181 to be built.
Anti-tank Mines: 65,457 laid; 102,000 to be laid.

Some of the delay in minelaying was caused by the disruption in the flow of mines resulting from the bombing of the Po bridges.[143] The work on defences also suffered from the diversion of skilled engineer units to supervise repair of the bridges and the construction of temporary ferries over the Po. Nevertheless, on 12th August von Vietinghoff directed Bessell to plan the move of his staff and two-thirds of his engineers to Green II by 1st September, leaving the rest to strengthen those vulnerable sectors in Green I about which his Corps commanders might be worried.[144]

As much less detail has survived concerning *AOK 14's* preparations, the evidence which is available suggests that the senior officers of this Army paid less attention to their sectors of Green I, including the vital Florence-Bologna axis, than did the Commander and Staff of *AOK 10* to theirs. Nonetheless an unspecified number of Panther turrets were being emplaced by 25th August, when Lemelsen informed his Corps that at some indeterminate future date they would also receive a number of obsolete 3.7–cm tank gun turrets, to be installed in rear of the more vulnerable sectors of Green I.[145]*

On the evening of 3rd August the two opposing Army Group Commanders were set upon divergent courses, as Alexander intended they should be. Alexander himself was getting ready to force the centre of the Gothic Line, cutting his way through Lemelsen's

---

* An 8th Army assessment of the German defence line, made in late July and based on air reconnaissance and Intelligence sources, judged that the defences of the Futa Pass (Route 65) were formidable but appeared 'outflankable and to have little depth'.[146]

AOK 14 and then trapping von Vietinghoff's *AOK 10* between the River Po and the Adriatic coast. Kesselring, on the other hand, was moving troops to shore up his Adriatic defences and was preparing to counter possible landings round either of his flanks: between Rimini and Ravenna, or in the Gulf of Genoa. Next day Alexander was to fly to Orvieto to discuss future operations with General Leese.

(x)

There was no anxiety among the Allied tactical air force commanders about the ability of the *Luftwaffe* to interfere.[147] June and July had not been encouraging months for the German Air Force in Italy. *Luftflotte 2's* Order of Battle contained 203 operational aircraft on 10th June, of which 90 single-engine fighters were in the far north to counter the Allied heavy day bomber raids into Austria and Germany. The long-range reconnaissance aircraft were at Bergamo. All these aircraft in both roles were directly under H.Q. *Luftflotte 2.** All the long-range bombers (Ju. 88s) had been transferred to France to oppose Operation 'Overlord'. This left 16 tactical reconnaissance aircraft, 64 ground-attack/dive-bombers (all F.W. 190s whose units had become operational again) and 20 night ground-attack aircraft (Ju. 87s) for the direct support of the German armies—a mere 100 aircraft of which 79 were serviceable on 10th June.

Luftflotte 2 continued to issue directives which belied the ability of its subordinate commands to carry out their tasks. On 11th June it announced that if Army Group C were forced to retreat to the Gothic Line the existing functions of the Commanding General of the *Luftwaffe* in central Italy (General der Flieger Ritter von Pohl) would be extended northwards. Subordinate to the Commanding General once the occupation of the Gothic Line was complete, *Jagdfliegerführer*, Northern Italy, would be responsible for air cover for the entire northern area and also for countering Allied bomber formations heading for the Reich. To enable the equipment, supplies and ground organisation of the G.A.F. to move north of the Apennines preparations were to be made for the dismantling of this organisation south of the Genoa-Rimini line, including Rimini airfield and leaving only what was necessary to maintain the small tactical air force. New headquarters were to be prepared for *Luftflotte 2* and for the Commanding General of the *Luftwaffe* in

---

* Under *Luftflotte 2's* direct control were also two Italian Republican Air Force fighter formations equipped with Italian aircraft.

Central Italy. *Jagdfliegerführer*, Northern Italy, was to take over the Fighter Control Centre which was then in Siena.

In another directive dated 23rd June *Luftflotte 2* again defined the tasks of its air forces, and took account of the prevailing concern for further Allied landings. Its long-range reconnaissance *Gruppe* was ordered to carry out photographic reconnaissance of the eastern and western sea areas and of Bizerta (Tunisia), and was also to give warning of preparations for, and approach to a landing, as well as the actual event. In tactical support of the German land forces night ground-attack aircraft, operating from the Forli–Ravenna area (*Map 4*) with advanced landing grounds near Florence, were to attack front line targets during the full moon period.* When his normal tasks permitted, *Jagdfliegerführer*, Northern Italy, was additionally to counter Allied bombing raids in the Lucca-Florence area, and Allied fighter operations in that of Siena-Arezzo, with great importance attached to the prevention of the latter.

On 23rd June *Luftflotte 2* also made provision for the setting up of a new Fighter Control Centre north of Verona (no doubt to assist in the interception of Allied bomber formations heading for the Reich). Apart from the construction of new airfields and A.L.G.s in the far north, all bomber airfields in Northern Italy were now to be prepared for fighter occupation as well, those in the areas of Milan–Piacenza–Forli–Ravenna–Vicenza having first priority. Airfields in the Arno valley were to be prepared for reconnaissance and night ground-attack aircraft, but all other G.A.F. installations south of the Apennines and around Rimini were to be demolished.

Even before these directives were issued, the steady wastage of aircraft and aircrews had shorn the G.A.F. of whatever influence it still exerted on events in Italy.† The movement north of units, which had begun at the end of May with the withdrawal of the long-range reconnaissance *Gruppe* to Bergamo, continued with that of the tactical reconnaissance aircraft, of which two *Staffeln* had moved to Florence by early July, the third being already at Iesi. The night-flying *Gruppen* moved first to Castiglione del Lago and then to Ravenna and Forli.

By 20th July, the number of aircraft in *Luftflotte 2's* operational units had shrunk to 150. The strength of the single-engine fighter

---

* This led to an intensification of night ground-attacks on Allied front-line units, Ju. 87s taking over more and more of the tasks of the obsolescent Italian aircraft such as the C.R. 42s.

† During the 36 days from 11th May to 15 June, 82 German, 191 Italian, two French and 15 unidentifiable aircraft (a total of 290) had been found abandoned on 14 captured enemy airfields.

force which was mostly in Northern Italy had fallen to 61 aircraft, but that of the long-range reconnaissance force had risen to 24 aircraft. In the tactical air force all the ground-attack dive-bomber F.W. 190s had been withdrawn, and though the force of night ground-attack Ju. 87s had risen to 50 aircraft these, together with 15 tactical reconnaissance aircraft, gave von Pohl only 65 aircraft, of which only 30 were serviceable for direct support of the German armies.

Not surprisingly little was seen of the G.A.F. by day in the forward areas. On 15th June about 30 G.A.F. fighters were encountered in the Pistoia area. Thereafter few were seen until the 29th when 25–30 Me. 109s and F.W. 190s were sighted in the Ancona area. Activity was a little more pronounced at night. From the night of 5th/6th June Me. 110 night-fighters appear to have operated nightly north of Rome, but after the 8th/9th these operations ceased abruptly. Ju. 88 bombers were reported over Anzio on the 8th/9th and 11th/12th June but these operations, obviously mounted from southern France, could not be sustained. Night ground-attack aircraft were active in the battle area; for example on 6th/7th July about 40 Ju. 87 sorties were flown against the Polish Corps south of Ancona, which meant some of the German aircraft flying up to three sorties each. The re-appearance of Ju. 87s as night ground-attack aircraft had been detected on 3rd/4th July, and by the night of the 8th/9th they were operating from an A.L.G. near Florence. Beaufighters attempted to intercept these nightly raids, and on the 8th/9th destroyed two aircraft. In this period 1st–16th July, losses in German night ground-attack aircraft amounted to seven, including two shot down by A.A. gunfire. In the period 17th–27th July few if any German aircraft were reported over the battle area, but on the night of 27th/28th two were claimed shot down against a known German loss of three.[148] On six later occasions before the end of the Fourth Phase one or more enemy aircraft were shot down over the battle area bringing the total to ten in the three weeks. These losses were a heavy drain on such a small force whose efforts were at most of nuisance value only.

In the north about 30 G.A.F. fighters were seen on 11th June but sightings in such numbers were few and far between. An unusual encounter was experienced by No. 322 Wing from Corsica on 8th June when its Spitfires engaged 20 Macchi fighters west of Parma and claimed two shot down and two damaged without loss. The same day the Spitfires of No. 251 Wing, also based in Corsica, destroyed a Ju. 88 further south in the Pistoia area—probably long-range reconnaissance aircraft. Enemy attempts to interfere with Operation 'Mallory Major' already described were few and ineffective.

In brief, the G.A.F.'s influence upon the land campaign in Italy had continued to decline. The defence of the Reich against the Mediterranean Allied Strategic Air Force's raids absorbed an increasing proportion of *Luftflotte 2's* efforts as the summer months passed by.

(xi)

In this and the previous chapter we have described the tactical air support, that is to say the direct air support, given to the Allied armies in their advance in Italy from Rome to Florence and for this purpose we have included, purely for convenience, the period dawn 17th July to dawn 6th August. In turning to what the Mediterranean Allied Air Forces were doing *north* of the battle area in Italy and *beyond* Italy's borders we will revert to dawn 5th June to dawn 17th July which gives us a manageable period of 42 days and nights.[149]

A general survey of air operations during this period would be helpful, but first a word about the weather. In spite of Italy's reputation as a holiday area with brilliant summer weather, air operations in June and July 1944 were severely hampered by low cloud, waterlogged airfields and strong cross-winds, which, on occasions, prevented aircraft taking off. The worst weather occurred in the second half of June which covered the battles of Lake Trasimeno and the Cecina river. The heavy day bombers were grounded on ten and the heavy and medium night bombers on nine occasions; the medium day bombers were also grounded on ten days. The light bombers had their problems with the weather, too, both by day and by night, and so did the fighter-bombers which nevertheless were never completely grounded.

The wide dispersal of M.A.C.A.F.'s coastal aircraft enabled it to take advantage of areas in which flying was possible, even on those day when the weather generally was very bad for flying and in some areas quite impossible, as it was in Malta on 17th, 22nd and 26th June. The consistent level of M.A.C.A.F.'s flying activities, even allowing for its greater choice of altitude over the sea, was remarkable.

During the 42 days this period represents the Mediterranean Allied Air Forces (including R.A.F., Middle East but excluding anti-shipping operations and attacks on ports) flew a total of 72,739 sorties, which is the equivalent of 1,732 every 24 hours (see Table II). This was only 75% of that achieved during 'Diadem' (12th May–4th/5th June). The weather was not only appreciably worse during the post-'Diadem' period but the longer range at which the Allied aircraft were required to operate had its effect.

The Allies lost a total of 695 aircraft, only 23 of which were lost by R.A.F., M.E. The Germans lost 136 aircraft (destroyed and missing cannot be segregated), 54 of them in the Balkans. Whereas the equivalent daily loss rate for the Allies during dawn 5th June–dawn 17th July was remarkably close to that for 'Diadem', for the G.A.F. it was only half, due to the decline in *Luftflotte 2's* operations.

In Table III it will be seen that up to dawn 17th July, in terms of bomb tonnage dropped, targets north of the battle area received well over four times those within it, and against targets beyond Italy's borders it was over five times the battle area figure.

We will concentrate first on bombing north of the battle area where, during the first 15 days (coinciding with the First Phase of direct air support), railway targets absorbed two-thirds of the 7,158·4 tons of bombs dropped. Most of the balance was expended on road and M.T. targets. Much less effort was devoted to targets of opportunity, dumps, towns, enemy headquarters and command posts and guns, but 707·3 tons of bombs were dropped on oil refineries, storage tanks and depots by the heavy day bombers of M.A.S.A.F. which also bombed Ferrara airfield on 10th June with 278·9 tons.

The general effect of the Allied air attacks during this period (dawn 5th to dawn 20th June) on the enemy's L. of C. is referred to on occasion in Kesselring's reports to *O.K.W.*[150] For example, his second report after the fall of Rome stated on 5th June that Allied air supremacy, and the damage inflicted on roads and bridges, were seriously jeopardising withdrawal to the Dora Line (*see Map* 1) and that it would be necessary for *AOK 14* to accelerate its retreat. On the 9th, Kesselring reported that air attacks were much impeding the 'feeding' of his right wing with tanks, anti-tank guns, and ammunition. In conjunction with the difficult terrain that must be traversed, they were also imposing heavy delay on the westwards movement of *AOK 10's* mobile formations. We have noted in the previous chapter that on 18th June, after he had been ordered to stand on the Albert Line, Kesselring spelt out for Jodl the effects of six weeks' non-stop exposure to air attacks. His reference on that occasion to the wear and tear on M.T. entailed by a journey of 120 miles to the main railheads is of special interest, as this was one of the impositions which the Allied Air Forces set out to enforce during 'Strangle', and subsequently by their attacks on railway communications in Central Italy. Kesselring could also have added that the toll of M.T. destroyed and damaged by Allied air attack was still significant. Altogether during these 15 days 1,894 M.T. and horse-drawn vehicles and nine tanks and nine armoured vehicles had been claimed destroyed and 1,648 M.T. and horse-drawn vehicles and four tanks damaged.

See Map 4

During the next 13 days north of the battle area (coinciding with the Second Phase of direct air support within it) the enemy's railway system continued to receive by far the greatest attention and absorbed 4,161·3 tons of bombs. The major role against railway targets was played by the medium day bombers of M.A.T.A.F. which contributed two-fifths of the total bombload dropped on these targets, most of the remainder being more or less evenly shared between the fighter-bombers of M.A.T.A.F. and the heavy day bombers of M.A.S.A.F. During the very bad weather 18th–20th June the enemy had taken full advantage of the conditions to repair as much as he could of his battered railway communications. Improved weather conditions on the 21st prompted the Allies to make up some of the leeway, and that night 56 Wellingtons, eight Halifaxes and three Liberators from M.A.S.A.F. dropped a total of 126·5 tons of bombs on the marshalling-yard at Ventimiglia (Liguria) with what were described as 'excellent results'. The following day, despite worsening weather, 554 heavy day bombers from M.A.S.A.F., with 513 fighters escorting them, dropped 1,152·1 tons of bombs on the marshalling-yards at Ferrara, Bologna, Modena, Parma, Casalmaggiore, Fornovo di Taro (including the oil storage plant) and Chivasso, the rail and road bridges over the Piave river north of Treviso, the rail bridges at Rimini and the Fiat factory at Turin (aero engine and motor vehicle works). The same day Lieutenant-General Ira C. Eaker, Air C.-in-C. M.A.A.F., extended M.A.T.A.F.'s responsibility for the disruption of the enemy's rail communications as far north as the Po river and north-westwards as far as the Genoa-Alessandria line. During the last few days of this period, on 8th Army's front, enemy rolling stock provided lucrative targets for the fighter-bombers. On 28th June, on the Rimini-Forli line, 200 trucks containing tanks, A.F.V.s, guns, P.O.L. and ammunition were attacked throughout the day with 'great success'. Claims for the day amounted to 21 wagons and two locomotives destroyed and 15 wagons damaged. On the 29th a further 75 wagons and two locomotives were added to the number destroyed and 66 wagons and six locomotives to those damaged. On 1st July, when the attacks were extended to the railways beyond Forli and Imola and as far as Ravenna, 400 wagons were found loaded with guns, armoured vehicles, P.O.L. and ammunition, and nine more wagons were claimed destroyed and 16 wagons and one locomotive damaged. Though M.T. and roads were next in terms of effort expended attacks on them were few, and of the comparatively small total of 613·3 tons of bombs dropped on them, two-thirds were by the fighter-bombers of M.A.T.A.F. Fuel and ammunition dumps against which the medium day bombers of M.A.T.A.F. and the light day bombers of U.S. XII T.A.C. played the major role received a total of 311·5 tons of bombs. There were also minor efforts against airfields, towns and guns but, surprisingly, miscellaneous targets absorbed 461·9 tons of bombs during operations like the raid on the Fiat factory on 22nd June by M.A.S.A.F.'s heavy day bombers, and several raids on oil refineries and oil storage tanks and depots by the heavy night bombers and Wellingtons.

In this period (dawn 20th June to dawn 3rd July) the Allied air attacks on the enemy's railway system in the north were having their effect, though they were not succeeding in keeping the main lines to Florence cut for more than brief periods. For example, on 22nd June Kesselring reported to *OKW* that trains from the north could get as far south as Montevarchi (between Florence and Arezzo) via Bologna, Prato and Florence, and that two sections of the track further south were also open.[151] In fact there were two gaps of about seven and a half and two and a half miles each between Florence and Terontola (just north of Lake Trasimeno) Next day he did however report that there was a gap on the Verona–Padua–Bologna stretch (about 10 or more miles, astride Ferrara); there appears to have been one between S. Giorgio di Piano and Bologna (about 10 miles) and another from Vernio to Florence (about 22½ miles), but the Florence–Montevarchi line was clear. On the Verona–Bologna direct line Kesselring reported that trains were being 'diverted' via Ostiglia–Crevalcore, and this could only mean either a diversion to Ferrara or transfer of freight to road transport between these points. On the 26th Kesselring was able to say that through traffic from the Brenner on the main line via Verona–Padua–Bologna–Prato–Florence and on to Montevarchi had been restored, but next day, the 27th, he added the qualification that south of Bologna there was a gap beyond Vernio (of about five and a half miles) on the Bologna–Prato line. On the 30th Kesselring's report to *OKW* shows that two gaps had appeared in the main line north of Florence, one on the Ferrara–Bologna stretch and another between Bologna and Prato. Such was the see-saw effect of the Allied air attacks on the enemy's rail communications in the north. As fast as the German repair gangs closed the gaps others were opened elsewhere by persistent Allied airmen.

In this same period claims of enemy M.T. and horse-drawn vehicles destroyed and damaged were of a very low order. As near as can be traced they amounted to 238 destroyed and 217 damaged. The reason was succinctly summed up by the German Air Historical Branch in its survey of operations in June:[152]

> 'It was no longer possible for movements by motor transport convoys to be carried out by day except at the risk of sustaining heavy losses . . . All changes in the dispositions of troops, supply movements in their entirety, and all other runs for the purposes of repair, provisioning and the like had to be crowded into the few hours of darkness. Hold ups and jams occurred frequently on the busy roads.
>
> Movements were also severely restricted at night as a result of intensive enemy air activity in which innumerable flares were used'.

In June 1944 enemy documents fell into Allied hands which had been prepared in June 1943 by the Italian Transport Directorate of that period, as a guide to the establishment of A.A. defences at crucial rail points in northern Italy.[153] H.Q. M.A.A.F. had already prepared target charts for 34 of the 46 vital rail points listed. Of the remaining 12, six were north of Milan in an area where no operations had been planned because of the mass of inter-connecting lines; three were minor targets on the Brenner line which photographic reconnaissance had shown to be unsuitable for heavy bomber attack; one was a hydro-electric power station, a low priority target at that time (June 1944); and two were bridges for which suitable alternatives were already targeted. By 27th June about half of the rail points had been attacked, principally marshalling-yards but including the bridges at Dogna (north of Udine), Avisio (south of Bolzano) and Bolzano (*Map* i). South-west of Ljubljana, the Borovnica viaduct had been cut twice by Partisans. What is interesting about this appreciation is that it not only confirmed the competence of Allied Intelligence in selecting vital points in the enemy's northern railway network for air attack, but it also completely ignored all but five railway bridges over the Po and in the Alessandria-Genoa area, the elimination of which would have interdicted all supply to the south by rail. This was the aim of Operation 'Mallory Major' which we have already described earlier in this chapter.

North of the battle area during the last 14 days in this period (dawn 3rd to dawn 17th July) railway targets received by far the greatest attention, involving 4,271 sorties (5,301·4 tons of bombs).[154] Every type of bomber was used but easily the greatest contribution came from the medium day bombers whose 1,645 sorties (2,762·9 tons) included the first five days' effort towards Operation 'Mallory Major'. Miscellaneous targets absorbed 1,479·1 tons of bombs which include 1,289·5 tons dropped by M.A.S.A.F.'s heavy day bombers and 145·8 tons by M.A.T.A.F.'s medium day bombers on oil storage tanks and depots, and steel and ammunition foundries and factories. The effort expended on M.T. and roads in terms of tons of bombs dropped was nearly double that expended in the previous fortnight, and the medium day bombers delivered well over three-quarters of the total of 1,179·8 tons dropped on these targets. Fuel and ammunition dumps absorbed 488·3 tons, and again the greatest contribution came from the medium day bombers of M.A.T.A.F. Smaller amounts were dropped on towns, airfields, guns, and troops, also enemy headquarters and command posts.

Confirmation from German sources of the destruction and damage caused in some of these attacks is of special interest. For example, on 6th July, when 114 U.S. Liberators dropped 254 tons of bombs on an oil storage site at Trieste, two oil refineries and an ammunition dump were set alight, and so were two steamers (of a total of 34,510 G.R.T.—see Chapter XII) both of which were burnt out.[155] On at least five occasions rail traffic was held up—on the night of the 5th/6th at Verona, on the 6th between Mestre and Venice, on the 9th south of Ostiglia; and on the 12th near Montesanto on the Ferrara–Porto Maggiore line—in some instances the blockages prevailed for several days. A dramatic effect was achieved by Italian saboteurs at Riola on the Bologna–Pistoia line, and though we are concerned here with air attacks it is a convenient place to describe this incident. On 10th July the brakes of two fuel-carrying trains were released in a tunnel and a collision followed. Seventeen trucks containing 79,165 gallons of petrol, 34,745 gallons of Diesel fuel and 264 gallons of gear-oil, and 2,646 lbs of grease, all destined for *AOK 14*, were set ablaze.

The participation of the heavy day bombers in attacks on targets north of the battle area in Italy depended to a large extent on the vagaries of the weather beyond Italy's borders.[156] The primary task of the heavy day bombers (of the United States Fifteenth Air Force which formed the U.S.A.A.F. element of M.A.S.A.F.) was to support the Combined Bomber Offensive, and this it did whenever the weather was suitable. The heavy and medium night bombers (of No. 205 Group, R.A.F.) followed suit. Before describing M.A.S.A.F.'s operations beyond Italy during the period dawn 5th June–dawn 17th July, it would be opportune to recall the choice of targets and their priorities to which M.A.S.A.F. conformed prior to and then after the changes which followed during this period.

See Map ii

Before 'Diadem' the Mediterranean Allied Strategic Air Forces had been operating to a directive issued by General Eaker in February 1944, which gave first priority to 'Pointblank' targets of the Combined Bomber Offensive; second priority to disruption of rail communications in Italy; and third priority to direct support of the land battle.[157] A fourth priority covered targets in the Balkans. During 'Diadem' direct support of A.A.I. was elevated to first priority.* It was not until 15th June, eleven days after the fall of Rome and hence the end of 'Diadem', that H.Q. M.A.A.F. issued a new directive to M.A.S.A.F. which defined its new priorities as:

Priority 1.   Special attacks made at the direction of M.A.A.F. H.Q. on targets the destruction of which would assist the land campaign in Italy, should the situation justify them.

Priority 2.   Special targets, attacks on which were designed to assist the progress of Operation 'Overlord'. These attacks like those under Priority 1 above, were only to be made on the instructions of M.A.A.F. H.Q.

Priority 3.   *'Pointblank' Operations (the Combined Bomber Offensive)*
(a) Oil production.
(b) Counter air force operations—the maintenance of the degree of destruction and dislocation of the enemy's aircraft production already achieved by renewed attacks whenever photographic reconnaissance cover indicated they were necessary.

Priority 4.   Communication targets, including those in the Balkans, as promulgated from time to time.

Priority 5.   Other industrial and economic targets to be notified from time to time.

Well before this directive was issued, it was clear that, in American Air Force circles, attacks on oil targets had become the first priority task for M.A.S.A.F. in support of 'Pointblank', contrary to existing M.A.A.F. directives.† Consequently in Italy, targets had frequently been chosen by U.S.A.A.F. staffs because they embraced oil refineries and oil storage facilities, examples being air attacks on 9th, 10th and 13th June on Porto Marghera (Venice) and on 10th June on Trieste. The new directive placed the tasks of M.A.S.A.F., in both strategical and tactical roles, in

---

* See Part I of this Volume (H.M.S.O. 1984) p.65 paragraphs 2 and 4.

† On 8th June General Carl Spaatz, Commanding General of the United States Strategic Air Forces in Europe and responsible for co-ordinating the strategic operations of the U.S. Eighth and Fifteenth Air Forces, issued an order to them that henceforth the primary strategic aim was to be the denial of oil to the enemy's armed forces. The assumption in U.S.A.A.F. minds in Italy that attacks on oil targets was the first priority task of M.A.S.A.F. was correct. Details of the origin of this change in strategic air priorities are given by Sir Charles Webster and Noble Frankland: *The Strategic Air Offensive against Germany 1939-1945* Vol. III (H.M.S.O. 1961) pp.42-7.

proper perspective, and the unofficial assumption that the enemy's oil refineries and oil storage facilities were first priority in M.A.S.A.F.'s contribution to the Combined Bomber Offensive had become official M.A.A.F. policy. As a result, for the rest of June and throughout July the enemy's oil refineries and oil storage facilities received by far the greatest attention from M.A.S.A.F's heavy day, and heavy and medium (Wellington) night bombers. Marshalling-yards and L. of C. leading to the Rumanian and Italian fronts took second place as shown in the Table below:

EFFORTS EXPENDED BY M.A.S.A.F.
BEYOND THE BORDERS OF ITALY
DAWN 5th JUNE–DAWN 17th JULY
(Sorties, with total bombloads dropped shown in brackets)

Country	Oil	M/Y&L. of C.	Factories	Airfields
Czechoslovakia	158(330.1)	Nil	Nil	Nil
Germany	451(1,008.7)	130(167.3)	688(1,943.1)	219(465.8)
Austria	1,206(2,394.6)	115(267.3)	331(678.9)	422(801.2)
Yugoslavia	556(1,189.2)	480(1,096.3)	22(47.9)	126(267.5)
Hungary	871(1,881.3)	602(1,317.0)	Nil	180(320.8)
Rumania	2,789(5,632.6)	988(2,309.3)	Nil	226(385.1)
Bulgaria	Nil	Nil	Nil	174(298.9)
France	67(119.4)	989(2,215.3)	Nil	Nil
	*220(517.0)			
	(*Attacks spread over both types of target)			
Totals	6,098(12,555.9) 3,284(7,372.5)		1,041(2,069.9)	1,347(2,539.3)
	Plus 220(517.0)			

German documents bear witness to the destructive and damaging effect of many of these attacks, but space precludes other than brief mention of a few examples. In Bulgaria, as a result of a day attack by U.S. Liberators on Karlovo airfield on 28th June, the workshops were destroyed and the technical school, barracks, four hangars and several buildings badly damaged, and well over 50 aircraft were destroyed or damaged.

In Hungary, on 14th July, 345 Fortresses and U.S. Liberators dropped 844 tons of bombs among the Fanto, Shell, Hungarian and Petfurdo oil refineries in Budapest and on the adjoining Farenovaros marshalling-yard; apart from other widespread destruction and damage the Shell oil refinery was forced to close down until further notice.[158]

In Rumania the destruction and damage inflicted by Allied air attacks on oil targets prompted the German Naval Staff War Diarist to record that in June the processing of mineral oil had fallen further in arrears.[159] In fact though in mid-June the crude oil yield was 6,000 tons per day, of this amount only 2,700 tons could be processed. Thus the supply of 'finished products' had decreased considerably. What the Diarist did not mention was the additional hazard even this low ebb of 'finished products' faced from the attention M.A.S.A.F. paid to transportation by rail and barge. Incidentally, when on 11th June 246 U.S. Liberators with 480 tons of bombs attacked oil storage, railway installations and oil delivery pipelines at Giurgiu (on the Danube) and the fuel plant at nearby Ruscuk, 1,968.4 tons of sugar were destroyed at Ruscuk. On 15th July a very heavy attack was made by 511 Fortresses and Liberators on four oil refineries at Ploesti with a total of 1,175 tons of bombs. One refinery was heavily damaged and at two others the destruction and damage was classed by the Germans as 'medium'—no doubt by the standards the Allies had by then established.

In France, on 25th June, when 157 U.S. Liberators dropped 356 tons of bombs on rail targets at Avignon, all rail routes were cut, some in several places, 400 carriages were badly damaged, and the water supply for locomotives was damaged too.[160] The Alfa factory was one of two works which were seriously damaged and a bomb severed the suspension bridge across the Rhône connecting Avignon with Villeneuve.

Two interesting instances (but by no means the first) of U.K.-based heavy day bombers assisting M.A.S.A.F. took place during this period.[161] In Rumania an attack on Arad marshalling-yard took place on 3rd July by 55 Fortresses of the United States Eighth Air Force operating from Italian bases after arriving there from Russia. Two days later these Fortresses attacked the marshalling-yard at Beźiers in France on their way to the U.K. This was the first 'triangular' shuttle by U.S. Eighth Air Force.

By 5th June U.S. Fifteenth Air Force had already received its full establishment of 21 Groups of heavy day bombers, containing a total of 84 squadrons, and seven Groups of fighters containing 22 squadrons and two reconnaissance squadrons.[162]* On the same date No. 205 Group R.A.F.'s operational strength consisted of three Wellington Wings with a total of six squadrons, one (R.A.F.) Liberator Wing with one squadron only, and one Halifax Path-finder squadron directly under Group control—a total of eight squadrons. On 16th June No. 31 (S.A.A.F.) Squadron with its

---

* The U.S.A.A.F. 'Group' was the equivalent of the R.A.F. 'Wing'. The number of squadrons in U.S.A.A.F. Groups and R.A.F. Wings varied according to role and circumstances, but the U.S.A.A.F. heavy day bomber Group normally consisted of four squadrons of eight aircraft each and the fighter Group of three squadrons of 25 aircraft each. The R.A.F. Wing was much more varied in make-up.

Liberators began to arrive at Celone (near Foggia) in Italy from the Middle East, and flew its first operational sortie on 25th/26th June under the temporary control of No. 240 Wing R.A.F. On 6th July H.Q. No. 2 (S.A.A.F.) Wing began to arrive from the Middle East and on the 8th so did No. 34 (S.A.A.F.) Squadron with Liberators, both units joining No. 31 (S.A.A.F.) Squadron at Celone. Both squadrons were ultimately to be under No. 2 (S.A.A.F.) Wing but it did not exercise operational control over its two South African squadrons until 19th July. No. 34 (S.A.A.F.) Squadron flew its first operational sortie that night. Thus by 19th July No. 205 Group R.A.F. had ten operational squadrons.

A re-organisation and re-equipment of No. 205 Group R.A.F. had been under discussion for some time. On 2nd July it was decided to eliminate the Halifaxes and Wellingtons and to convert the crews to Liberators of which there were to be three wings, each of two squadrons. It turned out to be a slow process as it was not until March 1945 that the Wellington wings were completely converted to Liberators.

TABLE I

Desert Air Force
Order of Battle as at 2nd August 1944[163]

Air Formation		Location[(1)]
Adv. H.Q. D.A.F.		Siena
M.O.R.U. 'A'		Crete
Ops 'A'		(with 5th Army)
M.O.R.U. 'B'		Cecina

Squadrons	Aircraft	
No. 600 (N.F.)	Beaufighter VI	Rosignano
No. 92 (one Flight) (F)	Spitfire VIII	Rosignano
No. 3 (S.A.A.F.) Wing		Pescara
No. 12 (S.A.A.F.) (M.B.)	Marauder II	Pescara
No. 21 (S.A.A.F.) (M.B.)	Marauder II	Pescara
No. 24 (S.A.A.F.) (M.B.)	Marauder II	Pescara
No. 223 (L.B.)	Baltimore IV & V	Pescara
No. 454 (R.A.A.F.) (L.B.)	Baltimore IV & V	Pescara
No. 7 (S.A.A.F.) Wing		Foiano di Chiana
No. 1 (S.A.A.F.) (F)	Spitfire IX	Foiano di Chiana
No. 7 (S.A.A.F.) (F)	Spitfire IX	Foiano di Chiana
No. 2 (S.A.A.F.) (F.B.)	Spitfire IX	Foiano di Chiana
No. 4 (S.A.A.F.) (F.B.)	Spitfire IX	Foiano di Chiana

TABLE I—*continued*

Squadrons	Aircraft	Location[1]
No. 232 Wing		Cecina
No. 13 (R.A.F.) (L.B.)	Baltimore IV & V	Cecina
No. 55 (L.B.)	Baltimore IV & V	Cecina
No. 18 (L.B.)	Boston III & IIIA	Cecina
No. 114 (L.B.)	Boston III & IIIA	Cecina
No. 239 Wing		Crete
No. 3 (R.A.A.F.) (F.B.)	Kittyhawk IV	Crete
No. 5 (S.A.A.F.) (F.B.)	Kittyhawk IV	Crete
No. 112 (F.B.)	Kittyhawk IV	Crete
No. 250 (F.B.)	Kittyhawk IV	Crete
No. 450 (R.A.A.F.) (F.B.)	Kittyhawk IV	Crete
No. 260 (F.B.)	Mustang IIIA	Crete
No. 244 Wing		Perugia
No. 145 (F)	Spitfire VIII	Perugia
No. 417 (R.C.A.F.) (F)	Spitfire VIII	Perugia
No. 601 (F)	Spitfire IX	Perugia
No. 87 (F)	Spitfire V, VIII & IX	Perugia
No. 92 (one Flight) (F)	Spitfire VIII	Perugia
No. 285 Wing		Malignano
No. 40 (S.A.A.F.) (Tac.R)	Spitfire V & IX	Malignano
No. 208 (Tac.R)	Spitfire V & IX	Malignano
No. 318 (Polish) (Tac.R) (one Flight)	Spitfire VB & C	Falconara
No. 683 (P.R.) (Det.)	Spitfire XI	Malignano
No. 287 Wing		Falconara
No. 241 (F)	Spitfire VIII & IX	Falconara
No. 318 (Polish) (Tac.R) (one Flight)	Spitfire VB & C	Falconara
A.O.P. Wing		
No. 651	Auster	(with 5th Corps)
No. 654	Auster	(with 10th Corps)
No. 655	Auster	(with 13th Corps)
No. 657	Auster	(with 13th Corps)

[1] *See Map 1*

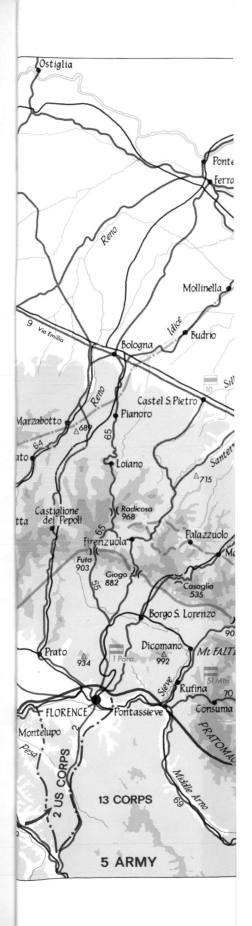

TABLE II

SORTIES FLOWN BY MEDITERRANEAN ALLIED AIR FORCES DAWN 5th JUNE—DAWN 17th JULY 1944
(EXCLUDING ANTI-SHIPPING OPERATIONS AND ATTACKS ON PORTS)

Command	Land Recce.	Fighters (Shipping protection shown in brackets)
M.A.A.F.[1][2] (excl. M.E.)	3,433[1]	27,089[4] (2,007)
H.Q. R.A.F. M.E.[2]	223[4]	1,495[4] (609)
TOTALS	3,656	28,584 (2,616)

Bombers and Fighter-Bombers (values shown as top / bottom of each split cell)

	France	Italy	Italy	Germany	Germany	Czecho-slovakia	Austria	Austria	Hungary	Hungary	Yugoslavia	Yugoslavia	Bulgaria	Rumania	Rumania	Alb.
	L. of C. & other Targets	L. of C. & other Targets	Airfields and L.G.s	L. of C. & other Targets	Airfields and L.G.s	L. of C. & other Targets	L. of C. & other Targets	Airfields and L.G.s	L. of C. & other Targets	Airfields and L.G.s	L. of C. & other Targets	Airfields and L.G.s	Airfields and L.G.s	L. of C. & other Targets	Airfields and L.G.s	L. of C. & other Tar.
H.B.	1,294 / —	2,623 / 101	193 / —	1,236 / 11	219 / —	158 / —	1,689 / —	312 / 27	1,366 / 31	154 / —	741 / 11	126 / —	138 / 4	3,509 / 33	226 / —	— / —
M.B.	— / —	6,330 / 543	3 / —	— / 51	— / —	— / —	— / 2	— / 83	— / 106	— / —	— / 306	— / —	— / 32	— / 125	— / —	— / —
L.B.	— / —	1,649 / 1,053	— / 3?	— / —	— / —	— / —	— / —	— / —	— / —	— / —	37 / —	— / —	— / —	— / —	— / —	— / —
F.B.	— / —	15,299 / 25	53 / —	— / —	— / —	— / —	— / —	— / —	— / —	26 / —	177 / —	4 / —	— / —	36 / —	— / —	53 / —
M.B. (H.Q. R.A.F. M.E.)	— / —	— / —	— / —	— / —	— / —	— / —	— / —	— / —	— / —	— / —	— / —	— / —	— / —	— / —	— / —	— / —
L.B. (H.Q. R.A.F. M.E.)	— / —	— / —	— / —	— / —	— / —	— / —	— / —	— / —	— / —	— / —	— / —	— / —	— / —	— / —	— / —	— / —
TOTALS	1,294 / —	25,901 / 1,722	349 / 32	1,236 / 62	219 / —	158 / —	1,689 / 2	312 / 110	1,366 / 137	180 / —	955 / 350	130 / —	138 / 36	3,545 / 158	226 / —	53 / —

(1) The sorties flown by 'M.A.A.F' include A.H.Q. Malta but *not* H.Q., R.A.F., M.E.

(2) The sorties flown by 'M.A.A.F.' and H.Q., R.A.F., M.E. have been taken from a single consolidated record amended by other documents as necessary and are considered reasonably accurate for our purpose.

(3) These figures do not include a total of 150 flare-dropping sorties, nor sorties flown during mining of the Danube.

(4) Estimated.

TABLE III

M.A.A.F. (INCLUDING MALTA BUT EXCLUDING H.Q. R.A.F. M.E.)
Distribution of Bomber and Fighter-Bomber sorties flown
and bombloads dropped (*excluding anti-shipping operations and attacks on ports*)
Dawn 5th June–Dawn 6th August 1944
(*excludes flare-dropping*)

Aircraft	Dawn 5th June–Dawn 20th June			Dawn 20th June–Dawn 3rd July			Dawn 3rd July–Dawn 17th July			Dawn 17th July–Dawn 6th August		
	Within the battle area	North of the battle area	Elsewhere than Italy	Within the battle area	North of the battle area	Elsewhere than Italy	Within the battle area	North of the battle area	Elsewhere than Italy	Within the battle area	North of the battle area	Elsewhere than Italy
Heavy day bomber		1,150(2,482.2)	3,586(7,205.8)		604(1,274.3)	3,385(7,176.2)		1,062(2,459.5)	4,197(9,496.7)		289(707.2)	5,115(11,612.3)
Heavy night bomber	5(13.4)	20(49.9)	43(108.9)		36(93.8)	67(161.2)		40(121.9)	40(120.4)		20(62.1)	114(296.1)
Medium day bomber	571(969.2)	1,950(3,332.9)		20(52.2)	1,140(1,913.5)		129(219.6)[2]	2,523(3,948.1)[2]		84(110.2)[2]	1,792(3,001.8)[2]	222(359.7)
Medium night bomber	73(146.8)	74(135.0)	254(422.2)		170(297.6)	216(281.6)		226(423.1)	235(466.4)		91(191.0)	243(380.5)
Light day bomber	150(114.7)	395(309.2)		66(48.3)	503(400.5)		276(216.0)[2]	259(195.6)	37(11.7)	89(70.3)[2]	321(261.8)	61(48.2)
Light night bomber	222(159.2)	117(71.4)		87(61.4)	226(144.5)		150(104.4)[2]	283(200.0)		196(144.5)[2]	285(215.7)	
Fighter-bomber day[1]	3,064(1,282.0)	1,819(772.2)	213(61.5)	719(323.6)	3,885(1,699.0)	38(7.9)	2,852(1,130.0)[2]	3,113(1,301.5)	74(16.4)	2,723(1,300.7)[2]	3,950(1,661.7)	251(77.1)
Fighter-bomber night		25(5.6)										
TOTALS	4,085(2,685.3)	5,550(7,158.4)	4,096(7,798.4)	892(485.5)	6,564(5,823.2)	3,706(7,626.9)	3,407(1,670.0)	7,506(8,649.7)	4,583(10,111.6)	3,092(1,625.7)	6,748(6,101.3)	6,006(12,773.9)

NOTES [1] The figures in respect of 'Fighter-bomber day' operations 'Within the battle area' and 'North of the battle area' are close approximations. They are considered accurate enough for our purpose. In aggregate they are true totals.

[2] These figures include the efforts expended in operation 'Mallory Major' and in support of the Polish Corps' advance on and capture of Ancona.

TABLE IV

OPERATION 'MALLORY MAJOR'

AIR ATTACKS ON BRIDGES OVER THE PO RIVER

Location	Type of Bridge	Date in July 1944																Total
		12th	13th	14th	15th	16th	17th	18th	19th	20th	21st	22nd	23rd	24th	25th	26th	27th	
Moncalieri	Rail	—	—	—	—	—	—	—	—	—	—	—	—	—	—	—	18(29.0)	18(29.0)
Chivasso	Rail	—	—	—	—	—	—	—	—	—	—	18(32.1)	—	6(14.3)	18(30.4)	—	23(41.1)	65(117.9)
Casale Monferrato	Rail	—	—	—	—	24(42.8)	18(32.1)	—	—	—	—	—	—	—	—	—	15(26.8)	57(101.7)
Torreberetti	Combined Rail/Road	—	—	—	—	24(38.4)	—	—	—	—	—	—	—	—	—	—	17(30.4)	41(68.8)
Bressana	Combined Rail/Road	—	—	—	—	37(65.2)	—	—	—	—	—	—	—	—	—	—	—	37(65.2)
*Piacenza	Rail	29(51.5)	24(42.8)	29(50.0)	—	47(83.5)	—	—	77(118.3)	22(30.8)	—	—	—	—	—	—	—	228(376.9)
	Road	30(53.4)	—	—	—	—	—	—	—	—	—	—	—	—	—	—	—	30(53.4)
*S.Nazzaro	Pontoon	—	23(20.1)	—	—	—	—	—	—	—	—	—	—	—	—	—	—	23(20.1)
*Cremona	Combined Rail/Road	40(70.9)	39(69.6)	—	3(5.4)	—	—	—	—	—	—	—	—	—	—	—	—	82(145.9)
*Casalmaggiore	Rail	27(47.9)	—	—	—	—	—	—	—	—	—	—	—	—	—	—	—	27(47.9)
	Pontoon	27(48.0)	—	—	—	—	—	—	—	—	—	—	—	—	—	—	—	27(48.0)
*Viadana	Pontoon	—	23(41.1)	—	—	—	—	—	—	—	—	—	—	—	—	—	—	23(41.1)
*Guastalla	Pontoon	—	22(38.4)	—	—	—	—	—	—	—	—	—	—	—	—	—	—	22(38.4)
*Borgoforte	Rail	15(16.1)	23(33.6)	—	24(35.7)	—	12(21.4)	—	15(26.8)	18(32.1)	—	—	11(14.7)	—	—	—	73(122.3)	191(302.7)
	Pontoon	15(16.0)	—	—	—	—	—	—	—	—	—	—	—	—	—	—	—	15(16.0)
*S.Nicolo	Pontoon	—	18(9.5)	—	—	—	—	—	—	—	—	—	—	—	—	—	—	18(9.5)
*S.Benedetto	Pontoon	—	12(6.6)	—	—	—	—	—	—	—	—	—	—	—	—	—	—	12(6.6)
*Ostiglia	Combined Rail/Road	38(60.7)	25(64.3)	—	32(46.4)	—	—	—	23(41.1)	48(75.0)	—	—	19(28.6)	—	—	53(88.2)	—	238(404.3)
*Sermide	Pontoon	—	19(17.0)	—	15(37.5)	—	—	—	—	—	—	—	—	—	—	—	—	34(54.5)
*Ficarolo	Pontoon	—	19(15.1)	—	24(20.6)	—	—	—	—	—	—	—	—	—	—	—	—	43(35.7)
*Pontelagoscuro	Rail	3(4.0)	60(95.0)	—	32(50.0)	—	—	—	—	24(42.8)	—	—	18(32.1)	—	—	—	—	137(223.9)
	Road	3(4.0)	—	—	33(51.7)	—	—	—	—	—	—	—	—	—	—	—	—	36(55.7)
*Polesella	Pontoon	—	—	—	24(21.4)	—	—	—	—	—	—	—	—	—	—	—	—	24(21.4)
*Corbola	Rail	—	—	21(18.7)	—	—	—	—	—	—	—	—	—	—	—	—	—	21(18.7)
	Road	—	—	21(18.8)	—	—	—	—	—	—	—	—	—	—	—	—	—	21(18.8)
*Taglio	Road	—	—	26(44.6)	—	—	—	—	—	—	—	—	—	—	—	—	—	26(44.6)
TOTALS		227(372.5)	307(453.1)	97(132.1)	187(268.7)	132(229.9)	30(53.5)	NIL	115(186.2)	112(180.7)	NIL	18(32.1)	48(75.4)	6(14.3)	18(30.4)	53(88.2)	146(249.6)	1,496(2,366.7)

* Targets listed in C.G. M.A.T.A.F.'s directive of 11th July 1944

NOTE Only the total sorties flown against and total bombloads dropped on each target each day are shown above. In some instances there were two or more attacks on the same day on the same target.

TABLE V

OPERATION 'MALLORY MAJOR'

AIR ATTACKS ON BRIDGES NORTH OF THE PO RIVER

Location	Type of Bridge	Date in July 1944																Total
		12th	13th	14th	15th	16th	17th	18th	19th	20th	21st	22nd	23rd	24th	25th	26th	27th	
Bozzolo	Rail	—	—	—	46(81.2)	—	—	—	—	—	—	—	—	—	—	—	—	46(81
Desenzano	Rail viaduct	—	—	—	18(32.1)	—	—	—	—	—	—	—	—	—	—	—	—	18(32
Peschiera	Rail	—	—	—	—	18(32.1)	—	—	—	—	—	—	—	12(28.6)	—	—	—	30(60
Mantua	North & East Rail	—	—	—	—	49(86.6)	—	—	—	18(32.1)	—	—	—	—	—	—	—	67(118
Verona	West Rail	—	—	—	—	—	—	—	—	—	—	—	—	—	—	19(30.4)	—	19(30
Legnago	Rail	—	—	—	—	—	—	—	—	—	—	—	—	—	20(30.4)	—	—	20(30
Rovigo	Rail	—	—	—	—	—	—	—	—	—	—	—	—	—	18(32.1)	—	—	18(32
TOTALS		—	—	—	64(113.3)	67(118.7)	—	—	—	18(32.1)	—	—	—	12(28.6)	38(62.5)	19(30.4)	—	218(385

NOTE Only the total sorties flown against and total bombloads dropped on each target each day are shown above. In some instances there were two or more attacks in the same day on the same target.

CHAPTER XI

THE PLAN IS CHANGED

(i)

See Map 8

ON 4th August Alexander and Harding met Leese on Orvieto airfield. So improvised was this meeting that it took place under the wing of a parked Dakota transport aircraft which gave them some shade from the hot August sun.[1] There were no staff present and so no record was kept of the arguments which led to one of the most dramatic and perhaps unfortunate decisions taken during the Italian campaign. Leese managed to persuade both Alexander and Harding that their well matured concept for forcing the centre of the Gothic Line should be jettisoned at the last moment in favour of a wholly undeveloped plan in which 8th Army would cross the Apennines and attack on the Adriatic coast, supported by subsidiary attacks by 5th Army on the Florence-Bologna axis. In effect, the real and deception plans were to be reversed, even though regrouping had already started for the original plan and the administrative build up at Arezzo to support the central assault west of the Apennines was almost complete. The arguments used by Leese must have been extraordinarily cogent to make Harding, if not Alexander, accept such a last minute change. It is far from easy to make so great an alteration in operational policy at so late a stage with forces as large as the Allied Armies in Italy without paying heavy penalties in terms of waste of preparatory effort and resources, of confusion and uncertainty at lower levels, and, above all, of loss of time, which with the approach of autumn—only two months away—was to prove a critical factor in the balance between success and failure. It is to the great credit of the very professional and experienced staffs of 8th Army and its subordinate Corps that these penalties were minimized.

As the meeting at Orvieto was arranged at General Leese's request and since the change of plan was based upon his initiative, we will probe his motives first, and then consider the standpoints of Alexander and Harding. Leese wrote two important demi-official letters to Major-General J. N. Kennedy, who was Director of

Military Operations in the War Office at the time.[2] The first is dated 1st August 1944. It starts with a summary of the heavy fighting south of Florence and then goes on to explain the regrouping for a central breach in the Gothic Line. He notes the marked improvement in the administrative situation which, by the middle of August, should enable him to 'deploy the whole Army' and 'build up 800 r.p.g. for the 1,000 guns' which he should have available for the assault. After commenting on his immediate intentions to close up to the Line, which he feared might 'be no easy task as there are quite good hill positions between Florence and the Gothic Line', he deals with the cover plan and its emphasis on two main points: 'the Polish Corps and the 5th Corps attack in the Adriatic sector' and 'a landing by American and French troops in the Genoa area'. If, in spite of this deception, the Germans concentrated north of Florence, 8th Army's task would be far more difficult. The Allies had successfully 'sold cover plans in the past' and he was hopeful. There is nothing of substance, however, in this letter to suggest any impending change of heart.

In his unpublished autobiography of his military career, Leese does not go very deeply into the reasons underlying the change of plan, but he is definite that his decision was made during a visit to an Observation Post with General Kirkman, then Commander of 13th Corps, when they viewed the mountain country which lay ahead of them.[3] Further evidence comes from Kirkman himself, who wrote in 1948 that he brought pressure to bear on Leese 'and pointed out much more forcibly than ever before that I thought the policy of continuing the thrust from Florence to Bologna the wrong one'.[4] We know from 13th Corps War Diary that this visit occurred at 9 a.m. on 3rd August.[5] Leese then lunched with Alexander, who was on his way to view Botticelli's 'Primavera' and other famous paintings, which 8th Indian Division had found hidden in the vaults of Sir Osbert Sitwell's house.[6] It seems probable that Leese expressed his misgivings to Alexander who almost certainly declined to discuss a change of plan without reference to his Staff. That evening Leese asked his 8th Army Staff for a short appreciation of why 8th Army should not attack on the Adriatic Coast instead of the Central Sector.[7] The G (Plans) appreciation was probably used by Leese as an *aide memoire*. It is headed 'Note on an attack in the East Coast Sector'.[8] The 'object' of the appreciation is strictly limited and stated as 'To break the Gothic Line and penetrate into the Po valley, with a secure L of C, before winter'; and the final assessment of the factors is headed 'The Proposed Course Reviewed', which suggests that the appreciation was confined to assessing the possibility of an attack on the east coast. The advantages were seen to be:

'(i) The initial attack should be easier from all points of view.
(ii) The enemy will probably be weaker.
(iii) We should be able to achieve surprise.
(iv) Terrain suits armoured action.'

And the disadvantages were clearly and fairly stated:

'(i) Although we may break the Gothic Line, a series of new lines
can be established
    e.g. Rimini–San Marino
         Cervia–Cesena
         Ravenna–Forli
all hinged on the main mountain features of the main Gothic
Line.
(ii) As we push the enemy back, we enable him to reduce his front.
(iii) It is easy for the enemy to manipulate his reserves [using Route
9, the Via Emilia].
(iv) If we are caught by winter in the Ravenna–Forli area, we will
get bogged down as it is a wet area.
(v) The present cover plan is working against us.'

After comparing the opposing force levels which showed that the
equivalent of nine divisions (i.e. 8 divisions and 3 tank brigades)
with 600–750 tanks would be attacking 'seven divisions, of which
two are weak and one unreliable' with 230 tanks in support, the
appreciation ended on the lame note that exploitation in the Po
valley would be limited by the port capacity of Ancona because
winter would close the trans-Apennine routes. This state of affairs
would continue until Venice was captured. There were no recommendations, which suggests that the Staff were either specifically
told not to make any or that they were to hesitant to do so. Their
note certainly did not provide adequate grounds for a major change
of plan.

Leese sets out very fully his motives for his change of plan in
the second letter which he wrote to General Kennedy on 7th
August, three days after the Orvieto meeting.[9] First of all, there
had been 'a change in the technique of German tactics during the
last few weeks. In country ideal for defence they have stubbornly
contested every yard of ground'. Against the present number of
German divisions it was 'well nigh impossible to get a break
through with armour'. Secondly the Germans had 'assessed correctly our present thrust line through Florence to Bologna'. They had
concentrated 'the majority of their divisions between Prato and
Sansepolcro'. Thirdly, the mountains north of Florence were some
30 miles deep. 'Success in mountain fighting depended primarily
on surprise and mobility'. 8th Army was unlikely to achieve
surprise; it would stand a greater chance of decisive success if it
fought in the lower ground where it could exploit its great strength

in tanks, artillery and aircraft. Fourthly, with the withdrawal of
the 'Anvil' troops, there would only be one instead of two parallel
thrust lines in the centre. It seemed 'vital to open a second thrust
line, if possible in less difficult country'. 'The gap between the
mountains and the sea on the Adriatic coast' had been chosen.

After stressing the paramount need for secrecy, he explains the
new plan in detail and acknowledges the tremendous administrative
and movement problems in switching a large part of the Army
back again, at short notice, to the Adriatic.

> 'But we are confident that we can do so. We are very hopeful
> that we can maintain the necessary security. All Corps Com-
> manders have complete confidence in the plan. It will appeal to
> the troops. It is a new adventure, and no longer a slog through
> the mountains of Central Italy'.

He then confesses:

> 'We realise that it is not an easy operation. It goes against the
> grain of the country. It is easy for the Germans to switch
> reserves. But in order to defeat the enemy we have got to fight
> another big battle somewhere; and we would far sooner fight
> this battle in the low ground than in the mountains.'

It will be observed that these were all valid military reasons
though unfortunately based upon two false assumptions, which
should be noted now as they were to help Kesselring survive the
autumn and winter in the Northern Apennines. As we have seen,
his concentration of divisions in the centre had been for the defence
of Florence, and was not a premeditated move to strengthen the
centre of the Gothic Line. Leese was wrong in assuming that the
fighting south of Florence was a pointer to German intentions. In
early August Kesselring was busy with counter-invasion precautions. Leese's second false assumption was that the east coast
would be much easier for 8th Army's main thrust than the
Northern Apennines, which are for the most part steep rolling hills
with only about 10–15,000 yards' depth of truly mountain country
along the watershed of the range.[10] The east coast might have
been easier if there had been enough amphibious shipping for
subsidiary right-hooks from the sea to loosen up the naturally
strong defensive positions which abounded on the ridges between
the many rivers flowing down from the Apennines into the Adriatic.
'Anvil' had absorbed almost every ship available in the
Mediterranean. The earliest Leese could expect any naval help
was the end of September and then there would only be enough
craft for one battalion group.[11] The unsatisfactory nature of the
topographical exchange which so attracted Leese was aptly summed
up after the war by General Heinz Trettner, the commander of
4th Parachute Division.[12]

'On the Adriatic front it was water that had to be included and taken into account as an obstacle; in the Apennines it was the mountains. Now water is very often incalculable, but mountains stay the same . . .'

There is a paucity of contemporary written evidence setting out Alexander's and Harding's views. In Alexander's papers there is a 'Note on the present situation and future plans' which is unsigned but dated 30th July.[13] It contains a careful assessment of the forces available to both sides and ascribes Kesselring's success in maintaining an unbroken front to the Allies' administrative difficulties and the defensive advantages of the terrain. It makes no mention of the Adriatic coast at all, and concentrates upon the concept of exploiting a breach in the centre of the Gothic Line to trap *AOK 10* between the bridgeless Po and the Adriatic. After acknowledging the strength of the Gothic positions and the fact that the Allies would 'be fighting uphill, which is always a laborious business' it says:

'We believe however that we can continue the battle until we do get a penetration deep enough and wide enough to make the position untenable and admit of exploitation. When that stage is reached we hope and think that the enemy will have considerable difficulty in extricating his troops especially on the flanks, and that, with the Po bridges broken behind him he will be in a very difficult position of which our troops can take full advantage by rapid exploitation to the line of the Po . . .'

There is no contemporary document showing why Harding changed his mind, but in March 1946 he prepared an account for the Central Mediterranean Force's History, in which he gives three reasons for the change.[14] The first is the withdrawal of troops for 'Anvil' which had two effects: the long period of uncertainty while the 'Anvil' decision was being taken had had 'a bad psychological effect on the troops, especially the French', which had enabled the Germans to recover their balance; and the loss of the seven 'Anvil' divisions, particularly the French mountain trained divisions, made it less likely that the Allies would be able to breach the heavily defended central mountain sector. His second and third reasons were more subjective:

'(a) 8th Army did not like the idea of fighting in mountains. They had no mountain trained troops; further their traditions were more of armoured battles and rapid movements on flat ground, supported by heavy artillery fire on fixed programmes. General Kirkman, of 13th Corps, was particularly depressed at the sight of the mountains behind Firenzuola.

(b) On the proposed plan 5 and 8 Armies would be attacking abreast and in close contact. Gen Leese was still very jealous of

Gen Clark over the capture of Rome when the two armies had fought more or less on the same axis. He . . . wanted to make quite certain that credit for the next Allied success . . . should go to him alone. This would be ensured if 8 Army fought its battle well away on one flank where there could be no question of 5 Army having had any effect on the result. Oliver Leese did not expect that 5 Army, in its now reduced state, would get even as far as it did in an attack on the centre of the line'.

Harding sums up by saying that although he and Alexander were 'still convinced that their own appreciation was militarily correct' it was no use trying to make 8th Army carry out a plan in which it had no confidence. They had 'to pay attention to such considerations, however unworthy'. It would be difficult 'to assure really close co-operation between the GOsC Fifth and Eight Armies' and this was crucial to the original plan.

Alexander, in his Despatch published in 1950, reinforces Harding's view on the last point:[15]

'Eighth Army's preference for the east coast was based . . . on reasons both strictly military and also psychological . . . in a case where the courses available were fairly equally balanced it was obviously preferable to choose that course which inspired the greater confidence in those who were to carry it out'.

He then rounds off his case by adding one further reason which was characteristically his own. He would be able to use his favourite strategy of:

'. . . the "two-handed punch" or, more orthodoxically expressed, the strategy of attacking two points equally vital to the enemy (i.e Ravenna and Bologna) either simultaneously or alternately in order to split the reserves available for the defence'.

The suggestion made in the American Official History that Alexander's decision was influenced by Churchill's predeliction for an advance towards the Middle Danube has no validity.[16] Whichever route 8th Army took, the advance would pass through the Bologna-Ferrara area.

No decision of this magnitude could be taken by the Army Group Commander without reference to 5th Army. The record of Alexander's daily movements shows that he visited Clark on 5th August.[17] We have no account of this meeting, but since Alexander did not overturn Leese's proposals we can assume that Clark did not produce any arguments which would have enabled him to maintain his original plan in the face of Leese's disquiet. In retrospect it can be seen that Leese won the argument by reinforcing his military case with emotional factors. The decision was taken without adequate staff examination of all the repercussions, or sufficient time for the senior commanders themselves to probe the consequences of such a major change in operational policy.

Next day, 6th August, Harding issued the formal instructions from Advanced H.Q. A.A.I.[18] The new operation would be code-named 'Olive'. While 8th Army was completing its preparations and carrying out its march to the east coast, both armies were to launch a series of attacks to secure the high ground north and north-west of Florence on 8th Army's front, and the Mt Albano and Mt Pisano hill masses on the north bank of the Arno in 5th Army's sector. The date of 'Olive' would be decided by Leese, and the preliminary operations in the centre would be timed 'so that the enemy has no time in which to re-position his reserves or regroup his forward formations before "OLIVE" is launched.' The date of preliminary operations should not be before 17th August because 'Anvil' would be given all available air support until then; 18th August would be the best date from the M.A.T.A.F. point of view. After capturing the preliminary objectives in the Arno valley, 5th Army was to 'regroup to produce the maximum strength' on its right, and be ready to advance across the Apennines to Bologna to take advantage of any enemy reaction to 'Olive'.

Changing plan at so late a stage took great moral courage. Had the change led to a brilliant military coup Alexander would have been applauded for a stroke of military genius. Most of the consequential problems fell upon Leese, the proposer; nevertheless, Clark's 5th Army underwent last minute changes as well. The two Army Commanders met on 7th August to sort out the implications, which centred largely on the use of 13th Corps, the only British formation that would remain west of the Apennines.[19] Timings were also discussed.

This conference between Army Commanders led to Alexander calling an Army Group co-ordination conference for 3 p.m. on 10th August at Tactical H.Q. 8th Army.[20] Security was so tight that no official records were kept. We have to depend upon the notes of Major-General G.P. Walsh, Chief of Staff 8th Army and the evidence of Clark's unpublished diaries given in the American Official History for this period of the Italian campaign. While Clark 'agreed that the new concept . . . seemed sound', he had misgivings about the lack of unification of command west of the Apennines.[21] In his view 13th British Corps should come under 5th Army for operations. This seems eminently sensible, but Leese could not agree. In his unpublished memoirs Leese says:

'I remember the conference so well. It took place in a charming glade on a hillside in the open, just General Alexander, Mark Clark, John Harding and myself [sic]. I can see now General

Alexander turning to me and asking me if I would agree to Mark Clark's proposition. I hesitated for some time. I knew at once that I would have to agree, and yet I struggled in my mind to think of some way to maintain the 8th Army intact . . .'[22]

Leese proposed that General McCreery, Commander 10th Corps, should become Clark's British Deputy Commander to look after 13th Corps at 5th Army H.Q. while Kirkman took charge of operations. Clark, however, felt that no compromise of this type was workable and Alexander ruled in his favour.[23] 13th Corps would pass to 5th Army command.

The most difficult problem at Army Group level was the reversal of the deception plan. Plan 'Ottrington' was already developing well and German attention was becoming focussed on the east coast. It was now necessary to redirect their interest to the Florence-Bologna axis.[24] Fortunately the battle for Florence had drawn many of the best German divisions into that sector. The new deception plan, 'Ulster', was designed to keep them there; an easier task than to persuade them to move. The concept as defined on 14th August was:

> 'To persuade the enemy that we intend to use our surplus armour in a feint on the ADRIATIC coast to divert his attention from the centre and then to make a frontal assault on the GOTHIC line and to thrust through the Futa pass to BOLOGNA'.

Steps were taken to allow dummy activity on the east coast to die down and, in certain instances, to be compromised as false to ensure the Germans accepted that the east coast concentration was bogus. Elaborate communication deception was then to be carried out simulating the continued presence of H.Q. 8th Army and its principal formations still in the central sectors west of the Apennines. Wireless silence was to be observed by all formations when they moved eastwards.

(ii)

The time factor and its consequential need for speed led to an unusual degree of concurrence in planning between Army Group and Army levels. The emphasis on secrecy led to the imposition of strict 'need to know rules' and as little as possible was committed to paper, making the planning of 'Olive' more complex than usual. 8th Army's opening directive, issued on 5th August, stated that only thirteen principal staff officers were to be told of the change of plan, and they alone were to handle 'Olive' papers.[25] During

6th and 7th August 8th Army planners worked under great pressure to produce an appreciation which Leese could use at a conference of his Corps Commanders, called for 9th August.[26] The object, as set out by the planners, was: 'To bring the enemy to battle under conditions most favourable' to 8th Army, which meant doing so 'as far north as possible, that is with the least extent of hilly country behind him . . .' They also stressed the need for deep and rapid penetration of the front, which would need minimum regrouping and good traffic control during the battle. They envisaged a three corps operation in which 5th Corps would be styled the 'pursuit corps'. It would need either one good two-way road and one adequate one-way road or three adequate one-way roads. This meant that the 'pursuit corps' should be given the coast road 'once the battle began to move'. They also noted that the Polish Corps' task would have to be limited, owing to its lack of further reinforcements.[27] 'The isolation and reduction of Pesaro' would probably be about as much as the Poles could undertake. The corps on the inland flank would be advancing through the hills and would probably lag behind the main advance. The Staff presented Leese with two alternatives: attack with three corps up, placing the Poles initially on the coast as far as Pesaro, 5th Corps in the centre, and 1st Canadian Corps on the inland flank; or attack two corps up, holding 5th Corps back until the Gothic Line had been breached. They left the decision on which course to adopt until the conference on 9th August, but they pointed out that the three corps attack would obviate the loss of time likely to occur in passing 5th Corps through in the pursuit stage; however it would create administrative difficulties in cramming the Corps Troops of three corps into the very constricted area from which the offensive would be launched. In an outline movement plan attached to their paper the planners suggested 25th August as a feasible date for the offensive.

See Map 9

The conference on 9th August crystallized the plan into a logical but unexpected shape.[28] Leese first dealt with the Polish Corps' tasks. The Deputy Corps Commander, representing General Anders, expressed the view that the Poles were unlikely to reach the Gothic Line before D day.* Leese suggested that this would

---

* British orders and narratives rarely differentiate between the two components of the Gothic Line: Green I and Green II. A study of contemporary documents suggests that 8th Army knew little, if anything, of Green II. Its reference to the Gothic Line relate to Green I. Photographic cover of the German defences was not as complete as had been achieved for 'Diadem'. The change of plan was followed by a period of bad weather which limited air photography.[29]

be an advantage since a surprise attack on the enemy's covering
positions behind the Metauro might result in his being unable to
man the main Gothic positions properly, as had happened with
the Hitler Line. He hoped the Poles could secure a bridgehead
over the Metauro and, if possible, reach the high ground just
south of the Gothic Line, but they were not to weaken themselves
so much that they could not deal with Pesaro. Leese then suggested
that a three corps attack had great operational advantages if
the administrative problems could be overcome and if detailed
reconnaissance revealed enough roads. He next asked for Corps
Commanders' views. Lieutenant-General C.F. Keightley, who had
just taken over command of 5th Corps, simply agreed;* but the
Deputy Commander of the Polish Corps made a decisive contribution to the discussion. The Poles had found 'that progress along
the coast road axis was generally slower than inland. The Germans
did extensive demolition and mining on the coast road but did not
pay so much attention to the inland routes'. There is no reference
to the views expressed by the Canadian Corps Commander. Leese
recast the plan of attack then and there to take account of the
Polish advice. The attack would be on a three corps front with
the Poles aiming to isolate Pesaro as suggested by the planners,
but 5th Corps and the Canadians would change places. 5th Corps
would still act as the main pursuit corps, and, in effect, would be
the main striking force as well. It would advance through the hills
on the inland flank directed, ambitiously, on Bologna and Ferrara.

8th Army's Operation Instruction to implement Leese's plan
was issued on 13th August.[31] It gave the Army object as 'To break
the enemy defences on the Adriatic coast and enter the valley of
the Po'. Two objectives were given: '(a) the general line of the R
Marecchia running west from Rimini; (b) Bologna-Ferrara'. The
Corps tasks from right to left were to be:

'*2 Polish Corps*
    To attack and seize the high ground NW of Pesaro, by-
passing the town itself. On completion of the above task to
revert to Army Reserve.

1 Canadian Corps
    To attack and seize the high ground west of Pesaro.
    To strike North to cut out the main road at Cattolica.
    To drive along the coastal axis directed on Rimini.

5 Corps
    To attack the Gothic Line on the left of 1 Canadian Corps.
    To drive on, on the inland axis west of Rimini, directed on
Bologna and Ferrara.

---

* General Allfrey handed over command of 5th Corps on 3rd August.[30]

To protect the left flank of the Army thrust by using 4th Indian Division in the hills'.

The target date for D day was not stated in the order but was given verbally to commanders as 25th August.

The crystallization of Leese's concept for 'Olive' was only the start of the immense organisational, engineering and administrative task of moving 8th Army over to the Adriatic coast in absolute secrecy. The Army Staff had done this in the reverse direction in March and April for the 'Diadem' offensive, but over a longer period. In the very broadest terms there were five distinct problems to be solved: first, the halting and amendment of the regrouping plan for the assault on the centre of the Gothic Line, which had already started and which would have to be reversed without causing loss of confidence and breaches of security amongst the lower formation staffs and the troops; secondly, adequate trans-Apennine routes had to be reconnoitred and strengthened to take the weight of tanks and S.P. guns as well as a volume of heavy military traffic for which they were not designed; thirdly, the actual move had to be conducted as smoothly as possible, and yet in such a way that units spent no more time in their east coast assembly areas than was absolutely necessary, thereby reducing the chances of a premature disclosure of 8th Army's move; fourthly, there were insufficient tank transporters to lift all the tanks and S.P. guns, and infantry formations were not fully mobile and would need time in which to ferry their marching men forward in formation 2nd Line transport; and fifthly, the whole force had to be supplied in its new locations and during the coming offensive.[32]

The extraction of formations and units was in many ways the easiest part of the plan, because the Lake Trasimeno-Foligno area, from which the main trans-Apennine routes diverged, was already being used by 8th Army for the concentration of both 5th Corps and 1st Canadian Corps for the original plan. The formations which had to be extracted from the front, were:

4th Indian Division from 10th Corps
1st Canadian Infantry Division ⎫
4th Division ⎬ from 13th Corps*
2nd New Zealand Division ⎪
25th Army Tank Brigade ⎭

The other formations needed to make up the 'Olive' force, apart from those of the Polish Corps, were:[33]

1st Armoured Division concentrating at Altamura, south-west of Bari.

---

* The operations of 13th Corps, 4th–18th August, are described in Section iv of this chapter.

46th Division at Bavagna ⎤
56th Division at Assisi   ⎦ near Foligno

5th Canadian Armoured Division moving up from the south.
7th Armoured Brigade resting near Lake Bolsena.

Tentative concentration areas were allotted in the rear of the Polish Corps. Armoured units would assemble around Iesi in the Esino valley, using Route 76 as their principal lateral artery; and the rest of the force, including its administrative echelons, would occupy the Macerata-Tolentino-S. Severino area just south of the Potenza river. 5th Corps would administer the reception areas on the far side of the Apennines, while 1st Canadian Corps initially looked after the assembly areas around Foligno until No. 1 District could assume control.

The limiting factor in the speed with which the moves could be completed was the engineer effort and bridging resources available to replace bridges blown during the German withdrawal and to strengthen those which had survived to take heavy loads, particularly tanks on transporters. Two principal routes were chosen for engineer development:[34]

> *Route A* (Southern) ran from Foligno on Route 77 to S. Severino and was to be raised to Class 30 standards for most of the wheeled traffic.*
>
> *Route B* (Northern) also from Foligno but using Route 3 and then Route 76 through Fabriano to Iesi would be raised to Class 70 for tank transporters and would be the principal route for armoured units which would concentrate forward in the valley of the Esino.

There would be a variation of *Route A* called *Route C* which branched off to Tolentino; and there was an extreme northerly *Route D* for 4th Indian Division from Perugia to Gubbio and across the mountains to Sassoferrato which was to be the responsibility of its own divisional engineers.

'A' Army Group R.E. was ordered late on 4th August to open the northern *Route B* from Foligno to Iesi for Class 70 traffic as soon as possible, and a few days later was ordered to open *Route A* from Foligno to Macerata for Class 30 traffic for which 46th Divisional Engineers were placed under command.[35]† The work, which was carried out in hot dusty weather, involved amongst

---

* Class 30 provided for armoured vehicles on their tracks, Class 70 when on transporters. For further details of Load Classes see Part I of this Volume (H.M.S.O. 1984) p.77*n.*

† 'A' A.G.R.E. had under command:
1210 G.H.Q. Troops R.E.
16 G.H.Q. Troops R.E.
South African Engineers 'Road Group'
46th Divisional Engineers.

other things the construction of forty Bailey bridges with a total length of 3,380 feet.

Shortage of tank transporters meant that the majority of tanks and other tracked vehicles would have to cross the Apennines on their tracks in spite of the wear and tear to both engines and tracks.[36] To keep them off the wheeled routes 1st Canadian Corps Engineers constructed a cross-country route some 120 miles long, which started from Ferentillo, north-east of Terni, and used secondary roads and tracks via Visso, Camerino, S. Severino, Villa Potenza (north of Macerata) and Filottrano to Iesi.[37] The tanks of 7th Armoured Brigade and 5th Canadian Armoured Division used this route on their tracks; indeed 5th Canadian Armoured Brigade tanks covered 400 miles in their approach march to Iesi with remarkably few vehicle breakdowns, which says much for the mechanical reliability of the American Sherman.[38]

The Engineers' tasks did not end with the opening of the trans-Apennine routes. They had to construct or develop airfields, roads and tracks on the east coast to support the coming offensive.[39] In addition it was necessary to develop the port of Ancona and to lay out new stores depots, workshops, camps and hospitals, all of which demanded great organisational skill as well as engineer effort and resources. An Engineer stores depot was established at Ancona on 18th August to which stores and bridging material were brought by road, chiefly from east coast dumps in the Sangro area. Forward of Ancona, Route 16, the main coastal road, was developed to two way Class 40 and one way Class 70. This involved the construction of a 420-foot nine span Bailey bridge and a causeway with two 80-foot Bailey spans over the River Cesano and, later, a 440-foot Bailey bridge and a causeway, with two Bailey spans of 110 and 270 feet respectively, over the Metauro river. All this work was carried out by 8th Army Troops R.E.

By 13th August reconnaissance and staff planning was far enough advanced for 8th Army to issue its orders for the main move to begin on 15th August, although some vehicles had set off as early as 12th/13th August. It was found that the need for formations to spend as little time as possible in their concentration areas east of the Apennines had to give way to the equally pressing need to use all available road space to maximum capacity. Movement tables were also complicated because *Route B* could not be opened for tank transporters until 18th August. Furthermore, the traffic was not all one way because tank transporters had to make several trips, and when returning empty had to be so timed that they did not clash with any forward moves of other columns of transporters or vehicle convoys.[40] Block timings were so arranged to give priority to the transporter moves upon which the whole movement plan hinged. Formations were allotted road space on the basis of 250 vehicles per hour by day and 200 by night. Wireless silence was enforced and all communication was by land line and despatch riders. No headlights were used, but the Provost provided verge lights in difficult sections of the road. No formation signs were displayed and detailed arrangements were made to camouflage units in their east coast locations. A special Regulating Movements H.Q. was set up at Foligno, staffed by selected officers from 8th Army Staff Duties and Movement Branches, which depended upon Army resources of Provost and Signals to control the traffic flow through the Foligno bottleneck and on light aircraft to patrol and report on the flow of traffic along the trans-Apennine roads.[41] 'Regmov' as this headquarters was called, opened on the morning of 15th August when the main movement began. The bulk of the programme was practically complete by 22nd August, except that 4th British and 2nd New Zealand Divisions were still waiting in their assembly areas round Foligno, ready to be called forward when they were needed. The move went as nearly according to plan as any operation of this size ever does. The density of traffic was such that little or no margin could be allowed between formation blocks. Fortunately, apart from one severe storm which made gradients and corners difficult and the decks of Bailey bridges slippery for transporters and heavy vehicles, the fine weather held and delays were no more than expected. Over 52,000 vehicles passed north-eastwards through the Foligno bottleneck with minimum confusion.

See Part I of this Volume (H.M.S.O. 1984) Maps 18 and 19

The administrative problems were by far the most taxing of those created by the 8th Army change of plan. The administrative lay-out of the British Lines of Communication had been built up and conditioned on the assumption that the main assault on the Gothic Line would be made on the Florence-Bologna axis with only 2nd Polish Corps, maintained independently under A.A.I. control, in the Adriatic sector.[42] The switch of 8th Army to the east coast naturally involved considerable changes in the administrative arrangements to sustain the new offensive, but forward planning still assumed that Bologna would be reached before the winter and that the advanced base for 5th and 8th Armies operating north of the Apennines would be established there.[43] Immediate requirements made it essential to enlarge the facilities offered by Ancona and the build up of stocks there became a matter of urgency. It must be stressed, however, that there was no intention of replacing Bologna as the main advanced base for operations in the Po valley and beyond. Ancona continued to be regarded only as a port of entry and the temporary depot area from which the offensive could be maintained in the short-term.

Immediately after the change of plan on 4th August the necessary administrative reorganisation began.[44] Temporary arrangements were made to provide the day to day needs of formations arriving in the assembly area round Foligno prior to their move across country to the Adriatic coast, and for the formations assembling in the east coast concentration areas. From 15th August No. 1 District assumed local command and responsibility for the maintenance of 8th Army Troops left west of the Apennines and took over the maintenance of troops waiting in the Foligno assembly area. It also assumed administrative control of No. 4 Roadhead at Arezzo as well as responsibility for the maintenance of 10th Corps around Bibbiena. When 13th Corps passed to command of 5th Army it would be supplied with British type supplies from the Arezzo depots which remained under command of 8th Army.[45] A special administrative staff was added to 5th Army, called *British Increment to 5th Army*, to help the Americans with the logistic support of 13th Corps.*

During August the build up of stocks in Ancona was pushed forward with the greatest urgency: 3,000 tons of supplies and 1,000 tons of fuel were to arrive per day by sea from the Heel ports, and the two supporting railheads of Assisi and Ortona were to take 1,400 and 1,200 tons per day respectively.[47] The depots at Ancona had to be enlarged to handle this flow, and a special oil storage and construction group was placed under command 8th Army to repair and reconstruct the oil storage facilities and to lay a 4-inch pipeline forward from Ancona behind the Army's advance.[48]

The administrative problem was also complicated by lack of space on the east coast. This was felt most severely by the Medical Services because suitable existing accommodation for hospitals proved to be scarce.[49] The casualty estimate made for the first ten days of the battle amounted to 18,500 sick and wounded, to deal with which only some 12,000 beds could be made available, even including hospitals in the Perugia area. Air evacuation of long-term sick and wounded had, however, started on 5th June and did much to reduce the discomfort of the journey rearwards and to increase the speed of evacuation to Base Hospitals at Naples and Bari.[50]

---

* A 'British Increment' was first formed when 10th Corps was attached to 5th Army for the Salerno landing. The object was twofold:
i. Since American logistics were run on entirely separate lines, a normal British staff system was set up to handle administration.
ii. To provide officers to advise any American General or staff section dealing directly with British units.[46]

Apart from dealing with the immediate problems of regrouping 8th Army, the administrative staffs were also planning the future arrangements for maintaining the Army after it had begun its advance through the Gothic Line into the Romagna.[51] Their plans entailed the early restoration of the railways Foligno-Fabriano-Falconara and Ancona-Falconara-Senigallia. It was hoped to open railheads in the Iesi area by 7th September to supply the forward depots or the next Army roadhead when one was established. From here it was planned to extend the railway on the Rimini-Bologna axis with a new forward railhead at Rimini if the offensive went well. Petrol pipelines with a capacity of 800 tons per day were being constructed from Ancona to Falconara, which it was planned to extend eventually to Rimini and Bologna. Consideration was also given to the future of Ravenna port, when captured. As its capacity was very limited it was planned to open it for supplies, petrol and aviation spirit only.

All the administrative problems and plans, which have been outlined above, kept A.A.I. and 8th Army administrative staffs fully stretched between 4th and 24th August, ensuring that the administrative build up was adequate for the opening phases of the offensive and that the administrative preparations for the pursuit phase were well advanced. The outcome of both the movement and administrative planning for 'Olive' was that the offensive would be practicable from 25th August, as 8th Army's operational planners had originally estimated.

Splendid feat of staff work though the preparations for 'Olive' proved to be, it must be observed that this prodigious effort and lavish expenditure of engineer and administrative resources was based on little more than an acknowledgement by Alexander that it was no use forcing a subordinate Army commander to accept a plan in which he had no confidence. It might have been better to change commanders rather than lose time and misuse resources in this way. This was not an option considered nor would it have been in keeping with Alexander's style of command which was based upon total loyalty to his subordinates and command by suggestion rather than by order.

(iii)

The first factor to be considered in the Air plan to support 'Olive' was how to deploy the Desert Air Force so that it could initially support 8th Army on the east coast, and subsequently 5th Army in the Florence sector, without prejudicing the deception plan designed to suggest that 5th Army's operations were the main Allied effort.[52] D.A.F. would not only have to conceal the moves of 5th and 8th Armies and the changes in administrative build up, but also its own changes in deployment. The prevention of enemy air reconnaissance, particularly photographic, was obviously a task of the first importance for D.A.F.* So too would be the prevention of injudicious use of air signals traffic and air support radio.

D.A.F. co-operated closely with the new 'Ulster' Deception Plan.[53] After the move on 18th August to the Adriatic sector of a small air planning staff with Main H.Q. 8th Army, W/T silence was to be maintained and all communications were to be by telephone and teleprinter, until Advanced H.Q. D.A.F. joined up on 28th or 29th August. Air support radio facilities were to remain in the central sector, and even added to, in order to foster the belief in German minds of heavy air activity in that sector. Meanwhile extra A.A.S.C. tentacles and rear links were sited as required for the main attack in the eastern sector, which were to remain silent until Operation 'Olive' was launched. Aircraft were not to use east coast airfields until D day. By D + 10 it was hoped that the attack would have made such progress that certain squadrons could move forward to the Fano area and others back westward to act in support of 5th Army.

The operational Air Plan was in two parts: firstly, the actual Air Support Plan for 'Olive'; and secondly, a special plan for dealing with Pesaro, which was recognised as the most strongly defended sector of the Gothic Line.[54] Fixing the date for the attack on Pesaro, however, was to prove difficult and, in the event became unnecessary when the Germans withdrew from the town prematurely.

The Air Support Plan itself was divided into three phases. In *Phase A*, which was to last the five days and four nights from dawn D – 7 to dusk on D – 3, there were four main tasks: the strategic isolation of the battle area; attacks on the enemy's supplies and movements; interruption of work on the enemy's defences; and direct air support for the Allied troops. The first task was to be accomplished by continuing the attacks on the enemy's railway communications, with special attention to the area bounded by a line joining Rimini-Rovigo-Ferrara-Bologna (*Map 4*) and the east coast. There were, however, to be no attempts at road blocking or cutting. The second task arose because of the enemy's known shortage of ammunition and petrol and his problem of internal distribution resulting from Allied air interdiction. In the third task, targets were chosen all along the Gothic Line, avoiding emphasis on the east coast. And in the fourth task, most of the effort

---

* In the event, during the period 9th–25th August, only two enemy aircraft were plotted by day over concentration areas in the eastern sector, but aircraft were plotted on several occasions at night.

available was allotted to the Poles for their preliminary operations as they closed up to the Gothic Line. Little was left for the normal support of 5th and 8th Armies, although they could not be entirely neglected if an appearance of normality was to be maintained.

By night in *Phase A* the air effort was necessarily to be on a small scale because of the demands of 'Anvil'. It was appreciated that most German movement on the ground would take place at night. Past experience had shown that it usually began at dusk because the Germans knew that detection by Allied air reconnaissance at that time would leave insufficient time for Allied aircraft to attack and return to land in daylight. Unfortunately there was insufficient night bomber effort at D.A.F.'s disposal to force the enemy to revert to daylight movement and so offer more lucrative targets to the day bombers and fighter-bombers. However, an unexpected bonus helped to improve the night air effort. By 20th August, the bombline in southern France had been pushed too far north and west for the U.S. Bostons of U.S. XII T.A.C. to operate effectively, so they were allotted an area in western Italy, thus freeing No. 232 Wing R.A.F. to concentrate on night intruder work in eastern Italy.*

In *Phase B*, which was to last from dusk on D – 3 to dawn on D day, the isolation of the battle area was to become tactical rather than strategic.[56] Almost the entire effort of D.A.F. was to be concentrated on the lateral reinforcement routes connecting the central and eastern sectors, particularly the trans-Apennine roads which abounded in defiles. M.A.T.A.F. was to support D.A.F.'s effort with as large a force of medium day bombers as possible at the time. It was argued that careful selection of targets could assist the deception plan and make it more difficult for the enemy to supply his troops on 5th Army's front. There was to be some direct air support for the Polish Corps but on a limited scale, and at 8th Army's request air attacks on some long-range guns were to be made. At D.A.F.'s request the heavy and medium night bombers of No. 205 Group R.A.F. were to support Operation 'Olive' from the night of D – 1/D day to the end of August. A most important feature of the planning for this pre-D day phase of air operations was the avoidance of any emphasis on the eastern sector in the frequency of air attacks and air reconnaissance.†

Phase C was to last from dawn on D day to D + 2. Because initially information of enemy gun positions, defended localities,

---

* It is clear from the files and documents available that the air planners had in mind *26th August* as 'D day' and *dawn or just before dawn* as 'H hour'. We have maintained the air planners' interpretation of 'D day' which turned out to be D + 1.[55]

† For example, to counterbalance the required additional photographic reconnaissance of the enemy's Adriatic positions, dummy P.R. missions were to be flown regularly in the area of the Futa Pass on Route 65 north of Florence.

headquarters, and reserve areas would not be plentiful or reliable, a large portion of D.A.F.'s bomber effort was to be on call and, in the opening stages of battle, air support for the troops would come from Cabranks of fighter-bombers. To meet these requirements two Rover David teams were to be allotted, one (No. 1 Rover David) to 5th Corps and the other (No. 2) to 1st Canadian and 2nd Polish Corps. Anticipated targets would be gun areas, forward defended localities, enemy headquarters, enemy movement in rear of the battle area, and targets of opportunity such as concentrations in the forward area. Furthermore there was the possibility of an air blitz being required, combined with a creeping barrage when a break through seemed imminent.* It was also essential that air support for 5th Army be maintained at the normal rate of effort, and desirable to continue the attacks on communications targets begun in Phase 'B'. As D.A.F.'s resources would be insufficient for all these tasks, M.A.T.A.F. was asked to make additional air effort available in this Phase as well. By night in Phase 'C' D.A.F.'s night bombers were to continue to intrude over 5th and 8th Armies' fronts attacking any enemy movement detected, and on the night of D + 1/D + 2 No. 205 Group R.A.F. was to attack the Pesaro sector and thereafter selected reserve areas, dumps and communications.

At Table I at the end of this chapter is an Order of Battle in which the deployment of the Desert Air Force on 25th August is shown, indicating the moves of squadrons from the central to the eastern sector. These mainly involved Nos. 239 and 244 (both fighter) and No. 285 (Reconnaissance) Wings.[57] The total strength of D.A.F. in Italy on 25th August based upon establishments was approximately 568 aircraft, of which around 75% or more were serviceable. When required, the medium day bombers of M.A.T.A.F.'s U.S. 42nd and 57th Medium Bombardment Wings (Marauders and Mitchells) in Sardinia and Corsica were to switch from support of 'Anvil' to 'Olive' for which they had the range.

An Order of Battle of *Luftlotte 2* in Italy dated 20th August gives a total aircraft strength of 121 with 74 serviceable:[58]

Role	Strength	Serviceability	Aircraft
Long-range recce	22	11	Me. 410; Ju. 88 & 188.
Tactical Recce	26	15	Me. 109.
Fighter	40	31	Me. 109.
Night ground-attack	33	17	Ju. 87
	121	74	

---

* On the lines of that carried out at El Hamma in Tunisia on 25th March 1943. See *Mediterranean and Middle East* Volume IV (H.M.S.O. 1966) pp. 345-9.

The only unit of interest in the Italian Republican Air Force was a new one formed through the intervention of General Ritter von Pohl and equipped with (on 20th August) 37 Me. 109G fighters. They were used chiefly against unescorted Allied medium day bombers, individual pilots making passes at the bomber formation. Generally speaking the *Luftwaffe's* influence on events in Italy, and its ability to affect them, continued to decline, and no compensating effort worthy of note was made by the Republican Air Force with which the *Luftwaffe* appears to have become disenchanted.

(iv)

See Map 8

While 8th Army was concentrating upon 'Olive' planning, A.A.I. and 5th Army were contending with the residual problems of maintaining pressure west of the Apennines, both for deception purposes and to develop 5th Army's operations in such a way that Clark would be able to exploit any weakening of German troops holding the Florence-Bologna axis which 'Olive' might cause. Clark had expected to start the first phase of the assault on the centre of the Gothic Line between 5th and 10th August by attacking across the Arno, through the New Zealand screen on the river, to seize the Mt Albano feature.[59] After consultation between A.A.I., 5th Army and 13th Corps, this plan was completely revised, and fresh orders were issued by Clark on 17th August.[60] His Army's main thrust was moved eastwards onto the Florence-Bologna axis, and the primary effort was to be by 2nd U.S. Corps.

5th Army's attack was to be in two phases: 2nd U.S. Corps would pass through the British troops holding Florence and would secure the high ground north of the city, whilst 13th Corps would take Mt Giovi (Pt 992) overlooking Dicomano and the Sieve valley. 2nd U.S. Corps would then develop operations on the axis of Route 65 towards Bologna. 13th Corps would do likewise on the Firenzuola-Imola road to its east. 4th U.S. Corps would hold the line of the Arno from the coast to a point five miles west of Florence. The boundary between 2nd U.S. and 13th Corps was to be some 6 miles east of Florence. 13th Corps' eastern boundary (which was also the new inter-Army boundary) ran roughly along the eastern edge of the Pratomagno massif.[61]

As 4th U.S. Corps could not hold such a wide front with only Task Force 45 and 1st U.S. Armoured Division, 6th South African Armoured Division (with 24th Guards Brigade still under command) was to be transferred from 13th Corps to Crittenberger's command.[62] Clark was particularly anxious to conceal the exact point of 2nd U.S. Corps' attack although the deception plan required him to draw attention to the central axis. Fortunately 2nd U.S. Corps could be held in bivouac areas well back from the front. Deception could be achieved by allowing the extensive regrouping to be noted which would imply an impending attack somewhere on 5th Army's front. The likely date of D day was also contained in these orders but will be discussed in another context.

We left 13th Corps on 4th August entering the outskirts of Florence and closing up to the Arno (*see Map 5*). That morning the rear-guards of 1st Parachute Corps were still holding two bridgeheads south of the river. To the west of the city, Empoli was strongly held, and to the east, the loop of the Arno from the south-east outskirts of Florence to Incisa had not yet been cleared. 1st Canadian Division had been brought up to relieve the New Zealanders in the Florence sector, starting 5th August so that they could move west to clear the Empoli bridgehead, and to enable 8th Indian Division to be pulled back (as was then intended) into Corps reserve.[63] 4th Division, which had closed up to the Arno near Florence, was given the task of clearing the river loop east of the city.[64]

Freyberg, commanding 2nd New Zealand Division, had intended to 'bounce' a crossing over the Arno west of Florence during the night 4th/5th August, but found he could not do so without shelling the city because the Germans still had 'spandaus on top of houses', and so he concluded that it was 'not on unless he [the German] was out of the town'.[65] Moreover, his Sappers reported that the construction of a low level crossing would be difficult. The alternative of a high level bridge would mean a 200-foot Bailey bridge which would take too long to build. He would have to leave the problem to the Canadians, while he relieved 8th Indian Division in the Empoli sector. The New Zealand operations, which took place between 10th and 13th August, were also designed to screen the deployment of 2nd U.S. Corps, which Clark originally intended to use to force the crossing of the Arno and to seize the Mt Albano feature. Although Clark's offensive was postponed, the New Zealanders successfully forced the Germans back over the river and cleared Empoli before they themselves were relieved by 85th U.S. Division, so that they could enjoy a brief rest before assembling in 8th Army's rear for Operation 'Olive'.

4th Division's task of clearing the loop of the Arno east of Florence involved capturing the 1,600-ft ridge on which stood the Incontro Monastery with its high tower and walled grounds.[66] Like Monte Cassino, this steep, wedge-shaped peak dominated all the countryside in the Arno's bend east of Florence. No force could hope to cross the Arno on 4th Division's side of the city, and none of the roads approaching the river from the south could be used for supply until 715th Infantry Division had been driven from the Incontro ridge. 4th Division's 28th Brigade closed up to Incontro during 5th August, but failed to carry the ridge in its attack that night. The reserve brigade (10th) was then committed. At dawn 8th August 4th Division attacked again, eventually clearing the ridge after a fierce battle which was costly to both sides. 2nd D.C.L.I. who carried out the main assault suffered 99 casualties.[67] The loss of Incontro unhinged the German positions in the loop and forced them to withdraw across the Arno, allowing 4th Division to close up to the river line opposite Pontassieve.

1st Canadian Division was relieved in front of Florence for 'Olive' by the ubiquitous 8th Indian Division on 8th August and the relief of 4th Division and 25th Tank Brigade by 1st Division from Army Reserve started during the night 8th/9th August.[68] Then on the night of 10th/11th August demolitions shook the city of Florence as rear-guards of 1st Parachute Corps withdrew to the line of the Mugnone canal which runs through the northern half of the city.[69] Shortly after dawn white flags were seen hanging from the windows of the houses along the Arno. Conditions in the city were such that General Kirkman decided to reverse his decision not to send fighting troops into the city. The people of Florence had been without food, with little water and no sanitation for five days, and had been confined to their houses by sporadic fighting as the German garrison, the local Fascists and the Partisans of the Tuscan Committee of National Liberation clashed in the streets. 8th Indian Division followed up the German withdrawal during 11th August until it found its further advance blocked by machine gun fire down the streets leading to the Mugnone canal crossings. Brigadier B. S. Mould, commander 21st Indian Brigade, was made Commander of Florence Garrison with responsibility for re-establishing the life of the city by co-ordinating military and civilian efforts to restore order, round up Fascists, and bring relief supplies to the unfortunate citizens.[70]

East of Florence 1st Division gained a foothold on the north bank of the Arno on 12th August; and, in Florence, 21st Indian Brigade gradually extended the area under British control.[71] Although Partisans reported a 'reign of terror' in the German held northern part of the city no further operations to force them back from the Mugnone canal could be undertaken because priority had to be given to regrouping for 'Olive'.[72] On 18th August 13th Corps came under operational command of 5th Army and three days later, 21st August, under 5th Army's administrative command as well.

The Allied landings started on the south coast of France on 15th August. Next day the final A.A.I. Operation Order for 'Olive' was issued.[73] Commander 8th Army was still responsible for setting D day, which he had done verbally for security reasons. 5th Army was to be at 24 hours' notice to attack north of Florence at any time after D + 5. Alexander himself would decide the exact time. Clark, however, in his final orders wrote: 'D day: Units will be prepared to attack on 72 hours' notice after 0001B August 25'.[74] Such are the problems of co-ordinating two different national staff systems even in important matters like security.

Thus, as the Allied forces developed their operations on the coast of southern France, both 5th and 8th Armies had formulated their plans to implement Alexander's changed strategy for the battle of the Gothic Line which would begin in the last instead of the first week of August. A precious three weeks had been lost.

(v)

See Map 4

On the German side uncertainty regarding the next Allied strike in the Mediterranean persisted right up to the moment it was delivered. In Part I of this Volume* we described the differing views expressed in the first fortnight of August by the Intelligence services which fed the High Command, and we showed how these were re-interpreted by the senior commanders in France and Italy, each intent on the threat to his own sphere of responsibility. As he believed that the Allies had enough resources to assault the Gulf of Genoa as well as southern France Kesselring was taking no chances, and on 10th August he listed for *OKW* the counter-invasion precautions he had already prepared.[75] Marshal Graziani, who had been in command of the Army of Liguria since 3rd August, was reinforced on the 8th by the H.Q. and Corps Troops of 75th Corps from *AOK 14*. Although it retained its status as Army Group reserve, 90th Panzer Grenadier Division was also placed under Graziani's command, strengthening his German component of 34th Infantry Division which was watching the coast west of Genoa, and 42nd Jäger Division deployed south and east of the port. A regiment of 15th Panzer Grenadier Division was placed on three hours' notice to move west or east from the Bologna area, pending the release of the whole division which was contingent on the withdrawal of *AOK 10* into the *Vorfeld* line covering Green I. A regiment of 1st Parachute Division was similarly earmarked for

---

* Part I (H.M.S.O. 1984) Chapter VI.

anti-invasion duties at five hours' notice, and the rest of this division, 98th Infantry Division and parts of 162nd Infantry Division were warned for action on the Adriatic as well as Ligurian coasts.

The first positive evidence of an impending amphibious operation came in a sighting report early on 12th August of two convoys heading for Ajaccio, Corsica. On the same day Kesselring was told by von Vietinghoff that a major frontal assault on the left wing of *AOK 10* was not expected, as there were no signs of any substantial build up behind the Poles, nor even of preparations for such an assembly in the form of repair work on demolished bridges.[76] Garnered as it must have been before 8th Army's engineers started work on the trans-Apennine routes, this information encouraged Kesselring to react to the convoy sightings with vigour and speed. With both his armies alerted, by the evening of the 12th one regiment of 1st Parachute Division had been ordered to Reggio to cover Parma from airborne landings and to be ready to strike towards Spezia. The rest of the division, and parts of 98th Infantry Division, were placed on 12 hours' notice to move to Genoa, and a regiment of 15th Panzer Grenadier Division was ordered to the Piacenza area as Army Group reserve. Artillery and Tiger tanks were moved from *AOK 14* to the Army of Liguria, and Lemelsen was instructed to strengthen his coastal sector with motorised infantry. As two regiments of 90th Panzer Grenadier Division had already moved towards Genoa on 11th August, it was fortunate for Kesselring that Alexander had changed his plan and was not about to strike at *AOK 14's* front north of Florence and Pistoia as originally intended.

OB Südwest was also fortunate in having reserves on which to draw, unlike Colonel-General von Blaskowitz, the commander of the impoverished Army Group G in southern France. We study his situation in the next chapter, and have noted in Part I of this Volume that Field-Marshal von Kluge, as *OB West*, was without orders for his Mediterranean front until 14th August. One of Hitler's staff (unidentified) had suggested on the 13th that Kesselring's armies should withdraw to Green I forthwith, in order to free more mobile reserves to counter the 'expected landings'.[77] As the Führer maintained that more time was needed for development of the Green Line's defences, the proposal was not pursued.

By then the Allies' air attacks on radar installations on the French Riviera, and the systematic demolition of the Rhône bridges, had convinced von Blaskowitz that an invasion of southern France was imminent. But from Italy Kesselring also reported the destruction of bridges, for instance that at Pontelagoscuro on 14th August, and at Rovigo the day before, when damage was also reported to shore batteries and ships in port at Genoa.[78] Kesselring was similarly non-committal about the first convoy sightings of 14th August, which we describe in Chapter XII. With no details, he assumed that the convoys were but the tip of an iceberg and would be joined by others from North Africa, Sardinia and Naples. On the morning of the 15th, when the 'Dragoon' landings had begun, he told Wentzell that the westerly course from Ajaccio might have been a feint and a force destined for Liguria might yet appear. In a different and personal context his comment that 'we must still expect surprises' was proved right, for he was unexpectedly summoned to Hitler's Headquarters as a possible candidate with Field-Marshal Model for the post of *OB West* in place of von Kluge, whose absence from his own headquarters on 15th August gave rise to suspicions that he had gone to negotiate with the Allies. Model succeeded him on the 17th and when Hitler subsequently observed that 15th August was 'the worst day of my life' he was probably thinking more of von Kluge and the disasters at Falaise, than the Allied landings in southern France.

Kesselring returned to Italy, and Allied operations in southern France took the course which will be described in Chapter XII. On 16th August *AOK 10* was warned that 'the overall situation in the West' would soon entail the withdrawal through the Brenner Pass of 15th Panzer Grenadier Division, and orders also to extract 3rd Panzer Grenadier Division for the West were confirmed to *AOK 14* on the 18th.[79] It was not however intended that these divisions should stiffen resistance to the Allied landings. The records of *OB West* show that they were destined '*ab initio*' for central France, and not for the Mediterranean coast. Their removal diminished the battle potential of *AOK 10* and *AOK 14*, but the staffs in Italy accepted that needs were greater in France. With customary energy Kesselring also accepted an extension of his responsibilities which was the first, and indeed the only, direct effect of the landings on the affairs of the Italian Theatre.

By the evening of 16th August it was clear that the invaders of southern France would not be dislodged. The Operations Branch of *OKW* drafted a directive for the withdrawal from the coast of *AOK 19* which was signed by Hitler and despatched 24 hours later.[80] No effort had been made to reinforce the Mediterranean front at the expense of the German forces opposing Eisenhower. It was the rapid advance of Eisenhower's forces, which posed the risk of encirclement for *AOK 19*, that gave Hitler the reason for authorising the evacuation of southern France by Army Group G. Kesselring was implicated because the Führer made him responsible for the defence of the Franco-Italian frontier, from its boundary with Switzerland down to the Ligurian Sea. As two divisions of *AOK 19's*

62nd Corps were to withdraw along the line of the French Alps, they were placed under Kesselring's command; and to safeguard their movement he was directed by Hitler on 20th August to keep the frontier passes open and free from attack by the French Maquis.

This mandate proved troublesome, because the Italian Partisans as well as the Maquis made vigorous efforts to block the passes from both sides of their borders. The bulk of 90th Panzer Grenadier Division was sent into the Alps by the Army of Liguria, but mounting pressure from Italians and French impelled Kesselring to inform *OKW* on 23rd August that Graziani must be reinforced by mountain troops. *AOK 10* had accordingly been instructed to release 5th Mountain Division from its front. With 3rd and 15th Panzer Grenadier Divisions also to be released for the West, both *AOK 10* and *AOK 14* were involved in extensive regroupings which provided the excuse for a number of local withdrawals. However this was not yet the occasion for a general retreat into Green I. On the grounds that it would free reserves for the West, Hitler mooted the possibility on 19th August, with the additional prospect of a further withdrawal into the *Voralpen* position once this was fully developed. Kesselring's staffs thereafter began to study the implications of reaching and crossing the Po, but we note later that on 28th August, when Hitler accepted Jodl's suggestion that retreat to the Green Line would free forces for counter-action elsewhere, it was not for the West that the release was envisaged, but rather to create a reserve against possible Allied landings in the northern Adriatic.[81] Thus the direct impact of the landings in southern France on German strategy for Italy was not particularly far-reaching, although the diversion of 90th Panzer Grenadier Division and the bulk of 5th Mountain Division to the Western Alps could be counted as a tactical bonus for the Allies in that these experienced troops were not on hand when Operation 'Olive' opened. But Alexander's change of plan meant that in the preceding weeks no advantage could be taken of the weakening of Kesselring's main front nor of his distraction with affairs in the Western Alps. The chance of collecting the one dividend paid to A.A.I. by the landings in southern France was thus lost.

(vi)

Before we finally set the stage for 'Olive' we must describe the preliminary operations of 10th Corps in the Northern Apennines and the Polish Corps on the east coast: the former because in them General McCreery, who was later to take over 8th Army from Leese, developed mountain warfare techniques which were to pay dividends in the autumn; and the latter because General Anders carried out his task of covering the move of 8th Army over the Apennines in an exemplary way.

We left 10th Corps engaged in the final stages of operations to seize Bibbiena in the valley of the Upper Arno as a base for further operations against its sector of the Gothic Line.[82]* When the plan was changed on 4th August the future role and composition of 10th Corps was radically amended. By this time, however, the Corps was already committed to an operation to secure the two mountain masses flanking the Upper Arno valley, the Alpe di Catenaia on the east and the Pratomagno on the west. McCreery appreciated, as early as 21st July, that 10th Corps' task in tackling the Gothic Line would be an outflanking movement through the mountains on a mule-pack basis.[83] He envisaged his Indian infantry working forward on foot while his Sappers, heavily reinforced with mechanical plant, blasting equipment and labour units, built tracks for jeeps and armour in their wake. The success of his operations would depend upon the speed with which his Sappers could open up these tracks, one of which would be needed for each division.† The advance on Bibbiena would give him an opportunity to try out the necessary techniques and gain valuable experience on which to base his plans for the advance on Bologna through the high country in front of him.[84]

See Map 10

McCreery planned to launch his trial offensive at the beginning of August with a converging attack on Bibbiena by his two Indian Divisions, each with a tank regiment in support.[85] 10th Indian Division, on the right, would advance across the mountains from Anghiari to clear the Alpe di Catenaia and approach Bibbiena from the south-east. 4th Indian Division, on the left, would advance initially through the hills on the eastern side of Route 71 as far as the Subbiano spur and Falciano, and then astride Route 71. The Corps' flanks would be protected by 9th Armoured Brigade to the

---

* See Chapter X p. 96–7.

† The scale of engineer reinforcement envisaged for the two divisional jeep tracks was:

Troops	Two sections Canadian Drilling Company R.C.E.
	Six labour companies
Equipment	6 trailer compressors
	4 portable drills and breakers
	8 water pumps
	8 D4 angledozers
	4 D6 angledozers
Explosive	600 'Beehive' charges
Transport	100 jeeps and 100 trailers

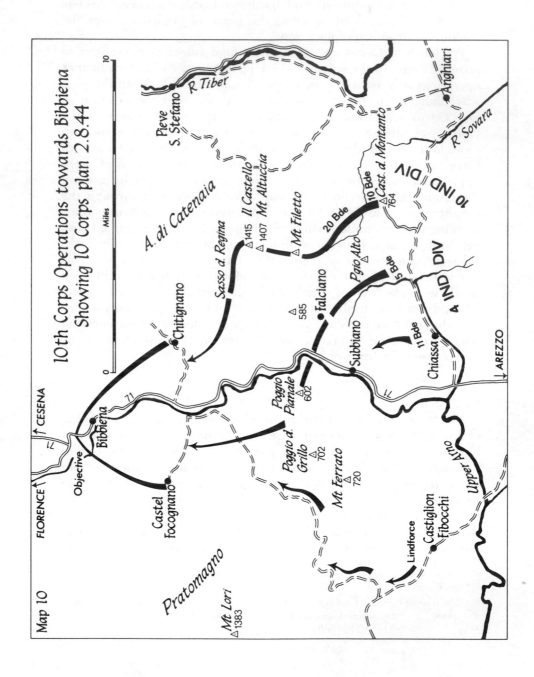

Map 10

10th Corps Operations towards Bibbiena
Showing 10 Corps plan 2.8.44

east and 'Lindforce' (an armoured reconnaissance force) to the west.

10th Indian Division had quite the hardest task as it had no road to help it. McCreery allotted it all the mountain artillery available, consisting of two mountain regiments and one jeep-drawn regiment. The divisional supply track was to run from a jumping off point north of the Anghiari-Chiassa lateral road at Castello di Montanto. Three field companies of the Divisional Sappers and Miners, two Italian labour companies, a Canadian drilling section, and three sections of a general transport company, were employed building this supply route.*

Preliminary operations to prepare the way for the Corps' attack started on 2nd August when 4th Indian Division advanced to secure the Subbiano ridge.[87] These operations progressed surprisingly well against weak opposition. By the end of the day 5th Indian Brigade on the right was secure on the Poggio Alto while, on the left, 11th Indian Brigade entered Subbiano. Lindforce operating on 4th Indian Division's left, west of Route 71, was in contact with 15th Panzer Grenadier Division holding Mt Ferrato in some strength. On 10th Indian Division's sector 20th Indian Brigade, which was to lead with one battalion from each of its fellow brigades under command, moved forward to Castello di Montanto ready to start the advance northwards. It was organised entirely on a mule and man-pack basis.

The success of 4th Indian Division in the Upper Arno valley led McCreery on 3rd August to reinforce his thrust on the axis of Route 71 by bringing 9th Armoured Brigade across from the extreme east flank to take over from Lindforce, which was disbanded.[88] Only 12th and 27th Lancers, with supporting arms, remained east of the Upper Tiber to watch the area between that river and the Polish Corps' left boundary. This all took time and the newly constituted 9th Armoured Brigade was not ready to participate in the battle until 5th August.

Meanwhile the main Corps' attack had opened on 3rd August. 10th Indian Division's 20th Indian Brigade in a silent night advance secured Mt Filetto and, continuing through thickly wooded country, occupied Mt Altuccia (Pt 1,407) by nightfall. This feature

---

* The building of this track proved to be a considerable engineering feat.[86] The alignment of the track involved a drop of 370 feet into the valley of the Sovara river followed by a climb of 2,300 feet to a maximum elevation of 3,750 feet over a distance of six miles. One field company, moving behind the leading battalion of 20th Indian Brigade from Castello di Montanto, constructed a mule track. This was improved and converted into a jeep track by a second field company, assisted by the Canadian drilling section and the Italian Pioneer companies. Behind these again worked a third field company constructing a track fit to take tanks. Work accomplished comprised five miles of mule track in 18 hours, six miles of jeep track which reached as far as Mt Filetto in 66 hours, and five miles of tank track in 36 hours.

had been held by 305th Infantry Division. Failure to hold it and Mt Filetto aroused displeasure at *AOK 10*.[89] The following day 2nd/3rd Gurkha Rifles carried Il Castello by assault, after a fierce hand to hand battle, and secured a foothold on the Sasso della Regina spur. On 4th Indian Division's front, 5th Indian Brigade moved forward from Falciano and secured the high ground to the west of Mt Filetto.[90] West of the Arno valley 11th Indian Brigade captured Mt Ferrato against light opposition and secured Poggio del Grillo. Kesselring was incensed by these failures.[91] *AOK 10's* Chief of Staff, Wentzell, replied he too 'was boiling with rage' and added that reinforcements from 15th Panzer Grenadier Division were being rushed up. 115th Panzer Grenadier Regiment counter-attacked Poggio del Grillo overrunning a company of 2nd Camerons; and another of its battalions went to the aid of 305th Infantry Division which was struggling to recapture Il Castello. 2nd/3rd Gurkha Rifles were able to hold the feature, but only by abandoning the Regina spur to help to repel these counter-attacks.[92] 20th Indian Brigade, in its turn, brought up reinforcements and re-established a foothold on the Regina spur during the night 6th/7th August, but were again forced to withdraw when their ammunition supply failed. The brigade then reorganised and consolidated around Il Castello. During these operations the Desert Air Force was hampered by poor weather.[93]

Only on the extreme left flank were further gains made.[94] Here 7th Indian Brigade was advancing in strength against light opposition on the Pratomagna and by 7th August had captured Mt Lori. It was at this stage in 10th Corps' offensive that 8th Army's change of plan forced the Corps to close down its operations for regrouping, which left McCreery only 10th Indian Division, 9th Armoured Brigade, 12th and 27th Lancers (armoured cars) and two newly arriving units, the Lovat Scouts and 4th/11th Sikhs, both mountain warfare trained. Just before its relief 4th Indian Division managed to retake Poggio del Grillo.[95]

The withdrawal of 4th Indian Division meant that 10th Indian Division had to take over both divisional sectors.[96] McCreery could no longer expect to continue full scale operations on a front which extended for some fifty miles with only one division, but it was essential that he should conceal the drastic weakening of 10th Corps and this demanded vigorous action by his remaining troops. He decided, therefore, to concentrate his infantry strength in sectors considered to be vital to the German defence and to cover the rest of his extended front with armoured car and tank patrols. On 9th August McCreery ordered his Corps to pass onto the defensive in its existing positions, concealing the withdrawal of the 4th Indian Division and the change of policy on the Corps' front by deep and aggressive patrolling.

On the German side the agreed switch of the corps headquarters of *AOK 10* took place on 8th August.[97] As a result, Feuerstein's 51st Mountain Corps which maintained command of 44th Infantry and 114th Jäger Divisions, also assumed that of 15th Panzer Grenadier and 715th, 334th and 305th Infantry Divisions. Herr and the staff of 76th Panzer Corps moved to the Adriatic wing and took over 5th Mountain and 71st and 278th Infantry Divisions in the line, with 1st Parachute Division in reserve on the coast. During the next fortnight *AOK 10* continually adjusted its forward positions as it withdrew gradually to the main Gothic defences further north.[98] These withdrawals were followed up, and by 25th August 10th Corps had moved up to the vicinity of Chitignano east and west of the Upper Arno. The vale of Bibbiena remained in German hands. Nevertheless, McCreery and 10th Corps Staff had gained valuable experience in mountain operations and were better able to judge the practicability of working through the roadless sectors of the Northern Apennines.

See Map 9 (Inset)

On the Polish Corps front, Anders' men had secured positions between the Misa and Cesano rivers by 4th August.[99] In the light of the change of plan agreed that day, Leese instructed Anders to press forward with all speed towards the Metauro river so as to cover the concentration of 8th Army in the Ancona-Iesi area and to safeguard Route 76 (redeployment *Route B*) from any long-range artillery interference by German guns positioned south of the Metauro. In response, Anders started to plan a fresh offensive to drive the Germans back over the Cesano and set 9th August as his target date for the resumption of his advance. The intervening period was devoted to intensive patrolling and preparations for a Corps' assault. This was to be carried out with the two infantry divisions abreast, 3rd Carpathian Division on the right nearest the coast and 5th Kresowa Division on the left, directed to take the La Croce feature, while the *C.I.L.* performed its normal role of protecting the inland flank of the Corps.

The attack went in as planned on the early morning of 9th August. 1st Carpathian Rifle Brigade, supported by 1st Polish Armoured Regiment, attacked to the west of Scapezzano towards the high ridge which connected this place with the La Croce feature.[100] By 10 a.m. the brigade had secured the first objective and then continued its advance north-eastwards along the ridge towards Scapezzano while 2nd Carpathian Rifle Brigade attacked it from the south-east. The enemy defended Scapezzano stubbornly all day but withdrew over the Cesano river under cover of darkness. The Kresowa Division's 5th Wilenska Brigade secured the La Croce feature by 10 a.m. and, continuing its thrust, reached and captured Monterado towards nightfall after a heavy day's fighting. On the Corps' left flank the *C.I.L.* reached the Corinaldo–Castelleone di Suasa ridge and 12th Podolski Regiment moved up through Corinaldo to reach the Cesano, south of Monteporzio, opposed only by rear-guards. A.O.C. D.A.F. made support of the Polish Corps his major concern. On 9th August guns were the prime target south of Fano; roads, M.T. and a suspected German H.Q. were minor tasks.[101]

During 10th August the Carpathian Division forced a crossing over the Cesano south of Mondolfo and established a small bridge-head, while a second bridgehead, south of Monteporzio, was secured by the Kresowa Division, but had to be abandoned owing to heavy artillery and mortar fire.[102]

278th Infantry Division, with four battalions in the line and supported by four batteries of artillery, as well as one armed with Hornets and one with assault guns, had fought very stubbornly and suffered heavy losses.[103] 303 prisoners were captured and over 200 enemy dead were counted on the battlefield. Eighteen guns, including eight 8.8-cm. guns were captured. Bad weather prevented any air support being given.

12th to 17th August was devoted to reorganisation, patrolling and preparations for the further advance to the Metauro river. The bulk of the *C.I.L.* was withdrawn during this period, their positions being taken over by a special force named 'Cavalry Force'.[104]* Anders protested about the loss of the *C.I.L.* but was told confidentially that the reason for its withdrawal was to allow 5th Corps to use its area for the 'Olive' concentration.[105] The Italians were only to be told that they were to be rested and refitted for the next offensive. He was, however, allowed to keep some of the Italian units for the time being.

Anders reopened his offensive towards the Metauro river on 19th August. His plan aimed at breaking through the enemy defences at Mondolfo and S. Constanzo on the coast, followed by a drive northwards towards the Metauro.[106] Through the breach made by this attack 2nd Polish Armoured Brigade was to thrust west via Cerasa towards Montemaggiore. The object of this thrust was to cut off and destroy 71st Infantry Division, which was positioned on 278th Infantry Division's inland flank on the high ground north

---

* The force consisted of Carpathian Lancers, 12th Podolski Reconnaissance Regiment, the British Household Cavalry Regiment (now returned from 10th Corps) and 7th Polish Horse Artillery Regiment. The '*Banda Maiella*' of about 400 Italian Partisans, was also put under command.

of Monteporzio and Mondavio, facing the Kresowa Division and Cavalry Force. These formations were instructed, initially, to tie down the enemy in front of them and, at the right moment, to concert their assault with the armoured thrust coming in from Cerasa.

The main assault by the reinforced 3rd Carpathian Division started at 10 a.m. on 19th August, with 2nd Carpathian Brigade on the right making for Mondolfo and 6th Lwowska Brigade (under command) directed on S. Constanzo on the left.[107] The Germans fought so doggedly that a way through for the armour was not cleared until the following morning. The Armoured Brigade was then fiercely opposed and the fighting continued throughout 20th August, the Germans holding on with great stubbornness to enable 71st and 278th Infantry Divisions to get back across the Metauro river. It was not until 10.30 a.m. on the 21st that the Polish armour cleared Cerasa, from where their advance continued slowly in the face of heavy resistance towards Montemaggiore. Meanwhile the Kresowa Division had launched its attack directed through Poggio and Piagge, with the Cavalry Force advancing on their left through Barchi. This advance made slow progress and it was not until nightfall on the 21st that the Kresowa Division linked up with the Armoured Brigade east of Montemaggiore.

On the coastal axis the Carpathian Division had continued its northerly drive from S. Constanzo and Mondolfo and reached the Metauro river line before dawn on 22nd August. By then 71st and 278th Infantry Divisions had made good their withdrawal across the Metauro and the whole of the south bank of this river between the coast and Fossombrone was in Polish hands. The Polish Corps had failed to destroy its opponents but it had inflicted very severe losses on 71st and 278th Infantry Divisions, destroying 20 S.P. guns, 22 anti-tank guns and six tanks.[108] 273 prisoners were captured and 300 dead were counted. All the ground south of the Metauro had been cleared, thereby giving 8th Army its required Start Line for its forthcoming attack on the Gothic positions.

During 19th–22nd August D.A.F.'s main occupation was with communications in the north. Bad weather made it difficult to give full support to Anders' offensive. On the 20th, however, the small effort available for air support within the battle area was devoted to the Polish Corps, and approximately 60 fighter-bomber sorties were flown against guns three miles south-west of Fano, and between 14 to 19 miles north-west of Senigallia.[109] Rail bridges and a road bridge W.N.W. of Senigallia were secondary targets. Next day this pattern was repeated but the guns attacked were by now only five miles south of Pesaro and within four miles west of Fano.

On 22nd August almost all 45 available fighter-bomber sorties were flown against guns within the same area.

With Anders' seizure of the covering position on the Metauro the stage had been successfully set for 'Olive'. A most difficult manoeuvre had been accomplished through meticulous staff work and efficient movement control. The ground needed for the concentration of 8th Army's formations prior to the assault had been captured on schedule and the necessary switch in the administrative arrangements to support the assault had just been completed. During the whole period which covered the move of the Army from west to east the Allied Air Forces had successfully prevented enemy air reconnaissance on a scale great enough to discover the massive movements which were going on. The carefully controlled security arrangements, including all aspects of camouflage and concealment, had apparently worked to perfection. All in all a masterpiece of staff planning had been achieved.

See Map 8

5th Army's preparations for its supporting offensive were also completed on time. Taking its front from west to east, 4th U.S. Corps was reinforced by 6th South African Armoured Division which took over the Empoli-Montelupo sector of the Arno Line on 22nd August.[110] 2nd U.S. Corps concentrated its assault force, comprising 34th, 85th and 91st U.S. Divisions, around Certaldo, while 88th U.S. Division took over the sector immediately west of Florence from British troops.

On 13th Corps' front Clark had intended to leave Kirkman's forward units where they stood and to pass his assault force through them when he opened his offensive. On 20th August 13th Corps detected a German withdrawal brought about by the extraction of 15th Panzer Grenadier Division from the line, and so it was decided to enlarge the small bridgehead over the river east of Florence before the main offensive started. One possible hazard facing 1st Division, which was to undertake the task, was the presence of an artificial lake held back by locks on a small tributary of the Arno between Florence and Pontassieve. If the Germans blew these, the assault troops could be cut off. On 21st August, the Sappers and Miners of 8th Indian Division crossed the river and managed to open the locks. After the first rush of water had subsided the Arno was left with only about two foot of water in places, allowing 1st Division to cross and develop the bridgehead. It was extended beyond Route 67 on the north bank and enabled the engineers to bridge the river without interference. 8th Indian Division found a ford just west of Pontassieve and crossed as well.

6th Armoured Division, east of the Middle Arno, also found opposition to its advance slackening. By 25th August it had reached the junction of Routes 67 and 70 east of Pontassieve and was nosing its way up the Sieve river valley.

Between 6th and 25th August M.A.T.A.F. (with the exception of D.A.F.) had been busy concentrating upon preparations for and then actual participation in the landings in southern France which we shall be describing in the next chapter. Here we will confine ourselves to a synopsis of D.A.F.'s air activity within the battle area, but before doing so we must first note two changes which took place in the control of and in the direction of tactical air operations in Italy.

In the first instance it will be recalled that by mid-July H.Q. No. 287 Wing (M.A.C.A.F.) was acting as a Forward Fighter Control on the east coast of Italy; No. 1 M.O.R.U. 'A' was supporting 8th Army in Central Italy; and No. 1 M.O.R.U. 'B', at Cecina on the west coast, was controlling the day and night fighters in 5th Army's area.[111] Just before 'Olive' was launched No. 1 M.O.R.U. 'A' joined H.Q. No. 287 Wing on the east coast at Falconara; No. 1 M.O.R.U. 'B' on the west coast was then split into two sections, one of them to provide a replacement for No. 1 M.O.R.U. 'A' at Crete (retaining its title as No. 1 M.O.R.U. 'A') and the other to remain on the west coast to control the day and night fighters with the new title of No. 1 M.O.R.U. (F.C.U. 'B').*

The second change arose from a new directive issued by C.G. M.A.T.A.F. on 6th August to A.O.C. D.A.F. and to come into effect on the 10th. Not only was Dickson to continue to be responsible for the air support of both 5th and 8th Armies, but also for air attacks upon enemy communications in the area bounded on the west by the Genoa–Pavia railway line, on the north by the Po river (both inclusive) and on the east by the east coast. Because from 10th August onwards U.S. XII T.A.C. and the medium day bombers of M.A.T.A.F. (the U.S. 42nd and 57th Medium Bombardment Wings) would be heavily committed in support of operations in southern France, only in an emergency or when the weather restricted air operations in southern France, would these forces be available to support the Allied armies in Italy; but targets in northern Italy would however be attacked whenever possible. M.A.T.A.F. would keep a very close watch on the enemy air forces and enemy communications in this area. But

---

* F.C.U. = Fighter Control Unit.

if, at any time Dickson required additional assistance for some specific purpose, he was to notify Cannon through D'Albiac (A.O.C., H.Q. T.A.F. (Italy)). In an emergency Dickson could contact H.Q. M.A.T.A.F. direct over the A.A.S.C. network.

We have mentioned a few instances of D.A.F.'s air activity in the battle area in support of 8th Army's preparations for 'Olive'. Air support for 5th Army was not neglected, small though it was. The approximate number of sorties flown and bombloads dropped in the battle area in Italy during dawn 6th to dawn 25th August compared with the approximate effort north of the battle area in Italy and that beyond Italy are shown at Table II.[112]

Weather played a disrupting part on several of the 19 days during which an approximate total of 1,761 sorties were flown and 873.7 tons of bombs dropped in the whole battle area. These were divided between 5th and 8th Army areas as follows:—[113]

Air Formation	5th Army		8th Army	
	Sorties	Tons of bombs	Sorties	Tons of bombs
M.A.T.A.F: (Medium day bombers)	79	129.7	—	—
D.A.F: (Light bombers —day)	18	12.8	12	9.4
(Light bombers —night)	7	4.8	28	17.5
(Fighter-bombers —day)	290	108.8	1,327	590.7
	394	256.1	1,367	617.6

The distribution of effort between 5th and 8th Armies again reflected the activity of the troops on the ground. 5th Army was not in as close contact with their enemies as 8th Army because until 5th Army took over command of 13th Corps all its troops were south of the Arno. Suppression of German artillery was thus less important than to 8th Army. This was reflected in the targets against which direct air support sorties were flown, the approximate sorties being:[114]

	German Artillery Targets	M.T. and Road Targets	Others	TOTALS
5th Army	77	177	140	394
8th Army	998	150	219	1,367

(vii)

In the second half of August there were some changes of emphasis in the German High Command's strategic thinking about the Italian Theatre. With the possibility of Allied operations in the Gulf of Genoa reduced, albeit not entirely eliminated, by the landings in southern France, the Operations Branch of *OKW* began to look to the Northern Adriatic as the next scene for a strike of strategic scale. Foreign Armies West (the Intelligence section for Europe at *OKH*) as usual, veered from one assumption to another. On 18th August Kesselring reported that 5th British Corps was now on 8th Army's eastern wing, that heavy bridging equipment and large quantities of supplies were being shifted to this wing, and that Allied aircraft were keeping the east coast under constant surveillance.[115] *FHW* cited these straws in the wind as evidence for a thrust towards the eastern sectors of the Green Line, where the terrain offered the best opportunities for an attempted break through into the Po valley, and supported this conclusion with reports from G.A.F. Intelligence that the Allied Air Forces operating 'in close support of the Eastern Mediterranean' were now controlled from Ancona, where an increased activity in ground organisation and installation of radar stations had been observed. On 20th August *FHW* suggested that the Polish Corps' current upsurge of pressure could well presage operations of a larger scale against the eastern wing of *AOK 10*. By the 25th, however, there were rumours of Allied regrouping east of Florence, and *FHW* tacked to the view that forces might be assembling in this area for a strike at Bologna.[116] Deception plan 'Ulster' received a useful fillip when, on the 26th, a 'good *Abwehr* source' reported that the (fictitious) British 14th Corps was concentrating north of Lake Trasimeno. With 'Olive' already launched, on this date *FHW* accordingly reiterated the assumption that a build up was in progress east of Florence.

OKW's Operations Branch had mulled over the Allies' options on 23rd August, and had decided that as landings in the Northern Adriatic could 'open the way to the Danube' they offered wider enticements than did the prospect of outflanking *AOK 14* by landing near Genoa. Subsequent reports that Churchill had met Tito during his August visit to Italy (which we will be describing in the next chapter) awoke suspicions that some operation was being concerted with the Yugoslavs, and fed a concern for the vulnerability of the Istrian peninsula which Jodl had nurtured since July. On 28th August he told Hitler that he believed that the Allies were planning to land on the Venice-Trieste coast, and suggested that Kesselring, who had already been directed to thin out his front, could create additional reserves behind his eastern wing if Army Group C were to withdraw to the Gothic Line.

The Führer raised no objection, for the priority hitherto accorded by *OKW* to the defence of this complex had declined. Allied successes in France, and the upheavals in the Balkans which we consider in Chapter XIV, claimed more attention from the German High Command and led to an acceleration of work on the *Voralpen* line, which drained off engineers and construction troops from Green I.[117] We have noted that on 13th and 19th August there had been talk at Hitler's Headquarters of a possible withdrawal of Army Group C, first to the Green Line and then to the Alps once the defences there were sufficiently developed. Contingency plans for a retreat to and beyond the Po were accordingly drawn up by *AOK 10* and *AOK 14*, under the code-name of Operation *Herbstnebel* ('autumn mist'). von Vietinghoff, who already on 1st August had authorised reconnaissance for a new defence line north of the Adige, called a conference of his commanders to discuss *Herbstnebel* on the 30th. Although it took place five days after 'Olive' had opened, it is clear from the records of *AOK 10* that preparations for the conference had begun before Leese launched his offensive.[118] *Herbstnebel* was finally vetoed by Hitler on 5th October, but its genesis in August meant that, when the Gothic Line was first attacked, the German commanders in the field were looking over their shoulders.[119] At *AOK 10's* level, resources had, moreover, been drawn away from the Gothic Line to improve its rear coastal defences known as the 'Water Line'. Specific attention was paid to the Rimini area, off which a mine barrage had been laid. *AOK 10's* Chief of Staff, Wentzell, inspected the shore defences on 17th August and reported that they had acquired a depth of up to about half a mile.[120] The construction of strongpoints was progressing well, and although Rimini airfield was inadequately protected from airborne assault Wentzell reckoned that the sector as a whole was 'ready for defence' against small scale enemy landings.

Another factor which affected German attitudes in the field was a misappreciation of the timing and kind of offensive which was coming. Kesselring and his commanders had become so used to the steady and apparently diffuse Allied pressure across the whole front since the battle of the Albert/Anton Line that they were not expecting another 'Diadem' type attack. On 20th August von Vietinghoff issued a detailed directive for training once the divisions were installed in the Green Line, which clearly anticipated a period of quiet during which newly arrived and inexperienced troops could be taught their business.[121] The directive also indicated that Bessell's work on the defences had borne fruit and had allayed many earlier misgivings about the siting of the line. When 'Olive'

opened on 25th August both von Vietinghoff and Heidrich, commander of 1st Parachute Division, were on leave, which reinforces
the supposition that no immediate offensive action was expected
of 8th Army.

As soon as transfers were demanded of them, Lemelsen and
Hauser asserted that there were clear signs of an impending assault
on the front of *AOK 14*. This was a routine reaction, and as the
number of prisoners taken by both German Armies in mid-August
was very meagre the information obtained from interrogation was
correspondingly fragmentary. In *AOK 10,* heavy traffic across the
Apennines in the areas of Sassoferrato and Pergola (i.e. movement
north to Fossombrone) (*Map 9*) was detected by 76th Panzer Corps
on 18th August, but this was linked to the shifting of supplies from
Ancona rather than to troop movements.[122] Also on the 18th, 51st
Mountain Corps was instructed by Wentzell to keep a close watch
on the road running north-east from Citta di Castello (Tiber valley)
as it could be that forces were being shifted eastwards from this
area and also from Florence.

This vague unease did not however prevent Kesselring from
deciding on 19th August that *AOK 10* must extract 5th Mountain
Division. von Vietinghoff fought to retain this strong formation,
for by this date it was clear that its battles with the Poles would
leave the exhausted 278th Infantry Division in no state to be
entrusted with defence of the vital east coast road. As Kesselring
would not change his mind, von Vietinghoff concluded after a
long discussion with his commanders that 76th Panzer Corps must
regroup.

See Map 11

On the evening of the 19th he directed that 1st Parachute Division
should come forward from reserve and move into the *Vorfeld* line
on the Metauro river. 278th Infantry Division was to pass through
the paratroopers and then sidestep into the inland sector earmarked
for 5th Mountain Division in the Red Line, which lay between
Vorfeld and Green I and which had been prepared for defence while
51st Mountain Corps was still on the Adriatic wing. These moves,
which were to be completed by 23rd August, would leave Herr with
1st Parachute Division (whose 4th Parachute Regiment returned to
the division on 22nd August) on the coast, 71st Infantry Division
just inland, and 278th Infantry Division in the mountains between
Urbino and Mercatello, roughly on the line of Route 73. At the
same time similar regroupings coupled with withdrawals were
authorised for 51st Mountain Corps, to enable Feuerstein to extract
15th Panzer Grenadier Division. It was these withdrawals which

enabled 13th Corps to secure its bridgehead over the Arno east of
Florence so easily.

In *AOK 14,* the loss of the Headquarters Staff of 75th Corps to
the Army of Liguria was accepted quite calmly, and on 11th August
Dostler's divisions were taken over by 14th Panzer Corps.[123] The
withdrawal of 3rd Panzer Grenadier Division, and its replacement
by 362nd Infantry Division, which had completed refit after its
mauling in the battle for Rome, was also taken in good part.
Complaining began when Kesselring accepted von Vietinghoff's
proposal of 22nd August that *AOK 10* should be given one of
AOK 14's mobile divisions to compensate for the loss of 15th Panzer
Grenadier and 5th Mountain Divisions, and to enable *AOK 10* to
keep a motorised formation in reserve.[124] Lemelsen and Hauser
learnt of this suggestion on 24th August, when they were moreover
informed that *OB Südwest* required the extraction from their front
of 26th Panzer Division, so that it could form a new Army Group
reserve. The prospect of losing two mobile divisions caused the
higher officers of *AOK 14* promptly to assert that they expected the
Allies to attack the sector held by 29th Panzer Grenadier Division,
a view reinforced on 25th August by reports that on leaving the
front 2nd New Zealand Division had been ordered to remove
all divisional markings. Nonetheless, Kesselring directed on the
following day that 29th Panzer Grenadier Division was to be given
to *AOK 10.* It was first planned that in exchange *AOK 14* should
receive 98th Infantry Division, coast-watching near Ravenna, but
by 27th August the choice had fallen on 334th Infantry Division,
which was now in 51st Mountain Corps' reserve and hence much
nearer to *AOK 14.*

These plans occasioned much discussion, but the orders made
to implement them were not couched in terms of any urgency, for
in the days before 'Olive' opened the staffs of *AOK 14* and *AOK 10*
were mainly pre-occupied with the problems of getting 3rd and
15th Panzer Grenadier Divisions back to Germany for refit, and of
moving 5th Mountain Division to Liguria. Main line communications north of Verona were constantly disrupted by Allied air
attacks, and those directed against the east-west lines south of the
Po were so destructive that on 23rd August Wentzell announced
that the entraining of 5th Mountain Division was a 'catastrophe'.[125]
It was also a useful diversion for 8th Army, for when Kesselring's
Operations Officer asked for news of *AOK 10's* left wing, the Chief
of Staff replied that although the latest reports were not yet to
hand he did not expect 'anything out of the way'. On the 24th
AOK 10 reported that the front was generally quiet; 71st Infantry
and 1st Parachute Divisions had observed lively traffic opposite
their sectors and some Allied warships, presumed light cruisers,

were spotted off Fano. Early on the 25th Wentzell told Kesselring that 'something' was rumoured to be happening in the Macerata area.[126] To Kesselring's query, 'Otherwise nothing of importance?' Wentzell replied 'Otherwise nothing. We must now watch carefully what he is doing on the Adriatic wing. When he sees Heidrich's men there he may take his forces further inland'. Movement orders issued on the afternoon of the 25th to the Corps of *AOK 10* still showed no sense of urgency, and envisaged that 51st Mountain and 76th Panzer Corps would both be installed in the Red Line by the morning of the 28th. 8th Army had achieved complete tactical surprise.

(viii)

See Map 4

We must now turn to air activity north of the battle area in Italy, and then to strategic air operations beyond Italy, during the period dawn 17th July to dawn 25th August. It will be seen in Table III, which contains the sorties flown by M.A.A.F. during this period on all kinds of missions other than anti-shipping operations and attacks on ports, that the daily sortie rate (1,736 per 24 hours) was about the same as the previous post-'Diadem' period.[127] Of the 17,193 bomber and fighter-bomber sorties (13,853 tons of bombs) flown against targets in Italy, 12,340 of them (11,353.6 tons) were flown north of the battle area. Of these latter sorties, during the first half of the period, two-thirds of the sorties flown (6,748) were against railway targets; M.T. and roads absorbed half the remainder. During the second half, the effort against railway targets fell to half of the sorties flown (5,592) and that against M.T. and roads fell too, dumps and guns in north-west Italy gaining favour in preparation for the landings in southern France.* Some targets were selected for their dual effect upon German forces in Italy and southern France. The impact of these attacks was frequently recorded by the German commanders, particularly on the two main rail routes running southwards from Verona to Bologna via Ostiglia and Rovigo.[128] The battle between German repair gangs and the Allied airmen was continuous with

---

* The approximate number of sorties flown and bombloads dropped in the battle area in Italy as compared with the approximate effort north of the battle area in Italy and with that beyond Italy from dawn 17th July to dawn 6th August, which represents the first half of the period under review, is shown at Table III in Chapter X. Table II at the end of this chapter gives similar information for the second half of the period under review, i.e. dawn 6th to dawn 25th August.

the latter maintaining the initiative and hence the upper hand. Agents' reports, radio intercepts and the pattern of bombing within the Po basin after the 'Dragoon' landings prompted Kesselring to report to *OKW* on 22nd August that the Allies were intent on destroying the east-west rail system in Italy to prevent the transfer of German forces from the Adriatic to the 'West Alpine Front'. As this front had to be reinforced, he warned *OKW* that if rail transport proved impossible lorries might have to be used to move parts of 5th Mountain Division westwards from Forli. In view of the urgent need to save fuel, *AOK 10* was nonetheless instructed that the bulk of the division must march by night to its assembly points at Bologna and Mantua, and then go by rail to Turin, marching between blocked sections of the line. Disruption of the main lateral routes became serious enough for Kesselring to refer to them specially in his daily reports to *OKW*. For instance, on 26th August, he reported that the main east-west railway had two ten mile gaps, between Imola and Bologna and at Reggio.

German records show clearly that Allied air attacks on their rail communications in northern Italy during the 39 days had achieved a considerable measure of success, not only in supporting the Allied armies in Italy but also, even if indirectly, Allied operations in southern France. The Germans recorded many Allied successes, but only a few examples must suffice. On 30th July the Po bridge at Pontelagoscuro was put out of action by Mitchells. On the last day of the month U.S. Thunderbolts destroyed a railway bridge east of Novara (west of Milan) and two road bridges near Piacenza. August 3rd saw some Baltimores and a Boston destroy a railway bridge in the upper Piave valley.[129] Several bridges were damaged during the next few days, and on 13th August the road bridge at Rovigo was destroyed. Eight days later Mitchells destroyed a rail bridge west of Parma. Next day (22nd August) Kittyhawks destroyed the bridge at Poggio Renatico and Marauders that across the Secchia river near Modena.

Beyond Italy poor flying conditions exerted an unwelcome influence on air operations, particularly during the 12 days from 29th July to 9th August inclusive, when the weather was almost continuously poor, grounding the day bombers of M.A.S.A.F. on five of the 12 days and its night bombers on seven of the 13 nights.[130]

The distribution of sorties (and bombloads which are given in brackets) among the four categories of targets attacked in each country is given in the table opposite.

In the course of all the tasks performed by M.A.S.A.F. in and beyond Italy during this period 297 Liberators and Fortresses from U.S. Fifteenth Air Force and nine Liberators and 25 Wellingtons from No. 205 Group R.A.F. were lost.

EFFORTS EXPENDED BY M.A.S.A.F. BEYOND THE BORDERS OF ITALY DAWN 17th JULY–DAWN 25th AUGUST

(Attacks on targets in Italy and France and on ports, mining in the Danube and supply and flare-dropping have been omitted).

Country	Oil	M/Y, L. of C. & Misc.	Factories & Depots	Airfields	Bomber losses
Germany	614 (1,258.5)	33 (7.9)	1,052 (2,267.3)	397 (920.5)	86
Czechoslovakia	686 (1,592.3)	2 (4.9)	—	161 (340.0)	27
Austria	335 (660.6)	64 (145.6)	777 (1,829.8)	331 (664.2)	76
Hungary	227 (494.6)	223 (523.2)	647 (1,482.1)	526 (1,078.9)	28
Yugoslavia	25 (51.9)	310 (703.0)	—	310 (589.8)	—
Bulgaria				1 (1.8)	—
Rumania	2,570 (5,356.6)	39 (88.4)	—	—	112
Albania	63 (162.4)		—	—	1
Greece		23 (61.6)	—	—	—
Poland	213 (487.5)		—	—	1
Totals	4,733 (10,064.4)	694 (1,598.6)	2,476 (5,579.2)	1,726 (3,595.2)	331

GRAND TOTALS = 9,629 (20,837.4 tons of bombs)

On 3rd August H.Q. M.A.A.F. issued a new directive to M.A.S.A.F., cancelling that of 15th June. The general function of M.A.S.A.F. now leaned more in favour of the Combined Bomber Offensive. The reduction of German sources of fuel, particularly petrol which was considered to be his 'most critical military supply' was accorded first priority. The targets were to be synthetic fuel plants, crude oil refineries and stores of refined products, and they were listed in order of importance based on total capacity with petrol targets forming the bulk of them. Second priority was given to the destruction of the remaining sources of supply of ball and roller bearings, and the 'policing' of those production facilities already damaged, the targets being listed in order of importance. M.A.S.A.F.'s remaining effort in support of the Combined Bomber Offensive was to be devoted to reducing the supply of certain major items of army equipment particularly tanks, armoured vehicles, M.T. and heavy ordnance, and here again targets were listed in order of importance.

To maintain the necessary degree of air superiority so that Allied offensive and defensive air operations of all kinds could be sustained without prohibitive loss, air attacks were to be directed as the Commanding General, M.A.S.A.F., deemed necessary against aircraft and their associated installations and against selected engine and aircraft factories. Particular emphasis was placed on factories producing jet-propelled and pilotless aircraft, and on fighter engine production such as that of the BMW 801 and DB 603, and on 'policing' major fighter airframe production facilities already damaged.* Heading the list of targets attached to the directive were the bases of the Me. 262 jet-propelled and Me. 163 rocket-propelled fighters and the factory which produced them together with the Me. 410.

'Priority 1' of the directive of 15th June, i.e. support of the land campaign in Italy, had not been dispensed with altogether. The new directive contained the proviso that other priorities must give way to employment of the strategic air forces in a tactical role in support of the armies when the situation demanded.

It is interesting to see what effect the new directive of 3rd August had on M.A.S.A.F.'s operations. The totals in the table below show the efforts expended on the four principal categories of targets before and after the issue of the new directive during the period dawn 17th July–dawn 25th August:—

---

* Some examples of German Aircraft using these engines are:

BMW 801	*DB 603*
F.W. 190	Me. 410
Certain marks of Do. 217	Certain marks of Do. 217
Certain marks of Ju. 88	Certain marks of Ju. 88

Oil	M/Y, L. of C. & Misc.	Factories & Depots	Airfields	Totals
Prior to 3rd August (17 days)				
1,878 (4,281.1)	292 (677.4)	1,668 (3,708.0)	614 (1,361.1)	4,452 (10,027.6)
3rd August onwards (22 days)				
2,855 (5,783.3)	402 (921.2)	808 (1,871.2)	1,112 (2,234.1)	5,177 (10,809.8)

The allocation of effort to oil targets, already higher than against any other target, increased considerably. Against factories and depots it fell away sharply but was doubled against airfields. The attacks on factories and depots before and after 3rd August were:—

	Prior to 3rd August	3rd August onwards
Aircraft/airframe/engine/factories & assembly	727 (1,580.2)	531 (1,229.9)
Ordnance depot	128 (261.7)	—
Armament factory	366 (828.1)	—
Tank factories	447 (1,038.0)	77 (179.4)
Chemical factory	—	133 (296.4)
Industrial area	—	67 (165.5)
Totals	1,668 (3,708.0)	808 (1,871.2)

The U.S. Eighth Air Force flew another shuttle mission using U.K., Russian and Italian airfields. On 6th August 76 Fortresses with 64 Mustang escort fighters flew to Russian bases, bombing the F.W. 190 fighter factory at Gdynia in Poland on the way.[131] Next day part of this force bombed an oil refinery at Trzebinia in Poland, returning afterwards to Russia. On the 8th the entire force left Russia, 36 of the Fortresses bombing Bizau airfield and another 36 Fortresses bombing Zilistea airfield, both in Rumania, on the way to Italy from where they eventually returned to the U.K.

Air attacks on oil targets in Rumania deserve a special mention here, first because it was during August that the last attacks were delivered on the Ploesti oil complex before it fell into Russian hands, and secondly because of the revelation produced by post-capture survey that the attack carried out on 1st August 1943, described by one German report as 'entirely without success' and thought by the Allies at the time to be inconclusive, was in fact the most successful of all the attacks. It destroyed the surplus plant and refining capacity. This is why the effect of the Allied raids of 1944 was catastrophic.*

This final offensive against Rumanian oil targets had started on 4th April.[132] Until the last attack on 19th August the offensive was

---

* See *Mediterranean and Middle East* Volume V (H.M.S.O. 1973) pp. 219–221.

pressed home despite the ingenuity of German counter-measures. The anti-aircraft defences had been considerably strengthened, and one German report referred to Ploesti and Bucharest as being 'ringed by A.A. guns and search-lights'. The fire-fighting services had been reinforced, and a heavy smoke screen installed around both targets. Special steps had been taken to protect the oil tanks, blast walls being built around each of them and sand-dams piled up between them to stop the spread of burning oil. Other measures were the hosing of tanks not hit to keep them cool and the use of fire-foam installations and portable fire-foam appliances. These fire-foam measures were the least successful as bombs damaged the foam installation pipelines and the water mains on which portable fire-foam appliances depended.

In the first ten days of May two additional fighter *Gruppen* were transferred from Hungary and Italy for the day fighter defence of Ploesti, and the night fighter defence force was reinforced. It must be observed that the clockwork regularity with which the Allied Air Forces timed their air attacks, both by day and by night with little variation, was an additional help to the Germans. It is clear, too, that the smoke screen was certainly effective. An analysis of the bombs falling on the refineries during 5th April–19th August shows that the percentage on target in the first of the July attacks, when the smoke screen was heavy, was only half that in August when the smoke screen operators deserted.

The effect of the Allied air attacks on the Rumanian oilfields during 4th April–19th August 1944 was a fall in production of crude oil to 51% of the January–April 1944 output. The amount processed fell to just over 40% (1,139,000 tons lost), and the production of petroleum dropped to 56% (approximately 370,500 tons lost). The total effort expended by M.A.S.A.F.'s heavy day and heavy and medium night bombers from 4th April to 19th August to achieve these results was:[133]

When oilfields and refineries were ancillary targets within the proximity of marshalling-yards and associated targets	When oilfields and refineries were the principal targets
4th April–7th/8th May	
2,909 (6,726)	Nil
8th May–3rd July	
331 (702)	1,550 (3,185)
4th July–19th August	
Nil	3,545 (7,632)
Totals 3,240 (7,428)	5,095 (10,817)
GRAND TOTAL 8,335 (18,245)	

The Allied air offensive against the Rumanian oilfields and refineries certainly achieved considerable success. On 23rd August the country's new Government accepted the armistice conditions of the Soviet Union and the Western Powers and by the end of the month the Ploesti oilfields and refineries were in Russian hands.[134] This enabled M.A.S.A.F., particularly U.S. 15th Air Force, to take a larger part in the offensive against synthetic oil plants in Germany itself thereafter.

(ix)

We will end this chapter with a brief description of the self-sacrificing efforts of the Special Duties units to supply the tragically unsuccessful insurrection of General Bor-Komorowski's Polish Partisan Army, which on 1st August rose in Warsaw to expel the Germans from the city.[135] Only three days before, on 29th July, the first hint of the imminent rising had come from the exiled Polish Government in London. This was quickly followed by appeals for air support consisting of the bombing of various Polish towns, with the environs of Warsaw as first priority, the landing of Polish squadrons in the Warsaw area and of the Polish Parachute Brigade in the city; substantially increased air supply over and above the routine Special Duty drops was also requested, particularly of heavy machine guns, anti-tank weapons, ammunition and grenades. Because of range air supply could only be undertaken from the U.K. or Italy, and this was a formidable task in itself. The Russians were much closer at hand for all needs but made no attempt to help the General; indeed for a time they refused to allow British and American aircraft engaged on air supply for Warsaw to force land on Russian-held territory. The Special Duty squadrons in the U.K. were fully occupied in supporting 'Overlord' and so it fell to M.A.A.F. to undertake this increased air supply for Warsaw.

During the round trip of some 1,750 miles, parts of the outward and inward flights would have to be in daylight, and at night (in early August) the moon would be full. Most of the territory to be flown over was German-occupied and night fighters were plentiful. Accurate identification of Partisan ground signals and dropping points would necessitate flying at only a few hundred feet over the target area, alive with search-lights and anti-aircraft guns of all kinds, and to prevent canopies being torn from containers the aircraft would have to reduce speed to 140 miles per hour by use of flaps and thus be unable to take evasive action during the process. Afterwards any aircraft crippled by flak would have little

chance of making the long homeward journey. And then there was
the weather to contend with. On top of all this was the question
of how much of the drop would reach the Polish Partisans? At
this time conditions in Warsaw were chaotic. Several parts of the
city were ablaze and the whole of it was covered with a canopy of
black smoke, penetrated here and there by tongues of flame, which
lit up the sky above and were visible 60 miles away. Beneath the
smoke large areas defended by the Germans were punctuated by
blocks and strongpoints held by Polish Partisans, and the chaos
was made worse by the fluctuations of guerilla warfare in which
the dispositions of each side constantly changed. There was ample
justification for the view held by Air Marshal Sir John Slessor,
Deputy Air Commander-in-Chief of M.A.A.F., that few aircraft
would get through and much of what was dropped would fall into
enemy hands. In his opinion this air supply task for the Polish
Partisan Army in Warsaw was not a reasonable operation of war,
and he pressed for the Russians to be persuaded to take it on.
The British Chiefs of Staff agreed with him but gave in to the
piteous appeals for help from General Bor-Komorowski, and on
the nights of 8th/9th and 9th/10th August Slessor laid on a trial
flight by aircraft of No. 1586 (Polish) Special Duties Flight.* It was
successful and the air supply effort was accordingly stepped up.

Unfortunately Slessor's predictions as to losses proved to be all
too accurate. During the nights from 12th/13th to 16th/17th August
17 out of 93 aircraft despatched to Warsaw were lost, three more
crashed on landing and many more were damaged. Operations
were therefore suspended, but, after protests from the Polish
authorities, Polish volunteers from the Polish Flight were allowed
to continue until operations were again suspended after four out
of nine aircraft had been lost on the nights of 26th/27th and 27th/
28th August. They were resumed in September when delayed-drop
parachutes, which allowed containers to be dropped above the
range of light A.A. fire, became available.

The following description of a supply dropping sortie over
Warsaw on the night of 20th/21st August, made by Flight Lieutenant R. Chmiel of the Polish Flight, gives some idea of the hazards
encountered:

> 'We had been ordered to carry out the sortie regardless of
> weather conditions. So, though the Met forecast was exception-
> ally despondent, we took off. It's funny how only the gloomy
> predictions come true: sure enough, right from the Yugoslav
> coast fog stretched from the ground to 6,000 feet above. Fog

---

* According to '*Destiny Can Wait*', The Polish Air Force in Second World War (London
1949) p. 220, seven aircraft of No. 1586 (Polish) S.D. Flight, carrying supplies, successfully
reached Warsaw and returned without loss on the night 4th/5th August.

was hardly the word for it—water vapour or steam would be more appropriate. We had no navigational aid from the ground; I tried map reading at first but even rivers were so obscured that we finally flew on solely with star 'fixes'.

We had similar weather all the way until we crossed the Carpathians and got over Poland, where we saw a Jerry fighter shoot down one of our Halifaxes—it crashed and burst into flames. (There had been, by the way, a lot of flak over Yugoslavia and the Danube, and they had done their best to bring us down). We pushed on and got a decent 'fix' by the time we reached the Pilica. After that we flew guided by the distant glow over Warsaw.

We dropped to some 700 feet, got through a very dense flak barrage near Sluzew and so over the Vistula. Fires were blazing in every district of Warsaw. The dark spots were places occupied by the Jerries. Everything was smothered in smoke through which flickered ruddy, orange flames. I had never believed a big city could burn so. It was terrible: must have been hell for everybody down there.

The German flak was the hottest I have ever been through, so we got down as low as we could—70 or 100 feet above ground; it was very low, but we had to get out of the line of fire. The flicks in the Praga and Mokotow suburbs lay down flat on the ground and kept us lit up all the time—there was nothing we could do about it. [The 'flicks' were the search-lights.] We nearly hit the Poniatowski Bridge as we cracked along the Vistula: the pilot hopped over it by the skin of his teeth.

Our reception point was Krasinski Square, so, when we got over the Kierbedz Bridge, we turned sharp to port and made ready for the run-up. The Square was nicely lit up. The whole southern side was blazing and wind was blowing the smoke south, much to our satisfaction. We dropped the containers and knew we had made a good job of it.

It was time to clear out. The pilot came down a little lower, keeping an eye for steeples and high buildings. The cabin was full of smoke which got into our eyes and made them smart. We could feel the heat from the walls of the burnt-out district.

We ripped along the railway leading to Pruzkow and Skiernie-wice. Some flak near Fort Bem tried to shoot us down. It came from an anti-aircraft train on the track, so we let go some bursts at it. We had a breathing space until flicks near Bochnia picked us up and the flak got uncomfortably near. We passed over the crashed bomber in the foothills; it was now burning out.

We got through all the usual flak on the way home and landed safely at base. The other Halifaxes—five of them—that had taken off with us never returned. The Home Army people signalled that a supply was received on Krasinski Square on the 20th August at the time we noted in our log book. So we knew that at least our flight had not been in vain.'

There were further losses as operations continued into September until they were stopped by bad weather. The last supply dropping mission appears to have taken place on the night of 20th September when five out of 20 aircraft despatched failed to return. Meanwhile Slessor's continued protests at last bore fruit and the Russians were persuaded to co-operate by allowing the U.S. Eighth Air Force in the U.K. to lay on shuttle supply dropping operations. Of 110 Fortresses despatched on 18th September 107 successfully released their containers over the target area and then flew on to their Russian shuttle bases. Two Fortresses were lost and one Mustang out of 137 long-range escorts.

Excluding other routine Special Duty missions over Poland, and so far as the available records show, air supply for the Partisans in Warsaw during August and September cost M.A.A.F. 31 aircraft out of 185 despatched—a loss rate of 17%. The saddest feature was the loss of over 200 trained pilots and aircrew, although happily some were later to be found safe in Russian hands.

TABLE I

M.A.T.A.F. ORDER OF BATTLE—25th AUGUST 1944

Excludes U.S. XII T.A.C. in Corsica supporting Operation 'Dragoon'

Air Formation	Role	Aircraft	Location(*)	Remarks
UNDER DIRECT CONTROL OF M.A.T.A.F.				H.Q. M.A.T.A.F. was located at Furiani in Corsica, and 'H.Q. T.A.F. (Italy)' in The Siena area in Italy.
			SARDINIA AND CORSICA	
U.S. 42nd M.B. Wing				
U.S. 17th Group 34th, 37th, 95th, 432nd Sqdns.	M.B. (Day)	Marauder I & II	Elmas (Sardinia)	
U.S. 319th Group 437th, 438th, 439th, 440th Sqdns.	M.B. (Day)	Marauder I & II	Villacidro (Sardinia)	
U.S. 320th Group 441st, 442nd, 443rd, 444th Sqdns.	M.B. (Day)	Marauder I & II	Decimomannu (Sardinia)	
3e Escadre F.F.A.F. I/22, I/19, I/2c (equivalent of Sqdns.)	M.B. (Day)	Marauder II	Villacidro (Sardinia)	
U.S. 57th M.B. Wing				
U.S. 340th Group 486th, 487th, 488th, 489th Sqdns.	M.B. (Day)	Mitchell III	Prunelli (Corsica) Alesani (Corsica)	
U.S. 321st Group 445th, 446th, 447th, 448th Sqdns.	M.B. (Day)	Mitchell III	Solenzara (Corsica)	
U.S. 310th Group 379th, 380th, 381st, 428th Sqdns.	M.B. (Day)	Mitchell III	Chisonaccia (Corsica)	
DESERT AIR FORCE				
			ITALY	
ADV. H.Q. D.A.F.			Chiaravalle	Siena area until 24th August
No. 7 (S.A.A.F.) Wing				
Nos. 1 (S.A.A.F.), 7 (S.A.A.F.) Sqdns.	S.E.-F.	Spitfire IX	Foiano di Chiano	
Nos. 2 (S.A.A.F.), 4 (S.A.A.F.) Sqdns	S.E.-F./F.B.	Spitfire IX	Foiano di Chiano	

TABLE I—continued

Air Formation	Role	Aircraft	Location(*)	Remarks
No. 285 Wing				
No. 241 Sqdn.	S.E.–F./TAC.R.	Spitfire VIII & IX	Malignano	OP. Chiaravalle 27th August
No. 40 (S.A.A.F.) Sqdn.	TAC.R.	Spitfire VB & C & IX	Chiaravalle	Falconara until 24th August / OP. Chiaravalle 26th August
No. 208 Sqdn.	TAC.R.	Spitfire V, VIII & IX	Malignano	
No. 318 (Polish) Sqdn.	TAC.R.	Spitfire V B & C	Malignano	Falconara until 23rd August
No. 683 Sqdn. (Det)	P.R.	Spitfire XI P.R.	Chiaravalle / Malignano	{ Detachment from M.A.P.R.W. { OP. Chiaravalle 26th August
No. 3 (S.A.A.F.) Wing				
Nos. 15 (S.A.A.F.), 454 (R.A.A.F.) Sqdns.	L.B.	Baltimore IV & V	Pescara	
No. 12 (S.A.A.F.) Sqdn.	M.B. (Day)	Marauder II & III	Falconara	
No. 21 (S.A.A.F.) Sqdn.	M.B. (Day)	Marauder III	Pescara	
No. 24 (S.A.A.F.) Sqdn.	M.B. (Day)	Marauder I & II	Pescara	
No. 30 (S.A.A.F.) Sqdn.	M.B. (Day)	Marauder III	Pescara	
No. 239 Wing				
Nos. 3 (R.A.A.F.), 5 (S.A.A.F.), 250, 450 (R.A.A.F.) Sqdns.	S.E.–F./F.B.	Kittyhawk IV	Crete (Italy)	Crete (Italy) until 24th August / OP. Iesi 26th August
No. 112 Sqdn.	S.E.–F./F.B.	Mustang III	Crete (Italy)	OP. Iesi 26th August
No. 260 Sqdn.	S.E.–F./F.B.	Mustang III	Iesi	Crete (Italy) until 22nd August
No. 244 Wing				
No. 92 Sqdn.	S.E.–F./F.B.	Spitfire VIII	Perugia	OP. Loreto 26th August
Nos. 145, 417 (R.C.A.F.) Sqdns.	S.E.–F./F.B.	Spitfire VIII	Loreto	OP. Loreto 26th August
No. 601 Sqdn.	S.E.–F./F.B.	Spitfire IX	Perugia	OP. Loreto 26th August
No. 87 Sqdn.	S.E.–F.	Spitfire VC & IX	Perugia	
No. 185 Sqdn.	S.E.–F.	Spitfire VB & C & VIII	Loreto	Perugia until 23rd August

Note: 'O.P.' = Completed move to and operating from

TABLE I—*continued*

Air Formation	Role	Aircraft	Location(*)	Remarks
No. 232 Wing				
No. 13 (R.A.F.), 55 Sqdns.	L.B. (Night)	Baltimore V	Cecina	
No. 18 Sqdn.	L.B. (Night)	Boston III, IIIa & IV	Cecina	
No. 114 Sqdn.	L.B. (Night)	Boston IV	Cecina	
No. 600 Sqdn.	T.E.-F. (N.F.)	Beaufighter VIF	Rosignano	Controlled by No. 1 M.O.R.U. (F.C.U)'B'
UNDER DESERT AIR FORCE				
No. 651 Sqdn.	A.O.P.	Auster III	Pergola (5 Corps) Scheggia	H.Q., 'A' and 'B' Flights 'C' flight
No. 654 Sqdn.	A.O.P.	Auster III	S.W. of Iesi (2 Polish Corps) S.E. of Iesi	H.Q., 'A' Flight 'B' and 'C' flights
No. 655 Sqdn.	A.O.P.	Auster III	S.E. of Florence (13 Corps) S. of Florence	H.Q., 'A' and 'B' flights 'C' flight
No. 657 Sqdn.	A.O.P.	Auster III	N.E. of Pergola (1 Canadian Corps) Corinaldo Trasimeno area	H.Q. 'A' and 'C' flights 'B' flight

(*) *See Map 1*

TABLE II

M.A.A.F. (including Malta but excluding H.Q. R.A.F, M.E.)
Distribution of bomber and fighter-bomber sorties flown and bombloads dropped
(excluding anti-shipping operations and attacks on ports)
Dawn 6th–Dawn 25th August 1944
(excluding flare-dropping)

Aircraft	Dawn 6th August–Dawn 25th August		
	Within the battle area	North of the battle area	Elsewhere than Italy
Heavy day bomber		772 (1,873.7)	6,394 (13,481.1)
Heavy night bomber		16 (42.8)	112 (273.1)
Medium day bomber	79 (129.7)	829 (1,267.7)	3,179 (5,267.4)
Medium night bomber		53 (126.8)	392 (703.4)
Light day bomber	30 (22.2)	409 (305.9)	225 (175.8)
Light night bomber	35 (22.3)	337 (234.0)	154 (118.9)
Fighter-bomber day*	1,617 (699.5)	3,176 (1,401.4)	2,579 (1,116.6)
	1,761 (873.7)	5,592 (5,252.3)	13,035 (21,136.3)

GRAND TOTAL = 20,388(27,262.3)

* The figures in respect of 'fighter-bomber day' operations 'Within the battle area' and
'North of the battle area' are close approximations. They are considered accurate
enough for our purpose. In aggregate they are true totals.

CHAPTER XII

'ANVIL/DRAGOON' AND CHURCHILL'S AUGUST VISIT TO THE MEDITERRANEAN

(i)

GENERAL Leese was not the only Allied leader trying to win support for a change of plan in the first week of August. Mr. Churchill began one last attempt to stop Operation 'Anvil' (now rechristened Operation 'Dragoon'), not in order to strengthen the Italian front but to bring reinforcements more quickly to General Eisenhower.* He had noted the success of the American advance southwards from Cherbourg into Brittany and saw the possibility of using the ports of Brest, Lorient and St. Nazaire to feed troops into North-West Europe more quickly than through Toulon and Marseilles.[2] Late on 4th August he held a Defence Committee Meeting to consider these new possibilities at which he tabled a draft telegram to President Roosevelt. The British Chiefs of Staff accepted the draft and agreed that they too should approach their American colleagues with his suggestion that the 'Dragoon' forces should be switched to the 'main and vital' theatre through the French Atlantic ports. General Wilson was also to be consulted upon the practicability of the proposal.

It is surprising that the British Chiefs of Staff were prepared to consider such a change only ten days before 'Dragoon's' D day of 15th August, but they were apparently under the impression that Eisenhower favoured the switch. Wilson's reply was not encouraging.[3] The American assault divisions were already embarking; the landing craft could not make the long passage into the Atlantic; but, by diverting shipping from other tasks in the Mediterranean, over half the force (25,000 men) could be lifted, and could be off

---

*As a precautionary measure, the code word 'Anvil' which had been in use for many months was changed to 'Dragoon', with effect from 1st August. 'Dragoon' will be used in all references subsequent to this date.[1]

173

the Brittany coast in the first week of September. The supporting air forces of U.S. XII T.A.C. could not be moved. The American Chiefs of Staff, as was to be expected, saw no merit in the suggestion at all.[4] They thought the change could only 'cause the utmost confusion everywhere'; the opening of the Breton ports was speculative; and, even if they became available, they would be used to capacity by troops already scheduled to move to France from America.

In building up his case Churchill put the idea personally to Eisenhower during a visit to S.H.A.E.F.,* which was still near Portsmouth, but received no support from him.[5] Eisenhower strongly opposed the suggestion when it was made to him officially by the Combined Chiefs of Staff, and on 8th August the President replied to the Prime Minister firmly rejecting Churchill's last effort to stop 'Dragoon'.[6] Wilson was authorised to sail the leading elements of the force on 10th August.

When it was clear to Churchill that there could be no change at this late hour, he decided that he must visit the Mediterranean to discuss post-'Dragoon' operations with the commanders on the spot and to prepare himself for the next Allied summit conference, 'Octagon', which was due to open in Quebec on 13th September.[7] He flew out via Algiers and arrived in Naples during the afternoon of 11th August, travelling under the pseudonym of Colonel Kent.

Churchill's visit was to last two and a half weeks during which he watched both the 'Dragoon' landings and the start of 'Olive', and was able to discuss and probe the major political and strategic issues arising in the Mediterranean with the principal Allied commanders and their staffs. The obvious decline of German military power in southern and eastern Europe was opening up not only military opportunities but also rivalries for post-war political power in the wake of an Allied victory. The main issues can be grouped under three headings: Yugoslavia, Greece and Italy, but first we look at the planning for 'Dragoon'. The actual invasion of the coast of southern France and subsequent advance inland were essentially Franco-American and so are sketched only in outline; very few British troops took part, even though 'Dragoon' was planned under General Wilson's overall direction and strongly supported by British naval and air forces.

(ii)

On 19th December 1943, H.Q. 7th U.S. Army at Palermo in Sicily had been warned that it would be required to provide a

---

*Supreme Headquarters Allied Expeditionary Force.

special staff to plan 'an operation of a similar size to HUSKY' (the invasion of Sicily) in which it had been the major component of Alexander's 18th Army Group.[8] Its commander, General George S. Patton, was about to return to England to join Eisenhower's forces gathering for 'Overlord', and its divisions and Army Troops had largely been dispersed either to 5th Army in Italy or back to 21st Army Group in the U.K. General Mark Clark was to be responsible for 'Anvil' planning as well as commanding his own 5th Army in Italy. The 'Anvil' planning staff was given the code-name Force 163 and was moved from Palermo to Bouzareah, near Algiers, where the Sicily landing had been planned in the spring of 1943.

The 'Anvil' planners inherited all but one of the difficulties suffered by their 'Husky' predecessors. They could be given no firm order of battle; the availability of assault shipping was uncertain; the target date for the operation varied from week to week; and initially they had no real commander, because Clark was deeply involved in the Italian campaign and was in the midst of preparing the landing by 5th Army's 6th U.S. Corps at Anzio.[*] The one advantage Force 163 was to enjoy in the future was the eventual gathering of all the principal headquarters concerned in the Naples area as soon as the time came to convert plans into executive instructions. This moment was some months off, but in the meantime Force 163 was close alongside Wilson's A.F.H.Q. in Algiers from which it received most of its direction.

See Map 12

Planning started on 12th January under Brigadier General Garrison H. Davidson, 7th Army's Chief Engineer.[9] The planners did not take long to discard the tentative A.F.H.Q. plan which envisaged, amongst other possibilities, a landing off the Hyères Roads, close to Toulon, in favour of the beaches less strongly defended but farther east between Cape Cavalaire and Agay Roads, just west of Cannes. Use of these beaches would avoid an approach between the off-shore islands of Porquerolles, Port Cros and Levant which were strongly defended.[10] They had other advantages as well. They were slightly nearer the fighter airfields in Corsica; the sea approaches, besides being easier, were known to be less heavily mined; and the German coastal defences were less well developed because the hinterland was easier to defend than other potential landing areas. Although great stress was laid on rapid exploitation inland, the planners concluded that ease of landing should take

*See *Mediterranean and Middle East* Volume V (H.M.S.O. 1973) p.643.

precedence over exploitation. A final decision could not be made until a force commander was appointed and the resources available to him were finalised by the Combined Chiefs of Staff.

The first moves in sorting out personalities came when Wilson decided with the concurrence of his Deputy, Lieutenant-General Jacob L. Devers,* that Clark should be relieved of his responsibility for 'Anvil' on 28th February.[11] Lieutenant-General Alexander M. Patch, who had established a high reputation in amphibious operations in the Pacific, was appointed to command 7th Army. Responsibility for operational control of 7th Army would rest with Wilson until Patch had advanced far enough north for Eisenhower to assume command of the 'Anvil' forces. With this ultimate link in view, Devers was in due course to establish a special head-quarters in Corsica, to be known as 'Advanced Allied Force H.Q. Detachment', which would become H.Q. 6th Army Group when the transfer to Eisenhower took place.

The forces available to Force 163 during planning waxed and waned in step with the strategic debate on 'Anvil'. They eventually settled at three U.S. divisions for the assault landings from the sea, one Airborne Task Force comprising one U.S. Parachute Regimental Combat Team, one U.S. Glider Regimental Combat Team and 2nd British Independent Parachute Brigade (the only British army formation taking part) for a supporting airborne landing, and seven French divisions in the follow-up echelons.†

The American army formations were highly experienced. 6th

---

*Devers was also Commanding General N.A.T.O.U.S.A. (North African Theatre of Operations, U.S. Army.)

†The forces made available to 7th U.S. Army were as follows.[12] Those formations marked with an asterisk'*'had been withdrawn from General Alexander's armies in Italy:—

6th U.S. Corps* (Major-General Lucien K. Truscott)

	Port of embarkation
3rd U.S. Division*	Naples area
36th U. S. Division*	Naples area
45th U.S. Division*	Naples area
1st Airborne Task Force	Rome area
1st U.S. Special Service Force*	Naples area

French Army B (General de Lattre de Tassigny)

1st French Corps (General Henri Martin)

5th French Armoured Division	Oran
2nd Moroccan Infantry Division*	Oran
4th Moroccan Mountain Division*	Oran
French Commando Group	Naples area

2nd French Corps (General de Larminat)

1st French Armoured Division	Oran
3rd Algerian Infantry Division*	Taranto/Brindisi
1st French Infantry Division*	Taranto/Brindisi
9th French Colonial Division	Corsica
Moroccan Goums—Two Groups of Tabors*	

Forces Françaises de l'Interieur (General Cochet)	The Maquis, Southern France

U.S. Corps had conducted landings at Salerno and Anzio, where Truscott had won his spurs as a Corps Commander, taking over during the darkest days of the Anzio fighting and leading it brilliantly in the subsequent break out towards Rome in June.* Its 3rd and 45th U.S. Divisions had landed in Sicily, and its 36th U.S. Division had joined the other two at Salerno. All three divisions had been fighting almost continuously throughout the Italian campaign. A stronger team could not have been chosen.

The participation of seven French divisions presented a number of difficult political and military problems in arranging a satisfactory command structure, which balanced justifiable French claims for a say in the second invasion of their country and the need for the most experienced and efficient headquarters organisation to command the operation.[13] General Wilson handled negotiations with a combination of sympathy for the French arguments and corresponding firmness in ensuring that military requirements were not overborne by political expediency. On 7th March he briefed General Giraud, who was then the French Commander-in-Chief in Algiers, on the operation and successfully persuaded him that the French divisions could not match the Americans in amphibious experience and that the initial assault landings should be entirely American, with the French divisions landing in the immediate follow-up. He was less successful in persuading Giraud to accept American overall command for two good reasons: the bulk of the force would be French, and the French Resistance movement would react more favourably to a French Commander. Wilson countered, pointing out that the French would not be dominant ashore for some time and that, for military efficiency in the initial phases, command must be exercised by an American. Giraud undertook to consult General de Gaulle. Negotiations dragged on for some weeks during which Giraud's post as Commander-in-Chief was abolished, leaving Wilson to deal direct with de Gaulle. On 15th April de Gaulle announced that General de Lattre de Tassigny would command French Army B with two subordinate Corps Headquarters for the seven French divisions allotted to 'Anvil'. He asked that de Lattre should be allowed to work out the command structure with Force 163. A happy compromise was reached whereby General de Lattre would command the first of the French Corps to land with the actual Corps Commander as his deputy, and subsequently take over of French Army B when sufficient French troops of the second French Corps had landed.

---

*Truscott himself had been attached to Mountbatten's Combined Operations H.Q. in 1942 and had commanded the American force which took Port Lyautey during the 'Torch' landings in Morocco. He subsequently commanded 3rd U.S. Division in the Sicily landings and at Salerno before being given command of 6th U.S. Corps at Anzio.

7th Army H.Q. would then operate temporarily as an Army Group headquarters.

There was less difficulty over the internal structure of Devers' and Patch's headquarters.[14] The ideal solution would have been to establish a Franco-American staff structure on the Anglo-American lines, but the French appreciated that language difficulties and lack of trained and experienced staff officers, who understood the American command and administrative systems, made this impracticable. Instead a liaison mission was attached to Devers' headquarters, but it was rarely at full strength due to a shortage of bilingual French officers with adequate operational experience. Rightly, most of the experienced officers were kept with French formations.

Each of the two French Corps of Army B was given two veteran divisions from Juin's French Expeditionary Corps and a novice armoured division which had been formed and equipped with U.S. equipment during and after the Tunisian campaign. 1st French Corps was under General Henri Martin, who had been in charge of 9th Colonial Division's invasion of Elba in June. 2nd French Corps was under General de Larminat, who had commanded Juin's 'Pursuit Corps' with success after 'Diadem'. And on landing in southern France, de Lattre would take under his command General Cochet's *Forces Françaises de l'Intérieur* with an estimated 24,000 Maquis.

On the Naval side, Admiral Sir John Cunningham, Commander-in-Chief Mediterranean, placed the very experienced Vice-Admiral H. Kent Hewitt U.S.N., in charge of planning the maritime side of the operation.[15] Hewitt had commanded the American naval forces in the North African and Sicilian landings, at Salerno and at Anzio, and he and his staff were in close touch with the 'Overlord' planners so that the Normandy experience could be used for 'Anvil'. No amount of experience could, however, overcome the problems of uncertainty about availability of assault shipping and landing craft, nor of the actual shortage of shipping in the Mediterranean which was not resolved until almost the last moment. 'Anvil' did not acquire a high enough priority in the allocation of naval resources until the beginning of July. Until then all Mediterranean shipping was bespoke for supplying the Italian Campaign. The 28 L.S.T. and 19 L.C.T. promised by the American Chiefs of Staff did not start arriving until the end of June; and assault shipping released by Eisenhower from 'Overlord', consisting of 6 L.S.I., 24 L.C.I. and 24 L.C.T. or L.C.T.(R), did not reach the Mediterranean until the end of July. The same thing applied to the availability of supporting warships, but here there was a distinct advantage in late arrival because it enabled well worked up ships, which had recently proved their value off Normandy, to participate in 'Anvil'.

On the Air side, planning had started under Air Vice-Marshal Sir Hugh Lloyd, A.O.C. M.A.C.A.F., in December 1943 and had led to the development of Corsica and Sardinia as potential air bases for 'Anvil'.[16] Air planning lapsed in the early months of 1944 and was not revived until early July, when Eaker made Cannon responsible for detailed planning with the naval and army staffs, and Brigadier General Saville, Commanding General U.S. XII T.A.C., was appointed Air Task Force Commander with responsibility for co-ordinating all direct air support, including carrier-borne operations by naval aircraft, and for the provision of air protection for the assault and airborne forces. Nevertheless, air operations in support of 'Anvil' can be said to have started with the massive air raid on Toulon on 29th April when 488 day bombers from M.A.S.A.F. dropped 1,117 tons of bombs on the port.[17] Between 1st April and 17th July, when the opening phase of the 'Anvil' preparatory programme started, just under 4,000 sorties were flown against targets in southern France.

Before sketching the Air Order of Battle and plan we must consider briefly the deception planning to which air operations are particularly sensitive because bombing patterns can betray intentions and conversely be used to deceive. Plan 'Ferdinand', the strategic deception plan for 'Anvil', set out to suggest that there would be no attack on southern France.[18] Instead all Allied forces in the western Mediterranean would be concentrated for a major effort in Italy. The Gothic Line would be turned by a landing in the Genoa area and a land attack up the Adriatic coast towards Ravenna. On 4th August Alexander changed plan and 'Ferdinand' had to be revised. The amended version, issued on 15th August, suggested that due to American successes in Normandy a French Army would be landed in southern France to ensure a French presence if the German Army collapsed.[19] An Allied Corps would still land in the Genoa area, but Alexander would now be attacking the centre of the Gothic Line. The amended version concluded that:

> 'The above story is not of course entirely consistent with that which we have followed up to date. It has, therefore, been made purposely as muddling as possible in order to confuse the issue and prevent the enemy from detecting any persistent scheme of deception.'

The Order of Battle of M.A.T.A.F. and M.A.C.A.F. Squadrons assigned to 'Anvil' and deployed in Corsica and Sardinia is set out in Tables I and II. The actual numbers of aircraft available can only be estimated from establishment figures. M.A.T.A.F.

had about 1,358 aircraft, including P.R. aircraft on loan from M.A.P.R.W. and Lightning fighters on loan from M.A.S.A.F.[20] M.A.C.A.F. had 310 aircraft, and there were 512 troop carriers for whose protection M.A.S.A.F. would lend two squadrons of Mustangs. British and American naval aircraft for the escort carriers amounted to 214 Seafires, Martlets and Hellcats.

M.A.S.A.F. could deploy around 1,000 Liberators and Fortresses with another 550 fighter escorts, and 64 R.A.F. Halifax and Liberators and 120 Wellingtons.[21] If further air effort was needed the Desert Air Force could provide another 500 aircraft at the expense of support to 5th and 8th Armies. All in all, there were well over 4,000 Allied aircraft available with a further 500 on call. In contrast to these figures it was thought the Germans might start off with 175 aircraft, possibly rising to 330 after a few days. This would enable them to undertake 215–235 sorties (80–85 by the bombers) daily, falling gradually to 150–165 by D + 5, and then declining rapidly to 75–90. This in itself would have represented comparatively minor air opposition to the Allies' great numerical air superiority. In the event hardly more than 100 German aircraft opposed 'Anvil' and their marginal influence faded within a matter of days. Greater precautions had to be taken to ensure that there was no repetition of Allied aircraft being shot down by Allied ships and army gunners, as had happened in previous amphibious operations in the Mediterranean. Special rules for control of A.A. gunfire were drawn up and strictly enforced. Very elaborate arrangements were made for the provision of day and night fighter patrols over the invasion beaches and assault shipping and craft, but they were only put to insignificant test and need not detain us.

Before we discuss the bombing plan it would be well to mention briefly that 'taken for granted' service so vital to all sea, land and air operations—air reconnaissance. Though 'Anvil' would hardly tax the invasion forces and their naval air support on the same scale as previous amphibious operations in the Mediterranean, this very fact pre-supposed the provision of maximum, comprehensive and effective air reconnaissance of every kind, from pre-invasion photographic reconnaissance and spotting for the naval guns on the approach, to increasing artillery and tactical air reconnaissance for the advance inland.

The bombing plan was divided into four phases: 'Preliminary Air Operations' from 17th July to 9th August (D – 6); Phase II from 10th August to 3.50 a.m. D day; Phase III from 3.50 a.m. to H hour (8.00 a.m.); and Phase IV from H hour until the fall of Toulon, whenever that might occur.[22] In all phases particular emphasis was placed upon reinforcing the strategic and tactical deception plans and avoiding the betrayal of the proposed assault area through bombing patterns.

In the preliminary phase there were three distinct air tasks: counter air force operations to keep the G.A.F. subdued; interdiction of the German armies' communications; and neutralisation of the German Navy's submarine bases. The third task faded after two very successful raids on Toulon on 5th July and 6th August which reduced the available U-boats in the Western Mediterranean from eight to one.[23]*

See Maps 12 and 13

The interdiction task, on the other hand, was a major effort, M.A.T.A.F. continuing its attacks in north-west Italy and on the Genoa–Cannes coastal railway system as well as attacking the railway bridges across the Rhône south of Valence. Meanwhile M.A.S.A.F. kept the trans-Alpine railway from Valence via Grenoble to Turin blocked and unusable against the possible shuttling of German reinforcements between Kesselring's and von Blaskowitz's Army Groups. Interdictory attacks on roads east of the Rhône and south of the trans-Alpine railway were forbidden in order to avoid drawing attention to the assault area. In counter air force operations the three main airfield areas were Marseilles-Toulouse and Udine, which became M.A.S.A.F.'s responsibility, and the Po valley, which became that of M.A.T.A.F.[24] Though not specifically planned, the fighter-bombers and strafing fighters played their part too.

During these 'Preliminary Air Operations' 2,188 sorties were flown and 3,958 tons of bombs were dropped by fighter-bombers as well as bombers. Railways accounted for the lion's share, namely 2,571 tons; roads 456 tons; airfields 346 tons; ports (mainly Toulon) and miscellaneous targets 291 tons.

Phase II of actual operations concentrated upon neutralising the main enemy coast defence batteries, lowering the morale of the German troops in the coastal divisions, and eliminating the German radars watching the assault area. Targets were attacked from Sète in the west to Genoa in the east to disguise the point of attack. In

---

*On 5th July 233 U.S. Liberators attacked, sinking *U.586* and damaging *U.466, 471, 642, 952, 967, and 969*. Only *U.230* was unscathed. On 6th August 146 U.S. Liberators repeated the performance destroying *U.471, 642, 952 and 969*. *U.230* put to sea on 17th August but went aground and was blown up by her crew. *U.466 and U.967* were repaired but were blown up by the Germans on 19th August as the French approached Toulon. This left only *U.407, 565 and 596* elsewhere in the Mediterranean.

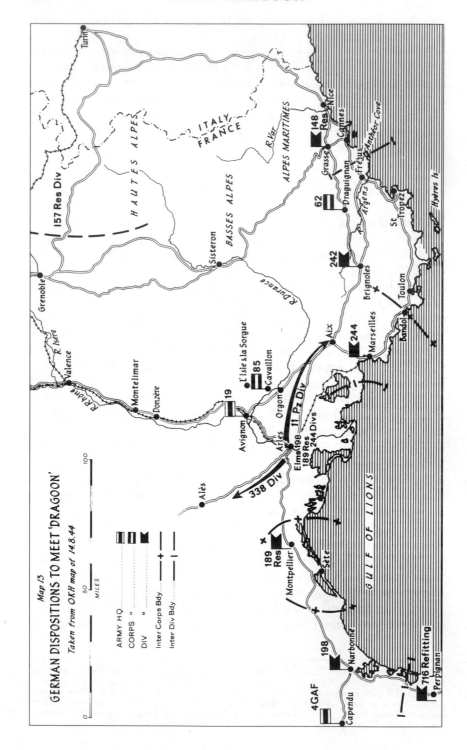

Map 13
GERMAN DISPOSITIONS TO MEET 'DRAGOON'

Taken from OKH map of 14.8.44

this Phase (from 10th August to 3.50 a.m. D day) because of early bad weather, air operations amounting to 2,350 sorties had to be crowded into four instead of five days. Of the 4,189 tons of bombs dropped 3,679 were expended on coastal batteries and artillery positions, other targets receiving minor attention. However, it was during this period that as part of the cover plan, 'Ferdinand', a further 1,047 sorties were flown against targets in the Genoa–Milan–Como area, most of the 1,717 tons of bombs dropped falling on guns around Genoa. On the 14th attacks were concentrated against gun and radar sites which could interfere with the landings, although two-fifths of the total effort were still in the Genoa area. Attacks on the radar sites did not prove fully satisfactory, but happily the most successful took place in the 'Dragoon' area where the radars were apparently knocked out. An added handicap for the Germans was the cutting of telephone and teleprinter links between *AOK 19* and Army Group G by Allied fighter-bombers.

In Phase III, starting just over four hours before H hour, the air effort was integrated with the naval gun fire support to crush the coastal defences in the assault area and to neutralise any German artillery which could bring fire to bear on the beaches and obstruct the attacking divisions' subsequent advance inland.[25] German airfields within close fighter range of the assault were also to be attacked. Particular emphasis was laid on the close control of air space by adherence to the allocated height bands and approach lanes for all aircraft, which are shown on *Map 14*. And in Phase IV and the continuing phase of air operations after H hour the air forces were to revert to the normal type of support tasks associated with major land battles: destruction of enemy strong-points holding up the advance inland; isolation of the battlefield by destroying any remaining bridges over the Isère and Durance rivers; attacks on German troop movements which might be detected; and continuing neutralization of German airfields.[26] M.A.S.A.F. was directed to concentrate on road bridges over the Rhône and at Sisteron on the Durance, and to attack beach defences in the assault area if need be.

The plan for landing the Airborne Task Force around Le Muy was complicated by lack of moonlight. A Pathfinder force was to drop at 3.23 a.m.[27] Then the 50th and 53rd U.S. Troop Carrier Wings with 413 Dakotas (flown out from England) and the 51st Wing, which was already in the Theatre, would alternately drop paratroops and launch gliders in successive operations. The main parachute drop was timed for 4.23 a.m., using 396 aircraft. The first glider wave of 71 aircraft towing 36 Waco and 35 Horsa gliders was to arrive at 8.14 a.m. The second parachute drop with 42 aircraft was to be at 6.10 p.m., and the main glider landings with 332 gliders would begin nine minutes later at 6.19 p.m. A total of some 500 tug aircraft and 480 Waco and 50 Horsa gliders were available for the whole operation. On D + 1 there would be a re-supply mission using 100 aircraft with delivery timed for 8.13 to 8.18 a.m.

Elaborate plans were made to avoid repetition of the Sicily airborne fiasco, when the airborne divisions were scattered over the island; many gliders were lost in the sea by casting off too soon, and Allied aircraft were shot down by their own side. For 'Anvil' every available navigational device and technique was used, including the positioning of special beacons on naval ships and on islands to mark the route over the sea. Night and day fighter cover was provided; safe lanes were designated; and special aircraft were used to jam and confuse the German radars and ground observers by scattering 'window'; exposed search-lights and active flak guns were bombed by intruding aircraft; and dummy paratroops were dropped between Marseilles and Toulon.

One other facet of the air planning should be mentioned. As in all previous amphibious operations in the Mediterranean great efforts were to be made to establish Allied fighter aircraft ashore as soon as possible. It was hoped to clear or construct 15 airfields by D + 25, to begin construction of all-weather airfields by D + 35, and to have four of these available by D + 50. It was assumed that the bulk of the Allied aircraft in Corsica would be flown onto airfields in southern France as soon as airfields were ready.

The most contentious areas in 'Anvil' planning lay in the administrative field because direct conflict with the Italian campaign was continuous at every level. Administrative problems were not so well defined nor as easy to quantify as the withdrawal of, say, a specific division on the operational side. Moreover, differences of opinion were less easy to resolve because of the inter-Allied and yet national basis of administration in Italy. Some of the difficulties were highlighted in a study made by the A.F.H.Q. Logistic Planners of the impact of the 'Anvil' decision.[28] Their paper, dated 2nd July 1944, showed that there would be a general reduction in the administrative support of Alexander's offensive caused not only by the withdrawal of American logistic units, but also by the absorption of Italian port capacity for 'Anvil' loading and subsequent supply at the expense of imports to sustain Allied troops left in Italy. They concluded that with extensive improvisation, including greater use of Italian labour and technicians and by combing the Middle East for more British administrative units and engineers, 8th Army could just be sustained in an advance through the Northern Apennines. The commitment to supply the large

civilian population in the Po valley would fall upon British administrative resources and might cause some reduction in the number
of divisions which could be supplied to exploit success northwards.
The figure might be as low as eight until the port of Venice was
captured and brought into operation. This bald appreciation,
however, disguised the constant push and pull between the administrative staffs which became polarised into a British versus American
contest, the British trying to ensure adequate support for the Italian
front while the Americans made full use of the priority accorded
to 'Anvil' after 2nd July. This was not a happy period for the
administrative staffs.

The combined naval, army and air plans were not developed
into their final form until all the headquarters concerned had
moved to the Naples area early in July. The capture of Rome had
enabled Alexander to move H.Q. A.A.I. closer to the Italian
capital, which freed the Palace of Caserta on the outskirts of Naples
for Allied Force Headquarters, and other buildings in Naples itself
for the Western Task Force staff, 7th Army's H.Q., XII U.S.
T.A.C. H.Q. and the French Mission.[29] General Devers' embryo
Army Group staff remained part of A.F.H.Q. until it moved to
Corsica on 30th July. The name Force 163 was dispensed with
when Patch's staff reached Naples. 6th U.S. Corps H.Q. was
located in Naples as well, and the headquarters of the three assault
divisions were established with their supporting Naval Task Force
staffs in the old citadel in the centre of Naples.[30] The lesson of co-
location of staffs, which had been learnt from bitter experience
during 'Husky' planning, was relentlessly applied at all levels.

The final plans, which emerged in the first week of August, are
set out diagrammatically on *Map 12*. The mission was 'To establish
a beachhead east of Toulon as a base for the assault and capture
of Toulon'; and then 'to capture Marseilles and exploit towards
Lyons and Vichy'.[31] The invasion force was organised into three
major elements and a number of special forces. The main assault
group, 'Kodak Force', consisted of 6th U.S. Corps plus one French
Armoured Combat Command from 1st French Armoured Division,
which would land as soon as a suitable beach had been cleared
and pontoon causeways had been positioned to disembark its tanks.
The objective of Kodak Force was the 'Blue Line' which ran in
an arc some 20 miles deep from Cape Bénat to a point just west
of Cannes, a distance of about 40 miles. 'Garbo Force', which
comprised an advanced detachment of H.Q. French Army B and
2nd French Corps (including the balance of 1st French Armoured
Division) was to start landing on D+1 and would pass through
6th U.S. Corps' western flank, making for Toulon. The third
element was the Airborne Task Force, 'Rugby Force', which

contained 2nd British Parachute Brigade. It was to land around
Le Muy, almost 20 miles inland from the beaches, to disrupt the
assembly of German reserves as they moved towards the beachhead. The Special forces were: 'Sitka Force', based upon 1st U.S.
Special Service Force, was to neutralise the German defences on
the islands of Port Cros and Levant on the western flank; 'Romeo
Force' of French Commandos was to destroy those defences on
Cape Nègre; and 'Rosie Force' of more French Commandos was
to blow up vulnerable points on the Cannes–St. Raphael road and
the Cannes–Fréjus road on the eastern flank. For sea transport
purposes Sitka Force and Romeo Force came under one heading,
Sitka. All the Special force operations would take place during the
night before D day. Most of 6th U.S. Corps was to be ashore and
up to the Blue Line by D + 1. Although 2nd French Corps would
start landing on D + 1 it would not be complete until D + 25; and
1st French Corps would start landing much later and would not
be complete before D + 40 because it depended upon the return of
shipping from the initial landings.

Admiral Hewitt's and Truscott's experience in previous
Mediterranean landings led to an unusual choice of H hour.[32]
Previously it had been considered essential to land in darkness to
reduce the vulnerability of the troops in the assault waves and of
the mass of shipping close inshore during the initial phases of the
landings. The proven effectiveness of naval gunfire support
(recently confirmed in 'Overlord'), the greater ease of getting
troops ashore at the right place in daylight; and having the whole
night for the final approach to the landing area, led to the choice
of 8.00 a.m. 15th August for H hour. As first light was 6.10 a.m.
there would be almost two hours in which the warships and the
air forces could neutralise the German defences. There was some
argument about delaying H hour until 9.00 a.m. to allow even
more time, but in the end 8.00 a.m. was accepted by the three
Services as a realistic compromise between their conflicting
requirements.[33]

Admiral Hewitt's naval plan divided his Western Task Force
into four naval attack groups each supported by a bombardment
group. In addition an Anglo-American escort carrier group with
seven British and two American escort carriers, under Rear-
Admiral T. H. Troubridge R.N. (H.M.S. *Royalist*), was to
reinforce the fighter cover provided by XII U.S. T.A.C. from
Corsican airfields. One naval attack group and bombardment
group was to land Sitka and Romeo Forces during the night before
H hour and subsequently to support the French advance along the
coast towards Toulon. Each of the other three carried and supported one American assault division.[34] The allocation of ships to each

force is given in detail in Captain S. W. Roskill's *The War at Sea*.*
The naval assault convoy routes and the air lanes are shown on
Map 14.

It is important to appreciate the scale of the Allied Naval effort
devoted to 'Dragoon'.† Some 881 ships and major landing craft
and 1,370 minor craft were allocated to the Western Task Force of
which 65% were American, 33% British and the balance came
from the French and other Allies. Amongst the bombardment
groups there were five battleships (one British) and 20 cruisers
(seven British) and there were four anti-aircraft cruisers (all
British), which was not far short of the 'Overlord' array of seven
battleships, two monitors and 23 cruisers.[36]

The picture would not be complete without mention of the
maritime air forces under M.A.C.A.F. which provided maximum
air protection against air, surface and submarine attack and all
the requisite air reconnaissance over the seas. An extra and
welcome task on 14th August was to provide fighter air/sea rescue
escort for a Dakota carrying Mr. Churchill from Naples to Ajaccio.
Next day he saw the landings from the deck of the destroyer
H.M.S. *Kimberley*, the Flagship of Admiral Sir John Cunningham,
Naval Commander-in-Chief, Mediterranean. General Wilson was
also present.[37]

Loading and sailing the 'Dragoon' convoys was complicated by
the wide dispersion of troops to available loading ports which could
not, like headquarters, be concentrated at the wish of the planners.
The Italian ports were already working to full capacity supplying
the Italian campaign. As many other Mediterranean ports as
practicable had to be used to reduce the impact upon 5th and 8th
Armies.[38] The general pattern for emarkation is shown in the
footnote on p.176. The four naval bombardment groups were
assembled at Naples for Sitka, and at Malta, Taranto and Palermo
for the divisional assault groups of Kodak Force, themselves
christened Alpha, Delta and Camel.[39] The Escort Carrier Group
concentrated at Malta.

Due to the relatively long sea passages, the varied speeds of the
many different types of ship involved had a major impact on
timing and convoy routing.[40] It was not possible to sail each attack

---

The War at Sea Volume III Part II (H.M.S.O. 1961) p.91.

The major British ships taking part were:[35]
Battleship: *Ramillies*
Cruisers: *Orion, Aurora, Ajax, Black Prince, Argonaut, Dido, Sirius.*
A.A. Cruisers: *Royalist, Colombo, Delhi, Caledon.*
Escort Carriers: *Khedive, Emperor, Searcher, Pursuer, Attacker, Stalker, Hunter.*

†Assault landings have been described in elaborate detail in this history for North Africa
(*Mediterranean and Middle East* Volume IV (H.M.S.O. 1966) Chapter V), Sicily (Volume V
(H.M.S.O. 1973) Chapters I and II) and at Salerno (Volume V Chapter VIII). Readers
interested in such plans for 'Dragoon' may refer to Roskill: *The War at Sea op.cit.*

group as a separate entity. Convoys had to be made up by types of vessel rather than the tactical use to which their loads were to be put. There were a number of slow, medium and fast convoys from each of the main embarkation ports, and each convoy was formed into sections at ten mile intervals, the first section in each case belonging to Camel Attack Group, the second to Delta and so on. A glance at *Map 14's* inset will show that this arrangement allowed the convoys to sail up the west coast of Corsica and to turn north-west at the appropriate moment, bringing each section into its planned final approach lane.

The convoy routing played an important part in the deception plan which was intended to suggest to the Germans that Genoa was the objective of any of the convoys which they might detect. All the convoys carrying the assault divisions and Special forces were routed as if heading for Genoa.[41] They were not to turn north-west towards the actual assault area until last light on D − 1. This was not quite possible for the slowest convoys which had to turn slightly earlier, but this risk had to be accepted, and, in the event, was screened from German view by a sea haze.

Other naval tactical deception measures were put in hand by a Special Operations group under Captain Henry C. Johnson U.S.N., whose task was to simulate diversionary forces heading for the Nice–Cannes area and the Bay of La Ciotat between Toulon and Marseilles.[42] The Special Operations force was divided into eastern and western groups, each of which was equipped with radio deception equipment, radar jamming devices and a variety of radar reflectors to simulate convoys 12 miles long and eight miles wide on surviving German radars. The eastern group had the distinction of being led by Lieutenant-Commander Douglas Fairbanks U.S.N.R., the film actor, and consisted of the British gunboats *Aphis* and *Scarab* of Western Desert Inshore Squadron fame, four M.L.S. and 12 P.T. boats. It was accompanied initially by the Fighter Direction Ship H.M.S. *Stuart Prince* and the Air Sea Rescue Ship H.M.S. *Antwerp* which were to act as marker ships for the troop carrier force. The western group, under Johnson himself in the U.S. destroyer *Endicott,* consisted of four M.L.s, eight P.T.s and 12 Air Sea Rescue craft. The Fairbanks' group had the additional task of landing the Rosie Force of French Commandos to cut the roads west of Cannes.

(iii)

See Map 13

In the last chapter we looked briefly at German reactions to the coming invasion in the light of its effect on the Italian campaign.

We now turn to the German situation in southern France where, under command of von Blaskowitz's Army Group G, General Friedrich Wiese's *AOK 19* had the task of defending the Mediterranean coast from the Italian to the Spanish frontier. On 4th August von Blaskowitz had informed *OB West* that since the Allies had landed in Normandy Wiese had lost so many formations to Army Group B that a successful defence of the southern coast could no longer be guaranteed.[43] By the 7th Hitler had nonetheless decreed that 11th Panzer Division, the one mobile division left to Army Group G, must move north. As the result of pleas from von Kluge this order was temporarily postponed on the 12th, but as 11th Panzer Division had to yield all of its operational Pzkw IVs and assault guns to the Normandy front its usefulness as a striking force was much reduced. Further inroads on the resources of Army Group G consisted in the removal, on 10th August, of the Staff and Army troops of *AOK 1* hitherto responsible for the defence of south-western France. On this date Wiese's 338th Infantry Division was also ordered to march north, and it was not until the late evening of 14th August that von Kluge obtained *OKW's* permission to halt the two-thirds of the division that had not already moved off.

Thus Wiese was left to defend a 400-mile coastline with eight relatively low-grade infantry divisions, plus the weakened 11th Panzer Division which until 13th August was stationed west of the Rhône. On that date von Blaskowitz, who had placed Army Group G on full alert the day before, reiterated his conviction that the Allies' systematic bombing of the bridges over the Rhône and the Var, and their attacks on radar installations east of the Rhône, portended imminent landings on the coast between the two rivers. *AOK 19* was accordingly authorised by *OB West* to redeploy 11th Panzer Division east of the Rhône, but by 15th August no bridge over this river was left standing south of Donzère, and 11th Panzer Division was only beginning to cross it by barge when the 'Dragoon' landings began.

With all lateral movement hampered by this river obstacle, Wiese's mandate to defend the coast was further prejudiced by responsibility for Marseilles and Toulon, given 'Fortress' status by 12th August and each claiming a division for its defence.[44] On 4th August *OKW* had moreover decreed that in the event of landings 157th Reserve Division of *AOK 19's* 62nd Corps must garrison the Franco-Italian frontier east of Grenoble.[45] As *Map 13* shows, 62nd Corps' sector, which was that chosen by the Allies for 'Dragoon', was held by 148th Reserve Division from the River Argens in the centre of the beachhead to the Italian frontier. The beaches west of the River Argens were held by detachments of 242nd Infantry

Division garrisoning Toulon, and the only other German formation wholly east of the Rhône on 15th August was 244th Infantry Division, garrisoning Marseilles under command of *AOK 19's* 85th Corps.*

The German coastal defences were much less formidable than those built under Rommel's dynamic leadership in Normandy. They lacked depth and had the additional weakness of being more extensive than could be properly manned with the troops available. Nevertheless the beaches were covered by an impressive array of artillery of all calibres, including heavy railway guns and guns from French warships scuttled in Toulon in 1942. Most possible landing beaches were obstructed by underwater obstacles and mines, which were never exposed in the tideless Mediterranean as they were at low tide in Normandy. The exits from the beaches were mined and in places concrete anti-tank walls and other obstacles had been built. The infantry positions had been carefully camouflaged with their concrete bunkers constructed within existing seaside villas, cafés and shops. Likely glider landing areas were obstructed with vertical poles, as in Normandy, but there is evidence that the French workmen skimped their job by deliberately failing to secure them properly, thus reducing Allied glider casualties.[47] The whole coast was well covered by radar stations. The main fortification effort had gone into the defences of Marseilles and Toulon. On 12th August Army Group G reported to *OB West* that Toulon's landward defences were complete, but those at Marseilles were held up by a shortage of mines and explosives.[48] The ports were prepared for demolition, but it had been agreed at the end of July that they should not be destroyed until actually threatened with capture.

---

* At the time of the invasion, the state of *AOK 19's* eight divisions from west to east was:

716th	Infantry, refitting in Perpignan after decimation in Normandy.	
198th	Reserve in Narbonne, recently reformed after losses in Russia.	4th G.A.F.
189th	Reserve in Montpelier, with weak elements moving towards the Rhône delta, to plug the gaps left by:	Corps
338th	Infantry, halted at Arles after one regiment had been lost to Normandy.	
244th	Infantry, defending Marseilles.	85th Corps
242nd	Infantry, defending Toulon. Both at 85% strength, many young troops lacking experience.	
148th	Reserve, from the River Argens to the Italian frontier; up to strength but lacking experience.	62nd Corps
157th	Reserve, in the southern Alps; also up to strength but no combat experience.	

N.B. Many of these divisions contained a large percentage of Poles, Czechs, Bohemians and 'rehabilitated' Russian prisoners of war. The designation 'Reserve', which was applied to formations performing garrison and training duties in occupied territories, had been dropped by H.Q. 62nd Corps on 9th August, but this was a change in nomenclature only.[46]

The vacillating views held by the German Intelligence staffs during the first fortnight of August have already been described in Chapter VI of Part I of this Volume, and in Chapter XI we saw how they were interpreted by Kesselring. In southern France German minds were made up by 12th August, when von Blaskowitz informed *OB West* that among the local population rumours were rife that 15th August would be the landing date.[49] It cannot therefore be said, as General Devers claimed after the war, that the Allies' success was based upon achieving complete surprise.[50]

Allied tactical deception measures did have some effect in confusing the German commanders during the night 14th/15th August, but, as they had so few mobile reserves with which to react, much of the Allies' Special Force's effort was wasted.[51] A low mist screened the passage of the main convoys from the few German reconnaissance aircraft which did try to penetrate Allied controlled air space. At 7.15 p.m. a sighting was obtained of two heavily escorted convoys of about 100 ships each, 60 miles west of Ajaccio, steering west and covered by 100–120 aircraft. These were probably the first slow convoys which had had to change course just before dusk. The next sightings came from the surviving coastal radars, which did detect the Special Force's electronic feints off the Bay of La Ciotat and off Nice at 1.30 a.m. on 15th August. The sightings served to alert the defenders, but had little effect on the higher echelons of command because communication between *AOK 19* and Army Group G had been cut, presumably by air attack. By 4.30 a.m. radar indicated one convoy approaching St. Tropez (probably Kodak Force), and another off Bandol, just west of Toulon, (certainly an electronic feint). Other sources in Italy reported that 150–200 troop carrying aircraft with gliders in tow had left Italian airfields and would arrive about 7 a.m. The dummy parachute drop near Marseilles did cause a minor flurry in which preliminary orders were given to start the demolition of the port but these were soon rescinded. The first finite reports of landings came at 5 a.m. when the start of the genuine parachute drop was reported at Draguignan, in which 100 aircraft were estimated to be involved (nearly 400 were, in fact, used). Thereafter successive reports of the Allies' preliminary bombardment and landings from the sea began to create a hazy picture of what was happening. At 9 a.m. the demolition of the minor ports of St. Tropez, Cannes and Nice began, and two regiments from 4th G.A.F. Field Corps, west of the Rhône, were directed to march on Brignoles to deal with the Allied airborne landings. Leading elements of 11th Panzer Division were over the Rhône, but the rest of the division was still crossing. Even at 1.40 p.m. *AOK 19* was still uncertain about the extent of the Allied landings in its report to Army Group G, and

by nightfall the situation was not much clearer because contact
had been lost with 62nd Corps. Only one Ju. 88 managed to
photograph the beaches in the assault area and its film did not show
any vessel much bigger than landing craft and minor warships. In
his tactical report to *OKW* for 15th August Kesselring construed
this to mean that larger landings were still to come, probably
between Cannes and St. Tropez but possibly on the Ligurian
coast.

For the German High Command, the problems of *AOK 19* were
quite overshadowed by those of *AOK 7* and 5th Panzer Army
trapped at Falaise, and by the added anxiety of von Kluge's
disappearance on 15th August. Early on the 16th contact between
OB West and his Chief of Staff, General Blumentritt, was re-
established at the H.Q. of 5th Panzer Army, when Blumentritt
assured his master that 'down there things were taking their
course'.[52] He estimated that at least a regiment had been air
landed and that there was enough Allied shipping to suggest that
three to four divisions were being put ashore. The eastward moves
of 11th Panzer Division and other reinforcements were in train,
and there was not, in Blumentritt's opinion, any need for von
Kluge to issue any special orders to *AOK 19*. Obtaining Hitler's
authority for the withdrawal of Army Group B behind the Seine was
a much more pressing requirement and there was no inclination to
reinforce *AOK 19* from other fronts in France. Nor were 3rd and
15th Panzer Grenadier Divisions to be sent to its aid, for Army
Group B was informed on 18th August that these divisions would
refit in Germany before being routed 'towards Paris'. By the 24th,
Model was planning to assemble both divisions in such a way as
to maintain contact between Army Groups B and G. Thus Wiese
was left to oppose 'Dragoon' with hopelessly inadequate forces,
which for lack of mobility could not concentrate quickly enough
even to worry the Allies.

During the next two days the scope of the Allied landings became
clearer, but it was not the rapid development of the southern
beachhead which led Hitler to authorise the withdrawal of *AOK 19*.
As we mentioned in Chapter XI, the directive to this effect was
drafted by *OKW's* Operations Branch on the evening of 16th August
and was despatched over the Führer's signature at 5.20 p.m. on
the 17th. The preamble stated that the 'development of the situation
of Army Group B' opened the possibility that *AOK 19* might be
cut off 'in the foreseeable future'. With the exception of the forces
remaining in Toulon and Marseilles, Army Group G was therefore
to disengage from the enemy and to make contact with the southern
wing of Army Group B. The Führer went on to order the
methodical withdrawal of all troops from southern France. The

bulk of 11th Panzer Division was to remain in the Rhône valley to protect it against further airborne landings and subsequently to act as *AOK 19's* rearguard. Having made the provisions noted in Chapter XI for the retreat of 148th and 157th Reserve Divisions of Wiese's 62nd Corps, and for their subordination to *OB Südwest,* the directive ended with the decree that Toulon and Marseilles, together with the other 'Fortresses' in southern and south-western France, were to be defended to the last man.

Hitler's orders did not reach von Blaskowitz until the morning of 18th August. In the interim, the Commander of Army Group G received at 11.15 a.m. on the 17th authorisation from Field-Marshal Keitel, Chief of *OKW,* to withdraw all troops and head-quarters stationed in south-western France. As Keitel's instructions anticipated those of the Führer, they excluded from this withdrawal the fighting troops of *AOK 19,* also all units manning fortress areas in southern and south-western France. Keitel's instructions and Hitler's directive were intercepted and in the hands of Allied commanders within a few hours of their despatch.[53]

(iv)

Seen from the Allies' standpoint the 'Dragoon' landings were a mixture of pride in the smoothness with which the intricate plan was carried through by the large air, naval and land forces involved and anti-climax in the lack of German resistance ashore. Put in its simplest terms 4,000 aircraft of M.A.A.F., a naval bombard-ment force not far short of the 'Overlord' scale, and three experi-enced American assault divisions overwhelmed the equivalent of one regimental group of four battalions (one an *Ost* battalion) of the German 242nd Infantry Division holding the assault area.[54]* By the end of D + 1 all three assault divisions were on the Blue Line, having captured 2,041 prisoners, many of whom were of non-German origin, with negligible loss to themselves. The German bombers made one fleeting appearance when four Do. 217s attacked shipping off the Camel beaches, using glider bombs. The control aircraft employed a new technique of staying over land so that it kept its victims between itself and the Allied ships fitted with jammers.[55] Twenty-two ships tried to jam the attack but failed. *L.S.T. 282* was hit and burnt out, and the Camel Group flagship, U.S.S. *Bayfield,* suffered a near miss. This was the only attack on Allied shipping during 15th August.

---

* 765th Grenadier Regiment held the assault section with 4th Battalion (*Osttruppen*) opposite 3rd U.S. Division, 1st Battalion opposite 45th U.S. Division, 2nd Battalion opposite 36th U.S. Division, and 3rd Battalion in reserve at Fréjus.

The airborne landings of Rugby Force were carried out with greater accuracy than had ever been achieved in previous operations in the Mediterranean or during 'Overlord', despite unfavourable conditions. The nine Dakotas carrying Pathfinders encountered dense fog.[56] With the help of radar and radio aids the aircrew dropped the Pathfinders accurately on the planned dropping zones around Le Muy at 3.31 a.m., 50 minutes ahead of the main parachute force, which had had to contend with dust clouds on take off, no moon during flight and fog up to 500 feet on arrival. The navigational marker ships proved successful and the Pathfinders 'Eureka' beacons enabled the 396 Dakotas to drop their paratroopers correctly, only 37 aircraft missing their targets.* There were only two per cent drop casualties in the whole airborne force. The first wave of gliders was delayed, and the second had to be recalled due to worsening weather. It eventually flew in, just ahead of the main glider force of 332 Dakota tugs and gliders which had completed its landings by 7 p.m. All told, about 9,000 men, 221 jeeps and 213 guns of various types were landed by air during D day.[58] No aircraft or glider was lost during the approach, but many gliders were wrecked on landing, causing about 148 glider force casualties. Supply dropping was less accurate, only 40 per cent being recovered, due to wind conditions and lack of time to search the area thoroughly.

The preparatory air and naval bombardments which should have begun at 3.50 a.m. (Phase III) were delayed by bad weather until 6 a.m. For an hour twelve groups of heavy day bombers and their escort fighters, all from M.A.S.A.F., and the entire resources of two U.S. medium day bomber wings from U.S. XII T.A.C. (in M.A.T.A.F.) attacked selected coast defences, guns and radar sites within the assault area. Then for half an hour, and to combine with naval bombardment, the air effort was switched to the landing beaches, each being covered by two or more waves of bombers. The air attacks ceased at 7.30 a.m. and the naval bombardment ships alone took on the task of pulverising the beach defences as the assault craft began their final run-in. Allied bombing in direct support of 6th U.S. Corps began at H hour (Phase IV), and continued relentlessly until the fall of Toulon which, as will be noted later, coincided with the end of tactical air support from Corsica.†

---

* Unfortunately many of these carried 2nd British Parachute Brigade which had a more scattered drop than the Americans.[57] Nevertheless the Brigade took all its objectives although an attack on Le Muy was repulsed.

† Targets attacked and efforts expended on them during Phases III and IV until dawn on 16th August are shown in Table III.[59]

The Beach and Administrative organisations were as successful as the operational troops. 6th U.S. Corps was ashore complete by midday D + 1.[60] General Patch and H.Q. 7th Army disembarked from Hewitt's command ship U.S.S. *Catoctin* that afternoon. And at 8 p.m. the troops of 2nd French Corps started landing through the American cleared beaches. At the first Staff conference held by H.Q. 7th Army ashore, changes were made in shipping priorities to bring in units and stores which would help the rapid exploitation of success. Expecting determined German opposition, the Administrative planners had given preference to ammunition rather than fuel.[61] Fuel soon became the critical item ashore. So rapid had been the unloading across the beaches that seven ships due to join returning empty convoys on 16th August and one due for 17th August left with a D day return convoy. On 17th August five empty convoys left and shipping settled down into a routine cycle of convoys sailing to the beachhead from Naples, North Africa and Corsica.

Naval statistics show that 86,575 men, 12,520 vehicles and 46,000 tons of stores were landed in the first three days. Allied Naval losses matched those of 6th U.S. Corps in their insignificance; one L.S.T. and eight minor craft lost, six landing craft damaged by gunfire; 19 damaged by mines or under-water obstacles; one minesweeper and one L.C.T. damaged in collision; and one craft damaged by a rogue Apex drone.* 7th Army's 'Report of Operations' gives the casualties suffered by 6th U.S. Corps and prisoners taken by the assault divisions at the close of 15th, 16th and 17th August respectively, as:[63]

3rd U.S. Division	264 casualties	1,600 prisoners
45th U.S. Division	232 casualties	929 prisoners
36th U.S. Division	800 casualties	2,800 prisoners

Churchill, cabling to Eisenhower to congratulate him on the near destruction of von Kluge's troops in the Falaise pocket in Normandy, expressed his feelings about the efficient but negative nature of the 'Dragoon' landings:

> 'You have certainly among other things effected a very important diversion for our attack at 'Dragoon'. I watched this landing yesterday from afar. All I have learnt here makes me admire the perfect precision with which the landing was arranged . . .'[64]

---

* The Apex drone was a remotely controlled landing craft filled with high explosive for the destruction of underwater obstacles on the beaches.[62]

See Maps 13 and 15

The swamping of the German coastal defences and their garrisons, and the absence of German counter-attacks of any significance, encouraged Patch on 16th August to hasten exploitation by 6th U.S. Corps and 2nd French Corps, whose disembarkation was rushed forward as fast as its shipping would allow.[65] The general 7th Army plan was for 6th U.S. Corps to extend its beachhead to the Durance river to cover the advance of 2nd French Corps on Toulon and Marseilles. Truscott, however, put in hand the assembly of an armoured task force under his Deputy Commander, Brigadier General Frederick B. Butler, the composition and tasks of which had been thought out during the training period before the troops embarked at Naples.[66] Task Force Butler consisted of a reconnaissance squadron, tank battalion, infantry battalion, field artillery battalion and companies of tank destroyers, engineers and logistic units; and its task was to be the rapid exploitation of any break through which might occur as the beachhead was expanded.

There were three principal axes which could be used for exploitation: the coast roads to Toulon and Marseilles which were allotted to 2nd French Corps; Route 7 through Aix-en-Provence to Avignon in the Rhône valley and thence up the east bank of the Rhône to Lyons, which was given to 3rd U.S. Division; and the Route Napoléon from Nice to Grenoble which was to be 36th U.S. Division's axis. 45th U.S. Division was given the roads between Route 7 and the Route Napoléon. Initially 36th U.S. Division was to secure the eastern flank of 7th Army until relieved by the Airborne Task Force which would be losing 2nd Parachute Brigade for return to Italy. By the evening of 17th August the German intention to evacuate southern France was known to 7th Army, and Truscott decided that so little resistance was being met in the centre of the beachhead that this was the most suitable sector from which Task Force Butler should attempt an armoured break through. So swift and successful were the advances of Task Force Butler and the rest of 6th U.S. Corps during 18th August that any thought of pausing on the Durance to protect French operations against Toulon and Marseilles faded. The operations of the two Allied Corps went ahead simultaneously, with the Americans thrusting west, north-west and north intent on disrupting any plans which the Germans might have for containing their beachhead while the French advanced on Toulon.

On the German side a plan was made for 11th Panzer Division to mount a counter-attack from south of the Durance but it was invalidated by the withdrawal order of 18th August. Thereafter, 85th Corps was instructed to screen the movement of 4th G.A.F. Field Corps from the Spanish frontier to the west bank of the

Rhône.[67] For this purpose, 338th and 244th Infantry Divisions were reinforced by 198th Infantry Division and other detachments thinned out from 4th G.A.F. Field Corps. On 19th August 11th Panzer Division was ordered to assemble between Arles and Orgon, and von Blaskowitz informed *OB West* of his intention that *AOK 19* should reach the general area south of Avignon by 23rd August. In accordance with Hitler's directive, 148th and 157th Reserve Divisions of 62nd Corps were placed under command of *OB Südwest* for defence of the Franco-Italian frontier.

In the American advance, which started early on 18th August, 3rd and 45th U.S. Divisions ran into opposition at Brignoles on Route 7 and Barjols in the Argens valley, both due north of Toulon on the Germans' first delaying position.[68] 36th U.S. Division was still involved in pushing back 148th Infantry Division from Cannes to Nice and could not start up the Route Napoléon until relieved by the Airborne Task Force. The main break through came with the advance of Task Force Butler, which met virtually no opposition as it thrust rapidly northwards from Le Muy. It mopped up the German 62nd Corps H.Q., which the Airborne troops had been engaging, and captured Lieutenant-General Neuling. It then thrust due north through Riez to reach Sisteron on the Route Napoléon in the afternoon of 19th August, having surrounded and forced the surrender of a detachment of 157th Reserve Division, which had been sent south from Grenoble to block the Route Napoléon at Digne. The local German commander and 600 prisoners were taken. By the end of 20th August Butler had seized Gap on the Route Napoléon, where another 1,000 prisoners and a large dump of demolition stores and rations were taken, and he had troops blocking Route 93 at the pass of Col de la Croix Haute only 33 miles south of Grenoble.

7th Army's intention, expressed in a field order of 19th August, was for 36th and 45th U.S. Divisions to follow Task Force Butler in a thrust directed on Grenoble, while 3rd U.S. Division covered the French flank by continuing its advance along Route 7 to Aix-en-Provence. Truscott soon recognised the possibility of turning Task Force Butler westwards to cut the German withdrawal routes up the Rhône valley. He first ordered Butler to reconnoitre the routes westwards to Montélimar, and early on 20th August he ordered him to move there at first light on 21st August with all possible speed.[69] Butler was to block all routes of withdrawal up the Rhône valley in that vicinity, and 36th U.S. Division would follow him. A classic encircling move was about to be attempted. The target was the five divisions of *AOK 19*, including 11th Panzer Division, which were known by then to be withdrawing up the Rhône valley. Allied air reconnaissance had shown a southward trend in German road and rail movements until 20th August. By 21st August it was flowing strongly in the reverse direction.

Meanwhile by 20th August 3rd U.S. Division had fought its way to the outskirts of Aix, covering the advance of 2nd French Corps on Toulon and Marseilles.[70] The French were supported by naval shore bombardments and by U.S. Marauders and Mitchells of M.A.T.A.F. which paid progressively more attention to the guns and defences of both ports. By 23rd August Toulon was under close siege and the French Resistance had risen in Marseilles. Both cities fell early on 28th August in spite of Hitler's orders to fight to the last man. Allied air attacks and German demolition teams had wrought havoc in both ports. Toulon accepted its first Liberty ship on 5th September and Marseilles on 15th September.[71]

Task Force Butler started its march to cut the German withdrawal routes at Montélimar at first light on 21st August, using Route 93 along the valley of the Drome river.[72] By dusk Butler was overlooking the Rhône valley from the high ground northeast of Montélimar and had established an artillery position at the village of Condillac within effective range of the roads both sides of the Rhône. Attempts to establish a block on the road were frustrated by German troops. At this stage neither side had enough troops in the area to block the road effectively or keep it open completely. The week long battle of Montélimar became a race between the arrival of German and American reinforcements. On the American side, regiments of 36th U.S. Division were fed into the battle as they arrived on three successive days from 23rd to 25th August. On the German side, 85th Corps, led by 11th Panzer Division and with 338th Infantry Division as rear-guard, fought its way past the American positions on Route 7 along the east bank of the Rhône, whilst 4th G.A.F. Field Corps withdrew on the west bank running the gauntlet of American long-range artillery fire.[73] At no time was 36th Division strong enough to block the Rhône valley with troops for any length of time. It had to depend on its concentration of eight battalions of artillery of various calibres to cripple the German columns as they made their escape up both banks of the river.[74] Shortage of gun ammunition limited the damage that could be done. The American supply columns were operating a 470 mile turn-round from the beaches. Supplies of food and fuel were as critical as ammunition and had to be rationed. By 27th August the divisional artillery was told to stop firing whenever it reached a level of 25 rounds per gun in reserve. Nevertheless the Rhône valley was strewn with the burnt out wreckage of German vehicles and equipment which had been destroyed by American artillery fire. Several train loads of equipment, including long-range railway guns, had also been caught in the trap and destroyed. Unfortunately the Allied air forces could play little part in the battle of Montélimar. The German withdrawal had been so fast that the Corsican-based aircraft were soon out of range, and airfields on the mainland were not yet ready to receive them.[75] By 28th August six airfields had come into use but this was too late.

Having escaped annihilation in the Rhône valley the divisions of *AOK 19* turned and fought whenever their evacuation routes were threatened.[76] Their losses, particularly in equipment, had been severe.* By the beginning of September a new race had begun.[77] The Germans fought hard to hold open a gap between 7th Army thrusting north through Lyons and 3rd U.S. Army advancing westwards from south of Paris. The gap finally closed on 11th September, and on the 15th Eisenhower assumed control of an Allied front which was continuous from the Channel to the Swiss frontier. By this time the German front had also closed, and presented a cohesive defence which Field-Marshal Montgomery failed to disrupt with his Operation 'Market Garden' launched on 17th September.

There is no denying the tactical success of 'Dragoon'. The landings were efficiently organised; the subsequent advance up the Rhône valley was ably executed; and the spoils, in terms of French territory liberated and German prisoners taken, were impressive. The figures of Germans trapped in south-western France and the amounts of equipment captured or destroyed cannot be assessed accurately, but there is no reason to dispute those quoted by General Devers.[78] He credits French Army B with taking 47,717 prisoners for the loss of 1,146 French killed, captured or missing, and 4,346 wounded, and 6th U.S. Corps with 31,211 prisoners for 3,000 Americans killed, captured or missing and 4,419 wounded. From 17th July to 28th August Allied bombers and fighter-bombers had flown 9,992 sorties against ports and other targets in southern France on which they had dropped 14,266 tons of bombs.[79] A further 4,530 sorties (5,505 tons of bombs) had been flown against ports   and   other   targets   west   of   and   including   the

---

* *AOK 19's* closing report for 30th August has not survived but Army Group G's war diary contains an entry commending 338th Infantry Division for its 'heroic and selfless efforts' covering the withdrawal of 198th Infantry Division over the Drome. In a report to *OB West* on 19th September von Blaskowitz says: 'Thanks to good leadership and the bravery of the troops, the divisions which were constantly attacked from the air, engaged by the French who were in full revolt, also at times under direct fire from the enemy on their flank, fought their way out to the north'.

Genoa–Milan–Como line in indirect support of 'Dragoon'. Against this formidable recital the German Air Force could only offer a few fighter sorties on 15th August and a handful of bomber sorties that night. Whatever unrecorded effort followed, by 19th August there was none as the G.A.F. had withdrawn from the scene. It is not so easy, however, to accept Eisenhower's claim, made in his *Crusade in Europe,* that:

> 'There was no development of that period which added more decisively to our advantages or aided us more in accomplishing the final and complete defeat of the German forces than did this secondary attack coming up the Rhône Valley'.[80]

The German defence of France south of the Loire was little more than a balloon which, if pricked, was bound to collapse. 'Dragoon' did not draw German forces away from Eisenhower as was intended; on the contrary, it enabled Hitler to shorten his western front. What would have happened if the 'Dragoon' forces had remained in Italy must remain a matter for speculation. Certainly the ports of Marseilles and Toulon were not over-used for the entry of U.S. Divisions waiting in the United States to join Eisenhower.[81] Only six disembarked through them; three in October and no more until a further three were landed in December. In the next chapter we return to the Italian front to describe what did happen there without the experienced 6th U.S. Corps, without the mountain trained troops of the French Expeditionary Corps, and with greatly reduced air support.

(v)

While 7th U.S. Army was carrying out its successful operations in the south of France, Churchill was adding his personal dynamic to the affairs of the Mediterranean. Before flying north to Corsica to witness the start of the 'Dragoon' landings, he concentrated on Yugoslav affairs, meeting Marshal Tito twice in formal session and at a number of less formal social occasions. The groundwork for these meetings had been laid in June and July, and it would be helpful to retrace its erratic course. Churchill had been actively trying to promote co-operation between the Royalist Government in exile and Tito's Partisans in Yugoslavia, known as the Yugoslav Army of National Liberation or Y.A.N.L. for short.[82]* He had some success when Dr. Ivan Subasic, Prime Minister of the Royal

---

* J.A.N.L. rather than Y.A.N.L. was used in British contemporary documents.

Yugoslav Government in London, had visited Vis and on 17th June had reached an agreement with Tito whereby the settlement of Yugoslav political differences would be postponed until after the war so that a united effort could be mounted against the German occupation forces.[83] This meeting was to have been followed up by an Anglo-Yugoslav meeting on 12th July under General Wilson's chairmanship and attended by both Tito and Subasic.[84] At the very last moment Tito backed out, on the excuse that the Yugoslav National Liberation Committee would not authorise his attendance. This may or may not have been the true reason; little time had been allowed for Partisan leaders to accept the idea of co-operation with the Royalists. The discourtesy, however, irritated the British.[85] Air Vice-Marshal Elliot, Commander of the Balkan Air Force, considered it monstrous that Tito should 'play merry hell with our common object and seek to defeat the Hun by refusing to take part in conversations at Caserta.' He should be told that conversations were needed without delay. Tito changed his mind and on 16th July sent Wilson a request for a new meeting 'within the next three days for purely military discussions'.[86] The first week of August was fixed for the renewed visit to Caserta.

Wilson held two meetings with Tito, on 6th and 10th August, which proved encouraging from the British point of view though less so for the Yugoslavs. On the positive side, agreement was reached that the best way of bringing pressure to bear on the Germans would be a co-ordinated attack on their communications by Y.A.N.L and the Balkan Air Force.[87] Tito was to ask his commanders for specific targets for the B.A.F. to attack so that a combined plan could be drawn up. (The operations were later called 'Ratweek'.) Attacks would last initially for one week and would be followed about a fortnight later by a further series of attacks. Tito also agreed that plans should be made to seize an island in the northern Adriatic to serve as an air base for operations over Slovenia.

The most unsatisfactory part of the meetings dealt with supply.[88] Tito's shopping list had included equipment for a complete armoured brigade, field and anti-tank guns, and 60 plane loads per day to supply Y.A.N.L. and 30 for the civil population. Wilson had to inform him that the most he could do from Mediterranean resources was to equip and train one armoured regiment with Stuart light tanks, and an armoured car squadron. He could also provide 84 75-mm pack howitzers. Tito asked what was the prospect of seizing a bridgehead on the Dalmatian coast through which his forces could be supplied by sea.[89] Wilson had to tell him that the necessary forces and assault shipping were not available at present. Nor could he promise to increase deliveries by air since the maximum possible was already being done with the air lift available.*

Reporting to London on 12th August, Wilson commented that Tito's request for more tanks was 'clearly part of his bid for post-war control of Yugoslavia'.[91] He was, however, impressed by Tito's frankness, bearing and ability throughout the discussions.

When it became apparent that Churchill would arrive in Italy soon after these meetings, Tito agreed to delay his return to Vis so that he could meet the British Prime Minister. Dr. Subasic was also asked to return to Italy to be available to exploit any success Churchill might have in encouraging the development of a united Yugoslav war effort. Churchill's two meetings with Tito went well. The first on 12th August was with Tito alone and the second on the 13th was *à trois* with Dr. Subasic present.[92] Politically, he sought to bring the two men closer together and obtained Tito's agreement to make a public announcement that he did not intend 'to impose Communism' by force on the Yugoslav people after the war. Churchill probed the possibilities of attracting more Serbian support and made it very clear that H.M. Government would not countenance the use of British supplies in continued fighting (other than in self-defence) with General Mihailovic's supporters.† Militarily, Churchill's mind had moved far ahead of the strictly practical discussions which had taken place during Wilson's conferences. With the successful exploitation of 'Olive' in mind, he sought Tito's views on possible Anglo-Yugoslav co-operation in a combined operation against the Istrian Peninsula, for which the opening up of a small port on the Yugoslav coast would be most useful.[93] Tito responded favourably, saying that he would be able to draw on considerable support from Croatia and Slovenia for such an operation. Churchill was gratified and left the details to be worked out at a staff conference between General Gammell and Tito. One positive step towards unity appeared to be the agreement between Tito and Subasic to accept the amalgamation of the Royal Yugoslav and Partisan Navies under the overall command of the Commander-in-Chief, Mediterranean.

Both Tito and Subasic attended Gammell's meeting on 13th August at which it was agreed that:

> '. . . in the event of Allied forces occupying Northern Italy, Austria or Hungary, Commander-in-Chief, Yugoslav Army of National Liberation, would place at the disposal of the Com-

---

* The difficulties which affected the delivery of supplies to resistance forces by S.D. aircraft are explained in Part I of this Volume (H.M.S.O. 1984) Chapter VII Section (v). Yugoslav Partisans received a very generous proportion.[90]

† General Draza Mihailovic was leader of the Serbian 'Cetniks'. For a broader outline of the situation see John Ehrman: *Grand Strategy* Volume V (H.M.S.O. 1956) pp.76–8 *et al.*

mander of such Allied forces all those facilities necessary to the Commander for the maintenance of his forces and the military security of his lines of communication, over which the Yugoslav Army of National Liberation exercised *de facto* control at the time . . .'[94]

In particular, it was agreed that the Allied Commander should exercise command and control of the port of Trieste and that British troops should guard their own Lines of Communication to Austria or Hungary through Ljubljana–Maribor–Graz and through Gorizia and Klagenfurt (*see Map 23*). Tito, however, only agreed to study a draft memorandum from the Supreme Allied Commander in which it was stated that the Allies intended to impose an Allied Military Government upon Istria. At the subsequent meeting that same evening with Churchill and Subasic, whereas Churchill said that the status of Istria should not be pre-judged, Tito made it clear that 'in no circumstances could he acquiesce in an Italian civil administration and requested that the Yugoslav authorities should be associated in the administration of the territory' by an Allied Military Government.[95] Tito also placed the question of Istria first in a letter, which he sent to Churchill just before this second meeting, stating that an organised Yugoslav civil administration already existed, where circumstances allowed, in Istria and the Slovene littoral.[96] The seeds of future difficulties between the Allies and Y.A.N.L. in Istria were being sown.

After these Anglo-Yugoslav conferences, Subasic returned with Tito to Vis for further talks.[97] They agreed to amalgamate the Yugoslav air forces on the same lines as the navies. This would be done by enrolling all Yugoslav airmen in the R.A.F.V.R., (as was the case with existing Partisan squadrons), whereas the navies would sail under the 'constitutional Yugoslav flag'. It was to take another five months before the practical details of the naval agreement were worked out. During the interval, lack of Royalist vessels rankled with Tito who felt that the British were withholding his due rights.[98] The Yugoslav Air Force became effective almost immediately, flying within B.A.F.'s overall command.

Churchill's most significant success in trying to promote a united Yugoslavia came at the end of August when King Peter dismissed Mihailovic and called upon his followers to join Y.A.N.L.[99] This was an important concession for Tito, although he was to remain as suspicious of Western intentions about the Cetniks as Churchill was to be of Tito's determination to fight the Germans rather than the Cetniks.[100]

(vi)

On return from watching the 'Dragoon' landings Churchill was conducted by Alexander on a tour of the recent battlefields of Cassino and then of the Allied positions along the Arno and around Florence, which lasted until the morning of 21st August.[101] It enabled him to meet and talk to all the principal commanders, including General Clark, who received him at 5th Army Head-quarters and left him under no illusion about the emasculated state of his Army or of the opportunities which, in his view, had been lost by mounting 'Dragoon'.* Just before the end of Churchill's tour, Field-Marshal Sir Alan Brooke and Marshal of the Royal Air Force Sir Charles Portal, who had followed him out to Italy, held some sensitive staff conferences with Wilson at A.F.H.Q. The sensitivity was due to Wilson having an integrated Anglo-American staff, which made it difficult to transact 'British-only' business. There had to be a careful inter-weaving of joint and separate meetings.[102] Thus on 20th August there was a 'British-only' meet-ing at 10 a.m. followed by a full staff conference with Americans present at 11.45 a.m., and a further 'British-only' meeting at 5.30 p.m. Brooke, Portal and Wilson then travelled north to meet the Prime Minister at the British Embassy in Rome for a further 'British-only' meeting next day.

The duplication of the staffing arrangements was a true reflection of the continuing divergence of Anglo-American views and policies in the Mediterranean. In preparation for these staff conferences a very detailed agenda had been drawn up by the British element of Wilson's staff which showed four 'British-only' worries.[103] The first and most pressing was the suspicion that with the successful launching of 'Dragoon' and Eisenhower's sweeping advance east-wards from Normandy, which was in full flood at the time, the Americans would insist on the transfer of the rest of 5th Army and the medium bombers of XII U.S. T.A.C. to France, making the Mediterranean a 'British-only' theatre. The second worry flowed from the first. Would the Americans be prepared to continue to be associated with British policies in the Mediterranean after Germany collapsed? The British in A.F.H.Q. believed that their policy should be to attract 'Maximum American support without undue pressure'. The Americans must be brought to recognise that there was 'an inescapable military commitment attached to relief operations and to agree that these should be undertaken by the British on their behalf'. In order to ensure the continuation of

---

* General Clark has set out his views in *Calculated Risk* (Harper & Brothers New York, 1950) p.367 *et seq*.

American support, responsibilities for such operations in Greece, Bulgaria and Rumania at present assigned to the British Commander-in-Chief, Middle East, should be transferred to the Supreme Allied Commander.

The third worry was the lack of progress in 'Rankin' planning for action to be taken if Germany collapsed unexpectedly.* Nothing had been decided about the general strength and dispositions of occupational forces, the extent of U.S. and Dominion participation in occupational duties, the organisation of U.N.R.R.A.† and relationships between the armed forces and the Allied Armistice Commissions.

Fourthly, what were the British long-term aims in the Mediterranean? Was there anything which should or should not be done in anticipation of the future? To what extent could the Americans be associated with securing British requirements? And in the last paragraph there was a plea for guidance on the probable transfer of troops from the Mediterranean to the Far East for the war against Japan and to the United Kingdom for demobilization.

Few of these questions could be answered during the meetings on 20th August because they depended upon the outcome of the 'Octagon' conference at Quebec and the general development of the Western Allies' political and military policies for dealing with a defeated Germany. The Anglo-American meeting at 11.45 a.m. dealt mainly with the transfer of 7th U.S. Army to Eisenhower, and the possible loss of the American medium bombers as well.[104] In Portal's view S.H.A.E.F. had 'as much tactical air support as they could profitably use' and might not press for transfers from M.A.A.F. Eaker said he understood that General Spaatz still intended XII U.S. T.A.C. to pass to S.H.A.E.F., but thought it might be possible to split Saville's command by transferring only the Mitchells to Eisenhower, leaving the Marauders in the Mediterranean.

The two 'British-only' meetings concentrated upon the future of the Italian campaign and the situation in Greece, and these two subjects were also the main topics at meetings held in Rome next day with the Prime Minister. We will look at these problems in the order in which Churchill tackled them: Greece first, and then the Italian campaign.

The story of British attempts to bring about unity both amongst the guerilla bands in the mountains and amongst the Greek politicians inside and outside Greece had not been a happy one.

---

* 'Rankin' was the code word for a sudden collapse of German resistance, anywhere in Europe.

† United Nations Relief and Rehabilitation Administration.

We can only summarise events here.* British military and political requirements were unfortunately incompatible. Military operations were being executed by Force 133† under G.H.Q. Middle East, through Liaison Officers of the Allied Military Mission attached to the guerilla bands.[105] The shorter-term military interest demanded British support of the large and widespread *E.L.A.S.* bands controlled by *E.A.M.,* a composite body of five Socialist parties and the Communist Party, for which it was a 'front'.‡ Longer-term British political interests required the establishment of a Greek government in Athens 'friendly to us and not dominated by Russia'.[107] This entailed supporting the exiled government of King George II of Greece in Cairo, and the less effective and much smaller non-communist guerilla bands in the mountains, the most important of which was *E.D.E.S.* led by General Zervas, a strong nationalist, whose main support lay in the Epirus in western Greece. The common denominator between these conflicting facets of British policy was the need for Greek unity to fight the Germans. Regrettably no leader of Tito's politico-military stature arose in any party of the Greek political spectrum inside or outside Greece and unity remained elusive. The fighting which broke out between *E.A.M./E.L.A.S.* and *E.D.E.S.* in October 1943 and continued until early February 1944, when an armistice was signed, showed that, although *E.A.M.* was the strongest group in the country, they could not gain their ends while the Germans remained in occupation.[108]

The search for Greek political and military unity was bedevilled by the much disputed views on the King's position. Early in April 1944 the Greek Army and Naval units in the Middle East rose in mutiny for a third time.[109] (Trouble had occurred already in March and July 1943).[110] In local British opinion the mutinies were essentially Republican in sympathy, although exploited by the Communists. They did, however, produce one positive result. On 12th April King George appealed for unity, announcing that he would submit to the result of a national plebiscite on the nature of Greece's future regime once peace had been restored.[111] He made no mention of a recent proposal for an interim Regency

---

* The story is developed more fully by John Ehrman: *Grand Strategy* Volumes V and VI (H.M.S.O. 1956).

† A Special Operations force described in Part I of this Volume *op. cit.* pp. 389–90.

‡ *K.K.E.:*   *Kommounistikon Komma Ellados* Communist Party of Greece.[106]
  E.A.M.:   *Ethnikon Apeleftherotikon Metopon,* National Liberation Front.
  E.L.A.S.:   *Ellenikos Laikos Apeleftherotikos Stratos,* Greek People's Army of Liberation.
  E.D.E.S.:   *Ellenikos Demokratikos Ethnikos Syndesmos,* Greek Democratic National
        League: the name covered both political and military wings.

which would have postponed his return to Greece, although it was the unanimous advice of all parties in Greece and recommended by the Cairo Government. Republican opinion was far from satisfied. Mutinies continued and spread to Greek ships in Malta as well as Alexandria. General Sir Bernard Paget, Commander-in-Chief Middle East, who had postponed using force against the mutinous Greek Army units, acted on 23rd April. After only slight opposition, in which one British officer was killed, the Greek units surrendered. There were no Greek casualties.

In the middle of this crisis M. Giorgios Papandreou arrived in Cairo on 15th April, having been smuggled out of Athens.[112] The King asked him to form a new Government. Papandreou's quest for Greek unity led to a conference attended by all political parties, which opened on 17th May near Beirut. The resultant 'Lebanon Charter', which provided for a unified army under a single government, including four portfolios specifically earmarked for the Left, was accepted with suspicious ease and was indeed repudiated by the *E.A.M.* Central Committee within a week. They made three new demands: they wanted part of the Greek Government to be established in 'Free Greece'; they must have the portfolios of War and Interior; and the constitutional issue must be settled.

The British Government had on several occasions in 1943 considered breaking entirely with *E.A.M.*[113] In mid-July 1944 the Joint Planning Staff again reported on the military aspects of such a breach. Although theoretically well placed to threaten the main German Lines of Communication, in practice *E.L.A.S.* had shown little initiative and such acts of sabotage as had been carried out had been under the leadership of British Liaison Officers. Without such leadership it was likely that *E.L.A.S.* 'would devote their energies almost entirely to the elimination of their rivals'. This in turn would lead to the breakdown of 'Noah's Ark', an operation then being planned, which was designed to harass and disorganise German troops in the event of a withdrawal from Crete, the Aegean Islands and Greece. Furthermore, Allied Liaison Officers now numbered 398 (350 of these being with *E.L.A.S.*), plus some 200 Greek assistants, all of whom would be endangered. The British Chiefs of Staff discussed the paper on 17th July.[114] They also heard a report from the head of the Allied Military Mission, Colonel the Honourable C. M. Woodhouse, who put the strength of *E.L.A.S.* at about 30,000 men. In contrast to the political wing, *E.A.M.*, the majority of those who joined *E.L.A.S.* he believed were patriots wanting to fight the Germans. He argued that:

'No Greek would willingly take up arms against us, provided we did not try to establish the King in power, and our commitment would be limited to the forces required in order to ensure free elections. These elections would reveal that *E.A.M.* had practically no support in the country and they would no longer be a threat to our interest'.

The Chiefs of Staff thereupon advised the Prime Minister that the flow of supplies and equipment to *E.L.A.S.* should be throttled, but no public denunciation of *E.A.M.* should be made.

At this point, when British policy hung in the balance, *E.A.M.* changed their attitude. The arrival of a Russian Military Mission, which flew secretly from Bari to *E.A.M.* Headquarters in late July, seems the probable cause since in mid-August *E.A.M.* agreed unconditionally to enter the Greek Government in Cairo, where it further agreed to send its representatives to take up the portfolios offered them at the Lebanon conference.[115]

The question of how many troops should be sent to Greece, if and when the Germans withdrew, in order to restore law and order and prevent a *coup d'état* had been reviewed by the Chiefs of Staff on 20th July.[116] On the assumption that it was 'of high military importance' that a friendly government should be firmly established and that *E.A.M./E.L.A.S.* should not have the opportunity to seize control, they concluded that there were two options. 'The only <u>certain</u> way' was to occupy the whole of Greece with 80,000 troops, supported by a small air contingent. The alternative was to occupy Athens and Salonika only, which would require 10,000 men, leaving the Greek Government to police the rest of the country. They doubted whether the Greek Government would be able to fulfil such a role; in the consequent unrest it might be necessary to despatch up to the full 80,000 men in an open ended commitment, possibly lasting many months.

Despite the Chiefs of Staff recommendation, the Prime Minister, supported by Mr. Eden, held to the view that the smaller force would be sufficient and on 8th August warned Brooke to prepare a force of 10,000, adding that '5,000 men in five days is better than 7,000 men in seven days'.[117] With the approval of the War Cabinet, orders were issued to General Wilson on 14th August to prepare such a force in conjunction with General Paget, Commander-in-Chief Middle East.[118] Air support was to consist of two to three squadrons with adequate replacement aircraft. Shortly afterwards the Prime Minister himself advised Wilson that intervention in Greece must be regarded as 'an operation of reinforced diplomacy and policy, confined to Athens with possibly a detachment at Salonika rather than an actual campaign.'[119]

At the 'British only' meeting at A.F.H.Q. on 20th August, it was agreed that the C.I.G.S. should advise the Prime Minister on two points: that the occupation of Greece should be carried out under the orders of a British Task Force Commander, reporting direct to the Supreme Commander, and that General Paget should prepare part of the force so as to reduce the demands on the Italian campaign.[120] The outline plan, code name 'Manna', envisaged 2nd Parachute Brigade (which it was hoped would shortly be released from 'Dragoon') being air landed in the Athens area in a surprise operation, in the wake of which the Greek Government would be established before *E.A.M.* could take the capital. A sea-borne force made up of the balance of the 10,000 men would follow-up to relieve the paratroopers for use elsewhere. There would be some delay in landing these troops, the time depending upon how many minesweepers could be made available to clear a passage to the Piraeus.

The final decisions were taken at the meeting of Brooke, Portal and Wilson with Churchill in the British Embassy in Rome on 21st August.[121] Wilson reported that by employing 2nd Parachute Brigade from Italy and 23rd Armoured Brigade from Egypt he might be able to scrape the '*ad hoc*' division of 10,000 men together without calling upon Alexander. General Paget was planning to occupy the Dodecanese Islands and Crete with his own resources. The Prime Minister endorsed the tasks of the force commander as:—

'a.   To instal the Greek Government.
 b.   To accept the German surrender.
 c.   To open the way for the introduction of relief'.

That evening Churchill met the Greek Prime Minister, M. Papandreou, who stayed to dine with him.[122]* The two men got on well together. Churchill had to be non-committal and could only say that the despatch of British forces to aid the reintroduction of the constitutional Greek Government into Greece was under examination. It would be helpful if the Greek Government were transferred from Egypt 'to some place in Italy in relation to the Headquarters of the Supreme Commander' as such a move 'would act as a warning to *E.L.A.S.* and encourage the loyal population of Greece'. As in Yugoslavia, the future constitutional position would be decided by the Greek people after the war.

So began the preparation of operation 'Manna'. The Soviet Union was not to be informed, but Churchill had cabled President Roosevelt on 16th August to inform him of the situation and to seek his agreement for the Anglo-American staffs at A.F.H.Q. to prepare and hold in readiness a British force to put into Athens should the Germans collapse or withdraw from Greece.[124] He also sought authority to use American transport aircraft in the Theatre for the lift of a parachute brigade, as speed would be essential.

---

* M. Papandreou was ostensibly in Italy to inspect 3rd Greek Mountain Brigade.[123]

Ten days later the President replied that he had no objection to the preparation of such a British force, nor to the use of American transport aircraft available to Wilson.

Both sets of 'British only' meetings on the future of the Italian campaign (at Caserta on 20th August and in Rome on 21st August) were dominated by the British fear of a continuing withdrawal of American troops, assault shipping and aircraft from the Mediterranean.[125] Brooke argued that any reference to an advance into Austria through the Ljubljana Gap would not be 'good tactics'. The destruction of the German forces in Italy could not but be regarded as the right policy. It was important to stress to the Combined Chiefs of Staff that this was the object of Alexander's campaign. He felt that one of the flaws in the case for an advance into Austria was the natural defensive strength of the country through which Alexander would have to fight.* The Americans could well argue that 'fifteen divisions could not be profitably used in the difficult country on the way'. It would hardly be practicable to advance through the Gap before the Spring of 1945. Wilson gave his view that the campaign in Italy should be a drive across the Po to the Venice–Verona line, followed by an advance to the Piave. This was a formidable task, and although it had previously been considered that the correct strategy would be to force this line on land, he now felt a better method would be to turn it with an amphibious landing on the Istrian peninsula using three divisions, of which two would require assault shipping. This operation would have the advantage of enabling the maximum use to be made of the support accorded by the Yugoslav Army of National Liberation. Like Brooke, he could not see the operation being mounted much before the spring of 1945 and by then it might not be necessary, unless Eisenhower was halted before the Siegfried Line. Admiral Sir John Cunningham warned of the difficulty in mounting such landings: British assault shipping was due to leave the Mediterranean for the Far East early in September and, in any case, there were no British L.S.T.s in the Mediterranean. 'Sufficient amphibious lift would be difficult to provide unless the Americans could be persuaded to put L.S.T.s into the Adriatic'.

Churchill had few doubts about the policy to be followed. The minutes of the Embassy meeting record his views which are worth repeating verbatim:[127]

---

* Brooke had used a similar argument to the Prime Minister against supporting Alexander's advance to Vienna on 23rd June, when he pointed out that 'if we took the season of the year and topography of the country in league against us, we should have three enemies instead of one'.[126]

'He hoped that when the Army had broken through the Apennine position and reached the Po, it would continue to develop its operations to Trieste and into Istria. He recalled that the President, at Teheran, had expressed interest in Istria and he hoped that he would be able to revive this interest. He was utterly opposed to the proposal that General Alexander's Army should move westward. He was also determined that its operations should not be hampered by the withdrawal of further forces. The Army in Italy was the most representative Army of the British Empire now in the field. He was prepared to go to extreme measures to ensure that the operations of this great Army should not be hamstrung. If the worst came to the worst and the Americans persisted in their desire to withdraw their troops from Italy into France he would be prepared to split the Command'.

At the end of this meeting the Prime Minister directed that planning an amphibious operation against Istria should be set on foot at once. Anticipating these instructions, Wilson had already directed his planners to consider how the campaign in north-east Italy might best be developed during the coming autumn, winter and spring, assuming that the Germans were able to effect prolonged resistance in north-west Europe.[128] In particular they were to consider the desirability and practicability of landing on the Istrian peninsula and to estimate the maximum size of land force which could be employed in a thrust through the Ljubljana Gap, bearing in mind the help that might be given by Y.A.N.L. to such a combined assault.

(vii)

We have already described M.A.T.A.F.'s and M.A.S.A.F.'s air operations in preparation for 'Dragoon' and 'Olive' in Chapter XI and the actual support of 7th U.S. Army's landings in southern France earlier in this chapter. These operations formed the foreground of the air picture of July and August. We must now complete the picture by looking at the background which included three separate groups of air and naval activity: the combined air and naval effort against the dwindling German controlled shipping and ports; the continued mining of the Danube, also a dwindling commitment as the Russian armies advanced; and the efforts of the Balkan Air Force in Yugoslavia, Albania and Greece, together with the Middle East Air Force's operations in the Aegean and M.A.S.A.F.'s contribution to the Combined Bomber Offensive. We will consider each in turn.

Air attacks on ships at sea and in port showed a marked increase between July and August, reflecting Allied interest in the coasts of southern France, the Italian Riviera and the head of the Adriatic in both their actual and deception plans for amphibious operations in August.[129] This increase in maritime air effort involved greater anti-shipping activity and sea reconnaissance. The most severe damage was inflicted upon German naval resources and merchant shipping during the heavy raids on Toulon, Genoa and Trieste. The statistics set out in Table IV show the increase of effort.

The breakdown of German merchant and naval vessels sunk by air attack was (Gross Registered Tonnage or Tonnage for naval vessels in brackets):—[130]

	Merchant Vessels				Naval Vessels			
	500 G.R.T. & Over		Under 500 G.R.T.		500 Tons & Over		Under 500 Tons	
	In Port	At Sea	In Port	At Sea	In Port	At Sea	In Port	At Sea
July	3 (58,146)	1 (1,259)	7 (925) 7 (a)	1 (427)	4 (5,695)(b)	—	13 (1,540) 30 (c)	8 (940) 3 (d)
August	9 (41,258)	—	17 (2,147)	—	9 (6,680)(e)	—	16 (575) 6 (f)	9 (1,000)

(a) Seven small vessels of unknown G.R.T. were sunk in port in addition.
(b) Includes two U-boats—*U.586* and *U.967*—sunk in port.
(c) Thirty small vessels of unknown tonnage were sunk in port in addition.
(d) Three small vessels of unknown tonnage were sunk at sea in addition.
(e) Includes four U-boats—*U.642, U.952, U.471* and *U.969*—sunk in port.
(f) Six small vessels of unknown tonnage were sunk in port in addition.

As will be seen from this table of losses the sinkings of German ships, naval vessels and craft in port greatly exceeded those in the open seas. Perhaps the most indicative statistic is that of the 13 merchant ships of over 500 G.R.T. sunk in July and August of which only one was successfully attacked at sea. All the rest were destroyed in port, three by the R.A.F., eight by the U.S.A.A.F. and one by unknown aircraft. Incidentally, three of those sunk in port were over 10,000 G.R.T.—S.S. *Duilio* (23,636 G.R.T.) and S.S. *Sabaudia* (29,307 G.R.T.) were sunk in and near Trieste on 6th July, and S.S. *Splendor* (12,173 G.R.T.), a tanker, was sunk in Savona on 8th August. The single ship sunk at sea among those over 500 G.R.T. was the S.S. *Agathe* (1,259 G.R.T.), the victim of rocket-firing R.A.F. Beaufighters on the night of 2nd/3rd July south of the Cyclades. The details of German shipping losses from surface action, submarines, air attacks, mines and other causes are given in Captain Roskill's *The War at Sea*, Volume III, Part II *op. cit.* pp. 108–9.[131]

Of the naval vessels sunk in port by air attack, we have mentioned the destruction of six U-boats at Toulon.[132] Of other vessels of over 500 tons sunk in port were the *Cornelio Silla*, an uncompleted cruiser of 3,362 tons, a freighter, a corvette, two minesweepers and a minelayer.

French warships are not included in the total of enemy naval vessels sunk in port. The French battleship *Strasbourg* (26,500 tons), which was scuttled in Toulon harbour in November 1942, was raised partially in the summer of 1944 and towed to another site in Toulon harbour. On 18th August 36 U.S. Mitchells attacked the *Strasbourg* and she eventually sank from a near miss.[133] A cruiser, the *La Galissoniere* (9,120 tons) and a submarine lying near the battleship apparently sank too. It was believed the battleship and cruiser were destined to be used as blockships.

By the end of August the number of German-controlled ports still operating in the Western Mediterranean had been reduced to Genoa and Savona from where supplies were sailed to Spezia and to a few minor ports on that stretch of the Ligurian coast.

The pattern of attacks on ports throughout the Mediterranean during July and August was as follows:[134]

Italian ports	—	1,132 sorties
French ports	—	639 sorties
Yugoslav ports	—	103 sorties
Greek and Aegean }	—	159 sorties (includes 134 by R.A.F., Middle East)

Anti-shipping operations at sea had consisted of protecting Allied convoys against enemy submarine attack as well as deliberate attacks on enemy shipping. August saw the first task draw to a close. The *U.596*, based at Pola, was fitted with a *Schnorkel*, a fact of which the Allies were unaware.* In spite of forewarning of her movements detection was so difficult that she was hunted for eight days without avail by sea and air forces during her passage to her patrol area. She arrived there on the 14th and put into Salamis on 1st September. Her destruction there together with the remaining German U-boats in the Mediterranean in September will be described later.

Other than the S.S. *Agathe* (1,259 G.R.T.) the sinkings of enemy merchant ships and naval vessels at sea by air attack were all below 500 G.R.T. or tons.[135] The Royal Navy's submarines did rather better. In the Western Mediterranean, of four vessels sunk one was a 500-ton coaster off Hyères by H.M.S. *Ultor*. In the Aegean three steamers were sunk, all over 500 G.R.T., the largest

---

* See Captain S. W. Roskill: *The War at Sea* Volume III Part I (H.M.S.O. 1960) p.18.

being the S.S. *Anita* (1,165 G.R.T.) off Andros by H.M.S. *Vox*. Surface craft accounted for quite a few ships. Among the largest were the anti-submarine vessel *UJ. 2211* (916 tons) and S.S. *Sarina* (547 G.R.T.) sunk on the night of 20th/21st July between Savona and Genoa, and the S.S. *Numidia* (5,335 G.R.T.) torpedoed on 17th August between Trieste and Pola.

Besides anti-submarine operations another maritime task came to an end in August. This was the protection of Allied convoys against enemy air attack.[136] The German anti-shipping strike force had been drawn northwards from its bases in southern France, initially by 'Overlord', and subsequently in an attempt to keep out of range of M.A.T.A.F.'s counter-air operations in preparation for 'Dragoon'. The main anti-shipping force became centred around the Lyons/Dijon area, and was out of range of the Allies' convoy routes along the North African coast. The last two anti-convoy operations were against UGS. 46 (65 merchant ships) on 11th/12th July and UGS. 48 (54 merchant ships) on 1st August. Both failed due to the Allies' successful use of smoke screening. After the first the Germans reported three aircraft missing out of 26 in the force, and four Ju.88s were missing at the time of the second. On 3rd August eight bombers of the Republican Italian Air Force tried to attack UGS. 48 off Benghazi with equally little success. Thereafter the Allied Mediterranean convoys were free to sail at will.

The end of German air attacks on Allied convoys robbed M.A.C.A.F.'s day and night fighters of lucrative targets. Nevertheless, they persevered and even though sometimes unsuccessful in interception they presented a serious hazard to enemy aircraft, chiefly day and night reconnaissance.[137] In July and August 18 enemy aircraft were shot down, 14 of them over Italy or Italian waters. This compares favourably with the total of 17 known to have been shot down in the same period by M.A.T.A.F. There was an obvious need to transfer some of M.A.C.A.F.'s North African based headquarters and units to more active areas and to disband those which had become redundant.[138] On 6th July H.Q. M.A.C.A.F. moved from Algiers to Caserta in Italy. On 13th July operational control of M.A.C.A.F.'s forces was taken over by the Combined Naval/R.A.F. War Room newly-built in Caserta Palace. To control the units left in North Africa No. 210 Group was reformed, and fighter defence was handed over to the French Coastal Air Force. By the end of August, so far as can be traced, there were 28 operational squadrons in M.A.C.A.F., which includes the co-belligerent Italian Air Force, the equivalent of two R.A.F. squadrons in aircraft strength. In A.H.Q., Eastern Mediterranean there were, again so far as can be traced, 15 squadrons. As will be seen in Part III Chapter XVII, this decline in maritime air strength was to gather speed during the next four months.

We must now turn to the disruption of enemy shipping of a different kind: the tugs, barges and other craft which plied the Danube carrying oil to the Reich from the Rumanian refineries. By mid-1944 the German counter-measures had had some success in reducing the effects of minelaying. The officer responsible for Danube transports informed Hitler on 10th July that by the previous day the joint efforts of the German navy and air force had cleared or detonated 510 mines, and though 202 vessels had been lost (130 of which had been sunk, including 27 tugs) it was hoped to raise 80–90% of those sunk. A further 172 vessels had been damaged. More barges and lighters were in use and more tank-trucks for transporting oil were in operation from Belgrade. However, renewed minelaying in the Danube began on the first night of July and air attacks on Danube ports and installations on the 3rd. During the whole month R.A.F. Liberators and Wellingtons of No. 205 Group R.A.F. flew 127 sorties to lay 428 mines on three dates, and Liberators and Fortresses from U.S. Fifteenth Air Force flew 145 sorties and dropped 328 tons of bombs on oil storage, dock gates and railway targets associated with the Danube.[139] Additionally Beaufighters of No. 255 Squadron in M.A.C.A.F. intruded over stretches of the river during the moonlight period, end June/early July. They had major successes on the nights of 29th/30th June and 8th/9th July. Eight oil barges were claimed destroyed and 102 other craft damaged. Despite minelaying and bombing and strafing attacks, the Germans recorded that in July 130,000 tons of fuel were transported to Germany as compared with the previous 'low' of 50,000 tons.

In August the R.A.F. Liberators flew 37 minelaying sorties laying 220 mines, and the U.S. Liberators and Fortresses flew 65 sorties during which they dropped 141 tons of bombs on Danube targets. The Magnetic Mines dropped in August included a delay mechanism which enabled them to lie on the river bed immune to detonation until the delay-time was at an end. This created a major difficulty for the German anti-mining organisation, and reports received at the time stated that in desperation the Germans accepted the risk of losing vessels, so shipping was no longer held up.* But the situation deteriorated on the Rumanian stretch of the river because the Germans had withdrawn the minesweeping elements from Rumania to combat the increased minelaying in

---

* This information might well have originated from the small Intelligence Group of the Royal Navy which was operating clandestinely in the Danube area during most of the May-October period of 1944.

the Hungarian stretch, and the extreme measure was adopted of drifting old vessels down river to explode the mines. The Russian occupation of the Rumanian oilfields at the end of August brought the Allied air forces' interruption of the Danube traffic to an end. Mining had clearly caused the Germans grave embarrassment.

The Balkan Air Force, unlike the Allied and German maritime air forces, was in a period of expansion during July and August, and, indeed, was the legatee of several of the squadrons bequeathed by the declining M.A.C.A.F. and R.A.F. Middle East.* By the end of July, excluding transport aircraft, B.A.F. totalled 11 squadrons and a flight.[140] Five more squadrons of some 80 aircraft were added during August but regrettably the number of aircraft fit to fly showed little improvement. 130 aircraft were serviceable at the end of July and 138 at the end of August. Low serviceability, due to aging and obsolescent aircraft, became the subject of a concerted drive in B.A.F. to raise it to 75% and to keep it there. Although officially established on 1st June, the Force did not start operations until 1st July.

On 20th July the German Air Force in *OB Südost's* theatre had a strength of 228 aircraft of which 169 were recorded as serviceable. By 20th August strength had risen to 242 but only 164 were recorded serviceable. General der Flieger Martin Fiebig, commanding *Luftwaffenkommando Südost*, laboured under two disadvantages not suffered by Air Vice-Marshal Elliot's B.A.F. His parish included not only the western Balkans, but Crete and the Aegean as well. Of his 228 aircraft 106 were either reconnaissance or obsolescent types fit only for limited coastal duties, leaving him with as few as 39 night ground-attack aircraft to support German anti-Partisan operations, and 58 day and 25 night fighters for the air defence of his vast area of responsibility. His second disadvantage was the advance of the Russian armies on his eastern boundary which by the end of August had drawn away most of his effort, leaving B.A.F. without air opposition. Fiebig was not to see this happen as he was succeeded on 20th August by General der Flieger Stephan Fröhlich, whose first task was to organise the airlift of German troops and equipment from the Aegean Islands which began at the end of the month and which we will describe in Chapter XIV.

July and August were months in which the newly formed B.A.F. Command cut its teeth in the unorthodox environment of the Balkans, in which nothing was certain, misunderstandings inevitable and everything was done against a background of political suspicion. The G.A.F. was the least of Elliot's worries. Allied air

---

* The July order of battle of B.A.F., and the squadrons added in August, are given in Part I of this Volume *op. cit.* pp.406–7. There is also a brief summary of the work of the Russian Air Force Detachment which began operations from Bari on 21st/22nd July.

force attacks on German occupied airfields, successful encounters between B.A.F. fighters and German aircraft supporting anti-Partisan operations, followed by the withdrawal of aircraft back to Hungarian airfields when Rumania left the Axis at the end of August, and when Bulgaria left in early September, all contributed to the reduction of German air opposition to negligible proportions.* During July *Südost* is known to have lost 17 aircraft in the air and 11 on the ground destroyed by the Allied air forces. In August the figures were eight and five, bringing the total for the two months to at least 41, but what proportion was the work of the B.A.F. is unknown.

B.A.F.'s air losses were significantly higher, at 28 in July and 54 in August for 2,509 and 3,437 sorties flown respectively.[141] In its final report on operations B.A.F. estimated that well over 50% of their casualties, and probably as high as 75%, was caused by flak. The German aim was to keep open their principal Lines of Communication which were, of course, B.A.F.'s primary target. They concentrated their static anti-aircraft defences at the most important centres of communication and at vulnerable points like major bridges. Such targets tended to fall to the lot of M.A.S.A.F. It was the mobile light and medium anti-aircraft weapons protecting convoys, trains and vulnerable stretches of line which caused most of B.A.F.'s casualties. The mountainous nature of the country contributed to the German gunners' successes. Some of B.A.F.'s aircraft strafing in the Montenegran valleys were to suffer the disconcerting experience of machine gun fire directed down on them from the hillsides above them and their targets.[142] There was to be another side to this coin when the appearance of mobile flak-towers and railway flak-wagons on previously inactive railway lines alerted B.A.F. to the probability of their future use for important German operational movements.

The most trying problem faced by B.A.F. was co-ordination with the Yugoslav Army of National Liberation.[143] Although R.A.F. Liaison Officers were established with radio links to H.Q. B.A.F. at selected Partisan Corps H.Q.s, it was still difficult to form an accurate picture of what was happening in the field. Guerilla commanders have a disinclination to stick to regular plans and, in any case, are forced to operate mainly by night. The constant cry of the Allied air force commanders was for more and better Intelligence. It was the need to settle such difficulties that

---

* For instance, M.A.S.A.F. bombed Zagreb airfield on 7th July destroying seven and damaging three German aircraft on the ground that day. On 20th July Spitfires and Mustangs of B.A.F. drove off seven Me. 109s and twelve He. 126s attacking the Partisans in Montenegro, and destroyed one Me. 109. Two days later they caught six Ju. 87s and a Do. 17 on Kraljevo airfield. (*Map 23.*)

prompted Elliot's efforts to bring about worthwhile military talks with Tito and his chagrin when Tito refused to attend Wilson's meeting of 12th July. The subsequent meetings did much to make amends and resulted in the successful 'Ratweek' operations in September, which we will be describing in Chapter XIV.

During July and August B.A.F.'s efforts to help Y.A.N.L. were on a 'catch as catch can' basis, harrying the Germans whose June offensive in Albania preceded strikes into north-western Greece and Montenegro. The German attacks had some initial success but no decisive results, and after the collapse of Rumania and Bulgaria Field-Marshal von Weichs (*OB Südost*) could make no further concerted attempts to subdue the Partisans as his few reserves were transferred eastwards.[144] B.A.F. also supported a number of small raids by Land Forces Adriatic, commanded by Brigadier G. M. O. Davy. None were large enough to be more than irritants for the Germans holding the Dalmatian coast and islands.

We should also note the sterling work done by B.A.F. in the evacuation of Yugoslav wounded. This was prized by the Partisans, not only on humanitarian grounds but more importantly because the need to carry their wounded with them, to save them from being slaughtered by the Germans, reduced the cross-country mobility so essential to their survival. During the peak months of 1944 B.A.F.'s evacuation figures were:[145]

June 1944	2,186 cases	August 1944	2,321 cases
July 1944	3,827 cases	September 1944	1,781 cases

The influx of these large number of casualties placed some strain on the medical resources in Italy, but by the end of July enough hospital beds had been found. The largest operation of this kind carried out by B.A.F. was on 22nd August, 1944, when 1,030 wounded were evacuated from a new air strip in Montenegro ('hacked out of mother earth').[146] The Dakotas, operating in five waves of six aircraft, flew 30 sorties in one day. The Senior Medical Officer B.A.F. described 'the pathetic sight' of the waiting men, 'obviously in an exhausted and starved condition . . .'.

The total air effort by B.A.F. in the ten months of its existence is recorded in Table V at the end of this chapter.[147]

(viii)

It is appropriate to end this chapter with a brief summary of the remarkable growth of air power in the Mediterranean, because during July and August the vastness of the area over which M.A.A.F. operated and the variety of air operations which it undertook, in terms of range, role and task, reached its zenith. Thereafter the German evacuation of southern France and the Aegean and their gradual withdrawal from the Balkans reduced M.A.A.F.'s area of responsibility and the variety of its operations. The chances of geography, the remarkable increase in strength, and the application of the principle of centralisation of control of air power by a series of able air commanders gave air operations in the Mediterranean and Middle East a uniqueness that can hardly be matched.

When Air Chief Marshal Sir Arthur Longmore took command of the R.A.F. in the Middle East on 13th May 1940, just before Italy entered the war, he found that he had 205 aircraft in Egypt available for operations, less than half of which were bombers with limited range and bomb capacity.[148] With the exception of the flying boats, which were confined to maritime tasks, the remainder were obsolescent biplane fighters and army co-operation aircraft. The few aircraft deployed elsewhere in the Middle East and Africa were equally obsolescent and the French air forces in Africa and Syria were soon destined to be lost to the Allied cause. Longmore's resources were demonstrably inadequate for support of operations in the Western Desert and at sea when war broke out, let alone for targets of strategic value. Longmore, however, had one great asset. All Allied air resources in the Mediterranean and Middle East were concentrated under his sole command and remained so in spite of several efforts by Naval and Army commanders to have this principle broken. Without centralised control he could not have achieved as much as he did with such slender resources.

When Tunis fell on 13th May 1943, three years to the day after Longmore's assumption of command in the Middle East, Air Chief Marshal Sir Arthur Tedder, who had succeeded him on 1st June 1941 and had later become Air Commander-in-Chief Mediterranean Air Command and Eisenhower's Air Deputy, was controlling 3,500 modern operational aircraft and air transports of the greatly expanded R.A.F., including Commonwealth and Allied Squadrons, and the powerful U.S. Ninth and Twelfth Air Forces.[149] His subordinate Air Commanders, operating from bases along the North African coast, could give the most effective air support to amphibious operations within single-engine fighter range of North Africa and Malta; could escort sea convoys the entire length of the Mediterranean; and could strike deep into Italian and Balkan territory against strategic targets. Tedder with overall control could switch the weight of attack and concentrate fighter defence at will when and where they mattered most. Longmore had the right but not the resources to do this; Tedder had both and used them to great effect.

A year later Tedder's efforts were far exceeded by the expanded
M.A.A.F. under General Ira Eaker.[150] The acquisition of air bases
in Sicily, central Italy, Sardinia and Corsica had given the Allied
airmen not only the ability to cover the length and breadth of the
Mediterranean but also a great area of southern, central and
eastern Europe, from southern France through southern Germany,
Czechoslovakia, Rumania, Bulgaria and Greece to the Aegean,
which is shown diagrammatically on *Map 16*. By July and August
1944 Eaker was controlling the operations of 5,000 modern operational and transport aircraft and could make the fullest use of the
inherent flexibility of air power, concentrating his effort sometimes
at short-range, sometimes at medium and at other times at long-
range, always with devastating results.

July started with the 'Mallory Major' operation against the Po
bridges in northern Italy.[151] Then the attack was switched to north-
west Italy and southern France in preparation for 'Dragoon'. In
August the whole weight of M.A.S.A.F., most of M.A.T.A.F.
and much of M.A.C.A.F. was directed to the support of the actual
landings in southern France, while D.A.F. continued 'business as
usual' in support of 5th and 8th Armies in Italy, and B.A.F.
developed its support of the Partisans in Yugoslavia with its Special
Duty aircraft penetrating deep into the Balkans. Air Headquarters
Eastern Mediterranean (under R.A.F., Middle East) with its
limited air resources attacked ports and shipping in and off Greece,
Crete and the Aegean islands. M.A.C.A.F. followed suit elsewhere
and also scoured the Western and Central Mediterranean for
enemy submarines and surface ships; and hand in hand with
A.H.Q., E.M. provided fighter and anti-submarine escort for the
Allied convoys as they traversed the length and breadth of the
Mediterranean. Beyond all these operations M.A.S.A.F. struck at
targets in Germany and central Europe in support of the Combined
Bomber Offensive, and to assist the Russian advance.

No Commander will readily confess to having enough of everything, but the air resources at Eaker's disposal were sufficient to
enable him to exploit range and flexibility in a way that could
hardly have been bettered. Much less would have been achieved
had all the Allied air resources not been concentrated in the hands
of one man as it had been since Longmore's day, with the exception
of the short but confused period during the earlier part of the
Tunisian campaign before Tedder was given overall command.
Allied air power could always be applied where it was needed most
at any given time, and yet the never-ending run of the mill air
commitments could still be met. In brief, unified control did make
it possible not to squander these vast resources.

TABLE I

M.A.T.A.F. ORDER OF BATTLE IN CORSICA AND SARDINIA ON 15th AUGUST, 1944

CORSICA				
	*U.S. 1st Group	3 Squadrons	Lightning (P38G, H & J)	T.E.-F.
	*U.S. 14th Group	3 Squadrons	Lightning (P38G & J)	T.E.-F.
	(*On loan from U.S. Fifteenth Air Force (M.A.S.A.F.) from D-3. Ceased operations with M.A.T.A.F. at last light on 20th August 1944)			
	No. 324 Wing R.A.F.	4 Squadrons	Spitfire IX	S.E.-F.
	No. 322 Wing R.A.F.	4 Squadrons	Spitfire IX	S.E.-F.
	No. 251 Wing R.A.F.	3 Squadrons	Spitfire IX	S.E.-F.
	U.S. 57th Group	3 Squadrons	Thunderbolt	S.E.-F.
U.S. XII T.A.C.	U.S. 79th Group	3 Squadrons	Thunderbolt	S.E.-F.
	U.S. 324th Group	3 Squadrons	Thunderbolt	S.E.-F.
	U.S. 86th Group	3 Squadrons	Thunderbolt	S.E.-F.
	U.S. 27th Group	3 Squadrons	Thunderbolt	S.E.-F.
	U.S. 47th Group	4 Squadrons	Boston IV (& A20B & G)	L.B.
	U.S. 415th Squadron		Beaufighter VI	T.E.-F.(N.F.)
	U.S. 111th Squadron		Mustang (F6A)	Tac.R.
	No. 225 Squadron R.A.F.		Spitfire VB & C	Tac.R.
	II/33 Escadrille F.F.A.F.		Spitfire V	Tac.R.
	Quatrième Escadre F.F.A.F.	3 Squadrons	Thunderbolt	S.E.-F.
	U.S. 321st Group	4 Squadrons	Mitchell III	M.B.
U.S. 57th Wing	U.S. 340th Group	4 Squadrons	Mitchell III	M.B.
	U.S. 310th Group	4 Squadrons	Mitchell III	M.B.
	†U.S. 23rd Squadron		Lightning (F5A, B & C)	P.R.
	†U.S. 5th Squadron		Lightning (F5A, B & C)	P.R.
M.A.T.A.F.	†No. 682 Squadron R.A.F.	(detachment)	Spitfire XI	P.R.
	(†On loan from M.A.P.R.W.)			
SARDINIA	U.S. 17th Group	4 Squadrons	Marauder I & II	M.B.
	U.S. 319th Group	4 Squadrons	Marauder I & II	M.B.
U.S. 42nd Wing	U.S. 320th Group	4 Squadrons	Marauder I & II	M.B.
	31e Escadre F.F.A.F.	3 Squadrons	Marauder II	M.B.
Escorts for airborne operations	*Note* The following squadrons lent by U.S. Fifteenth Air Force (M.A.S.A.F.) as escorts for airborne operations operated from Italy and were *not* under the operational control of M.A.T.A.F.:			
	U.S. 325th Group	3 Squadrons	Mustang (P51B, C & D)	S.E.-F.
	U.S. 31st Group	3 Squadrons	Mustang (P51B, C & D)	S.E.-F.

TABLE II

M.A.C.A.F. ORDER OF BATTLE IN CORSICA AND SARDINIA ON 15th AUGUST, 1944

CORSICA	No. 326 Squadron F.F.A.F.	Spitfire V & IX	S.E.-F.
	No. 327 Squadron F.F.A.F.	Spitfire IX	S.E.-F.
U.S. 63rd	No. 328 Squadron F.F.A.F.	Spitfire V & IX	S.E.-F.
Fighter Wing	U.S. 417th Squadron	Beaufighter VI	T.E.-F.(N.F.)
	*U.S. 415th Squadron	Beaufighter VI	T.E.-F.(N.F.)
	U.S.N. (ten aircraft)	Hellcat (F6F-3)	S.E.-F.(N.F.)
SARDINIA	†U.S. 346th Squadron	Airacobra I	S.E.-F.
	U.S. 347th Squadron	Airacobra I	S.E.-F.
	U.S. 345th Squadron	Airacobra I	S.E.-F.
	No. 272 Squadron R.A.F.	Beaufighter X	T.E.-F.(C)
	U.S. 414th Squadron	Beaufighter VI	T.E.-F.(N.F.)
U.S. 63rd	No. 256 Squadron R.A.F.	Mosquito XII & XIII	T.E.-F.(N.F.)
Fighter Wing	No. 153 Squadron R.A.F.	Beaufighter VI	T.E.-F.(N.F.)
	No. 458 Squadron R.A.A.F.	Wellington XIV	G.R.
	No. 36 Squadron R.A.F.	Wellington XIV	G.R.
	No. 17 Squadron S.A.A.F.	Ventura V	G.R.
	4S Squadron F.F.A.F.	Walrus	G.R.
	No. 14 Squadron R.A.F.	Marauder I, II & III	G.R.
	U.S.N. (five aircraft)	Avenger	A.S.
	(*On loan from M.A.T.A.F.*)		
	(†*Moved to Sardinia from Italian mainland after 15th August*)		

Note This Order of Battle excludes M.A.C.A.F. squadrons available to support 'Dragoon' but not based in Corsica or Sardinia.

TABLE IV

SORTIES FLOWN BY M.A.A.F. IN ANTI-SHIPPING OPERATIONS
JULY–AUGUST 1944

Month	Target	M.A.A.F. (including Malta but not R.A.F., M.E.)		H.Q., R.A.F., M.E.	Totals on target each month
		R.A.F. (including Allied units)	U.S.A.A.F.		
July	Ships at sea	740	80	266	1,086
	Ports	486	421	90	997
August	Ships at sea	1,271	211	144	1,626
	Ports	471*	521	44*	1,036
Totals	Ships at sea	2,011	291	410	2,712
	Ports	957	942	134	2,033
GRAND TOTALS		2,968	1,233	544	4,745

* Excludes flare-carrying sorties.

TABLE V

BALKAN AIR FORCE
MONTHLY RECORD OF SORTIES FLOWN AND TONNAGE OF
BOMBS DROPPED
1st JULY 1944 TO 8th MAY 1945

Month	Sorties	Tonnage bombs
1944		
July	2,509	132.2
August	3,437	276.8
September	3,698	479.9
October	3,416	429.9
November	4,604	341.6
December	4,653	760.6
1945		
January	2,460	394.8
February	4,690	1,085.0
March	3,954	1,086.6
April	4,546	1,561.1
May (1st–8th)	373	101.3
TOTALS	38,340	6,649.8

NOTE: Although it will be seen that the peak of effort by B.A.F. was reached in February 1945, the number of *Offensive Sorties* flown and tonnage of bombs dropped during the month of April 1945 by Squadrons operating directly under B.A.F. constitute a record for the period July 1944 to April 1945. In previous months a large percentage of the effort by B.A.F. was contributed by *Special Duty Squadrons* operating directly under or loaned to this H.Q. During the month of April 1945, however, only 427 S.D. sorties were flown.

CHAPTER XIII

BREACHING THE GOTHIC
LINE

(i)

THE first factor to appreciate in studying 'Olive' is the balance of forces engaged. The three Corps of 8th Army in the Adriatic sector could deploy three armoured divisions, seven infantry divisions, and four independent armoured brigades.[1]* The infantry battalions totalled 71, all up to a strength

---

* Outline Order of Battle of 8th Army on *25th August 1944* was:

   5th Corps (Lieutenant-General C. F. Keightley):[2]
     1st Armoured Division (Major-General R. A. Hull): 2nd Armoured, 18th Infantry, and 43rd Gurkha Lorried Infantry Brigades.†
     4th Division (Ward): 10th, 12th and 28th Infantry Brigades.
     46th Division (Major-General J. L. I. Hawkesworth): 128th, 138th, 139th Infantry and 25th Tank Brigades.
     56th Division (Major-General J. Y. Whitfield): 167th, 168th, 169th Infantry and 7th Armoured Brigades
     4th Indian Division (Holworthy): 5th, 7th, 11th Indian Infantry Brigades.
     1st Army Group R.A.
     C.I L. (*Corpo Italiano di Liberazione*).
   10th Corps (McCreery):
     10th Indian Division (Reid): 10th, 20th, 25th Indian Infantry Brigades, one regiment 9th Armoured Brigade.
     9th Armoured Brigade Group (less regiment)
     2nd Army Group R.A.
   1st Canadian Corps (Burns):
     5th Canadian Armoured Division (Hoffmeister): 5th Canadian Armoured, 11th, 12th Canadian Infantry Brigades.
     1st Canadian Division (Vokes): 1st, 2nd, 3rd Canadian Infantry Brigades.
     21st Tank Brigade.
     1st Canadian Army Group R.C.A.
   2nd Polish Corps (Anders):
     3rd Carpathian Division (Major-General Duch): 1st, 2nd Carpathian Rifle Brigades.
     5th Kresowa Division (Major-General Sulik): 5th Wilenska, 6th Lwowska Infantry Brigades.
     2nd Polish Armoured Brigade.
     Army Group P.A.
   Army Reserve
     2nd New Zealand Division (Freyberg): 4th N.Z. Armoured, 5th, 6th N.Z. Infantry Brigades.
     † 3rd Greek Mountain Brigade.

Commanders given in full only when newly appointed or making their first appearance in this Volume.

† These two brigades had undergone training at the M.E.F. Mountain Warfare Training Centre.[3]

of 845 officers and men, with the exception of the seven Polish battalions whose reinforcement continued to be difficult.[4]

See Maps 8 *and* 11

By 25th August, the 'Olive' D day, 8th Army was disposed as follows:[5]

> *Right*   Between the coast to exclusive Montemaggiore on the Metauro lay 2nd Polish Corps, with 5th Kresowa Division in the line and 3rd Carpathian Division in reserve about Senigallia.
>
> *Centre Right*   From inclusive Montemaggiore and 4 miles to the south-west was 1st Canadian Corps, its 1st Canadian Division, with 21st Tank Brigade under command, in the line and 5th Canadian Armoured Division in reserve. Under command of the Canadian Corps also was the divisional artillery of 4th Division, brought forward to strengthen the Canadian artillery for the opening phase of the attack.
>
> *Centre Left*   From east of Fossombrone to the boundary with 10th Corps in the hills, which ran north and south through Urbania on Route 73, was 5th Corps. Its divisions were still moving north towards the Metauro, with 46th Division on the right and 4th Indian Division on the left. In reserve were 56th Division, 1st Armoured Division, 7th Armoured Brigade and 25th Tank Brigade. 4th Division, except for its artillery with the Canadian Corps, was still in the Foligno area waiting to be called forward to join 5th Corps.
>
> *Left*   Between 5th Corps and the Upper Arno valley lay 10th Corps with its 10th Indian Division operating in the Upper Arno valley towards Bibbiena and 9th Armoured Brigade, now comprising only 12th and 27th Lancers (armoured car regiments) watching and patrolling the mountain area between the left of 5th Corps and the Tiber valley.

The Canadian Corps' front was covered by the Polish Cavalry Force patrolling the south bank of the Metauro, temporarily under Canadian command.[6] 5th Corps was similarly covered by elements of the *C.I.L.* and in Army Reserve north of Siena, waiting to be called forward, was 2nd New Zealand Division with under its command 3rd Greek Mountain Brigade, which had just arrived from the Middle East.[7]*

---

* 3rd Greek Mountain Brigade: 1st, 2nd and 3rd Greek Mountain Battalions and with 3rd Greek Artillery Regiment under command.

On the German side things were very different. 76th Panzer Corps, which was to bear the brunt of the fighting, had initially only three divisions: 1st Parachute Division on the coast; 71st Infantry Division immediately inland; and 278th Infantry Division, which was relieving 5th Mountain Division in the hills, on the Corps' western flank.[8] von Vietinghoff could reinforce 76th Panzer Corps' front from several sources under his own control. 51st Mountain Corps had five divisions covering the 80 miles of mountains from the inter-Corps boundary at Belforte to the inter-Army boundary at Mt Giovi (Pt 992), north-east of Florence. Corps Witthöft, which was responsible for coastal defence behind 76th Panzer Corps' Adriatic flank, had 162nd (Turkoman) Infantry Division coast-watching in the Rimini–Ravenna sector and 98th Infantry Division in support further inland. *AOK 10*'s first plans to exchange 98th Infantry Division for 29th Panzer Grenadier Division (Lieutenant-General Fries, replaced by Major-General Polack on 30th August) were ratified by Kesselring on 25th August. Of the potential reinforcements represented by Kesselring's Army Group Reserve, General Baade's 90th Panzer Grenadier Division was still underpinning the Army of Liguria in the Maritime Alps. 26th Panzer Division, now commanded by Colonel (later Major-General) Crasemann, was under orders from 24th August to assemble near Bologna in Army Group reserve, and was just beginning to withdraw from *AOK 14*'s front north-west of Florence when 8th Army opened its offensive.*

The best indicators of an army's potential in a defensive battle of the type *AOK 10* was about to wage are the strength of its infantry battalions, its holdings of anti-tank weapons and tanks, and the condition of its artillery and ammunition supply.[9] We have available the weekly strength returns submitted to *OKW*, *OKH* and *OB Südwest* by *AOK 10* on 20th August, which grade the

---

* The outline Order of Battle of *AOK 10* on 25th August was, east to west:

76th Panzer Corps (Herr)
    1st Parachute Division (Heidrich)
    71st Infantry Division (Raapke)
    278th Infantry Division (Hoppe), relieving 5th Mountain Division (Schrank) of which
        the bulk was *en route* to Army of Liguria.

51st Mountain Corps (Feuerstein)
    114th Jäger Division (Bourquin)
    305th Infantry Division (Hauck)
    44th Infantry Division (Lieutenant-General Hans-Günther von Rost)
    334th Infantry Division (Böhlke), under orders to move into *AOK 10* reserve.
    715th Infantry Division (Colonel Hans von Rohr)

Corps Witthöft
    162nd (Turkoman) Infantry Division (von Heygendorff)
    98th Infantry Division (Major-General Alfred Reinhardt)

Venetian Defence Sector (Gall)
    Fortress battalions, engineer detachments, Italian Bersaglieri battalion.

infantry battalions and give the state of medium anti-tank weapons and field artillery. The infantry state shows:

Battalion Grading	51st Mountain Corps	76th Panzer Corps (including 5th Mountain Division)	Corps Witthöft	Total
Strong (over 400)	4	8	11	23
Medium (below 400)	13	8	2	23
Average (below 300)	13	11	2	26
Weak (below 200)	8	1	—	9
Total	38	28	15	81

Provided 51st Mountain Corps was pinned down by 5th Army and 10th Corps, 8th Army would have almost a 2 to 1 superiority in battalions and a $3\frac{1}{2}$ to 1 superiority in actual infantry strengths.

A return of 27th August gives the number of serviceable tanks and medium anti-tank weapons in the Corps of *AOK 10*. 76th Panzer Corps held a total of 95 such weapons (including 14 assault-guns and five 'Rhinoceros' equipments) of which 62 were serviceable. It also held 33 Panther tanks of which 20 were serviceable on the 27th, and nine Panther turrets were emplaced in Herr's sector of the Gothic Line. If Kesselring committed 26th Panzer Division on the Adriatic front it would bring with it a further 50 tanks. 51st Mountain Corps had no tanks but held 140 medium anti-tank guns of various types of which 111 were serviceable. *AOK 10*'s total muster, including 26th Panzer Division and the Gothic emplacements, was 92 tanks and 235 medium anti-tank weapons against which 8th Army could deploy 1,276 cruiser and infantry tanks (1,089 Sherman and 187 Churchill).[10] In addition it had 278 Stuart reconnaissance tanks (a conversion originally devised in the Middle East) and a fully stocked reserve of tanks ready to replace battle casualties. It also held 1,055 anti-tank guns.[11]

British commanders, while anxiously seeking an opportunity to deploy this vast force of armour, were at the same time concerned as to the relative inferiority of Allied tank armour and gun power compared to the German equipment which might be encountered. 21st Army Group had naturally received the latest, most powerful, Marks of tanks and anti-tank guns before the invasion of

Normandy. A comprehensive review written by B.R.A.C.*
A.F.H.Q. in July concluded that the Sherman, although a good
cruiser tank was undergunned, while the available Marks of
Churchill or Infantry tank were both undergunned and inadequately armoured for the 'heavy assault role'.[12]† Numbers of the
Sherman 76-mm gun tank were due to reach Italy in August and
the first were issued to 2nd Armoured Brigade (on the scale of one
per troop), but this did not satisfy 8th Army's desire for the
Sherman 17-pdr tanks and for 'Heavy Churchills' mounting the
75-mm gun.[13] Alexander raised the problem of up to date equipment with Churchill during his visit to Italy in August, but the
Prime Minister's intervention could do little but speed up the
arrival of the new Discarding Sabot ammunition to boost the
performance of the 6-pdr gun.[14] A.A.I. had already taken intermediate measures to upgun the Churchill. During the early summer
a local conversion had been devised and carried out on 106 tanks,
replacing (what must be presumed to have been) the low velocity
6-pdr Mark II gun by the 75-mm gun taken from unserviceable
Shermans.[15]‡ For 'Olive' the two 8th Army Tank Brigades operated with a 'mix' of Churchill 6-pdr and Sherman or Churchill 75-
mm.[16] The heavy Churchill did not begin to reach 8th Army in
any number until late autumn and the Sherman 17-pdr until 1945.
It will be seen, however, that equipment worries do not appear to
have influenced the aggressive use which 8th Army intended to
make of its armoured divisions.

In artillery the superiority of 8th Army was even more marked.
It deployed 1,122 guns,§ whereas *AOK 10*'s return of 20th August
shows that the number of field guns held by its divisions totalled
351, of which only 132 were with 76th Panzer Corps.[17] There is,
however, no contemporary evidence that the air interdiction of the
Po bridges had created an artillery ammunition shortage. Fuel
shortages are mentioned in reports of German commanders but
not ammunition. In 8th Army levels of artillery ammunition were

---

* Brigadier, Royal Armoured Corps.

† A comparison of British and German tanks and the performance of tank and anti-tank
guns is given by Major L. F. Ellis: *Victory in the West* Volume I (H.M.S.O. 1962) pp. 545–9,
where also will be found a definition of Discarding Sabot ammunition.

‡ Whereas the Churchill 75-mm (Mark III/IV) was a local conversion, the conversion of
the Sherman to mount a 17-pdr gun was carried out in the U.K. It was designated by the
letter 'C' after the Mark.

§ The totals of 8th Army artillery and anti-tank equipment were made up as follows:

Artillery	Anti-tank guns
863 25-pdr field guns	716 6-pdr
228 4.5-in. and 5.5-in. medium guns	190 17-pdr
31 7.2-in. heavy guns	149 3-in. S.P. M.10

very adequate, although, as we saw in Part I of this Volume,* there was a growing shortage of British and American artillery ammunition world wide. The first warning of an impending cut-back in supply was given to A.F.H.Q. by the War Office on 17th August.[18] 'Olive' was not affected. If a break through had occurred, consumption would have dropped and there would have been no crisis in the post-'Olive' period. Petrol would have become the critical item of supply.

Linked with artillery was air defence and tactical air support. *AOK 10* could expect neither, and received little of either. *Luftflotte* 2 had been downgraded to the status of a local *Luftwaffe* Command in Italy with General der Flieger Max Ritter von Pohl as its commander.[19] von Pohl seems to have been a man of some mettle who tried to offer a semblance of air opposition. On fourteen occasions his fighters and fighter-bombers tried to intervene over the battlefield in daylight during which he lost six Me. 109s. On nine other occasions he tried intrusion by night, losing six Ju. 87s to Allied Beaufighters. These efforts were insignificant in effect and in comparison with the Allied air operations, which went on remorselessly, hindered only by the weather which became a critical factor in *AOK 10*'s chances of blocking 8th Army's way into the Po valley. Although the Allied air forces were also supporting operations in southern France, there was still a very considerable tactical air effort available to support 'Olive'.[20] The scale of effort is best judged by the size of the figures for bomber and fighter-bomber effort during the 28 days of 'Olive'. M.A.A.F. inflicted upon *AOK 10* 6,471 tons of bombs with 8,507 sorties. D.A.F. provided 70% of the bombload and 90% of the sorties.

The outline plan for 'Olive', which we discussed in Chapter XI, was for the Polish Corps to mask the initial advance of 8th Army over the Metauro river and then thrust up the coast towards Pesaro; the Canadian Corps would attack in the centre, and 5th Corps, named the 'Pursuit Corps', would advance on the inland flank. Leese hoped to achieve such a surprise that he could 'gatecrash' the Gothic Line before 76th Panzer Corps could man its sector properly.[21] He left 5th Corps to solve the problems of advancing on a narrow front, protected by 4th Indian Division in the hills on the western flank. Once through the Gothic Line Leese hoped to maintain momentum and to break through as quickly as possible into 'the good tank country' which lay beyond Rimini.

The casting of commanders and troops to tasks was carefully thought through. Anders and his Poles had been operating on the

* Part I (H.M.S.O. 1984) Chapter VIII Section viii.

Adriatic coast for many weeks and were fully conversant with its tactical peculiarities. The limitation of their objective to Pesaro was well judged because they were tired and could not have undertaken much more. Burns' Canadians had had the experience of breaching the Hitler Line in June and were thus an obvious choice to breach the strongly fortified sector of the Gothic Line between Pesaro and the Apennine foothills. Leese had also taken particular care in selecting dynamic commanders for 5th Corps in its role of 'Pursuit Corps'.[22] Lieutenant-General Keightley, its Commander, and Major-General Hull, who had taken over 1st Armoured Division on 14th August and would lead the exploitation of any breach made in the German line, were both armoured commanders with considerable experience of tank warfare in the mountainous country of Tunisia. 4th Division was an experienced, well tuned formation under its Commander, Major-General Ward, who had led it with distinction during 'Diadem'. The newcomers, 46th and 56th Divisions, were well commanded too: Major-General Hawkesworth lived up to his nickname 'Ginger' in 46th Division, and Major-General Whitfield was chosen personally by Leese for 56th Division. 4th Indian Division, like 4th Division, was experienced and forcefully led by Major-General Holworthy.

There was one weakness in 5th Corps which Leese could do little about. The headquarters staffs of the Corps H.Q. and three of its Divisional H.Q.s were not 'run in'. H.Q. 5th Corps had not undertaken a major offensive operation for almost a year because it had been confined to the quiet Adriatic sector. H.Q. 1st Armoured Division had not been in action since the Tunisian campaign, and its subordinate brigades and units had been assembled piecemeal in July and August. And 46th and 56th Divisions had only recently returned from the Middle East.*

The general feeling prevalent in 8th Army before 'Olive' was that the war was snowballing to its close. This created a sense of optimism in officers and men alike which was reinforced by Leese's pre-battle addresses to senior officers, on 23rd August to 5th Corps and 24th August to the Canadian Corps.[24] The Canadian Official Historian described the latter as 'a brilliant eighty-minute *résumé*'. Leese did not belittle the difficulties of the ground but in his

---

* The backgrounds of the two fresh infantry divisions in 5th Corps Order of Battle were:[23]

46th Division had been resting in the Middle East since March 1944 and returned to Italy early in July where it took over the equipment of 5th Division (moving to the Middle East) and completed its concentration in the Foligno area about 25th July.

56th Division had also returned from a rest period in the Middle East, taking over the equipment of 78th Division (moving to Egypt for rest and reorganisation). 56th Division was due to complete its concentration in the Assisi–Perugia area about 8th August.

determination to build up the morale and confidence of his Army he gave the impression that this would probably be 8th Army's last great battle in which its superiority in armour, artillery and air support would be decisive. In his Order of the Day to 8th Army he wrote:

> 'Now we begin the last lap. Swiftly and secretly, once again, we have moved right across Italy an Army of immense strength and striking power—to break the Gothic Line.
>   Victory in the coming battles means the beginning of the end of the German Armies in Italy.
>
> *Let every man do his utmost,*
> *and again success will be ours.*'[25]

Keightley's pre-battle directive to 5th Corps' divisional commanders stressed the probable disintegration of the German Army and advocated a combination of 'violence and ferocity' in attack.[26] He emphasised the need for concentration of artillery and armour, the maintenance of momentum and the prerequisite of flawless traffic control. His Planning Instruction reflected the current view of how the offensive would develop.[27] It said:

> 'The object of Operation 'Olive' so far as 5th Corps is concerned is to smash the Gothic Line in conjunction with the rest of Eighth Army, and, having entered the valley of the Po, to destroy all enemy forces there.'

His plan was in three phases: first, rush the Gothic defences before the Germans could man them; second, force the Gothic Line if it was not rushed in the first phase; and third, exploitation of success, which would consist of a deep and rapid advance with the aim of encircling and destroying the whole left wing of the German Army. 46th and 4th Indian Divisions would lead in Phase I; 56th Division would be added for Phase II; and for Phase III 56th Division would advance on Bologna while 1st Armoured Division, followed by 4th Division, would head for Ferrara on the Po.

At the next level down Hull sent his commanders in 1st Armoured Division a short letter in which he said:

> '. . . There will be no time for a Div exercise so I am sending you these notes on certain points that I consider especially important. The end of the war with Germany is, I consider, in sight, but just as in a race, it is essential to keep going flat out till the very end . . .'[28]

He stressed the need for high standards of march discipline and traffic control; of junior leadership; of tank gunnery; of quick consolidation by the infantry; and ended with a short peroration on team work. Lack of a Divisional exercise had been caused by the late arrival of essential components of the Division which was outside 8th Army's control but should be noted because it had serious effects later on the Division's performance.*

In the ranks of 8th Army the euphoric feeling that this last great offensive would be a 'walk-over' is expressed in many personal accounts. One of the more colourful is by J. S. Lucas of the Imperial War Museum staff, who was a company runner in 56th Division at the time:[30]

> 'There is no doubt in my mind that the hope of our High Command, of a lightning advance against minimal opposition up to the gates of Vienna, was interpreted by the rank and file as the certainty that to reach the Austrian capital within a week was well within the capability of the 8th Army . . . I heard of, but never saw, military signposts with the legend, "DUST— drive carefully or you won't see Vienna".'

There were, none the less, three interrelated command and staff worries about the future: the weather, the number of rivers and canals in the supposedly good tank country of the Po valley, and the size of the River Po itself. Views on the probable effects of autumn weather were many and varied.[31] Rainfall statistics were reassuring but meteorological experts pointed out that the weather in northern Italy rarely conformed to the average. Such unpleasant thoughts were nevertheless brushed aside by most commanders on the grounds that the weather affected friend and foe alike, and it was no use allowing the possibility of bad weather to hold up the final destruction of the German Army with the end of the war so clearly in sight.[32] Although the plains of the Po valley held a fatal fascination for the commanders and staff of 8th Army, they were not blind to the obvious problems posed by the many blue lines, representing water obstacles, which criss-crossed their maps. A great deal of thought had gone into developing suitable obstacle crossing devices for both dry and wet gaps. This work is described in Appendix 6 Part III of this Volume. At the beginning of 'Olive' 1st Assault Regiment R.A.C./R.E. (under command of Lieutenant-

---

* The Divisional assembly took place in the following sequence:[29]

9th–14th June	—H.Q., Divisional Troops and 2nd Armoured Brigade disembarked from Tunisia and assembled at Altamura in the Heel of Italy.
21st July	—Orders received to reform the Division on a two infantry brigade basis adding 66th Brigade, which was being formed from Gibraltar and other Mediterranean garrisons, and 43rd Gurkha Lorried Infantry Brigade from the Middle East.
2nd August	—43rd G.L.I. Brigade arrived in the divisional area.
15th August	—43rd Brigade equipment completed.
15th August	—Move of Division to forward concentration area at Porto Recanati started.
18th August	—18th Brigade (which used to belong to 1st Armoured Division) returned from 1st Division in exchange for 66th Brigade.
23rd August	—2nd R.H.A. and 23rd Field Regiment R.A. joined Division.

Colonel R. E. H. Drury R.A.C.) was ready to support 8th Army, with two ARK/AVRE squadrons and one Sherman dozer squadron.[33]* 3rd Hussars had begun training with amphibious Duplex Drive tanks. And the Chief Engineer 8th Army was assembling a special Po Task Force, organised to build two Class 40 Bailey pontoon bridges across the Po near Pontelagoscuro. 8th Army was also planning to reorganise 3rd, 4th and 7th Hussars into 9th Armoured Brigade, under Brigadier R. B. B. Cooke, to handle all amphibious tanks and later the armoured personnel carriers called 'Kangaroos'.

At the outset of the battle the conduct of operations on the German side was also hampered by misappreciations. Kesselring was affected by what has aptly been called his 'Anzio Syndrome', which led him to believe that the opening of an Allied ground offensive in Italy must presage or cloak other intentions.[34] In the case of 'Diadem' he had feared that the first assault was designed to screen landings on the west coast. When 'Olive' opened he was equally reluctant to rate it as a major offensive. Early on 27th August he told Wentzell of *AOK 10* that in his view:

> '. . . this whole thing is only a large scale diversion, because in the West the enemy is afraid that we might thrust at his flank with three or four divisions and thus wreck the whole invasion of southern France.'[35]

As he did not then believe that Allied pressure on 76th Panzer Corps would be sustained, Kesselring would not immediately commit such reserves as he could muster, and the reinforcement of *AOK 10* was rendered even more piecemeal by the Allied airmen's total domination of its lateral communications. The failure of the German field Intelligence to appreciate that an Allied assault was imminent was another factor common to the opening of 'Diadem' and 'Olive'. The latter caught *AOK 10* with von Vietinghoff and Heidrich on leave, and with 278th Infantry Division in the process of relieving 5th Mountain Division in the sector to be attacked by 5th Corps. Analogies between May and August 1944 could not however be drawn where Kesselring's supply situation was concerned. By the summer, the Combined Bomber Offensive had imposed severe restrictions on the use of fuel, and the mobility of the German divisions in Italy was further reduced by shortages in towing equipment and spare parts, particularly tyres.[36] The

---

* ARKs and AVREs were modified tanks, the former used for bridging and the latter as assault engineer vehicles. They are described in detail in Appendix 6 Part III of this Volume.

reinforcements they received from depots in Germany were of lower calibre, and the threat to the eastern and western provinces of the Reich tempered the mood of the troops. Constant improvisation and making-do helped to maintain morale, and on 18th August von Vietinghoff reported that his troops were 'thoughtful, but they were confident of victory and willing to fight.'[37]

See Map 1

This is an appropriate stage at which to set out changes in the control and nature of tactical air operations as they affected 'Olive'.

Advanced H.Q. D.A.F. operated from Siena until 24th August, and then from Chiaravalle (south-west of Falconara) next day, in preparation for 'Olive', before moving on to Senigallia at the end of the month.[38] A major change in the air command developed during September. As the 'Dragoon' forces approached their junction with Eisenhower's armies, and the moment for 5th Army's offensive drew near, a redeployment of air squadrons from southern France and Corsica back to Italy began. At midnight 14th/15th September control of U.S. XII T.A.C., which was to become solely responsible for supporting 7th U.S. Army in the Rhône valley, passed to Eisenhower's U.S. Ninth Air Force. A new headquarters, at first called U.S. 'X' or 'X-Ray' T.A.C. was formed under Brigadier General Benjamin W. Chidlaw at Cecina to support 5th Army, and to relieve the Desert Air Force of the additional responsibility which it had been practicable to handle during 5th Army's preparatory period, but could not continue once both Armies in Italy were on the offensive.*

However, it was not until 20th September that Air Vice-Marshal Dickson, A.O.C. D.A.F., could relinquish responsibility for providing air support for both 5th and 8th Armies. Thus for most of 'Olive' the tactical air support for both Armies was provided mainly by D.A.F. and controlled by Dickson, with the exception of the U.S. medium day bomber effort.†

---

* The name of Chidlaw's command suffered several changes. 'X' was first changed to 'X-Ray' to avoid confusion with the U.S. X or 10th T.A.C. Then the transfer of the headquarters staff of U.S. XII Fighter Command from M.A.C.A.F. changed the name to U.S. XII F.C. This was not the final name. It became U.S. XXII T.A.C. on 19th October and remained so thereafter.

Chidlaw received the U.S. 62nd and 87th Fighter Wings from M.A.C.A.F. and the U.S. 47th Light Bombardment Group and the U.S. 27th, 57th, 79th and 86th Fighter Groups from U.S. XII T.A.C. It took time for the move back to Italy to take place. As a stop gap U.S. XII T.A.C. Thunderbolts, still in Corsica, were used to support 5th Army by staging at Cecina and Tarquinia.

† H.Q. M.A.T.A.F. did not return to Italy from Corsica to be alongside H.Q. A.A.I. once more until 24th September.

The development of Army/Air co-operation techniques involved the expansion of the Rover David teams. In 8th Army 2/5 A.A.S.C. now controlled two Rover teams: Rover Paddy for 5th Corps and the original Rover David for the Canadian Corps. The main innovation was the creation of a Rover Frank team which was entirely responsible for dealing with German artillery. It consisted of an air force controller and an army counter-battery officer who worked side by side in conjunction with H.Q. 8th Army R.A. At midnight every 24 hours a new target list was agreed. Each mission detailed for a counter-battery target called up Rover Frank on its way out to confirm that the target was still valid; if not, Rover Frank provided an alternative. The first targets attacked by the Rover Frank system were on the Canadian front on 18th September. The system was further developed by adding Forward Observation Officers to the Rover teams. These F.O.O.s could direct artillery on to those targets which were either too close to our own troops or unsuitable for air attack for some other reason. They could also order, with minimum delay, coloured smoke shell to mark targets which were difficult to identify from the air.

Air support control for 5th Army was the responsibility of 'Fifth Army Air Support Control Section'.[39] The Commander of the British No. 9 A.A.S.C. with U.S.A.A.F. and R.A.F. air controllers formed an advanced air support control known as Rover Joe which began operations in support of 2nd U.S. Corps on 11th September and extended them to Cabranks on the 19th.*

The complicated story of the Mobile Operations Room Units resolved itself when on 1st September U.S. 62nd (Fighter) Wing took over the defensive fighter control on the west coast from No. 1 M.O.R.U. (F.C.U. 'B') which then faded out of the picture and on the 21st assumed air operations control duties in central Italy, in support of 5th Army, from No. 1 M.O.R.U. 'B'. Four days later No. 1 M.O.R.U. 'B' was absorbed by No. 1 M.O.R.U. 'A' at Fano on the east coast to form plain No. 1 M.O.R.U. once more. It provided both air operations control facilities in support of 8th Army and defensive fighter control on the east coast. Thus, by 25th September, the U.S.A.A.F. and R.A.F. were providing these facilities within their own national areas.

---

* When 8th Army began its attack on the night of 25th/26th August, 5th Army A.S.C.S. became responsible for meeting requests for air support for the British 13th Corps (under 5th Army). The British No. 9 A.A.S.C. provided the wireless links, but to mask the fact that 13th Corps was operating under 5th Army the link between their two headquarters was by landline via the British No. 2/5 A.A.S.C.

(ii)

See Map 17

The month long 'Olive' offensive is easiest to follow with a brief *résumé* of the outcome before studying the detail of its battles which are complex and overlapping. Moreover, it is helpful to break them into four phases though these were not seen as such at the time. Three of the four phases started with the successful breaching of one of the Gothic Line positions and ended with a severe check in front of the next German line of resistance. In the first phase (25th August to 7th September) 8th Army overran Green I with surprising ease and was checked by the defeat of 1st Armoured Division in the first battle of Coriano and of 56th Division at Croce, both within Green II. In the second phase (8th to 11th September) 5th Corps fought to regain the initiative in deteriorating weather and with a marked increase in casualties as 76th Panzer Corps struck back. In the third phase (12th to 17th September), Green II was breached in the second battle of Coriano. Fierce and costly fighting carried 8th Army over the Marano river and up to the River Ausa, on the north bank of which reared the final ridge of hills before the plain of the Romagna, and upon which *AOK 10* was to establish its last defensive position—the Rimini Line— covering the Po valley. In the fourth phase (18th to 21st September), this line was breached too, but with equally heavy casualties and in ever worsening weather. 8th Army at last saw the 'promised land' through sheets of sleeting rain as it crossed the wide bed of the Marecchia river to enter the flat Romagna on 21st September.

See Map 11

During 25th August, while 8th Army was putting the finishing touches to its preparations for its rolling advance over the Metauro that night, each level of staff in *AOK 10* was grappling with different problems, oblivious of the massive Allied concentrations lying behind the thin Polish and *C.I.L.* screen.[40] The Army Staff was making preparations for the conference on the *Herbstnebel* contingency plan for withdrawal to the Po and beyond, which was to be held at H.Q. *AOK 10* in five days time: their eyes were certainly not fixed on *AOK 10*'s sector of the Gothic Line. At Corps level the staffs were immersed in the complications and improvisations caused by the decision to withdraw 5th Mountain Division and to side-step the tired 278th Division into its place. And at divisional level all staffs were busy with preparations to continue their phased withdrawal from the Gothic *Vorfeld* on the Metauro towards an intermediate position, the Red Line, which lay some six miles south of Green I. The initial advance of 8th Army went undetected as a major offensive because it appeared to be the routine follow-up of 76th Panzer Corps' retreat from the *Vorfeld*.

The three Corps of 8th Army advanced through the Polish and *C.I.L.* screen about an hour before midnight on 25th August and by dawn were thrusting rapidly north-west from bridgeheads over the Metauro.[41] Some of their intense preliminary bombardments of known defensive positions caught the Germans in the open on their way back to the Red Line. Most of the fire, however, landed upon vacated positions, which Leese described, when writing to the A.C.I.G.S. on 8th September, as 'a pity'.[42] For three days the advance across the whole 8th Army front went ahead as planned, with increasing resistance being felt during 27th and 28th August as the leading divisions fought to drive the Germans back from the Red Line to the Foglia. The Poles on the Adriatic coast were delayed for a time by 1st Parachute Division on the Mt Bellila ridge; and the Canadians had some very hard fighting during 28th August to clear their axis of advance through Monteciccardo, against opposition from 71st Infantry Division and parts of 1st Parachute Division. Further inland 5th Corps was delayed more by lack of roads and difficulties in traffic control than by the opposition of 278th Infantry Division. 46th Division on 5th Corps' right managed to keep pace with the Canadians,* but 4th Indian Division on the left, with rougher country to contend with and the open flank to watch, were some distance behind when German resistance south of the Foglia began to slacken late on 28th August. By the end of the third day, 29th August, all three Corps of 8th Army were on the Foglia and able to examine Green I for them-selves. What they found was to be described, at first hand, by General Leese in the same letter to the A.C.I.G.S:

'You may like to hear a few words about the Gothic Line. It is very much stronger than we had expected. The valley was 2–3

---

* *Outline Order of Battle of 46th Division* (Major-General J. L. I. Hawkesworth)[43]
   128th Infantry Brigade
   2nd, 1st/4th, 5th Hampshire Regiment
   138th Infantry Brigade
   6th Lincolnshire Regiment, 2nd/4th King's Own Yorkshire Light Infantry, 6th York and Lancaster Regiment.
   139th Infantry Brigade
   2nd/5th Leicestershire Regiment, 5th Sherwood Foresters, 16th Durham Light Infantry.
   R.A.C. 46th Reconnaissance Regiment.
   R.A. 70th, 71st, 172nd Field Regiments; 58th A/Tk Regiment; 115th L.A.A. Regiment.
   R.E. 270th, 271st, 272nd Field Companies; 273rd Field Park Company.
   M.G. 9th Manchester Regiment.
   Additional Troops
   25th Tank Brigade
   North Irish Horse, 51st R.T.R., 142nd R.A.C.; 142nd Army Field Regiment (S.P.) R.A.

miles broad. The FOGLIA river at this time of year was not a serious obstacle, though the water-meadows were marshy. It would have been a difficult advance across the valley as one would have had to compete with two or three miles of open country, in which every house and tree had been razed to the ground to improve the field of fire. Minefields were anything from half to three-quarters of a mile in depth, and there was an anti-tank ditch along most of the front. Luckily we had surprised the enemy so much by the speed of our advance that he had left all his notices up, saying "*Minen*" with a skull and cross-bones; and "*Gasse*" or "*Minen frei*", denoting a safe lane!

To turn now to the infantry defences covering the anti-tank ditch. The nearer one got to PESARO the more complete were these defences. The frontage consisted of a series of Spandau posts, each surrounded by deep belts of low wire. The wire obstacles were far the most formidable that we have come across in ITALY. In each post there were two concrete Spandau pits let into the ground. Behind these positions there was a deep belt of tactical wire along the whole front, with further defences covering that. In certain cases *Flammenwerfer* [Flame-throwers] were dug in at ground level in forward posts. The weakness of the position lay in three things. Firstly, the high ground over-looking the river from the south gave excellent observation over the whole position. Secondly, the general line of the F.D.Ls. ran along the main road. This would have been of great assistance in forming any artillery plan. Thirdly, there was no depth to the position at all: everything was in the shop-window.

The only attempt to provide depth was by means of "Panther" turrets. About 24 [sic] of these had been let into the ground anything between a mile and two miles behind the main position. They were well-sited to cover roads, re-entrants, and any tanks crossing the sky-line. But they were not protected by infantry positions and would have been easy meat to an infantry attack by night. There were several turrets, together with their huge iron casemates, waiting to be let into concrete pits in the ground. It was interesting to find these and to realise in what great supply they must be.'

To the Chiefs of Staff of *AOK 10* and 76th Panzer Corps, the seriousness of 8th Army's intentions was demonstrated by the heavy bombing of Green I during 26th and 27th August. Kesselring was more sceptical as we have seen, although he did recommend on the evening of the 26th that von Vietinghoff be recalled from leave.[44] Before the Army Commander returned on the 28th, his Chief of Staff, Wentzell, had a hard time trying to convince Kesselring and Röttiger that unless 76th Panzer Corps was speedily reinforced it would be unable to withstand the major assault on Green I which Wentzell reckoned was imminent.[45] However, by the evening of the 27th Kesselring had agreed that 29th Panzer

Grenadier Division would be more speedily released for committal with 76th Panzer Corps if it were relieved by 334th Infantry Division from 51st Mountain Corps, instead of by 98th Infantry Division as first planned. 98th Infantry Division was, therefore, ordered to move down from the Rimini area to take over the sector of Green I earmarked for 71st Infantry Division. Wentzell also induced Kesselring to place 26th Panzer Division at the disposal of *AOK 10*, subject to the approval of Army Group before any part of it could be committed. Meanwhile Herr was authorised to pull back his divisions to the Red Line during the night of 27th/28th August, as was 51st Mountain Corps to facilitate the extraction of 334th Infantry Division.

For the Commander and Staffs of *AOK 10*, all previous uncertainties about events on the Adriatic wing were resolved by the capture on 28th August of Leese's pre-'Olive' Order of the Day to 8th Army. The distribution list on one of the documents captured with it gave away significant parts of the order of battle and the message itself showed Leese's intention to breach the Gothic Line as the first step in the destruction of the German forces in Italy. The Order of the Day was closely scrutinized to see if it gave any suggestion of a possible amphibious operation, but the absence of any clues was not taken as reliable evidence that the threat no longer existed. Without, it appears, explaining that the message emanated from the Commander of 8th Army, Kesselring informed *OKW* only of the captured distribution list and the indication that the Allies 'intended to break through on the Adriatic wing with strong forces'.[46] As we noted in Chapter XI, Jodl believed that the Allies were planning to land at the head of the Adriatic, and *OKW*'s diarist states that the release of reserves for such an eventuality was a determining factor when Hitler agreed that Army Group C could fall back to the Green Line. In his ratifying directive of 29th August, issued to *AOK 10* and *AOK 14*, Kesselring announced that the withdrawal would begin on the night of the 30th, with *AOK 14* first moving into the *Vorfeld* Line and there establishing contact with *AOK 10* in the Red Line.[47] The extraction of 334th Infantry Division from 51st Mountain Corps' front was to be accelerated, and Lemelsen was warned that, in view of the situation on *AOK 10*'s eastern wing, he might have to relinquish 29th Panzer Grenadier Division before *AOK 14* reached *Vorfeld*. These were the only references to the effects of 'Olive', and the Armies were instructed that on concluding their planned withdrawal into the Green Line they would there revert to 'conclusive defence'.

On the surface strategic planning for Army Group C was unruffled by the revelation of 8th Army's intentions; underneath, however, lay the fact that Kesselring had already authorised by the evening of 28th August the withdrawal of 71st Infantry and 1st Parachute Divisions across the Foglia into Green I.[48] His decision had been prompted by the heavy losses suffered by both divisions during the day, and was accompanied by Röttiger's promise of three A.A. batteries for 76th Panzer Corps to give its defences in Green I some measure of protection against air attack. von Vietinghoff was also authorised to commit two battalions and an artillery battery of 26th Panzer Division, and the first regimental group of 98th Infantry Division was to be sent forward as quickly as possible. A race began between *AOK 10* trying to man and settle into the defences of Green I and 8th Army crashing through before it could do so.

8th Army's initial advance went so well that anticipatory steps for breaching the Gothic Line were taken by Army and Corps H.Q. from 26th August onwards. As already described, each Corps had started its advance with about half its resources deployed.[49] All three Corps were planning to bring up their reserves before they reached the Foglia. 3rd Carpathian Division was brought up ready to pass through 5th Kresowa Division; 5th Canadian Armoured Division came into the line on the left of 1st Canadian Division during the night 28th/29th August; and the leading brigade of 56th Division, with 7th Armoured Brigade, was moving forward to come into the line between 46th Division and 4th Indian Division as the latter became more and more stretched covering 8th Army's western flank. The most important warning order went to 1st Armoured Division on 27th August, alerting Major-General Hull to be ready to move forward.[50] 8th Army also ordered 2nd New Zealand Division, with 3rd Greek Mountain Brigade under command, to complete its crossing of the Apennines and be assembled at Iesi ready for operations by 30th August.[51] 4th Division was left at Foligno for the time being.

Special measures were taken by 8th Army to ensure that the maximum concentration of artillery would be within range to saturate the defences of Green I, each Corps having an A.G.R.A. in support.[52] As it was anticipated that the Canadians would make the principal assault on Green I they were given 2nd New Zealand and 4th Divisions' artillery in support. 5th Corps stengthened its own artillery support by bringing forward the artillery of 56th and 1st Armoured Divisions ahead of their parent formations. And the Royal Navy provided a small inshore bombardment force of two destroyers and a gun-boat which was later augmented with another destroyer and a second gun-boat.

The most devastating fire support came from the Allied air forces which began a systematic bombardment of Green I on 8th

Army's front from 26th August until the attack was launched. Wentzell and Herr complained bitterly that many of the minefields forward of Green I had been 'simply lifted from the air' which meant hurried relaying, and that fortifications had been continuously 'plastered by bomb carpets'.[53] By dusk on 29th August approximately 1,600 tons of bombs had been dropped in direct support of 8th Army since dawn on the 26th, two-thirds of them by D.A.F., and one-third on three successive nights by the Strategic Air Force on 1st Parachute Division's defences in the Pesaro area.[54] From first light on 26th August onwards D.A.F. devoted its maximum effort in support of 8th Army by using the medium and light bombers principally to harass the enemy with fragmentation and small bombs, while the fighter-bombers attacked guns, troops, strongpoints and defended positions. Rover Paddy supported 5th Corps, and Rover David 1st Canadian and 2nd Polish Corps. Tactical and artillery reconnaissances were flown constantly, and on the 26th some Dixie sorties were flown against road movement. Though careful watch was kept on roads for enemy reinforcements, only scattered movements were seen.

See Maps 17 and 18

By the evening of the 29th it seemed to Leese that the enemy had either been taken by surprise and was not ready to man the Gothic Line, or that he had decided to withdraw altogether from Italy.[55] Thus encouraged he decided to keep to his plan and to try to 'gatecrash' the German line. There was no appreciable pause for reconnaissance. The three Corps pushed strong fighting patrols over the Foglia straight away and each division followed up with companies and then battalions wherever infiltration seemed possible. At midday 30th August Leese stopped the general air attacks on the German positions to allow greater tactical freedom of action to the assaulting divisions, which, thereafter, depended for direct air support on the Rovers controlling Cabranks over the battlefield.[56]

Burns directed his two Canadian divisions to seize a shallow bridgehead over the Foglia during the night 30th/31st August about a mile beyond the lateral road on the north bank, thus establishing themselves on the southern ends of the spurs running down from the twin peaks of Mt Peloso (Pt 253) and Mt Luro (Pt 289), which formed the watershed between the Foglia and Conca rivers and dominated the Canadian and Polish sectors.[57] On these prominent features were the small towns of Tomba di Pesaro and Monteluro. 1st Canadian Division attacked at 4 p.m. on the 30th and 5th Canadian Armoured Division an hour and a half later. At first all went well and by 6 p.m. Canadian Corps H.Q. was considering the possibility of taking Mt Luro that night and pushing on to the Conca without a pause. This optimism proved misplaced. With 26th Panzer Division coming into the line, 76th Panzer Corps began to fight back more effectively.[58] After a hard night's fighting, none the less, the Canadians had secured adequate footholds over the Foglia and could start a methodical destruction of their sector of Green I.

31st August was a highly successful day for 1st Canadian Corps. Using its great concentration of artillery to best effect, and its infantry and tank co-operation working well, both of its divisions made steady progress up the bare spurs leading to Tomba di Pesaro and Monteluro. By the end of the day they were within 1,200 yards of the watershed, with Green I successfully breached. A sizeable batch of prisoners had been taken from 71st Infantry, 1st Parachute and 26th Panzer Divisions. 67th Panzer Grenadier Regiment of 26th Panzer Division had been committed piecemeal in counter-attacks and had been driven back like the rest of the German troops opposing the Canadians on to the reverse slopes of the Tomba di Pesaro–Monteluro ridge.

The Poles, on the Canadians' right, were not yet due to open their offensive to bypass Pesaro, but 5th Corps had been almost as successful as the Canadians. Its problem was rather different because in its sector Green I depended upon the natural defensive strength of the hills overlooking the Foglia. There was no continuous line of fixed defences as such.[59] All major tactical features had been fortified, mined and wired with lay-back positions thought out, and sometimes dug, behind them. There were wide gaps between positions which could be covered by fire from a distance because, although steep in places, the hills were coverless rolling grasslands. Two main groups of these hill defences existed on 5th Corps' front.[60] In 46th Division's sector there was a complex generally referred to as Montegridolfo, upon which nestled the three villages of Montegridolfo, Mondaino and Saludecio about 1,200 feet above the Foglia's flood plain. These villages blocked the winding hill roads, leading generally northwards across the ridges to Morciano di Romagna on the River Conca, which were to form 46th Division's axis of advance. In 4th Indian's sector a long ridge ran north-westwards from the bend in the Foglia valley around Mt della Croce (Pt 320) through Montecalvo-in-Foglia to Tavoleto on the watershed some 1,400 ft above the Foglia. Once through Tavoleto the road ran down a continuation of the same ridge to Montefiore Conca and to the crossing over the River Conca south of Croce village, which was to gain sudden notoriety later in these battles. This ridge road was 4th Indian's axis of advance.

5th Indian Brigade was the first to cross the Foglia on 5th Corps' front. Led by 3rd/10th Baluchis in a silent approach march and crossing during the night 29th/30th August, it seized Mt della Croce, the stepping-stone to Montecalvo, with deceptive ease.[61] The Baluchis had to withstand several counter-attacks by 71st Infantry Division, but managed to hold their prize with the help of tanks of 6th Royal Tank Regiment, which reached them after daybreak, while the rest of the brigade wound its way across the river into positions from which Montecalvo could be attacked. In the early hours of 31st August a concentric attack was launched: 3rd/10th Baluchis attacking frontally from Mt della Croce and 4th/ 11th Sikhs from the south-east. 1st/9th Gurkhas, mounted in jeeps, tried to make a wide turning movement further east to get behind the German positions but were stopped accidentally by troops of 56th Division who had cut across their route. The attack had to be modified but after a hard day's fighting 5th Indian Brigade was in possession of Montecalvo. 4th Indian Division had breached its sector of Green I in two days.

46th Division was equally successful. It crossed the Foglia during the morning of 30th August and attacked Montegridolfo with two brigades up: 139th Brigade attacking up the two spurs which run up from the river to the high ground, and 128th Brigade trying to turn the position by advancing along the lower eastern slopes.[62] The infantry had difficulty in working their way forward against persistent shell, mortar and machine gun fire. Tanks sent over the river found themselves in difficulties in minefields. It was not until dusk that the two brigades were assembled ready to start fighting their way up the spurs in front of them. During the night 30th/ 31st August they secured a firm foothold on the first ridge above the river; and next day secured Montegridolfo, Mondaino and the highest peak of the ridge Pt. 374, halfway between the two villages, thanks to a brilliantly successful attack by 1st/4th Hampshires in which Lieutenant G. R. Norton won the V.C. for dealing with three German concreted weapon emplacements. 46th Division had also breached its sector of Green I in two days.[63]

At 3.25 p.m. on 31st August Colonel Runkel, the Chief of Staff 76th Panzer Corps, confirmed to *AOK 10* that his Corps 'no longer had the Green Line in its hand'. von Vietinghoff was then at the front, learning from Herr and his divisional commanders why this had happened with such dismaying speed.[64] The reasons listed by the Army Commander on his return included 8th Army's massive resources in artillery and tanks, and the destruction of minefields by Allied bombing. Preceding a reference to the reduced strength of 71st Infantry Division, the list was headed by the statement that 26th Panzer Division 'had not been familiar with its positions'. It had begun to move piecemeal into the line between 1st Parachute and 71st Infantry Divisions during the night 29th/30th August. There was no time for reconnaissance, and its commander, Crasemann, recollected after the war that his troops had 'just muddled their way into the line', where they found that air and artillery bombardment had already obliterated many of the positions they should have occupied. None the less, *AOK 10* could claim in its final report for 31st August that 26th Panzer Division had imposed temporary checks south of Tomba di Pesaro, and at Mondaino.

Reinforcements for 76th Panzer Corps now in the line included a battalion of Panther tanks, attached to 1st Parachute Division, and the leading regiment of 98th Infantry Division. To add to the troubles of *AOK 10*, the southwards move of this division had been delayed by chaos on the railways and by shortage of fuel for its transport by road. The gains made by 5th Corps on 31st August caused von Vietinghoff to scrap the plan for 98th Infantry Division to relieve 71st Infantry Division. Exhausted though the latter was, it remained in the line and 98th Infantry Division took over the right of its sector. Although *AOK 14* was instructed on 30th August to accelerate the release of 29th Panzer Grenadier Division regardless of the arrival of 334th Infantry Division, the motorized formation was not expected to reach Herr's front before 4th September.[65] Army Group, therefore, accepted Wentzell's proposal that the move of 100th Mountain Regiment to rejoin its parent 5th Mountain Division should be stopped at Forli, whence the regiment would return to 76th Panzer Corps. Another formation on the move by the night of 31st August was 20th *Luftwaffe* Field Division from *AOK 14*. Reflecting *OKW's* pre-occupations rather than those of *AOK 10*, this formation was initially required to transfer to the rear Adriatic coastal zone and there act as Army Group reserve.

In his own reports to *OKW*, Kesselring began on 31st August to refer to 8th Army's assault as a *Grossangriff* or major offensive.[66] When visiting *AOK 10* on 1st September he admitted that he had recognised too late that the Allies were forming a *Schwerpunkt* on the Adriatic wing. This confession, which would be fully justified by the fighting of the next three days, was borne out by Wentzell's comment to a member of *OB Südwest's* staff: 'Now we are approaching the point of no return, but as always 24 hours too late'.

To return to the Allied side, the last day of August was a successful one for D.A.F. which devoted almost its entire effort to direct air support for 8th Army.[67] Of the estimated 333 sorties flown by the bombers and fighter-bombers that day, some 229 were against targets west of Pesaro; nearly half were despatched by Rover David (with 1st Canadian and 2nd Polish Corps). *AOK 10's* War Diary for 31st August recorded that the left wing of

76th Panzer Corps had been subjected to 'particularly heavy' attacks from fighters and fighter-bombers.

At a conference at 8th Army Headquarters during the afternoon of 31st August Leese co-ordinated the actions of the Canadian and Polish Corps.[68] Burns was to secure the Tomba di Pesaro–Mt Luro ridge next day, with the Poles protecting his eastern flank by attacking almost due north along Mt Luro's eastern spurs. Burns gave 1st Canadian Division the task of taking Mt Luro (Pt 289) and exploiting to cut the Via Adriatica near Gradara, just south of Cattolica; he directed 5th Canadian Armoured Division to capture Tomba di Pesaro and exploit to the River Conca, seizing a bridgehead over the river.

1st and 2nd September were proud days for 1st Canadian Corps. In spite of fatigue in the dust laden atmosphere and stifling heat which enveloped the battlefield in the first days of September, morale was unquestionably high as every man sensed that he was writing an important page in Canadian history. The Canadian Official Historian quotes an apt contemporary description:

> 'In places the dust lies like powdered snow to a depth of 3 to 4 inches. It is impossible to see a moving tank. You are only aware of its presence by the turbulent cloud of dust which accompanies it . . .
>
> The most remarkable thing is that in all this filth, fatigue and bodily discomfort, the same old time-worn humour and perpetual good nature persist'.

1st Canadian Division's plan was to strike at Monteluro with a force designed for exploitation as well as for the initial break in. 21st Tank Brigade would lead the assault closely supported by 2nd Canadian Brigade. Mixed groups of British tanks and Canadian infantry were formed and the two brigade headquarters were located side by side from which either the armoured or infantry brigade commander could direct the battle depending upon which arm—tanks or infantry—was predominant at the time.* The assault could not be launched, however, until 5th Canadian Armoured Division had taken and cleared Mt Peloso (Pt. 253) and Tomba di Pesaro which dominated the approaches to Mt Luro from the south. 3rd Carpathian Division was to cross the Foglia and attack via S. Germano, exploiting towards the coast to cut off the retreat of 1st Parachute Division's garrison in Pesaro.[70]

5th Canadian Armoured Division's attack on 1st September did not start in the most propitious way. 11th Canadian Brigade was

---

* 21st Tank Brigade had trained and fought with 1st Canadian Division throughout the Italian campaign and they knew each other very well.[69] They had exercised together using live ammunition and artillery supporting fire just before 'Olive'. They were thus able to 'marry-up' quickly and effectively for the attack on Mt Luro.

to lead, using as infantry for the first time 4th Princess Louise Dragoon Guards, from 12th Canadian Brigade, supported by Lord Strathcona's Horse.[71]* The Princess Louise took some time to come forward as they were scattered in the traffic congestion behind the front. When they reached the forward area they ran into heavy and prolonged German harassing fire. It took most of the morning to reassemble and make the final artillery and tank co-operation arrangements. They attacked Mt Peloso eventually at 1 p.m. and caught the paratroopers of 4th Parachute Regiment out of their trenches, apparently assembling for counter-attack. The Strathcona's tanks inflicted heavy losses on the German troops whom they found crouching behind what little cover was available; bulldozers had to be used to bury the many dead. The Princess Louise also suffered heavily, reaching the last rise 200 yards from the summit with only 40 men for the final rush which was over heavily ploughed land. Fortunately the Germans had had enough and were falling back. The watershed between the Foglia and the Conca was in Canadian hands. In the early evening 11th Canadian Brigade cleared the almost empty ruins of Tomba di Pesaro.

21st Tank Brigade and 2nd Canadian Brigade launched their assault at 6 p.m. on Monteluro, which had been softened by heavy air and artillery bombardments all afternoon. The New Zealand divisional artillery played a prominent part in the fire plan. When the leading troops reached the summit they found the intricate and deep system of trenches, M.G. posts and anti-tank gun positions abandoned. As the tank/infantry groups were already married up the pursuit started in the failing light, and, inspite of some confusion during the night, a useful break through was achieved. By the following evening, 2nd September, 1st Canadian Corps was up to the line of the River Conca and the Poles had entered Pesaro, which had been abandoned by 1st Parachute Division in a hasty withdrawal back to Cattolica. By dawn on 3rd September 1st Canadian Division had established a bridgehead over the Conca due north of S. Giovanni.

It is difficult to trace what happened on the German side to cause this sudden collapse. Heidrich, 1st Parachute Division's experienced commander, had not rejoined his division.[72] There had been difficulty in tracing him and when he was found in Dresden he did not return with any alacrity. Colonel Schulz, his deputy and commander of 1st Parachute Regiment, was also handicapped by the absence of the commander of 3rd Parachute Regiment who was hurt in a car accident, returning from leave

---

* 4th Princess Louise Dragoon Guards had been converted to infantry from armoured cars to form the new 12th Canadian Brigade which was to give 5th Canadian Armoured Division a second infantry brigade.

with Heidrich on 4th September. With or without Heidrich 1st
Parachute Division was notoriously slow in reporting to higher
formations, so for much of 1st September *AOK 10* had no clear
picture of developments in this sector. That evening it informed
OB Südwest of heavy and costly fighting near Tomba di Pesaro. At
3 a.m. on 2nd September Kesselring authorised a withdrawal for
76th Panzer Corps which took Herr's eastern wing back to the
Conca, but it seems that Schulz had anticipated this order by some
hours.[73] At 10 a.m. on the 2nd Herr reported to von Vietinghoff
by telephone that Allied armour had already reached Gradara. He
attributed the collapse of the coastal sector to lack of co-ordination
within 1st Parachute Division. Assuming that 4th Parachute Regiment was still firm on Mt Luro, 3rd Parachute Regiment had
apparently 'marched off' during the night, leaving a wide gap into
which 21st Tank Brigade had plunged. The situation of 1st Parachute Regiment on the coast was not then clear, and Herr feared
it might be cut off before it and the other parachute units could
re-establish contact with each other and with 26th Panzer Division.
It was not until 6.30 p.m. on the 2nd that Schulz managed to
report fierce fighting for Gradara. One battalion of 1st Parachute
Regiment had indeed been encircled and had been ordered to fight
its way out. 76th Panzer Corps' evening report completed the
picture. Thanks to the 'sacrificial' defence of the Gradara-S.
Giovanni area by 26th Panzer Division, 3rd and 4th Parachute
Regiments had made good their retreat and had re-established
contact with 26th Panzer Division. 1st Parachute Regiment had
escaped with the loss of the headquarters and one company of the
surrounded battalion. Several of the Parachute Division's anti-
tank guns had been abandoned, together with the 8.8-cms of its
attached Flak battery, but most of its field artillery and mortars
were safely back over the Conca. The worst losses had been
suffered by 4th Parachute Regiment opposing the Canadians on
Mt Luro.

While *AOK 10* awaited news from 1st Parachute Division on 1st
September, its senior officers had speculated anxiously about 5th
Corps' operations against Montegridolfo and Tavoleto. Here 290th
Grenadier Regiment of 98th Infantry Division, fighting alongside
71st Infantry Division, was reported to be standing up well to its
first engagement, but Wentzell wanted this sector reinforced.[74] He
argued that as the British usually made sure of the high ground
before going for the plains, they would secure the Montegridolfo-
Morciano di Romagna-S. Clemente axis before turning their attention to the coast. Kesselring's Chief of Staff, Röttiger, insisted that
Herr must also watch his coastal wing, and that a rallying line
should be established running inland from Cattolica. Kesselring

seems to have favoured Wentzell's view, for, when he authorised withdrawal for 76th Panzer Corps early on 2nd September, he stressed that the range immediately west of Mt Maggiore must be strongly held and defended. In and forward of a line running from the Foglia, below Auditore, along this range to Morciano and thence to the coast near Cattolica, Herr was to offer stubborn resistance in order to block 8th Army's advance and thus to gain time for the consolidation of Green II. In this part of *AOK 10's* sector Green II ran from the outskirts of Riccione on the coast to S. Clemente north of the Conca and then swung south over the river to Morciano di Romagna and Montefiore Conca, thence along the foot of the prominent Gemmano ridge.

See Map 18

The successful capture of Mondaino and Montegridolfo encouraged Keightley to widen the base of his offensive.[75] On 1st September 46th Division brought up 138th Brigade, which had been in reserve so far, and committed it with the support of 142nd Royal Tank and 46th Reconnaissance Regiments to an advance in the lower ground east of Montegridolfo on the inter-Corps boundary with the Canadians. 128th and 139th Brigades were to clear the rest of the Montegridolfo-Mondaino feature, which they had taken the day before, and continue their advance northwards along the high ground. And the leading brigade of 56th Division, 169th Brigade, was to take over the left sector of 46th Division west of Mondaino.* 7th Armoured Brigade would follow.

Progress was slow everywhere on 1st September because the Germans had not abandoned hope of holding at least the rear positions of Green I. 138th Brigade's advance was delayed by inadequate tank crossings over the Foglia and did not start until midday. 128th Brigade on Montegridolfo had to fend off counter-attacks and 139th Brigade had to clear German troops who had infiltrated back into Mondaino. Heavy and sustained fighting took

---

* *Outline Order of Battle of 56th Division* (Major-General J. Y. Whitfield).[76]

167th Infantry Brigade
8th and 9th Royal Fusiliers, 7th Oxfordshire and Buckinghamshire Light Infantry.
168th Infantry Brigade
1st Welch Regiment, 1st London Scottish, 1st London Irish Rifles.
169th Infantry Brigade
2nd/5th, 2nd/6th, 2nd/7th Queen's Royal Regiment.
R.A.C. 44th Reconnaissance Regiment.
R.A. 64th, 65th, 113th Field Regiments; 67th A/Tk Regiment; 100th L.A.A. Regiment.
R.E. 220th, 221st, 501st Field Companies; 563rd Field Park Company.
M.G. 6th Cheshire Regiment.

Additional Troops
7th Armoured Brigade
7th Hussars, 2nd and 8th R.T.R. (7th Hussars came under command 3rd September to replace 6th R.T.R. operating under 4th Indian Division).

place all day as 139th Brigade struggled to wrest control of the
triangle of roads just north of Mondaino, where 71st Infantry
Division tried to block any further advance towards Saludecio and
Montefiore Conca. 56th Division's 169th Brigade, on the other
hand, had a successful day and drew level with 139th Brigade. In
4th Indian Division's section 5th Indian Brigade was relieved by
11th Indian Brigade in front of Tavoleto, and 7th Indian Brigade,
at last, managed to close up to the Foglia opposite Auditore on
the north bank.

In the air, 1st September was the occasion for a general 'blitz'
on the German defences just ahead of the advancing troops, and
this accounted for an estimated 494 bomber and fighter-bomber
sorties flown by D.A.F. in support of 8th Army, during which
about 335 tons of bombs were dropped.[77] Rover Paddy supporting
5th Corps launched Cabranks on 16 targets, and the fighter-
bombers also answered a request from 1st Canadian Corps to attack
an enemy headquarters seven miles west of Pesaro. Ninety of
D.A.F.'s Marauders and 92 of its Baltimores bombed guns and
defended positions west of Pesaro. It was a highly successful day
in Army/Air co-operation. Inspite of the increasing opposition
experienced by 5th Corps during 1st September, Canadian successes
created the impression that a break through was imminent.[78]
Keightley issued a 5th Corps Operation Order on 2nd September
which started by saying:

> 'The enemy have been badly mauled by 1 CANADIAN CORPS
> and it is appreciated that there is a possibility of a break through
> on that front during 2 September'.

His intention was to be prepared to exploit a break through on
the Corps' right flank. He gave each of his divisions a centre line:

> 1st Armoured Division: S. Maria de Monte—S. Andrea (on the
>   Conca)—Coriano.
> 46th Division: Montegridolfo—Morciano.
> 56th Division: Mondaino—Montefiore Conca—north-west to
>   Montecolombo.
> 4th Indian Division: Tavoleto—north-west to Montescudo.

46th Division was to secure a crossing for 1st Armoured Division
over the Conca and to cover it by seizing the S. Clemente ridge.
1st Armoured Division would pass through its right flank and lead
the Corps pursuit on the right, not starting before 4 a.m. 3rd
September. 56th Division was similarly to pass through the left of
46th Division and lead the Corps pursuit on the left. 46th Division
would come into Corps Reserve after its ten days hard fighting.

Events during 2nd September suggested that the chances of a
break through were indeed bright. 138th Brigade of 46th Division

found less opposition in its advance through the lower ground east of Montegridolfo.[79] By early afternoon 46th Reconnaissance Regiment was on the Ventena stream (a tributory of the Conca) one mile south of Morciano, in contact with the Canadians. The advance continued through the night and by dawn 3rd September 6th York and Lancasters were on the Conca north-east of Morciano, where the Conca bridge was being covered by artillery fire to prevent its demolition. In the afternoon 6th York and Lancasters, now under 128th Brigade, which had taken command of the right sector, crossed the Conca, followed by 2nd Hampshires, and by dusk they had established a bridgehead on the spurs leading up to S. Clemente. Meanwhile 2nd/4th K.O.Y.L.I. of 138th Brigade fought its way into Morciano and captured the bridge intact at about 10 p.m. Opposition on Montegridolfo had by now collapsed, enabling the rest of 46th Division to advance rapidly to Morciano. Two battalions of 128th Brigade were brought forward in troop carriers. Nevertheless, the troops were beginning to feel the strain of the long advance with very short breaks followed by the recent stiff fighting; but believing that the Germans were giving up the line of the Conca 46th Division's Commander, General Hawkesworth, called upon 128th Brigade for one more effort before the division was relieved by 1st Armoured Division the following day.[80] They were to press on to seize the bridge over the Marano at Ospedaletto (*Maps 18 and 19.*)

During the night 3rd/4th September 6th York and Lancasters secured S. Clemente and 128th Brigade passed through, heading up the ridge towards Coriano.[81] By dawn on the 4th, 46th Reconnaissance Regiment was at Castellealc half way along the ridge and 1st/4th Hampshires, working up a parallel ridge to the east, was level with them. Increasingly heavy artillery fire stopped any further progress by 128th and 138th Brigades, but 139th Brigade crossed the Conca west of Morciano and took the ridge overlooking the river without much difficulty. Turning west along it the brigade ran into strong opposition in front of the hill-top village and road centre of Croce. This was the situation when the leading tanks of 1st Armoured Division crossed the Conca, heading for Coriano.

Before looking at 1st Armoured Division's actions to exploit on 5th Corps' right we must go back to look at 56th and 4th Indian Divisions' operations designed to bring 56th Division through for exploitation on 5th Corps' left.

See Map 18

169th Brigade of 56th Division could make little progress on the ridge running between Mondaino and Tavoleto during 2nd

September, but that night 76th Panzer Corps pulled back to the Mt Maggiore ridge.[82] General Whitfield, commander of 56th Division, now decided the time had come to advance on a two brigade front in order to exploit the 'break through . . . occurring' on the Army's right flank[83] He planned to pass 167th Brigade through on the right, directed upon Montefiore Conca and then onto the eastern end of the Gemmano ridge overlooking the Conca from the south, while 168th Brigade would advance through difficult country to seize the western half of the Gemmano ridge. 169th Brigade would come into divisional reserve. The Division was directed to seize crossings over the River Conca as quickly as possible at Montecolombo (*Map* 19). It should be observed, however, that two formidable obstacles blocked its approach to the river and its intended crossing place: the Mt Maggiore–Montefiore Conca feature which was 1,100 feet high, and the Gemmano ridge of 1,200 feet.

Whitfield's plan could not be put into operation until 4th Indian Division had taken Tavoleto, which dominated 168th Brigade's Start Line and axis of advance.[84] For this, however, 11th Indian Brigade had to take over from 5th Indian Brigade, which was tired after eight days of marching and fighting, so it was decided to delay 168th Brigade's attack on Mt Maggiore. 167th and 11th Indian Brigade's attacks were successful when launched during the night 3rd/4th September. 289th Grenadier Regiment of 98th Infantry Division was driven off Mt Maggiore with heavy loss by 167th Brigade and 71st Infantry Division lost Tavoleto to the Indians. 7th Indian Brigade also successfully crossed the Foglia at Auditore and, after taking the strongly fortified village, came up alongside 11th Indian Brigade west of Tavoleto. Both Indian Brigades now faced the formidable Pian di Castello ridge which blocked their advance as obviously as Gemmano stood between 56th Division and the Conca crossing at Montecolombo. However, as we shall see, expectations of success continued high and on the evening of 4th September General Whitfield decided to bypass Gemmano and to advance through 46th Division's bridgehead just east of Croce, so preparing the way for exploitation on 5th Corps' left flank with an advance over cross-country routes to the Marano.[85]

On 2nd September the Desert Air Force gave 8th Army direct air support on a heavy scale even if the estimated total of 407 sorties fell short of the previous day's effort.[86] Considerable movement of enemy M.T. and guns north-westward across the Conca was reported by air reconnaissance. To deal with it, Dixie operations against enemy movement on 5th Corps front were laid on early in the morning and then on 1st Canadian Corps front an hour before noon. Rover Paddy was in continuous operation all day in support of 5th Corps. What had become a rare event was the appearance of enemy fighters in the forward area, four Me. 109s attacking a Kittyhawk at 5 p.m. and two other fighters damaging a Spitfire an hour later west of Pesaro.

Next day, 3rd September, thunderstorms grounded D.A.F.'s fighter-bombers in the morning and the medium and light bombers all day. However, the discovery of about 200 M.T. of all types, some towing guns, just north of the Marano enticed special fighter-bomber missions to deal with them. Rover Paddy also operated to help 5th Corps, and air attacks were made on a defended area south of Rimini to meet a request from 1st Canadian Corps. Early that morning enemy fighters appeared again in the forward area and two paid for their efforts by falling to the guns of No. 145 Squadron. That same night No. 600 Squadron's Beaufighters shot down four Ju. 87s in the Ancona-Rimini area.

On 4th September both of 5th Corps' pursuit divisions were poised to take advantage of a German collapse on the Conca as Keightley had planned in his Operation Order of 2nd September. Two extracts of the 8th Army daily Intelligence Summaries point to the general attitude prevailing at the time:[87]

> *'1900 hours 2 Sep '44*
> . . . There is now no question of further riverline withdrawals with short delaying actions of the type the enemy has so far done on the Adriatic coast. In a fluid battle in more open country that must ensue after our bridgehead over the Conca, he will undoubtedly use his armour more, but firm infantry resistance, even from parachutists, is becoming more and more difficult . . . The latest photographs have shown nothing prepared on any of the river lines between us and the Po valley, at least this side of the Savio river . . .'

> *'1900 hours 3 Sep '44*
> Still there is no sign of further major reinforcements, a violent contrast with the Cassino days when every battalion that could be spared was hunted up . . .
> The immediate future holds out good hopes. We have the initiative over his armoured rear-guards tonight and it seems likely that tomorrow may find the most forward enemy behind the Marano . . .'

Within 24 hours a new German defensive line was detected on air photographs running inland from Rimini towards the Republic of San Marino.[88] Reconnaissance aircraft also spotted large scale movement northwards from Coriano which seemed to suggest that 26th Panzer Division was pulling back to this new line. 5th Corps Intelligence Staff commented, 4th September, 'we may confidently expect to gain a bridgehead across the Marano by tonight'.

See Map 17

The German defensive preparations on what was to become known as the 'Rimini Line' were thus detected in ample time. 8th Army, however, was still unaware of the existence of Green II upon which 76th Panzer Corps had been ordered to stand. This was probably because Green II was little more than a reconnoitred line on German staff maps, there not having been the time or resources to give it actual defence works before 'Olive' opened. Its strength, none the less, lay, not in fortifications, but in the well selected natural features and in the fact that it was being manned by fresh German divisions which had not been reduced in the fighting for Green I. Moreover, north of Morciano, Green II lay some distance west of the Conca river and so the Canadians and 46th Division had been able to cross with deceptive ease.

There are several instances in German military history of a Chief of Staff grasping the reins on behalf of, and on some occasions inspite of his commander at the critical moment of a great battle. On 3rd September Major-General Wentzell, Chief of Staff *AOK 10*, acted in this way with the full support of von Vietinghoff and the praise of Kesselring.[89] He set off on a tour of the front to sort order out of chaos and to re-establish communication with 76th Panzer Corps and its divisions which had become more and more tenuous due to Allied air action. During his tour he took two crucial decisions which were to check 8th Army's sweeping advances and turn the battle into a costly struggle of attrition. The results of his tour are set out in the report he made to Röttiger, Kesselring's Chief of Staff, over the telephone when he got back to H.Q. and *AOK 10* that night.

The first of his two decisions was his confirmation that 100th Mountain Regiment should come into the line of the Gemmano feature in rear of Green II which, unbeknown to him, 56th Division was to attempt to bypass. He had nothing but praise for Reinhardt's leadership of 98th Infantry Division and the excellence of his battalion commanders who were fighting their first major battle. He also confirmed that 71st Infantry Division would stay in the line until the mountain regiment was in position. Reinhardt would then take over on the right of 26th Panzer Division, with 100th Mountain Regiment under his command and with one regiment of 98th Infantry Division acting as a reserve for 26th Panzer Division.

Wentzell was far less complimentary about 26th Panzer and 1st Parachute Divisions when he toured their fronts in the afternoon, visiting S. Clemente and Mt Gallera (Pt 143), the former being in Green II and the latter in its rear. The Canadian operations over the Conca were only just starting so he did not witness the hard fighting which occurred that evening when 5th Canadian Armoured Division pushed 1st Parachute Division out of Misano in Green II and approached Mt Gallera; and 1st Canadian Division also followed the retreating 1st Parachute Division up to the Green II line in the southern outskirts of Riccione. Wentzell's general impression was that Crasemann, commanding 26th Panzer Division, 'lacked the energy which would make men stand firm'; and that 1st Parachute Division was 'disconcertingly adrift without Heidrich', who did not rejoin his division until the next day. Sensing that the critical sector lay at the junction of these two ill led divisions, Wentzell took his second well judged decision: to commit the leading regiment of 29th Panzer Grenadier Division, 71st Panzer Grenadier Regiment, to the defence of the Coriano ridge in depth behind Green II. Mindful of the over-hasty deployment of 26th Panzer Division in Green I von Vietinghoff had agreed with General Polack, commanding 29th Panzer Grenadier Division, that his troops should be properly deployed and not rushed into unreconnoitred positions. Wentzell's choice of the Coriano ridge fulfilled this condition. 71st Panzer Grenadier Regiment had ample time to settle into its blocking position with 8 tanks and 4 Pak 7.5-cm which had accompanied it from *AOK 14*. Wentzell, moreover, decided that in view of the currently 'unsure' nature of the leadership of 1st Parachute and 26th Panzer Divisions Polack must himself take command of 71st Panzer Grenadier Regiment. This would help to bring things under control, and as an experienced gunner Polack could also supervise the artillery concentration which Wentzell ordered there and then to form for the defence of the Coriano sector.

On his way back to H.Q. *AOK 10* Wentzell called at that of 76th Panzer Corps, making himself 'unloved all round' (his own words) by demanding that Herr abandon all thoughts of further withdrawal and hold the Allies at bay until 29th Panzer Grenadier Division was fully installed.[90] He also gained Ritter von Pohl's assurance of maximum anti-aircraft support in this 'decisive battle for Italy'. Both Kesselring and von Vietinghoff endorsed Wentzell's arrangements, and Röttiger placed 29th Panzer Grenadier Division at the full disposal of *AOK 10*, with none of the qualifications which had so hampered the first committal of 26th Panzer Division. The two key features in the German defence—Gemmano and Coriano— were in trustworthy hands. Kesselring felt sufficiently reassured to spend most of 4th September visiting *AOK 14*.

With all his divisions now installed in the *Vorfeld* line of Green I, Lemelsen had nothing alarming to report, but when Kesselring learnt on his return of further ground lost by 76th Panzer Corps he raged at von Vietinghoff on the telephone.[91] Herr was severely criticised for failing to make better use of his artillery, and for the performance of 26th Panzer Division which was described as 'miserable'. The replacement of Herr and Craseman was mooted but not pursued, because von Vietinghoff stood by his subordinates. The higher officers of *AOK 10* were used to Kesselring's outbursts, and went ahead with their primary task of scraping up reserves. Feuerstein was warned that 51st Mountain Corps might have to give up 44th Infantry Division. Von Vietinghoff also told Herr late on 4th September that he could reconnoitre a new main line which was to run from the coast south of Rimini along the general course of the Ausa river.* Italian and German construction battalions were allotted to 76th Panzer Corps for its development, and by 8th September it was reckoned that 10,000 Italian labourers could be rounded up for work. On the 4th, when Army Group agreed that the port of Rimini could be prepared for demolition, the German Naval Staff War Diary recorded that Kesselring had decided to remove 90th Panzer Grenadier Division from the French frontier, so that it would be available to check any break through towards the Po.

At High Command level, as we note later, the pros and cons of Operational *Herbstnebel* were now being weighed in their strategic and economic context. In the field, 76th Panzer Corps was able by and large to hold its positions on 5th September, and although the course of Green II had been bent in places, it seemed to the staff of *AOK 10* that the front was showing encouraging signs of stability. In a better humour, Kesselring agreed that the sectors of Green I not under threat could be combed out for reinforcements. He would not however sanction the release of 44th Infantry Division, and instead ordered *AOK 14* to send 356th Infantry Division from 1st Parachute Corps' sector above Florence to reinforce the coastal wing of *AOK 10*. Its move was given priority over that of 20th Luftwaffe Field Division, which on approaching Forli had been assigned to Corps Witthöft for defence of the Cesena-Ravenna sector. *AOK 10* was instructed on 6th September to use 356th Infantry Division for the release of the remnants of 71st Infantry Division, which would refit in the northern Adriatic sector, and for that of 100th Mountain Regiment which Kesselring wanted to reunite with 5th Mountain Division on the French frontier, where French Moroccan troops had been identified. *AOK 14* was warned that it might also have to surrender 16th SS Panzer Grenadier Division. In the event Lemelsen won his fight to retain this formation, but by 10th September he had lost two battalions of Tiger tanks to *AOK 10*, plus a battery of *Nebelwerfer*

---

* There is a discrepancy between British and German records here: compare 5th Corps Intelligence Summary, issued early 4th September p. 253.[92]

and one of new 8.8-cm Pak 43 (anti-tank guns).[93]* The progressive reinforcement of *AOK 10's* front at the expense of *AOK 14's* resources in weapons, as well as in manpower, was weakening the latter's ability to withstand 5th Army, which was exactly what Alexander had hoped would happen.

While these German troop moves were taking place 1st Armoured Division began its move forward. On 30th and 31st August it had received executive orders to concentrate south of the Ceseno between Senigallia and Castelleone (*Map 9*) by 3rd September[95]†

Its approach march, which began on 31st August, was marred by unrealistic staff estimates. In spite of 8th Army's enjoyment of almost total freedom from German air reconnaissance, the tanks of 2nd Armoured Brigade were moved during darkness on three successive nights, including the final approach over the Conca.[97] Thus on the night 1st/2nd September the tanks reached the north bank of the Ceseno on their transporters at 3 a.m. They were unloaded there and set off on their tracks at 2 p.m. for the Foglia, which they reached between 8 a.m. and 2 p.m. next day (3rd September), having driven all through the night over little more than a bulldozed mountain track with sharp bends and steep gradients. These caused frequent frustrating halts and almost continuous driving in low gear. 2nd Armoured Brigade's historians comment that the route would have been bad enough in daylight, but at night in choking dust it put too heavy a strain on both drivers and tanks, many of which broke down.‡

See Map 17 and 19

The final advance over the Conca started at 1.30 a.m. on 4th September and was carried out under equally difficult conditions,

---

* The 8.8-cm Pak 43 was described by MI 10 as an 'exceptionally good weapon' with low silhouette and efficient traverse. German authorities quote the same performance as for the Hornet/Rhinoceros S.P. gun and the 8.8-cm Kwk 43 in the Tiger tank: firing A.P.C.B.C. shell they could penetrate about 136-mm of armour at 2,000 yards.[94]

† *Outline Order of Battle of 1st Armoured Division*[96] (Major-General R. A. Hull)
  2nd Armoured Brigade
  The Queens Bays, 9th Lancers, 10th Hussars.
  Infantry: 1st King's Royal Rifle Corps.
  18th Infantry Brigade
  1st Buffs, 9th King's Own Yorkshire Light Infantry, 14th Sherwood Foresters.
  Reconnaissance: 4th Hussars.
  R.H.A.: 2nd Regiment; 11th (H.A.C.) Regiment (S.P.)
  R.A.: 23rd Field Regiment; 60th A/Tk Regiment; 42nd L.A.A. Regiment.
  R.E.: 1st, 622nd, 627th Field Squadrons; 631st Field Park Squadron; 27th Bridging Troop.
  Additional troops
  43rd Gurkha Lorried Infantry Brigade
  2nd/6th, 2nd/8th, 2nd/10th Gurkha Rifles.

‡ 2nd Armoured Brigade tank state between 31st August and 3rd September shows the loss of 22 Sherman tanks on the approach march.[98] Many more fell out at the time but were repaired by regimental Light Aid Detachments and Brigade Recovery Teams.

including traffic congestion, as the brigade made its way through the rear echelons of 46th Division. Movement was extremely slow and it was an hour after dawn before elements of the brigade's covering force, consisting of 1st K.R.R.C. supported by 10th Hussars and 11th (H.A.C.) R.H.A., began to cross the Conca. By 10.30 am the divisional reconnaissance regiment, 4th Hussars, had contacted 46th Division around S. Clemente and sent forward patrols to Castelleale, where they reported coming under considerable fire. At about the same time the 1st K.R.R.C./10th Hussars group reached the S. Clemente ridge and also found that any attempt to advance further was met by heavy fire from the parallel S. Savino-Coriano ridge two thousand yards away to the west.

At the divisional orders group at 8 p.m. on 3rd September Brigadier R. W. Goodbody, commanding 2nd Armoured Brigade, had been told that his task was to lead the division over the Conca and to cover its deployment on the north bank prior to passing through 46th Division. He was aware that he might meet opposition north of S. Clemente but it was hoped that 46th Division would be up to the River Marano by the time his brigade crossed the Conca. He planned to establish a firm base in the S. Savino area preparatory to passing through 46th Division if and when it had seized crossings over the Marano. The only infantry he would have with him were his motor battalion, 1st K.R.R.C.[99] 18th Brigade and 43rd Gurkha Lorried Infantry Brigade were a long way back in the divisional order of march.

The check to 4th Hussars and the 1st K.R.R.C./10th Hussars group on the S. Clemente ridge showed that 46th Division was certainly not on its way to the Marano. 1st Armoured Division would have to fight its own way forward. Brigadier Goodbody was then faced with an entirely new situation for which a plan had to be made on inadequate and, as events showed, inaccurate information. He issued new orders at midday with the intention of passing through 46th Division's forward posts and advancing well south of Coriano to the high ground just east of Marano from which he would seize crossings over the river. The brigade was to advance two up, with 10th Hussars right and the Bays left, each with a company of 1st K.R.R.C. 9th Lancers and the rest of 1st K.R.R.C. were held in reserve to exploit, once crossings over the Marano had been seized. The Start Line was to run along the ridge road running south-west from S. Clemente. Unfortunately there were no more infantry immediately available to support the tanks so no change could be made in the composition of the attacking force.

The attack started at 3.45 p.m., five hours after 2nd Armoured Brigade had reached 46th Division's forward posts.[100] 10th Hussars on the right advanced towards Coriano and were greeted with very heavy anti-tank and artillery fire. The Bays suffered a worse experience as they advanced towards S. Savino. They were met by high velocity fire from the ridge in front of them and were shelled from their left rear by German artillery, whose Observation Posts on Gemmano overlooked their axis of advance. In the ensuing fight, which lasted until dark, both regiments manoeuvred uncertainly as they tried to work their way down the forward slopes of the S. Clemente ridge before they could start climbing the Coriano ridge. Not only was the sun in the eyes of their tank crews, but three nights without proper rest was telling on the drivers. A number of tanks were accidentally bogged, some over-turned and many shed tracks in the very difficult going which was steep and loose. The prospect of gaining a decisive success faded with daylight and both regiments were ordered to pull back behind the S. Clemente ridge for the night, having achieved nothing except to confirm the strength of the German opposition on the Coriano ridge, not yet identified as Polack's 29th Panzer Grenadier Division.

10th Hussars and the Bays still had 49 Sherman tanks left between them at the end of the day, and 9th Lancers, who had not been engaged, could muster 32.[101]* The brigade's losses, in fact, were not unduly high because many were due to mechanical faults caused initially by the long approach march, without pause for maintenance, and exacerbated by difficult going in the battle area. These tanks could be recovered. A much more serious deficiency was the absence of infantry to take over from the tanks after dark and to continue the battle next day. 1st K.R.R.C. had been in action with the tanks all day, and only 1st Buffs, leading 18th Brigade, were near enough to give any help.[102] 2nd Armoured Brigade, therefore, spent another tiring night leaguered just behind the S. Clemente ridge. Only a thin screen of K.R.R.C. and 1st Buffs was on the ridge to hold the gap between S. Clemente and 139th Brigade on the Cevolabbate ridge, overlooking the Conca, where 56th Division was beginning to develop its operations to take Croce.

The check at Coriano on 4th September did not deter 5th Corps from pressing on with its plan to break through to the Marano

---

* The Sherman tank states of 2nd Armoured Brigade for the evenings of 3rd and 4th September were:

	3rd September	*4th September*
The Bays	45	19
9th Lancers	47	32
10th Hussars	44	30
H.Q. Squadron	5	5
	141	86

with an essentially armoured attack.[103] 1st Armoured Division directed 2nd Armoured Brigade to seize the S. Savino-Coriano ridge first thing the next morning, and to exploit to the Marano at Vecciano. At the same time 56th Division was to thrust through Croce to the river on the left.

2nd Armoured Brigade's plan was based upon the assumption that the S. Savino end of the Coriano ridge was lightly held.[104] 9th Lancers were to lead with a company of 1st K.R.R.C. advancing from Cevolabbate, north-west to S. Savino. The advance started at 7 a.m. and by about 9 a.m. a patrol of 9th Lancers managed to enter S. Savino. The leading squadron was engaged in the cemetery 400 yards south of the village. A second squadron fought its way to the cemetery by 1.30 p.m., and both squadrons found themselves closely engaged by German troops armed with *Faustpatronen** and by snipers. With insufficient infantry on hand to clear the area the advance was checked until, after repeated requests for infantry, 1st Buffs were sent forward in the late afternoon. The Lancers then overran the cemetery killing 60 of the defenders and capturing another 60. That night 18th Brigade took over the S. Savino sector from 2nd Armoured Brigade and attacked the village itself with only partial success. 14th Foresters captured the commander, headquarters and 46 of 98th Infantry Division's reconnaissance battalion, but as the night wore on the Germans won back most of the village and forced the Foresters to retire again to the cemetery, where the brigade consolidated its positions before dawn.

56th Division had meanwhile brought 167th and 168th Brigades over the Conca during 5th September preparatory to an attack that night to secure a Start Line for 7th Armoured Brigade between S. Savino and Croce.[105] Each brigade was to use only two battalions so that their third battalions could join 7th Armoured Brigade. Like 2nd Armoured Brigade, it was to exploit to the Marano which seemed so near and yet was to prove to be so far away.

Orders issued for 56th Division's first battle for Croce stress the continuing feeling amongst higher commanders that 76th Panzer Corps was beaten and on its way back to the next major river line, if not the Po. Regimental historians, however, emphasise that officers and men at battalion level had no such illusions, and on the night 5th/6th September were confirmed in their view that the Germans were far from beaten.[106] The attack on Croce led to violent and confused fighting in which losses on both sides were heavy and Croce changed hands several times.[107] When dawn

---

* Anti-tank grenade launchers.

came German artillery began to demonstrate the significance of
Gemmano which overlooked the battlefield from only two thousand
yards to the south. General Whitfield had been conscious that this
might happen, but, if the Germans had been falling back as
expected, their interference with his advance would not have lasted
long.[108] The intensity and accuracy of the fire forced him to change
plan and seek ways of dealing with Gemmano.

Whitfield's first step was to break up 7th Armoured Brigade's
exploitation groups. Most of its tanks were moved to the Croce-S.
Savino line to help the infantry repel a succession of determined
German counter-attacks which came in during 6th September.[109]
7th Oxford and Buckinghamshire Light Infantry were sent with a
squadron of 8th Royal Tanks to help 44th Reconnaissance Regiment clear Gemmano. By evening they seemed to have had some
success. The village of Gemmano was occupied and the battalion,
though under attack, felt 'confident'. The same evening 167th
Brigade reported Croce secure with 168th Brigade equally secure
on its right.

The Canadian Corps also had only limited success in exploiting
the failure of the Germans to hold the Conca. 5th Canadian
Armoured Division had swung northwards towards Besanigo, on
the ridge running parallel to the Coriano ridge only about
1,000 yards to the east.[110] Besanigo was taken on 5th September,
but no further progress was possible until the Germans could be
driven off the Coriano ridge. 1st Canadian Division, on the coast,
was held up just south of Riccione by 1st Parachute Division,
which had been reinforced by a blocking group provided by 162nd
(Turkoman) Infantry Division from Corps Witthöft.[111] Losses,
which so far had been reasonable for the great achievement
of breaching Green I, were now beginning to mount without
compensating successes. 1st Canadian Brigade alone lost more than
300 men in the four days between crossing the Conca and reaching
the outskirts of Riccione.

German losses were also high. When touring 76th Panzer Corps'
front on 7th September von Vietinghoff learnt that none of the
embattled battalions of 98th Infantry Division had a fighting
strength of more than 100 men. 1st Parachute Regiment could
muster 862 men, but 3rd and 4th Parachute Regiments were down
to 370 and 153 respectively. The infantry regiments of 26th Panzer
Division were in somewhat better shape with 788 and 503 men
apiece, and the battalions of 29th Panzer Grenadier Division had
an average strength of 250–300. Herr's strength returns would be
boosted by the further reinforcements which were on the way, but
their arrival was an uncertain factor because of the damage done
by the Allied air forces to the Germans' lateral communications.

Apart from the heavy fighting at Croce two other important things happened on 6th September. Leese decided to regroup, and the weather broke. Looking ahead, Leese appreciated that he would have to mount a co-ordinated Army assault on the recently detected Rimini Line on which he judged *AOK 10* would make its last attempt to stop 8th Army breaking out into the Po valley.[112] Before such an attack could be mounted 76th Panzer Corps would have to be driven off the dominating high ground of Gemmano-Croce-Coriano, which Leese took to be part of the forward defences of the Rimini Line, whereas, in fact, they were key features in the general Green II Line which *AOK 10* was still intent on holding as a main position. Both clearing the high ground and regrouping would take time and that time was to be increased by the weather.

It rained hard throughout the night 6th/7th September and most of 7th September during the first battles for Croce. The billowing white dust of the early days of the offensive turned quickly to a slippery slime; hard fields became glutinous mud; and Sapper-made diversions and bulldozed tracks sank into quagmires wherever they lay through undrained hollows, across streams or at approaches to river crossings. Any hopes of still reaching the Marano quickly were literally washed away and Leese's initial regrouping moves were delayed as the Sapper-built bridge over the Foglia was destroyed by the flood waters.[113] Only essential operational and supply vehicles could be allowed on the roads and tracks.[114] The first phase of the 'Olive' offensive was over. Green II had yet to be overrun and the new Rimini Line was emerging as 8th Army's primary concern. Leese hoped to reopen his offensive on 10th/11th September.

Direct air support during the last five days of the first phase of 'Olive' was affected by weather except for the two critical days of the first battles for the Coriano ridge.[115] The summary of D.A.F.'s effort shows the pattern:

September	Sorties	Bomb tonnage	Remarks
3rd	166	72.5	Thunderstorms reduced flying.
4th	312	205.2 }	1st Battle of Coriano.
5th	367	209.8 }	
6th	214	92.2	Poor weather
7th	25	17.8	Bad weather reduced flying to a few F.B. sorties.

(iii)

Kesselring had paid a price in checking 8th Army's offensive not only in casualties and loss of equipment but also, as Alexander hoped, in weakening *AOK 14* and absorbing potential reserves. Of the German formations, which by 8th September had been or were being drawn towards 8th Army's battle, four (26th Panzer, 29th Panzer Grenadier, 20th Luftwaffe Field and 356th Infantry Divisions) had been ceded by *AOK 14*.[116] 98th Infantry Division and a blocking group of 162nd (Turkoman) Infantry Division had been transferred from Corps Witthöft on the Adriatic coast, 100th Mountain Regiment had been turned around at Forli, and 90th Panzer Grenadier Division was moving towards the Po from the Franco-Italian frontier.

See Map 8

Alexander had intended to launch 5th Army's offensive towards Bologna when he judged that the German forces holding the Florence sector had 'been sufficiently weakened by the movement of reserves to meet Eighth Army's attack on the East Coast'.[117] 5th Army was to be ready to attack 'at 24 hours notice at any time after Eighth Army's D + 5', i.e. 30th August.* In his plan issued on 17th August, it had been Clark's intention to make his principal effort on the main Florence-Bologna road (Route 65) which crossed Green I at the Futa Pass.[118] Here the approaches were relatively easy but correspondingly heavily fortified. Intelligence reports later suggested that Il Giogo Pass to the east on the road to Firenzuola, although more difficult, was less well defended and lay on the inter-Army boundary between *AOK 14* and *AOK 10*. On 4th September Clark recast his plan for 2nd U.S. Corps.[119] Keyes was to advance with 34th and 91st U.S. Divisions west and east of Route 65, apparently heading for the Futa Pass.† He was then to bring up 85th U.S. Division to make the main effort against Il Giogo Pass. 88th U.S. Division would be in reserve, ready to pass through either 85th or 91st U.S. Divisions. 13th Corps

---

* A.A.I. Operation Order of 16th August p. 141.

† *Outline Order of Battle of 5th Army, 4th September 1944:*
  2nd U.S. Corps (Keyes):
     34th U.S. Division (Major-General Charles Bolté)
     85th U.S. Division (Coulter)
     88th U.S. Division (Major-General Paul W. Kendall)
     91st U.S. Division (Major-General William G. Livesay)
  4th U.S. Corps (Crittenberger)
     1st U.S. Armoured Division (Major-General Vernon E. Pritchard)
      Attached: 370th Regimental Combat Team, 92nd U.S. Division.
     6th South African Armoured Division (Poole)
      Under command: 24th Guards Brigade
     Task Force 45 (Brigadier General Cecil L. Rutledge)
  13th Corps (Kirkman)[120]
     6th Armoured Division (Major-General H. Murray)
     1st Division (Major-General C. F. Loewen)
     8th Indian Division (Russell)
     1st Canadian Armoured Brigade
     6th Army Group R.A.

would protect 2nd U.S. Corps' eastern flank by developing its operations on the axis of the Borgo S. Lorenzo-Faenza road. Kirkman was to make his main effort on his western flank to give maximum support to 2nd U.S. Corps at Il Giogo Pass. He was also to maintain contact with 8th Army on his eastern flank. Anticipating acute supply difficulties in the mountains, 2nd U.S. Corps was provided with nine Italian mule companies each with 260 mules, and 13th Corps had six Indian and five Italian mule companies together with five specially equipped Jeep transport platoons.

The situation on 5th Army's front had not remained static since 25th August. We have seen that on 29th August, with Hitler's sanction, Kesselring authorised the gradual withdrawal of both his Armies into Green I.[121] On the following day *AOK 14* began to move into *Vorfeld*, and 5th Army followed up all along the front. 4th U.S. Corps crossed the Arno on 1st September between Pisa and Montelupo, led by 1st U.S. Armoured Division, and for three days met little opposition. Lucca was entered on 5th September and the whole area south of the River Serchio had been cleared. 6th South African Armoured Division, operating under 4th U.S. Corps, crossed the Arno between Montelupo and Empoli and cleared the Albano massif, reaching Monsummano on 5th September. Instructions were then issued by 4th U.S. Corps that no further advance was to be made towards Pistoia to avoid jeopardising the surprise which Clark hoped to achieve when 2nd U.S. Corps opened its offensive north of Florence. 4th U.S. Corps was to hold the line of Serchio river-Mt Pisano-Mt Albano with minimum troops while planning to follow up any further withdrawal the Germans might make.

In 13th Corps' sector north and east of Florence its three divisions followed up the German withdrawal into the Apennine foot-hills.[122] Hardly had 2nd U.S. Corps started on 4th/5th September to move into its new assembly areas north of the Arno behind 1st Division and 8th Indian Division than the Germans began to withdraw again; this time back to Green I proper through a number of intermediate delaying positions, to allow the release of 356th Infantry Division and possibly 16th SS Panzer Grenadier Division to *AOK 10*. On the night of 7th/8th September 1st Division and 8th Indian Division occupied the line of hills from Mt Giovi (Pt 992) westward to Mt Morello (Pt 934) and so brought 13th Corps onto the watershed overlooking the valley of the Sieve river, beyond which the main Apennine ridges rose steeply to the Green I positions. The task of screening 2nd Corps completed, 1st Division could be shifted eastward to take over 13th Corps' left flank. 'We are all set', Clark had written in his diary on 7th September, 'for the thrust over the mountains toward Bologna'[123]

8th September was an important day of decisions on the Allied side. Alexander visited Leese at 8th Army H.Q. to hear his plans for continuing the 'Olive' offensive, and then went on to see the Canadian Corps before recrossing the Apennines, where he was in touch with General Clark.[124] In a personal signal to the C.I.G.S. on 9th September he explained that 8th Army could not continue its advance until the Gemmano-Coriano high ground had been taken, and that 8th Army would need time to regroup and build up for a full-scale attack on the Rimini Line. 'For these reasons' he signalled, 'I have decided to unleash Fifth Army'.

As we shall see, however, it was evident by 9th September that 5th Corps' attempts to clear the high ground on 8th Army's inland flank were proving slow and costly. The new plan, which Leese drew up on this date, acknowledged that he could not afford to wait.[125] He therefore shifted the weight of his attack to the right flank and transferred the role of 'Pursuit Corps' to 1st Canadian Corps, which he reinforced with 4th Division (supported by 25th Tank Brigade) and 2nd New Zealand Division. He planned to neutralize the dominant high ground on his inland flank, firstly, by a liberal use of smoke as he had done at Cassino, and, secondly, by forcing the Germans to disperse their artillery by attacking simultaneously all along 8th Army's front. The outline plan contained in his Chief of Staff's papers makes the point:

'If at all stages we were to consider that the high ground facing 5 Corps must be captured before 1 Cdn Corps could advance it would mean that, inspite of our great superiority in tanks and guns, we would be limiting the rate of our advance to the . . . speed . . . it would be possible to maintain in the difficult country on the 5 Corps front'.

See Maps 17 *and* 20

Leese visualised a three phase offensive to complete the destruction of von Vietinghoff's Adriatic defence lines.[126] His corps were to be grouped as follows:

5th Corps (LEFT)	*1st Canadian Corps (RIGHT)*
1st Armoured Division	1st Canadian Division
46th Division	5th Canadian Armoured
56th Division	Division
4th Indian Division	4th Division
7th Armoured Brigade	2nd New Zealand Division
Regiment, 25th Tank	3rd Greek Mountain Brigade
Brigade	21st Tank Brigade
7th Hussars (less squadron)	25th Tank Brigade
	(less regiment)

In *Phase I* both corps would attack the Coriano position using 5th Canadian and 1st Armoured Divisions side by side, supported by the artillery of both corps, together with pre-arranged air strikes. The attack, timed for the night 10th/11th September, was to be on a north-westerly axis with the Canadians taking Coriano itself and 1st Armoured Division clearing the rest of the ridge on the Canadians' southern flank between Passano and S. Savino. At the same time 46th Division, with 4th Indian on its left, would be clearing the Croce-Gemmano high ground to protect the Army's western flank and to clear German observation off its main axis of advance. The key feature of the western flank was now identified as Montescudo, which was 1,550 feet high and overlooked both Croce and Gemmano from the west.

In *Phase II*, 4th Division would pass through 5th Canadian Armoured Division and, in conjunction with 1st Armoured Division, would seize the next ridge to the west, referred to as the Ripabianca ridge, overlooking the Marano. 56th Division was to take any features vital to defence between 1st Armoured and 46th Divisions. The culmination of this phase would be the seizure of bridgeheads over the Marano by 1st Canadian and 4th Divisions supported by the Canadian Corps Artillery, moved as far forward as possible.

In *Phase III*, the Canadian Corps with 1st Canadian Division (right) and 4th Division (left) would breach the Rimini Line by destroying 76th Panzer Corps' defences on the S. Fortunato ridge. 5th Canadian Armoured Division was to be ready to exploit to the Marecchia river and into the Po valley beyond.

The reopening of 8th Army's offensive was subsequently postponed from 10th/11th to 12th/13th September, presumably due to delays in regrouping exacerbated by bad weather.[127] During the regrouping period the Coriano and more distant S. Fortunato ridges were to be kept under continuous air attack, and Naval fire support was to be available to the Canadian Corps.[128]

Leese commented that:

> 'I relied for success on decisive and determined break-in action by the Canadian Corps in the coastal sector, and by sustained offensive action by 5th Corps on the left, in order to pin down the enemy all along their corps front'.

General Harding, in a follow-up signal of 10th September confirmed General Alexander's verbal instructions to Clark.[129] 5th Army would 'develop their operations with a view to launching their main attack on the Gothic Line on 13 Sept or as soon as possible after'. 8th Army was 'to drive enemy north of Marano river and be prepared to launch their main attack against the enemy position running south-west from Rimini approximately 24 hours after Fifth Army launched their attack on the Gothic Line'. Priority for air support was given to 5th Army up to 15th September, but Clark was expected to keep his demands to an essential minimum for 14th and 15th September. After the 15th Alexander would decide priorities as the offensive developed.

It remained for 5th Corps to secure the dominant features overlooking 8th Army's left flank which it had first tried to take on 6th September as the rain started. The operations undertaken by 5th Corps to wrest Gemmano and subsequently Montescudo from the tenacious grip of 100th Mountain Regiment and supporting units of 71st and 98th Infantry Divisions were to prove slow and costly. We must look briefly at these and then at 5th Army's final approach to Green I.

See Maps 17 and 19

We left 5th Corps' operations on the evening of 6th September. Plans made the following day show that optimism was still high: 56th Division was to establish a firm front by consolidating on Gemmano and extending its gains to the spur immediately west of Croce, referred to in most accounts as Il Palazzo spur [130] Its reserve brigade, 169th, would then thrust through and in a night attack would seize the prominent hill villages of Montecolombo and Montescudo and thus secure the whole ridge overlooking the Conca from the north. During the 7th, however, 167th and 168th Brigades had to fight hard to retain Croce and, heavy rain having delayed the move of 169th Brigade, it was the Germans on Gemmano who attacked first during the night and drove 7th Oxford and Buckinghamshire L.I. group out of Gemmano village and down to the lower slopes.[131] This was followed on the 8th by a series of fierce attacks on 56th Division's front north of the Conca. The attackers around Croce were 117th Grenadier Regiment of 98th Infantry Division, which had previously been fighting under 1st Parachute Division's command in the coastal sector; and on Gemmano they were Austrians of 100th Mountain Regiment. South of the Conca, 56th Division's 169th Brigade then launched a counter-attack, and Gemmano village was retaken during the afternoon.

Keightley had already decided that he must devote his main effort to the clearance of the high ground on his left flank, if possible on the night of the 8th/9th.[132] His intention was that 56th Division should hold fast on Il Palazzo ridge while it cleared first the Gemmano and then the Montescudo features. 4th Indian Division was to support it by working northward from Pian di

Castello to take Mt S. Colomba.* In two days' hard fighting 169th
Brigade managed to force 100th Mountain Regiment back off the
eastern half of Gemmano, but could not clear the western end.[133]
The rest of 56th Division in the Croce sector continued to repel
counter-attacks throughout 9th September until the German effort
was spent and their attacks ceased that evening. Both sides had
suffered heavy casualties. To the south, bad weather and resolute
resistance by 278th Infantry Division had slowed the advance of 4th
Indian Division.[134]† By 9th September they had finally managed to
clear the Pian di Castello ridge, but were still some three difficult
mountain miles south of their objective.

General Keightley's orders for the 9th reflected the decisions
taken by General Leese that same day (see pp. 265–6) which
planned for the re-opening of the Army offensive on 10th/11th, later
delayed until 12th/13th, September. Keightley distributed his tasks
as follows: 1st Armoured Division was to prepare for the Army
attack on Coriano and the advance to the Ripabianca ridge.[135]
56th Division was to provide a firm base for 1st Armoured Division
between S. Savino and Croce, from which he stressed there must
be no withdrawal; 169th Brigade, he assumed, would have cleared
the Gemmano feature before it was relieved by 46th Division. The
task of 46th Division was to cross the Conca below Montecolombo
village and secure Montescudo. 4th Indian Division was to help
by taking Mt S. Colomba and, crossing the Conca, to take Gaiano,
south-west of Montescudo. The assumption that Gemmano would
be cleared was made despite the knowledge that the enemy held
well protected positions in caves and shelters and that there
had been a noticeable increase in his artillery fire.[136] The Corps
Commander's view was not shared by the Commander of 169th
Brigade, who forecast hard fighting in which even well established
positions would be difficult to hold. This was to prove the more
accurate assessment.

12th September came without either 46th Division or 4th Indian
Divisions clearing Gemmano, let alone crossing the Conca.[137] In
bitter fighting throughout 10th and 11th September 46th Division
lost, retook and lost again the dominant Pt 449 on top of Gemmano
ridge. 4th Indian Division, hampered by muddy crumbling tracks
reached, but could not clear, the village of Onferno below

---

* There are two 'Monte' Colombos, one either side of the Conca in the battle area.
Mt S. Colomba is the mountain feature on the western end of the Gemmano ridge,
Montecolombo the village on the Croce-Montescudo ridge. (*See Map 20.*)

† The Division had also to guard an open west flank, deploying two battalions in the
hills south-west of Pian di Castello. The nearest patrols of 10th Corps were some 10 miles
to the south-east.

Mt S. Colomba. 5th Corps' front line south of the Conca was virtually unchanged by two days of costly fighting.

See Maps 8 and 21

On the other side of the Apennines, 5th Army's approach to Green I accelerated as 1st Parachute Corps withdrew into its defences. 2nd U.S. Corps advanced over the Sieve river during 10th and 11th September against little or no opposition.[138] During the afternoon of 12th September the leading regiment of 91st U.S. Division, heading for Il Giogo Pass, met with increasing fire as it approached the pass. It was thought that the two major features on either side, Monticelli to the west and Mt Altuzzo to the east, were not strongly held and that 91st U.S. Division might be able to seize the pass without the help of 85th U.S. Division which was moving up behind ready to develop operations on its eastern side. Quickly mounted but abortive battalion attacks against both features during the night 12th/13th September soon ended these hopes. 4th Parachute Division was ready to oppose 2nd U.S. Corps.

13th Corps on the Americans' right had side-stepped during 9th September, as planned, to let 2nd U.S. Corps pass through.[139] Kirkman then began his advance towards Green I with his three divisions abreast. On his western flank 1st Division advanced astride the road which runs from Borgo S. Lorenzo on the Sieve over the Casaglia Pass to Marradi and eventually to Faenza on the Via Emilia. It was narrower and less well surfaced than Route 67, the only other good road across the Apennines in the Corps' sector, which was given to 6th Armoured Division on the Corps' eastern flank. This road ran from Dicomano on the Sieve up to the Muraglione Pass and then on to Forli in the Po valley, hardly armoured country. Moreover air photographs showed that Route 67 was strewn with major demolitions. All exits from Dicomano had been obstructed and in the first ten miles to the north of the town twelve gaps had been blown in the road, two of which were over 300 feet long in corniche sections where diversions were impossible. In the centre of the Corps' front 8th Indian Division, organised on a jeep and mule-pack basis, was to advance through the steep roadless country to seize the Alpe di Vitigliano, some 3,700 feet high, from which it could turn either east or west to help outflank troops of 715th Infantry Division resisting the advance of 1st Division and 6th Armoured Division.

Like 2nd U.S. Corps, Kirkman's divisions met little opposition in their advance over the Sieve and up to 715th Infantry Division's outposts in front of Green I, which stood just below the main passes. By the end of 12th September all three divisions were in contact with these outposts.

During this second phase of 'Olive' the operations of the Desert Air Force were again badly disrupted by waterlogged airfields.[140] Despite the weather 12 Ju. 87s operated over 8th Army's battle area during the night 8th/9th September causing 146 casualties on the ground. The approximate D.A.F. sortie rate in support of 8th Army was:

	Sorties	Bombs
8th September	77	50 tons
9th September	226	189 tons
10th September	243	177 tons
11th September	298	216 tons
12th September	272	149 tons

The main highlights of D.A.F.'s operations during this period were the close air support of 5th Corps' operations against Gemmano and Croce and the start of the softening up of the S. Fortunato ridge in anticipation of Leese's assault on the Rimini Line. During 9th September D.A.F. kept half-hourly Cabranks in the air for nine hours over 56th Division's sector. 11th September saw the first heavy air attacks on the S. Fortunato ridge. They were part of a mission by 94 D.A.F. Marauders which bombed guns behind the feature and others south of Rimini. They were requested by 1st Canadian Corps, as was an attack by 44 Baltimores on guns in the Rimini area. On the same day Air Vice-Marshal Dickson directed that the Mustangs should temporarily cease long-range armed reconnaissances, and he banned flying north of the Po river in order to give 8th Army as much support as possible and to increase attacks on communications immediately behind the German front line.

References in British War Diaries suggest that the direct air support in the Gemmano-Croce sector was not very effective because the defenders were using 'caves and shelters, making bombing and shelling difficult'.[141] On the other hand local civilians reported that, while these attacks did not cause many casualties, German equipment did suffer. A bomb exploded an ammunition column near Gemmano, killing 200 men, and the reconnaissance battalion of 29th Panzer Grenadier Division was caught on the move in daylight, losing most of its heavier anti-tank weapons.[142]

Direct air support for 5th Army during this period was strictly limited.[143] Since 27th August Air Vice-Marshal Dickson had had the undivided support of three U.S. fighter groups in Corsica for operations in Italy, including air support for 5th Army. On the 31st No. 7 (S.A.A.F.) Wing (fighter-bombers of D.A.F.), which had operated from Foiano della Chiana (south of Arezzo) since mid-July, began to operate mainly in support of 5th Army, and it was reinforced on 11th September by two R.A.A.F. fighter-bomber squadrons which remained at Foiano until the 20th.

On 9th and 11th September M.A.T.A.F.'s Mitchells (based in Corsica) took part in Operation 'Sesame' which was designed to neutralize strongpoints at selected places in Green I in the path of 5th Army's offensive. These enemy defences consisted of gun emplacements, machine guns and troops guarding the Futa and Il Giogo Passes, and their camps, stores and supplies. During the 15 days prior to the beginning of Operation 'Sesame' on the 9th, D.A.F. was able to operate in support of 5th Army on 12 of them, weather grounding the aircraft on three occasions. The average bomber and fighter-bomber effort during those 12 days was some 60 sorties per day, which included U.S. XII T.A.C.'s contribution from Corsica on six days. On the 9th, however, the sorties rose to 226 of which 162 were by M.A.T.A.F.'s Mitchells in Operation 'Sesame'. Unfortunately their attacks on the areas of the Futa, Il Giogo and Casaglia Passes gave advanced warning to Lemelsen that 5th Army was more interested in 1st Parachute Corps' defences in the Futa Pass than in 14th Panzer Corps' sector north of Lucca. The latter had so far received most American attention, as Clark's deception plan intended.[144] Operation 'Sesame' was suspended on 10th September for reasons not recorded and continued on the 11th with 96 sorties. In direct air support 5th Army received approximately:

	Sorties	Bombs
9th September	226	181 tons
10th September	149	95 tons
11th September	259	271 tons
12th September	373	307 tons

By 12th September, when 2nd U.S. Corps was within striking distance of the target areas, bombing was lifted over the watershed into the valley of the Santerno around the important lateral road through Firenzuola. The Mitchells concentrated on targets west of and at Firenzuola, where the U.S. Marauders operated as well. The Germans recorded some of the effects of this air activity, 4 Parachute Division's rear-guards getting special mention. Moreover, *AOK 14* complained in its evening report of 12th September that 1st Parachute Corps, which was then holding a covering position a few miles south of Green I, had been exposed to numerous air attacks on its artillery and anti-aircraft gun sites, as well as the positions in the main and rear defence lines.[145]

(iv)

In spite of the delays and failure to clear the high ground during the second phase of 'Olive', which, in reality, was an interlude between breaching Green I and finally destroying Green II or, in British eyes, driving in the German covering position in front of the Rimini Line, confidence and optimism still prevailed in 8th Army. Casualties had undoubtedly risen dramatically in the week since 1st Armoured Division had tried to break through at Coriano. They were, however, in keeping with the normal pattern of any great offensive: break in, dog-fight and break out. After initial success in the opening phases, there usually follows a period of bitter attritional fighting until a break through can be achieved. The Germans had certainly suffered severely. Moreover, British tank losses had not been heavy (93 damaged beyond repair) and all had been replaced.[146]

See Map i *(front end paper)*

In view of the continuing Allied optimism, it is worth noting that, for a brief period, a retreat over the Po was actively debated at *OKW* and led in the first half of September to a spate of deliberations on the *Voralpen* position, known also as the 'Blue Line'.[147]* On 4th September Kesselring sent *OKW* his list of priorities for construction of defensive works. He gave the Blue Line from the Swiss frontier to Verona and the line of the Adige first priority, with lay-back positions on the Brenta, Piave, Tagliamento and Isonzo rivers. On 12th September Hitler decreed that from the head of the Tagliamento a new line of fortifications was to adjoin 'Blue' on the 'German soil of Carinthia and Styria', extending eastwards to north of Ljubljana and west of Varazdin in Yugoslavia. A week later Keitel signed orders for the construction of additional defences in eastern Slovakia, thus creating, on paper, a line of fortifications to protect the Greater German Reich against attacks from the south and from the south-east.

Whatever its state of development, in early September the Blue Line held the attraction for Hitler that its occupation by Army Group C could release forces to the western and eastern fronts with which he was then primarily concerned.† In an appreciation dated 2nd September Jodl conceded this advantage, for he reckoned

---

* See p. 61.

† After the war General Warlimont, Jodl's deputy until 5th September 1944, claimed that the breaching of Green I came as a 'very painful surprise' to the Führer. This may have been the case, but the contemporary records of *AOK 10* provide no evidence of High Command recriminations on this score, nor of any fresh tactical orders issued by Hitler.

that Kesselring could hold the *Voralpen* position with 15 divisions in line and four in reserve. In Jodl's view the release of forces would, however, be offset by other factors, notably the serious loss to the German economy represented by the abandonment of Italy's northern provinces, of whose valuable resources in raw materials, industry and agriculture he had just been reminded by his logistic staff.[148] A retreat of such scale would also uncover the route to Vienna, and allow Allied air bases to advance nearer to the Reich.

Hitler was not immediately convinced, and on 5th September he called for a report from Kesselring on how the withdrawal of Army Group C could be carried out. Having discussed ways and means with the German Naval Commander in Italy, Kesselring and Vice-Admiral Löwisch replied to *OKW* and *OKM* respectively. Unfortunately the text of the Field-Marshal's report is not available to us, but the naval records indicate that it 'supported' the views of Löwisch, who himself favoured withdrawal and whose recommendations were accepted by *OKM*.

On 14th September Jodl's Operations Branch announced that in view of the present situation in central Italy, and of probable future developments, all the resources of the territories lying south of the Blue Line were to be 'drained off for the *Wehrmacht* and the Reich'. With Hitler still undecided, the activation of Operation *Herbstnebel* thus awaited a casting vote which, to the German staffs in Italy, polarised the choice between an enforced withdrawal to the Po and one which could, albeit with difficulty, be prepared in advance. Kesselring did not himself raise the issue with *OKW* until 20th September. The final outcome, described in Chapter XIV, was negative for in the end the balance was tipped against *Herbstnebel* by its political and economic implications.

At tactical level, German success in holding Gemmano, and in blocking 56th Division and 1st Armoured Division at Croce and Coriano, gave the staffs of *AOK 10* and 76th Panzer Corps some hope that they could hold the general line of Green II with the help of 356th Infantry Division.[149] This formation, which was not expected to be fully in the line before 15th September, was placed under Herr's command on the 13th, together with 20th Luftwaffe Field Division which was to defend the Rimini area and eventually relieve 26th Panzer Division for refit. 8th Army's 48 hour delay in launching its assault reduced what Wentzell and Runkel referred to as the 'thirsty period' before the arrival of these reinforcements. During his inspection of Herr's divisions on 7th September von Vietinghoff learnt that mines were short but ammunition supplies were adequate, and there was universal praise for the support given by artillery and *nebelwerfer*. Strengths were reduced, particularly that of 98th Infantry Division as we have noted. However, von

Vietinghoff told Kesselring on his return that Reinhardt was a tower of strength and that 26th Panzer Division seemed to have recovered its equilibrium. Heidrich had pulled 1st Parachute Division together, although he complained that his recent reinforcements were inadequately trained. The paratroopers regarded the Canadians as élite opponents, and Kesselring was reminded by von Vietinghoff that it was not 'the number of men which was decisive, but artillery fire. When he [the British] has chosen his point of assault he concentrates his artillery and shells everything to pieces'.

During 12th September 76th Panzer Corps reported that its gun positions were under systematic counter-battery fire and in the evening, when 40 Allied warships were spotted off the coast near Senigallia, 26th Panzer Division reported that the fire was becoming heavier.[150] Further west 51st Mountain Corps reported growing pressure on 715th Division north of Borgo S. Lorenzo and Dicomano although its opponents had not been identified. *AOK 10's* operations officer described 12th September as the curtain rising on the 'Second act of Rimini'. Kesselring's operations staff were also hearing the overture to the battle for Bologna on 5th Army's front.

See Map 20

8th Army's offensive to clear Green II and to destroy the Rimini Line opened at 6 p.m. on 12th September with an Army artillery bombardment by 700 guns on the Coriano-S. Savino ridge, which lasted for five hours on 5th Corps' front and a further two on the Canadian front. It heralded what Alexander has described as 'the beginning of a week of perhaps the heaviest fighting on both fronts that either Army had yet experienced'. The attacks that night were completely successful.[151] 1st Armoured Division attacked first with its two infantry brigades abreast between S. Savino and Passano, striking the boundary between 26th Panzer and 98th Infantry Divisions.[152] The artillery programme had been fired in five identical bombardments, each of 15 to 20 minutes duration: a short sharp burst of five minutes almost immediately after the end of each shoot was intended to catch those German troops who were bold enough to emerge from their slit trenches in the intervals, which were otherwise only filled with general harassing fire.[153] The fifth bombardment was fired at 11 p.m. when the infantry began the long approach from their Start Line on the S. Clemente ridge. Two and a half hours later the Gurkha battalions of 43rd G.L.I. Brigade on the right and the British battalions of 18th Brigade on the left were secure on the ridge between the two villages.* Passano was cleared by the Gurkhas quite early, but the garrison of S. Savino fought on until the afternoon when two battalions of 98th Infantry Division and one of 26th Panzer Division surrendered to 18th Brigade.[155] 789 prisoners passed through 1st Armoured Division's P.O.W. cages that day.

11th Canadian Brigade led 5th Canadian Armoured Division's attack which started at 1 a.m. on 13th September.[156] Fighting for Coriano was more localised and prolonged than at Passano and S. Savino. It was not until 9 a.m. on 14th September that the village was finally cleared. Nevertheless, 2nd Armoured Brigade started to pass through the infantry in 1st Armoured Division's sector and 4th Division started to move through 5th Canadian Armoured Division during the afternoon of 13th September.[157] The break through for which Leese had been working for so long seemed to be in the making. Unfortunately 1st Armoured and 4th Divisions were unable to apply enough pressure. 2nd Armoured Brigade tried once more to exploit without sufficient infantry to support its tanks, and also with too little daylight left.[158] Its advance began at 5 p.m. with 9th Lancers leading and 1st K.R.R.C. following up. The ground between S. Savino and their objective on the Ripabianca ridge was extraordinarily difficult. It was made worse by mines and anti-tank guns which had survived on the reverse slopes of the S. Savino-Coriano ridge. German artillery fire was also heavy and accurate, the leading squadron losing six tanks in ten minutes by shelling alone. As darkness fell the brigade was forced to leaguer having achieved very little. 4th Division was even more unlucky. Its leading brigade was so heavily shelled during its approach march that its advance had to be delayed until the following morning.

The delays experienced by 2nd Armoured Brigade and 4th Division were regrettable, because the morale of 76th Panzer Corps was starting to flag under the weight of 8th Army's attack and the scale of its artillery and air support.[159] *AOK 10's* final report for 14th September stated that because of a marked drop in the troops' 'inner will to resist' Herr's front had been torn apart, and could only be restored with the greatest difficulty. The day's telephone conversations showed that a few units were beginning to desert, and this rare and disturbing phenomenon for the senior German officers was reflected in the unusually high number of prisoners

---

* The Gurkha attack was planned in meticulous detail from air photographs which were exceptionally good, enabling officers to visualize exactly how many hedge lines they had to pass before reaching their objective.[154] 2nd Armoured Brigade does not seem to have been so lucky.

taken by 5th Corps and the Canadian Corps during 13th and 14th September.*

Kesselring's report to *OKW* of 14th September spoke of the 'strong impression' which 8th Army's 'completely unilateral superiority' was making on the much reduced units of 76th Panzer Corps, and of their feeling of helplessness *vis-à-vis* the Allied air forces.[161] von Vietinghoff told him the next day that as the result of air attacks many gun crews had been buried with their weapons, and those who could be dug out were 'completely dazed and confused'. To screen the gun positions from bombing an appeal was made for more smoke, of which 8th Army was making lavish use to blind the German artillery observers and thus prevent effective counter-bombardment. But Kesselring could not help, for *AOK 10* was informed on 16th September that no suitable German smoke was available in sufficient quantity. Coincidentally, the British were reported on the following day to be dropping smoke canisters from the air for the first time, but this was, in fact, for target marking and not for screening purposes.

Repairing the damage done to Green II at Coriano was not helped by the tardy arrival of 356th Infantry and 20th Luftwaffe Divisions, which, as usual, had to be fed into the line piecemeal. Where possible this was done by the fresh troops taking up new positions just behind the front so that the exhausted units could fall back through them. The process was going on during the 15th and 16th September, enabling 8th Army to make progress all along the front, in some places catching German units 'on the wrong foot' during reliefs. In broad terms 356th Infantry Division relieved the remnants of 98th Infantry Division, and 278th Infantry Division extended its front northwards to help extract the last battle group of 71st Infantry Division. On 15th September *AOK 10* authorised the precautionary manning of the 'Rimini Line' by two regiments of 162nd (Turkoman) Infantry Division. It was also hoped to employ 20th Luftwaffe Field Division in this sector, but 76th Panzer Corps was so short of local reserves that various battalions of this division had to be attached on arrival to the front line formations.

---

* The rate of prisoners entering 8th Army's P.O.W. cages during 'Olive' is given at intervals in 8th Army's Intelligence Summaries:[160]

Dates inclusive	Intake	Cumulative Total	Approx. daily rate	
26 Aug–2 Sep	1,275	1,275	160	Breaching Green I
3–6 Sep	1,431	2,706	360	1st Coriano and Croce
7–12 Sep	916	3,622	150	Pause for regrouping
13–19 Sep	3,154	6,776	450	2nd Coriano
20–22 Sep	1,394	8,170	465	Rimini Line

The principal reinforcement on the horizon was 90th Panzer Grenadier Division, which late on 14th September Kesselring ordered forward from the Po valley to Forli to form a reserve for *AOK 10*. This powerful division could not join the battle for several days, nor could some 4,000 infantry replacements promised to the Italian Theatre by *OKW*.

For four days, 14th to 17th September, 8th Army fought its way forward over the Marano and up to the Ausa on which the Rimini Line was based. German resistance, and consequently the fierceness of the fighting, increased each day. 5th Corps was helped by the poor performance of 356th Infantry Division, which took time to find its feet in unfamiliar surroundings; and the Canadian Corps was impeded by the improved performance of 1st Parachute Division under Heidrich's personal command, and by the continuing resilience of 29th Panzer Grenadier Division.[162] No longer the 'Pursuit Corps', 5th Corps could settle down to hard methodical fighting instead of always looking for opportunities for exploitation which rarely existed. In his execution of the task of clearing German observation on the inland flank Keightley was to win the Army Commander's praise. In a report written immediately after the battle on 26th September, Leese said that '. . . great strides had been made by 5th Corps. General Keightley had handled his divisions very well'.[163]

As 5th Corps' operations on the inland flank helped to clear the way for the Canadian Corps we will deal with its operations first. Keightley modified his plan for 14th September by ordering 1st Armoured and 56th Divisions to clear the Ripabianca-Sensoli ridge overlooking the Marano and then to establish bridgeheads over the river, 1st Armoured aiming for Case il Monte and 56th for Mulazzano on the far side of the river.[164] 46th Division was to give up its attempts to clear Gemmano and hand the task over to 4th Indian Division so that it could cross the Conca and concentrate upon rooting the Germans out of their dominating positions at Montecolombo and Montescudo.

All four divisions were equally successful in driving back the German line which was thoroughly disorganised. 1st Armoured Division's infantry were on the Ripabianca ridge overlooking the Marano in the early afternoon of 14th September. 56th Division burst through the reconnaissance battalions of 44th Infantry and 114th Jäger Divisions, which had hastily been sent to hold Sensoli to cover the deployment of 356th Infantry Division. Both battalion headquarters were captured together with some 200 stragglers from 98th Infantry Division. 46th Division secured Montecolombo taking about another hundred prisoners. The Germans on Gemmano realised that their position was becoming untenable with the loss of Montecolombo and began to thin out during the night 14th/15th September. By dawn on 15th September the whole feature was in 4th Indian Division's hands. Later in the day Mt S. Colomba was found to be deserted.

Operations during 15th and 16th September followed a similar pattern with 5th Corps' divisions continuing to profit by German confusion. 1st Armoured Division's Gurkha battalions crossed the Marano and secured the division's objective around Case il Monte. 56th Division crossed as well and cleared Mulazzano against increasing opposition, which was not subdued until late on 16th September. 46th and 4th Indian Divisions were more strongly opposed by remnants of 98th Infantry Division, 100th Mountain Regiment and the last battle group of 71st Infantry Division as they fought for time to allow 278th Infantry Division to pull back over the Conca, and for the balance of 356th Infantry Division to reach the front. This mixed force fought with extraordinary determination to hold the Montescudo high ground, engaging British tanks at close quarters with *Faustpatronen* and defeating repeated attacks by British infantry from the very strong natural positions which they were holding. 128th Brigade of 46th Division made two abortive attacks during 15th September. When it mounted its third attack that evening the Germans slipped away, their task completed, as 278th Infantry Division had side-stepped and joined hands with 356th Infantry Division. The gallant remnants of 71st and 98th Infantry Divisions were thus able to leave the line, although 100th Mountain Regiment could not be extracted until after 76th Panzer Corps had finally disengaged on 20th September.[165] Developments on 5th Army's front were soon to curtail 98th Infantry Division's much needed rest and refit, but in the meantime the release of these German units enabled 46th Division to draw alongside 56th Division north of Marano during 17th September. 4th Indian Division paused, allowing priority to 46th Division on the congested roads, before it advanced to clear probable German Observation Posts from the commanding heights of the rock fortress of San Marino itself. By dawn on 17th September 5th Corps stood ready to play its full part in 8th Army's assault on the Rimini Line on the far side of the Ausa.

The Canadian Corps' operations started well, but did not have the opportunity to profit so much from German confusion.[166] 3rd Greek Mountain Brigade, which was given a narrow sector near the coast in order to gain operational experience, and was supported by New Zealand tanks, British anti-tank guns and Canadian machine guns and mortars, moved forward to protect the flank of 1st Canadian Division as it crossed the Marano on 14th September. The Canadians by swift action seized a bridge intact, which made the crossing easier than the subsequent fighting for the long low ridge between the Marano and Ausa on which stand the villages of S. Lorenzo in Correggiano and S. Martino in Monte l'Abbate. The former was held by 29th Panzer Grenadier Division and the latter by 1st Parachute Division, and both were covered by artillery observation from S. Fortunato, north of the Ausa. The fields either side of the ridge were flat and afforded no cover as they had just been harvested. Throughout 14th September 3rd Canadian Brigade tried to secure a foothold in both villages, losing heavily in the attempt. 4th Division passed through 5th Canadian Armoured Division and successfully crossed the Marano at Ospedaletto, where its Sappers bridged the river during the night and enabled the division to secure the high ground around S. Patrignano north of the river next day.

1st Canadian Division, well supported by the Churchill tanks of 21st Tank Brigade, fought hard throughout 15th September to clear S. Lorenzo and S. Martino, and by evening appeared to have done so. *AOK 10's* final report for the 15th stated that all three battalions of 29th Panzer Grenadier Division's 71st Panzer Grenadier Regiment had been decimated in the fight for S. Lorenzo, which was lost after a day-long struggle.[167] Much reduced, 29th Panzer Grenadier Division had to retreat, but a muddled take over between Canadian units during the night left S. Martino temporarily unoccupied. Heidrich's paratroopers took advantage of the mistake and when daylight came the Canadians found that they had lost an essential part of their Start Line for the advance across the Ausa and eventual attack on S. Fortunato in the Rimini Line.

16th and 17th September were no better days for the Canadian Corps. The Greek Mountain Brigade was held up near Rimini airfield, and every endeavour made by 1st Canadian Division to retake S. Martino failed, with heavy losses. 4th Division on the inland flank made better progress, operating in close conjunction and slightly ahead of 5th Corps. Major-General Ward, commanding 4th Division, appreciated that he could not advance from S. Patrignano to the Ausa without clearing German observation off the Cerasolo ridge on his left, immediately south of the Ausa, which would not be reached by 1st Armoured Division for some hours. With Keightley's agreement, 4th Division crossed the inter-corps boundary and at first light attacked Cerasolo which it secured, enabling Ward to establish his division along the Cerasolo-Frisoni ridge overlooking the Ausa before midnight on 17th September.

By the end of 17th September 8th Army was ready to cross the Ausa and overcome the last known obstacle standing between it and the plain of the Romagna. There were now more substantial grounds for optimism because the growing number of prisoners taken pointed to cracks in the morale of 76th Panzer Corps, and 5th Army's offensive against the Futa and Il Giogo Passes could be expected to pin down potential reinforcements for the left wing of *AOK 10*. Nevertheless, Alexander had his doubts.[168] Cabling the C.I.G.S. on 17th September he observed:

> 'The enemy continues to put in reinforcements and there is not the least sign of any intention on his part to withdraw: on the contrary there is every indication that he intends to fight it [out] where he stands.'

During the five days (13th–17th September) of the second battle of Coriano, the direct air support for 8th Army in daylight amounted to an estimated 2,035 bomber and fighter-bomber sorties during which some 1,341 tons of bombs were dropped. A total of 359 sorties (452.8 tons of bombs) were flown by M.A.T.A.F.'s U.S. Marauders and Mitchells and all the rest by D.A.F. On three nights a further 97 sorties were added in which about 67 tons of bombs were dropped.[169]

On the 13th, morning and afternoon, the main focal point of attention for the medium and light bombers was the S. Fortunato feature where guns and defended positions received about 135 tons of bombs in 154 sorties. The fighter-bombers flew an estimated total of 256 sorties. The Germans recorded that 15th Panzer Grenadier Regiment was pinned down at Coriano by the 'murderous' artillery and air attacks, and a relief by the tanks of 29th Panzer Grenadier Division resulted in 19 of them being put out of action by Allied aircraft.[170] Though an attempt by fighter-bombers to destroy 26th Panzer Division's H.Q. was in vain, other fighter-bombers managed to attack troops in the 'wadis' around Montescudo to some effect.

Next day, the 14th, a special air operation was mounted to reinforce D.A.F.'s effort against the Coriano defences. Only the Mitchells could be made available from M.A.T.A.F., but with D.A.F.'s Marauders and Baltimores they provided 189 of the estimated 402 sorties flown and three-quarters of the total bombload dropped (some 316 tons) in support of 8th Army that day.*

*	Sorties	Bomb tonnage dropped
Medium day bombers—		
M.A.T.A.F.'s Mitchells	105	145.4
D.A.F.'s Marauders	48	72.4
Light day bombers—		
D.A.F.'s Baltimores	36	21.8
	189	239.6

D.A.F.'s Marauders are included because their attacks on guns in the vicinity of Rimini indirectly assisted the operation. *AOK 10* recorded that on the 14th casualties in 29th Panzer Grenadier Division were very high, due mainly to the weight of Allied artillery and the bombardment by '35 waves' of bombers, part of an observed total of 250 aircraft which had pounded all of Herr's left wing causing severe damage to men, weapons and equipment.

Next day, the 15th, bad weather prevented M.A.T.A.F.'s medium day bombers (Sardinia and Corsica) from operating in support of 8th Army, and only a few of D.A.F.'s Marauders could do so—probably against defended positions in the Rimini area—together with the Baltimores. The total daylight effort in support of 8th Army on the 15th amounted to an estimated 254 sorties with 96 tons of bombs dropped. That night 27 of D.A.F.'s Bostons and Baltimores were out over the battle area.

Though the weather on the 16th brought low cloud in the afternoon, D.A.F., with the support of M.A.T.A.F.'s U.S. Marauders, just managed to reach the 400 sortie mark (271 tons of bombs). Enemy movement on the roads received its usual attention but traffic was moderate.

Mid-morning on the 17th, cloud interfered with air operations and during the afternoon it prevented flying in 5th Corps' sector. Despite the weather, however, and thanks to comparatively massive support from M.A.T.A.F.'s Mitchells direct air support for 8th Army reached an estimated 566 sorties (438 tons of bombs). Specially planned close air support was flown during the morning to cover the Canadian Corps' attack on the S. Fortunato ridge which we will describe shortly.

Enemy aircraft had appeared on several occasions during this five-day period and on the last day (the 17th) one pilot of an Me. 109 baled out; the enemy recorded only one Me. 109 lost that day and that it fell 'to A.A. fire'.

(v)

See Map 21

As 8th Army cleared the Coriano ridge on 13th September, Clark's 5th Army had opened its assault on Il Giogo Pass. *AOK 14* had been so reduced by its transfers to *AOK 10* that only two divisions were available to resist the 2nd U.S. and 13th Corps' attacks.[171] When these opened, 4th Parachute Division was still south of Green I, with each of its three regiments covering the objective of a complete American division. 10th Parachute Regiment faced 34th U.S. Division south-west of the Futa Pass; 11th

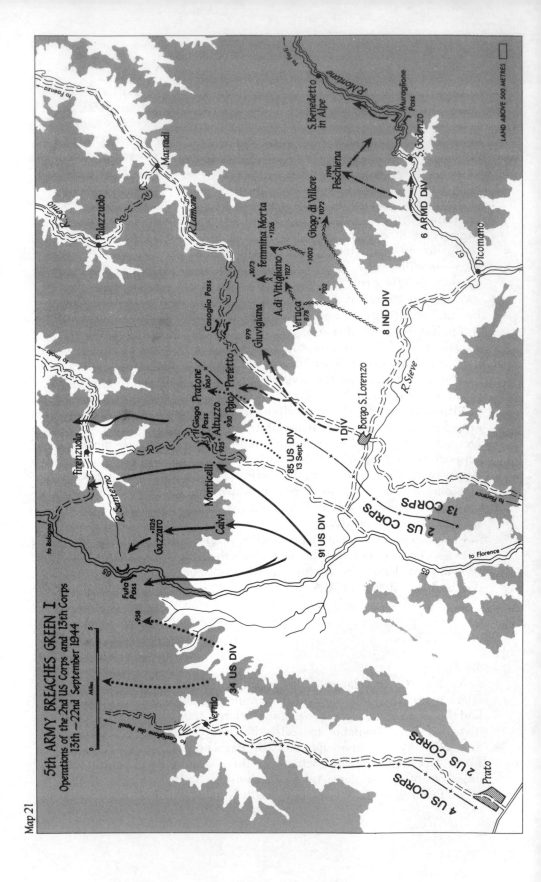

Map 21

5th ARMY BREACHES GREEN I
Operations of the 2nd US Corps and 13th Corps
13th – 22nd September 1944

Parachute Regiment faced 91st U.S. Division between the two passes on Mt Calvi and at Monticelli overlooking Il Giogo Pass; and east of this pass 12th Parachute Regiment faced 85th U.S. Division south of Mt Altuzzo and the adjoining Mt Verruca (Pt 930). 715th Infantry Division similarly faced 13th Corps with its three regiments up: 735th Grenadier Regiment on the Casaglia Pass opposing 1st Division; 725th Grenadier Regiment in the centre against 8th Indian Division; and 1028th Grenadier Regiment against 6th Armoured Division on Route 67. Apart from over-extension, the Germans suffered a number of other disadvantages. On 10th September 715th Infantry Division, which was controlled by *AOK 10*, had taken over part of the sector in Green I previously earmarked for 356th Infantry Division. It found the installations so poorly sited that 51st Mountain Corps recommended that the 'main line' be re-developed to run along the Mt Patrone ridge. Work was begun at once on *AOK 10's* side of the inter-Army boundary, which ran east of Il Giogo Pass road, but *AOK 14* did not respond to appeals to extend the new line westwards. Thus the boundary, a notoriously weak spot in any defensive position, was ill-secured from the start of the battle. Neither 715th Infantry nor 4th Parachute Divisions were particularly well endowed with artillery, whereas 2nd U.S. Corps was heavily reinforced, with each division supported by the equivalent of a British A.G.R.A.[172] 34th U.S. Division had 10th British A.G.R.A. to support it, while the other divisions each had a U.S. Field Artillery Group equipped with 155-mm howitzers and 4.5-inch guns. In addition 2nd U.S. Corps was provided with the 423rd Field Artillery Group with two battalions of the large 240-mm howitzers, three sections of 8-inch guns and two battalions of 155-mm guns. These heavy weapons were available for counter-battery fire and for dealing with concrete bunkers and other strongly reinforced defences.

2nd U.S. and 13th Corps were not the only enemies with whom the German troops had to contend. The Italian Partisan bands in the Apennines had grown in strength, activity and effectiveness during the summer. Their operations had become such a menace to *AOK 14* that Lemelsen argued his case for the retention of 16th SS Panzer Grenadier Division less on the weakening of 14th Panzer Corps than on the need to deal with the Partisan threat to his communications through the Apennines—a threat which was dramatised when the commander of 20th Luftwaffe Field Division was ambushed and killed by Partisans on 12th September.[173]

16th SS Panzer Grenadier Division was the strongest division left in *AOK 14*, with an 'actual' strength on 1st September of nearly 14,000 men. That of 4th Parachute Division was about 10,200 and that of 715th Infantry Division nearly 11,000, but these 'actual' totals bore little relation to fighting strengths which were usually 50% lower. 715th Infantry Division was graded III (suitable for defence only) by *AOK 10*, with two of its seven battalions graded 'medium' and the rest 'average'. 4th Parachute Division had recently been reinforced with very young recruits, who had fired no live ammunition until they reached the division. On 13th September their Corps Commander, Schlemm, suggested that they could best be used to control the Corps pack transport because the Italian muleteers had deserted under the 'very unpleasant' air attacks.

2nd U.S. Corps' main assault, which started on 13th September, turned out to be something of a preliminary operation in that the exact locations of 91st U.S. Division's troops, which had made the abortive attempt to seize the heights dominating Il Giogo Pass to the east and west the day before, had to be established and the whereabouts of the carefully camouflaged German defences discovered.[174] 85th U.S. Division deployed two regiments and advanced through 91st U.S. Division, with Mt Altuzzo and the neighbouring peak of Mt Verruca to the east of the pass as regimental objectives. 91st U.S. Division redeployed and used one regiment against Monticelli. By the end of the day neither could report any real success but two things had been established: where the forward German positions were located, and that the Germans had no intention of treating Green I as just another delaying position.

For the next two days 2nd U.S. Corps tried literally to blast 4th Parachute Division out of its position in front of Green I. Its operations were a story of small and continuous infantry attacks upon specific German positions after every weapon in range had been used to soften the objective. Only small groups of infantry could be used because of the precipitous and tangled nature of the ridges leading up to the main Apennine watershed, just below which the actual positions of Green I were located. Platoon and company attacks were more frequent than battalion operations. Where possible direct fire of anti-tank guns, tanks and tank destroyers was used to deal with pillboxes and bunkers. Heavy calibre 8-inch guns and 240-mm howitzers were used in precision shooting to deal with positions out of range of, or too strong for, the smaller calibre weapons. In the end it was the infantry section which had to close with and destroy or capture the garrisons, using grenades and small arms. To increase the attritional effect of these operations, harassing artillery fire was laid on the reverse slopes and attacks by fighter-bombers were directed at preventing supplies reaching the German positions. Many prisoners complained that they had received no food or supplies for three or four days.

During the night of 14th/15th September 4th Parachute Division went back into Green I proper, and by the end of the following day there was still no sign of its giving way on any of the features under attack. American losses had been heavy but the attritional effect on the Germans could not be assessed. General Clark decided to widen the attack during 16th September by taking advantage of some success which 13th Corps had had against 715th Infantry Division.[175]

1st Division, advancing astride the road to the Casaglia Pass, initially gave 85th U.S. Division heavy artillery support, firing four to five hundred rounds per gun during 12th and 13th September which caused serious transport problems arranging re-supply.[176]* Kirkman had always envisaged his operations going more quickly at first than the Americans' but thereafter slowing down. In his Operation Instruction of 9th September he had said:

> 'The American technique . . . is a very careful positioning of their forces prior to the start, based on a plan in considerable detail . . . once the advance starts it aims at advancing at great speed regardless of the enemy's reactions . . .
>
> Our own technique is to carry out detailed planning only when we have gained information by reconnaissance of the enemy's main defences. Our methods are more flexible, though more subject to delay'.

By 15 September 1st Division had secured the heights commanding the approaches west of the road with an attack by 1st Hertfordshire Regiment, supported by 116 guns, but had failed to clear those to the east of the road.

8th Indian Division had, in the meanwhile, achieved a remarkable success in the roadless country east of 1st Division's thrust. Only three-foot wide mule tracks led to the dominating features of Mt Veruca,† Mt Citerna (Pt 702) and Mt Stelleto (Pt 1,002), which were stepping-stones to the Alpe de Vitigliano and Mt Femmina Morta, the Apennine watershed.[178] Attacking mostly by night and using the spurs rather than the re-entrants, the

---

* *Outline Order of Battle of 1st Division* (Major-General C. F. Loewen)[177]
  2nd Infantry Brigade
  1st Loyal Regiment, 2nd North Staffordshire Regiment, 6th Gordon Highlanders.
  3rd Infantry Brigade
  1st Duke of Wellington's Regiment, 2nd Sherwood Foresters, 1st King's Shropshire Light Infantry.
  66th Infantry Brigade
  2nd Royal Scots, 11th Lancashire Fusiliers, 1st Hertfordshire Regiment.
  R.A.C. 6th Lancers
  R.A. 3rd, 52nd, 53rd Field Regiments; 81st A/Tk Regiment; 26th L.A.A. Regiment.
  R.E. 23rd, 238th, 248th Field Companies; 6th Field Park Company.
  M.G. 2nd/7th Middlesex Regiment.

† Not to be confused with Mt Verruca on 2nd U.S. Corps' front.

Indians hustled 725th Grenadier Regiment out of its prepared positions, which it was not strong enough to man properly in such massive country when attacked by a force able to disregard the more obvious approaches. 21st Indian Brigade, on the left, climbed an almost vertical cliff face and cut its way through barbed wire on the top to storm the peak of Mt Citerna during the night 12th/ 13th September. By the end of 13th September it was temporarily held up one thousand yards short of the bare crest of the Alpe de Vitigliano. On successive nights (13th/14th and 14th/15th) the brigade stormed both Mt Veruca and the Alpe de Vitigliano, killing or capturing most of the garrisons. 17th Indian Brigade which had been committed a day later on 21st Brigade's right, advanced to capture Mt Stelleto against shelling and mortaring only. Thus by the end of 15th September 8th Indian Division was overlooking the Casaglia Pass from the Alpe di Vitigliano and was well poised to secure the watershed at Mt Femmina Morta, opening the way into the Lamone river valley, down which the road wound its way to Faenza.

6th Armoured Division's operations went more slowly, both because 8th Indian Division had been given priority of movement on Route 67 and because of the numerous demolitions on this road. Most of the Division's effort went on clearing the high ground either side of Route 67 to enable the divisional and corps engineers to work on it.[179] This was helped by the fact that von Vietinghoff authorised the withdrawal of 715th Infantry Division on the night of 14th/15th September to new ridge positions, which brought 1028th Grenadier Regiment back to Mt Peschiena (on the watershed north of the Muraglione Pass) which 1st Guards Brigade found was firmly held.

Clark's method of widening the base of 2nd U.S. Corps' offensive was to order 85th U.S. Division to commit its reserve regiment through 1st Division to attack Mt Pratone, the main watershed feature to the east of Mt Altuzzo and Mt Verruca, on which its other two regiments were stalled.[180] On 16th September hard fighting on this widened front led to no apparent success, but 4th Parachute Division was weakened by high casualties and the stolid defence of its 12th Parachute Regiment began to crack. An attack by 338th U.S. Regiment during the night of 16th/17th September penetrated the German defences on Mt Altuzzo, and in the words of *AOK 14's* War Diary at last brought the Americans 'through and over' this sector of Green I. All along 2nd U.S. Corp' front German resistance began to falter, not least because Mt Pratone lay on *AOK 10's* side of the inter-Army boundary and Feuerstein, commanding 51st Mountain Corps, insisted that 715th Infantry Division must again withdraw because *AOK 14* had lost Mt Altuzzo.

Mt Pratone fell on the afternoon of 17th September and by evening 85th U.S. Division was secure on the watershed east of Il Giogo Pass. Twenty-four hours later 91st U.S. Division secured the watershed to the west and both divisions started to exploit their success, pushing down the reverse slopes towards the Santerno river valley to outflank the German defences of the Futa Pass.

1,145 bomber and fighter-bomber sorties had been flown in support of 5th Army during the five days, 13th–17th September, and 796 tons of bombs had been dropped.[181] Over half the sorties flown and about a third of the bombload dropped had been by D.A.F.*

During these first vital days of 5th Army's offensive the attention of Kesselring and his Chief of Staff had been held by the battle for Green II on 8th Army's front. In consequence, *AOK 14* received little help from the higher command and such counter-measures as were taken at Army level could not save 4th Parachute Division from near decimation. On 14th September Trettner was reinforced by the independent Infantry Demonstration Brigade, but Kesselring, who had earmarked this unit for *AOK 10*, would not agree until the 22nd that it could remain with *AOK 14*.[183] He was equally reluctant to allow Lemelsen to keep 16th SS Panzer Grenadier Division, and it took a personal visit from the Army Chief of Staff, Hauser, to persuade *OB Südwest* on 16th September that the division should move into the line between 65th and 362nd Infantry Division, thus enabling the latter to close up to the eastern wing of 1st Parachute Corps. The moves could not have any effect before Il Giogo was lost, and Kesselring made few attempts to co-ordinate operations on the inter-Army boundary. Frequent loss of contact between the inner wings of 1st Parachute and 51st Mountain Corps led to retreats for which each Army command blamed the other and exacerbated relations between *AOK 10* and *AOK 14*, which had never been warm. By 17th September it was obvious that a wedge had been driven between 4th Parachute and 715th Infantry Divisions, and von Vietinghoff decided on his own initiative to move one regiment of 44th Infantry Division across to support 715th, which 'was floundering in the mountains'. The impact of this measure was, however, blunted by the fact that Allied air forces had two days previously destroyed a major road bridge on the Firenzuola-Imola road, delaying all lateral reinforcement. Kesselring's Chief of Staff, Röttiger, predicted with accuracy on

---

* Together with the direct air support given to 8th Army on 13th September, that given to 5th Army brought the total for the day across the whole width of Italy to an estimated 826 bomber and fighter-bomber sorties during which about 579 tons of bombs were dropped.[182] D.A.F. provided no less than 72% of the total sorties and about half the total bombload.

19th September that if the divisions on the boundary could not maintain contact a 'festering sore' would develop, but at that time von Vietinghoff was immersed in the struggle for the Rimini Line and Lemelsen's attention was split by his concern (expressed to Kesselring on 14th September) lest 5th Army develop another thrust further west. This was what the Allied deception plan had intended, and in the days to come 5th Army would benefit from the lack of unified control in the centre of the German front which contributed to the loss of a large sector of Green I.

(vi)

See Map 22

On 16th September Leese revised his plan for the destruction of the Rimini Line.[184] Instead of giving the Canadians sole responsibility for the breach he gave verbal orders to both Corps Commanders to attack with their infantry divisions on a wide front, while holding their three armoured divisions (1st, 2nd New Zealand and 5th Canadian) in reserve ready for pursuit. There would not be simultaneous assault; divisions would cross the Ausa as they reached it and would begin their own battles to clear the last ridges of high ground before the plains of the Romagna.

Keightley issued his orders to 5th Corps next day, directing 56th and 46th Divisions to rush the Germans off the ridge running north-east and south-west of the village of Ceriano beyond the Ausa river.[185]* 1st Armoured Division was to come into reserve, preparatory to exploiting to the Marecchia if the infantry divisions were successful in gnawing a hole. In the meanwhile it was to take over from 4th Division at S. Patrignano so that the latter could concentrate on its own attack over the Ausa; and it was also to help 4th Division 'by neutralising by fire from all weapons' the German defenders of Mt dell'Arboreta on the north bank of the Ausa, to prevent them interfering with 4th Divisions's crossings. 4th Indian Division would, as usual, protect the western flank, but on this occasion would have the additional task of clearing German troops from the Republic of San Marino.[186]† Allied sources

---

* Ceriano should not be confused with the Coriano of the previous battles.

† In mid-August 1944 Kesselring announced that San Marino's neutrality would be respected, with German military requirements limited to right of passage for supply vehicles and medical services.[187] On 2nd September *AOK 10* however warned that it might not be possible to exclude its territory from forthcoming operations, and on the 7th Kesselring was asked to establish the 'political conditions' whereby 76th Panzer Corps could plot rear positions on the high ground. *OB Südwest* agreed that 'we cannot lose any battles for the sake of this little state', but on the available German evidence 278th Infantry Division offered only token resistance when the capital was entered.

record that 278th Infantry Division held a line running north-east from Borgo Maggiore (a suburb of the main town).[188] 2nd Camerons (11th Indian Brigade) had 36 casualties forcing their way into San Marino itself on 20th September and picked up 20 German dead and 54 prisoners. Out of respect for the Republic's neutrality Allied Military Government was not proclaimed, and the Republic was to be evacuated by Allied troops as soon as the military situation allowed.

In the Canadian Corps' sector Burns accepted a plan by Ward for 4th Division to cross the Ausa without a pause during the night 17th/18th September, and also Vokes' contention that his 1st Canadian Division should first close up to the Ausa in daylight of 18th September as the area around its positions at S. Lorenzo was 'still thick with enemy'.[189] His 1st Canadian Brigade would press forward east of S. Martino in conjunction with the Greeks on the coast to give the impression that the main Canadian effort was directed at Rimini. The actual main effort would be by 2nd and 3rd Canadian Brigades over the flat bare fields west of S. Martino (still in the hands of Heidrich's paratroopers), and aimed at capturing the dominant S. Fortunato ridge on the far side of the Ausa. Final brigade objectives were 2nd Brigade (right), the village of S. Fortunato and the rest of the ridge running north towards Rimini; and 3rd Brigade (left), the southern half of the ridge. If the attack was successful both 4th Division and 1st Canadian Division would exploit to seize crossings over the Marecchia. The principal feature of the Canadian attack was to be the intense artillery and air bombardments which preceded it. Four divisional artilleries (1st and 5th Canadian, 4th British and 2nd New Zealand Divisions) and the 1st Army Group Royal Canadian Artillery carried out intense preparatory shoots, and were ready to support the actual attacks with a high percentage of smoke to blind the German observers on the S. Fortunato ridge while the infantry were advancing over the dangerously open fields below.

The air plan was designed to soften up the German defences on the ridge with concentrated fighter-bomber attacks.[190] There were to be two phases each lasting one hour. In the first phase three wings of fighter-bombers (six aircraft every five minutes) were to bomb and strafe both the forward and reverse slopes of the ridge. In the second phase, while the Allied infantry attacked the forward slope, the fighter-bombers were to concentrate on the reverse slope. Bomblines were to be marked by coloured smoke laid by aircraft. Although precise details are not available it is probable that the total fighter-bomber effort actually flown in these attacks on the S. Fortunato ridge on the 17th was not far short of and might well have exceeded 200 sorties, involving some 90 tons of bombs or more and many hundreds of thousands of rounds of ammunition of various types.

In this last of 8th Army's battles before it emerged in the plain of the Romagna, 4th Division led the way and was the most successful. In its attack across the Ausa on 17th/18th September Ward used the technique of battlefield illumination at night, first introduced into operations by 5th Corps and now adapted by the Canadian C.C.R.A.[191]* Anti-aircraft search-lights were deployed a few thousand yards in rear of the front, playing their beams on cloud to provide general Artificial Moonlight, while others were deployed on high ground and to the flanks, with the dual purpose of blinding the defence while keeping the assaulting troops in the lower ground cloaked in darkness. Helped by this illumination 4th Division successfully crossed the Ausa and managed to secure a bridgehead half a mile deep around S. Antimo, two miles short of the ridge road running north-east along the S. Fortunato feature. Ward would have gained more ground on his northern flank if it had not been for the irritating minor obstacle of the Budriolo stream which skirts round the southern end of the S. Fortunato ridge. His right hand brigade captured a bridge intact but could make little progress during daylight. When night came Ward repeated his Artificial Moonlight attack, bridged the Budriolo for tanks and rushed the main ridge around S. Aquilina. By noon on the 19th, 4th Division had a firm footing in the Rimini Line and was within half a mile of the main ridge road. *AOK 10's* War Diary for 19th September testified to the effectiveness of the illumination technique (likened by Wentzell on the telephone to that of the Nazi Rallies at Nuremberg) by pointing out that in addition to impeding regrouping and the bringing up of supplies, it had further impaired the morale of the troops, already strained by weeks of attritional warfare.[192]

5th Corps and the rest of the Canadian Corps had less to show and far higher casualties for operations on 18th September. 56th and 46th Divisions were held up trying to clear Mt Olivo and Colle di Montelupo (Pt. 244 on *Map 20*).[193] By the end of 18th September 56th Division's 168th Brigade seized a small bridgehead over the Ausa just south-west of Mt dell'Arboreta. Keightley decided that he would need more weight to force the Ausa and to step up the pace of operations, in order to conform with the advance of 4th Division on the right. He ordered 56th Division, after consolidating its bridgehead south-west of Arboreta, to push on and seize the Ceriano ridge and the high ground to the north

---

* The device had been developed with success by 21st Army Group in Normandy during the previous July.

of Ceriano, Pt 203. 1st Armoured Division was to use its infantry to take Mt dell'Arboreta and hold 2nd Armoured Brigade ready to move forward to capture Pt 153. (This height was on the northern end of the 'Ceriano ridge' and stood on a road leading directly to a bridge over the Marecchia).

That night, 18th/19th September, 1st Armoured Division's 18th Brigade attacked and secured Mt dell'Arboreta while to its left 168th Brigade expanded its bridgehead. Next morning all troops had to fend off persistent counter-attacks. No tank crossing of the Ausa could be found in 56th Division's sector so permission was given for supporting tanks to use the single ford in 1st Armoured Division's sector, opposite Arboreta, and these tanks eventually helped to stabilise the situation. Meanwhile, unnoticed it seems by the Germans opposing 168th Brigade, two tank/infantry groups under 7th Armoured Brigade (8th R.T.R. with 7th Oxfordshire and Buckinghamshire L.I. and 2nd R.T.R. with 2nd/5th Queens) managed to work their way up onto the Ceriano ridge road between the Scuole track junction and Pt 186, but could make no progress towards Pt 203, 1,200 yards to the west.[194] 1st Welch (168th Brigade) also managed to cross the river south of Il Palazzo and began to clear a way forward onto the ridge east of Ceriano. 56th Division intended to pass 169th Brigade through to continue the advance to Pt 203 during that night, 19th/20th September.[195]

At 2 p.m. earlier the same day orders were issued to 2nd Armoured Brigade to advance, in conjunction with 56th Division on its left, to capture the high ground of Pt 153 at dawn on the 20th.[196] Before the leading group (the Bays, 1st K.R.R.C. and 11th (H.A.C.) R.H.A.) had crossed the river the timing was brought forward and the Brigade was ordered to attack that evening.* Heavy shelling, which caused infantry casualties, and extremely bad tank going north of the river so delayed 2nd Armoured Brigade's approach that the attack had to be postponed until next morning. In Brigadier Goodbody's view, there would have been a chance of success had he been able to put in a quick attack that evening before the Germans had settled down on the Ceriano ridge. When however he pushed out patrols to Pt 153 during the night they found that the ridge was strongly held.

The Brigadier's assessment was nearer the truth than he realised. It was on the 19th that the redoubtable General Baade, Commander of 90th Panzer Grenadier Division, took over 356th Infantry Division's sector, at the instigation of Herr and von Vietinghoff, who had told Kesselring that the British strength in armour and their

---

* The most probable explanation is that an intercept of a German signal credited 56th Division with the capture of Pt 203.[197]

own lack of anti-tank weapons were fraying the nerves of the infantry.[198] They had lost ground between Ceriano and S. Aquilina where there was a 'deep hole'. With his own division coming forward piecemeal, Baade assumed command of a miscellany of units including the remnants of 100th Mountain Regiment, some Panther tanks and (to counter the British tanks) an independent battalion of 8.8-cm Pak. The lead elements of 361st Panzer Grenadier Regiment (90th Panzer Grenadier Division) were in the battle group which in the early hours of the 20th counter-attacked and drove back 7th Oxford and Buckinghamshire Light Infantry from the Ceriano road. They then continued south-west and closed with the leading battalions of 169th Brigade who, during the night, had passed through 168th Infantry Brigade's 1st Welch near Ceriano village, and were moving on to consolidate the line gained on the ridge before attacking Pt 203.[199] Fighting for the village continued throughout the day, but it was noon on 20th September before news of the German challenge reached H.Q. 56th Division. It was not realised that Pt 203 was still in German hands until *1.10 p.m.*

The realities of the new situation, however, quickly became apparent to 2nd Armoured Brigade.[200] As the Bays moved forward to their Start Line soon after first light on 20th September they came under fire from their left and left rear from weapons on the Ceriano ridge between Ceriano village and the Scuole road junction. By 7.30 a.m. two squadrons were trying to work their way up the re-entrant leading to Pt 153. The amount of fire coming from the main ridge on their left confirmed that it was strongly held, and that if they tried to press on over the Scuole crest they would come under murderous fire from both front and left flank. Goodbody ordered the Bays to clear up the opposition on their left and while they were doing this brought forward 9th Lancers from the Ausa. By 9.30 a.m. there was less opposition from the left, but any attempt to move towards the objective of Pt 153, a mile to the north, was met by accurate fire which picked off any tank which tried to cross the skyline. The Bays had had considerable casualties and were reinforced by a squadron of 9th Lancers in fire positions. Goodbody represented the situation by radio to H.Q. 1st Armoured Division, but on 5th Corps' instructions, also by radio, was ordered to start his attack on Pt 153 in 15 minutes (i.e. at 10 a.m.). This was too early for 9th Lancers who could not get into position in time. When the attack did go in at 10.50 a.m. Goodbody's worst fears were realised. General Baade's 8.8-cm guns behind the crest destroyed all but three of the tanks in the two leading squadrons of the Bays. The tank crews were machine gunned as they baled out. There was no cover and few hull-down positions, and by 11.30 a.m. the attack had disintegrated with only

600 yards gained and the Bays reduced to 18 tanks. Fortunately before it was renewed the true position of 56th Division's troops around Ceriano became known and a battalion of 18th Brigade was sent forward to take over the ground reached by the tanks. By the end of the day Baade's men still maintained their grip on 5th Corps' approach to the Marecchia.

Keightley intended to renew the attack that night with 56th and 1st Armoured Divisions but all operations were brought to a halt by rain, which started at midday and that evening turned into what the 9th Lancers War Diary describes as:

> 'the most devastating deluge of rain . . . within ten minutes, not a vehicle could move, for the whole country was transformed into a quagmire . . . There was nothing to do—or even attempt to do—so all tanks closed down . . .'[201]

Rain continued throughout 21st September, making many roads impassable except for jeeps with chains on their tyres. Some improvement in the weather began on 22nd September.[202]

While 1st Armoured and 56th Divisions were fighting the battle of Ceriano, 46th Division was working its way through the hills on the left and 4th Indian Division pushed through the Republic of San Marino. It was during the fierce fighting which followed the crossing of the Marano, during the night 17th/18th September, that Rifleman Sher Bahadur Thapa of 1st/9th Gurkhas won a posthumous Victoria Cross for great gallantry in action.

On 5th Corps' eastern flank operations had not started well when 1st Canadian Division began its attack at 4 a.m. on 18th September.[203] 2nd Canadian Brigade was prevented from developing its attack properly by being unable to clear the German paratroopers off the S. Martino feature and suffered heavy losses in trying to do so. 3rd Canadian Brigade on the left did manage to cross the flat ground from S. Lorenzo to the Ausa and then discovered the river, 'a definite tank obstacle and held in strength'. The brigade also found itself out in the open under close observation from S. Fortunato and, to make matters worse, it was attacked by mistake by Allied aircraft. All attempts to cross the river were foiled and the brigade dug in where it was to await nightfall, 'sweating and bleeding', as the Canadian official historian describes their predicament, 'in the low ground under direct observation for the rest of the day'.

The D.A.F.'s direct support of 8th Army on 18th September was 624 sorties (538 tons of bombs), the lion's share of which was used on another 'softening up' of the S. Fortunato ridge in support of 1st Canadian Division's attack.[204] The direct support programme was again divided into two phases. The first took place between 6 and 7 a.m. when three entire Wings of fighter-bombers bombed and strafed both the forward and reverse slopes. In the second phase, as a heavy artillery concentration came down on the forward slope, the bombing and strafing was confined to the reverse side, where a lucky hit by No. 145 Squadron blew up an ammunition dump in a house. When the Canadian attack faltered 8th Army cancelled requests for further bombing. It is worth recalling that it was on the 18th that Rover Frank operated for the first time against enemy guns. In conjunction with the Counter-Battery Officer of 1st Canadian Corps, Rover Frank was allotted eleven missions involving attacks on gun areas which were proving troublesome to the advancing Canadian troops.

During the night 18th/19th September 3rd Canadian Brigade with 48th Royal Tanks under command, helped by Artificial Moonlight on 4th Division's front, crossed the Ausa and by daylight had made adequate crossings for tanks, using Sherman dozers, fascines and an ARK.[205] The leading battalions pressed on to the lateral road beyond the river and at 6.30 a.m. started to climb the S. Fortunato ridge, with S. Fortunato and Covignano villages as their objective; shelling by both sides was intense, barrage bringing down counter-barrage. Renewed air attacks added to the dust of the general inferno, and yet when these ceased and the barrage lifted the German infantry could be seen emerging from their dug-outs and re-manning their weapons. The whole attack faltered and by dusk of 19th September 3rd Canadian Brigade was back behind the lateral road from which it had started that morning, except on the right where one battalion managed to retain a precarious foothold on the ridge. 48th Royal Tank Regiment's Churchills had rendered useful support.

4th Division, on the Canadians' left, had had a successful night. By dawn on 19th September they were half-way up the S. Aquilina spur and that afternoon they cleared S. Aquilina, taking 85 prisoners from 20th Luftwaffe Division.

1st Parachute Division abandoned S. Martino on 19th September, thus freeing 2nd Canadian Brigade's approach to the northern end of the S. Fortunato ridge, defended by 1st Parachute Regiment.[206] The rest of the ridge was held by 29th Panzer Grenadier Division, reinforced by a regiment from 162nd (Turkoman) Infantry Division, and by the bulk of 20th Luftwaffe Division, brought into the line to relieve the remnants of 26th Panzer Division. On the Canadian side, before dusk on the 19th, Vokes ordered 3rd Canadian Brigade to exploit its foothold on the ridge by bringing up its reserve battalion. 2nd Canadian Brigade were to try infiltrating through the German positions during the night to take the villages of S. Lorenzo in Monte and Le Grazie in their rear. If successful 2nd Canadian Brigade was to exploit to the Marecchia. 1st Canadian

Brigade and 3rd Greek Mountain Brigade were to keep up their pressure on the approaches to and around Rimini.

During the night 19th/20th September 1st Canadian Division reaped the rewards of its hard, bloody fighting of the last three days. The German records confirm that 314th Grenadier Regiment of 162nd (Turkoman) Division broke and scattered under attack by the Royal 22e, the reserve battalion of 3rd Canadian Brigade, who fought up the steep slopes in the dark and then turned their attention to the remnants of 15th Panzer Grenadier Regiment of 29th Panzer Grenadier Division. The Germans were rooted out of two large villas on the top of the ridge. By 9 a.m. the Commanding Officer reported the villas secure and that a company was pursuing the retreating garrison westwards. 2nd Canadian Brigade was equally successful. Inspite of delays caused by *Nebelwerfer* fire and minefields it captured the S. Fortunato ridge. Throughout the morning of 20th September both Canadian brigades had to withstand heavy shelling and counter-attacks, but then German resistance cracked and they were able to drive the survivors of 71st Panzer Grenadier Regiment out of S. Lorenzo.

4th Division made steady progress also during the night 19th/20th and had to withstand the same spate of counter-attacks and heavy shelling when dawn came. 1st Canadian Corps had bitten a large hole in the strongest sector of the Rimini Line.

On the German side the news of these developments was slow to reach Corps and Army. When von Vietinghoff spoke to Kesselring at 9.10 a.m. on 20th September he had little to report beyond the impression that in 90th Panzer Grenadier Division's sector the risk of break through seemed for the time being to have been averted.[207] Within two hours, however, he had learnt of the *débâcle* on the S. Fortunato ridge, and Kesselring was informed that 'something unpleasant had happened in the north' where Allied tanks had broken through. With his artillery positions now exposed to Allied fire Herr had been forced to take his guns back across the Marecchia, whence they could no longer give support to the infantry. Herr had therefore sought authority for all of 76th Panzer Corps to abandon the Rimini Line that night. Kesselring would not immediately concur and insisted on discussing the pros and cons with his staff. As the morning wore on the situation worsened, and at 1.20 p.m. Wentzell informed Röttiger that the two regiments of 29th Panzer Grenadier Division could muster only some 300 men between them. 162nd (Turkoman) Infantry Division had virtually disintegrated, and Baade had told Herr that he doubted whether the infantry in his sector could resist much longer, let alone counter-attack. For these reasons Wentzell maintained that the withdrawal of 76th Panzer Corps across the

Marecchia was imperative, and would be aided by the rain, which was now falling all along the front, as this would reduce interference from the air. Röttiger promptly sought out Kesselring who sanctioned the withdrawal. In the eveing Kesselring expressed qualms about his decision because Herr would be moving into open country and thus 'might let the whole thing slide'. von Vietinghoff replied that in Herr's view, with which he agreed, the plain would be quite favourable for defence, particularly in bad weather. Herr proved to be a better prophet than Kesselring.

At 3.15 p.m. on 20th September von Vietinghoff issued the executive order to break off the battle which had lasted since 'Olive' began, almost a month before on 25th August. 51st Mountain Corps was to withdraw to Green II to shorten its front and to collect reserves, and 76th Panzer Corps was to take up positions behind the Marecchia called the '*Adelheid Line*', which ran from the Adriatic coast at Viserbella to the south-eastern side of Santarcangelo and thence to the Marecchia river at Poggio Berni and on to Verucchio (*Map* 17). The withdrawal went off smoothly thanks to the weather, which ruled out air activity that night, and the effective use of search-lights. The remaining port installations and naval guns were blown up in Rimini and the port was evacuated on 21st September. At 10 a.m. that day the first Canadian troops crossed the Marecchia at S. Martino in Riparatta and spent the day expanding their bridgehead.[208] Rimini was occupied by the Greek Mountain Brigade during the morning and during the afternoon 4th Division crossed the Marecchia on the other flank of the Canadian Corps front at S. Giustina. 5th Corps found the battlefield of Ceriano deserted on the morning of 21st September except for a few abandoned German guns and bits of equipment. By dawn on the 22nd patrols from 5th Corps' divisions were up to the river all along the Corps' sector. 5th Corps Intelligence Summary for 22nd September remarks that 'the total lack of air reconnaissance' (due to weather) on 21st September made it difficult to locate the new German positions.

The sorties and bombloads of D.A.F.'s direct air support to 8th Army in the battle for the Rimini Line were:[209]

	Bomber & Fighter-bomber Sorties	Bomb Tonnage
18th September	624	537.8
18th/19th September	96	304.3
19th September	321	108.8
20th September	328	86.9
21st September	Nil	Nil
Totals (4 days)	1,369	1,037.8

Viewing the effect of recent heavy fighting and of the high level of Allied air activity over 8th Army's battle area, von Vietinghoff, on the evening of the 17th, had come to the conclusion that a newly-committed division could be burnt out 'within three or four days'. The even higher scale of direct air support which 8th Army enjoyed on 18th September must have appeared to confirm his view. He called the 18th 'a hard day' for Herr's left wing which was exposed to unremitting air attacks. If the effort that night (the 18th/19th) put in by No. 205 Group's Liberators, Halifaxes and Wellingtons in a devastating attack on troops and supplies in the Rimini area is added, then in the 24 hours the estimated totals of 720 sorties and not far short of 850 tons of bombs must have seemed intolerable.

It was fortunate that 8th Army's requests for direct air support began to decline during 18th September, initially because the two sides were so closely engaged and then due to the break in the weather on the 20th. The strain of the last fortnight's, and not least the previous day's effort, was beginning to have its effect on D.A.F.'s pilots, aircrew and serviceability of its aircraft.

Probably the greatest contribution made by D.A.F. in the destruction of the Rimini Line was in helping to suppress the German artillery. The historians of 29th Panzer Grenadier Division wrote:

> 'Our field guns and other heavy weapons took severe punishment from the enemy's heavy and systematic air attacks. At times they were virtually paralysed, for aircraft hung overhead and could be directed at will to attack one troop that was firing, or any other form of activity'.

(vii)

See Map 21

On 5th Army's front, the gaps which had been cut in Green I on the German inter-Army boundary by 17th September were rapidly exploited by 85th U.S. Division and 8th Indian Division. The former entered the Santerno valley with its three regiments abreast.[210] Endeavouring to check this advance, Lemelsen on 18th September ordered 362nd Infantry Division to move to the eastern wing of 1st Parachute Corps. But the lateral move was difficult and slow, and on *AOK* 10's side of the boundary the piecemeal arrival of 132nd Grenadier Regiment of 44th Infantry Division could not stabilise the front of 715th Infantry Division. With that of 4th Parachute Division penetrated in several places, Kesselring agreed on 19th September that during the next night 1st Parachute

Corps would withdraw its left wing and centre to new positions north of Firenzuola, which 2nd U.S. Corps entered on 22nd September.

The American advance from Il Giogo Pass made the Futa Pass untenable. Although *AOK 14* commended the dogged resistance of 334th Infantry Division, it was forced to withdraw to avoid encirclement by 91st U.S. Division to the east, and 34th U.S. Division to the west. The pass was opened to American traffic late on 22nd September, enabling 2nd U.S. Corps to start building up supplies for the next phase of its advance on Bologna.

8th Indian Division's successes in the centre of 13th Corps' front were crowned on 18th September by the seizure of Mt Femmina Morta, which dominated the Casaglia Pass, and eased the advance of both 1st Division and 6th Armoured Division.[211] The latter, helped by 19th Indian Brigade, pushed forward on its left and occupied Mt Peschiena, the guardian peak of the Muraglione Pass, on 21st September. Although there were occasional sharp clashes with the enemy the main obstacles during the Corps' advance came from the rain and mist and the difficult terrain. What appeared five miles across country by map could prove an exhausting day's journey for men and mules, or for the evacuation of casualties.

See Map 8

On the western flanks of 8th and 5th Armies, 10th and 4th U.S. Corps maintained as much pressure as they could with the limited resources available to them. By late August 10th Corps had been left with only 10th Indian Division and 9th Armoured Brigade, which comprised three armoured car regiments (Kings Dragoon Guards and 12th and 27th Lancers) who worked mainly on foot.[212]* Despite its lack of resources 10th Corps kept up its operations so realistically that up to 18th September Kesselring would not accept any of von Vietinghoff's suggestions that 51st Mountain Corps should withdraw to provide reserves, and it was not until the 20th that Feuerstein was finally authorised to retreat to Green II. 10th Indian Brigade entered Bibbiena on 28th August. The Pratomagno massif was cleared at the same time. By 3rd September the Corps was in contact with Green I all along its front. On 12th September a major regrouping was ordered by 8th Army to provide more reserves for the Adriatic front. 10th Indian Division and H.Q. 9th Armoured Brigade, with 27th Lancers, departed on 19th September.† By the time this reorganisation was complete 51st

---

* On 11th September the Household Cavalry Regiment replaced 12th Lancers.

† H.Q. 9th Armoured Brigade was to be allotted a new role, see p.234.

Mountain Corps was falling back to Green II, the Rimini Line having been lost on 20th September.

4th U.S. Corps' operations were on a larger scale as it had under command from east to west: 6th S.A. Armoured Division, operating northwards from Pistoia with its main axis on Route 64; 1st U.S. Armoured Division in the Serchio river valley, but with reservations on its use in case it was needed by 2nd U.S. Corps for exploitation in the Po valley; the first regimental combat team of the Brazilian Expeditionary Force, fighting for the first time in Italy, in the hills above Lucca; and Task Force 45 on the coast.[213] The main strength of 4th U.S. Corps lay in its artillery which was used in extensive harassing shoots to simulate a much larger force.

Between 12th and 20th September 6th S.A. Armoured Division did most of the fighting because of the restrictions placed on the American armour. Their Armoured Brigade, largely dismounted, had the hardest role, holding 362nd Infantry Division in the mountains due north of Pistoia until it began to move eastward on 18th September. On 22nd September demolitions were heard to the north and it became clear that a withdrawal was in hand. It was in fact the start of their opponents' retreat to Green II.

On the rest of 4th U.S. Corps' front 1st U.S. Armoured Division probed forward into the Serchio valley until, on 20th September, following the break through at II Giogo, orders were received to transfer its Combat Command A to south-east of Prato, in readiness to exploit. On the coast Task Force 45 closed up to Green I, south of Massa.

It will be recalled that after 14th September the intensity of air support in 5th Army's area was drastically reduced by the bad weather, and then kept down by the needs of 8th Army. On the 18th another spell of bad weather set in on 5th Army's front, but the Spitfire fighter-bombers operating from Foiano di Chiana (*Map 1*), which were the only aircraft available to support 5th Army, managed to fly an estimated 112 sorties dropping 25 tons of bombs on a variety of targets, particularly guns and troops north-west and south-west of Firenzuola.[214] Next day, the 19th, the effort was virtually identical although some motor transport appear in the list of targets. Thereafter the worsening weather prevented further air support to 5th Army until 22nd September.

(viii)

'Olive' can be said to have ended as 8th Army crossed the Marecchia on 21st September in pouring rain. It had reached its 'promised land', but was to find mud rather than the milk of good tank 'going' and frustration rather than the honey of rapid exploitation. Leese could rightly claim in his report, written immediately after the offensive on 26th September, that 8th Army's achievement was 'a great one'.[215] It had crossed the Apennines secretly and on time. It had gate-crashed 'the powerful Gothic Line defences at very small expense and before the enemy was ready'. Moreover it had defeated eleven German divisions in sustained battle and had broken into the plains of the Romagna. On the debit side he had to admit that casualties, particularly amongst the infantry, had been so great that 1st Armoured Division had to be broken up, two infantry brigades reduced to cadre, and all infantry battalions brought down from four to three rifle companies. We will be looking in greater detail at these measures in the next chapter. Leese made no claim that the early onset of the autumn rains had robbed 8th Army of victory because at this stage it was not apparent that victory had eluded his Army. There was every reason to hope that 5th Army's advance through the centre of the Apennines would unhinge the German defence and send 8th Army rolling forward to the Po. Indeed, General Kirkman wrote to Leese on 22nd September optimistically forecasting that he would 'get wheels through to the plains' by 1st October, a week earlier than he had originally forecast.[216]

In assessing 'Olive' we will first look at its impact on the German High Command and upon Kesselring's Army Group C. At *OKW* the decisions taken by Kesselring during the fighting seem to have been accepted without demur, and his strategy for the longer-term was not the subject of directions from Hitler until 23rd September when 'Olive' was over. The possible enforcement of *Herbstnebel* became a very live issue for the commanders of *AOK 10* after the second battle of Coriano and the crossing of the Marano by 8th Army on 15th September. They had an ally in Kesselring's Chief of Staff, Röttiger, but *OB Südwest*, who had also to think of *AOK 14* and the Army of Liguria, would not be rushed. At a staff conference held at von Vietinghoff's headquarters on 16th September, when he appreciated that the Allied build up north of Florence did not as yet compare with their concentration on the Adriatic wing, Kesselring insisted that *AOK 10* must stand firm and take 'very sharp measures' to meet any signs of desertion.[217] During a brief and inconclusive discussion of *Herbstnebel* von Vietinghoff drew attention to the technical problems involved and the shortage of engineers to tackle them. The shortage also prevailed at *AOK 14*, whence Lemelsen told Röttiger on 13th September that the opening of 5th Army's offensive was forcing him to bring back engineers already deployed at the Po so that they could work on Green II, as yet largely undeveloped on his Army's front.[218] Despite the thorniness of what von Vietinghoff described as the 'long road back to the Po'. Röttiger, none the less, tried on 17th September to persuade Kesselring that the time had come to seek a 'big decision' from *OKW*.[219] He believed that it must be brought home to the High Command that unless Army Group C was substantially reinforced withdrawal might be forced upon it under conditions in which it would be extremely difficult, if not impossible, to execute.

Also on the 17th, von Vietinghoff sent Kesselring a written appreciation which made the same point on behalf of *AOK 10*. Pointing out that his divisions were engaged in attritional warfare of 'the first order', he asked *OB Südwest* either to approve the release of 44th Infantry Division to feed the battle on the Adriatic wing, or to find 'another solution'. Kesselring sanctioned the release, but in respect of long term planning Röttiger was again ahead of him. On 19th September the Chief of Staff put personally to Jodl the question whether the Army Group must risk possible destruction by continuing to accept battle 'under present conditions', or could begin a gradual and phased withdrawal across the Po. Kesselring took up the cudgels the next day. He informed *OKW* that in view of the heavy losses sustained by both his Armies he must 'shorten his front'. Unless large reinforcements were immediately forthcoming, retreat to Green II along the whole front was inevitable, with 'transition' to the start of *Herbstnebel* and retreat to the lower Alps as the probable consequence. Hitler sanctioned the front-shortening on the 21st, and Röttiger was sent to *OKW* to discuss the wider issues on the 23rd.

By this time, it can be presumed, Hitler had studied further papers produced by Jodl's staff on the pros and cons of retaining northern Italy. We know of Röttiger's meeting with the Führer only that Kesselring's 'intentions' were reported, with the result that *OB Südwest* was instructed to conduct his operations on the assumption that the Northern Apennines and the Western Alps would be held.[220] There must be no major withdrawal without the Führer's authority, but 'local freedom of action' was allowed. Kesselring could also plan any 'dispersals' which would speed up withdrawal if this became necessary, but the *Herbstnebel* demolition programme must be curtailed for lack of explosives. On 26th September *OKW* promised 20,000 replacements for the Italian Theatre by early October, which would go a long way to meet Kesselring's demand of 23,800. It seems, therefore, that, although Hitler had not yet decided to veto *Herbstnebel* for the economic and political reasons he would later adduce, he was prepared to meet Kesselring's contention that he must be reinforced or withdraw by providing the reinforcements. Thus 8th Army had mauled some of the best German divisions in Italy, but it had not imposed a withdrawal of strategic scale.

It was not in fact Alexander's primary objective to force a major withdrawal upon Kesselring. The destruction of Army Group C was more important and this he hoped to achieve south of the Po. *AOK 10*'s losses were certainly very high in both men and equipment, and German records show that its morale had dropped to a worryingly low level which was reflected in the number of tank crews, who usually had the highest morale, abandoning their tanks and deserting.[221] Producing comparative British and German losses is notoriously difficult for any great Second World War battle because they lasted so long and both sides' statistics were compiled with differing time frames and using differing classifications. In the month of September, according to an *AOK 10* return, which included 51st Mountain Corps, German equipment losses totalled just under 100 tanks and 124 medium anti-tank and assault guns. The Germans claimed over 600 British tanks destroyed. Although this was an exaggeration, the German analysis of their means of destruction is interesting. They were, in order of effectiveness:

Tank guns	32.3%
Close Combat weapons	21.2%
Anti-tank guns	19.5%
Artillery	17.1%
Assault guns	7.2%
Other weapons	2.7%

These percentages can be compared with those which 76th Panzer Corps claimed were the causes of the loss of their own tanks up to 15th September:

Artillery	33%	
Technical defects	26%	(blown up when abandoned).
Tanks and anti-tank guns	15%	
Captured and other unknown causes	15%	
Trapped in bad 'going'	11%	(also blown up when abandoned).

Such figures explain the contemporary feeling that the Allied tanks were less effective as tank killers than the German. The British had to depend more upon their artillery than their tank guns. By the end of September 15 Tigers had been lost but by mid-month none to the British weapons. Two somersaulted down a slope during a night withdrawal and two were stuck in bad 'going'. Most Panthers were lost from technical defects. 8th Army's Artillery Branch History comments on the 4th/12th September period that one feature was 'the persistent use of German "Tigers" and "Panthers" in a defensive role . . . It was profitable to hunt these large SP Guns [sic] by means of Air OP . . . working to 5.5 in or preferably 7.2 in guns'.[222] This method resulted in a number of successes. The German tactical handling of their heavier tanks in ones and twos in support of their infantry and concealed by buildings, haystacks and hedgerows made them difficult targets for British tanks and anti-tank guns.

British records show that 5th Corps lost 9,000 men plus 6,000 sick; the Canadian Official Historian places his Corps' losses at just under 4,000, with a further 1,000 sick in 1st Canadian Division but no record being given for sick in 5th Canadian Armoured Division.[223] 8th Army lost an average of 745 officers and men per day in the second, third and fourth phases of 'Olive', and a total in the order of 13,000 for the whole offensive, although Leese placed it slightly higher at 14,000.[224] He also reported that 210 tanks were irrecoverable.* The break down of casualties amongst British formations, as opposed to Canadian and Indian, is given in an 8th Army memorandum dated 21st September:[225]

Armoured Formations	*Officers*	*O.R.s*
1st Armoured Division	90	1,021
21st Tank Brigade	33	270
25th Tank Brigade	17	76
	140	1,367
Infantry Formations		
4th Division	39	798
46th Division	155	2,199
56th Division	195	2,783
	389	5,780

Although 'Olive' was intended to be a battle in which the British armoured formations would play a decisive part, it turned out to be one in which the infantry divisions paid the greatest price. Amongst the Infantry the greatest casualties were caused by German artillery fire. By Italian campaign standards there were unusually few mines used, possibly because of difficulties in moving them south across the Po, but stocks of German artillery ammunition seemed inexhaustible and the gunners' ability to use it appeared much less affected by counter-battery fire and air attack than in previous battles in this campaign.[226]

The relative intensity of the fighting in the four phases of 'Olive' is well illustrated in the casualty returns of 5th Corps:[227]

1st Phase	25th August to 7th September:	1,069
2nd Phase	8th to 12th September:	3,033
3rd Phase	13th to 17th September:	3,167
4th Phase	18th to 22nd September:	1,813
	Total	9,082

---

* The tanks irrecoverable were: 130 Sherman, 60 Churchills, 20 Stewarts, total 210.

The measure of damage inflicted and sustained by the two sides is most clearly reflected in the totals of personnel casualties:[228]

76th Panzer Corps   16,000
8th Army   14,000

Herr's Corps 'gave as good as it got'. 8th Army's entry into the Romagna had been bought at a painful price which Britain and Canada could ill afford.

If we bear in mind the preponderance of material on 8th Army's side and the massive air support it received, the results of 'Olive' in terms of destruction of *AOK 10* must be deemed disappointing. What went wrong? In retrospect it can be seen that subjective arguments swayed objective reasoning, resulting in loss of time, effort and resources, questionable tactics, and unfortunate casting of formations to roles. These are hard words which must be fully substantiated. There was in addition a further mistake, the idea that the Adriatic coast could afford better 'going' than the central sector, but this cannot be assessed properly until we see in the next chapter how 5th Army fared in the central sector.

There can be no gainsaying the loss of time, effort and resources. At least three weeks were lost by switching to the Adriatic. The staff and regimental effort devoted to the move might well have been better spent preparing for the original central breach. While operations were never actually halted by administrative shortages, Bailey bridging became a critical item, enforcing the use of bull-dozed diversions and fords which gave way every time it rained and thereby indirectly slowed operations. Moreover, the strain on supply transport of the long turn-rounds until new road and railheads could be re-established on the Adriatic coast was consider-able and was to have a cumulative effect as winter approached. More importantly, loss of time and resources meant a correspond-ing gain by the Germans for the consolidation of their Gothic Line defences and for the ferrying of adequate stocks of ammunition over the Po. As we have seen, British and Canadian losses mounted as the German artillery began to make such effective use of the good observation always available on the inland flank. Finally there can be little doubt that 8th Army lost the last of the summer weather by its march over the mountains.

Initially the tactics of 8th Army were almost entirely based upon the belief that the Adriatic coast would prove suitable for armoured warfare. The advance to and through Green I was a masterpiece in tactical surprise and went exactly as Leese planned. 76th Panzer Corps was not allowed time to settle down in its defence. Then the attempt was made to exploit in the grand manner with the 'Pursuit Corps', 5th Corps, headed by the untrained 1st Armoured

Division, trying to break through in the easily defended Coriano-Gemmano sector. The assumption that there was nothing in front of 5th Corps and that Gemmano could be ignored proved to be erroneous. Losses started to rise steeply from that moment onwards as German reinforcements arrived and began to take full advantage of the hills in the west, which rose in tiers like theatre seats to provide a better view of the stage. By the time that the emphasis was switched to the Canadian Corps' sector and 5th Corps started fighting well, as an orthodox corps, the chances of a breach, which had seemed possible on 9th September, had vanished. All that could be hoped for was the general collapse of German resistance under the pressure of vastly superior artillery and air bombardment applied across the whole front.

The fault in casting stemmed directly from Leese's vision of the armoured battle which he wanted to fight. He chose the right man in Keightley to lead 5th Corps, but the Corps Staff and three of its divisions were not such happy choices. For such a battle the staff and troops have to be at the peak of their form, understanding instinctively what is practicable and what is not, and knowing how to co-operate equally instinctively with one another. 5th Corps Headquarters had not handled armour since the Tunisian campaign, and neither it nor 1st Armoured, 46th and 56th Divisions had taken part in 'Diadem'. They needed time to settle down and to get into their stride again: after the battles of Croce and Gemmano they did so, but by then it was too late. Leese, writing to the A.C.I.G.S. in the War Office on 8th September, commented:[229]

> 'A certain amount of this delay . . . has been due to the "growing pains" of 56th Division and 1st Armoured Division . . . It is extraordinary how difficult it is to make new troops realise the inter-dependence of tanks and infantry until they have gained the knowledge by bitter experience in battle'.

It would not be right to criticise the selection of these divisions unless there had been an alternative. McCreery's 10th Corps, which had advanced through the mountains from Cassino northwards might, with 4th, 8th and 10th Indian Divisions, have been as effective as Juin's F.E.C. in unhinging the German mountain flank and reversing the observation advantage. Moreover, 6th Armoured Division was fully experienced in hill, if not mountain warfare and would have been a better choice than the *ad hoc* last minute grouping of three brigades which was all that 1st Armoured Division could really claim to be. There is, however, no evidence that 10th Corps was ever considered because the type of battle contemplated did not call for another F.E.C.; nor perhaps would it have been morally right to impose the toughest fighting on the three Indian Divisions, even though each Indian brigade contained a British battalion and their gunners were largely British.

In retrospect it can be seen that Leese's battle never existed. A mountain corps rather than a pursuit corps was what was needed. Above all, divisions in their stride, and not divisions coming back after a long rest, were an essential pre-requisite for quick success whatever tactics were used. Nevertheless, 8th Army came very close to a break through on a number of occasions during the offensive. Had it not been for German endurance and the fortuitous intervention of the weather at critical moments, A.A.I. would probably have wintered in the ancient towns of northern Italy instead of in the dark discomfort of the Apennines and the clawing mud of the Romagna.

von Vietinghoff summed up the feelings of the German soldier in a report to *OB Südwest* on 20th September:[230]

> '*All* soldiers hope that the use of the new weapons [e.g. V-weapons] will bring about a rapid and basic change in the situation. This hope is fostered by articles in the Press, and if it is not soon realised morale will drop . . .
>
> The physical and mental demands of a battle of material are such that the soldier can only do his duty to the limits of human endurance. He fights because he is ordered to do so, and for his very existence. Our inferiority in material is very bitter to him especially the total absence of the *Luftwaffe*'.

During 'Olive' the limits of German soldiers' endurance were tested over and over again. It is to their great credit that with few exceptions their morale did not break in spite of 8th Army's material advantages.

(ix)

See Map 4

We have woven the story of the tactical air effort into the accounts of the land battles. We must now turn to strategic air operations within and beyond Italy for the period 25th August to 22nd September. Sorties flown by M.A.A.F. are contained in Table I; the sorties and bombloads for the Italian battle area compared with the effort north of the battle area and beyond Italy are shown at Table II, and the breakdown of effort between targets attacked in Italy is given at Table III. Targets attacked elsewhere are given at Table IV. These tables will be found at the end of the chapter.

The weather began to make an increasing impact on air operations as autumn approached. During the summer specific periods of bad weather could be noted, but by September interruption in flying became much more general, although the reduction of flying due to weather was not yet critical. The average sortie rate was 1,710 every 24 hours which was only slightly below the previous period, but air reconnaissance appears to have suffered considerably.[231] Aircraft losses dropped from a daily average of 17–18 during the summer to 14, the total loss during the 28 days being 383. The *Luftwaffe* lost 171 during the same period; 27 in Italy (18 in the air and nine on the ground) and 144 in the Balkans (29 in the air and 115 on the ground).

On 3rd September H.Q. M.A.A.F. issued a directive affecting the selection of targets, principally those of strategic importance. As a general policy no further attempts were to be made to destroy basic public utilities such as dams, water purification and electric power plants in enemy-held territory other than in Germany, Hungary, Austria and Bulgaria.

Within Italy itself the return of H.Q. M.A.T.A.F., and the restoration of the arrangement which existed until early July of each tactical air force supporting its own national army, made it necessary to re-define the areas of responsibility of U.S. 'X' T.A.C. (as it was then) and D.A.F. for operations against enemy communications.[232] H.Q. M.A.T.A.F. foresaw the necessity and on 12th September issued a directive in advance. The dividing line between the two main areas of responsibility was to be the inter-Army boundary as far north as the Parma-Rimini railway line and then the railway line Ferrara-Ostiglia-Verona.

In air operations which took place north of the battle area in Italy, 63% of the sorties flown and 75% of the total bombload dropped were to maintain the dislocation of the railway system.[233] Roads and road transport came a poor second, and little was left for administrative installations and dumps. The enemy's constant changing from one route to another during successive Allied air attacks cannot be described in detail, but his experience on his main north-south route will be quoted as an example. This route, it will be recalled, ran from the Brenner via Trento to Verona. Thereafter it divided with the main route crossing the Po at Ostiglia and an alternative route crossing the Po at Pontelagoscuro. On 28th August Kesselring reported a break north of Trento and a diversion south of Ferrara. Next day he reported two fresh breaks in the north. On 2nd September he referred to only one break in the north and to one not far short of Bologna which was repaired next day. On the 4th, however, he reported that widespread Allied air attacks throughout northern Italy had disrupted communications and delayed troop movements. Not until the 9th could he report a clear line from the Brenner Pass to Vernio other than for the break across the Po at Ostiglia. On the 15th there was a fresh break north of Trento and another south of Ostiglia which was repaired by the 19th, but that day a diversion was necessary between Ostiglia and Bologna. It is possible that after 28th August the Germans mostly discounted the Rovigo route because of the attacks on the Pontelagoscuro rail bridge over the Po river, just north of Ferrara, by M.A.S.A.F. on 26th, 27th and 29th August, and on 5th September when the Germans recorded the bridge badly damaged. If this was so, then the see-saw nature of the contest between the damage and destruction caused by Allied air attack on the one hand and the determined and energetic attempts at repair by the Germans on the other must have been confined to the main route via Ostiglia for a time.

On 21st September, the last full day of air operations covered by this chapter, there came into effect a M.A.T.A.F. directive addressed to the Commanding Generals of U.S. 42nd (Marauder) and 57th (Mitchell) Medium Bombardment Wings, and of U.S. 'X' T.A.C., and to the A.O.C. D.A.F. No fighter escort was henceforth to be provided for Marauders and Mitchells (including D.A.F.'s Marauders) operating over Italy unless specifically directed by H.Q. M.A.T.A.F. With the decline in the size and activity of the German fighter force and lack of replacements of aircrews, aircraft and supplies, the *Luftwaffe* could no longer challenge the Allied bomber formations. The Allied fighter-bomber activity in the Po valley afforded reasonable protection.

In strategic air operations bad weather cancelled bomber operations on five days during the second half of the period covered by this chapter, but the transport of supplies to southern France on two of them exploited better weather elsewhere. There was no such compensation during the five nights the strategic night bombers were grounded by the weather. Table IV shows the effort expended by M.A.S.A.F. on targets in each of the enemy occupied countries involved excluding, of course, targets in Italy. Also excluded are the efforts expended on ports, flare-dropping, mine-laying in the Danube, evacuating P.O.W., delivering supplies to France and supply-dropping over Warsaw. It will be noted that although oil was still the primary target, attacks on German Lines of Communication to the Balkans and to the Russian front absorbed a much greater proportion of M.A.S.A.F.'s effort. This was primarily due to the deletion of the Rumanian oil-fields from the target list after they had fallen into Russian hands. Bombing in Rumania was stopped on 24th August pending clarification of the situation there. The effort released was re-directed against L. of C. targets in Hungary and Yugoslavia to disrupt the enemy's retreat from Greece, Rumania and Bulgaria, and against airfields and harbours in Greece to hamper evacuation from the Aegean and Crete.

This changing pattern was belatedly acknowledged in a new directive issued by M.A.S.A.F. on 13th September, which left the overall priorities of the directive of 3rd August unchanged, but provided new target lists. M.A.S.A.F.'s remaining effort was to be directed against L. of C. targets in the following order of priority:

    a. Interdiction of main exit rail routes from Italy east of the Swiss border.

    b. Interdiction and interruption of communications to Hungary with emphasis on those in the east.

    c. Communications in Czechoslovakia.

    d. Communications in Austria.

    e. Communications in Yugoslavia.

The proximity of Yugoslavia to the Italian Theatre, the greater interest of H.Q. A.A.I. in the discomfiture of *OB Südost's* troops in the Balkans and the belated issue of the directive might have been responsible for the large expenditure of effort against the Yugoslav L. of C. The Balkan Air Force selected the targets there and passed them to M.A.T.A.F., informing M.A.S.A.F. simultaneously, so as to save time.

The thirteen oil installations attacked were the Odertal and Blechhammer north and south synthetic oil refineries in Germany, the Bohumin and Privozer oil refineries and Bratislava oil district in Czechoslovakia, the Moosbierbaum, Lobau and Schwechat oil refineries in Austria, the Szoeny, Shell and Magyar oil refineries in Hungary and the Oswiecim oil refinery in Poland.[234]* Only Oswiecim could match the long haul M.A.S.A.F. habitually used to undertake to bomb selected oil installations among the eleven in Rumania, now in Russian hands.†

When Rumania finally changed sides a special airlift to ferry out Allied P.O.W. was quickly arranged which took place in three phases on 31st August, 1st and 3rd September. 1,166 prisoners were lifted out in 55 Fortress sorties, of which 1,061 prisoners belonged to the U.S. Fifteenth Air Force and 36 to No. 205 Group R.A.F. A further 303 U.S airmen were released by Bulgaria and sent overland to Turkey and then to Cairo. They were then air-lifted to Italy by another 22 U.S. Liberators and three Fortresses.

---

* The locations of the more important of these targets are shown on Map 1 of *The Strategic Air Offensive Against Germany* Volume III (H.M.S.O. 1961), Sir Charles Webster and Noble Frankland.

† On 4th September *OKL's* Chief of Staff informed all *Luftflotten* including *Luftflotte* 2, that due to the loss of Rumanian oil a cut in fuel quotas for that month was unavoidable. Within 10 days stocks of fuel for the evacuation of personnel from the Aegean islands began to run short and fuel deliveries for the *Kriegsmarine* reached an all-time low.

In Greece M.A.S.A.F. made heavy attacks on the three principal airfields in the Athens area, starting on 13th/14th September, but these were part of the lead up to 'Manna' and will be described in the next chapter.

A point worthy of note in this period of strategic air operations was the introduction of the 'Gee' navigation system into No. 205 Group's area of operations, and there was also the arrival in the Group of three more aircraft fitted with H2S radar.[235] Unfortunately the H2S proved unreliable and suffered from lack of spares to keep the sets operational.

Throughout September the contraction of M.A.A.F. continued apace. Excluding the decline in the maritime air resources which is discussed in Part III Chapter XVII of this Volume there was a continuing drain, chiefly on the remaining strength of R.A.F., M.E.[236] It lost three fighter squadrons to the Balkan Air Force, another to the Desert Air Force, and a radio counter measures squadron was disbanded. The Balkan Air Force did best from the chopping and changing during the month, gaining four squadrons and a wing headquarters, as well as an air headquarters formed on 1st September to exercise control over R.A.F. units in Greece for Operation 'Manna'. We have mentioned the loss of some of M.A.T.A.F.'s formations and squadrons to the U.S. Ninth Air Force, and with them we must also include the transfer of the 31st and 34th Fighting French Air Force Marauder Groups to U.S. Ninth Air Force, which meant the loss of six squadrons of these valuable medium day bombers from M.A.T.A.F's resources.*

---

* The 31st and 34th F.F.A.F. Groups had been part of the U.S. 42nd Medium Bombardment Wing.

TABLE II

M.A.A.F. (INCLUDING MALTA BUT EXCLUDING H.Q., R.A.F., M.E.)
DISTRIBUTION OF BOMBER AND FIGHTER-BOMBER SORTIES AND BOMBLOADS DAWN 25th AUGUST TO DAWN 22nd SEPTEMBER 1944
(Excluding anti-shipping operations and attacks on ports)

Aircraft	Within the battle area	North of the battle area	Elsewhere than Italy
H.B. (day)	NIL	1,051 (2,541.3)	7,587 (17,259.0)*
H.B. (night)	71 (162.1)†	201 (546.3)†	81 (206·1)‡
M.B. (day)	2,935 (3,727·5)	2,185 (3,528·9)	577 (915·0)
M.B.(night)	186 (665.2)	523 (1,511.4)	220 (434.7)‡
L.B. (day)	825 (609.3)	174 (144.2)	110 (98.1)§
L.B. (night)	329 (227.6)	599 (413.0)	18 (15.6)
F.B. (day)	7,386 (3,018.2)	4,134 (1,776.0)	1,418 (544.5)
TOTALS	11,735 (8,469.9)	8,867 (10,461.1)	10,011 (19,473.0)
GRAND TOTAL	30,613(38,404.0)		

* Excludes 324 recorded sorties on supply missions to France; 24 plus recorded sorties on Special missions, details unknown; 88 recorded sorties bringing back P.O.W. from the Balkans and via Egypt.
† Excludes 120 flare-dropping sorties in Italy and elsewhere.
‡ Excludes mining of the Danube.
§ Excludes 52 recorded sorties on supply missions to France.

TABLE IV

STRATEGIC AIR OPERATIONS BEYOND ITALY: DAWN 25th AUGUST TO DAWN 22nd SEPTEMBER 1944

Country	Oil	M/Y, L. of C. and Misc.	Factories & Industrial Areas	Airfields	Total	Losses in Aircraft
Germany	577 (1,280.6)	2 (4.5)	166 (329.4)	256 (595.1)	1,001 (2,209.6)	38
Czechoslovakia	132 (269.5)	84 (189.0)	299 (738.3)	252 (584.5)	777 (1,781.3)	18
Austria	334 (809.6)	—	184 (364.7)	—	498 (1,174.3)	17
Hungary	207 (445.5)	2,442 (5,601.1)	—	—	2,649 (6,046.6)	7
Yugoslavia	—	1,964 (4,693.2)	—	55 (102.8)	2,019 (4,796.0)	5
Rumania	—	258 (549.0)	—	115 (229.7)	373 (778.7)	4
Greece	—	—	—	443 (818.9)	443 (818.9)	2
Poland	96 (210.5)	27 (79.0)	—	—	123 (289.5)	9
Totals	1,326 (3,015.7)	4,777 (11,115.8)	649 (1,432.4)	1,131 (2,331.0)	7,883 (17,894.9)	100

CHAPTER XIV

SUCCESS BECKONS IN THE MEDITERRANEAN

(i)

IN early September 1944 the defeat of Germany before the end of the year seemed a strong possibility. In John Ehrman's words: 'Both in the west and in the east the crust seemed suddenly to have yielded, and . . . it was difficult to gauge if anything lay behind'.* In north-west Europe, 21st Army Group entered Brussels on 3rd September and Antwerp the following day, suggesting that the northern route to Germany's industrial heartland of the Ruhr might be quickly forced open by Montgomery's coming airborne operation, 'Market Garden', designed to seize crossings over the Maas and Rhine. In Italy, 8th Army's offensive had opened strongly and that of 5th Army was developing, but it was in eastern Europe that Germany's fortunes had suffered their most dramatic change. Rumania had accepted the Allies' armistice terms on 23rd August and declared war on Germany two days later. Having asked Moscow for peace terms, Finland severed diplomatic relations with the Reich on 2nd September; Bulgaria, on whom the Soviet Union declared war on the 5th, promptly sought to escape the consequences by similarly breaking off relations with Germany prior to a formal declaration of war on 8th September.[1] It was of primary importance to Hitler that Hungary should not follow suit; in early September the German military contingent there was extensively reinforced to reassure the Hungarians that they had a bulwark against the Russians whose advance to the oil and mineral resources of western Hungary the Führer was determined to prevent.[2] Neither the Germans nor the Allies could be certain in which direction the Russians would thrust next: to their traditional objective of the Dardanelles; into Macedonia to cut off the German Army Group E in Greece and the Aegean; to Belgrade to help Tito secure the Yugoslav capital; or into Hungary to unhinge the German defence of the Greater Reich?

---

* History of the Second World War *Grand Strategy* Volume V (H.M.S.O. 1956) p.377.

It was against this background that the Balkan Air Force began its 'Rat Week' operation on 1st September, and the Allied war leaders met for the second time in Quebec for the 'Octagon' conference in mid-September. In this chapter we will look at the German position in the Balkans and the first steps taken by the British to interfere with and to follow up the withdrawal of *OB Südost's* forces which began at the end of August. Then we will look at those 'Octagon' decisions which affected the Mediterranean, before returning to 5th and 8th Armies' continuing efforts to force *OB Südwest* to abandon the Northern Apennines.

(ii)

'Rat Week', which was planned during Marshal Tito's visit to Italy in early August (Chapter XIII), proved to be fortuitously well timed. It started within a week of *OB Südost* being authorised on 26th August to begin thinning out the German garrisons on the Aegean and Ionian Islands, and also to prepare for a north-wards shift of his forces from southern and central Greece.[3] The collapse of Rumania, followed closely by the Russian invasion of Bulgaria, posed an obvious threat to the safe withdrawal of Colonel-General Löhr's Army Group E, garrisoning Greece and the Aegean, which could be aggravated by the proposed combined attacks of the Balkan Air Force and the Yugoslav army of National Liberation on its withdrawal routes through Yugoslavia. In this wild country, ideally suited to guerilla warfare, General de Angelis' *Pz AOK 2* was already over-stretched.

The object of 'Rat Week' was:

'To stop for a period of one week beginning 1st September 1944
   a.   Enemy traffic through Yugoslavia.
   b.   Enemy traffic between garrisons in Yugoslavia.'[4]

For the operation Yugoslavia was divided into sectors in which Partisan commanders with their British Liaison Officers were made responsible for selecting targets.[5] Those targets, mainly key bridges and marshalling-yards, too strong for the Partisans to tackle suc-cessfully, were to be attacked by the air forces and, where B.A.F. aircraft did not possess the necessary punch or range, strikes were to be made by the powerful and far-ranging U.S. Fifteenth Air Force. Neutralising attacks were also to be carried out on German airfields around Belgrade and Nis. Careful photographic reconnais-sance of all targets was flown and special refuelling and re-arming arrangements were made at Brindisi and on the island of Vis. A close watch was kept on coastal shipping by the Royal Navy and

B.A.F. to stop attempts to by-pass the rail interdiction by sea. General Wilson set the tone of the operation on 1st September in a message to all the commanders in the Mediterranean, saying that it was vital, at a time when the war in Europe was reaching its climax, that they should all play their full part in making the German collapse immediate and final. They should act with determination and speed 'since it is the pace that kills'.[6] Risks were to be taken and the Partisans were to be encouraged to act with the greatest boldness everywhere to complete the confusion into which the German forces seemed to be falling.

See Map 23

The targets attacked fell into four groups: rail communications along the Sava valley from Zagreb to Brod and Belgrade; the Belgrade area itself with bridges to the north and east, including the Danube bridges; the vital Belgrade–Nis–Skoplje–Salonika–Athens railway line, and its alternatives via Mitrovica, by which Army Group E would have to withdraw from Greece; and a conglomeration of tracks between the Sava and the Adriatic coast supplying the garrisons of *Pz AOK* 2. The tonnage of bombs dropped reflects the importance attached to each group:

Zagreb–Belgrade	950 tons	U.S. Fifteenth
Belgrade area	675 tons	Air Force
Belgrade–Skoplje	1,760 tons	
Sava to Adriatic	300 tons	B.A.F.[7]

'Rat Week' achieved its immediate aims. The Partisans cut the Zagreb-Belgrade line nearly every night.[8] The Sava bridges were repeatedly damaged by B.A.F. and the Danube bridge at Pancevo was destroyed, causing considerable German embarrassment later during the Russian advance on Belgrade. The two vital Belgrade–Athens lines were later reported by *OB Südost* to be blocked about 60% of the time during September, and the most important of the Sava to Adriatic lines, Brod–Sarajevo–Mostar, was cut for 70% of the month. In the air–neutralisation attacks German records show only two aircraft damaged at Nis on 1st September, but on 3rd September 20 German aircraft were destroyed and four damaged on the ground and another destroyed in the air by strafing Lightnings near Belgrade. On 8th September another 56 German aircraft were destroyed and one damaged on the ground and two more destroyed in the air, all most probably by strafing Mustangs attacking airfields north-west and north of Belgrade. As a result the remaining German aircraft seem to have been withdrawn from Yugoslavia to Hungary.[9]

M.A.S.A.F. made a dramatic intervention on 6th September in support of 24th Partisan Division, attacking Leskovac, south of Nis, which is described by Brigadier Fitzroy Maclean who was watching:[10]

> '. . . looking up, we saw at a great height row upon row of bombers steadfastly following their appointed course, their polished wings gleaming in the sunlight . . ., the whole of Leskovac seemed to rise bodily into the air in a tornado of dust and smoke and debris, and a great rending noise fell on our ears. When we looked at the sky again, the Forts [sic], still relentlessly following their course, were silvery dots in the distance . . .'

The attack had been made by 111 Liberators of the U.S. Fifteenth Air Force which dropped 223 tons of bombs on the town.[11]

(iii)

See Maps 23 and 24

The end of 'Rat Week' coincided with Bulgaria's declaration of war on Germany and the beginning of active participation of Bulgarian troops in the development of the Russian threat to Löhr's withdrawal routes from Greece. It was clearly time for *OB Südost*, Field-Marshal von Weichs, to give thought to the total evacuation of Greece by Army Group E. For reasons soundly based upon staff calculations he was in no hurry to seek the necessary authorization from Hitler, who had his own geo-political reasons for leaving this issue in abeyance during September.[12] Militarily, von Weichs wanted to buy as much time as possible to clear Germany's very considerable assets in men and equipment deployed on the Aegean islands. For instance Crete was garrisoned by 22nd Infantry Division and Fortress Infantry Division 133. The former was one of the strongest and best equipped divisions left in the *Wehrmacht*. Its infantry companies averaged 100 men; it was fully motorised; and it had its complete establishment of artillery, S.P. anti-tank guns and flak weapons.[13] General Friebe, who took over the division in April 1944, came from the Eastern Front and was astounded at the strength of his new command in a 'fairly pointless outpost in the Mediterranean'. von Weichs' account of the 'Great Withdrawal', written in 1945, gives the garrison of Crete as 34,000 Germans and 6,500 Italians and the garrisons of the Dodecanese, including Rhodes, as another 23,300 Germans and 7,350 Italians. Discounting the Italians, von Weichs was faced with ferrying some 57,000 German troops to the mainland with about 100 Ju. 52 air transports and the few ships still available to the *Kriegsmarine*.

Another military reason for delay was the difficulty of withdrawing large bodies of troops northwards through Macedonia and Albania. As we have seen, very limited use could be made of the only main rail link between Salonika and Belgrade in September, owing to damage by Allied air attacks and Partisan raiding. von Weichs, therefore, needed time to move Army Group E through this bottleneck. And a third reason for not hurrying was the lack of British interference in early September with the evacuation of the Aegean.

Hitler's geo-political reasons stemmed from the general German conviction that the Western Powers would sooner or later fall out with Russia to Germany's advantage. This wishful thinking, and the hope that, if his subjects held on, the new V-weapons would eventually turn the tables in their favour, were fostered by propaganda to buoy up resistance in the field. At *OKW*, it seemed in September 1944 that *OB Südost's* theatre offered particular scope for Anglo-Russian rivalry.[14] Foreign Armies West declared on the 3rd that in the Balkans the 'political struggle' between the Powers was gaining in intensity. Allied strategic options were obscure, but from such items as Churchill's visit to Italy and the abandonment of Mihailovic in favour of Tito, *FHW* concluded that the British, albeit anxious about the growing power of the Russians, did not feel strong enough to do more than keep a foot in the Western Balkans by supplying both Nationalist and Communist movements. With this view apparently confirmed by the otherwise inexplicable lack of British air and naval interception during the first stages of the Aegean evacuation, Russia's declaration of war on Bulgaria was greeted by Hitler as 'surely heralding a rise in tension between Germany's enemies'. According to the *OKW* diarist, the Führer reckoned on 8th September that the Red Army would thrust into eastern Thrace to cut off the Dardanelles. He also surmised that in this event Army Group E might not be attacked by Soviet forces, but would be left to act as a buffer against a British advance from Greece. No such thrust had developed by the 14th, however, when it seemed more likely that the Russians would strike westwards from Bulgaria. As this would obviously threaten the L. of C. of Army Group E, Hitler shifted his ground. He now saw it as British policy to let German troops remain on the Aegean islands as a 'sort of police force' to check the spread of Bolshevism, and also to let German elements remain in Greece where they could block the advance of the Red Army and counterbalance the Communist *E.L.A.S.* guerillas.

This new theory had a practical effect, for having asserted that the *Wehrmacht* was not a police force, Hitler promptly sanctioned the complete clearance of the Dodecanese and Aegean islands. In the ratifying directive which was signed and issued by Jodl on 15th September the task of determining priorities for air and naval transport was allocated to *OB Südost*. He was to give first place to fighting troops and their most valuable equipment, such as tanks and assault and anti-tank guns, together with fuel and ammunition of types in short supply. In the political context, Jodl suggested that the currently 'passive' attitude of the British towards the withdrawal of German troops from the islands and southern Greece pointed to Soviet designs on the whole of the Balkans. It was not in German interests to prevent conflicts between Communist and Nationalist factions in the areas being evacuated, as these might lead to similar disputes between the Anglo-Saxons and the Russians. Every opportunity was to be taken to fan factional disputes even after German troops had actually withdrawn.

For Field-Marshal von Weichs, the overriding need of the moment was to gain time for clearing the southern and western sectors of his theatre, so that he could concentrate against the threat from the East. As we shall see, mid-September marked the end of British 'passivity' where the Aegean evacuation was concerned, but the clearance went determindly on as von Weichs needed all the troops and equipment he could muster for protection of the L. of C. of Löhr's Army Group E, and to keep open its eventual withdrawal route up the Salonika–Belgrade railway line. As soon as Rumania collapsed on 23rd August, he had been authorised by *OKW* to form a front for defence of this route, and three divisions (1st Mountain, 4th SS Police and 11th *Lufwaffe* Field) had accordingly been moved from anti-guerilla operations in Serbia, Macedonia and Greece.[15] The defection of Bulgaria on 8th September left von Weichs (as he wrote in January 1945) with an eastern flank which was open from the Aegean to the Hungarian border. His front, which until mid-August had faced seawards along the Adriatic and Aegean coasts, had to be turned inside out to face east. On 9th September von Weichs extended the sphere of command of Army Group E to include Macedonia, and with Albania added two days later Löhr was made directly responsible for the protection of his own withdrawal routes.[16] To meet his commitments, 11th Luftwaffe Field Division was moved to the Macedonian border and 41st Infantry, 117th and 104th Jäger Divisions were pulled out of the Peloponnese and Epirus areas of Greece. As von Weichs had on the one hand to guard against a Soviet thrust into Serbia from Rumania, and on the other to protect the southern part of his eastern flank from the Bulgarians, his new front was extended northwards to Turnu Severin on the Danube well to the east of Belgrade, and southwards down the Struma valley to Salonika. Defence of the southern sector was entrusted to 22nd Infantry Division, but as it was moved from Crete principally by air it arrived on the mainland without transport or heavy weapons, which had to be reprovided from such reserve stocks as existed in Greece. Left to defend Croatia, the front of General de Angelis' depleted *Pz AOK 2* was also turned inland, and by the third week in September most of the main offshore Dalmatian Islands had been evacuated by their German garrisons. The evacuation of Corfu was authorised by *OKW* on 18th September.

In the Aegean, British attacks on German air/sea transports were mounted after 15th September, but their land forces showed what Foreign Armies West described on the 26th as 'very striking caution' in occupying island or mainland territories which had been relinquished.[17] With neither the British nor the Russians conforming to Hitler's expectation of a race for the Dardanelles, the final incentives to pull out of Greece were provided by von Weichs' own concern for his theatre's transport problems and for the vulnerability of his eastern flank. By about 22nd September it was apparent that the Bulgarian Army would give vigorous support to its new masters, who were withdrawing their own troops from Bulgaria for re-deployment in the Danube basin. On 27th September von Weichs reckoned that the Russians were building up for a two-pronged attack on Belgrade, which would probably be accompanied by a supporting drive by Tito's Partisans.[18] Further reinforcements were sent towards Belgrade from Greece and from *Pz AOK 2*, and on 2nd October *OKW* asked *OB Südost* whether the time for the evacuation for Greece could be set.[19] He and Löhr agreed next day that it could start on 10th October, and with Hitler's approval orders ratifying the abandonment of Greece, southern Albania and southern Macedonia were at once issued to Army Group E. Flights to and from the islands and Salonika were to continue for as long as fuel stocks lasted and enough Greek airfields remained in German hands.

The airlifting of troops and equipment from the islands had in fact begun to peter out at the end of September, due more to shortage of fuel than lack of air bases.[20] The last Ju. 52 left Crete on 28th September and flights to Salonika were finally discontinued on 23rd October. Crete, Rhodes, Leros, Cos and Milos could not be fully cleared and the first three were designated 'Fortresses'.[21] Their garrisons were instructed to hold out to the last round if attacked, in order to pin down Allied forces which might be used elsewhere. On 26th October Army Group E and Admiral Aegean reported that a total of 22,400 Army and 4,095 naval personnel remained on the five islands, with some 13,700 on Crete, about 6,000 on Rhodes, 5,000 on Leros, 1,000 on Cos and under 1,000 on Milos. An *OKW* map dated 29th December gave slightly lower totals for the Germans, and showed that about 12,000 Italians had also been left behind.[22]

The story of the German evacuation of Greece belongs to Chapter XV. We must now look at the reasons for apparent British 'passivity' up to mid-September and their actions thereafter until the German withdrawal from Athens began, triggering Operation 'Manna'.

(iv)

See Map 24

German bewilderment about British policy in south-eastern Europe was matched by British difficulty in assessing when the Germans would withdraw and, indeed, why they had not already done so in view of the massive Russian threat to their rear. German hopes of an inter-Allied clash in the Balkans distorted their views on the priorities of Allied strategy in the Mediterranean, and they also failed to appreciate the paucity of forces at Wilson's disposal after 'Dragoon'.[23] Their notional order of battle for Allied forces, cluttered with non-existent formations, gave the impression of ample reserves, whereas none were readily available. Intervention by major forces in Greece had never been contemplated by the Allies.* The most that the British intended to commit, as has been explained in Chapter XII, was a small force which was to be dispatched *after* the German withdrawal.

Ever since Mr. Churchill's visit to Italy in August planning for Operation 'Manna' had been going on apace. One of the most important questions to be resolved was a delineation of Allied as opposed to British responsibilities. There had been a long history of American objections to military involvement in Greece, for while Washington was happy to be associated with the introduction of relief supplies for the Greek population, which in some areas was near starvation, they had no desire to be drawn into military operations which they believed should be left entirely to British initiative.[24] Negotiations, carried out by the British Joint Staff in Washington to reach an acceptable conclusion, culminated on 8th September in the issue of a formal C.C.S. Directive: General Wilson was to act in his capacity as Senior *British* Commander for operations in Greece, for which he would nominate a British Commander with a British and Greek force under him.[25] He would

---

* For decisions on Allied strategy in the Mediterranean taken at the Teheran Conference in November 1943 see Ehrman: *Grand Strategy* Volume V *op. cit.* pp.173–83.

act as Supreme *Allied* Commander for the introduction of relief
supplies, the control of which was accordingly to be transferred to
A.F.H.Q. from the Middle East Command. The co-ordinating
authority, Allied Military Liaison Headquarters (Balkans), would
operate under an American Deputy Commander.* The employment of American forces in the Balkans would be limited 'strictly
to relief and rehabilitation essential to relief in Greece, Yugoslavia
and Albania'.[26] The word 'Allied' was only to be used in procla-
mations concerning relief and rehabilitation; all others were to be
signed by a British Commander. U.S. transport aircraft (as had
been agreed) could be used for ferrying airborne forces into Greece,
if they could be spared from other operations under Wilson's
command, but operations in Greece must not interfere with those
in Italy or southern France.

On 22nd August Lieutenant-General R. M. Scobie was
appointed Commander Land Forces, Greece, with Brigadier-
General Percy L. Sadler as U.S. Deputy Commander for relief
and rehabilitation.[27] Scobie's headquarters was designated H.Q.
Force 140 and was formed from H.Q. 3rd Corps in the Middle
East. Scobie arrived at A.F.H.Q. from the Middle East with a
small planning staff a week later, followed by the remainder of
H.Q. 3rd Corps and part of the Greek General Staff from Cairo
during the first week of September. Besides such national forces
as the Greek Government could put under his command, General
Scobie was allocated:[28]

> 2nd Parachute Brigade; to be despatched from Italy by sea and
> air.
> 23rd Armoured Brigade; to be despatched from the Middle
> East, where, following the advice of the War Office, General
> Paget had dismounted the brigade to train as infantry.
> Force 133 in Greece, comprising Allied Liaison Officers operating
> with the guerilla forces.

On the naval side, Rear-Admiral J. M. Mansfield, Flag Officer
Commanding 14th Cruiser Squadron, was responsible as the Naval
Force Commander for the planning and safe arrival of the seaborne
force to Flag Officer Levant and Eastern Mediterranean
(F.O.L.E.M.) at Alexandria, whence half the naval forces were to
come.[29] The remainder were to be from Naples and the Heel
ports of Italy. The number of cruisers and attendant destroyers,
Mansfield was informed, would depend upon circumstances at the
time. 5th Minesweeping Flotilla (sailing from Malta) was specially
allotted to clear a passage from the west through the very extensive
minefields between the southern Peloponnese and Crete which

---

* A.M.L. was to operate until U.N.R.R.A. could take over.

barred the entrances into the Aegean Sea, but for these operations it would be under the orders of the Commander-in-Chief Mediterranean and would only afterwards transfer to F.O.L.E.M.'s forces. It was intended that Mansfield would turn over the local naval command to the Greek Naval Commander-in-Chief soon after the arrival of the forces in Greece.

The responsibility for planning the R.A.F. contribution to 'Manna' rested with Air Vice-Marshal Elliot as Commander, Balkan Air Force.[30] For this purpose he worked closely with the Air Officer Commanding, Royal Air Force, Middle East, who was providing a large proportion of the air resources and continued to be responsible for their maintenance. The tasks of the air forces to be sent to Greece were: to defend Athens and possibly Salonika later; to co-operate with the land forces in Greece as required; and to co-operate with the Italy-based Allied air forces in preventing German formations from withdrawing intact from Greece with their arms and equipment. For these tasks a small local head-quarters, A.H.Q. Greece, was set up. Air Commodore G. W. Tuttle was appointed to command with a force, as initially planned, of an R.A.F. wing of two fighter, one night and two reconnaissance squadrons.[31]

The work of the Force Commanders was made difficult by the wide dispersal of the authorities involved. Scobie's own H.Q. 3rd Corps was at Salerno, not too far from the Greek Government and A.F.H.Q. at Caserta.[32] Fortunately Admiral Mansfield had an office near Scobie at Salerno which he could use when not at sea, but he was unable to carry out an intended visit to F.O.L.E.M., Vice-Admiral Sir Edward Rawlings, at Alexandria. H.Q.s B.A.F. and Land Forces Adriatic, whose light raiding forces were soon to be in demand, were at Bari on the Adriatic. H.Q. Force 133, which controlled the British Liaison officers with the Greek guerilla bands, remained in Cairo but sent a liaison section to work with Scobie's staff.[33]

The chain of command for 'Manna' planning followed the established pattern of three independent land, sea and air head-quarters operating as a joint command.[34] Once in Greece, however, Scobie, as representative of S.A.C. Mediterranean, would co-ordinate local land and air operations, although Elliot remained responsible to Air Commander-in-Chief M.A.A.F. for any external operations. The relationship of Air H.Q. Greece to Scobie was similar to that of the command of a supporting tactical air force.[35] Air Commodore Tuttle had been personally selected by Air Marshal Slessor.[36]

A further difficulty in planning was that, unlike most operations, the commanders had no control over D day, which depended on the date on which the Germans withdrew from Athens, or upon their inability to offer organised resistance.[37]

General Scobie's directive, which was approved by Wilson on 5th September, although not formally issued until the 24th, read:[38]

> 'Your primary task, after securing the Athens area (including a suitable airfield), will be to establish and maintain law and order in that area and thereby facilitate the establishment of the Greek Government in Athens, in order to make possibile the introduction and distribution of relief supplies'.

He was given a number of subsidiary tasks: accept any German surrenders; enforce any armistice terms; help the naval forces to open up Greek ports for the entry of relief supplies; assist the Greek Government to maintain law and order; and ensure the equitable distribution of relief.

The Outline Plan, as issued to Scobie after approval by Wilson on 31st August, was to drop the Parachute Brigade near the Athens airfield of Kalamaki on the same day that 'Arkforce', 23rd Armoured Brigade, arrived by sea at the Piraeus.[39] Having seized the Athens port and airfield, he would establish law and order in the capital, so that the Greek Government could be brought in from Salerno and the inflow of relief supplies could be started. 2nd Parachute Brigade was to be relieved in due course by 3rd Greek Mountain Brigade from 8th Army.* 23rd Armoured Brigade was warned to be ready to sail from Egypt on 7th September; 2nd Parachute Brigade was to concentrate at Taranto on 8th September and to be ready to drop by 10th September. One store ship with ten days' supplies for Force 140 was to sail from Alexandria, and further shipments of R. E. stores and civil relief supplies were organised. The rest of the force was to be at 48 hours notice from midnight 13th/14th September.

Meanwhile there was growing anxiety in Whitehall as to future Russian intentions. A flurry of signals passed during 12th and 13th September between Caserta, Cairo, London and Quebec while a possible change of policy was being debated. On 12th September Mr. Eden expressed his concern to the Prime Minister, who with the British Chiefs of Staff had arrived in Quebec for 'Octagon'. He felt it was 'highly desirable that the British Force should enter Greece as soon as possible to counterbalance the presence of Russian troops in Bulgaria'.[40] He appreciated that Wilson would have no reinforcements available for 'Manna' while the 'Olive' offensive continued in Italy. He proposed, therefore, the alternative of establishing the Greek Government in the Peloponnese which it

---

* 3rd Greek Mountain Brigade's gallant action during the 'Olive' offensive leading to the occupation of Rimini on 21st September earned it also the title of the 'Rimini Brigade'.

seemed would be evacuated first. He was sceptical about *E.A.M.'s* promises of collaboration. If British troops did not follow the German withdrawal from the Peloponnese, *E.L.A.S.* would fill the vacuum and would be very difficult to dislodge; whereas, if British troops landed straight away, the authority of the Greek Government could be established progressively in other areas as they were left by the Germans. Simultaneously, it was reported from Caserta that M. Papandreou believed that the Russian entry into Bulgaria had upset the calculations on which *E.A.M.* had entered his Government, adding 'Collaboration [with *E.A.M.*] will become more difficult in proportion as they think Russia and not Great Britain may call the tune in Greece'.[41] And from Cairo Mr. Warner, British Chargé d'Affaires to that part of the Greek Government left in Egypt, cabled to the Foreign Office urging swifter British military intervention.[42] He feared that the *'ELAS wholesale massacres at Pyrgos'* meant that they would pay scant attention to their members in the Greek Government, and could foreshadow a 'general blood bath' unless firm action was taken at once. It was most unlikely that the Greek population would believe that the British could do nothing to avert the tragedy and it was 'a significant and sinister feature' that the Allied Military Mission was already being blamed.

These cables made their impact in Quebec. Within twenty-four hours Churchill had cabled Wilson asking him to plan a descent on the Peloponnese 'so that we can decide whether to do it or not'.[43] The British Chiefs of Staff sent a parallel and more finite signal asking Wilson to report whether he could carry out an operation to install the Greek Government in the Peloponnese, and, if so, whether the descent on Athens could be remounted subsequently.[44] Wilson replied to the Prime Minister on 15th September: 'I will of course put in hand immediately planning for the occupation of the Peloponnese, but I hope the measures described below will achieve the purpose which you have in mind'.[45] He then pointed out that the Peloponnese had probably been evacuated already south of the line Nauplia–Tripolis–Kiparissia and that the Germans appeared to be holding Corinth, the Isthmus of Corinth and the south shore of the Gulf of Corinth, including Patras. He had, therefore, dispatched a commando and light naval force to Cythera ('Fox Force'—to be described) which would reconnoitre as far north as the port of Nauplia and the islands of Poros, Aegina and Salamis which covered the approaches to the Piraeus and Athens. He had arranged for the Greek Government to infiltrate Commissioners into the Peloponnese, and into the Ionian and Aegean Islands, each accompanied by a British field officer and a small Greek military escort. With the agreement of the Greek Government he was also placing General Saraphis (Military Commander of *E.L.A.S.*) and General Zervas (Leader of *E.D.E.S.*) with their respective guerilla bands under Commander Force 140, General Scobie. Efforts were being made to bring these officers out of Greece to meet Scobie so that he could ensure that the bulk of their forces were used against the German withdrawal and not in the Athens area.

Wilson concluded his cable by saying that for several reasons he was anxious to keep the main body of Force 140 intact for the descent on Athens. Its strength was no more than adequate for the occupation of Athens and, were it to be dissipated, he had no other forces available. If Force 140 was landed in the Peloponnese its overland advance on Athens could be blocked by German demolitions and re-embarkation would take time. Finally any further westward advances by the Russians would precipitate the total German evacuation of Greece and enable 'Manna' to be launched in ample time to forestall the Russians. His last paragraph rounded off with, 'in discussion with me yesterday the Greek Prime Minister said he was strongly averse from returning to any area of Greece other than Athens'.

In a parallel cable, Mr. R. W. A. Leeper, the British Ambassaor to the Greek Government, expressed his and Harold Macmillan's support for Wilson's plan.[46] They were sure that the Greek Government would enjoy greater authority in Athens than in a small Peloponnese town, where it would be out of contact with the developing situation. This political support convinced Churchill and the Chiefs of Staff, who cabled to Wilson on 16th September, telling him to go ahead with his improvised re-entry into the Peloponnese, keeping Force 140 intact.[47]

Intelligence reports on the German evacuation from the Southern Aegean had been building up since late August and by 6th September had confirmed a flow of arrivals from Crete and the Islands at Tatoi airfield, and heavy rail movement from Athens northwards.[48]* Wilson, however, felt he had no means of exploiting the situation except by employing a force of British cruisers and escort carriers (released from 'Dragoon' and already in the Eastern Mediterranean) to 'intensify the enemy's difficulties in the Aegean'. He also decided to implement the final stage of 'Noah's Ark', and on 9th September issued orders for Greek Partisan forces to attack the main German escape routes with the aim of checking the withdrawal and 'killing the maximum number of German troops'.[49]†

---

* The build up of Intelligence is set out by F. H. Hinsley: *British Intelligence in the Second World War* Volume 3 Part 2 (H.M.S.O.) forthcoming.

† See p.207

Soon afterwards Wilson took the first steps for launching 'Manna': clearance of a passage through minefields in the Cythera Channel at the western entrance to the Aegean which depended in turn on the destruction of the coast defence guns and radar on the island of Cythera.[50] Plans for the necessary raid on Cythera had been prepared by Land Forces Adriatic (L.F.A.) and on 12th September he ordered that it should be launched as soon as possible. After a reconnaissance party of the Long Range Desert Group had reported that the island was clear, the raid was replaced by a landing to establish an advanced naval base for coastal forces and for general reconnaissance up the eastern coast of the Peloponnese. Fox Force (Lieutenant-Colonel R. J. F. Tod commanding 9th Commando and certain other Special troops) sailed for Cythera on 14th September.[51]

On 15th September Wilson assumed direct responsibility for all operations on the Greek mainland, the Ionian Islands and the islands in the approaches to Athens.[52] Meanwhile the measures which he had put in hand to provide 'maximum harassment' by sea and air had begun to take effect,[53] but the forces employed suffered from a number of handicaps, some of which are worth mentioning as they may help to explain the British 'passivity' which had bewildered the Germans.

For months past the Germans had been largely dependent upon air transport to maintain their Aegean garrisons on a quiet routine basis. Such deep inroads had been made into German controlled shipping that they had no alternative but to increase their air transport effort to carry out the evacuation when Hitler authorised its start on 26th August.[54] Attempts to intercept the routine traffic had not been very successful: the size of the area in relation to the numbers of German aircraft operating and to the limited air resources of R.A.F. Middle East, the long ranges at which the R.A.F. aircraft were forced to operate and the poor radar conditions experienced in the Aegean gave the German aircrew advantages over the R.A.F. intruders which they exploited to the full. Their lightly armed Ju. 52s flew sometimes as low as 50 feet over the sea at 110–140 miles per hour. This placed the faster R.A.F. Beaufighters at a tactical disadvantage. The Ju. 52s were usually airborne in the twilight periods of dusk and dawn when they were most difficult to detect. At the end of August, R.A.F. Middle East held just two Beaufighter squadrons which were of practical use to oppose the evacuation of German troops from Crete.* Had it not been for the services of the Fighter Direction Ship, *Ulster Queen*,

---

* For the first three nights one squadron only was operational. The arrival of the second raised the aircraft available from 4 to 7 or 8. They usually operated singly.

with her G.C.I. Type 277 radar sets, they would have been even less effective.[55] It is now known that a force of 107 Ju. 52s was available on 20th August to the German air command.[56] The numbers of other types pressed into service is unkown.

The most significant weakness in the force provided by the Royal Navy was the lack of night flying aircraft on the escort carriers, needed both for protecting the force during the dangerous twilight hours and for night interception.[57] Of the potential targets, small merchant vessels cried out for attack by long-range R. P. fighters, but only one squadron (on the *Emperor*) had long-range Hellcats and none had Rocket Projectiles.[58]

The force of seven British escort carriers, released from 'Dragoon', reached Alexandria on 1st September.[59] Here their aircraft complements were slightly modified to give a total of 20 fighter-bombers per ship (Hellcats, Martlets and Seafires)* although the numbers carried on operation were often below establishment. On 9th September Admiral Cunningham, Commander-in-Chief Mediterranean, placed the force of escort carriers and destroyers under Rear-Admiral Escort Carriers, Rear-Admiral T. Troubridge. It was to be augmented by cruisers from 15th Cruiser Squadron, earmarked for 'Manna', and a division of Hunt Class destroyers. Force 120, as the whole force was known (ships at sea whether as groups or singly used the call-sign Force A), operated from 9th September to 15th November; Troubridge was to be relieved by Commodore G. N. Oliver with the title Commodore, Escort Carriers (COMEC) on 6th October. The first elements to sail were the cruiser *Royalist* (Flag), escort carriers *Hunter*, *Khedive*, *Pursuer* and *Searcher*, and ten destroyers (eight British, the Greek H.H.M.S. *Navarinon* and the Polish *Garland*).[60] Force A remained at sea until 20th September, its composition fluctuating from time to time. Other ships which took part in its operations included: cruisers, *Black Prince* and *Aurora;* escort carriers, *Emperor* and *Attacker;* A.A. cruiser *Colombo*. Troubridge's task was to penetrate the German defences of the Aegean and to intercept their evacuation by sea.[61]

Force A began operations south of Crete on 12th September, moving through the Kaso Strait, east of Crete, after dark to carry out raids on shipping and returning each dawn.[62] On 15th September Troubridge decided that his force had provoked so little response from the *Luftwaffe* that it seemed safe to enter the Aegean.

---

* For our purpose we have continued to use the designation 'Martlet' for the later version known as 'Wildcat' in the U.S. Services.

For the next five days he disrupted German sea communications in the Southern Aegean, strafed sea and road traffic in Crete and, in a strike of 45 aircraft, sunk four ships in Rhodes harbour and destroyed a mine store. *U.407*, the last U-boat to be sunk at sea in the Mediterrean, was despatched after a grim ten hour hunt by destroyers.* Naval aircraft also covered Land Forces Adriatic's approach to Cythera Island and the sweeping of the Cythera Channel into the Western Aegean on which 5th Minesweeping Flotilla was at work.[63] Leaving the *Colombo* and two destroyers to maintain a nightly blockade of Cretan harbours, Force A withdrew to Alexandria for replenishment on 20th September; *Royalist* and the destroyers had been refuelled at sea by the carriers but this proved very slow.[64] Time was also needed to sweep a passage through the inner ring of minefields between the Cyclades and the Dodecanese to give access to more northern waters.

During Troubridge's first penetration of the Aegean over 500 sorties had been flown. Eight aircraft had been hit by German flak that was often intense and accurate; none was lost, which Troubridge attributed to operating experience gained during 'Dragoon'. Force A claimed a total 'bag' of one submarine and 16 vessels of all types sunk (including three useful *KT* freighters), 12 vessels damaged, four aircraft destroyed and one damaged, and some 80 M.T. destroyed or damaged on land. On three nights the *Royalist* had attempted to direct Beaufighters onto the stream of air traffic between Crete and Athens, but no intercepts had resulted.

The fighter direction ship *Ulster Queen* left Alexandria on 25th September and based herself on Cythera Island, taking up a position north of Crete at dusk each evening.[65] She had been supplied with Intelligence assessments of the airfields and routes being used by German evacuation aircraft which had been deduced from P.O.W. interrogation three months previously. In spite of the staleness of this Intelligence she found that the routes suggested were still being used. In her nine days north of Crete *Ulster Queen* tracked 269 aircraft: 69 on the Athens-Maleme route, 171 on the Athens-Heraklion route, and 29 others, principally seaplanes from Suda Bay. The Beaufighters of Nos. 46 and 108 Squadrons R.A.F. under her control made contact on 46 of these tracks.[66] The Germans recorded that four of their aircraft were shot down and one damaged by fighters, two shot down by A.A. fire and ten failed to return. They lost two more aircraft on 4th October but the Beaufighters responsible were not under control of *Ulster Queen*. German tactics changed with experience. For the first few days their aircraft were flown off in batches of 5 or 6 at a time and kept

---

* See Captain S.W. Roskill: *The War at Sea* Volume III Part II (H.M.S.O. 1961) p.107.

under 300 feet. Height was then varied with some aircraft flying between 1,000 and 6,000 feet with a probable preference for the 5,000 to 6,000 band. The types of aircraft were also varied from the slow Ju. 52s to the faster Ju. 88s, He. IIIs and Do. 24s, which had less economic payloads.

To open up a route to better 'pickings' in the Central and Northern Aegean F.O.L.E.M., Admiral Rawlings, on 25th September despatched *Black Prince,* the escort carrier *Stalker,* and two destroyers to cover the sweeping of the Cynaros Channel.[67] It took three days to clear an eight mile passage. The force then moved north to carry out a prolonged bombardment of the staging port of Syros, and to allow ranging naval aircraft to destroy, amongst other craft, five Siebel ferries in dock in Tinos. Unexpected difficulties, however, continued in clearing the Cynaros Channel.* Force A sailed again from Alexandria on 30th September, but Admiral Troubridge found his operations still confined to the Southern Aegean where, owing to *Ulster Queen's* successes, the heavy bombing of Athens airfields by M.A.S.A.F., and his own previous exploits, German sea and air movement had been reduced 'to a mere trickle'. After bombarding, bombing and strafing airfields and other targets on various islands, including installations at Heraklion and Maleme on Crete, Troubridge took his ships back to Alexandria to refuel, leaving the cruiser *Aurora,* an escort carrier and three destroyers to cover the minesweepers.

It was on 5th October that 5th Minesweeping Flotilla (Fleet Minesweepers), equipped with the heavier gear needed, was released from Cythera for Cynaros. They completed the clearance of the Cynaros Channel early on the 7th, when two destroyers were ordered to patrol northward to cover the route up the eastern coast of Greece to Salonika. This was none too soon as on 30th September Hitler had endorsed Army Group E's decision to confine the bulk of available shipping to this run.[69]

The intervention of M.A.S.A.F., which is set out in detail in the table over page had started on the night 13th/14th September.[70] Eleusis, Tatoi and Kalamaki airfields suffered three heavy attacks in mounting crescendo within 48 hours. 59 Wellingtons and 24 Liberators attacked on the first night, followed next night by 60 Wellingtons and 24 Liberators all from No. 205 Group R.A.F. and next day, 15th September, by 109 Fortresses and 167 Liberators of

---

* 35 fathoms of chain between mine and mooring wire proved difficult for the light gear of the small vessels of the 162nd Minesweeping Flotilla to tackle.[68]

Date	*Eleusis		Tatoi		Kalamaki	
	Aircraft	Bomb tons	Aircraft	Bomb tons	Aircraft	Bomb tons
13th/14th September	9 RAF Liberators	24.1	8 RAF Liberators	21.4	7 RAF Liberators	18.7
	3 RAF Halifaxes	Flares	3 RAF Halifaxes	Flares	3 RAF Halifaxes	Flares
	15 RAF Wellingtons	34.7	23 RAF Wellingtons	36.5	21 RAF Wellingtons	37.8
14th/15th September	12 RAF Liberators	32.1	5 RAF Liberators	8.9	7 RAF Liberators	12.5
	2 RAF Halifaxes	Flares	2 RAF Halifaxes	Flares	2 RAF Halifaxes	Flares
	22 RAF Wellingtons	46.7	14 RAF Wellingtons	25.0	24 RAF Wellingtons	43.6
15th September	54 U.S. Liberators	115.6	113 U.S. Liberators	227.7	109 U.S. Fortresses	133.6
TOTALS	117	253.2	168	319.5	173	246.2

* See Map 24.

Fifteenth U.S. Air Force. The photographic interpreters estimated that 77 German aircraft had been destroyed (60 being Ju. 52 transports) and another 20 damaged.[71] The *Luftwaffe's* Quartermaster, however, recorded the loss of only 28 transport aircraft and 13 others damaged, but three others lost in the air. Eleusis and Tatoi were made unserviceable for a time but Kalamaki was back in use within 24 hours.*

M.A.S.A.F.'s attacks were not renewed until 24th September because priority was given to the interdiction of German communications behind their Hungarian front. In the interval the Germans not only replaced their losses, but increased their evacuation sorties by over 100%.[73] Immediately after M.A.S.A.F.'s 13th to 15th September raids, the German effort fell from 100 sorties to 60 per day. By 24th September, when M.A.S.A.F. attacked again, a peak of 220 sorties per day had been reached. 252 U.S. Liberators then struck the three airfields with just over 400 tons of bombs destroying, according to German records, 30 more Ju. 52s and damaging four, and almost halving the sortie rate to 120. Recovery this time was much slower. This was not helped by *Ulster Queen's* intervention two days later. The sortie rate flickered between 80 and 160 per day until 4th October when M.A.S.A.F. intervened for the last time with a series of smaller raids. 39 of its Mustangs strafed

* Two additional causes of loss or damage to *Südost's* Ju. 52 force are worthy of mention. On the night of 7th/8th September Wellingtons from the Middle East destroyed three and damaged a fourth Ju. 52 on Maleme airfield.[72] On 15th September 15 'transports' were among 26 German aircraft damaged by land forces in *Südost's* area.

Greek airfields in daylight on 4th October; and 35 Lightnings and 55 Mustangs repeated the process on 6th October when strikes were made against airfields in the Salonika area.[74] At least 14 aircraft were destroyed but how many were transports is not known. As a final effort on the night 9th/10th October 19 Wellingtons dropped 40 tons of bombs on the Athens airfields. Evacuation flights to the Athens area died away, and those to Salonika fell to an average of about 40 a day until 23rd October, when air traffic was stopped. After its port installations had been demolished and the harbour fouled by mines the city of Salonika was officially evacuated by the Germans on 31st October, 36 hours before their last rear-guards crossed the border from Greece into Macedonia.[75] By that time some 67,000 Germans of all three Services had been brought off the islands by sea and air; the airlift included 1,000 tons of supplies and a further 28,000 tons were transported by sea, together with some 1,700 vehicles, 314 guns and a few tanks.

Meanwhile traditional British improvisation was allowed full rein in the Peloponnese.[76] Fox Force landed on Cythera Island in the early hours of 16th September as Churchill was cabling his agreement to Wilson's plan. It found itself drawn steadily northwards in response to urgent appeals by British Liaison Officers to prevent civil war between the *E.L.A.S.* guerillas and the German-armed Greek Security Battalions, who were ready enough to surrender but only to British forces.* By the beginning of October Fox Force had established an uneasy peace in the Peloponnese almost up to the Gulf of Corinth, using a combination of politico-military tact, firmness and individual initiative on the part of all ranks.† Following further orders from A.F.H.Q., it established an advanced naval base on Poros Island off the most easterly tip of the Peloponnese, and began to plan assaults to clear the German batteries off the islands of Aegina and Fleves, which covered the sea approaches to Athens and the German minefields obstructing them.

The improvised nature of operations at this time was also well demonstrated by the activities of Major the Earl Jellicoe's 'Bucket Force' which was a reinforced squadron of the S.B.S.‡[78] On 21st

---

* The Security Battalions' leaders were described by Colonel Woodhouse as 'collaborators' rather than 'quislings'.[77] The Greek Prime Minister had announced, before leaving Italy, that members who did not desert would be treated as criminals.

† Fox Force had the enthusiastic support of the Greek Government's Commissioner for the Peloponnese who said it averted much bloodshed.

‡ Originally known as the Special Boat Squadron, the S.B.S. became in 1945 the Special Boat *Service*.

September the Balkan Air Force proposed to A.F.H.Q. that Jellicoe should seize Araxos airfield, which lies on the Gulf of Corinth to the west of Patras, to provide air cover for the 'Manna' force in the Athens area and a forward base for air attacks on the German Lines of Communications in Greece.[79] It was also hoped to secure the surrender of the German garrison of Patras, opening the way to operations north of the Gulf.

See Map 23

Wilson's Chief of Staff, General Gammel, who visited H.Q. B.A.F. that same day to brief the Adriatic commanders, enquired whether Corfu could be forced to surrender. Brigadier Davy, Commander L.F.A., suggested this would be best done as part of a plan to land at Sarande in Albania, which would endanger the German withdrawal from the island.[80] The suggestion met with the approval of General Wilson, who had already determined to modify his orders on trans-Adriatic operations in a new directive which was to be issued on 26th September: the weight of effort by Land Forces Adriatic was to be switched by B.A.F. from Yugoslavia to Greece and Albania, and L.F.A., working in conjunction with General Scobie, was to plan its operations to destroy or induce the surrender of German forces in the Ionian Islands, on the west coast of Greece and on the mainland. The actual directive mentioned 'the desperate straits of the Germans', but Wilson was also influenced by Yugoslav successes in the Dalmatian Islands and, no doubt, by Tito's secret departure for Russia, which will be described later in this chapter.

On 22nd September reconnaissance patrols sent to Greece by Jellicoe reported an attack on Araxos practicable, and news arrived from Force 133 that Patras had been evacuated by the Germans.[81] This report was later proved to be false. The Bucket Force operations, however, began straight away. Araxos airfield was seized by parachute drop on the afternoon of 23rd September and the seatail arrived in landing craft during the 26th. In the meantime contact was made with the Germans still holding Patras with, it was thought, some 800 of their own troops and 1,600 Greeks of the Security Battalions. Bucket Force was soon involved in local politics as it tried to negotiate the surrender of the Germans and the Security Battalions in Patras while acting in co-operation with the latter's *E.L.A.S.* opponents. Using the R.A.F. Regiment squadron which had been landed originally for the defence of Araxos airfield, Jellicoe harassed the German evacuation of Patras as much as possible with the slender British resources available: 100 troops with no weapon heavier than two 6-pdr anti-tank guns. The Greek troops came out to surrender to the British and could only be interned on a spit of land nearby without adequate food, clothes or shelter, none of which Bucket Force could provide. As they could not be allowed to go free there was no alternative. The Germans completed their evacuation of Patras by 4th October. Jellicoe and the local *E.L.A.S.* Commander entered the city together at 8.30 a.m. Time-fuses left ticking in prepared demolitions in the main quay were successfully withdrawn and the third largest port in Greece was liberated almost undamaged. The initial welcome was tumultuous and genuine, but Patras did not feel itself free, and tension remained high. A company of 2nd Highland Light Infantry was flown in; a curfew was imposed; and joint patrols of British troops and *E.L.A.S.* guerillas were deployed to maintain order. For the moment the situation was contained.

Thus at the beginning of October, two small British raiding forces were advancing on Athens: Fox Force was moving up the east coast of the Peloponnese, and Jellicoe, now promoted Lieutenant-Colonel and appointed Allied Commander North-West Peloponnese, was approaching Corinth from the west with Bucket Force. The Germans had fallen back to the line of the Corinth Canal and the islands south of the Piraeus covering the sea approaches to Athens.

As Supreme Allied Commander, Wilson came under strong pressure, originating with the Foreign Office, to act with boldness in support of the Greek Government. 'We are being accused', signalled the Chiefs of Staffs on 21st September, 'of abandoning Greece to the Russians and Communists'.[82] Wilson was forced to defend the policy of not undertaking 'Manna' until the Germans had left Athens. All that could be done was to hasten their withdrawal. Apart from Fox Force and Bucket Force, the only way of doing this was to generate as much opposition as possible to the Germans through the Allied Military Missions with the Greek Partisan bands. In this he had some success. Generals Saraphis and Zervas were spirited out of Greece for a meeting at A.F.H.Q. which was also attended by Papandreou, and by Wilson, Scobie and Leeper on the British side.[83] The meeting went surprisingly well. The Caserta Agreement, which resulted from it, offered some hope of a united Greek effort against the Germans, instead of internal strife, and the eventual re-creation of a Greek national army:*

'1. All guerilla forces operating in Greece place themselves under the orders of the Greek Government of National Unity.

---

* The record of the meeting is dated 26th September.[84] It was made public on the 28th after the two Generals had safely returned to Greece.

2.   The Greek Government places these forces under the orders of General Scobie who has been nominated by the Supreme Allied Commander as GOC Forces in Greece.

3.   In accordance with the proclamation issued by the Greek Government, the Greek guerilla leaders declare that they will forbid any attempt by any units under their command to take the law into their own hands. Such action will be treated as a crime and will be punished accordingly.

4.   As regards Athens no action is to be taken save under the direct orders of General Scobie, GOC Forces in Greece.

5.   The Security Battalions are considered as instruments of the enemy. Unless they surrender according to orders issued by the GOC they will be treated as enemy formations.

6.   All Greek guerilla forces, in order to put an end to past rivalries, declare that they will form a national union in order to co-ordinate their activities in the best interests of the common struggle.

7.   In accordance with the powers conferred on him by the Supreme Allied Commander after agreement with the Greek Government, General Scobie has issued the attached operational orders'.

In the attached orders Scobie gave Saraphis and Zervas the same operational zones as allotted to them under the February armistice agreement which were set out clearly on a new map. Both Commanders were to be responsible for harassing the German withdrawal and eliminating German garrisons.* They were both responsible to Scobie for law and order in their territories, for prevention of civil war and killing of Greeks by Greeks, and for assisting in the establishment of the legal civil authority and distribution of relief supplies.

On the same day, 26th September, General Scobie reported at the Supreme Allied Commander's Conference that his 'Manna' forces were concentrated and ready to move.[86] He asked for further direction on a number of points, one of which was that a representative of the German Commander in Athens had approached the *E.L.A.S.* commander in Attica suggesting that, in order to preserve the city from damage, arrangements should be made whereby the British would not enter Athens until two to three hours after the Germans had left. Scobie was directed to inform the *E.L.A.S.* commander that the British would accept the German garrison's surrender if it marched south into the Lavrion peninsula with its arms. All that now stood between 'Manna' and

---

* One effect of the Caserta Agreement was a noticeable improvement in the relationship between British forces and *E.L.A.S.*, but it is impossible to say whether it helped to step up the actual harassment of retreating German troops. The claims of the A.F.H.Q. Special Operations History for 'Noah's Ark' are quite modest and seem to be borne out by the admittedly post-war account of *OB Südost*.[85]

Athens was the continued presence of a substantial German force which showed no sign of marching to Lavrion.

(v)

See Map 23

While Fox and Bucket Forces were penetrating the Peloponnese, Yugoslav Partisan reports and air reconnaissance showed that the Germans had begun the evacuation of the southern Dalmatian Islands.[87] In an attempt to cut off and harry the retreating forces, Land Forces Adriatic organised a succession of small operations against the islands of Brac, Korcula and Solta:

Brac	11th to 19th September	43rd (Royal Marine) Commando reinforced by one troop (4 × 75-mm howitzers) Raiding Support Regiment.
Korcula	14th to 17th September	2nd Highland Light Infantry reinforced by one battery (8 × 25-pdrs) 11th Army Field Regiment R.A. and one flight R.A.F. Regiment.
Solta	19th to 23rd September	43rd (Royal Marine) Commando with a battery from 11th Army Field Regiment R.A.

Partisan units co-operated with British troops in all these operations.

A number of significant trends became apparent during these successful but minor forays. The Partisan commanders showed a marked aversion to working with British infantry as they had plenty of their own. They had little artillery and no knowledge of how to use it. On Brac and Korcula they began to appreciate how much artillery could help them and their demands for British gunners grew as the days went by.

The Korcula operation illustrated another trend. The Partisan Chief of Staff on Vis would not authorise the operation without Tito's personal sanction. This was reasonable enough, although it caused delay. Permission when it came was subject to the provision of a written undertaking signed by the British Commander that no permanent occupation of Yugoslav soil by British troops was contemplated. Tito's sensitivity to the use of British troops, particularly on the mainland of Yugoslavia, was to grow as the German evacuation of the Dalmatian coast progressed. The Partisans had no desire to see anyone but themselves liberate their homeland or occupy it afterwards.

The most worrying development was the attitude adopted by Tito himself. As the Russians advanced into the Balkans he and his Partisan commanders became more secretive and less co-operative.[88] On 16th September General Wilson told Tito that he would like Brigadier Maclean to accompany him when he gave up his temporary refuge on Vis and returned to the Yugoslav mainland.[89] Tito let it be known that he would leave in about ten days time. On the same night (18th/19th September) he left Vis secretly in a Russian Dakota for Russia. His staff maintained he had gone to Serbia. Six weeks were to elapse before A.F.H.Q. could re-establish direct contact with him through Maclean, who returned to the mainland with the Partisan General Headquarters. Tito's recourse to Soviet support may have been purely pragmatic, but his apparent ingratitude to Wilson and his mode of departure from Vis exasperated his erstwhile hosts. For the time being Wilson had little need to work closely with Tito, because, as we have seen when describing the birth of Jellicoe's Bucket Force, he had switched operational priorities from Yugoslavia to Greece and Albania. This lessening of interest in Yugoslavia was to be only temporary. By the time that relations had been re-established between Tito's headquarters and A.F.H.Q. in late October the Yugoslav leader was able to negotiate from strength in Belgrade rather than as a fugitive on Vis.

The effect of Wilson's switch of priorities to Greece and Albania was felt soon after Tito's disappearance when preparations for a German evacuation of Corfu were reported.[90] There were only two escape routes open to the Corfu garrison; through the Greek port of Igoumenitsa, which was about to fall into Zervas' hands; or through the Albanian port of Sarande, to which Brigadier Davy had already called attention. A force based on 2nd Commando was assembled to harass the Germans in Sarande and to assist the Albanian Partisans. The initial intention had been to stay 24 hours, or 48 hours at the most. After landing on 22nd September, however, the situation seemed so favourable that the Commander of 2nd S.S. Brigade (present as a spectator) obtained authority to reinforce with 40th (Royal Marine) Commando and 25–pdr guns from 111th Army Field Regiment, in order to attack and capture Sarande. Then the weather broke and it was not until 9th October that the attack could be launched. It led to the capture of the port, some 600 German prisoners being taken by the British; later the total taken in the area by British and Albanians rose to about 1,000. The two Commandos suffered 81 casualties. Co-operation with the Partisans was reported to have been excellent, and they had fought hard and well.

As soon as Sarande had fallen surrender leaflets were dropped on Corfu. On 12th October white flags were seen and 40th Commando crossed to take the surrender. Only a few German stragglers remained, as the rest of the garrison had been successfully evacuated through Greece while Sarande was under attack. Attempts to follow up the German withdrawal northwards through Albania were foiled by extensive demolitions carried out by their rearguards. However, several Long Range Desert Group patrols were dropped in the Albanian mountains and carried out a number of successful demolitions and ambushes, besides directing R.A.F. air strikes onto enemy targets. Their presence and activities encouraged the Albanian Partisans to attack the Germans which they were previously disinclined to do.

The situation at the beginning of October can be summed up by saying that Land Forces Adriatic was nibbling at the German withdrawal from Solta in the north-west to Corinth in the southeast, trying to carry out operations for which larger forces should have been used if Allied strategic policy had permitted. The efforts of the officers and men of the various raiding forces were often outstanding, but out of scale in relation to the size of the German forces in the Balkans. The only thing which can be claimed is that some local embarrassment was inflicted on German evacuation plans which went on unhurried, with an eye to Russian and not to British operations.

(vi)

Across the Atlantic, Churchill and the British Chiefs of Staff had arrived in Quebec for the 'Octagon' Conference, which lasted from 12th to 16th September. The full story of 'Octagon' is told by John Ehrman.* We will confine ourselves to its Mediterranean aspects. The general tone of the conference is illustrated by Churchill's opening remarks, as recorded in the minutes of the first plenary meeting:[91]

> 'Since "Sextant" the affairs of the United Nations had taken a revolutionary turn for the good. Everything we had touched had turned to gold, and during the last seven weeks there had been an unbroken run of military success'.

The greater part of the discussion was concerned with plans for the eventual collapse of Germany in Europe and the redeployment of Allied resources to the Far East for the final defeat of the Japanese. Debates on the Mediterranean were mainly confined to resolving three strategic issues: Eisenhower's possible need for the transfer of American divisions from 5th Army to North-West Europe; Wilson's requirement for American L.S.T.s for operations

---

* *Grand Strategy op. cit.* Volume V Chapter XIII.

at the head of the Adriatic; and Admiral Mountbatten's request for Indian divisions from Italy for an amphibious assault on Rangoon which was, if possible, to be mounted before the monsoon in March 1945.* Before the conference Churchill and his military advisers had expected the Americans to insist on the first, refuse the second and be neutral on the third, which was an entirely British affair.

At the first meeting of the Combined Chiefs of Staff on 12th September British anxieties were quickly set at rest.[93] General Marshall stated and re-stated under friendly British cross-examination that the Americans had no intention of withdrawing formations from 5th Army until the outcome of Alexander's offensive was known; and Admiral King offered to leave the American L.S.T.s used for 'Dragoon' in the Mediterranean for a possible landing in Istria, provided a decision was taken by mid-October. At the second and final plenary session Churchill again questioned Marshall's interpretation of 'Alexander's present offensive'.[94] Marshall confirmed that he understood this 'included the invasion of the Po valley'. Churchill also thanked Admiral King for the offer of L.S.T.s for Istria. King, in reply, made it clear that these would be sailed subsequently for the Rangoon operation, neatly placing the onus of decision in any conflict between the Mediterranean and Indian Ocean squarely on the shoulders of the British Chiefs of Staff.

The relatively easy way in which the Americans agreed to leave their L.S.T.s in the Mediterranean for an amphibious operation in the northern Adriatic helped to conceal a deep gulf which existed between the British themselves: with the Prime Minister on the one hand, and the British Chiefs of Staff and Wilson on the other.[95] In the pre-conference discussions the Prime Minister had taken exception to Wilson's view, supported by the Joint Planners, that an amphibious operation against Istria would neither be desirable nor practicable with the resources available in the Mediterranean before the spring of 1945. The Chiefs of Staff supported Wilson in a forthright minute dated 7th September which said:[96]

> 'It is only on the assumption that Germany is still fighting in November and that Kesselring's army has been able to hold us up on, say, the line of the Piave, that an amphibious assault on Istria would be necessary. Since this assault must interfere with one or all of (a) "Overlord" (b) "Dracula" or (c) the Pacific, we feel certain that the U.S. Chiefs of Staff will argue that it should not be undertaken and that we should wait for "Rankin" conditions to permit our entry into Austria. We can see no

---

* No hint of any withdrawal of Indian divisions reached the Commanders and Staffs of A.A.I. until 28th September, when Wilson advised Alexander of the possibility.[92]

strong military counter-arguments to this and consider that it must be accepted'.*

But Churchill had some strong political points to make when he met the Chiefs of Staff next day: 'It seemed wrong to base our plans on the assumption that Germany was about to collapse. Their resistance in the West was stiffening . . .' He was very anxious 'that British forces should forestall the Russians in certain areas of central Europe. For instance, the Hungarians had expressed the intention of resisting the Russian advance, but would surrender to a British force if it could arrive in time. It was most desirable for political reasons that British forces should enter Yugoslavia and advance north and north-east into central Europe, even if "Rankin" conditions did not occur'.[97]

The American willingness to leave L.S.T.s in the Mediterranean weakened the Chiefs of Staff's military arguments, allowing Churchill to build up his political case, as the minutes for the first plenary meeting at 'Octagon' record:[98]

'It would never do for our armies to remain idle. He had always been attracted by a right-handed movement, with the purpose of giving Germany a stab in the Adriatic armpit. Our objective should be Vienna. . . . An added reason for this right-handed movement was the rapid encroachment of the Russians into the Balkans and the consequent dangerous spread of Russian influence in this area.'

Wilson was sent planning guidance by the Combined Chiefs of Staff that evening (13th September):[99]

'a. There will be no withdrawal of major units from Fifth U.S. Army until the outcome of present Italian offensive is known.
b. For planning the capture of Istrian Peninsula you may count on having amphibious lift now in Mediterranean. You should submit this plan to Combined Chiefs of Staff at the earliest date and in any event not later [than] 10th October.'

(vii)

See Maps 8 and 25

The likelihood of a trans-Adriatic operation being practicable depended upon a decisive success by A.A.I. in the Northern Apennines, either by routing Kesselring's armies where they stood, or by forcing them to withdraw in haste over the Po and back to the *Voralpen* Line. The point of German collapse did not seem far

---

* The codeword 'Dracula' referred to the Rangoon operation. For 'Rankin' see p.205*n*.

off on 21st September. Herr's 76th Panzer Corps had scrambled back over the Marecchia in pouring rain, just saving its artillery; Schlemm's 1st Parachute Corps had been forced to abandon both the Futa and Il Giogo Passes; and a breach was appearing in the German line on the boundary between *AOK 14* and *AOK 10*, which was drawn just west of the gorge through which the Santerno river and the road to Imola wind their way towards the Via Emilia (Route 9) in the Po valley.[100]

General Clark had two options: to continue his main thrust astride Route 65, aiming for Bologna, or to divert part of 5th Army's effort in a subsidiary thrust down the Santerno valley.[101] Such a diversionary operation seemed to offer four advantages: the shortest route to cut the Via Emilia in the Po valley, less well developed German defences, the chance of helping 8th Army by cutting in behind *AOK 10*, and the possibility of throwing Kesselring off-balance by a thrust down the German inter-Army boundary. The only difficulty was the limited capacity of the Firenzuola-Imola road, which could not carry the supply traffic of much more than one American division. In view of the rapid progress being made by 85th Division in its advance from Il Giogo Pass to Firenzuola, however, the opportunity seemed worth taking. Without changing the direction of 2nd U.S. Corps' main thrust, Clark ordered Keyes to use 88th U.S. Division to prize open the German inter-Army boundary by attacking north-eastwards astride the Santerno valley. 34th, 91st and 85th U.S. Divisions would continue the drive on Bologna with the immediate objectives of seizing the next major ridge north of Firenzuola: Mt Bastione by 34th U.S. Division, Mt Oggioli by 91st U.S. Division and Mt Canda by 85th U.S. Division.[102] 88th U.S. Division was given additional pack mules, and Combat Command A of 1st U.S. Armoured Division was made available to 2nd U.S. Corps to exploit success in the Po valley if 88th U.S. Division achieved a surprise break through. 13th Corps seems to have been left to support 88th U.S. Division's right flank as no fresh orders were issued to Kirkman.[103] Its objective was still Faenza. 1st Division had the additional task of securing and opening up the Borgo S. Lorenzo—Marradi road to form the main Corps' axis until lateral communication could be established with Route 67.

The deep belt of mountainous country either side of the Santerno valley was to prove some of the most difficult terrain encountered by 88th U.S. Division in the Italian campaign. The valley itself was particularly narrow and winding, with high mountains either side which did not start decreasing in size until they were within a few miles of Imola. For instance, Il Giogo Pass is 2,900 feet high, and yet Mt Battaglia, which stands on the last major ridge before Imola, is still 2,400 feet. The road in the valley was barely two way. It had a metalled surface, but its foundations were designed for light civilian traffic and not for heavy American trucks. As far as Castel del Rio there were no lateral roads leading into the mountains and very few tracks. Thereafter the valley became slightly less constricted but still offered little scope for manoeuvre almost to Imola.

88th U.S. Division opened its offensive at 5 a.m. on 21st September with a regiment advancing along the mountains on each side of the Santerno.[104] The third regiment was held initially in reserve, waiting to clear the Imola road into Castel del Rio when it was practicable to do so. For the first three days, despite bad weather, no significant resistance was met and the advance went well. 350th U.S. Infantry Regiment reached Mt. della Croce on the eastern side of the valley by nightfall on 23rd September. At much the same time 349th U.S. Infantry Regiment thrust its way forward to Mt la Fine on the west side of the valley. The western flank of the division was well covered by 85th U.S. Division, but to the east the division's rapid lunge towards Mt della Croce outstripped 13th Corps' advance down the parallel Senio valley, where units of the German 51st Mountain Corps were fighting to hold the mountains around Palazzuolo. A three mile gap opened up on the 350th's eastern flank through which German patrols successfully harassed its supply route and managed to capture most of one of its battalion command posts. This gap was to grow as 88th U.S. Division's advance progressed. By the evening of 26th September it was almost five miles wide and necessitated the deployment of two infantry battalions of 1st U.S. Armoured Division's Combat Command A to protect the flank and supply routes.

The initial impetus of 88th U.S. Division's advance caught the Germans just as *AOK 14* was trying to stabilise its front after the loss of Il Giogio Pass had forced 1st Parachute Corps to retreat north of Firenzuola. 51st Mountain Corps of *AOK 10* had begun to pull back towards Green II during the night of 20th/21st September, at which time it was planned that Feuerstein would release 44th Infantry Division to reinforce 76th Panzer Corps on the Marecchia.[105] Operations on the inter-Army boundary were still unco-ordinated by Kesselring, but the American threat to Imola was recognised by some of his subordinates. On 20th September, before 88th U.S. Division had begun its thrust, *AOK 10's* Chief of Staff, Wentzell, had told Kesselring's Chief of Staff, Röttiger, that he thought it wise to hold the bulk of 44th Infantry Division on the Via Emilia until they saw how the situation developed. If the Allies took the 'militarily correct' decision to strike towards Imola

instead of northwards to Bologna, *AOK 10* could be in really serious
danger. As noted in Chapter XIII, one regiment of 44th Infantry
Division had been released to 51st Mountain Corps on 17th
September. It arrived piecemeal, and with 715th Infantry Division
was under such pressure from 13th Corps that 51st Mountain Corps
could not bunch up towards the Imola road as it withdrew to
Green II, which it had been directed to do on 20th September.
88th U.S. Division plunged into a widening gap on the inter-Army
boundary.

To the west of this gap, the start of 5th Army's renewed offensive
found 34th and 91st U.S. Divisions opposed respectively by 334th
Infantry and 4th Parachute Divisions of *AOK 14*. 85th U.S. Division
was opposed by 362nd Infantry Division, which had begun on 18th
September to move to the eastern wing of 1st Parachute Corps
from the centre of 14th Panzer Corps, where it was relieved by
16th SS Panzer Grenadier Division.[106] Moving units laterally across
the grain of the country was a slow and dangerous business, and
on the morning of 22nd September Röttiger was informed by
Hauser of *AOK 14* that the Americans were forging down the
Santerno valley.[107] At the same time Wentzell reported for *AOK 10*
that the side-stepping of 715th Infantry Division of 51st Mountain
Corps into Green II had been dislocated by the speed and weight
of its opponents' assault.

That afternoon Kesselring conferred with von Vietinghoff and
Lemelsen at his tactical headquarters for the first time since 5th
Army had begun to attack in mid-September. The agreed counter-
measures were sound enough, but they were 'too little too late'
for *OB Südwest* was strangely slow to tackle the pressing issue of a
unified command on the inter-Army boundary. In confirmation of
preliminary orders already issued over Röttiger's signature on 20th
September, Kesselring agreed during the conference that Lemelsen
could take 1st Parachute Corps and part of 14th Panzer Corps back
to Green II.* The Army Commanders were told that the central
gap must at all costs be closed, and as von Vietinghoff maintained
that this must entail the further reinforcement of 51st Mountain
Corps he was authorised to commit a second regiment of 44th
Infantry Division to the mountains west of the Santerno. Earlier
plans for the transfer of this formation to 76th Panzer Corps were
dropped, and in their place Kesselring undertook to provide *AOK
10* with a rear reserve consisting of a regimental group of 94th
Infantry Division, to be brought down to the Po from north-eastern
Italy. After the conference 51st Mountain Corps was instructed to

---

* As has been explained in Chapter X Section (ii) which deals with the planning of
Green I and II, we do not know the exact course of Green II on *AOK 14's* front.

offer resistance on a line which ran along the spurs south-west and south-east of Castel del Rio and merged into Green II north of Palazzuolo. 1st Parachute Corps was authorised to withdraw to Mt Canda which guarded the Radicosa Pass on Route 65, and the inter-Army contact-point was to be at Belmonte, south-west of Mt la Fine to which was assigned 134th Grenadier Regiment of 44th Infantry Division.

Next day, 23rd September, Kesselring was forced by the speed of the American advance to settle the command issue. Neither von Vietinghoff nor Lemelsen wished to be saddled with responsibility for closing the gap and argued accordingly.[108] By the end of the day Kesselring had decided to give it to *AOK 14*, informing Lemelsen that on the arrival of its third regiment in the area of Castel del Rio all of 44th Infantry Division would be placed under command of 1st Parachute Corps. The inter-Army boundary was shifted from west to east of the Santerno and was to run from Mt Carzolano to Mt Faggiola and Mt Battaglia and thence to the eastern edge of Imola. *AOK 14* was thus able to concentrate on resisting 5th Army while *AOK 10* opposed 8th Army. As *AOK 10's* rear was endangered by the threat to Imola, and as 1st Parachute Corps was already over-extended, Kesselring's decision was ill-judged. It led to constant complaints from Lemelsen, who on 24th September was told by *OB Südwest* that *AOK 14* must help itself by transferring another entire division to its eastern wing.[109] As the lateral shift of one of von Senger's formations would take too long, Lemelsen decided that 334th Infantry Division, progressively relieved by 16th SS Panzer Grenadier Division, should move in three nights into the line between 362nd and 44th Infantry Divisions. 334th Infantry Division was one of *AOK 14's* best formations, but its troops were very tired after days of dogged fighting against 34th U.S. Division. Their move added to the burdens of the Corps Commander, Schlemm, who was as concerned for his centre as for what Lemelsen described on 24th September as the 'unforeseeable consequences' of an American break through to Imola. Within three days this threat was worrying *AOK 10* more than *AOK 14*.

During 24th and 25th September 88th U.S. Division continued to probe forward, bringing up artillery and supplies, and generally making ready to attack the line of mountains stretching west and east of Castel del Rio: Mt. Pratolungo to the west and Mt Carnevale to the east of the Santerno, with Mt Cappello and Mt Battaglia lying in depth behind Mt Carnevale.[110] In order to allow 88th U.S. Division to attack on a narrower front, 85th U.S. Division took over the defence of Mt la Fine, which had been frequently counter-attacked by battalions of both 362nd and 44th Infantry Divisions without success. 88th U.S. Division was to attack with its deployment unchanged. General Kendall sent a special message to 350th U.S. Infantry to emphasise the need for a swift advance into the Po valley before the Germans could move troops to parry the thrust. 88th U.S. Division's objectives were: 349th U.S. Infantry, Mt Pratolungo and then the road running north-west out of Castel del Rio to Pezzolo; 351st U.S. Infantry, Castel del Rio itself and then Mt Cappello to the north-east; and 350th U.S. Infantry, the long ridge running from Mt della Croce via Mt Carnevale to Mt Battaglia. H hour for the attack was 6 a.m. on 26th September.

On the German side, 44th Infantry Division commanded by General von Rost went under command of *AOK 14* on 24th September.[111] Its second and third regiments were installed piecemeal as they arrived on Mt Pratolungo and on the western slopes of Mt della Croce. 44th Infantry Division was an Austrian formation with the title and traditions of the old Imperial regiment known as *Hoch and Deutschmeister*. The higher German commanders felt that in Italy it did not always live up to its fine traditions, but in this instance their criticisms made little allowance for the way in which it had been bandied about between *AOK 10* and *AOK 14* as it came into the line. Due to the commanders' haverings over its deployment it never managed to settle down, and the situation on the new inter-Army boundary remained as precarious as ever.

By the evening of 24th September 715th Infantry Division had been driven off the high ground east and north of Palazzuolo in a series of attacks launched by 1st Division of 13th Corps. Although it had managed to establish a weak defensive line north-westwards to the inter-Army boundary, von Vietinghoff informed Kesselring that the division was now too depleted to offer any real check to the Allies' advance.[112] He had therefore decided to re-commit 98th Infantry Division, which was part refitted after its gruelling battles with 5th Corps during 'Olive'. Described by Wentzell as 'only a torso', Reinhardt's division was to come into the line of 51st Mountain Corps on the right of 715th Infantry Division.

88th U.S. Division's attack was too much for 44th Infantry Division.[113] 349th U.S. Infantry seized Mt Pratolungo, decimating one of its regiments and capturing a battalion headquarters; and by the end of the second day's fighting had reached the high ground overlooking its objective, the Castel del Rio—Pezzolo road. In the centre 351st U.S. Infantry cleared Castel del Rio during the morning of the second day, but 88th U.S. Division's major breach in Green II occurred on the eastern side of the valley where 350th U.S. Infantry attacked down the new German inter-Army boundary with exhilarating success. On the second day a chance contact was made with an Italian Partisan band, who led its 2nd

Battalion by a covered route onto the crest of the dominant Mt Battaglia where it dug in during the afternoon, under orders from General Keyes to hold its ground until 351st U.S. Infantry could come up on its left. The key to Imola had been seized, and the German inter-Army boundary again threatened to open up rather like a loosened zip fastener, 1st Parachute Corps pulling back northwards and 51st Mountain Corps north-eastwards.

88th U.S. Division's effort was not made in isolation from the rest of 5th Army. The presence of very active bands of Italian Partisans was having an effect as well. The three main force divisions of 2nd U.S. Corps had started to thrust northwards towards their mountain objectives (34th U.S. Division, Mt Bastione; 91st, Mt Oggioli; and 85th, Mt Canda) on 24th September.[114] In tough fighting all three were successful and high casualties were inflicted on 362nd Infantry Division and 4th Parachute Division, whose 12th Parachute Regiment was already decimated. With Kesselring's consent 1st Parachute Corps' divisions fell back during the night of 26th/27th September to positions just north of the Radicosa Pass. As they were closely pursued they had again to withdraw on the following night to a line which ran east and west through Monghidoro on Route 65. By this time 350th U.S. Infantry was digging in on Mt Battaglia, and, as 44th Infantry Division had been driven out of Castel del Rio, Schlemm decided to commit the lead regiment of 334th Infantry Division 'finally to resolve his Corps' problems on the inter-Army boundary'.

13th Corps' operations during this period were less spectacular as it was facing the main body of 51st Mountain Corps, which was withdrawing more methodically than the troops on its western wing, and was less easily persuaded to abandon the strong positions held by the very experienced 305th Infantry Division.[115] The division had extended its right to relieve its hard pressed neighbour and by 25th September dominated the communication centres of Palazzuolo, Marradi and S. Benedetto in Alpe from the north. Thus 1st Division, after taking Palazzuolo, found its further advance blocked by 305th Infantry Division in strong defensive positions based upon Mt Gamberaldi: a feature some 2,700 feet high and almost unapproachable from the south, due to its steep rocky face commanded by German machine guns and mortars. Its 2nd Brigade made five attempts by day and night during 25th and 26th September to secure the summit, but all failed.[116] 66th Brigade had meanwhile managed to open up a narrow track from Borgo

S. Lorenzo via Mt Carzolano to Palazzuolo, enabling jeeps to bring up supplies more easily. It then moved 1st Hertfordshires in a long night march over slippery mountain tracks to seize Mt Toncone, about a mile north of Mt Gamberaldi, during 26th/27th September. Next night 6th Gordons of 2nd Brigade followed in their footsteps and attacked in darkness and rain, from the west, only to find that Mt Gamberaldi had been abandoned by its German defenders.

The loss of Mt Battaglia to 350th U.S. Infantry was beginning to affect the whole of 51st Mountain Corps' front as the German commanders sought ways of assembling reserves to check the now obvious thrust to Imola.[117] 577th Grenadier Regiment (305th Infantry Division) was sent westwards to help 715th Infantry Division retake Mt Battaglia. The consequential regrouping enabled 1st Division to make further progress.

On 24th September the paramount need to protect 2nd U.S. Corps' flank had caused General Kirkman to recast his plan.[118] The new version depended as before on supply routes. The Borgo S. Lorenzo—Marradi road was not suitable for the support of more than one division and had been allocated to 1st Division. He therefore ordered that, once the Marradi crossroads were secure, this division would step left to Palazzuolo and would work down the Senio valley. 8th Indian Division would take over the advance down the Faenza road, its line of supply being Route 67 to S. Benedetto in Alpe and then the lateral track to Marradi. Sappers were to give priority to the development of these two axes.*

8th Indian Division, which had not met with much difficulty in its encounters with 715th Infantry Division as it advanced across country on 1st Division's right flank, experienced a very different reception when it tried to prize the Germans out of Mt Castelnuovo (Pt 629), covering Marradi; its new opponents were 305th Infantry Division.[120] 17th Indian Brigade assaulted Mt Castelnuovo on 25th September but was unable under sustained German fire to cross the sharp ridges covered with brushwood and shale. Next day rain made the mountain sides almost impassable even to mules. On the 27th, under wet and bitterly cold conditions, the brigade began a wide outflanking move to the east. On the 29th Mt Castelnuovo was found abandoned as 305th Infantry Division had drawn back to release troops for the battle of Mt Battaglia. The same day, 1st Division began a laborious advance down the Senio valley road to

---

* The Marradi-Palazzuolo road was reportedly open for maintenance on 29th September, but 1st Division's War Diary says that units of 3rd and 66th Brigades were still on a pack mule basis.[119]

gain contact with 88th U.S. Division on Mt Battaglia, and 8th Indian Division prepared to nose its way down the Lamone valley.

On 13th Corps' extreme eastern flank, 6th Armoured Division cleared S. Benedetto in Alpe on 24th September and pressed on astride Route 67 for another few miles to Bocconi which it reached on the 26th.[121] The occupation of Mt Fuso, overlooking the road to the north, caused losses amongst the infantry from exposure, the first suffered by A.A.I. that winter.

See Map 8

On 5th Army's western flank 4th U.S. Corps continued to apply an even pressure across the front, taking advantage of each German withdrawal brought about by Lemelsen's need to find more reserves to bolster 1st Parachute Corps' front.[122] Although Crittenberger did not launch any specific offensive, his troops by the end of the month had pushed their way through Green I except on the coast. Beginning on 21st September the whole of 1st U.S. Armoured Division, less Combat Command B, was transferred to 2nd U.S. Corps and was used dismounted, as we have seen, to protect 88th U.S. Division's exposed eastern flank. 1st U.S. Armoured Division's place was taken by another *ad hoc* group, called Task Force 92, based upon Combat Command B. 6th South African Armoured Division, with its brigades on a very wide front, continued for a time to push up the three available main roads running through the Apennines in its divisional sector, until it became apparent that the Divisional Engineers could not open up so many heavily demolished roads simultaneously. Route 66 was, therefore, handed over to Task Force 92, which released 24th Guards Brigade for the reinforcement of 11th South African Armoured Brigade in the more important task of protecting 2nd U.S. Corps' western flank on the Castiglione dei Pepoli road. By the end of September the Guards were abreast of the leading elements of 34th U.S. Division.

Tactical air operations during the period 21st–27th September were punctuated by bad weather.[123] On the 21st all aircraft were grounded and in the following six days, during a period of critical fighting, only 558 fighter-bomber sorties were flown and some 158 tons of bombs dropped. D.A.F. fighter-bombers flew twice as many sorties in support of 5th Army as did those of U.S. XII F.C., the bomb tonnage being only marginally greater because the U.S. Thunderbolts carried twice the bomb-load of the R.A.F.'s

Spitfires.* A further spell of bad weather began on the evening of 27th September and lasted until the end of the month, bringing air support almost to a standstill. The absence of Air O.P.s also severely limited the effectiveness of the Allies' artillery.

While bad weather reduced Allied air effort and so made it easier for the Germans to redeploy to meet various crises, attacks by Partisans became more frequent and more successful in impeding movement and telephonic communications between the German formations.[125] So irritating did these attacks become that 16th SS Panzer Grenadier Division was authorised by H.Q. *AOK 14* on 29th September to root out and destroy the 'Red Star' Partisan Brigade's base area at Marzabotto, east of Route 64, on condition that there was to be no violation of the existing regulations for operations against Partisans. The savagery of the operation, however, was reflected in *AOK 14's* tactical reports of 2nd October and in the proportion of 718 Partisans killed to only 456 taken prisoner. Despite this ruthlessness the Partisan threat to Army Group C's rear areas continued to grow.

On 27th September, when 5th Army's approach to the Via Emilia was described as 'strategically very unpleasant' in the War Diary of *AOK 10*, Kesselring again sought the Führer's permission to implement the *Herbstnebel* contingency plan for withdrawal across the Po.[126] Before we look at the results of his approach and the final desperate attempts by his divisions to stop 5th Army reaching Imola, we must see how 8th Army's operations on the Adriatic coast were developing.

(viii)

See Map 8

The difficulties of conducting military operations in the Romagna were at first obscured from 8th Army Staff by the atrocious weather in the last ten days of September and by the success of 5th Army's thrust towards Imola. 8th Army Intelligence Summaries from 21st September onwards confidently foretold a German strategic withdrawal from the Apennines.[127] As each day went by and no withdrawal started, this was ascribed to the German need to extricate their troops from north-western Italy before allowing *AOK 10* to start its retreat to the Po. It was General Leese's intention,

---

* On 20th September when U.S. XII Fighter Command (later U.S. XXII Tactical Air Command) became a tactical air command to support 5th Army it had only the six squadrons of the U.S. 57th and 350th Fighter Groups and one night fighter squadron in Italy.[124] As a stop-gap additional air support was arranged by two U.S. Thunderbolt Fighter Groups based in Corsica, staging at Cecina and Tarquinia in Italy for refuelling and briefing.

expressed at a conference with his Corps Commanders on 16th September, that, after 8th Army had crossed the Marecchia, he would exploit with his three armoured divisions (2nd New Zealand on the coast, 5th Canadian in the centre and 1st Armoured inland). Meanwhile the rest of the Army would regroup. The precise form of the regrouping was left until the Rimini Line had been overrun. In general terms 1st Canadian Corps was to head for Ravenna and Ferrara on the axis of the Via Adriatica (Route 16), while 5th Corps advanced astride the Via Emilia (Route 9) towards Bologna and a junction with 5th Army.

It was now that the Desert Air Force suggested a new tactical policy.[128] Noting the many river lines which 8th Army would have to cross in its advance to the Po, Air Vice-Marshal Dickson proposed that all bridges on the Savio and later on the Reno rivers should be destroyed with three purposes in mind: to make the Germans stand and fight if they were inclined to withdraw; to embarass their withdrawal if, nevertheless, they tried to do so: and in either case to disrupt their supply system. The attacks on the Reno river had the additional purpose of severing communications between *AOK 10* and *AOK 14*. Although the proposals were accepted Leese and the 8th Army Staff were far from enthusiastic about them because they doubted if the effort was worth the loss of immediate air support for 8th Army operations. Moreover, 8th Army was still optimistic about the imminence of a German withdrawal and felt that the loss of the Savio and Reno bridges might hinder its own troops' advance more than the Germans' withdrawal. Leese insisted, for instance, that the southern road bridge in Cesena should be left intact for 5th Corps' use when it reached the Savio.

The Savio bridge bombing programme started on 22nd September and lasted four weeks. It was not a success, partly because of the weather and also because of the extraordinary efforts made by the German Engineers to counter its effects. At first the targets numbered ten bridges. As the attack developed the Germans constructed foot bridges and more road bridges over the river and began to use fords when the weather allowed. They also adopted the Allies' technique, used earlier at Cassino and on the Garigliano, of keeping the most important crossings under smoke screens. By the end of the first week the road bridges in use had grown to twelve. On 1st October pontoon bridges began to appear and by 13th October there were so many bridges that the D.A.F. had to confine attacks to those crossings thought strong enough to carry tanks, S.P. guns and other heavy equipment. The Germans had to contend not only with Allied air attacks but with periods of spate which washed away many of their temporary bridges. By

15th October they had begun to blow up some of their own bridges in preparation for withdrawal. As 8th Army approached Cesena on 16th October all heavy bridges had been destroyed either by bombing, spates or demolition except the southern road crossing in Cesena which Leese had reserved, hopefully, for 5th Corps. Its fate will be mentioned in the next chapter. 8th Army Staff concluded that, while the air attacks on the Savio bridges inconvenienced the Germans, the meagre results confirmed their view that they were not worth the loss of direct air support to the forward troops.

The report on the Savio bridge bombing produced some interesting findings. The medium and light bombers dropped 93 tons of bombs in 67 sorties on two permanent bridges without success. The fighter-bombers flew 609 sorties, dropping 284 tons, and could claim six permanent road bridges destroyed, two possibly destroyed and one damaged but still standing. In the fighter-bomber attacks the 1,000–lb bomb was shown to be infinitely preferable to the 500–lb bomb even though fewer could be carried. The Mustang proved the best aircraft for the job as it could carry two 1,000–lb bombs whereas the Spitfire normally only carried one 500–lb. German flak also had its effect. At first when there was little A.A. fire it took an average of 30 bombs to acquire a hit. Later it reduced accuracy to 150 bombs per hit.

For the first few days after crossing the Marecchia 8th Army advanced with its armoured divisions leading. In the Canadian Corps' sector the New Zealand Division passed through 1st Canadian Division's bridgehead astride the Via Adriatica, crossing the Uso on 26th/27th September without difficulty.[129] 3rd Greek Mountain Brigade was then brought up to widen the New Zealand front for its advance to the Fiumicino which, despite skilful German delaying tactics, was reached on 28th September.

5th Candian Armoured Division passed through 4th Division's bridgehead on 23rd September, advancing with one brigade up due to lack of roads, and reached the Fiumicino about the same time as the New Zealanders, having suffered unexpectedly high casualties.[130] The Fiumicino turned out to be a river of ill repute as far as the Canadians were concerned. Whether it or the smaller Uso was the Rubicon of Roman times is uncertain, but there is no doubt that in September 1944 it was the Fiumicino which demonstrated the treacherous nature of the Romagna rivers. In an attempt to beat imminent floods, 11th Canadian Brigade hurried troops across. On the left a company of the Irish Regiment of Canada waded the river in the early hours of 28th September without adequate anti-tank support and was trapped by a superior force from 26th Panzer Division. Before reinforcements could reach it most of the company had been taken prisoner. A little further north a second battalion just failed to rush the bridge in Fiumicino village before it was blown. Then the rain started again and in a few hours turned the river into an impassable muddy torrent. It was no flash flood. The rain poured down for the next ten days, washing away all fords and temporary bridges over the Uso and Marecchia rivers in the Canadian Corps' sector. Only the ancient Ponte di Tiberio outside Rimini survived. Conditions were naturally just as bad on the German side. The Chief of Staff 76th Panzer Corps reported the withdrawal over the Fiumicino on 29th September as 'indescribable', with men drowned and several guns literally washed away.[131]

Operations in 5th Corps' sector went more slowly for a number of reasons. Its axes of advance were still through the Apennine foot-hills which provided many excellent defensive positions for the usual German delaying tactics.[132] Its opponents were relatively fresher than those of the Canadian Corps, because 90th Panzer Grenadier Division had only recently entered the Adriatic battles and some troops of 114th Jäger Division had temporarily been freed from the Central Apennines to reinforce 278th Infantry Division. In addition 5th Corps was in the process of reorganising its divisions to overcome the shortage of reinforcements in the Italian Theatre. We will be discussing this reorganisation in the next chapter.

5th Corps had to fight hard to cross the Marecchia on 22nd and 23rd September. 1st Armoured Division, in its last action before it was to be disbanded, fought its way into Santarcangelo on 24th September and was then relieved by 56th Division which advanced astride the Via Emilia towards Savignano on the Fiumicino. 46th and 4th Indian Divisions too had a long hard fight, much of it at close quarters, to secure the prominent ridge beyond the Marecchia south of Poggio Berni (*Map 17*). At one time during 24th September, 4th Indian Division appeared in danger of losing its bridgehead over the Marecchia to some vicious counter-attacks, probably mounted by troops from 278th Infantry Division. The Germans fortunately started to thin out during the afternoon, enabling the left wing of 5th Corps to continue its advance to the Fiumicino on 25th September.

The Fiumicino treated 5th Corps no better than the Canadians. The centre of German reistance was at Savignano and on the ridge running south-westwards from the town.[133] 56th Division opened its attack on the town and the ridge during the night 27th/28th while 46th and 4th Indian Divisions were struggling to close up on its western flank. 169th Brigade led the attack using all three of its battalions. In spite of a barrage fired by five field regiments with additional medium artillery superimposed, which lasted for an hour and a half, 90th Panzer Grenadier Division stood firm and the attack failed. Only one company of 2nd/6th Queens managed to reach the top of the ridge and another secured the bridge over the Fiumicino in the western outskirts of the town. When dawn came both companies were ordered to withdraw as their positions were untenable in daylight. The company on the ridge did so successfully. In the town the platoons around the bridge tried to stay concealed in the houses until darkness would allow them to escape. One platoon did survive the day, but the rest were captured and the bridge was blown by the German defenders. It had been hoped to renew the attack on the Savignano position on the night 29th/30th September but the rain made it impracticable.[134] During the night, the Germans took the opportunity to slip back over the river. Operations by 46th and 4th Indian Divisions brought them to positions from which they too could prepare to cross the river. Attempts to do so by 46th and 56th Divisions during 30th September and 1st October failed. The rain, which had lifted briefly during 1st October, came down again in torrents. The Bailey pontoon bridges over the Uso became impassable and vehicles bogged down across the whole Corps' front. In places artillery positions were swamped before the guns could be extracted. Operational activity was reduced to patrolling over the river, the west bank of which was found to be well fortified and mined.

The period covered by 8th Army's advance to the Fiumicino, 21st–27th September, coincided with 5th Army's offensive towards Imola. The direct air support given 8th Army amounted to some 969 sorties (403.7 tons of bombs dropped) which was almost double that given to 5th Army, the operations of which were potentially more rewarding.[135] As on 5th Army's front no flying was possible on 21st September and in the following six days weather was indifferent. U.S. XII F.C. contributed only three sorties on 8th Army's front. In addition to the fighter-bomber effort, D.A.F.'s Marauders flew 220 sorties (374.1 tons of bombs) and 93 of its Baltimores added a further 74.3 tons, bringing the total daylight effort on 8th Army's front for the seven days to 1,282 sorties with 852.1 tons of bombs dropped. By night the Baltimores and Bostons added a further 40 tons. German aircraft only appeared twice by night and three times by day, singly or in very small numbers.

In the centre of the Allied front the skeletal remains of 10th Corps had been grouped into small *ad hoc* forces, based upon three dismounted armoured car regiments and three, sometimes four, independent infantry battalions.[136] McCreery sought to maintain contact with the centre of 51st Mountain Corps as it withdrew to

Green II in the high Apennines astride Route 71. His Corps
Engineer resources were concentrated largely on the task of opening
up the main road and putting it into good repair against the rain
and mud of the approaching winter.

S. Piero in Bagno was entered unopposed on 25th September.[137]
Contact was not re-established with the Germans until entry into
Sarsina two days later, Route 71 being reported undamaged as far
as this small town. It was then found that 51st Mountain Corps
was occupying a tenuous line of posts north of Green II, some 15
miles from Cesena.

While the Canadian and 5th Corps had been closing up to the
Fiumicino, Leese and 8th Army Staff were still watching for signs
of the early withdrawal by *AOK 10* predicted by Intelligence.[138] On
25th September, however, when Leese issued one of his rare written
instructions in the form of notes for a conference with his Corps
Commanders, he set out plans to meet two sets of circumstances:
Case A, the Germans continued to withdraw, and *Case B*, they put
up a determined resistance, necessitating a strong co-ordinated
Army thrust. Before the month was up he had decided that the
German line must be forced and had initiated plans to regroup
for an Army attack on a three Corps front, bringing the Polish
Corps into the line on the Adriatic coast.[139]

We need not go into the details of Leese's regrouping proposals
because on 27th September Alexander received a signal from the
C.I.G.S. informing him that Leese had been selected to take over
the Army Group in Burma and was needed at once.[140] Lieutenant-
General Sir Richard McCreery, commander of 10th Corps, was to
be promoted to command 8th Army. The date of hand over was
agreed for 1st October. McCreery inherited the problems of the
Romagna, which were just beginning to make themselves felt as
8th Army lay bogged along the line of the Fiumicino in the first
week of October. Whether Leese's *Case A* or *B* would prove to
reflect German operational policy depended upon the success or
failure of Kesselring's second approach for Hitler's authority to
initiate the *Herbstnebel* plan, to which we must now return.

(ix)

See Map 8

By noon on 27th September, when Kesselring asked *OKW* for
the second time for authority to implement *Herbstnebel*, 5th Army
had almost broken through in its thrust towards Imola and was

about to force the main body of 1st Parachute Corps to retreat on
the Bologna front. 8th Army had not paused since Herr's 76th
Panzer Corps had fallen back to the Marecchia and was now over
the Uso on its way to the Fiumicino. *OB Südwest* based his case
for withdrawal over the Po upon the fact that his armies were under
such heavy pressure from ground and air; that reinforcements were
not keeping pace with losses; and that, if 5th Army did break
through to Imola-Bologna, not only would this cause 'very grave
difficulties' for *AOK 10*, but it could also endanger the movements
of the Army of Liguria if the Allies were to thrust over the
French Alps towards Turin, or to put troops ashore on the
Italian Riviera.[141] Unless Alexander's offensive could be checked,
Kesselring considered that Army Group C should fall back to the
Italian Alps as gradually as possible. It should make an early start
to take advantage of whatever fine autumn weather was left before
winter began.

Hitler replied on the same day, announcing more positively than
on previous occasions that he could not sanction *OB Südwest's*
proposal for two main reasons: it would entail the loss of the
economic resources of northern Italy, and it would damage the
internal morale of the Reich. He also doubted the practicability
of *Herbstnebel* now that the weather had broken, and preferred to
promise an increased allocation of weapons to the Italian Theatre
rather than save military resources by abandoning the Italian
commitment altogether. His decision was made final on 5th October
when Jodl informed Kesselring that 'for political, military and
economic reasons' the Führer had decided that the Apennine front,
and with it upper Italy, must be defended not only until late
autumn but indefinitely. *OB Südwest* was to ensure that 'every last
German soldier under command was imbued with this intention'.

Kesselring summoned Lemelsen and von Vietinghoff to his
headquarters on 28th September to inform them of the Führer's
reactions to his proposal. von Vietinghoff had already anticipated
him by circulating to his corps and divisional commanders on 6th
September a message which set out 'why we must fight so stubbornly down here in Italy'. He explained that it was a matter of
strategic necessity to hold northern Italy for as long as possible, in
order to safeguard its resources for the Reich and to ensure that
Army Group C remained self-supporting. There was no military
benefit in falling back to the *Voralpen* Line, as this would only
increase the Army Group's supply problems and give to the enemy
all the advantages of terrain and of airfields which would be closer
to the front and to the Reich. *AOK 10* must therefore conduct its
operations so as to ensure that the Allies incurred high casualties
for every inch of ground that they gained, and must follow the

tactical prescription of 'depth and more depth; reserves and more reserves'.

On the available evidence Lemelsen was less communicative to his subordinates, but his immediate problems won a number of reinforcements for *AOK 14*. Kesselring decided on 27th September that 1st Parachute Corps was to receive a reconnaissance and a *Luftwaffe* guard battalion from northern Italy, also 100th Mountain Regiment which was diverted from rejoining 5th Mountain Division in Liguria.[142] Having authorised the eastwards move of two further reconnaissance battalions from 14th Panzer Corps, *OB Südwest* held out hopes that 94th Infantry Division, which was refitting on the Adriatic coast, would be allocated to 1st Parachute Corps. However when the Army Commanders met on 28th September von Vietinghoff laid claim to this division for *AOK 10*, and as Kesselring would not make up his mind it was of no early benefit to either Command.[143] It was his wider purpose at this conference to inform his generals of the reasons for Hitler's refusal to permit the implementation of *Herbstnebel* and of the consequential need for continued defence of their present fronts. Destruction south of the Po was to be avoided by 'skilful tactics' and *AOK 10* was conceded room to manoeuvre on its coastal wing, but *OB Südwest* insisted that in the centre both Armies must stand firm and prevent a break through to the Via Emilia.

von Vietinghoff reacted the more decisively, for he had finally lost patience with 51st Mountain Corps' tendency to blame *AOK 14* for every disaster on the inter-Army boundary. When he learnt late on 27th September that there were troops on Mt Battaglia whose 'steel helmets indicated that they were American', first von Vietinghoff and then Wentzell took Feuerstein to task and made him responsible for clearing the Battaglia area.[144] By this time more troops were opposing 88th U.S. Division, thanks to the poor flying weather which had restricted Allied air interference with German lateral movements. The leading regiment of 98th Infantry Division was now in the line reinforcing 715th Infantry Division which, together with 305th Infantry Division, had been authorised to pull back its front so that 577th Grenadier Regiment of 305th Infantry Division could participate in the counter-attack. From *AOK 14's* side of the boundary it was planned to strike at Battaglia from the west with 755th Grenadier Regiment of 334th Infantry Division, which took over on 28th September part of 44th Infantry Division's sector in the mountains east of the Imola road. Elements of 362nd Infantry Division were side-stepped to help hold the road itself and the area west of it, because one regiment and a battalion each of the other two regiments of 44th Infantry Division had already been destroyed by the Americans during their advance down the Santerno valley. On the morning of 28th September von Vietinghoff made it plain to Feuerstein that failure to close the gap between *AOK 10* and *AOK 14* would lead to a court martial to apportion blame. Mt Battaglia must be retaken, and, disregarding the inter-Army boundary, General von Rohr, commanding 715th Infantry Division, was to make sure that firm contact with *AOK 14* was regained in the area of S. Margherita which lay to the north of Mt Battaglia. von Rohr was also made responsible for securing a viable defence line on the ridge running from S. Margherita to Casola Valsenio in the Senio valley.

See Map 25

The defence of Mt Battaglia was an American epic. 350th U.S. Infantry were just digging in during the afternoon of 27th September when the first German attempts to regain the mountain started.[145] The enemy had several advantages. Although Battaglia was 2,400 feet high and offered commanding views over the surrounding country, it could also be infiltrated via the deeply indented courses of the many streams running down from its summit towards the Senio. The top of the mountain was bare except for an old castle ruin, and the only route by which supplies could be brought up and casualties evacuated ran along a narrow ridge to the south-west. Moreover, the 2nd Battalion, which was digging in on the summit, was far ahead of 1st Division to the east and 351st U.S. Infantry attacking Mt Cappello to the west; until the latter was taken on 30th September it was devoid of flank support. To make things more difficult the foul weather reduced observation, blinding the American artillery observers and grounding their observation aircraft.

As the leading regiment of 334th Infantry Division was pinned down at Mt Cappello before it could reach Mt Battaglia, the first attacks on the mountain were delivered by a battalion of 577th Grenadier Regiment of 305th Infantry Division which came in from the east.[146] Fighting in driving rain, the Americans managed to hold their half dug positions. During the night they were heavily shelled and at dawn were attacked again, losing some of their forward posts and only just preventing the Germans from overrunning the summit.

Mt Battaglia became a '*point d'honneur*' for 577th Grenadier Regiment, which was reinforced with a battalion from 334th Infantry Division on 29th September. The previous afternoon 577th Grenadier Regiment had attacked again, using flame-throwers and explosive pole-charges in an attempt to throw the Americans out of the castle ruins. They came very near to doing so. The defenders were almost out of ammunition when towards evening a mule train reached them with ammunition and the first food they had received since they seized Mt Battaglia.[147] The escorting infantry company entered the fight and turned the scales. And so the fight went on throughout the 29th and 30th September. The fourth attack launched on 29th September actually penetrated the castle during hand to hand fighting on the crest, and the following day a German soldier wielding a flame-thrower managed to scramble into the castle again. Fighting was so close that the American artillery could do little to help, and the low mist and the echoes of the ravines, which distorted the readings of the American sound-rangers, made harassing fire ineffective.

While the duel was being fought out on Mt Battaglia, von Rohr was successfully consolidating the S. Margherita-Casola-Valsenio line.[148] In consequence Mt Battaglia lost much of its real, though not psychological importance, to the German defence. On 29th September *AOK 10* authorised 51st Mountain Corps to continue its attempts to blast the Americans out of the castle, but also stated that it was not to be a 'big affair' as unnecessary casualties were to be avoided. 577th Grenadier Regiment mounted its eighth and last attack on 1st October with engineers of 715th Infantry Division. Its men again penetrated the castle but by then the rest of 350th U.S. Infantry had joined the tired 2nd Battalion and the American position was secure. The weather also cleared momentarily enabling the American artillery to become fully effective. The field artillery battalion supporting 350th U.S. Infantry fired 3,398 rounds that day. German shelling on Mt Battaglia continued for a few more days.

The Americans had won the struggle for the feature but their advance on Imola had been checked. *AOK 10's* War Diary for the beginning of October was prefaced with the words:

'After many vain attempts it has been possible to re-establish contact on the Army boundary and thus to form a connected front, in which we hope to foil the enemy's efforts to break through the mountains to the Via Emilia'.

Clark had already appreciated that once 88th U.S. Division's secondary advance upon Imola had been checked by a concentration of German troops he must abandon the drive as the limited capacity of the L. of C. would not carry reinforcements.[149] In order to allow General Keyes to concentrate his forces for the capture of Bologna, Clark therefore directed 13th Corps to shift its left flank westward and to take over the high ground east of the Imola road. His decision can be dated by 13th Corps instructions, issued on 29th September. The first move, the transfer of 1st Guards Brigade (from 6th Armoured Division) to relieve 88th U.S.

Division, began with the arrival of the Guards advanced party on Mt Battaglia on 1st October.

88th U.S. Division had not broken through to Imola, but it had drawn upon itself a remarkable number of troops from Lemelsen's *AOK 14*, thus weakening the German defenders in front of 2nd U.S. Corps' main thrust towards Bologna. These were reduced to elements of 16th SS Panzer Grenadier Division opposite 34th U.S. Division, 4th Parachute Division oppostie 91st U.S. Division on Route 65, and 362nd Infantry Division less several major detachments on the west side of the Santerno valley opposite 85th U.S. Division. Clark had every reason to hope that by shifting his emphasis back to Route 65 he would be able to blast his way through the last 200 miles of mountains to Bologna. Keyes set 1st October as D day for his next thrust.[150]

In summing up 'Olive' in the last chapter we left one question unanswered. What would have happened if the two Allied Armies had attacked side by side in the centre of the front as Alexander had originally intended before Leese pressed him to undertake 'Olive' instead? The combined offensive would have opened three weeks earlier in much better weather. 5th Army's breaching of Green I in a week's fighting and 88th U.S. Division's rapid break through to Castel del Rio showed that it was far from impossible to attack through the centre of the Northern Apennines without Juin's mountain troops, as Leese and Kirkman believed. By 27th September Kesselring was brought for the second time to the point of seeking *OKW's* authorisation to implement *Herbstnebel*. What would have happened if the two Allied Armies had struck the junction of *AOK 14* and *AOK 10* instead of just one U.S. Division? In early August both German Armies would, of course, have been in better shape than was the case in late September, but the extra three weeks of fine weather would probably have tipped the balance irrespective of which thrust lines were chosen by the Allies. The relatively easier going on the Adriatic coast was not sufficiently easy to offset the loss of time.

(x)

See Map 8

The hand-over notes which General Leese wrote for General McCreery on 29th September are still preserved.[151] He had reached the decision that determined German opposition must be expected and had accordingly ordered the Polish Corps to start moving forward from the Pesaro area to come into the line in the coastal sector. The bad weather had resulted in the Poles' move being postponed. The whole tenor of the notes, however, reflects his optimistic belief that 5th and 8th Armies would link hands in a matter of days and that the combined advance to the Po was imminent. Corps' axes, boundaries and objectives were set out. The Poles were directed to the Po at Ariano and the Canadians were to advance via Budrio to Ferrara where they would force a crossing. They had been specially trained for an assault crossing of the Po. The New Zealand Division had also studied the Po crossings and expected to be placed under Canadian command for the operation.

In the event the Po was not reached for another seven months. These hand-over notes serve as an epitaph to Leese's command of 8th Army and illustrate a persistence in the use of unsuccessful tactics. His judgement throughout his command can be faulted more often than praised. There was a suspicion at the time that he had been promoted out of 8th Army because a change was needed after the heavy casualties and disappointments of 'Olive'. A careful check of contemporary files has revealed no evidence to support this theory. On the contrary, Mountbatten asked for an officer with recent experience of high command in Europe to take over the Army Group in Burma for the coming offensive there.[152] Leese was genuinely selected as the best man available for the job. There is no hint in Alexander's papers that he was glad of a change of Army Commander. Brooke's correspondence with Alexander does however show growing disappointment with Leese's performance as early as July. He wrote:[153]

> 'There is one other respect in which Oliver is a serious disap-
> pointment to me lately. I may be wrong but he gives me the
> impression of stickiness and lack of thrust . . . 8th Army has
> advanced sedately up the leg of Italy following closely in Kessel-
> ring's retreating footsteps. Both the 5th Army and even the
> Poles seemed [sic] to have shown greater enterprise and to have
> left the 8th Army behind.'

We can only judge Leese on his record which, in Italy, was not very flattering, and was made less so by his having to follow Montgomery without the latter's staff, most of whom returned with him to 21st Army Group. Leese was essentially an emulator rather than an innovator. He tried to copy Montgomery in personal style and military technique without the professional qualities which made Montgomery so successful. He carried on the system of a small tactical headquarters divorced from Main H.Q. 8th Army but lacked a de Guingand as Chief of Staff to act as a go-between to ensure, by anticipatory action, that the two command elements of 8th Army were always synchronised and in sympathy with each other.[154] Some of the staff muddles during Leese's battles were caused by the officers at Main H.Q. not being fully in the mind of those at Tac H.Q. Nevertheless, the Main and Rear H.Q. Staffs showed great professionalism in 8th Army's two moves across the Apeninnes and in its efficient administration under the most trying logistic conditions.

Leese's period in command of 8th Army spanned three distinct types of operation: the set-piece opening phase of 'Diadem' which was fought as a attritional battle until a break through was achieved in the Liri valley, thanks to the successful operations of Juin's French mountain troops in the hills to the south and Anders' Poles on Mt Cassino to the north; the advance to Rome and from Rome to Florence; and the 'Olive' offensive, designed to roll through the Gothic Line before it could be manned effectively by the Germans. In the first phase of 'Diadem' Leese was fighting the type of battle upon which he had built his reputation. His 30th Corps in North Africa had been Montgomery's battering ram at El Alamein, Mareth and Wadi Akarit, and with this experience behind him he was well suited to command 8th Army in the last battle of Cassino, which he handled well. In the Western Desert all wide ranging manoeuvre and mobile operations had been the prerogative of General Sir Brian Horrocks' 13th Corps. When the advance from Cassino started, 8th Army, under Leese's direction, showed his lack of experience in handling such operations. The traffic jams in the Liri valley were not fortuitous. They must be ascribed to the inability of Leese and his staff to think through the problems of mobile warfare in the unfavourable Italian terrain. As we have seen, 8th Army had the unhappy tendency of trying to pass its armoured divisions through the infantry at the wrong moment, and of being unable to handle the intricate organisational problems involved. The speedier advance of the American 5th Army showed what could be done in much the same type of country.

In the pursuit north of Rome Alexander and Harding were probably most at fault in failing to drive the two German armies apart when *AOK 14* was in disarray and *AOK 10's* flank was wide open. Leese cannot, however, be exonerated entirely. 8th Army moved ponderously, displaying little finesse and dynamism. It was a pedestrian performance. The country was certainly very difficult, but there was too great an acceptance of the difficulties and too little effort to overcome them.

The 'Olive' offensive did not lack imagination or originality. Alexander and Harding must take responsibility for agreeing to the change of plan. Nevertheless, it was not only Leese's concept of the offensive but also his handling of the resulting battles which were questionable. The over-optimism, which he engendered, could be forgiven in that the war seemed to be racing to its close.

His misconception of the type of battles which should have been fought is less easy to defend. After the demonstration by the French Expeditionary Corps during 'Diadem' of the importance of clearing the mountain flank, and the ease with which this could be done by infiltration due to the sheer size of the features that made them difficult to defend, it is surprising that he placed so much reliance on the use of armoured divisions in the heavily rivered coastal plain. The validity of this argument will only become apparent when we have described his successor's change of tactics.

These criticisms of Leese's handling of 8th Army must be set against its record of continuous success, operating under the most difficult conditions in country which favoured the defender. 8th Army never lost a battle under his command, nor could it claim a resounding victory.

CHAPTER XV

FRUSTRATION IN ITALY
OCTOBER 1944

(i)

THE Allies' hope of a German collapse in the autumn of 1944, which had been so bright in August and September, began to flicker in October although it was not finally snuffed out until November. In Western Europe Montgomery's operation to break through into Germany north of the Ruhr had failed at Arnhem, and cumulative supply difficulties, caused by German retention of the Channel ports and the Scheldt approaches to the port of Antwerp, began to hamstring Eisenhower's efforts to win a decision before winter. On the Eastern Front the Russians were slowing down as well. In the far north the German 20th Mountain Army was making good its escape from Finland into Norway.[1] In the Baltic provinces two Armies of Army Group North were bottled up in the Kurland peninsula west of Riga, but the first Soviet attempt to break through into East Prussia had failed when the Russian troops who crossed the border on 16th October were dispersed by German counter-attacks. In Poland, the last embers of Polish resistance in Warsaw were dowsed by 2nd October; and in Hungary, Admiral Horthy's attempts to reach an accommodation with the Russians resulted in his own deportation and replacement by a pro-Nazi puppet in the middle of the month. In the Balkans, von Weichs was to lose Belgrade during October. Löhr's Army Group E suffered no Russian interference in its gradual withdrawal from Greece, Macedonia and Serbia except for a short-lived threat to Kraljevo north-west of Nis.[2] In Italy, the Allies' ambitions suffered a progressive decline as the prospect of fighting an unbroken *Wehrmacht* under autumn and eventually winter conditions, so near the apparent end of the war, became evermore likely. Five major factors contributed to the changes which occured in the psychological as well as physical conditions of the Italian Theatre, turning the happy optimism of the pre-'Olive' period into the frustrating drudgery of the autumn and winter battles. We will discuss each in turn before turning

to the operations themselves, because they provide a common
background to all that was to happen in the next three months.

The first factor was the impact of autumn weather on the Italian
topography which, even in summer, favoured the defender. 5th
and 8th Armies were operating in entirely different terrain, but
the weather was common to them both. Neither fully appreciated
how early in the autumn they were to be impeded by weather,
which had two effects: in the air it reduced the potency of Allied
air support, and on the ground it immobilised all arms, except
the infantry, who had to continue fighting in appalling conditions
without the full support of the heavier army weapons.[3] Although
all the forward troops suffered chilling from the rain and discomfort
from the mud, it was the infantry who suffered most and whose
endurance was seriously affected. Regimental histories and personal
accounts of this period emphasise the problems of relieving the
infantry in the line for short periods to dry and warm them, to
give them dry and mudless clothing, and to feed them with really
hot meals. Strangely, despite all the rain, there was even a shortage
of palatable drinking water, because streams were so filled with
mud that the filters of the unit water trailers failed and unit water
trucks found great difficulty in reaching the Sapper water points
in the brigade and divisional echelon areas. Brews of tea, in which
the British and Indian soldiers always found solace, were apt to
be mugs of mud when they managed to find enough shelter to
boil the water. Bogged transport meant long hauls on men's backs
of fighting necessities like ammunition, food and water. Even the
mules found the going too difficult at times as they slipped on the
steep slopes of the Apennines or sank into the glutinous mud of
the valleys. The wounded fared worst. They suffered much longer
carries by struggling stretcher bearers, longer rides in twisting,
turning and exposed jeep ambulances, and slower bumping rides
further back in lurching ambulances. It was not that the distances
had increased; it was the longer time taken to cover the same
distances which caused the acute discomfort of the casualty evacuation chain.

See Map 8

The second factor was the peculiar topography of the Romagna
which 8th Army entered when it crossed the Marecchia on 22nd
September. In the next fortnight, while it advanced steadily to the
Fiumicino, the Romagna's true nature was born in upon every
member of 8th Army—rear echelons as well as forward troops. It

could hardly have been more unsuitable, especially in winter, for an over-mechanised force like 8th Army, intent on making sweeping armoured thrusts. It would not have been an easy area in summer; in winter its peculiarities turned it into superb defensive country for the tired but experienced troops of *AOK 10*.

The Romagna in Roman times had been a vast marsh between the Apennines and the Po. Drainage schemes had been started in the 12th Century and had been continued up to the outbreak of war in 1940.[4] They have, of course, been restarted since the Second World War, and the massive damage inflicted on the drainage systems during the fighting has been repaired, so making it difficult for visitors to appreciate 8th Army's problems to the full. Most of the original drainage schemes involved confining the rivers and major streams between high banks to reduce floods, and canalizing their courses to allow a swifter discharge of water during spates caused by heavy rain higher up in the Apennines. Over the centuries silting occurred, which raised the river bed above the level of the surrounding land. East of the Via Emilia the flood banks of the main rivers rose between 15–30 feet above the plain.[5] Not only were these rivers formidable obstacles to movement and observation, but their flood banks provided the German defenders with ready-made mounds into which they could dig their weapons to command the flat countryside, and into which they could tunnel shelters and dug-outs, proof against artillery and air bombardment.*

The courses and methods of outflow of the many rivers, which streamed down from the Apennines in a generally north-easterly direction, were important to the development of operations of both sides in the Romagna.[6] The most northerly rivers, the Idice, Sillaro, Santerno and Senio which flowed into the plain between Bologna and Faenza, had all been diverted artificially into the Reno or, in the case of the Lamone, through the marshlands just to the south. The Reno ran from the Apennines west of Bologna and swept in a great arc round the north of the city to enter the Adriatic just south of Lake Comacchio, the very large shallow lagoon between the Po and the city of Ravenna. The Reno thus made an ideal defensive line south of the Po on which the Germans could hold the Allies temporarily while they withdrew the bulk of their troops over that vast obstacle. At the end of September von Vietinghoff had established within *AOK 10* a special staff named *Wehrmacht* H.Q. Reno–Po.[7] With General Bessell appointed as its Senior Engineer Commander on 4th October, it was the two-way

---

* The Italian names for the many types of river, stream and watercourse used on contemporary maps were, in descending order of magnitude: *Fiume* (River), *Canale* (canal), *Rio* (stream), *Torrente* (mountain torrent), *Scolo* (drain), and *Fossa* or *Fosso* (ditch).

task of this headquarters to ensure the continued passage of troops
and supplies southwards over the two rivers, and also to construct
the necessary defensive works and prepare the additional bridges
and ferries which would enable the divisions to cross in the reverse
direction 'should the contingency arise'.

The next two rivers to the south-east, the Montone and Ronco,
were united in a common outflow appropriately called the *Fiumi
Uniti* which emptied into the Adriatic south of Ravenna. [8] The
more southerly rivers, which 8th Army was in the process of
crossing in October, flowed directly into the Adriatic. The main
rivers were, however, only part of the tactical problem. Between
them the plain was criss-crossed with irrigation dykes and ditches,
some large enough to be termed canals and others, though smaller,
still created effective tank obstacles. Along the coast much of the
ground had been reclaimed. Some of the dykes drained naturally
into the sea, but many could not do so and depended upon
continuous pumping. Widespread flooding could follow the cutting
of the flood banks—either in an attempt to prepare bridge
approaches for an assault crossing or as a result of deliberate
German policy.[9] It could also be caused by simply stopping the
pumps. In a comment on the extension of flooding south and east
of Ravenna on 4th October, 8th Army remarked that it had begun
to take the place of troops in this sector.[10]

Throughout the Romagna there were only two major axes of
advance open to 8th Army: the Via Adriatica (Route 16) on the
coast through Ravenna, and the Via Emilia (Route 9) leading
directly to Bologna through the ancient cities of Cesena, Forli,
Faenza and Imola. Both routes were embanked and free from
flooding, and between them there was an extensive network of
roads and agricultural tracks, but few of these had any real
foundation and most were only one-way, certainly for military
traffic. There were few bridges over the major rivers except on the
main roads; and the lateral roads connecting those bridges which
did exist, ran along the tops of the flood banks. South of the Via
Emilia the roads were primitive and tended to lead into the foot-
hills, whereas 8th Army needed axes parallel to its line of advance.

Two other features of the Romagna affected 8th Army's operations. The whole plain was densely populated and covered with
small farms and villages, which afforded excellent cover for German
snipers and became all the stronger when reduced to rubble by
artillery. Secondly, most farmers double or treble cropped their
land. Besides growing crops of various types on the ground, they
grew vines which were suspended between the pollarded fruit trees
as much as 15 feet from the ground. From 8th Army's point of
view, as the attacking force, the vines obscured the view of tank

commanders in their turrets; the supporting vine wires became festooned round the tanks tracks and were strong enough to immobilize a tank temporarily until its tracks could be freed with wire cutters; and, as most of the rows of trees and vines were spaced about 30 yards apart, the German defenders could enfilade one row with machine guns to drive the attacking infantry away from their supporting tanks and the next with anti-tank weapons to deal with unsupported tanks. Moreover, most of the tree lines ran parallel to the rivers and ditches and hence at right angles to the line of advance, thus obscuring the front of the attacking troops while exposing their flanks to concealed weapons.

A further tactical problem was the unexpected speed with which river spates could arrive after rain had fallen in the mountains. Bridgeheads would be established on the far banks of rivers by infantry wading across. Suddenly the water would begin to rise behind them and make it impossible to pass anti-tank guns across in support, leaving the infantry vulnerable to counter-attack by German tanks and S.P. guns. Several unfortunate incidents, large and small, were to occur from this cause as 8th Army fought its way through the Romagna. Eventually ways were found of dismantling the 6-pounder anti-tank gun so that it could be man-handled across swollen streams to give the infantry some immediate protection.

It soon became apparent to the Chief Engineer 8th Army that it was more important to use all available Sappers to overcome the immediate problems of the Romagna than to keep the Po Task Force inviolate for an operation which looked singularly unlikely to occur for some weeks, if not months.[11] On 3rd October the force was disbanded, subject to 48 hours notice of recall, and the special bridging and engineer equipments were put into a dump at Fano. The troops so released were used to grapple with the multifarious engineering problems of continuing 8th Army's advance through the Romagna.

5th Army's topographical difficulties were of a different kind. The weather and consequently the mud were common to both fronts, but 5th Army, including the British divisions of 13th Corps and 6th South African Armoured Division in 4th U.S. Corps, had also to endure the increasing cold in the mountains and the difficulties of keeping themselves supplied with the basic necessities of life. British troops were in battle dress and greatcoats, as mountain warfare clothing had not arrived.[12] Supplies reached forward troops largely by precarious jeep, mule and manpack chains. The cry went up for more and more mules. 5th Army had established a training school for Italian muleteers, which raised in all 15 pack transport companies.[13]* The Royal Army Service Corps, which in October already held 22 pack companies, also raised eight new Italian companies during the winter, which did splendid work. At the end of the supply chain there were often long carries which only men could undertake.[15] Pioneer units were moved forward from their usual work in the base installations to help with these carries and with road repair.

After the failure to break through to Imola at the end of September, General Keyes introduced a system of rotation of units within divisions which enabled him to keep his four divisions in the line with adequate reserves, while accepting the fact that men could not go on fighting day after day in the stark conditions prevailing in the Apennines.[16] Each division was to hold one regiment out of the line and rotate regiments on approximately five day cycles. Thus each cycle of 2nd U.S. Corps' operations would start with fresh troops to employ in co-ordinated attacks against the successive ridges which it appeared the Germans were preparing to hold.

The defensive strength of the Northern Apennines grew no less as 5th Army pushed its way over the watershed.[17] Indeed, as we have pointed out in the last chapter, the height of the peaks on the northern side of the watershed was very little lower than those of the watershed itself until the mountains fell away sharply just south of Bologna. The mountain rivers flowed northwards on 4th and 2nd U.S. Corps' fronts and north-eastwards in 13th Corps' sector. All of them descended through steep gorge-like valleys which offered little room for deployment and which were overlooked by rocky, steep and sparsely covered spurs and ridges on either side. Apart from Route 65 such main roads as there were clung to the valley bottoms and there were very few lateral roads between the valleys. The spurs were often capped with well-built farm houses, which continued to serve as strongpoints even when reduced to ruins.

Thus on both Army fronts the Germans held the defensive advantage of terrain and of cover from the weather, in that the farms and villages behind their front were still largely undamaged. A crucial difference between the two sides lay in their attitude to the weather. The Allies prayed for the clouds to part and for the sun to shine so that the ground would dry out to restore some of their mobility, their clothes would dry enough to reduce personal

---

* See Part I of this Volume (H.M.S.O. 1984) p. 27 for a brief introduction to animal pack transport in Italy and the loads needed to support a formation operating in the hills. Numbers in A.A.I. service on 31st October were: *British*: about 13,500 mules. *U.S. Army*: about 3,400.[14]

discomfort and the Allied Air Forces could reappear overhead. The Germans prayed that rain would ground the swarms of Allied aircraft and keep Allied infantry and tanks floundering in mud. The Germans' tactical advantages were no less marked in the autumn of 1944 than they had been in the previous autumn and winter, when they defended Cassino and the Gustav Line so successfully. These advantages could only be overcome by a prolonged period of fine weather, or, as this was most unlikely, by a lavish expenditure of artillery ammunition to carry the infantry forward in spite of the conditions.[18] As the infantry of both Armies tired with the worsening weather, still more ammunition was needed. Unfortunately there was a growing shortage of both necessities—infantry and artillery ammunition—in 5th as well as 8th Army, to which we will now turn. The lack of reinforcements and a growing dearth of ammunition make up the third and fourth causes for growing pessimism on the Italian front.

We referred to the problems of British infantry reinforcements in Part I Chapter VIII of this Volume and told how a programme for the conversion of redundant anti-aircraft artillerymen into infantry was instituted in Italy and the Middle East in the spring of 1944 to help meet a predicted shortfall for September 1944; of a world wide deficiency of 42,000, 21,000 would be in the Mediterranean Theatre. The retraining of gunners as infantry, and other measures put in hand at the same time, did enable 8th Army to enter the 'Olive' offensive with its divisions largely up to strength.[19] By 10th September its high casualties were beginning to cause alarm. Alexander asked A.F.H.Q. to increase the flow of infantry reinforcements, saying that otherwise he would have to cannibalize 56th and 78th Divisions. On 17th September he reiterated to A.F.H.Q. that the battle was nearing its crisis and it was essential to send every available man forward. Wilson offered 850 infantry reinforcements with a further 300 retrained Gunners on 24th September. These men, though welcome, could not make good 8th Army's losses which had been running at about 300 per day for a month and showed no signs of abating. The War Office was also approached but could not help.

In the meanwhile Alexander's staff had been working on ways of overcoming his immediate operational problems by reorganisation. On 22nd September Alexander accepted his staff's proposals that all infantry battalions should be reduced from four to three rifle companies, with a drop in established strength from 36 officers and 809 men to 30 officers and 700 men; that two infantry brigades should be reduced to cadre; and that 1st Armoured Division should be broken up into its constituent parts which would be used to reinforce other formations.[20] The brigades selected for reduction to cadre were 168th Brigade of 56th Division and 18th Brigade of 1st Armoured Division. 43rd Gurkha Lorried Infantry Brigade was transferred to 56th Division as a temporary replacement for 168th Brigade. 2nd Armoured Brigade was made an independent armoured brigade and 1st Armoured Division's Divisional Troops were turned into 8th Army Troops for general employment. Subsequently, as a result of a review of manpower carried out by A.A.I., A.F.H.Q. and the War Office in October, it was decided in November to break up permanently:[21]

> 1st Armoured Division (less 2nd Armoured Brigade)
> 168th Infantry Brigade (ex 56th Division)
> Two Guards battalions:
> > 3rd Coldstream Guards
> > 5th Grenadier Guards
> Two infantry battalions:
> > 9th King's Own Yorkshire Light Infantry
> > 10th Battalion Rifle Brigade
> 25th Tank Brigade (to form an R.A.C./R.E. Assault Brigade)
> Royal Artillery:
> > Two Medium Regiments
> > One Field Regiment
> > One A/Tk Regiment*

A proposal that 56th Division should be broken up was not accepted by the War Office. Its future was to be reviewed in the New Year. In the event the division was saved by the South Africans providing a second infantry brigade for 6th South African Armoured Division, thus releasing 24th Guards Brigade for 56th Division.[22]

One principle was maintained inviolate throughout these reorganisations. Men were not transferred from one division to another unless it was unavoidable. In these cases general officers were sent to explain the reasons to the men concerned.[23] The lessons of the mutinies at Salerno, caused by unexplained cross-postings, were fresh in all commanders' minds.† In the case of the A.A. Gunners, care was taken to post them as far as possible to infantry battalions associated with their home areas: North Country, West Country, Scottish, Irish and so on. Amongst the infantry themselves care was also taken not to re-badge unless there were valid reasons for doing so, which could be explained to the men concerned. The roots of the British regimental system ran very deep and could not be disturbed without risk.

---

* War formed units were disbanded, Territorial Army units placed in suspended animation, and Regular and Supplementary Reserve reduced to cadre and returned home.

† See *Mediterranean and Middle East* Volume V (H.M.S.O. 1973) p. 422.

Battle casualties were not the only causes of reduction in unit strengths. Two other causes must be mentioned: the 'Python' scheme for the repatriation and replacement of servicemen with long overseas service, and the problem of desertion. Python had been started in January 1943.[24] At that time men with over six years continuous overseas service could claim repatriation. Numbers were small because it only affected regulars who were overseas at the outbreak of war. By November 1944 the qualifying period for the Mediterranean Theatre had been reduced to four and a half years. Large numbers of men had been despatched to the Middle East from May 1940 onwards and were now serving in Italy. In consequence the numbers for repatriation rose steeply and modifications had to be made to the original Python scheme. Under the existing rules a man once repatriated under Python could only serve in north-west Europe, unless he volunteered to serve elsewhere. Some servicemen would have preferred to stay in the Mediterranean if they could be given home leave first. The 'L.I.L.O.P.' (leave in lieu of Python) scheme was introduced for those willing to stay and who possessed 'such particular technical qualifications or such highly specialised local knowledge as a Python replacement from the U.K. would not be able or could not be expected to acquire in a reasonable time'.[25] Successful applicants were given 61 days home leave. Problems of war-weariness were tackled by another scheme called 'L.I.A.P.' (leave in addition to Python) and was introduced in November 1944, allowing men with not less than three years and not more than four years unbroken overseas service the chance of a month's home leave.[26] In order to ensure absolute fairness L.I.A.P. was decided by a ballot run by a committee composed of an equal number of officers and other ranks who were not themselves eligible for leave. Commanding Officers were, however, entitled to veto successful applicants charged with serious crime or when men were under suspended sentence. 3,000 places were allotted to the Central Mediterranean Forces of which 2,000 were for A.A.I.[27] The first draft left Italy by sea on 15th November. Alexander and Robertson agreed that priority should be given to fighting troops.

The problem of desertion was not new. Most of the field commanders believed that it had been exacerbated by the abolition of the death sentence for desertion but appreciated that its re-introduction was politically impracticable. General Wilson, writing early in 1944, doubted whether abolition was the cause.[28] He pointed out that comparative figures with the First World War were unobtainable but he noted that the crime of the self-inflicted wound had become almost unknown and thought it would certainly re-appear if the death penalty was re-introduced. He gave several causes for desertion: 5% were criminals who had no intention of fighting; some were nervous cases who should never have been allowed into the line at all; some had been overseas too long; some had been sent to strange regiments where they had no friends; but the majority, in his view, deserted 'because they have been in the line too long or consider they have had too much continuous fighting'. This view was confirmed by Lieutenant-Colonel John Sparrow (later to become Warden of All Souls' College Oxford), who discussed the problem with field commanders at all levels and with the Staffs of A.A.I. and 8th Army during a special investigatory tour of the Italian Theatre in July 1944.[29] These discussions, together with interviews with psychiatrists, defence and prosecution lawyers and with 16 prisoners awaiting trial, led him to conclude that the chief cause of desertion was prolonged action which was greatly increased by close contact with the enemy. He also classified deserters and absentees into two broad classes: the 'deliberate' who preferred prison service to the dangers of the line, and the 'involuntary' nervous breakdowns who would often welcome a second chance to prove themselves. The second category was by far the larger, and could be ascribed to war-weariness.[30]

In Italy commanders had begun to express renewed concern about desertion and absence without leave during the winter of 1943/44. With the reopening of the successful 'Diadem' offensive and the return of better weather, it was hoped that the problem would diminish. That it did not do so is shown by the monthly figures for convictions for Desertion and Absence Without Leave for United Kingdom troops gathered by the Theatre's historians at the end of the war.[31] The desertion and absence figures are taken together because the difference between them is a fine one and favours the offender in that the intention never to return has to be proved in convictions for desertion. The combined figure shows the true extent of the problem:

1944							
	Jan	349	Cassino and Anzio		Oct	905	Battles of Romagna rivers
	Feb	207			Nov	1,200	
	Mar	521			Dec	1,211	
	Apr	583	Regrouping	1945	Jan	1,127	Retraining
	May	495	'Diadem'		Feb	616	
	Jun	994					
	Jul	779	Advance to Gothic Line		Mar	404	Final offensive
	Aug	628			Apr	153	
	Sep	944	'Olive'		May	242	

These figures show a steadily rising trend up to the start of 1945, which was to be expected from the combination of a high level of offensive operations and the cumulative effect of war-weariness in divisions which had fought through the Tunisian, Sicilian and Italian campaigns since the autumn of 1942.

Alexander was in correspondence with the Adjutant-General, Sir Ronald Adam, in June 1944, who informed him that the Secretary of State for War was preparing a memorandum to the Prime Minister on the subject of desertion.[32] It was 'a political question and not easy to put across'. The Secretary of State, while refusing to recommend the death penalty, would try to have the amnesty question (discussed below) dealt with firmly. Adam would also try to establish that service prior to desertion would not count towards demobilization. A man's service would start afresh after the completion of his sentence.

In October the Government's demobilization plan was given wide publicity in the Army Bureau of Current Affairs pamphlets.[33] McCreery was soon writing to Alexander about the encouragement the plan would have for would-be deserters. The points system, upon which it was based, added length of service to age to produce each man's release group. The A.B.C.A. pamphlet showed that the only penalty for desertion in these computations was loss of the months spent absent and in prison or detention. McCreery's calculations demonstrated that the average deserter might drop eight places in the release group spectrum but as there were 75 Release Groups the resulting postponement of his release would be very short. Added to this factor was the conviction amongst most soldiers that there would be an amnesty for offenders as soon as the war was over. McCreery asked for a firm declaration of Government policy that there would be no amnesty; that all men convicted would serve their sentences unless suspended to enable them to be sent to a non-European theatre of war (e.g. the Far East); that men under suspended sentence should not qualify for demobilization until they had earned full remission, which they could only do after posting to a non-European theatre, and that automatic review of sentence should stop and only be undertaken in special cases.

Alexander supported McCreery's proposals in a renewed approach to A.F.H.Q. at the end of October, urging that strong immediate action was needed.[34] It was not until 14th December that a clear Government statement was made in the House of Commons, when Churchill announced:

> 'So far as concerns the present Government, it is not the intention to grant any general remission of sentences. Offences such as desertion which comprise the bulk of these sentences, involve at the best an added strain upon man-power of this country, and at the worst forfeit the lives of other soldiers who

have filled the places of these deserters. Such very serious offences are happily rare . . .'[35]

The figures suggest that the Prime Minister's statement had little effect as the January total showed only a slight decline although the intensity of operations fell after 2nd January. It was not until an announcement was made that any soldier who deserted after 1st February 1945 would forfeit all prior service for release that a significant drop in desertions did occur.[36] The figures are not conclusive because reduction of operational activity was also having its effect.

The Prime Minister's statement that 'such offences are happily rare' could be supported in percentage terms in that there were just under a million men on the ration strength of the British Central Mediterranean Forces. The desertion/absence figure, at worst, was about 0.1%.[37] As far as the commanders were concerned the offence was certainly not insignificant. The difference in the two points of view lay in the fact that most of the deserters were from the infantry, who, of all arms, suffered most prolonged hardships, and who had to close with the enemy without the benefit of armoured protection. Within the infantry the most experienced and hence over-worked divisions lost most. An extract of a table produced by the historian of 8th Army's 'A' Branch, which shows the desertion/absence figures by formations and by months from August to December 1944 inclusive, is reproduced below:[38]

British Infantry Formations	Deserters/Absentees over five months August to December 1944
1st Division	626
4th Division	664
46th Division	1,059
56th Division	990
78th Division	927 (October, November and December only)
1st Guards Brigade	81
24th Guards Brigade	102
British Armoured Formations	
1st Armoured Division	95
6th Armoured Division	220
2nd Armoured Brigade	30
7th Armoured Brigade	4
9th Armoured Brigade	13
25th Tank Brigade	3

Three things stand out: the bulk came from the infantry divisions as expected. Even the resting of divisions in the Middle East did not reduce the problem, since 78th Division had the highest monthly figures of all divisions when it returned to the front in October. The armoured formations were scarcely affected, 6th Armoured Division's 220 (judging by comparative figures produced by Colonel Sparrow) probably came mostly from the infantry for which there are no separate figures.[39]

Set in the context of other crimes, desertion and absence were by far the most prevalent, as is shown by the following breakdown of all court martial convictions in 8th Army from 1st January to 30th September 1944.[40]

Desertion	878	} 1,289
Absence without leave	411	
Cowardice	3	}
Sentry offences	53	
Mutiny	7	
Striking or threatening		} 368
a superior officer	131	
Disobedience	147	
Insubordination	15	
Neglect of orders	12	

The American divisions of 5th Army were suffering similar reinforcement difficulties as battle casualties during the Gothic Line fighting outstripped the reduced flow of American replacements. On 6th October Clark signalled General Devers, who was still Commanding General of the North African Theatre of Operations (N.A.T.O.U.S.A.) and responsible for the allocation of replacements, saying that his four infantry divisions had been losing 550 men per day since the beginning of the month.[41] Heavy fighting was continuing. Without additional replacements his infantry strength would drop by 5,000 for every ten days' fighting after 10th October. 'Infantry Rifle Companies will thereby be reduced so seriously as to create an extreme operational handicap.' Clark's plea fell on deaf ears probably because Devers, reflecting higher American policy, was more concerned with the operations of 7th Army in the Belfort Gap than with the Italian campaign: he had not, as Clark sharply pointed out, been able to visit the Italian front for about two months.[42] Clark signalled again on 9th October asking him to divert shipments of reinforcements destined for 7th Army to Italy with equally little success.[43] On 15th October Alexander intervened with a signal direct to Eisenhower:[44]

> 'I know you realise and appreciate what we have done and are doing here to keep German Divisions from being transferred to

the Western Front. But the time has now arrived when my Armies will not be able to continue the offensive much longer. This is mostly due to the fact that all Divisions are very tired and completely lack fresh replacements. Especially is this the case with American Fifth Army. I have done everything through official channels to get replacements but I have not succeeded. My last chance is to appeal to you personally. Anything you can do to help Clark will be to our mutual advantage. Lemnitzer has left today by air for General Devers' Headquarters with full details of Clark's requirements.'

Eisenhower did not hesitate. He replied next day agreeing to release 3,000 replacements for the Mediterranean if they could be flown there quicker than from the United States.[45] This proved to be the case and so they were flown from France to Italy.

The principal material shortage in Italy was ammunition. We have discussed the earlier crisis in the ammunition field in Part I Chapter VIII of this Volume, when it was only a British and Mediterranean Theatre problem. By October it had become an Allied and world-wide cause for concern.[46] As early as the end of 1943 stocks had appeared so high that production in both Britain and America had been cut back and the labour saved in Britain was transferred to aircraft production. By October 1944 the original estimates, upon which production was based, were proved inadequate by the upsurge of expenditure in France and Italy as the autumn battles became more bitter and by the clear indication that the war would not end in 1944. The Defence Committee (Supply) considered the British position in October and decided to increase production, but no benefits from the decision could be felt in the field until the spring. It was with relief that the Defence Committee noted in January that production was beginning to rise.

In the meantime the ammunition situation caused concern at all levels. The Deputy Chief of Imperial General Staff wrote to 21st Army Group and A.F.H.Q. on 14th October explaining that expenditure of 25-pdr ammunition was exceeding production by $1\frac{1}{2}$ million rounds per month and medium artillery ammunition expenditure was 40% higher per month than production.[47] He calculated that 25-pdr ammunition would be in adequate supply, providing existing expenditure did not rise, but there would be a crisis in medium shell unless the Armies were more economical and reduced expenditure rates.

Inspite of D.C.I.G.S.'s assurances about 25-pdr ammunition,

the crisis was already affecting 8th Army. The staff had made the monthly allocation to the Corps of 8th Army on the basis of:[48]

25-pdr   9 days at 100 rounds per gun per day (r.p.g.p.d.)
          22 days at 65 rounds per gun per day
Mediums   31 days at 55 rounds per gun per day

When the actual ammunition allocation was received from A.F.H.Q., based on War Office delivery estimates, 8th Army decided to introduce as from 13th October a low basic rate of 40 and 30 r.p.g.p.d. in order to build up an Army reserve which might be allocated, on demand, for specific operations. At the end of October the allocation had to be further reduced to 25 and 15 r.p.g.p.d. McCreery henceforth treated ammunition supply as a major factor in future planning. The American ammunition supply situation in 5th Army was no better.[49] On 14th October Clark was warned by his logistic staff that if current expenditure continued he would be forced onto the defensive due to shortage of ammunition by 10th November.

Alexander, with his extensive battle experience, which included fighting as a regimental officer and later as a brigade commander in the Guards Division in almost all the major battles in France in the First World War, sensed the coming failure of his efforts to defeat Kesselring between the Northern Apennines and the River Po as early as 21st September, when he wrote to the C.I.G.S. about the reduction of his forces and his difficulties in finding replacements.[50] He was fighting:

> 'the battle of Italy with about 20 divisions, almost all of which have had long periods of heavy fighting this year, and some for several years, against the 20 German divisions committed to the battle front, with the prospect of 4 more German divisions and probably 2 Italian divisions joining in the battle at a later stage.'

He continued:

> 'We are inflicting very heavy losses on the enemy and are making slow but steady progress, but our losses are also heavy and we are fighting in country [in] which it is generally agreed that a superiority of at least three to one is required for successful offensive operations. It will be small wonder therefore if we fail to score a really decisive success when the opposing forces are so equally matched.'

He complained about delays in sending out equipment for the six combat groups of the Italian Army which were being formed, and trusted that recent proposals for the expansion of the Polish Corps

would be implemented more quickly.* He also rejected a War
Office proposal that he should exchange one British infantry division and an armoured brigade for the balance of 31st Indian
Armoured Division from the Middle East, rightly questioning how
he was expected to accept 'the dead loss . . . of a whole British
infantry division'.†

(ii)

See Map 23

It was at this time, when success in Italy was seen to hang in
the balance, that Alexander began to consider plans for capturing
the Istrian peninsula which the Combined Chiefs of Staff had
asked to have by 10th October, in accordance with the 'Octagon'
decisions.‡ On 2nd October a meeting was held at H.Q. A.A.I.,
attended by Wilson, at which the practical problems of mounting
this theoretically desirable operation were probed by the responsible
commanders for the first time. In his notes for the conference
Alexander made a number of significant points which influenced
Wilson's reply to the Chiefs of Staff.[54] He pointed out that he
needed 'fourteen days of fine weather to drive Kesselring back to
the line of the River Po'. Should the unfavourable weather continue, Kesselring would be able to retire 'in his own time', his
probable intention being to stabilise his front on the Adige river.
In order to contain German divisions in Italy, A.A.I. must advance
to the Adige, and to do this he could not afford to release any of
his divisions. Moreover, all his divisions, except 78th Division,
were tired out and would need two months out of the line during
the winter. A halt must, therefore, be called once the Adige was
reached. He estimated that he might cut the Via Emilia near
Bologna by 15th October and reach the Adige between the middle
and end of November. His divisions could not be rested, re-trained

---

* A.F.H.Q. had agreed with the Italian Government that the *C.I.L.* should be replaced
by an expanded force of six battle groups, which would move forward between late October
1944 and early January 1945.[51] In mid-October equipment for four of the groups had still
to be despatched from the U.K.
Difficulties over the supply of Polish reinforcements have been explained in Chapter X
pp. 55–6. By late September sufficient numbers had reached Italy to form a third brigade
for both infantry divisions.[52] During October A.F.H.Q. decided that an armoured division
(of one armoured, one infantry brigade) should also be raised. Alexander believed that this
Polish force would 'pay a big dividend'.

† Nothing more was heard of this proposal but when Alexander suggested on 30th
October that 6th Armoured Division should be accepted by the Middle East in exchange
for 5th Division, to increase the infantry divisions available to A.A.I., his request was
turned down at the behest of C.-in-C. Middle East, who needed infantry just as badly for
internal security duties.[53]

‡See Chapter XIV pp. 340–1.

and re-equipped before mid-February at the earliest. Thus trans-Adriatic operations could not take place before that date and would have to wait for the right weather. He believed that even if the Germans withdrew to the Italian and Austrian Alps they would still try to deny Fiume and Trieste to the Allies. As he would need fewer Allied troops to hold the shorter line of the Adige he would have enough divisions for an offensive on the Italian front to be launched concurrently with a trans-Adriatic offensive, using one of his Armies on each front. The trans-Adriatic operation would require not less than six divisions, and landing craft would be needed to switch divisions between the two fronts, depending upon the progress made as operations developed. He estimated that craft to lift two divisions should be retained and he would also like an airborne division.

When the possibility of an amphibious operation across the Adriatic was considered at the Supreme Allied Commander's conference next day, opinion hardened against a landing in Istria.[55] Admiral Sir John Cunningham stressed the problems of mine-sweeping in the area and the consequent dependence on light naval support only. He pointed out the maintenance problem caused by lack of suitable mounting ports in north-east Italy. Since Ancona was being fully utilised by 8th Army, landing craft would have to make a 500 mile voyage from the Heel ports in uncertain Adriatic weather. General Wilson argued that, even if the Germans withdrew through Yugoslavia and did not attempt to stand on the River Sava, they would almost certainly hold on to Trieste and Fiume, bearing in mind the dividends paid by their successful retention of ports in north-west Europe. He assumed also that A.A.I.'s advance would be slow and that it would not be able to force the Adige in 1944.

As an alternative operation in the Adriatic the meeting considered landings in the Split and Zadar areas on the Dalmatian coast. A few suitable beaches did exist, but the sea approaches were difficult and the bad roads running inland through Dalmatia made these areas of doubtful value, except in unopposed conditions. Admiral Cunningham, however, saw considerable merit in landing at Split and Zadar, where the maintenance problems for the Royal Navy would be easier than in Istria. He was supported by Wilson who saw the object of the Dalmatian landings as the seizure of a secure deployment area south of Zagreb, and the development of airfields there from which to attack Austria. Doubts were raised that it might all take too long, but it was finally decided that the Mediterranean Joint Planners should examine the time factor for an unopposed advance through Dalmatia: the landings to take place in early February; and the force finally deployed to be up to six divisions. The Commanders-in-Chief were also of the opinion that if the trans-Adriatic operation had to be mounted before the end of the year then fresh formations must be provided.

The new and disturbing factor to emerge from these meetings was that little could be done to open up a front across the Adriatic on a major scale before February, much later than participants of the 'Octagon' Conference anticipated when they agreed that assault shipping could be held in the Mediterranean for such an operation.

Three weeks after the 'Octagon' Conference Churchill set off once again (accompanied by Eden and Brooke) for the 'Tolstoy' Conference with Stalin in Moscow. They staged through Italy on the way out and on the way back, and were thus able to discuss with the Mediterranean Commanders the formation of future operational policy. The meeting on the way out was held on 8th October. Alexander was given the dubious honour of making the opening statement, telling Churchill that all was far from well on the Italian front.[56] Speaking very frankly, he said that all his divisions had been committed and were tired, and his Armies were now in an awkward position, stuck halfway through the Apennines with poor Lines of Communication behind them. Moreover, the weather had broken and, even if he did get into the Po valley proper, he was sure he would find it unsuitable for major operations at that time of year. Allied material superiority in armour and air power had been neutralized by the weather. The Germans were also tired, but they had an easier job as the defenders in country which suited their horse-drawn transport better than his mechanised formations. In his view the Italian campaign was being allowed to waste away by bad strategy. He suggested that it should be revived by the despatch of three U.S. divisions to Italy instead of France where, he understood, there might be difficulty in their reception.

The subsequent discussion was long and rambling. Brooke doubted the validity of the Istrian project because he did not think the Americans would agree to divert three divisions to Italy. There was a danger of them arguing that if formations could be withdrawn from the main front in Italy they should be sent to France instead of across the Adriatic on a 'Balkans venture'. No alternative operation to turn Kesselring's flank could be suggested by Admiral Cunningham; beaches between Ancona and Trieste were unsuitable and the waters shallow and heavily mined. Churchill decided to side with Alexander by approaching the President for extra divisions. He ended the meeting by saying that he would reflect on the matter during his journey to Moscow and would cable the British Chiefs of Staff and the President from Cairo, which was his next stop.

After the meeting Wilson despatched his official reply to the British Chiefs of Staff (repeated to the U.S. Chiefs of Staff) on 9th October which concluded with four points: he could not pull out formations from the Italian front if he was to keep Kesselring pinned down; he would need three fresh divisions as soon as possible if he was to mount an amphibious operation aimed at Trieste before the end of the year; he would also need an airborne division and a large proportion of the necessary air lift for an assault on Trieste; and he would need to retain the administrative and amphibious resources already in the Theatre.[57]

The President's reply to Churchill's plea for three divisions arrived on 17th October.[58] As expected, it was negative. The heart of his argument lay in the words: 'German actions in North Italy are more dependent on Russian advances that on our operations in Italy'. He continued:

> 'All of us are now faced with an unanticipated shortage of manpower and overshadowing all other military problems is the need for quick provision of fresh troops to reinforce Eisenhower in his battle to break into Germany and end the European war.'

His opinions, it is worth noting, were remarkably similar to those of the British Chiefs of Staff, cabling independently from London but taking, as they said, a purely military view.[59]

The reply from the U.S. Chiefs of Staff on 21st October was less austere than might have been expected.[60] They asked for the return of American assault shipping from the Mediterranean beginning about 1st November, but they recommended that Wilson should be left with enough ships and craft to lift about one division. While they insisted that the bulk of these ships should be British they were prepared to make up the balance with American ships until further British ships could be released by Eisenhower from the English Channel. They made no mention of any withdrawal of American divisions.

Meanwhile Alexander had returned to his headquarters and on 10th October had set in train the first phases of planning for the winter's operations with a letter to both his Army Commanders which he opened with the words 'There appears to be no certainty that the war against Germany will end this year'.[61] His sights were now set on reaching the Adige before he called a halt for the winter. 13th Corps and 6th South African Armoured Division were likely to stay with 5th Army until the River Po was reached. The destruction of Kesselring's armies was still his aim and, as long as the Germans remained in possession of north-eastern Italy and the ports of Trieste and Fiume, the best way of achieving this aim was 'a powerful drive through north-eastern Italy combined with a major amphibious operation across the Adriatic'. If the plan for future operations developed in the way Alexander envisaged, 8th Army would carry out the trans-Adriatic thrust while 5th Army undertook the overland advance through north-eastern Italy. He would probably form a separate force of defensive troops under direct control of A.A.I. to hold the northern flank between Lake Garda and the Swiss frontier, freeing 5th Army to concentrate on its overland offensive. Whatever happened, both Allied Armies would have to fight their way through hilly and mountainous country and over many water obstacles. Winter training for divisions as they were withdrawn from the line would be concentrated on these types of operations. In addition three of 8th Army's divisions would be given amphibious training.

On 21st October, however, when Wilson and Alexander met Churchill and Brooke, now on their way back from Moscow, they were unable to report significant progress on the Italian front.[62] Owing to the lack of an adequate number of assault formations, the onset of winter, the critical replacement situation, and the equally critical ammunition situation, they felt it would not be possible to advance beyond the line Ravenna–Bologna before calling a halt. Even this line might not be reached. On the other hand encouraging developments in the Balkans and, in particular, the German withdrawal from the Dalmatian coast invited 'energetic exploitation in support of the battle in Italy'. They advocated an offensive-defensive stand on the Italian front so that six divisions could be withdrawn to start preparations for a trans-Adriatic operation.

Wilson signalled on 24th October, asking the Combined Chiefs of Staff to approve this programme and to allocate the necessary landing craft to the Theatre.[63] At the same time he expressed the belief that immediate steps should be taken to exploit the critical situation of German troops in the Balkans. With this object he had issued orders that priority in air supply should be given to the Partisans in northern Yugoslavia over those in northern Italy, and that bomber squadrons of D.A.F. and of M.A.T.A.F. should be diverted to support the Balkan Air Force.*

During the autumn the position of the Italian Partisans in North Italy deteriorated steadily and by early November it had become clear to A.F.H.Q. that radical new measures must be taken to aid them.[64] First as regards air supplies: A.F.H.Q. had agreed to an allotment of 600 tons for the month of October but, due to the

---

* For implementation of these orders, see p. 447; also Part III of this Volume Chapter XVI.

weather and various technical difficulties only 73 tons were delivered. A.A.I. then protested that anything under 250 tons per month would jeopardise the entire Italian Resistance movement and would compel the withdrawal of some of its Missions; 550 tons was the true monthly requirement, even for scaled down winter conditions.[65]* It was the Air Force view, as put by Air Marshal Slessor, that operations in northern Italy were both inefficient (as few sorties were successful) and costly (in that casualties were unduly high), and it may be noted that Commander Balkan Air Force chaired the Special Operations Committee which co-ordinated air supplies.[66] Nevertheless no disagreement with its recommendations was reported at the S.A.C. conferences until 7th November, when Lieutenant-General McNarney (the new D./S.A.C.) stressed the military value of the Italian Partisans and argued—successfully—on behalf of A.A.I.'s larger target.[67]† It is also significant that at the same meeting the supply situation in Yugoslavia was reported to be very favourable.

On 23rd October Alexander issued a revised directive to his Army Commanders, based on the knowledge that far from gaining formations he was to lose 4th Indian Division, and 3rd Greek Mountain Brigade, to 'Manna' Force.[68]‡ Plans were to be made on the assumption that the Russian advance into Hungary and the operations of Tito's Partisans would force the Germans to abandon the whole of the Dalmatian coast and its immediate hinterland. Split, Sibenik and Zadar would be occupied by British Commandos and light forces which would develop communications inland in conjunction with the Partisans. If these operations were successful then:

> '. . . it should be possible to develop the ports and road and
> rail communications from them, under the cloak of opening up
> the country, and under the protection of our light forces and
> the Partisans. As soon as these preparations are sufficiently
> advanced our main bodies will be brought in as quickly and
> secretly as possible for an advance on Ljubljana and Fiume'.

This was the general concept. 8th Army's front would be taken over by a Corps H.Q. directly under A.A.I. so that H.Q. 8th

---

* For difficulties in supplying the Italian Partisans see Part I of this Volume (H.M.S.O. 1984) pp.390–91. And for a general account of Allied military relations with the Italian Resistance see Part III Appendix 7.

† General Joseph T. McNarney had taken over from General Devers as Deputy Supreme Allied Commander. He had visited Alexander on 25th October to discuss supply to the Italian Partisans.

‡ The withdrawal of 4th Indian Division and 3rd Greek Mountain Brigade had been announced at the Supreme Allied Commander's routine meeting of 10th October.[69]

Army could concentrate on planning and preparation for this trans-Adriatic operation. The target date was still February, but if it could be mounted earlier so much the better.

The new element in this directive was an estimate that offensive operations would have to stop during November to release divisions for training, re-equipment and recuperation. On the other hand it was considered essential to seize Bologna and Ravenna as bases for 5th Army's 1945 offensive into north-east Italy. The question was how these two desirable objectives could be attained. The plan suggested was for 5th Army to suspend operations and withdraw two divisions at a time to the Florence area for rest, thus simulating the Army's exhaustion. 8th Army would continue operations designed to seize Ravenna. As soon as the German mobile divisions had been drawn away from Bologna to check 8th Army, 5th Army should bring its divisions back from Florence quickly and secretly and re-open its offensive as soon as weather permitted. If this plan failed the best winter line south of Bologna–Ravenna would be taken up; it was of great importance to secure Forli in order to open up Route 67. Rest and re-training would then be given priority. A Commander-in-Chief's conference was arranged for 29th October at which these plans were to be discussed. We must now turn back to look at the operations of 5th and 8th Armies during October which had caused Alexander and Wilson to limit their objectives to the Bologna–Ravenna line instead of the Adige.

(iii)

See Maps 8 and 26

5th and 8th Armies continued their offensives in the Northern Apennines and in the Romagna throughout October, always on the watch for signs of a general withdrawal resulting from external pressures, such as the Russian advance into the Balkans, but conscious that the Germans would not otherwise yield ground unless compelled to do so by hard fighting.[70] 2nd U.S. Corps' operations can be described as the grinding of a relentless mincing machine with four to six day cycles based upon General Keyes' policy of the systematic rotation of regiments within divisions. 8th Army, under its new commander, General Sir Richard McCreery, began to show more originality in its operations and to manoeuvre as far as the weather would allow. It was helped by the German sensitivity to an American break through to Bologna. As 2nd U.S. Corps' advance progressed through the mountains, first, 29th Panzer Grenadier Division was transferred piecemeal from the Romagna to the Apennines, then 90th Panzer Grenadier Division

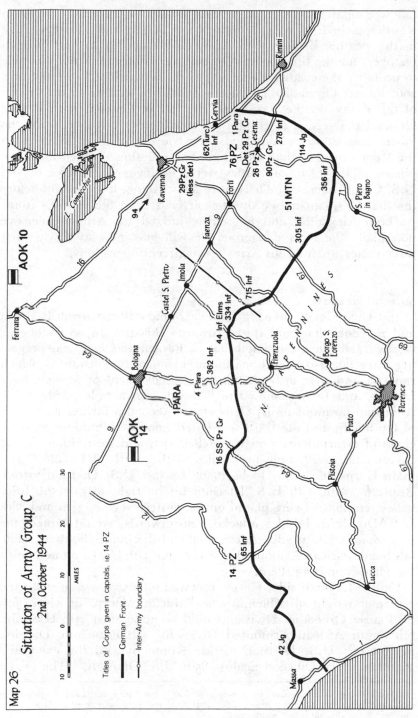

Map 26 Situation of Army Group C
2nd October 1944

Titles of Corps given in capitals. ie 14 PZ

— German Front
—○— Inter-Army boundary

MILES
10   0   10   20   30

followed in the same manner, and finally 1st Parachute Division was despatched, its arrival south-east of Bolgna and a further break in the weather bringing 5th Army's offensive to an end on 26th October, for the time being. On each occasion 8th Army was able to profit by the gradual departure of these divisions from its front: 29th Panzer Grenadier Division's departure leading to the arrival of 8th Army on the Savio and the fall of Cesena; 90th Panzer Grenadier Division's withdrawal starting its advance from the Savio; and 1st Parachute Division's transfer enabling it to reach the Ronco quicker than expected. The milestones which mark the phases of the October battles were, however, the cycles of 2nd U.S. Corps' offensive. There were five of these, three fought before the first German mobile division arrived from 8th Army's front. As both Alexander and Kesselring judged 5th Army's offensive potentially the most dangerous we will look now at Keyes' first three cycles, then at 8th Army's concurrent operations.

See maps 26 and 27

2nd U.S. Corps gave up its diversionary thrust towards Imola and reopened its main thrust towards Bologna on 1st October.[71] Corps Intelligence estimated that 1st Parachute Corps was preparing three defensive positions in succession across Route 65 which ran east and west through the three small towns of Monghidoro, Loiano, and Livergnano. The first was just a mile north of the American positions on 1st October; the second a further four miles to the north; and the third was based upon a forbidding ten-mile chain of escarpments which stretched east and west either side of Livergnano, itself some four miles to the north of Loiano.* The main Corps effort was to be made by 91st U.S. Division astride Route 65 with 85th U.S. Division on its right astride the Idice valley, emphasis being placed on the eastern sector. 34th and 88th U.S. Divisions, besides attacking northwards, would protect the immediate western and eastern flanks of the main offensive, while 6th South African Armoured Division and 13th Corps pinned down the forces opposing them.

On the German side, Keyes' renewed offensive was to strike the centre and right of Schlemm's 1st Parachute Corps in which 16th SS Panzer Grenadier Division would be up against 34th U.S. and 6th South African Armoured Divisions, 4th Parachute Division against 91st U.S. Division astride Route 65 and the exhausted 362nd Infantry Division against 85th U.S. Division.[72] The mixed

---

* For example at Livergnano the escarpment was 3 miles long and 1,800 feet high. Mt delle Formiche, the highest feature, was 2,092 feet and presented a sheer face to any approach from the south and south-east.

groups of 44th and 334th Infantry Divisions were still trying to hold 88th U.S. Division in the Santerno valley north of Castel del Rio, but on the afternoon of 1st October 51st Mountain Corps broke off the fight for Mt Battaglia, where 1st Guards Brigade was now relieving 88th U.S. Division. Nevertheless, the Mountain Corps continued to harass the defenders of Mt Battaglia to such an extent that 5th Army did not record the cessation of German attacks until 12th October.[73] The only reinforcements in the line when 2nd U.S. Corps attacked was a *Luftwaffe* guard unit in the centre of 4th Parachute Division's front which cracked on the first day (1st October) and let 91st Division into Monghidoro.[74] German attention was still focussed on the Imola thrust line and remained so until 4th October.

2nd U.S. Corps' attack on 1st October started in early morning mist. Then the skies cleared and the Americans could use the full weight of their artillery and air support.[75] 91st U.S. Division alone expended 10,587 rounds of gun ammunition in its initial attack. The fine weather lasted just 24 hours but in that time Schelmm's hold on the Monghidoro Line had been so shaken that he was forced by midday 2nd October to seek authority to withdraw slowly to the Loiano Line. The main damage had been inflicted by 85th U.S. Division on the shaky 362nd Infantry Division whom Röttiger, Kesselring's Chief of Staff, complained had 'not so much fought as run away'. On 3rd October the advance quickened as Schlemm fell back and by the end of 4th October 91st U.S. Division was in contact with the new German position at Loiano. 85th U.S. Division had been making even better progress against 362nd Infantry Division and the remnants of 44th Infantry Division in the sectors east of Route 65 and was slightly ahead of 91st U.S. Division.

Lemelsen had by this time appreciated that it was via Bologna, rather than Imola, that 5th Army would seek to break through to the plains of the Po. He argued that more must be done to help 1st Parachute Corps, and on 3rd October Kesselring agreed that *AOK 10's* 98th Infantry Division should come forward to relieve the remnants of 44th Infantry Division. 94th Infantry Division was finally allocated to 14th Panzer Corps, so that von Senger (whose only other divisions consisted of 42nd Jäger and 232nd Infantry Divisions, the latter *en route* from the Army of Liguria) could release 65th Infantry Division. This formation was instructed on 4th October to move battalion by battalion into the sector of 4th Parachute Division, whose troops were reported to be completely exhausted and nearing the end of their tether. However a trainload of replacements for Trettner's division was nearing Bologna, and it was planned that after their absorption and a brief period of

refit 4th Parachute Division would return to the line for relief of
362nd Infantry Division, which in the meantime was given a
narrower sector to defend. *AOK 14* also anticipated that the installation of 94th Infantry Division on the western wing of 14th Panzer
Corps would enable 16th SS Panzer Grenadier Division to close
up eastwards for more direct participation in the main battle. Thus
by 4th October the strengthening of the German front south of
Bologna had begun.

During this first cycle of 2nd U.S. Corps' offensive Alexander
decided to reinforce Clark with his only fresh division.[76] On 2nd
October 78th Division, which had just arrived back from the
Middle East and was concentrating around Fano in 8th Army
reserve, was placed under command of 13th Corps; it was to take
over 88th U.S. Division's sector in the Santerno valley so that the
latter could develop its operations northwards on 85th U.S. Division's right flank. The relief was not easy, nor could it be carried
out as quickly as it was hoped, due to the difficulties of bringing
up the British units on the narrow Firenzuola approach road,
already cluttered with American units and supply traffic supporting
88th U.S. Division. It had only been repaired to the standards
needed for the powerful American six-wheel-drive trucks and in
many places was almost impassable to the standard British two-
and four-wheel-drive vehicles. Inspite of loans of U.S. trucks, 78th
Division found it a slow business moving its units forward from
Firenzuola where they began to assemble on 5th October.* One
major hazard was the crossing of the Santerno at S. Andrea, just
south of Castel del Rio, where the Germans had blown out the
arches of a high level road bridge of viaduct-type construction. An
American low level bridge with steep approaches formed such a
severe bottleneck that it was decided to span the gap with a high-
level 500–ft Bailey bridge on the original piers, but this was a
major engineering undertaking which could not be completed
before 13th October.† In the meanwhile the relief of 88th U.S.
Division went ahead as fast as road conditions would allow. 38th
Brigade arrived at Firenzuola on 5th October and started moving

---

* *The Order of Battle of 78th Division* has been set out in Chapter IX p.42n. The
following changes had occurred: the division was now commanded by Major-General R. K.
Arbuthnott. In *38th Infantry Brigade*, 6th had been replaced by 2nd Battalion Royal
Inniskilling Fusiliers.[77]
Additional Troops
   12th Canadian Armoured Regiment
   66th and 78th Medium Regiments R.A.

† One of the highest Bailey bridges ever constructed, the S. Andrea bridge, did not ease
traffic flow on the Castel del Rio road as much as hoped, due to fears for its stability.[78]
Most vehicles were using chains on their tyres to get them through the mud and these had
to be removed to reduce vibration when crossing the bridge. 78th Division estimated that
they could not move across more than one battalion group a day.

into the line that night to relieve the Americans on Mt Cappello. Beyond Castel del Rio the brigade had to use mules borrowed from 13th Corps. It took three nights for the three battalions of 38th Brigade, with a battalion of 11th Brigade under command, to complete the relief by 8th October so that 88th U.S. Division could strike northwards in the third cycle of 2nd U.S. Corps' offensive.

While 78th Division had been taking over in the Santerno valley, the second cycle of the American offensive had opened on 5th October.[79] Sensing that the German defences were weaker opposite 85th U.S. Division than in 91st U.S. Divisions' sector astride Route 65, where the newly arrived German 65th Infantry Division would be identified north of Loiano, Keyes decided to shift the weight of his attack to the ridge of mountains separating the Idice and the Sillaro valleys in 85th U.S. Division's sector. The bulk of the Corps and Army artillery, and the lion's share of 5th Army's direct air support were concentrated in support of 85th Division, while the other divisions of 2nd U.S. Corps were ordered to press forward wherever it was practicable to do so. Any optimism that Schlemm's withdrawals may have engendered in 5th Army did not last long. In the first cycle four miles had been gained in as many days; this time only three miles were won in the centre and a mile on either flank. Throughout the cycle the weather remained wet and overcast which favoured infiltration but reduced artillery and air support.

Although the German line held, Kesselring and von Vietinghoff were becoming anxious and critical of *AOK 14's* conduct of operations in general, and of Schlemm's handling of 1st Parachute Corps in particular. This Corps' frequent withdrawals also incurred displeasure at *OKW*. We noted in Chapter XIV that on 5th October Kesselring was informed by Jodl that by order of the Führer the Apennine front was to be defended 'indefinitely', and the signal to this effect which was sent to Schlemm by Lemelsen on the 6th emphasised that the task must find its first expression in bringing the front of 1st Parachute Corps to a halt.[80] Jodl's message stirred Lemelsen into visiting the Corps on 7th October, followed by Kesselring two days later. *OB Südwest* was clearly dissatisfied with Schlemm's tactics, for he directed that *AOK 14's* policy of rigid linear defence and counter-attack must be changed to defence in depth. Counter-attacks involving any considerable body of troops were discouraged because they were too wasteful and were usually robbed of effect by the delays imposed by difficult terrain. More significantly, Kesselring gained the impression, communicated to *AOK 10's* Chief of Staff on the evening of 10th October, that Schlemm had 'too much on his plate'. He decided that 98th, 334th and the remnants of 44th Infantry Division were to transfer from command of 1st Parachute Corps to *AOK 10's* 51st

Mountain Corps, and that from 12th October the inter-Army boundary would run along the watershed east of the Idice river, and then north to Ozzano on the Via Emilia. *AOK 10* was willing enough to re-absorb the well-regarded 98th and 334th Infantry Divisions, but after a personal visit on 12th October von Vietinghoff reported to Kesselring that they and 44th Infantry Division had been badly handled by Schlemm.[81] In von Vietinghoff's view they had been burnt up too quickly by an unapproachable and ruthless Corps Commander, who had insisted that newly-arrived troops mount counter-attacks before they had had time to settle down, and who exhibited none of the 'sensitivity' needed in the present tactical situation. Possibly because he was a General of the *Luftwaffe*, no recorded steps were taken to remove Schlemm, but he learnt on 20th October that Göring proposed to give him command of a new Parachute Corps in the west and that he would be replaced in Italy by Heidrich of 1st Parachute Division. Meanwhile, shifting the inter-Army boundary was not much help to the hard-pressed divisions remaining with *AOK 14*. This became evident when Kesselring was forced on 12th October to order *AOK 10* to return 29th Panzer Grenadier Division to 1st Parachute Corps.

The third cycle of Keyes' offensive which lasted from 10th to 16th October was the hardest yet fought and the most bitterly resisted. The weather cleared for the whole phase and allowed the Americans full use of their material superiority, but the cave-riddled escarpments of Livergnano afforded the German defenders the strongest position since they lost Green I.[82] Keyes made no change in his divisional sectors and still kept his emphasis east of Route 65. 78th Division had released the whole of 88th U.S. Division, which was free to force its way northwards to come into line with 85th U.S. Division. As 38th Brigade and 1st Guards Brigade were fully occupied holding Mt Cappello and Mt Battaglia, 78th Division was to follow up as soon as it could bring additional troops forward.[83]* In order to create a Corps reserve more suitable for mountains than 1st U.S. Armoured Division, Keyes ordered its Combat Command A to relieve two regiments of 34th U.S. Division west of Route 65, so that they could be moved into the centre of the Corps' front ready for use if a break through occurred in the fourth cycle.

It took the whole of the third cycle for 91st and 85th Divisions to take their immediate objectives, the village of Livergnano and the escarpment above it from 65th Infantry Division, and Mt delle Formiche from a mixed force of 65th, 362nd and 94th Infantry

---

* 1st Guards Brigade was under Divisional command for administrative purposes only.

Divisions.[84] The weight of artillery support used can be judged by 91st U.S. Division's expenditure of 24,000 rounds of artillery ammunition between 12th and 14th October. The only substantial gains came in 88th U.S. and 78th Divisions' sectors. The Americans secured Mt delle Tombe in the bend of the Sillaro river; and the last German counter-attacks on Mt Battaglia were beaten off on 78th Division's right flank, while on the left 11th Brigade started to attack north-eastwards.[85] Its object was to protect 88th U.S. Division's flank by securing Mt La Pieve which dominated the area north of the Santerno.

Repeated two-battalion attacks on three successive days failed to loosen 334th Infantry Division's hold on Mt La Pieve. On 14th October one company did establish itself amongst the rubble of buildings on the crest, but was driven off by flame-throwers. On the 15th support was given by Canadian tanks, heartening for the infantry until the leader broke down and blocked the narrow track. The brigade reserve battalion was committed for a final attempt during the night 15th/16th October, the attack being timed late so as to leave less time for counter-attack before dawn. The battalion was at first successful in clearing the upper slopes under intense fire, but was then checked by a sheer cliff, covered by mortar and small arms fire. One small party did scramble to the top, only to be forced off after heavy loss. 334th Infantry Division was still in possession of Mt La Pieve as Keyes' third cycle ended early on 16th October.

Statistically the end of this cycle had an ominous ring about it which could not be ignored by Clark or Alexander. The trends demonstrated by figures for casualties suffered by the four U.S. Divisions, set against miles gained on the road to Bologna, were not encouraging.[86]* Total U.S. battle casualties since 1st October numbered 6,329. 2nd U.S. Corps could not continue to sustain such casualties for much longer. Losses of junior officers were disproportionately high and impossible to make good by battlefield commissions because the supply of experienced non-commissioned officers was just as critical. Losses amongst field officers were worrying as well. In 88th U.S. Divisions, for instance, only four of its infantry battalions were still commanded by Lieutenant-

---

* Figures for the 34th, 85th, 88th and 91st U.S. Divisions were:

	U.S Casualties	Miles towards Bologna	German prisoners taken
1st Cycle (1st to 4th October)	1,734	4	858
2nd Cycle (5th October to 9th October)	1,474	3	1,119
3rd Cycle (10th October to 15th October)	2,491	$1\frac{1}{2}$	1,689

Colonels. On the other hand the figures of German prisoners taken showed an encouraging increase from cycle to cycle. Nevertheless, there were now six German divisions crowded around 2nd U.S. Corps' salient, blocking the direct route to Bologna, and the leading elements of a seventh, 29th Panzer Grenadier Division from *AOK 10,* had been identified by 85th U.S. Division on its front at the end of the third cycle.[87] General Clark was warned by his Intelligence Staff on 15th October that 90th Panzer Grenadier Division might be on the way as well. In his diary he wrote 'this seems more than we can stand'. The battle for Bologna was at a critical point; one more American effort might result in the figures for German prisoners taken mounting to a point that marked the beginning of a German collapse, if only the weather would stay fine for a few more days.

The effect of weather on air operations is well illustrated by the estimates of sorties flown and bombs dropped in the three cycles:[88]

Cycle*	Weather	Sorties flown	Tons of bombs dropped
1st	2 good, 2 bad days	907	432.5
2nd	5 bad days	132	58
3rd	2 dull/fine , 4 bad days	712	1,969.5

* There was no air support by night in 5th Army's battle area except for 21 sorties by
  Bostons in the first cycle.

Two Air 'firsts' occurred during this period as well as one major air operation. So far as records show, the Napalm fuel tank incendiary bomb was used for the first time operationally in Italy on 3rd October. It consisted of a 110-gallon jettisonable long-range tank, filled with a mixture of petrol and Napalm with an all-up weight of about 700 lbs. On 7th October the first recorded Rocket Projectile attacks on land targets in Italy took place. Previously they had proved most successful against shipping. And on 12th October, despite bad weather, Operation 'Pancake' was launched with the aim of flattening the German defences guarding Bologna. Supplies and equipment were to be destroyed; the enemy forces concentrated in the approaches to the city were to be annihilated; and the battle area was to be isolated as far as possible. M.A.S.A.F. and M.A.T.A.F. dropped 1,500 tons of bombs in close on 1,000 fighter-bomber sorties. M.A.S.A.F.'s heavy day bombers were alloted ten targets but the effort on each varied greatly. For example, of the 1,135 tons of bombs with which 697 of M.A.S.A.F.'s Liberator and Fortress sorties ringed Bologna, 355.9 tons were dropped by Fortresses on a bivouac two miles south of Bologna, and Liberators dropped 163.3 tons on a munitions factory and 108 tons on a stores depot. Two barracks, three other stores depots, an ammunition depot and workshops shared the rest. One hundred Liberator and Fortress sorties were aborted because of the weather. For the same reason M.A.T.A.F.'s Marauder force of 75 aircraft was grounded. A force of 141 U.S. Mitchells from M.A.T.A.F. did manage to operate and dropped 226.8 tons of bombs on bivouacs, fuel dumps and barracks south-west of and in Bologna. On the other hand the U.S. fighter-bombers bombed a variety of targets strung out from just south of Bologna to eight miles north-east of Firenzuola with a total of 57.1 tons, while 18 Kittyhawks bombed railway bridges seven miles north-west of Bologna. Rover Joe also had a very successful day.

Evidence from German records of the damage caused by Operation 'Pancake' is scanty. However, in his tactical report to *OKW* for 12th October Kesselring stated that roads from the front to Bologna had been extensively damaged by the day's activity. That evening, 1st Parachute Corps' Chief of Staff told Hauser that supply columns were experiencing great difficulty in moving up the cratered roads, and added that German artillery support had been much impeded and restricted by the air attacks. U.S. 2nd Corps was more impressed. The Corps reported the operation 'eminently successful' and that it 'aided materially the advance of Fifth Army in taking important terrain'. The aim of paving the way for a break through to Bologna, however, was not achieved.

Before looking at the concurrent events on 8th Army's Adriatic front we must turn briefly to events on the fronts of 4th U.S. Corps, 6th South African Armoured Division and 13th Corps. All three, at this stage of 2nd U.S. Corps' offensive, were succeeding in their primary role of pinning down their German opponents. Only 65th Infantry Division moved from 4th Corps' front, but this was after relief by 94th Infantry Division from Istria. The other German reinforcements came from divisions whose refitting was cut short.

6th South African Armoured Division, its artillery reinforced by a medium regiment from 10th A.G.R.A. and a detachment of three American heavy guns, and with Combat Command B of 1st U.S. Armoured Division attached, was placed directly under H.Q. 5th Army on 6th October for its major task of thrusting north towards Bologna, covering 34th U.S. Division's flank.[89] C.C. B took Route 64, 24th Guards Brigade advanced astride the Setta valley road, while the South Africans tackled the high ground in between. Their opponents, 16th SS Panzer Grenadier Division, were referred to in the Guards' War Diary as 'a very different formation from the infantry divisions whom we have opposed till now.'

It had taken 11th S.A. Armoured Brigade four days severe

fighting to clear the Mt Vigese feature (Pt 1090) by 6th October. After two abortive attacks had been launched against Mt Stanco, General Poole decided that a divisional assault would be mounted on 13th October. 12th S.A. Motor Brigade took over the assault, with the Guards and 11th S.A. Armoured Brigade supporting its eastern and western flanks respectively. 139 guns took part in the preliminary bombardment, divisional artillery alone firing over 10,000 shells. This time there was no failure. By 15th October the Guards were far enough down the Setta valley to form a firm link between the South Africans and the western flank of 2nd U.S. Corps. C.C.B had only cleared the Reno valley down to Porretta Terme (see also *Map 8*) and so the South African Division at the end of Keyes' third cycle was holding a 15 mile front running from the Setta river south-westwards via Mt Stanco to Porretta.

With the loss of Combat Command B and 6th S.A. Armoured Division, 4th Corps was reduced to the strength of little more than a reinforced division with which to hold a 50 mile front, stretching inland from the coast below Massa.[90] Its troops were organised in three *ad hoc* Task Forces, their aim being to secure the Allied front and tie down the Germans.

On 2nd U.S. Corps' eastern flank Kirkman's intention was for 13th Corps to advance towards the Via Emilia down four river valleys:[91] 78th Division astride the Santerno aiming for Imola, 1st Division the Senio for Castel Bolognese, 8th Indian Division the Lamone for Faenza, and 6th Armoured Division (less 1st Guards Brigade on Mt Battaglia) the Montone for Forli on Route 67.[*] It was hoped that 1st Division would be able to relieve 1st Guards Brigade on Mt Battaglia when it drew level in the Senio valley and when the Palazzuolo road could support the traffic. This would allow the Guards to rejoin 6th Armoured Division, giving it the infantry resources it needed to make progress on a wider front.

In assessing the apparently slow progress made by 13th Corps, several factors must be taken into account: its four divisions were operating on a 24 mile front whereas 2nd U.S. Corps had its four divisions packed into 11 miles; its role was one of pinning rather than destroying its opponents and so it was not allocated the level of artillery or air resources given to 2nd U.S. Corps and 8th Army; and its supply problems were extraordinarily difficult.[†] At the

---

[*] Chapter XIV p.348 explains the lines of supply of 1st Division and 8th Indian Division at the end of September. The reserve brigade and all supplies and stores of 8th Indian Division were some 25 miles back in the Sieve valley.[92]

[†] As an example of conditions on Mt Battaglia, to supply 1st Guards Brigade it took 100 men and 150 mules working a nightly 16 hour turn round, along a narrow causeway, registered by German mortars and swept by gales.[93] Brigade stretcher bearers, reinforced by 200 Italian Pioneers, were strung out at 400 yard intervals but even with this limited carry it would normally take a casualty 3½ hours to reach the Advanced Dressing Station.

beginning of October it had light Pack Transport Companies carrying its vital supplies forward. Three more Italian companies were transferred from 8th Army at about the time of the arrival of 78th Division and were immediately pressed into service, but needed to be reinforced and re-equipped before they could give of their best. Where roads could be used, the British divisions were hampered by the low power and lack of all-wheel drive of their British trucks.

Great as were the engineering problems of restoring the roads after German demolition, 13th Corps had to depend on its own resources and did not have the backing of Army Troops, in the allotment of which priority was given to the main effort by 2nd U.S. Corps.[94] Divisional Anti-Tank and Light Anti-Aircraft regiments were used to help in road and bridge construction together with the Pioneers and, when available, infantry working parties. Route 67, from Dicomano to S. Benedetto, for instance was opened for one way traffic in 13 days by 6th Armoured Divisional Engineers and Artillery, working day and night; while 13th Corps Engineers, following up close behind, developed the road to two way Class 40 traffic. Corniche stretches were reconstructed partly by blasting, and partly by timber cribbing.

Hard though conditions were on 13th Corps' front, some of the slowness of operations stemmed from lack of enthusiasm for its task in the Corps Headquarters. Kirkman had been one of the advocates of the switch of 8th Army over to the Adriatic coast for the 'Olive' offensive because he could see no future in operations in the Apennines. As always the attitudes of the commander and his staff are reflected in the subordinate formations. Colonel W. M. Cunningham, Alexander's Military Assistant, recorded in his diary for 11th September:[95]

> 'John [Harding] is quite depressed by 13 Corps HQ's outlook on life. There is no doubt that in the sixth year of war everyone is very tired . . . 13 Corps HQ has been fighting continuously as a HQ since December 1940 . . . Now they are very despondent and feel that they can't push on much further . . .'

The war was not going to end as soon as expected and the prospect of winter battles in the Apennines did not appeal to those who had experienced the previous winter in front of Cassino.

Each division of 13th Corps had a prominent mountain feature in front of it. We have described 78th Division's abortive attacks on Mt La Pieve between 13th and 16th October. 1st Division was faced with an equally dominant and difficult feature in Mt Cece (or on some maps Ceco), which overlooked its centre line in the Senio valley. The fighting serves as an example of the type of operation being undertaken by 13th Corps at this time.

Mt Cece offered every obstacle to the attacker and advantage to the defender since it was not only steep and inaccessible, but it also consisted of a number of mutually supporting peaks, all of which had to be occupied if any were to be safely held.[96] One approach from the south was along a knife-edge ridge, which rose very sharply to the summit,, and the other from the south-west needed the use of both hands to climb it. Most of the fighting took place in torrential rain which turned the limited tracks into muddy slides, several feet deep in places, and made the steep slopes so slippery that it was difficult for armed infantry to maintain their footing. The steepness of the slopes had two other adverse effects. They provided excellent cover for German reserves on the reverse slopes, and they gave the British Gunners difficult problems of crest clearance. 1st Division's historian remarks:

'Crest clearance in this area was an artillery nightmare. Some guns of the Divisional artillery could not clear Mt Cece, and others could only clear the feature on certain lines'.

Matters were made worse by the difficulty of finding gun positions. There was little flat ground, and those places which were at all practicable were also subject to sudden flooding. The Gunners learnt from bitter experience always to check that they could get out of a position before occupying it; and in many cases guns had to be winched into and out of the only available sites.

The battle for Mt Cece lasted for six days and nights, in the course of which four separate attacks were launched. 3rd Brigade made the first attempt using a single battalion on 3rd October. The summit was gained, but, as so often happened in the fighting in the Apennines, could not be held against determined counter-attacks by 715th Infantry Division, backed by heavy mortar fire. The assault was renewed next day with supporting fire from Canadian tanks and a subsidiary infantry assault from the left flank. The positions gained there were then used to launch a night attack in which two platoons from each battalion reached the summit but again were unable to consolidate.

2nd Brigade was brought up as reinforcement and a compara-tively fresh battalion of 3rd Brigade, 1st Duke of Wellington's Regiment, was detailed to lead the attack which was to be launched on 6th October, this time with two battalions echeloned in depth. Heavy rain had eased off by 8.30 p.m. when the battalion started to climb the western slopes, but the ground was still slippery and the leading troops fell behind the barrage. Exhausted by the climb and without the benefit of the barrage the battalion failed in its attempt to rush the crest and was driven off the actual summit by German infantry emerging from sheltered positions on the reverse slope. It clung onto the positions it had gained just below the summit throughout 7th October and the following night. In the early afternoon of 8th October, when the Germans seemed least alert, they stormed the crest in a silent attack using only their weapons. Despite heavy casualties, including the death of the Commanding Officer, the D.W.R. held their gains until the reserve battalion reached them and consolidated the position.* To complete the capture of the whole feature it was necessary to relieve the tired and depleted units on Mt Cece with the reserve brigade, 66th Brigade. Owing to the limited capacity of the L. of C. from Borgo to Marradi and Palazzuolo, (also supporting 8th Indian Division) only a battalion a day could be brought forward in addition to supplies.[98] It then took three days hard fighting, 14–16th October, for 66th Brigade to clear the two remaining spurs.

8th Indian Division had made limited progress on its front. It had stormed Mt Cavallara on 7th October, but was then stopped on Mt Casalino whose summit it had to share with the Germans until the west bank of the Lamone had been cleared.[99] 6th Armoured Division entered, but failed to clear Portico on 8th October.[100] Lack of infantry made further progress impossible. 13th Corps was virtually brought to a halt on the line Mt La Pieve–Mt Cappello–Mt Battaglia–Mt Cece–Mt Casalino–Portico in mid-October.

(iv)

See Map 28

While 2nd U.S. Corps was grinding its way through successive German positions, 8th Army was settling down under its new commander to tackle the problems of advancing over the Romagna river lines and through the inundations deliberately caused by German interference with the flood control and irrigation systems. McCreery's first decision was to place the emphasis of his operations on and to the south of the Via Emilia. His command of 10th Corps in its advance from Cassino northwards through the Central Apennines had given him confidence in the ability of his experienced divisions to operate in hill country.[101] Prospects in the waterlogged plain were dismal, while the high ground could be expected to dry out quicker. Moreover, only one relatively weak German division, 356th Infantry, had been identified in the hill sector. It seemed possible that a quick, secret thrust down the

---

* Private R. H. Burton, 1st D.W.R., was awarded the V.C. for his outstanding courage during the assault and in the repulse of counter-attacks.[97]

Savio valley to the Via Emilia would outflank the German forces opposing the main body of 8th Army and position the force for an advance north-west towards Bologna.[102] Both the timing and the final direction of the thrust (whether towards Cesena or further west) were to be dependent on the progress of 5th Corps, which itself was working westward through the foot-hills. McCreery gave positive form to this change of tactical policy on 6th October in a signal to his Corps Commanders, stating that he had decided to develop a thrust down Route 71, using the Polish Corps.[103] The Corps' move was to begin on 10th October; it would take over 10th Corps' sector and troops, and at least one Polish infantry brigade was to be in action by 13th/14th October.[104] H.Q. 10th Corps was to be withdrawn to Arezzo.

While McCreery was developing his new policy, 5th and Canadian Corps prepared to cross the Fiumicino. Their operations were timed to start on the night 5th/6th October when heavy rain brought the Fiumicino up in flood, forcing a postponement of the crossings north of the Via Emilia.[105] 10th Indian Division, which relieved 4th Indian Division on 3rd October, and 46th Division found the ground drier in the southern half of 5th Corps' sector and were able to continue operations successfully in the Apennine foot-hills. 10th Indian Division crossed the headwaters of the Fiumicino on 6th October near Sogliano and stormed the key feature in its sector, Mt Farneto, early on 7th October. 46th Division crossed the river during the evening of the same day and secured the main hill ridge on the far bank around Montilgallo. Determined German counter-attacks to regain the two features persisted for the next two days.

At *AOK 10*, where it had been appreciated on 4th October that 8th Army was regrouping in the hills, an air reconnaissance report of the 6th that Ancona was full of ships and landing craft caused von Vietinghoff to alert his Corps to the possibility of outflanking landing operations.[106] It was proposed to Kesselring that 1st Parachute Division should defend Ravenna. 29th Panzer Grenadier Division, which had just begun to withdraw to rest areas, was turned around for concentration north-east of Forli whence it could be committed either on the coast or south of Cesena. However by 8th October the loss of Mt Farneto, and the general increase of pressure by 13th Corps, had resulted, first, in Herr's decision to employ 15th Panzer Grenadier Regiment to counter-attack 10th Indian Division, and then in Wentzell's agreement that all of 29th Panzer Grenadier Division should be sent into the line between 356th Infantry and 114th Jäger Divisions (*see Map 26*). The Panzer Grenadiers disliked their new task as they felt that their mobility and fire power were largely wasted in the hills, where they were opposed by 'small and catlike' Indians who were skilled in mountain warfare.[107] Fuel was short and supply difficult as there were only two usable bridges across the Savio, one at Cesena and another seven miles to the south. Badly needed rest and refit was lost for no very good purpose. No sooner had the Division reached and temporarily stabilised the Mt Farneto sector than it was warned of impending withdrawal. On 9th October von Vietinghoff decided that 29th Panzer Grenadier Division, being geographically the nearest of his mobile formations, must be sent westwards to help check the American drive on Bologna. As Army Group conceded, the release could only be effected if 76th Panzer Corps undertook a phased withdrawal into a new and shorter line covering Cesena.[108]

As a first step, Herr was authorised on 9th October to pull back within 36 hours to a line which ran behind the Rigossa Canal and extended to Gatteo a Mare on the Adriatic coast. Leaving outposts forward, 76th Panzer Corps was to prepare to defend this line. As usual its staff had thought ahead and had plotted a second set of positions on the last main ridges covering the Savio crossings and the approach to Cesena, and a third line for close defence of the town. At the start of the withdrawal 278th Infantry Division went temporarily into reserve near Cesena, as a preliminary to relieving 29th Panzer Grenadier Division. To enable Herr to concentrate his efforts on the defence of the Via Emilia, von Vietinghoff planned that the coastal sector and the Via Adriatica should be handed over to the Commander Venetian Coast, General Anton Dostler, who was instructed to concentrate all available forces for the countering of possible landings and the prevention of a strike up the coast. At the time, Dostler disposed only of local defence units and 162nd (Turcoman) Infantry Division, but it was intended that 1st Parachute Division should pass to his command once the other divisions of 76th Panzer Corps had reached the Savio. On 10th October Herr was warned by von Vietinghoff that there must be no concerted withdrawal to this river unless and until heavy pressure by 8th Army made it imperative. In view of the Allied Air Forces' interdiction of the Savio bridges Herr could start moving his longer range Corps artillery and A.A. guns back over the river, and start to prepare crossings for his Tiger tanks. Other aspects of the withdrawal could be planned and 'thought through', but the divisions must not yield any ground unnecessarily.

Thus when the main 8th Army offensive began with the Canadian Corps joining in with 5th Corps on 11th October, 76th Panzer Corps was moving into the Rigossa Canal line with 1st Parachute Division on the coast, 26th Panzer Division between the Via Adriatica and the Via Emilia, 90th Panzer Grenadier Division

astride the Via Emilia, and 114th Jäger Division immediately south
of it. 278th Infantry Division had reached Cesena while 29th Panzer
Grenadier Division, whose 15th Panzer Grenadier Regiment was
still pinned down in the Farneto sector, was preparing to release
its other units. On the higher Apennine flank 8th Army was
opposed by 356th Infantry Division which was now under command
of 76th Panzer Corps, and by parts of 305th Infantry Division of
51st Mountain Corps.

On 7th October, in development of his policy of turning the
German river defence lines by working through the hills, McCreery
issued orders for regrouping.[109] 1st Canadian Corps would relieve
56th Division, two brigades of which had been dangerously weakened in recent fighting for Savignano on the Fiumicino, and would
take over from 5th Corps the responsibility for the thrust along
the Via Emilia towards Cesena. This would leave 5th Corps free
to concentrate on turning the Germans' delaying lines. Burns
brought up 1st Canadian Division to relieve 56th Division, switched
the New Zealand Division from the coast to relieve 5th Canadian
Armoured Division north of the railway, and replaced the New
Zealanders on the coast with an *ad hoc* group, built round 3rd
Greek Mountain Brigade and dismounted Canadian tank units,
the whole being under command of H.Q. 5th Canadian Armoured
Brigade. It became known as 'Cumberland Force' after 5th
Canadian Armoured Brigade's commander.[110] Burns gave 1st
Canadian Division a narrow sector astride the Via Emilia, from
1,000 yards south of the road to the railway on its northern side.
It was to maintain pressure on the Germans while the New
Zealanders protected its northern flank and Cumberland Force
kept contact with the Germans on the Via Adriatica. The idea of
operating in the flat waterlogged plain did not appeal to the
Canadian commanders even though the ground astride the Via
Emilia was slightly higher and better drained than the rest of their
sector. Burns wrote in his diary:

> 'All divisional commanders pointed out the very bad going and
> expressed the opinion that we might be drifting into the carrying
> on of an offensive in similar conditions to those of last autumn
> and winter, when the hard fighting and numerous casualties
> resulted in no great gain.'

The Canadian offensive could not start until regrouping was
completed on 11th October. 5th Corps did not pause. 10th Indian
Division still had one brigade tied down by counter-attack on Mt
Farneto on 7th/8th October but its reinforcement by 43rd Gurkha
Lorried Infantry Brigade (transferred from 56th Division) enabled
it to continue the attack.[111] 10th Indian Infantry Brigade was
directed to by-pass Mt Farneto on the right and thrust north on

8th October to take Mt Spaccato, detaching one battalion to work round the left towards Montecodruzzo. The following day 25th Indian Brigade would launch a supporting attack from the far right. The Mt Spaccato operation was carried out in two phases: 2nd/4th Gurkha Rifles secured and held an intermediate feature in heavy fighting. 1st Durham Light Infantry then passed through; although the depth of the mud defeated the mules, and radio and ammunition had to be manhandled forward, the battalion succeeded in infiltrating the German positions and established themselves on Mt Spaccato before dawn on 10th October. As usual seizing the crest was only a third of the battle. Throughout 10th October the Durhams beat off successive counter-attacks, some at close quarters, and had to withstand heavy shell and mortar concentrations. Reinforced by two comapanies of 2nd/4th Gurkhas, they clung on until the Germans, under pressure from south and east, gave up and started to withdraw during the night 10th/11th October.

The benefits of the capture of Mt Spaccato were felt on the left of 10th Indian Division at Montecodruzzo and by 46th Division at Longiano ridge, both of which were securely held by 11th October.[112] 5th Corps suspected the existence of another position behind the Rigossa Canal and General Keightley made plans to reinforce his Corps in its attack on this line if it were found to be necessary.[113] He decided to bring 4th Division, which had been put under Corps command early in October, back into the line. It was to be positioned between 10th Indian and 46th Divisions, with the ultimate intention of using it to relieve 46th Division at a later stage. This forward planning was a feature of H.Q. 5th Corps which had by this time become, through bitter experience, a highly professional staff.

During the first ten days of October poor weather reduced air support in 8th Army's battle area very considerably. There was no flying on the 2nd and 8th and the only reasonable break in the weather came on the 7th when 427 sorties were flown during which 137 tons of bombs were dropped.[114] A squadron of Thunderbolts from U.S. 79th Fighter Group joined in and concentrated most of their efforts on the Savio road bridges. Considerable direct air support was given to 8th Army's advance across the Fiumicino towards Longiano and Spaccato. For example, a threatened counter-attack on the left flank was broken up and dispersed by Spitfire fighter-bombers under Rover control. Pre-arranged attacks by the fighter-bombers made at the request of 5th Corps included 16 batteries; they also attacked 18 strongpoints for 5th Corps (supported by Rover Paddy). These were followed by a 'blitz' on the Longiano area and strafing of troop concentrations there.

The totals for the ten days were only just short of 1,100 sorties, and 423 tons of bombs. The sole night excursion was on 1st/2nd October when D.A.F.'s Bostons and Baltimores flew 39 sorties.

1st Canadian Division's advance down the Via Emilia was given a good start by 56th Division, which had been probing across the river ever since it had lost its first bridgehead at Savignano on 28th September.[115] During 10th October a thinning out of 90th Panzer Grenadier Division's forces was detected and that night patrols were established on the far bank which enabled 56th Divisional Sappers to build a 120-ft Class 40 Bailey bridge over the river. The bridge was ready for 1st Canadian Division early on 11th October when the command of the sector passed to 1st Canadian Corps. 56th Division withdrew for a well earned rest, leaving its artillery and Sappers to help 10th Indian and 46th Divisions.*

5th Corps continued its drive to turn the Germans' defence positions and had another very successful four days.[116] On the left flank, showing great physical endurance, Gurkha battalions of 43rd Lorried Infantry Brigade pressed north through Montecodruzzo in successive night actions to reach Mt Chicco early on 14th October. The following day a brigade of 10th Indian Division joined with 46th Division to hustle the Germans off the remaining ridge positions on the right. Their opponents were 356th Infantry Division, 278th Infantry and parts of 29th Panzer Grenadier Division which it was relieving, and 114th Jäger Division. The penetration brought 5th Corps to within striking distance of Cesena and obviated the need for Keightley to bring 4th Division into the line immediately.

The progress of 5th Corps, taken in conjunction with the build up of German forces south of the Via Emilia, caused McCreery on the 12th to change his plans for the Polish Corps, then concentrating at S. Piero in Bagno, and to direct it down the side road to Galeata rather than along Route 71; it was still to aim for Forli.[117] He expected the attack to be launched on the 15th but, due to delay in getting mule transport forward, it was postponed to the 17th.† Evidence of the hopes attached to the forthcoming Polish operations is contained in a signal which Alexander sent to the C.I.G.S. on 16th October:[118]

> 'I hope that they will come as a surprise to the enemy. He has weakened that part of his front, and it offers a fair chance of a break through behind the forces opposing Eighth Army'.

---

* The Sappers' Savignano Bailey bridge was christened the 'Itsonitsoff' due to the many changes of plan in the first ten days of October while McCreery developed his new tactical policy.

† Command of the sector passed to the Polish Corps on 14th October.

During 11th and 12th October the Canadian Corps advanced along the Via Emilia and the railway line to Bologna against moderate opposition.[119] 1st Canadian Division, with one brigade up, seized a small bridgehead over the Rigossa Canal on 12th October and in the next two days fought its way into the strongly fortified town of Bulgaria, using techniques of house fighting learnt at Ortona the year before. The Canadian tanks blasted the buildings with H.E. shell and then raked them with machine gun fire while the Canadian Infantry broke in to finish the job. 90th Panzer Grenadier Division reported it had suffered severe casualties. The New Zealanders had a harder fight in more difficult going, and for a time were well behind 1st Canadian Division's right flank. They caught up on 15th October, crossing the Rigossa Canal and entering Gambettola without opposition from 26th Panzer Division, as Herr's formations had withdrawn during the previous night to their planned positions north of the canal. The Canadian Corps' advance was being helped by 5th Corps' successes and by German worries about the American advance on Bologna. During the evening of 13th October Herr had been warned that he might be required to pull one of 90th Panzer Grenadier Divions's regiments out of the line into *AOK 10* reserve for possible transfer to the right wing of 51st Mountain Corps.[120]

On the Adriatic flank of 8th Army, Cumberland Force not unnaturally made little headway against 1st Parachute Division rear-guards until they withdrew of their own accord on 15th October to the Rigossa Canal.[121] Cumberland Force followed up with only its three dismounted armoured regiments because orders had been received for the Greek Brigade to make ready to return to Greece.

5th Corps' progress between 11th and 15th October was accompanied by several days of passable flying weather which enabled the Desert Air Force to step up its attacks on the Savio bridges and give 8th Army more constant direct air support than had been possible in the first ten days of October. Unserviceable landing grounds remained a restriction during the first three days, but on the 13th they were all serviceable other than those of the medium and light day bombers. Over 100 of the 329 sorties flown by the fighter-bombers were against pre-arranged targets on 5th Corps and 1st Canadian fronts.[122] Rover Paddy operated Cabranks for both Corps, the targets being strongpoints, guns and *Nebelwerfer*. Some Tiger tanks were attacked in Gambettola. Tactical, photographic and artillery reconnaissance aircraft were all busy. Nearly 100 tons of bombs were dropped. Though the effort on the 14th was limited because of the weather the Indian Official Historian mentions the 'excellent' support given to 10th Indian Division, and in particular the Gurkhas' fight to hold their positions on Mt

Chicco when, directed by smoke shells laid by artillery, fighter-bombers broke up German attempts at reinforcement and knocked out troublesome mortars.[123] Next day, the 15th, the weather was fair and the effort considerable, German artillery being the main targets for pre-arranged attacks.

Just under 1,000 sorties were flown in the five days, during which 317 tons bombs were dropped. Poor weather and unserviceable landing grounds at night prevented the light night bombers operating.

The loss of its ridge positions caused 76th Panzer Corps to retreat into its third defence line for the close protection of Cesena.[124] On 16th October Herr told von Vietinghoff that the new line was 'quite advantageous' for defence, but without 15th Panzer Grenadier Regiment of 29th Panzer Grenadier Division he doubted whether he could hold Cesena, whose loss would entail withdrawal to the Savio within 48 hours. 5th Corps' plan to prevent a German stand was both simple and direct.[125] Two ridges ran north-westwards towards Cesena on the eastern side of the Savio. Each served as a divisional centre line, and each was dominated by a key hill feature. The axis through Mt Romano was alloted to 46th Division and that through Montereale to 10th Indian Division. 10th Indian Division was also to seek crossings over the Savio from its junction with the Borello river northwards. Once Cesena had been taken both divisions would swing westwards over the river, with their boundary running north-west through Acquarola. 4th Division was to be ready to come into the line on the right of the Corps' front at 24 hours notice from 6 a.m. on 15th October.

138th Brigade led 46th Division initially until checked and counter-attacked in front of Mt Romano on 15th October.[126] 139th Brigade passed through but made no further progress. 10th Indian Division used 25th Indian Brigade for the whole advance. It tried to infiltrate the German positions at Montereale but was stopped as well. A co-ordinated Corps' attack by the two divisions on the night 16th/17th October led to the capture of both features after stubborn fighting and to the Germans falling back to Celincordia and Acquarola which they managed to hold for a futher 36 hours. As we shall see, by the early evening of 18th October 76th Panzer Corps had been authorised to conduct a fighting withdrawal behind the Savio. The only permanent bridge still standing was the one which 8th Army had specially reserved in the southern half of Cesena, and so to cover their crossing of the Savio the German divisions took up intermediate positions around the southern outskirts of the town to protect this bridge.[127] Rear-guards of 114th Jäger Division remained on the eastern bank of the Savio until early on 20th October. The War Diary of 46th Division describes the tempo of German resistance during the last days of the battle for Cesena: 'a pretty tough battle' on 15th, 'stiff opposition' on 16th, 'stubborn fighting' during the night 16th/17th, 'resistance slackening' on 17th and 18th, and only 'slight opposition' on 19th October.

5th Corps' turning movement certainly helped the Canadian Corps astride the Via Emilia, but the latter's divisions were also inflicting serious losses on 90th Panzer Grenadier and 26th Panzer Divisions and parts of 1st Parachute Division.[128] After crossing the Rigossa Canal, 1st Canadian Division widened its front and approached the Pisciatello river with two brigades up, 1st Canadian Brigade on and to the south of the Via Emilia and 2nd Canadian Brigade astride the railway. 2nd New Zealand Division side-stepped northwards to give the Canadians more room. 2nd Canadian Brigade had the greater success. It managed to seize a small bridgehead over the river near the railway during the night 17th/18th October (when 5th Corps was battering at Celincordia and Acquarola). The familiar disaster of infantry stranded on the far bank in daylight without tank support was just averted by an officer of 12th Royal Tank Regiment who refused to accept an Engineer report that a nearby ford was too soft for tanks. With Churchills safely ensconsed in the Canadian bridgehead, Ponte della Pietra was attacked and cleared, allowing the Canadian Sappers to build an 80-ft Bailey on the village's original bridge site. 90th Panzer Grenadier Division again suffered heavily in the fighting; two battalions of its 200th Panzer Grenadier Regiment were overrun.[129] Next day, 19th October, opposition slackened as it did on 5th Corps' front.

On the German side, the staffs had been arguing about 76th Panzer Corps' conduct of operations since 16th October.[130] Doubting that he could hold Cesena, Herr had already prepared his next defensive line behind the Savio code-named 'Erika', and a second main position on the Ronco called 'Gudrun'. He and his Chief of Staff, Runkel, pressed for freedom of manoeuvre to both lines, but Runkel was told by Wentzell on the 16th that no such latitude could be expected from 'up there', signifying *OKW*. He was sharply reminded that 8th Army had taken just as much punishment as his own Corps. Interrogation of British prisoners had given the encouraging impression that by defending every inch of ground *AOK 10* had imposed a 'centimetre offensive' on its opponents which was very wearisome to them. It is worth noting that by mid-October the Germans had discovered 8th Army's break up of 1st Armoured Division and the reduction of units to cadre to supply reinforcements.

Wentzell's robust attitude did not survive the fighting of 17th

October when everything seemed to go wrong, not only for 76th Panzer Corps but also for the right wing of 51st Mountain Corps, which was under such pressure from 5th Army that von Vietinghoff decided that evening that it must be reinforced by all the units of 90th Panzer Grenadier Division which were still with 76th Panzer Corps. To add to its troubles, *AOK 10* learnt by the end of the day that what Wentzell described as the 'entire Polish Corps' had surfaced south of Galeata, where there was 'not one German soldier to be seen' since 305th Infantry Division had stripped this part of its front as a preliminary to relieving 98th Infantry Division. Wentzell was exaggerating the thinness of Hauck's front, but the sudden appearance of the Poles was a disagreeable surprise for *AOK 10* and forced consideration of the switch of 98th and 305th Infantry Divisions. It also affected Kesselring's reactions to the argument, put forward again and again on 18th October by von Vietinghoff and Wentzell, that to insist on 76th Panzer Corps continuing to stand east of the Savio would not only expose it to the risk of encirclement but would also jeopardise the German defence south of Bologna.

The paramount need of reinforcement of the Bologna front had already prompted Kesselring to propose to *OKW* on 17th October the abandonment of territory on *AOK 10's* eastern wing as a price which must be paid if Bologna, and with it the 'decisive' parts of the Po valley, were to remain in German hands.[131] The High Command was predictably unsympathetic, contending that there was no case for *AOK 10* to give ground as it was still one of the best equipped Armies in the *Wehrmacht*. To satisfy their superiors and to the annoyance of their subordinates, *OB Südwest* and his Chief of Staff accordingly put up a day-long show of obduracy until the appearance of the Poles gave them just sufficient excuse to act unilaterally.[132] Soon after midnight on 19th October Kesselring sent a signal to von Vietinghoff warning him to pay particular attention to the vulnerability of his Army's centre and to take appropriate measures for a fighting withdrawal of *AOK 10's* eastern wing behind the Savio. According to *OKW's* diarist, Hitler agreed later on the 19th that 76th Panzer Corps could shorten its coastal front in order to find additional forces for the battle south of Bologna.

Before it was ratified by signal, Kesselring's consent to Herr's withdrawal had been obtained over the telephone during the evening of 18th October. von Vietinghoff lost no time in authorising 76th Panzer Corps to pull back to the Savio, with the rider that Cesena must be held for as long as possible. The withdrawal was not excused by any successes achieved by 8th Army, but by the need to reinforce 1st Parachute Corps and the right wing of 51st

Mountain Corps. All remaining units of 29th and 90th Panzer Grenadier Divisions were to be extracted by regrouping during the withdrawal. Special orders were also issued for further flooding of the Via Adriatica sector, and H.Q. Reno–Po was instructed to reconnoitre a new defence line east of Bologna. Known in due course as the 'Genghis Khan' position, this was to merge into existing positions along the Reno, with a forward line along the Idice river. Preparations for the flooding of the rice fields around Argenta and the Po estuary were also to be set in hand forthwith. On 18th October 51st Mountain Corps was additionally informed of *OB Südwest's* orders that the departure from the Bologna area of trains carrying commodities earmarked for removal to Germany was to be speeded up. Provided that facilities for through traffic were maintained, other rail installations forming part of Bologna's central network could then be 'released for demolition'.

The effects of Kesselring's decision to allow *AOK 10* to shorten its line were soon felt by 5th and Canadian Corps on 18th October. 5th Corps issued orders for 10th Indian Division to halt after it had taken the Acquarola spur and turn westward to secure a bridgehead over the Savio.[133] 46th Division was to clear the high ground south of Cesena, when 4th Division would take over and force the river crossing.* 139th Brigade had a sharp fight for the approaches to Cesena on the 19th but broke through, taking 70 prisoners. 16th Durham Light Infantry, passing under command of 4th Division, strove to reach the still intact bridge, which 5th Corps artillery was keeping under fire to impede its demolition.[134] Patrols of 4th Division did succeed in reaching the bridge on the 20th only to see it blown up before their eyes.

Failure to secure the bridge intact was irritating but not unexpected or disastrous. Keightley had directed 10th Indian Division to cross the Savio and secure a bridgehead stretching north from Mt Cavallo.[135] The Division had already established a patrol base in the angle between the Savio and the Borello. There was thus an opportunity to repeat McCreery's successful tactics by turning the Erika Line on the Savio from the south.

While there was every prospect of 10th Indian Division surprising 356th Infantry Division, which was very thinly spread in its hill sector of the Erika Line, there were major supply and communication problems to be overcome.† The combined efforts of the

---

* 46th Division was due for rest having been in almost continuous operation for two months.

† Only a jeep track ran forward from Sogliano al Rubicone; the road to it was one way; three brigades and the artillery of two divisions already depended on it. The new route ran south from Sogliano to Mercato Saraceno on Route 71 (*Map* 28 *Inset*) and then north up the Savio.[136]

Divisional, Corps and Army Engineers opened up a fresh supply route from Sogliano south-west to Route 71 and thence up the Savio, much of the work being carried out under artillery harassing fire. While the work was going on 20th Indian Brigade slipped a battalion over the Borello undetected on the evening of the 20th and secured a bridgehead. Meanwhile, 25th Indian Brigade at Acquarola had moved quickly westwards and crossed the Savio at Roversano, where it had enlarged and secured a bridgehead against counter-attack by 21st October.

In Cesena 4th Division set about acquiring a bridgehead at the demolished bridge site against considerable opposition.[137] Early on 20th October 2nd Royal Fusiliers crossed the river, chest deep and laden with equipment, and took the Germans by surprise. Their situation next day was dangerous, supported only by the reinforced divisional artillery and close air cover, but the following night the two remaining battalions of 12th Brigade forced a crossing and a chain of ARKs was run into the river which allowed tanks to follow.* With their help the bridgehead was held but it was soon apparent that it would not be easily expanded against German opposition in the built-up area. North of Cesena the Canadian Corps was not so successful.[139] A two-company bridgehead could not be sustained and had to be withdrawn. Cumberland Force followed up the German withdrawal on the coast, reaching a point just north of Cesenatico on 21st October. The German line ran due west from the coast to the Savio.

During the six days 16th to 21st October there were two days when the weather seriously interfered with flying in 8th Army's battle area. On three other days, the 16th, 19th and 21st, a reasonable amount of flying was possible, and on the 20th the weather was described as 'excellent'.[140] At night D.A.F.'s light night bombers operated once, on 19th/20th. On the 16th the main task was to support 8th Army's drive towards Cesena, bombing targets including guns on 5th Corps' and 1st Canadian Corps' fronts. At the

---

* The ARK crossing of the Savio was a classic operation by the Assault Engineers.[138] The infantry waded the river which was some four feet deep to secure a shallow bridgehead. The site chosen for the ARKs, selected from air photographs, was at a point on the river where the Germans had ramped down the banks to make a tank ford, without success, as a tank was bogged in midstream. To build the bridge the first ARK entered the river, dropped its rear ramp on the home bank and its forward ramp into the river; the second ARK climbed over its back, dropping its rear ramp onto the first ARK's forward ramp and so on, the third ARK dropping its ramp on the far bank.

The bridge was completed at 6.15 a.m. on 21st October. Trouble started when the second ARK started to list and lost a ramp pin, dropping the ramp into the river where it became jammed in the ramp of the first ARK. It took until 9 a.m. to free the ramp. The gap was then filled with a fascine dropped in by an AVRE. The second ARK later received a direct hit and had to be repaired with rubble and sand-bags. When night fell the river rose, submerging the ARKs and widening the water gap. As soon as the water fell sufficiently a fourth ARK was added to the bridge which served its purpose until a Bailey and a folding boat bridge were opened late on 24th October.

request of 8th Army, an enemy command headquarters five miles east of Cesena and an artillery headquarters eight miles east of Forli were attacked. Rover Paddy operated Cabranks in support of 5th Corps. Between 17th–19th the weather closed in and unserviceable landing grounds hampered flying. But D.A.F.'s Baltimores bombed gun positions three miles north of Cesena at the request of 1st Canadian Corps on the 18th and gun batteries and *Nebelwerfer* were among the pre-arranged targets on 5th Corps' front, where some Baltimores also joined in.

Cabranks operated continuously for all three Corps. The remarkable change in the weather on the 20th enabled 381 sorties to be flown in 8th Army's battle area, including some by the medium and light day bombers. A third of the effort was flown against targets on 5th Corps' front, where 4th Division noted the considerable bombing and strafing in defence of its small bridgehead across the Savio.[141] Thirty-six Baltimores bombed gun positions near Cesena and 18 Mitchells bombed a stores depot at Imola to bring the total load of bombs dropped that day in 8th Army's battle area to 174 tons. But for the landing on some of D.A.F.'s airfields of several of M.A.S.A.F.'s heavy day bombers because of shortage of fuel, or damage after raids outside Italy, the effort would have been greater. The period finished on a high note, because, despite poor weather in the afternoon of the 21st, the fighter-bombers attacked 11 gun batteries on 5th Corps' front, and eight on 1st Canadian Corps' front.

In the six days a total of 1,281 sorties were flown and 513 tons of bombs dropped in support of 8th Army; not to mention the tactical and artillery reconnaissances which flew day in and day out, directing the Allied guns.

(v)

See Map 27

While 8th Army was fighting the battles for Cesena, Clark and Keyes were mounting the fourth cycle of the 5th Army offensive, orders for which had been issued on 13th October during the struggles for the Livergnano escarpment, Mt delle Formiche and Mt delle Tombe.[142] Clark had to act in the knowledge of the reinforcement problems, which had resulted in Alexander's appeal to Eisenhower related earlier in this chapter, and of restricted ammunition supplies. 2nd Corps did, however, possess one last resource, if not a very sure one.[143] The veteran 34th U.S. Division had been in action since 1942 and was, in the words of the U.S. Army historian, Ernest F. Fisher, 'suffering from the chronic

malaise of battle weariness'; surviving 'old hands' had been clamouring for repatriation and tended to infect replacements with the
same loss of morale. Its troops had been fighting their way
northwards, covering 91st U.S. Division's western flank, but, even
without the regiment left in its old sector to help 1st U.S. Armoured
Division, which had taken over, it was numerically strong. The
sudden introduction of this division in the Mt delle Formiche
sector, which the Corps' Intelligence Staff suggested was a weak
spot in the German front, might produce just the element of
surprise needed to start the collapse of the German defence of
Bologna, only 9 miles away.

Keyes' plan was based on 34th U.S. Division breaking through
on a narrow front to seize the next dominant feature on the eastern
side of Route 65, Mt Belmonte. 91st U.S. Division would support
its attack by continuing to exert pressure down Route 65, in
conjunction with 1st U.S. Armoured Division west of the road.
85th U.S. Division would support 34th U.S. Division's eastern
flank. 88th U.S. Division, its forces concentrated on a reduced
frontage, was directed upon the Mt Grande hill mass. Once this
was secured it would strike for the Via Emilia, in conjunction with
13th Corps. 78th Division (13th Corps), Clark had arranged, would
extend its left flank and take over the Gesso area from 88th U.S.
Division.[144] Its immediate object remained the capture of Mt La
Pieve.

The fourth cycle of 2nd U.S. Corps' offensive started on 16th
October in poor but not atrocious weather.[145] The veteran 34th
U.S. Division did not do so well as the much less experienced
85th and 88th U.S. Divisions, which had arrived in Italy only
shortly before 'Diadem'. Although 34th U.S. Division was allotted
the support of all the Corps artillery and a saturation air assault
against German positions on Belmonte, including the newly introduced Napalm 'bomb', its performance was disappointing to Keyes
and Clark. Their criticism can perhaps be modified by two factors
which were not appreciated at the opening of the assault. 71st
Panzer Grenadier Regiment, supported by the artillery of 29th
Panzer Grenadier Division, had reached Mt Belmonte in time to
settle into its positions and was ready to repeat the blocking
operation 29th Panzer Grenadier Division had carried out so
successfully at Coriano six weeks earlier; and on 14th October
General Lemelsen had been taken ill.[146] During his five-day absence
acting command of *AOK 14* was assumed by General von Senger
from 14th Panzer Corps, who promptly took energetic action for
the regrouping and strengthening of 1st Parachute Corps.

34th U.S. Division's drive to secure Mt Belmonte was stopped
on its fourth day by a combination of 29th Panzer Grenadier

Division's tanks and S.P. guns and a concentration of German artillery fire which seemed to match the American fire 'round for round'.[147] Mt Belmonte remained in German hands, and 34th U.S. Division halted to regroup. Little more than a mile was gained north of Livergnano by the end of 19th October and Route 65 remained firmly blocked. Both 1st U.S Armoured and 91st U.S. Division had experienced a marked increase in German artillery fire. Keyes noted the presence of 16th SS and 29th Panzer Grenadier Divisions in the area of Route 65 and, fearing that a major German spoiling attack might be launched west of the road, he ordered the divisions to assume an 'aggressive defence'.

85th and 88th U.S. Divisions had a better tale to tell. 85th U.S. Division advanced on the eastern side of the Idice valley, taking German posts in quick succession, and had reached a point by 19th October from which it was well positioned to help both 34th U.S. Division on Mt Belmonte and 88th U.S. Division's thrust to Mt Grande. In 88th Division's sector all three of its regiments, by dint of persistent effort, had crossed the Sillaro and, on 19th October, were converging upon Mt Grande.

On the German side, it was exhilarating for von Senger to find himself back in the ring after months of inactivity in the unassailed western sectors of the Gothic Line. As soon as he was in Lemelsen's chair, he made plans to block 2nd U.S. Corps' thrust to Bologna by denuding his former front, on the grounds that 14th Panzer Corps was so weak anyway that further stripping could not do much harm.[148] After he had toured the front of 1st Parachute Corps on 15th October, von Senger proposed to an acquiescent Kesselring that in addition to 362nd Infantry Division, whose relief by 29th Panzer Grenadier Division had been agreed on 12th October, the equally exhausted 4th Parachute Division should also leave the line. For its relief, 16th SS Panzer Grenadier Division would side-step eastwards, as would 94th Infantry Division which was placed under commaned of 1st Parachute Corps. Pending the complete transfer of 29th Panzer Grenadier Division from *AOK 10,* its units were fed on arrival into the line between 65th and 362nd Infantry Divisions. The American offensive then reopened on 16th October as we have seen, and created an even stronger German defence south of Bologna by pinning in the line both the troops who were to be relieved and their relievers. von Senger also, and most effectively, raised the fire-power of this sector by moving into it every artillery battery on which he could lay his hands. Although short of suitable radio equipment the gunners tried to emulate the British technique for concentration of fire, and on 19th October (when Lemelsen returned to duty) von Senger told Kesselring that during the past few days the number of guns brought into position east and west of Route 65 had been doubled. This concentration was quickly felt by 1st Armoured, 91st and 34th U.S. Divisions, and resulted in the preparations to fend off a counter-offensive. Thus von Senger was largely instrumental in stopping the Americans' direct thrust on Bologna.

The German success astride Route 65 was not equalled by the formations opposing 85th and 88th U.S. Divisions. Once again there was weakness on the inter-Army boundary, which ran from Monterenzio to Ozzano almost exactly on 85th U.S. Division's thrust line.[149] To the Americans' advantage, contact on the boundary between 362nd Infantry Division of *AOK 14* and 98th Infantry Division of *AOK 10* was frequently lost as both were almost exhausted. By 18th October 362nd Infantry Division (whose planned relief by 29th Panzer Grenadier Division was delayed by the opening of 2nd U.S. Corps' fourth cycle, as we have seen) was so spent that the Army Group agreed that 42nd Jäger Division must move to the eastern wing of 1st Parachute Corps from the front of 14th Panzer Corps. This decision had no immediate effect, however, because the Jäger Division had to await piecemeal relief by parts of 148th Reserve Division and of the unreliable Italian Monte Rosa Division, transferred from the Army of Liguria.[150] From *AOK 10's* side of the boundary, von Vietinghoff had decided on 15th October that 98th Infantry Division should change places in the line with 305th Infantry Division, using a regiment of 90th Panzer Grenadier Division as a short-term 'bridging loan'.[151] He intended thereby to give a quieter sector to 98th Infantry Division, but it was pinned before it could move and had thus to bear the brunt of 85th and 88th U.S. Divisions' attacks. On 17th October its commander, Reinhardt, reported that the fighting strength of his infantry regiments was down to 100, 140 and 290. Although it would fight well later, the 'bridging loan' regiment was slow off the mark, and to shore up Reinhardt's front Feuerstein moved 100th Mountain Regiment over from 334th Infantry Division. The exchange of 98th Infantry Division with 305th Infantry Division was just about to begin when the Poles were identified, causing Feuerstein and his Chief of Staff to beg von Vietinghoff to cancel the plan. Initially reluctant to agree, the Army Commander was persuaded on 19th October to accept the argument that the impending transfer of the rest of 90th Panzer Grenadier Division from 76th Panzer Corps would adequately stiffen Feuerstein's right wing. 305th Infantry Division was accordingly left *in situ* to oppose the Poles, less one regiment which had earlier gone to the aid of 715th Infantry Division and was now sent to reinforce 98th Infantry Division.[152] Also on 19th October, General Baade arrived at the front to supervise the insertion of his 90th Panzer Grenadier Division into the line between 98th and 362nd Infantry Divisions. This convergence to block the American thrust towards Castel S. Pietro on the Via Emilia would take time to complete, so there was still a chance that 85th and 88th U.S. Divisions might be too quick and would once more tear open the boundary between *AOK 10* and *AOK 14*.

The concentration of German troops and artillery in the centre to defend the direct route to Bologna, and 34th U.S. Division's failure to take Mt Belmonte, persuaded Clark on 19th October to develop the fifth, and, as it turned out, last cycle of 5th Army's offensive with attacks on both flanks.[153] He was specially interested in exploiting the right flank 'where 85th and 88th Divisions . . . had uncovered a weak point' on the German inter-Army boundary. Keyes was to mount a three phase operation: 88th U.S. Division to take Mt Grande, supported by 85th U.S. Division, and then come into reserve after relief by 78th Division on Mt Grande; next 1st U.S. Armoured and 91st U.S. Divisions to fight their way through the German defences covering Mt Adone; and finally 91st U.S. Division to open the way to Bologna by taking Mt Adone, the western bastion of Route 65's final defences. 34th U.S. Division, it was hoped, would by then have taken Mt Belmonte, the eastern bastion. Only the first phase need concern us because the second and third did not take place.

The Mt Grande hill mass consisted of three prominent features. Mt Grande (Pt 602) itself was in the centre with Mt Cuccoli (Pt 482) on its south-western spur and Mt Cerere (also Pt 602) on its south-eastern spur. 85th U.S. Division was already on the lower slopes of Mt Cuccoli and 88th Division was similarly placed on Mt Cerere. During 19th October heavy air and artillery bombardments were carried out on Mt Grande itself. 157 fighter-bomber sorties were used and 42 targets were heavily engaged by by combined artilleries of 85th and 88th U.S. Divisions and all 2nd U.S. Corps artillery in range. The weather was fine but had deteriorated by nightfall. Driving rain helped to cover 88th U.S. Division's night attack which met little opposition. By dawn on the 20th it was on the summit of Mt Grande earlier than anyone expected, including the Germans who were neither prepared to defend nor counter-attack this key feature.

General Clark was naturally delighted with 88th U.S. Division's feat which was reminiscent of the seizure of Mt Battaglia, but he was also well aware that a German counter-offensive would not be long delayed. Identifications from 98th Infantry Division, from the leading regiment of 90th Panzer Grenadier Division and from the remnants of 44th Infantry Division, which were under 98th Infantry Division's command, were obtained amongst the German prisoners and dead. The arrival of the rest of 90th Panzer Grenadier Division was expected. Fighter-bombers were directed throughout 20th and 21st October to strafe all approaches to Mt Grande, and the American artillery fired a steady harassing programme to break up any attempted assembly of German troops. The swift capture of Mt Grande had saved ammunition which could now be used to protect it.

On the rest of 2nd U.S. Corps' front no significant progress had been made, so on 22nd October Clark directed Keyes to abandon the second and third phases of the fifth cycle and instead to exploit success in the Mt Grande sector by capturing the heights which formed the last possible defensive position before the Via Emilia.[154] At the same time he was to prepare to meet a German counter-offensive west of Route 65. 13th Corps was to concentrate its main effort on the northern side of the Santerno to support the thrust by 2nd U.S. Corps to Castel S. Pietro. In preparation for this final effort Keyes ordered 34th and 91st U.S. Divisions and 1st U.S. Armoured Division to regroup and form a six regiment reserve, which might be used either to repel attack or to exploit north-east of Grande.

The attack by 85th and 88th U.S. Divisions started on the evening of 22nd October, but only on the right was any progress made, where a hill village north-east of Mt Grande was occupied. It was swiftly cut off and the leading battalion of 351st Infantry lost almost three companies during the subsequent fighting. Torrential rain, which fell on the 26th, washed out the bridges over the Sillaro and frustrated Keyes' plans to reinforce 88th U.S. Division.

Both sides were approaching the end of their endurance. On 24th October Feuerstein's Chief of Staff reported that the troops of 90th Panzer Grenadier Division and 98th Infantry Division were so tired that they were falling asleep on their feet; nevertheless help which was to tip the balance against the Americans was on the way.[155] von Vietinghoff had intended on 20th October to move Heindrich's 1st Parachute Division from the coast to shore up Herr's front on the Savio by relieving the battered 114th Jäger Division. The precarious situation north-east of Mt Grande led him to decide on 23rd October that 1st Parachute Division must 'migrate' further west. Answering Herr's protests, von Vietinghoff insisted that the presence of Heidrich, *AOK 10's* 'most reliable commander', was needed to prevent an American break through to Castel S. Pietro.[156]

There was no such break through. New life was given to the German defence by the news that Heidrich's men were to be brought into the line between 90th Panzer Grenadier and 98th Infantry Divisions.[157] A battalion of 4th Parachute Regiment was in action by 25th October. As the rain poured down more German reinforcements reached the front line and the exhaustion felt by Americans at all levels increased. It might have been possible by continued robust leadership to have summoned up further reserves of energy had it not been for the supply problems created by a week's continuous rain. The combination of physical exhaustion, dearth of replacements, shortage of ammunition, over-extension of engineer resources and deteriorating living conditions on the cold mist-shrouded mountain sides spelt the end of 5th Army's attempt to reach the Po valley, after so successfully breaching the Gothic Line and coming to within five miles of the Via Emilia. On 26th October Clark ordered 2nd U.S. Corps to go over to the defensive and dig in on the most suitable positions available.

There was another reason why General Clark called a halt to offensive operations for the time being. It will be recalled that Alexander had sent an appreciation to 5th and 8th Armies on 23rd October in which he postulated the best way of taking Bologna was for 5th Army to feign exhaustion until the German mobile divisions had been drawn back to 8th Army's front, when it would launch a surprise attack with rested divisions and accumulated stocks of ammunition.[158]* With this appreciation in his hands Clark saw no reason to ask his tired divisions to continue the offensive. Instead he cancelled a plan to move the reserve regiments of 91st U.S. Division across to the Mt Grande sector. 2nd U.S. Corps dug in upon Mt Belmonte, which 34th U.S. Division had at last taken and upon Mt Grande. 78th Division had secured Mt Spaduro completing the arc of mountain bastions pointing towards Bologna from the Reno valley in the west to the Santerno valley in the east.

The American battle casualties in the fourth and fifth cycles from 16th to 26th October totalled 3,572 of which all but a tiny percentage can be attributed to 2nd U.S. Corps.[159] From the start of the offensive on 10th September the four infantry divisions spearheading the attack had suffered 15,716 casualties, most of them in the fighting arms. The effect of these losses at divisional level is shown by the figures for 88th U.S. Division. Although it had been so successful, it ended the fifth cycle 115 infantry officers short and a total of 1,243 officers and men under strength, inspite of a steady flow of returning wounded and sick from hospitals and of new replacements.

On the flanks of 2nd U.S. Corps there was equally hard fighting under similar conditions of deteriorating weather.[160] 6th South

---

* See p.386.

African Armoured Division fought doggedly forward. Just as 24th Guards Brigade was taking up positions to attack Mt Sole its operations were abruptly halted by the torrential rains of 26th October. The bastion of Mt Sole remained in 94th Infantry Division's hands. To the south-west of the South Africans, C.C.B of 1st U.S. Armoured Division advanced along Route 64, where the positions vacated by 94th Infantry Division on its transfer to 1st Parachute Corps were gradually taken over by 232nd Infantry Division, brought down from Genoa for subordination to 14th Panzer Corps.

The main features of 13th Corps' operations during the fourth and fifth cycles of 2nd U.S. Corps' offensive were repeated extensions of its left flank to cover 88th U.S. Division on the east, and hard fighting by 78th Division to clear the mountains between the Santerno and Sillaro rivers.[161] Following 13th Corps' orders of 16th October, 6th Armoured Division, less 26th Armoured Brigade, moved across from Route 67 to come into the line between 78th and 1st Divisions in the Santerno valley. 6th Armoured Division re-assumed command of 1st Guards Brigade on Mt Battaglia and used its 61st Brigade to relieve 78th Division's 38th Brigade on Mt Cappello. 26th Armoured Brigade was given the reconnaissance regiments of 6th Armoured, 8th Indian and 1st Divisions and an Army field and a medium regiment to maintain contact with the Germans astride Route 67. These moves freed 78th Division to concentrate upon its task of relieving the Americans as they advanced north and of securing, first, Mt La Pieve, which had defied them so far, and then Mt Spaduro which lies due north of La Pieve. 1st Division and 8th Indian Division were to maintain pressure in their sectors to prevent their opponents sending help to the Bologna front.

Owing to the bad state of the roads, 6th Armoured Division was not able to free 78th Division to renew its attack on Mt La Pieve until the night of 18th/19th October, corresponding to 2nd U.S. Corps' fourth cycle.[162] By then 88th U.S. Division's operations north of the Sillaro had become so menacing that the Germans abandoned the mountain without a struggle, but they did not fall back far. La Pieve is at the junction of two ridges, one leading due north to Mt Spaduro and the other due east to Mt dell'Acqua Salata. Although only required by 5th Army to take Mt Spaduro, 78th Division's Commander, Major-General Arbuthnott, appreciated that the one could not be held without the other. 38th Brigade and 36th Brigade were given Mt Spaduro and Mt dell'Acqua Salata as their respective objectives, leaving

11th Brigade in reserve holding a firm base for the Division at Gesso. In between the two ridges there was a lateral spur on which stood the fortified farmhouse of Casa Spinello. The whole complex formed one of those interlocking and mutually supporting positions which the Germans were so good at exploiting. The main ridges themselves were dark toned, stony, devoid of trees and habitation except for a few thick walled, stone farmhouses on the crests, and utterly desolate in the mists and rain of autumn. Mt Spaduro was a massive horseshoe shaped feature some 1,200 feet high and a thousand yards in length. Mt dell'Acqua Salata was just as high and no less forbidding. The lower slopes of both were deeply indented with gulleys and deep ravines. 334th Infantry Division, commanded by General Böhlke, who was in high esteem in *AOK 10,* defended both features.[163]

78th Division's attack on the two mountains started during the night 19th/20th October as 88th U.S. Division began its attack on Mt Grande. [164] 1st Royal Irish Fusiliers led 38th Brigade's assault on Mt Spaduro. They bypassed Casa Spinello and managed to haul two companies up an almost impossible cliff to secure the crest. When dawn came it was found that the Germans in Casa Spinello could prevent any reinforcement in daylight. Both companies were overrun during the morning by counter-attacks, after they had exhausted their ammunition. The Germans reoccupied the crest and marched away forty prisoners. 5th Buffs led 36th Infantry Brigade's attack on Mt dell'Acqua Salata, but were checked by heavy fire short of the crest. Both brigades were ordered to resume the following night, the capture of Acqua Salata being made the first objective. This 36th Brigade successfully secured, led by 8th Argyll and Sutherland Highlanders, who kept so close to the artillery barrage that they were among the Germans before they realised that it had lifted. 38th Brigade then launched 2nd London Irish against Mt Spaduro, but the attack was disrupted by fire from Casa Spinello. The battalion tried again in the evening, having lain concealed in one of the gullies all day, but without success. A two-brigade assault was then planned to eradicate the opposition on Mt Spaduro; it was timed for 23rd/24th October.

On the remainder of 13th Corps front, the prior claims of the fight against 2nd U.S. Corps resulted in several local German withdrawals, which opened up the Savio valley to 6th Armoured and 1st Divisions. Such was not to be the fortune of 8th Indian Division, which met some of the stiffest opposition it had experienced in the Northern Apennines as it fought its way northwards through the mountains between the Sintria and Lamone rivers.[165] There were notable struggles, including hand to hand fighting for the ridges, which the Germans eventually abandoned in their local withdrawals. The division took Mt Giro on 23rd October and by late October it had three brigades in the line, each with two battalions up, so making administration extraordinarily complex and difficult.

The alterations made on 22nd October in 5th Army's plans for 2nd U.S. Corps' fifth cycle were accompanied by changes in 13th Corps' instructions.[166] 78th Division was no longer to relieve 2nd U.S. Corps on Mt Grande but, after taking Mt Spaduro, was to develop a strong thrust towards the plains on the right flank of 88th U.S. Division's advance from Mt Grande. Keyes would give the Division running rights for one brigade on the Sillaro valley road. 78th Division's sector would be narrowed by side-stepping 6th Armoured and 1st Divisions, the former taking over the whole of the Santerno valley and the latter relieving 1st Guards Brigade on Mt Battaglia and assuming responsibility for the high ground between the Santerno and Senio valleys. In front of 13th Corps there loomed the Vena del Gesso, which was a line of chalk escarpments running across the grain of the country similar to the Livergnano escarpment on the road to Bologna. Kirkman decided that the best way to deal with this was to outflank it via Mt dell'Acqua Salata. His instruction ran: 'As 78 Division's advance progresses, 6 Armoured Division will develop their operations to turn the Vena del Gesso . . .'

38th Brigade reopened its attack on Mt Spaduro on 23rd October with the capture of Casa Spinello farm, taken after fighting from room to room, during which one German was found to have been posted in the cellar to fire upwards through the floorboards![167] The Germans expected the next attempt on Mt Spaduro to come from Casa Spinello and were caught by surprise when a combined attack by 38th and 11th Brigades came from the opposite direction, reached the crest and secured the eastern end of the ridge. At midnight 11th Brigade committed a fresh battalion and cleared the northern extremities of the feature. Casualties were heavy on both sides. Attempts to exploit petered out in the heavy rain which had stopped 2nd U.S. Corps' offensive.

Plans for 13th Corps to thrust forward towards the Via Emilia after the fall of Mt Spaduro were stillborn.[168] 6th Armoured Division was compelled to withdraw the two rifle companies which it had put on Mt Taverna, after their supply line had been cut by swollen streams. 1st Division, at the limits of supply, had to concentrate its engineers to open a route from Palazzuolo to Mt Battaglia. 8th Indian Division pushed down the Faenza road to S. Cassiano and on the far right entered Tredozio. 26th Armoured Brigade's reconnaissance regiments kept contact with the Germans astride Route 67 until the Polish Corps took over. We will be describing the Polish Corps' operations when we return to the events on 8th Army's front, after looking at major changes which were taking place in the German command structure. We leave 5th Army with all its divisions, British as well as American, going over to the defensive on 26th October.

Flying weather during the fourth and fifth cycles of 5th Army's offensive was described as 'showers' or 'thunderstorms' and air support suffered accordingly.[169] In the five days, 16th to 20th October a total of 566 sorties were flown and 298 tons of bombs were dropped. The weather from the 21st to 26th, can only be described as disastrous from an Allied air support point of view, 148 sorties being flown and a meagre 70 tons of bombs dropped.

On 19th October the U.S. XII Fighter Command, which supported 5th Army, was retitled 'U.S. XXII Tactical Air Command' (U.S. XXII T.A.C.). It retained this title until the end of the campaign.

(vi)

As we have seen the German command structure first began to show signs of strain around 10th October when Schlemm's handling of 1st Parachute Corps was criticised by Kesselring and von Victinghoff alike. We have also seen that during Lemelsen's absence between 14th–19th October AOK 14 was competently run by von Senger, who by his own account received 'flattering congratulations' from the Field-Marshal.[170] On 21st October the possibility that von Senger might take over on the right wing of AOK 10, with Schlemm shunted off to the Western Apennines, was mooted in telephone conversations. AOK 10's War Diary recorded that Army Group was considering the transfer to this Army's command of the three divisions of AOK 14 which were defending the direct approach to Bologna. The implication that Kesselring was dissatisfied with the present state of affairs on the inter-Army boundary came through the diarist's careful reference to the need to ensure unified control of a sector which would 'play a major role in future operations'.

During 23rd October Kesselring took two organisational decisions.[171] The whole of 1st Parachute Corps would pass to AOK 10 at 6 p.m. on 24th October, and the headquarters of 51st Mountain Corps was to change places with H.Q. 14th Panzer Corps, the exchange probably reflecting Kesselring's increased confidence in von Senger. It was greeted glumly by Feuerstein, whose diarist recorded that 51st Mountain Corps had to relinquish

command of 'tried and tested divisions, which for months had
been at the centre of the battle', and in their place take over a
motley collection of formations on the western wing of *AOK 14*,
whose boundary to *AOK 10* was re-aligned on the old boundary
between 1st Parachute and 14th Panzer Corps.[172] *AOK 10* thus
acquired responsibility for the whole of the active front, leaving
AOK 14 to contend only with the emasculated 4th U.S. Corps. As
a sop to Mussolini's frequent demands that the Italian divisions
be employed against the Allies, Kesselring also decreed on 23rd
October that by the end of the month *AOK 14* would be subordinate
'in tactical matters' to Marshal Graziani, and would absorb the
predominantly Italian Corps Lombardia.*

Having set these measures in train, Kesselring spent the afternoon of 23rd October touring the front. His car collided in the
dark with a towed gun and he was taken unconscious to a Base
Hospital at Ferrara.[174] As he was unlikely to be able to re-assume
command for some time *OKW* appointed von Vietinghoff as acting
OB Südwest. Lemelsen would assume acting command of *AOK 10*.
His replacement at *AOK 14*, General Heinz Ziegler, was injured
in a Partisan ambush after a month in office, and after another
month of temporary command by Herr from *AOK 10* General Kurt
von Tippelskirch arrived in December.[175]

It is to the great credit of the German divisions that none of
these unsettling events were reflected in their operations. Their
strategy was still rigidly controlled by Hitler. When von Vietinghoff
boldly proposed on 24th October that within the next three weeks
AOK 10 should conduct a fighting withdrawal to the Genghis Khan
position, the Führer decreed the next day that it was the continuing
task of Army Group C to ensure that 'at every point' Italy was
defended as far to the south as possible.[176]

The reasons for this stance were economic rather than military.
Before *Herbstnebel* was vetoed on 5th October, Hitler's advisers had
stressed that if Army Group C withdrew to the *Voralpen* line it
could no longer 'live off the country' and would become dependent

---

* By 29th October Graziani's Army of Liguria, rechristened *Armeegruppe Graziani* and
retaining its German Chief of Staff Major-General Walter Nagel, commanded:[173]

75th Corps
　On the Franco–Italian frontier and in north-west Italy, with 34th Infantry, 5th
Mountain and 157th Reserve Divisions, plus the 3rd Regiment of the Brandenburg
Division and 4th Alpine Battalion.

AOK 14—with under command:
Corps Lombardia
　On the Ligurian coast, with the Italian San Marco and Littorio Divisions and parts
of 148th Reserve Division.

51st Mountain Corps
　Opposite 4th U.S. Corps, with 232nd Infantry Division and parts of 148th Reserve
Division; also Fortress Brigade 135, the Italian Monte Rosa Division, and elements of
42nd Jäger Division not yet transferred to *AOK 10*.

on supplies from Germany; also that such a withdrawal would terminate Italy's economic contribution to the Reich. The fallacy of both arguments was soon to be demonstrated, but at the time they appealed strongly to those who were struggling to maintain the German war machine. In December 1944 the *Qu* section of *OKW's* Operations Branch recorded that between Italy's capitulation in September 1943 and 10th October 1944 1,500,000 tons of uncategorised commodities had been removed to Germany; nearly half a million tons of foodstuffs were then awaiting transport, plus 700,000 tons of materials collected by and for Speer's Ministry of War Production.

The loss of resources from France, and from eastern and central Europe, enhanced the value to Germany of such spoils as could still be garnered from Italy. But by the Autumn of 1944 the economic benefits to be reaped from keeping Army Group C south of the Po were declining, and the self-sufficiency of the *Wehrmacht* was becoming a fiction. Out of 97,927 tons of essential supplies delivered to *OB Südwest's Qu* staff in October, 35,658 tons came from the Reich, 23,106 tons from the Army Group's own reserve depots in Italy, and only 39,052 tons from the Italian economy. As the 1944 harvest was 'favourable' the Armed Forces did not go hungry, but in early December *OKW* acknowledged that the amount of food that could still be shipped to the Reich would fall far short of expectation. Foodstuffs had now to share half of the available transport space with goods for war production, and an improvement on the present monthly estimate of 100,000 tons for both categories of export was not anticipated.

The lack of transport which crippled the clearance programme was aggravated by air damage and sabotage by Partisans, and by the overall shortage of coal. As Italy was not self-sufficient in fuel large quantities of coal had to be imported from the Reich to keep the trains running and the factories in production. In April 1944 coal imports had stood at 476,000 tons, but this scale could not be maintained due to the loss of coalfields in the West and East, and to the autumn imposition by Switzerland of strict controls on the through-traffic of goods trains.[177] There had been 91,000 railway wagons in Italy in February; by October 1944 these had shrunk to 56,000, with 21,000 lost through Allied air action and retreats, and 14,000 claimed back by the Reich.[178] Thus the capacity of the Italian railway system to meet military needs, let alone those of the civilian German agencies, was already greatly reduced before the Allied Air Forces began in November to concentrate their attacks on the main lines in and out of Germany, bringing traffic almost to a halt. We will be describing these attacks in Part III of the Volume, Chapter XVI.

Dogged efforts were still made to accomplish what *OKW* described on 12th November as the 'bringing back of large quantities of goods which were of great importance to the home economy'.[179] 112,000 tons of uncategorised goods were exported from Italy in October, but it is difficult not to conclude that this level of economic benefit weighed less than the military advantages which would have accrued if Hitler had sanctioned the activation of *Herbstnebel*. By so doing, he would have shortened Kesselring's front and saved divisions for operations on the Eastern or Western fronts; he would also have transferred to the Allied command in the Mediterranean the embarrassing load of feeding the great industrial cities of the Po valley, when it needed all available shipping space for military supplies to carry its armies into Austria and to transfer resources to the Far East.

After the war von Vietinghoff wrote of his first experiences as acting *OB Südwest* that he very soon realised that 'Hitler made all the decisions'; also that the political and economic situation in the northern areas of his theatre was much more complex that it appeared from the battlefield.[180] What he did not learn for some months was that, with the knowledge of Kesselring and Rudolf Rahn (the Reich's Ambassador to Mussolini's Fascist Government), SS General Karl Wolff, who was senior SS and Police Commander in Italy as well as the administrator of the non-operational zones in the north, had begun in October to seek ways and means of establishing contact with the Allies in Switzerland. This was not the first attempt to approach the Western Powers, for in the late summer of 1944 overtures were made by various individual Germans who were convinced that the war was lost. Their efforts were unsuccessful, because they were generally based on the theme that Europe would be saved from Russian Communism if the Germans opened the Western Front, which was quite unacceptable to the Allies. Nor had any of the approaches been made by military leaders. After the failure of the Plot of 20th July the generals were well aware that they were too discredited in Hitler's eyes to influence his policies, and that if discovered or suspected of 'talking peace' behind his back they would be branded as traitors. It might therefore seem surprising that Wolff's initiative was supported by Kesselring, who was a most loyal servant of the Führer. The Field-Marshal's post-war evidence indicates that he had no thought of military capitulation, and was determined to avoid it by seeking a political end to the conflict.[181] As he felt by the autumn of 1944 that the time had come to work for this, he squared his conscience as a soldier and his oath to the Führer by deciding that Wolff's activities could 'pave the way' for the Reich Government to enter into political negotiations at the appropriate moment.

Far-fetched though the idea seems in retrospect, the Italian Theatre offered some unique advantages for such probes in that both Switzerland and the Vatican could be used as channels for communication. It also had its own German political hierarchy under Rahn and its own SS organisation under Wolff, who thought that Italian intermediaries might develop another contact point with the Allies through the Partisan Committee of National Liberation. By mid-October Wolff and an SS Colonel called Eugen Dollmann, who had numerous Italian contacts and spoke their language, were in touch with Cardinal Schuster, the Archbishop of Milan. They persuaded the Cardinal to send a secretary to Switzerland at the end of the month, who sought out Allen Dulles, the American Chargé d'Affaires and representative of the Office of Strategic Services in Berne. The proposal was put to Dulles that Kesselring and Wolff should sign a document confirming that the Germans would abstain from destroying non-military objectives in northern Italy in exchange for an undertaking that the Partisans would also abstain from acts of hostility or sabotage against the *Wehrmacht*. Dulles relayed the proposal to Rome, but it was rejected. Any chances of its subsequent revival were diminished by Alexander's proclamation in mid-November that with the onset of winter, the Partisans should scale down their operations.*

Although this first probe was both limited and abortive, the naming of Kesselring and Wolff by a Prince of the Church suggested to the Americans in Switzerland that something was afoot in high Nazi circles in Italy which they had not yet encountered in any other theatre. Gero von Gaevernitz, Dulles' adviser on German affairs, began to make his own probes in the reverse direction. These were inconclusive, but the gradual emergence of Switzerland as a centre whence 'peace feelers radiated in all directions' would be of material assistance to Wolff and his emissaries when the negotiations went into higher gear in February 1945. Until then the probes were only exploratory. Nothing came of a second effort in October when an Italian industrialist, who had been arrested by Mussolini but allowed on German instigation to escape to Switzerland, made contact with the British authorities in Zurich. In doing so he caught the attention of SS General Harster, another of Wolff's subordinates in northern Italy. The Italian was told on 25th October to pass on the news that Harster was authorised by Himmler to test British reactions to a hazy scheme for the cessation

---

* For further details see Part III of this Volume *Appendix 7*.

of German hostilities in Italy in exchange for Allied support against the Russians. The British promptly declined to pursue the matter as they lacked faith in German intentions, a sentiment shared in this instance by the Americans.

Nonetheless, channels had been opened and Rahn began to take his own diplomatic soundings in Switzerland, albeit not until November on the evidence of his memoirs. He had 'many talks' with Wolff which convinced him that they were of like mind in their desire to end the war. The diplomat did not however adopt a leading role, as he apparently felt that it was 'symbolically correct' that the first promising steps towards peace should be taken by a senior SS officer.

Wolff was very ready to assume the mantle of peace-maker, and at the end of 1944 found a useful go-between in the person of Baron Luigi Parrilli, an Italian businessman with contacts in the SS and a self-appointed mission to save northern Italy from destruction. All we need to remember of October's peace feelers is that they awoke the interest of Dulles and von Gaevernitz, and that Kesselring and Rahn were both aware of Wolff's activities. Whether their knowledge was shared by Himmler is obscure, but it seems unlikely that the Reichsführer was left in the dark as Harster had his own links with senior SS personalities in Berlin such as Kaltenbrunner and Schellenberg.

It was not until 8th March 1945 that Wolff met Dulles face to face, and we must leave interim developments in what would then be christened by Dulles as Operation 'Sunrise' until we return to the subject in Part III of this Volume, Chapter XVIII. We now revert to the tactical situation of *AOK 10*, whose assumption of responsibility for the Bologna sector coincided with von Vietinghoff's decision to extract 1st Parachute Division from the front of 76th Panzer Corps. This move made a major impact on the operations of 8th Army.

(vii)

See Map 28

We left 8th Army as it entered Cesena and had secured three bridgeheads over the Savio: one seized by 4th Division in Cesena itself, which was strongly contested by the Germans, and two taken by 10th Indian Division in the hills to the south; these would serve as ideal starting points for another Indian turning movement through the Apennine foot-hills, this time to outflank the potential German defence lines: Erika on the Savio and Gudrun on the Ronco.

When McCreery studied Alexander's directive of 23rd October on future plans he came to the conclusion that it did not allow enough time for two things: for the Americans to withdraw their five divisions in rotation to the Florence area for rest and to get them back into the line by 15th November; and for the Germans to thin out their Bologna front after detecting the withdrawal of the American divisions and the increased pressure of 8th Army.[182]* He suggested delaying the Bologna offensive for a week or two to lull the Germans into a false sense of security and to avoid failure through being over hasty. His own plan was to continue operations with the Polish and 5th Corps while he rested the Canadian Corps and 2nd New Zealand Division for about a month so as to be fresh and ready to support 5th Army's next attack on Bologna when it started. He estimated that 8th Army could keep fighting until as late as 15th December, which he considered a more likely date for the end of active operations for the year than Alexander's 15th November.

McCreery's most difficult problem, as his Army closed up to and crossed the Savio at the end of the third week of October, was how to regroup in such a way as to release the Canadian Corps and to create an Army Reserve.[183] 1st Armoured and 56th Divisions had been reduced to non-operational status due to lack of infantry reinforcements; 46th Division had only just been withdrawn for rest; and 4th Indian Division and 3rd Greek Mountain Brigade were on their way to Greece. McCreery decided that he would first withdraw the New Zealand Division into Army Reserve, relieving them with 5th Canadian Armoured Division on 23rd October, and then withdraw the whole of the Canadian Corps for rest starting on 28th October. It would be replaced by an *ad hoc* force of armoured car and dismounted armoured regiments, with artillery and engineers, called 'Porter Force', which would cover the waterlogged area from just north of the Via Emilia to the coast. He would then depend upon 5th Corps and the Poles to maintain pressure on the Germans with a repetition of their outflanking manoeuvres. However, once the hill features across the Savio had been taken, the plain opened out in a wide arc around Forli and denied 5th Corps the chance of turning German positions astride the Via Emilia.[184] This would have to be done by the Poles, working through the mountains.

The Polish Corps' operations did not prove as rapid as McCreery would have liked or the Germans feared. Deployment was extraordinarily difficult in its mountainous sector and was made more so by having to advance initially across the grain of the country

* For directive see pp. 385–6.

to reach the Bidente and Rabbi valleys, down which Anders was to thrust towards Forli.[185] In order to reach these two valleys the Poles had to advance from their forward assembly area near S. Piero in Bagno on Route 71, and open up the secondary road north-west over the tangle of hills between the Savio and Bidente and then over the watershed into the Rabbi valley at Strada S. Zeno. Anders gave the task of opening up this preliminary axis of advance to 5th Kresowa Division and intended to pass 3rd Carpathian Division through for the main attack towards Forli. Three *ad hoc* groups of British troops under H.Q. 1st Armoured Division ('Wheeler Force', 'Elbo Force' and 18th Infantry Brigade) screened the assembly of the Polish Corps, and then protected its eastern flank while maintaining touch with 5th Corps in the Savio valley.

The Kresowa Division passed through Wheeler Force on the night 17th/18th October with 5th Wilenska Brigade leading. The advance was slow but steady as its battalions cleared the peaks either side of the road. On 19th October Galeata was taken and by 22nd October most of the hills overlooking Strada on the River Rabbi had been secured. The same day, however, in order to co-ordinate the Polish attack with the advance of 5th Corps and the Canadians, McCreery modified the Polish Corps' line of advance: the main effort would now be directed not west of the Rabbi, but west of the Bidente, and would be made quickly, independent of action to secure the covering heights to westward.[186] Forli remained the final objective. 5th Kresowa Division, protecting the western flank, had secured a footing on Mt Colombo on 23rd October, but it was not until 25th October that 3rd Carpathian Division, moving from the Adriatic coast via Arezzo, was able to get a brigade forward of Galeata.*

As the Polish Corps widened its front so H.Q. 1st Armoured Division's front was squeezed up.[188] Wheeler Force was withdrawn and disbanded as soon as 5th Kresowa Division's advance began, and from 24th October 18th Brigade acted as the link between the Poles and 10th Indian Division on the flank of 5th Corps.

Down in the plain the Canadian Corps started a deliberate as distinct from an opportunist crossing of the Savio on the night 21st/22nd.[189] In pouring rain and with heavy artillery support 2nd Canadian Brigade secured two shallow bridgeheads two and three miles north of Cesena, which were held despite armoured counter-attacks launched by 26th Panzer Division before any Canadian supporting arms could be got across the rising waters and soft

---

* 3rd Carpathian Division's axis was changed again when 8th Army's boundary was shifted westward on 2nd November and the Division took over Route 67 from 26th Armoured Brigade.[187]

banks of the Savio. The Canadian infantry had to depend upon artillery defensive fire and their own tank hunting platoons, armed with PIATs and Hawkins grenades, to fend off the German tanks which fortunately were confined to tracks firm enough to take their weight. During one of these counter-attacks Private E. A. Smith of the Seaforth Highlanders of Canada won the V.C., destroying a Panther at 30 yards range and driving off its supporting infantry with his tommy gun. No bridges could be built; nor could there be any air support with the cloud base almost on the ground. In normal circumstances 2nd Canadian Brigade would have been in desperate straits. During 23rd October, however, 8th Army detected signs of a German withdrawal from the Erika Line. McCreery directed the Canadians not to mount any further attempts to widen their bridgeheads, which had already cost 191 casualties. By daylight on the 25th a Bailey bridge had been completed, but next day the Savio rose and swept away all crossings in the Canadian sector.

In 5th Corps' sector 4th Division could make no progress in and to the south of Cesena.[190] 10th Indian Division was once more successful, attacking from its bridgehead across the Borello. A foothold was secured on Mt Cavallo which could not be exploited in daylight. After reinforcement by a second brigade, the crest was won by dawn on 23rd October. The remainder of the divisional objective to the north was secured unopposed on the 24th.

The German withdrawal detected by 8th Army was caused by the need to extricate 1st Parachute Division.[191] von Vietinghoff agreed on 23rd October that 76th Panzer Corps could 'disengage a little' that night, a euphuism for another withdrawal which brought its divisions nearer to the main Gudrun Line on the Ronco. von Vietinghoff had formulated a larger plan of pulling back *AOK 10* to the Genghis Khan Line, running south of Bologna to Lake Comacchio. Late on 23rd October all his Corps Commanders, and H.Q. Reno–Po, were directed to start work on preparing this line for defence, giving priority to positions on the Idice river which were to be ready by 15th November.*

Talking to Herr in guarded terms on the telephone, von Vietinghoff stressed that in view of the three weeks that must elapse before *AOK 10* could get back to the 'eel pond' (Lake Comacchio) 76th Panzer Corps must not be over-hasty in retreat. However, the 'eel pond' soon proved to be something of a mirage, for when von Vietinghoff sought *OKW's* sanction for his plan, on

---

* On *OKW's* situation maps for the Italian Theatre at the end of 1944 the line was shown as starting in the mountains north-west of Vergato; ran north-east and crossed Route 65 north of Pianoro; crossed Route 9 just east of Bologna; followed the Idice to the lower Reno near Molinella, then the Reno east towards Argenta; and finally skirted the southern tip of Lake Comacchio.[192] (*See Map 8*).

24th October, it was rejected.[193] The Führer replied on the 25th
that he would countenance the weakening of the Adriatic front
implicit in the release of 1st Parachute Division, but he would not
sanction a concerted 'voluntary withdrawal'. 76th Panzer Corps
must stand on its present line, yielding ground only if and when
8th Army launched another major offensive.

The main position which was thus to be defended by Herr's
divisions and the formations under Dostler's command on the
coast was defined by *AOK 10* on 24th October as running from
Bagno on the Rabbi to Mt Velbe (Pt 469) between the Rabbi and
the Ronco, then along the western side of the Ronco valley through
Meldola and north along the Ronco.[194]

The speed and entirety of the sudden German collapse on the
Savio was initially ascribed by 8th Army to the success of 10th
Indian taking Mt Cavallo, whereas it was caused by the extraction
of 1st Parachute Division without relief and the consequential
necessity to close the gap by 278th Infantry and 26th Panzer
Divisions edging northwards respectively as they fell back to the
Ronco.[195] 5th Corps met little opposition except from rear-guards,
mines and booby traps as its divisions advanced towards the Ronco
during 24th and 25th October. 4th Division took over the Via
Emilia from the Canadians, who were preparing to hand over the
remainder of their sector to Porter Force, and after a rapid advance
took Forlimpopoli at about noon on 25th October. It then closed
up to the river that evening, looking for crossing places between
the Via Emilia and Selbagnone about three miles upstream. 10th
Indian Division met equally little opposition as it too reached the
river at Meldola, which lay on the axis of 3rd Carpathian Division.
On 25th October the latter division was just beginning to enter
the battle in the Bidente valley. The Germans had withdrawn less
precipitately in front of the Poles, who had also to face the
administrative difficulties mentioned earlier.[196]

The sudden German withdrawal from the Savio to the Ronco
naturally engendered some optimism in 8th Army.[197] 'Something
bigger' than a mere readjustment of the German line might be
under way. Certainly it was not a moment for hesitation. Both
5th Corps' divisions attempted to 'bounce' crossings during the
night of 25th/26th October. 10th Indian Division was successful in
seizing two small bridgeheads either side of Meldola. 4th Division
suffered disaster in attempting to secure two bridgeheads as well.
2nd Duke of Cornwall's Light Infantry (10th Brigade) tried to cross
at a partially damaged footbridge north-west of Selbagnone, while
a supporting squadron of 51st Royal Tanks crossed at the only
suitable ford a mile upstream. Rain was falling heavily and the
river was beginning to rise. Two companies managed to cross

during the night, which was so dark and squally that the Artificial Moonlight was largely ineffective. They managed to secure their objectives by dawn and were preparing to expand their bridgehead when the leading tank of the supporting squadron was hit, effectively blocking the ford. Then 278th Infantry Division began to counter-attack with tanks, which systematically destroyed the buildings held by the infantry. The survivors tried to swim back, helped by a smoke screen. D.C.L.I. losses numbered 17 killed and wounded and 128 missing, including the two company commanders.

1st Kings Royal Rifle Corps (directly under divisional command) made the other attempt to cross near Ronco village on the Via Emilia.[198] On reaching the river in the evening a fighting patrol was sent over with an engineer reconnaissance party to occupy the first block of houses on the far bank and to look for crossings. It was intended to reinforce, if the patrol proved successful. When this was reported to Divisional Headquarters just after midnight by a liaison officer, orders were given that the battalion was to cross and seize Ronco 'without fail'. The battalion's plan had to be hastily revised and early on 26th October two companies were over the river. Two platoons of a third company crossed at another ford about a mile up-stream. 4th Hussars' tanks found it impossible to climb the flood banks and so no British armour reached the far side of the river, which began to rise rapidly, cutting off the infantry in the bridgehead. The inevitable German counter-attack began with the support of 'a heavy tank or S.P. Gun' which worked methodically down the street occupied by the stranded companies. An attempt was made to withdraw to the river bank but by then the current was too fast for any but the strongest swimmers. Various attempts were made to rescue the survivors without success. Seven platoons were lost in this unfortunate affair, which only served to demonstrate 76th Panzer Corps' apparent determination to stand on the Ronco. The K.R.R.C. lost 114 all ranks. General Hoppe, Commander of 278th Infantry Division, congratulated his regiments in a special order of the day, claiming 280 prisoners; a high figure which may have included other prisoners taken during his division's withdrawal (*AOK 10* records show 264).[199]

The weather on 8th Army's front was just as bad during the next few days as it was on 5th Army's front; it brought all operations to a halt as most of the temporary R.E. equipment bridges over the rivers behind 8th Army were washed away.[200] On 26th October the Via Emilia became impassable when a Bailey across a large crater just west of Cesena collapsed. The only way to reach Forlimpopoli was by a long diversion south, doubling the normal distance. Both 46th and 56th Divisional Engineers had to be concentrated to keep essential supply routes open, and for three days operations came to a standstill on most of 5th Corps' front. The worst obstacle became the Savio over which there was only one high level Bailey and that had been constructed across the gap in the southern road bridge in Cesena. Under weight of heavy traffic the stone piers of this ancient bridge began to give way. Traffic over it had to be restricted to light loads until 29th October when a new Class 70 bridge was opened on the site of the Via Emilia bridge.

During this compulsory pause in operations the Canadian Corps was withdrawn, and in 5th Corps 46th Division was moved forward to relieve 10th Indian Division for a short but well earned rest, starting on 31st October. The Polish Corps, less affected by flooding, but in no less difficulty with demolished mountain roads and washed out diversions, was making steady progress on 8th Army's western flank.[201] Reconnaissance troops of 3rd Carpathian Division made contact with 10th Indian Division at Gualdo (four miles south of Meldola) in the Bidente valley on 26th October, and its 2nd Carpathian Brigade took Mt Velbe (Pt 469) east of the Rabbi on 28th October. To the west of the river 5th Kresowa Division took and held Predappio on the 27th. Their advance threatened to outflank the German defenders of Meldola but *AOK 10* (unaware as yet of the presence of the Carpathian Division) felt that the right wing of 76th Panzer Corps was comfortingly protected by the mountains and by their own demolitions.[202]

During 8th Army's advance from the Savio river to the Ronco the weather limited direct air support in 8th Army's battle area to 450 sorties in the five days, 22nd to 26th October, a meagre 162 tons of bombs being dropped.[203] As already mentioned, there was almost no air support on the 22nd and none on the 23rd. Then, surprisingly, a break in the weather on the 24th brought ideal flying conditions in which to carry out 4th Division's plan to 'blind' the German positions overlooking the Savio bridgehead by repeated air attack. Thus 24 Baltimores were airborne bombing the village of Bertinoro west of Cesena. Meanwhile the fighter-bombers attacked pre-arranged targets, including guns and mortars, directed by Rover Frank at 1st A.G.R.A. during 16 missions on 5th Corps' front, five on the Canadian Corps' front and six on the Polish Corps' front. This was the day Advanced H.Q. D.A.F. (Ops) began operating from Rimini. Within less than 24 hours the bright weather was snuffed out like a candle, and after some pre-arranged targets had been attacked in the morning of the 25th all flying had to cease. Throughout the period the light night bombers were also grounded except for one mission north of the battle area.

We must leave 8th Army on the Ronco poised to renew its offensive as soon as the weather would allow. Neither 5th nor 8th Army had made the progress they expected or hoped for. Allied morale suffered a decline after the euphoria of August and September. The end of the war had seemed so near that it engendered an enthusiasm in men to be in at the kill. In October the end seemed just as inevitable but much further off. Alexander and his commanders looked upon the capture of Bologna and Ravenna, which should be accomplished before a halt was called for winter rest and refitting, as prerequisite for the final offensive in 1945. In both Allied Armies, however, officers and men were beginning to show increased symptoms of war-weariness. Not all the advances in weapon, vehicle and aircraft technology which have taken place in the twentieth century, could overcome the adverse effects of winter weather on a European battlefield; and the German soldier was just as difficult to defeat in the winter of 1944/45 as he had been in front of Cassino in 1943/44.

(viii)

See Maps 23 and 24

At the beginning of October the German evacuation of Greece was sufficiently advanced to bring the reoccupation of the country into the forefront of affairs in London, Caserta, Salerno and Bari. On 7th October Wilson sent to the British Chiefs of Staff the first of a series of weekly situation reports, which forms a suitable starting point for the events that culminated in the launching of operation 'Manna'.[204] In the Aegean, German garrisons still held Milos, Lemnos, Cos and Leros. Sea evacuation of Crete and Rhodes had been stopped but some air evacuation was still in progress. The Germans had withdrawn from Patras and possibly Corinth. The Canal had been blocked by landslides and demolitions, and most of the German controlled shipping had left the Piraeus for the north, suggesting that the evacuation of Attica had begun. As there were thought to be 20,000 German troops in Athens their withdrawal was unlikely to be complete much before mid-October. Fox Force, with B Squadron Greek Sacred Regiment, was established on Poros and had been directed to attack Aegina and the neighbouring island of Fleves. Colonel Jellicoe's Bucket Force, which had occupied Patras, was now pushing on to Corinth, its advance to be reinforced by the rest of 2nd Highland Light Infantry. The task of accepting German surrenders in the

Aegean had been entrusted to Headquarters Raiding Forces under G.H.Q. Middle East Command.* So far the Greek Government Commissioners had been well received wherever they had appeared and their instructions had been obeyed by *E.L.A.S.* Elsewhere *E.L.A.S.* bands were less well behaved. In Thrace no Commissioner had yet arrived. Rumours were rife that the Russians and Bulgarians would occupy Thrace until the Armistice. This was causing much disquiet to the Greek Government, and was making the occupation of Salonika more pressing than hitherto.

Two equal and opposite anxieties dominated the minds of the commanders and staffs involved in handling the military and political aspects of affairs in Greece at the beginning of October. On the one hand, there was the fear that 'Manna' would be launched too slowly and enable *E.L.A.S.* to fill the vacuum left by the German evacuation of Athens; and on the other, there was the suspicion that the Germans might decide to hold on to Athens and prevent the Greek Government re-establishing itself in the capital. The latter was the predominant feeling at the turn of the month. Papandreou had originally objected to establishing his Government in the Peloponnese, preferring to wait until he could enter Athens in the wake of the 'Manna' re-occupation of the city. By 25th September he had begun to fear that the situation was moving so rapidly that the continued absence of Ministers from Greece would dangerously weaken their authority.[206] Papandreou wanted to issue a decree calling up certain classes for regular military service, feeling that, if he waited until Athens was evacuated by the Germans, he would be accused of raising an army for political purposes. He could not issue such a decree from Salerno, but the Araxos/Patras area, which was now in the hands of Bucket Force would offer a suitable alternative on Greek soil. As the days went by and the Germans showed little sign of leaving Athens anxiety about the military assumptions upon which 'Manna' was based began to grow. On 5th October the Commanders-in-Chief Mediterranean discussed the possibility that resources at present earmarked for the operation could be better employed elsewhere in Greece.[207] Air Marshal Slessor observed that unless 'Manna' were launched within the next few days the airborne plan would anyway have to be recast; it had been intended to fly in two lifts per day but, as October advanced, the available daylight hours decreased to a point where only one lift would be possible. Admiral Cunningham suggested that forces should land at Missolonghi on

---

* A Squadron, Greek Sacred Regiment was at this date under command. On 4th October the M.E. decided to expand operations northward in order to harass the enemy, maintain law, and distribute civilian relief. The new H.Q., Force 142, was known as Allied Military Forces in the Greek Aegean. It was based on Chios.[205]

the northern shore of the Gulf of Corinth, which should be swept by the Royal Navy. Wilson emphasised the importance of installing the Greek Government ashore as early as possible. The meeting ended with directions to the Joint Planning Staff to make a preliminary examination 'of the uses to which the "Manna" resources might best be put on the assumption that Athens was held as a fortress . . .'. Two days later Wilson announced that the Greek Prime Minister had agreed to go to Patras and instructed Scobie to arrange his landing there on 11th October.

Anxieties about German intentions seem to have been resolved for General Wilson on 9th October by Intelligence. He cabled the Chiefs of Staff the same day that D day for 'Manna' was to be 15th October.[208] His reasons for setting this date were not given but early that day Special sources had reported that there were no Germans in Corinth and few in Athens.[209] H.Q. B.A.F. was shortly to receive information giving details of the German evacuation together with reliable evidence that Athens would be clear by 15th October. Anxieties now swung from having to root out the Germans to doing everything possible to speed up the arrival of the 'Manna' forces in Athens.

Wilson's decision to set 15th October as D day for 'Manna', with H hour at 5 a.m., cleared away uncertainty and enabled Scobie, Mansfield and Tuttle to start taking executive action.[210]* As the drop of 2nd Parachute Brigade was to precede the arrival of Arkforce at the Piraeus we will look at the Air plans and operations first and then turn to the approach by sea of the main and follow up forces. It had been intended that both parachute and sea-borne landings should take place in the Kalamaki airfield/port of the Piraeus area, from which the advance into Athens would be made. The successes of Bucket and Fox Forces in the Peloponnese led to a modification of this plan and in effect these two forces became the advanced elements of the air and sea-borne landings. The actions of these small forces influenced events as they unfolded.

Commander Land Forces Adriatic, Brigadier Davy, assessed the situation after Bucket Force's entry of Patras, and mindful of A.F.H.Q.'s original instructions to take operational and administrative risks, recommended to H.Q. B.A.F. on 6th October that he should push his patrols in two directions: via Corinth and Megara, towards Athens, and across the Gulf of Corinth to threaten the main German withdrawal route from Athens at Levadia.[211] When, however, A.F.H.Q. was consulted General Gammell coun-

---

* H hour was the time at which the first naval unit, 5th Minesweeping Flotilla, was to pass the rendezvous position, Point 704, approximately 5 miles east of the island of Hydra.

selled caution, being anxious about the internal security situation in Patras which had 'most explosive possibilities'. Jellicoe should 'be very chary of going beyond Megara' and his patrols across the Gulf of Corinth should be 'eyes and not fighters'. To free Jellicoe, arrangements were in hand to fly in Brigadier J. P. O'Brien Twohig (Commander of the Vis, or Adriatic Brigade, as it was shortly to be renamed), to take over internal security in the Peloponnese.[212] On the political side L.F.A. were to treat the Peloponnese bands of *E.L.A.S.* 'with complete trust and confidence' in the spirit of the Caserta Agreement, however difficult that might be. They were to avoid taking sides at all costs. Force 140, signalling on 9th October, confirmed this view.[213] Scobie felt a firm grip should be kept on the Peloponnese in view of the impending arrival of the Greek Prime Minister in Patras. He did not like the idea of an adventure which could lead to an unnecessary reverse.

Davy, therefore, having cancelled the Levadia reconnaissance, authorised Jellicoe to detach a field squadron of the R.A.F. Regiment to oversee the surrender of the Security Battalion in Sparta and Gythion, and to advance with the rest of his force on Megara and Athens.[214] The leading troops of his Special Boat Squadron reached Megara on 9th October, having crossed the Corinth Canal on an improvised ferry. The Germans were still holding the high ground six miles east of the village. An attempt to send patrols round their northern flank failed, but it was found possible to cross by caique to the east side of the Gulf of Salamis. The way had been paved for 2nd Parachute Brigade to enter Athens more quickly from the west rather than to drop on Kalamaki for an advance from the south-east.

During the afternoon of 11th October Air Vice-Marshal Elliot issued new verbal orders for 2nd Parachute Brigade in the presence of General Scobie.[215] The Brigade was to secure Megara airfield. If the flank-guard which was expected to cover the German withdrawal route from Athens to Thebes withdrew or was weakened, the Brigade was to advance rapidly on Athens, but was not to incur heavy casualties. Brigadier C. H. V. Pritchard, 2nd Parachute Brigade Commander, decided to secure the airfield with a company drop on 12th October, followed by the rest of the brigade and re-supply drops next day.[216]* Unfortunately the wind

---

* *Troop Carrier Forces Available*:
51st Troop Carrier Wing U.S.A.A.F. was to make available 100 Troop Carrier aircraft for lifting 2nd Parachute Brigade on three successive days and for a further four days 50 Troop Carriers would be available for transporting supplies and personnel. The Wing would also provide 30 Hadrian gliders, plus reserve, to carry supplies, ammunition and equipment during the initial assault. Two groups of fighters of Fifteenth Air Force (approximately 100 aircraft) were to escort the Carriers from the coast of Greece to and from the target area.[217]

was just too strong on 12th October and the company of 4th Parachute Battalion, which dropped, suffered many casualties by men making bad landings. The Germans, who shelled the dropping zone, caused few losses. Then the weather worsened, preventing the main drop until 14th October.

In the interval Jellicoe had been freed from his internal security responsibilities by the arrival of Brigadier Twohig, and on 13th October L.F.A. ordered him to investigate the situation in Athens as 'the Germans were believed to have left'. Jellicoe embarked his men in caiques. The only transport they had were two bicycles captured from the Germans at Megara. He landed west of Athens and, donning Brigadier Twohig's red tabs, bicycled into the city with one of his officers to report to the Greek Military Governor. The rest of his force followed on foot and entered the city in the early hours of 14th October, about the same time as the leading elements of Fox Force came in from the east.

We left Fox Force having established the advanced coastal craft base on Poros and about to reconnoitre Aegina and Fleves. On the night 11th/12th October, while the cruiser *Argonaut* carried out a diversionary bombardment, patrols were landed on Aegina, which reported that this island had been evacuated and probably Fleves as well.[218] Detachments were sent to both islands to destroy the guns while the rest of Fox Force embarked that night in two L.C.T.s, a schooner and a few caiques and sailed for the Piraeus. Early on 14th October the force was in sight of the port, dodging amongst numerous floating mines, many of which could be seen on the surface. As the harbour was also reported to be heavily mined they landed nearby. The Commandos were given a rousing reception from the people of the Piraeus as they pushed their way through the streets to secure Kalamaki airfield and then advanced towards Athens. The Mayor of Athens organised the provision of buses to ferry the troops forward. That afternoon Bucket and Fox Forces with the company of 4th Parachute Battalion from Megara and members of the Greek Sacred Squadron mounted a ceremonial parade amongst a seething crowd of jubilant Athenians. As a precautionary measure Fox Force placed guards on the principal public buildings and municipal services like the power station which was still working, and the telephone exchange, which was providing a limited service.

At sea the naval armada, which was described by Admiral Mansfield in his report as 'the heterogeneous collection of ships stretching to the horizon', was making for its rendezvous off the east coast of the Peloponnese (Pt 704, 5 miles off Hydra). Admiral Mansfield flew his flag in the *Orion*, which acted as headquarters ship during the voyage.[219]* The escort carriers of Force 120 (Commodore G. N. Oliver) had been active in the Aegean from 3rd to 12th October, attacking shipping and shore lines of communication by day, while the Fighter Direction Ship H.M.S. *Ulster Queen* controlled land-based night fighters during the night.[221]† On 15th October the carrier force (H.M.S. *Royalist*, *Stalker*, *Emperor*, *Attacker*, *Ulster Queen*, *Colombo* and destroyers) moved to an area from which they could provide defensive patrols and offensive close air support for 'Manna' if called upon to do so.

Arkforce sailed from Alexandria on 13th October in the *Black Prince* and the *Aurora* with Brigadier R. H. B. Arkwright (23rd Armoured Brigade) in the former.[223]‡ On the same day Scobie and his 3rd Corps Staff embarked at Naples in the *Orion*, accompanied by Mr. Harold Macmillan, Resident Minister in the Mediterranean; and the Greek Government, accompanied by Mr. Leeper, embarked at Taranto, in the L.S.I. *Prince David*. The *Ajax* also embarked troops from the Heel ports, whence came the sea-tail of 2nd Parachute Brigade, A.H.Q. Greece and other Air elements. The *Sirius*, uncluttered with troops, joined the Taranto ships to provide naval gunfire support in case Aegina and Fleves had not been taken by the time the force arrived off Poros. The Greek cruiser *Averoff*, flying the flag of the Greek Naval Commander-in-Chief, Vice-Admiral Voulgaris, sailed with Arkforce loaded with M.T. which was to be discharged at the Piraeus, before the Greek Government were transferred to her from *Prince David* for a ceremonial entry. The Greek admiral was to have no operational responsibilities until 'Manna' was over.

---

* The principal naval units taking part were:[220]

Cruisers	Escort Carriers
H.M.S. *Orion*	H.M.S. *Stalker*
Ajax	*Attacker*
Aurora	*Emperor*
Black Prince	Fighter Direction Ship
Sirius	H.M.S. *Ulster Queen*
Royalist	Greek Cruiser
Colombo	H.H.M.S. *Giorgios Averoff*

† The earlier operations of the *Ulster Queen* are covered in Chapter XIV pp. 330–1. Similar attempts to interrupt the Rhodes–Salonika traffic between 15th and 17th October had no success.[222]

‡ The carriage of Arkforce in cruisers involved:

	Troops	Vehicles	Stores
Aurora	746	26 jeeps	32½ tons
Black Prince	882	11 jeeps	36 tons
Ajax	688	13 jeeps	60 tons

plus 26 Pressmen

Housing and feeding so many additional men for the voyage reflected great credit on the ships' supply staffs.

All the various groups of ships involved arrived punctually on their specified times at the rendezvous.[224] Mansfield's plan was for 5th Minesweeping Flotilla, reinforced with 28th Minelaying Flotilla, to sweep ahead of the main force from Poros into the Piraeus. Unfortunately 28th M.L. Flotilla had already sailed to the Piraeus with Fox Force, and, unknown to Admiral Mansfield, was not available to help sweeping. 5th Minesweeping Flotilla started to sweep northwards from the rendezvous at 5.30 a.m. and was followed at 7.30 a.m. by the *Orion* leading the rest of the cruisers in single line into the Channel, which was just five cables wide and marked by Dan buoys only on one side. The escort carriers *Attacker* and *Stalker* provided air cover from Force A with Seafires, which shot down the only enemy aircraft, a Ju. 88, to interfere during the day. At 8.40 a.m., the sweepers ran into a densely laid shallow minefield off Aegina. Two Greek sweepers were mined and sunk almost at once, and shortly afterwards the *Larne*, carrying the Senior Officer of 5th M.S. Flotilla, was mined and severely damaged. The main force of cruisers was stopped in a most uncomfortable position in the narrow channel with unswept mines on either side. Had the weather not been clear and calm disaster could well have occurred. Mansfield decided at 9.15 a.m. to turn and to withdraw to the south to await the completion of sweeping. As the main force started to withdraw a second minesweeper, the *Clinton*, was mined and damaged, followed by a minelayer which was sunk. The *Clinton* made Poros under her own steam. While the *Orion* was turning at 10.40 a.m. an explosion was seen at the south end of the line of ships off Poros. The Dutch water-tanker *Petronella* had strayed out of the swept channel and sank in three minutes after being mined. This loss could have been serious if the Germans had blown the Marathon Dam which supplies Athens with water. Fortunately, although they had placed 80 tons of explosive in the dam, Greek Partisans had managed to remove it and had thrown it in the water before the demolition could be carried out.

Sweeping continued for some hours. By early afternoon only a narrow channel had been cleared through to the Piraeus. Mansfield ordered several groups including the *Averoff* to spend the night in the swept area around Poros. He then followed astern of the minesweepers with *Orion*, *Ajax*, *Black Prince*, *Aurora* and six destroyers, adjusting speed to deal with many floating mines with gunfire. The *Orion* reached her pre-arranged berth at the Piraeus at 5.20 p.m. just as it was getting dark. An electric sign blazed on the shore saying 'Welcome to Greece'. Admiral Mansfield observed 'We had very nearly come to Grief!' Arkforce had arrived on D day; the *Averoff* was to make her stately entry later, after suitable arrangement had been made for the reception of the Greek Government.

The Piraeus was not as badly damaged as had been feared.* Mansfield commented on the improvisation needed to get the troops ashore:

> 'In the event, no unloading of an expedition could ever have been more unlike the planned arrangements, more *ad hoc*, or more entirely successful.'

Brigadier Arkwright landed at 6.30 a.m. on 16th October and took charge of all troops already in the Athens area.[225] His own troops started landing at 8 a.m. and by 11 a.m. his three 'infantry' battalions were all ashore.†

The reception accorded to all British troops was rapturous and spontaneous but too emotional to last.[227] Arkwright's most difficult task was to establish a firm hold on the vulnerable points in the city, while at the same time making arrangements for the arrival of the Greek Government and General Scobie with his Headquarters' Staff. The *Averoff* attempted to off-load her cargo of vehicles and equipment before returning to Poros to pick up the Greek Ministers waiting there in the *Prince David*. Her main derrick broke down so she had to carry out her ceremonial duties with her quarterdeck looking like a car park.

M. Papandreou, accompanied by his Ministers, General Scobie, Admiral Mansfield and Air Commodore Tuttle, made his official entry into Athens on 18th October. The ceremonies included the rehoisting of the Greek Flag on the Acropolis, singing the *Te Deum* in the Cathedral, laying wreaths on the Unknown Warrior's tomb and a major address by Papandreou to the people of Greece, which was well received. On the same day the first five Swedish relief ships were brought safely into the Piraeus anchorage by the Royal Navy and the first merchant ship, a collier, berthed near the power station. Responsibility for unloading had now passed to H.Q. 3rd Corps. Life was returning to a quasi-normality in the capital. Operation 'Manna' had been completed successfully with the re-occupation of Athens and the return of the Greek Government to its capital. The delay in unloading caused by the minefield on D day was retrieved by the evening of 17th October, when 5,000

---

* Free of mines and other obstructions, it was possible to bring large craft into immediate use; tugs and lighters were in ample supply and a floating crane was available.

† Arkforce consisted of H.Q. 23rd Armoured Brigade, plus a large administrative increment which it was intended to pass to 3rd Corps command. The combat units consisted of: 23rd Armoured Brigade, 40th, 46th and 50th R.T.R., 463rd Battery R.H.A., 11th K.R.R.C., 1238th Field Company R.E.

When the brigade was converted to infantry 46th R.T.R. was split up, one squadron going to each of 40th and 50th R.T.R. and one remaining under Regimental Headquarters, re-equipped with armoured cars.[226]

personnel, 400 vehicles and 1,000 tons of stores had been landed. The commanding officer of 5th Minesweeping Flotilla reported that 100 mines in all had been swept from the main channel by 21st October.

On 17th October Wilson held a special meeting at A.F.H.Q. to consider future policy in the Balkans, the aims of which General Gammell defined as, firstly, to harass the German withdrawal and prevent the escape of as many as possible, while at the same time building up a position for future operations in the Northern Adriatic, and, secondly:

> 'To establish conditions in Greece of a kind which would make it possible to reopen the country for relief purposes.'[228]

The troops of Land Forces Adriatic were specially organised and equipped for harassing operations and might, in conjunction with the Navy, be able to open up ports through which Tito could be supplied in pursuit of the first aim. As regards the second, to ensure the stability of Greece, it would be necessary to enter Salonika on the heels of the Germans. Originally it had been estimated that the Germans would not leave Salonika much before 5th November, but this date seemed likely to be advanced and so Gammell recommended that a force should be prepared at once for despatch. There were, however, difficulties in finding the troops for both purposes. L.F.A. could not be released for further operations in Yugoslavia until replaced, and 2nd Parachute Brigade was needed back in Italy. The decision had already been made to withdraw 4th Indian Division and the Greek Mountain Brigade from A.A.I. He proposed therefore to replace all the present specialised formations (L.F.A. and 2nd Parachute Brigade) with a longer-term garrison of 4th Indian Division, which was in need of rest after its hard fighting on the Italian front throughout the summer, and the Greek Mountain Brigade. The first Indian Brigade Group would be released by the end of October for dispatch from Taranto to Salonika. L.F.A. troops in the Peloponnese could be relieved by the second Indian Brigade Group or the Greeks, and the third Indian Brigade Group could relieve 23rd Armoured Brigade. In the meantime a reinforced Commando should establish a base on Skiathos Island, off Volos, ready to occupy Salonika at short notice. One or two of 2nd Parachute Brigade's battalions should also be moved by sea to Skiathos, possibly in H.M. Ships, to support the Commando.

Admiral Cunningham was none too happy about these proposals. He supported the idea of an advanced base at Skiathos from which a small assault force could be mounted in suitable craft. A channel could then be swept properly behind it for a follow-up force in larger vessels. He did not think his cruisers should be exposed to mines in what was essentially a political operation. There were 60 miles of channel to be swept and there was an L.C.I. lift available for 2,000 men. He explained also that 15th Cruiser Squadron was being used to accelerate the clearance of the Aegean Islands, but that Crete, Rhodes, Cos and Leros were presenting difficulties.

Wilson issued orders on 20th October to implement Gammell's plan. 4th Indian Division and 3rd Greek Mountain Brigade were placed under command of 3rd Corps for planning purposes forthwith, and under operational command from their arrival in Greece.[229] The first Indian Brigade would be ready to sail from Italy in two echelons, the first on 2nd November and the second on 7th November. 2nd Parachute Brigade and L.F.A. troops should be released as soon as they could be spared.

Scobie's initial deployment of his available military resources was in four groups:[230]

> *23rd Armoured Brigade* with 6th Parachute Battalion added, was responsible for Athens and 'showing the flag' in Attica.

> *2nd Parachute Brigade* (less two battalions) with 9th Commando and a detachment of S.B.S. under command, was to establish an advanced base on Skiathos for the reoccupation of Salonika.[231]

> *H.Q. Vis Brigade* with 2nd H.L.I. and detachments of the R.A.F. Regiment, was responsible for Patras and the rest of the Peloponnese.

> *Special Boat Squadron* with 4th Parachute Battalion under command, was to pursue the Germans northwards until they were over the Greek/Yugoslav border. The Germans were to be harassed from the flanks and major actions avoided.[232]

23rd Armoured Brigade worked its way steadily through its area of responsibility, disarming the Security Battalions, opening up minor ports for relief supplies, acting as arbitrators in local disputes and in general providing a thin but respected British presence.[233] 2nd Parachute Brigade pushed patrols by road and sea up the coast towards Salonika (*Map 23*). The roads were so thoroughly demolished by the German rear-guards that most of the advance was made in small craft. Skiathos was found unsuitable as a base and so the patrols crossed over to the Kassandra Peninsula and set up a base 40 miles south-east of Salonika. Meanwhile an enterprising detachment of S.B.S. were embarked in caiques in order to reconnoitre ahead by sea, and had reached the outskirts of the city on 30th October.[234] Transport into Salonika was found 'in the shape of 4 fire engines plus accompanying silver helmeted firemen!' F.O.L.E.M. was to underline the value of the reports on landing facilities, mines and enemy defences, sent back by this unorthodox small force. The problems of the Athens reoccupation were repeated. The extensive mining of the sea approaches prevented the arrival of the main bodies of the brigade until the sweeping could be completed. This took until 8th November and even then the final approach was not cleared sufficiently for the larger vessels to enter the port. All troops were ferried ashore in smaller craft. The first landings were made early in the day and Brigade H.Q. was soon established in the German consulate. The welcome was not as enthusiastic as in Athens because *E.A.M./E.L.A.S.* had been in control of the city for some days. They were not uncooperative but relations could only be described, at best, as correctly cordial.

On land the Special Boat Squadron with 4th Parachute Battalion followed up the German withdrawal on the axis Thebes–Lamia–Larissa and north-west to the frontier at Florina.[235] The Germans had a long start and had destroyed the roads behind them with great thoroughness. There were some contact just before the Germans crossed the frontier but there the pursuit was halted.

At sea Force A with the cruiser *Royalist* (Flag), the escort carriers *Attacker, Emperor* and *Stalker* and four destroyers operated in the Northern Aegean from 15th to 24th October.[236] The Force was withdrawn to carry out operation 'Manna', but Mansfield agreed to reduce fighter cover from the carriers to maintain attacks on German troops withdrawing through northern Greece. By 19th October Commodore Oliver had under his command six cruisers, the *Ulster Queen* and the *Colombo*, three escort carriers and ten destroyers. On 22nd October Oliver became Senior Naval Officer Northern Aegean with a semi-permanent operational headquarters at Chios. Force A attacked what few enemy ships were to be found and concentrated more upon German withdrawal routes out of Greece. Carrier aircraft struck whenever the weather permitted at rail and road transport in the Volos area and then turned their attention to the Larissa–Salonika line where five trains were immobilised on the last day of operations. Four aircraft had been lost but all the pilots were rescued. The bag claimed was:[237]

Destroyed by ships: 1 destroyer
                                     1 transport
                                     4 smaller craft

Destroyed by aircraft: 8 locomotives
                                     40 rail wagons
                                     62 road vehicles
                                     2 smaller vessels (coaster and barge)
                                     2 aircraft

Damaged by aircraft: 2 locomotives
                         55 rail wagons
                         82 road vehicles
                          6 small vessels
                          1 bridge
                          1 tunnel
                          1 water tower

Captured by ships: 382 prisoners of war

Ships and aircraft of Force A also took a hand in the clearance of German garrisons on the Aegean islands; some, after bombardment, surrendered to seamen landing parties, others gave up without a shot being fired.

By the end of October military operations against the Germans were virtually over except for the containment of German garrisons on islands such as Crete, Rhodes and Milos, where they were obeying the Führer's order not to surrender. Scobie's troops were left with the crucial task of re-establishing the Greek Government in its homeland. In theory this should have been a diminishing responsibility as the Greeks managed to put their own house in order. At the end of October there was some optimism that this might happen. In a cable to the Foreign Office dated 31st October Mr. Leeper summed up the political situation:[238]

> 'So long as the bulk of the population in Athens is pre-occupied with money and food questions party politics take a back place. This means no political party is prepared to dispute the authority of M. Papandreou. The latter's problem is to decide in what way and to what extent he will exercise this authority. For the moment he will probably be guided by the following considerations:
> (a) The extent to which Britain can accelerate and increase supplies.
> (b) Prospect of early monetary stabilisation.
> (c) Time by which he can secure equipment for four classes of regular army which are being called up.
> It is too soon for me to be accurately and adequately informed on the true state of feelings in Athens let alone in the provinces . . .'

In the assessment, which he then gave of the situation, he felt that in Athens the Communists were well organised but had 'a very limited hold over the minds of the population'. 'The presence of British troops', he argued, 'offers a much greater attraction than any political ideology and Communists have been careful not to go against current popular feelings and have confined their activities to staging demonstrations to impress British troops'. Within the Government the Communists and their allies professed loyalty to

Papandreou and the British, on the assumption that the Russians intended to play no part in Greek affairs. Outside Athens *E.L.A.S.* behaved as they wished and it appeared unlikely that *E.A.M.* could, even if they tried, exercise any effective control. The appearance of British troops even in small numbers, he believed, could remedy the situation. He ended on the optimistic note:

> 'Fundamentally therefore, we need not take it too tragically. Provided we build up a satisfactory volume of supplies we can await the moment when the remedy can be applied'.

On 25th October Mr. Eden visited Athens.[239] He was accompanied by Mr. Macmillan and Lord Moyne (Resident Minister in Cairo) and they were joined by the three Commanders-in-Chief Mediterranean (Slessor, representing the Air forces) for a prolonged series of conferences with Scobie and Papandreou. Three crucial problems began to emerge from the general chaos and uncertainty of the immediate post-'Manna' period.[240] These were: roaring inflation, which was declared by the Greek Minister of Finance to exceed the worst period in Germany after the First World War; the difficulties of landing and distributing desperately needed relief supplies, which were exacerbated by lack of transport, demolished roads, railways and ports, inadequate numbers of Allied personnel to handle the distribution, and the unreliability of *E.A.M./E.L.A.S.* in country districts; and how to call up and equip a Greek national army and police force to replace the private armies of the guerilla leaders. These three problems were closely inter-connected and, although identified in October, their handling belongs to the next chapter (starting Part III of this Volume) which deals with the frustration of British policy generally throughout the Balkans.

(ix)

Throughout the period 22nd September (when 8th Army crossed the Marecchia river) to the end of October the Allied Air forces, like the Armies, had to fight against the relentless deterioration in what was then described as the worst October weather in Italy in living memory.[241] This was accurately reflected in the sorties flown and aircraft lost. The 35,206 sorties represented a daily rate of 880 every 24 hours, which was little more than half the 1,710 sorties per day in the last week of August and the first three weeks of September. The analysis of sorties for the period are set out at the end of this chapter in Tables I and II—Table I for the total sorties flown and Table II for the breakdown of bomber and fighter-bomber efforts within the battle area, north of it and beyond Italy's borders. The Allies lost 421 aircraft, which is an average of 10.5 every day and compares unfavourably with 14 per day lost in the previous period when the sorties rate was twice as high, and was almost entirely due to weather. During the 40 days of the period flying was restricted for over half the flying time available. An analysis of the days when there was no flying or flying was restricted shows:—

	Day		Night	
	No flying	Restricted	No flying	Restricted
M.A.S.A.F. Heavy Bombers	18	5	21	1
M.A.T.A.F. Medium Bombers	23	7	NA	NA
Desert Air Force	5	17	33*	Not known
U.S. XXII T.A.C.	4	18	26	Not known

* Includes 12 occasions when landing grounds were unserviceable.

This analysis does not tell the whole story. Some days would start with reasonable flying weather and would deteriorate later and vice versa. Landing grounds also took time to dry out and so clear skies did not necessarily mean that air operations would be possible straight away. M.A.T.A.F.'s medium bombers (U.S. Marauders and Mitchells) had to stay in Corsica because of difficulty in constructing airfields for their use in the Florence and Ancona areas. D.A.F.'s Marauders at Pescara were plagued with airfield unserviceability and, because of difficulties in preparing Iesi for their use, were unable to operate from 27th September until 26th November. Shortage of P.S.P. (Pierced Steel Planking) was one of the causes of airfield unserviceability. Efforts were made to increase shipments from the United States, from North Africa and from surplus stocks in France, but improvements in supplies took time.

The direction of strategic air operations under M.A.S.A.F. was redefined on 19th October by H.Q. M.A.A.F., its new directive superseding that of 13th September, 1944.[242] It incorporated a U.S.S.T.A.F.* directive for the 'Employment of the Strategic Air Force' of 23rd September and the instructions were adapted to meet the requirements of the Mediterranean and Middle East Theatres. The overall mission remained the support of the Combined Bomber Offensive and the direct support of land and naval forces when needed. The enemy's fuel, particularly petrol, was the

* U.S.S.T.A.F. was the agency under the command of General Spaatz for co-ordinating the strategic air operations of the United States Eighth (U.K.) and Fifteenth (Italy) Air Forces.

primary objective of strategic operations, followed by the supply of certain items of ground equipment which were listed. However, two special tasks were the attack from time to time of the enemy's railway system, and in Italy, because of the situation there, the Brenner route had to be kept closed and nothing was to be allowed to interfere with this process other than the weather.

The efforts expended by M.A.S.A.F. beyond the borders of Italy are shown in the table overpage.

It will be noted that oil targets received proportionately more attention than previously. On the other hand communications received less but the bombload was more evenly spread across the map, partly due to targets in Austria and Greece being attacked on a larger scale.

Allied losses in these attacks were 153 heavy day bombers (Liberators and Fortresses), four heavy night bombers (R.A.F. Liberators and Halifaxes) and eight medium night bombers (Wellingtons), but it has not been possible to break down these figures into territories over which they were lost.

In Greece the airfields at Eleusis, Kalamaki and Tatoi (Athens area) were again bombed on 24th September, and Greek airfields were strafed by M.A.S.A.F.'s fighters on 4th and 6th October.[243] Both subjects have already been covered in Chapter XIV p.332-3.

A departure from the routine tasks of the U.S. Liberators and Fortresses was an experiment in bombing at night. On 28th/29th October 12 Fortresses were sent to Munich to bomb the west marshalling-yard. Two night later (30th/31st October) six Liberators were sent to bomb Klagenfurt marshalling-yard. Eight of the Fortresses found their target and dropped 17 tons of bombs on it, and three of the Liberators successfully dropped just over five tons on theirs.

Another departure from routine arose from a plea from the Supreme Allied Commander to the Air Commander-in-Chief to support operations in the Balkans on a greater scale.* As a result, on 26th October, H.Q. M.A.A.F. directed that No. 205 Group was to concentrate its whole effort on fulfilling tasks required by A.O.C. B.A.F., first priority being given to tasks in Yugoslavia including supply-dropping. A.O.C. B.A.F. decided that No. 205 Group would be best used primarily for supply-dropping both by day and night, and for bombing isolated communication targets.

Several air formations disappeared from the strategic air scene. On 30th September the Mediterranean Allied Photographic Reconnaissance Wing was disbanded, its duties being taken over

---

* See p.384.

EFFORTS EXPENDED BY M.A.S.A.F. BEYOND THE BORDERS OF ITALY
DAWN 22nd SEPTEMBER–DAWN 1st NOVEMBER 1944

Sorties (bombloads in brackets)

Country	Oil	Railway	Factories & Indust. Areas	Airfields	Misc. & Targets of Opportunity	TOTALS
Germany	786 (1,668.5)	538 (1,111.1)	438 (959.2)	119 (241.3)	3 (7.1)	1,884 (3,987.2)
Czecho-slovakia	292 (715.5)	49 (119.0)	183 (376.8)		32 (59.9)	556 (1,271.2)
Austria	355 (723.1)	456 (968.6)	516 (1,042.0)	3 (5.7)	55 (104.7)	1,385 (2,844.1)
Hungary		737 (1,506.9)		137 (304.7)	72 (135.6)	946 (1,947.2)
Yugoslavia		374 (960.9)			4 (7.1)	378 (968.0)
Greece		134 (292.6)		271 (453.5)		405 (746.1)
TOTALS	1,433 (3,107.1)	2,288 (4,959.1)	1,137 (2,378.0)	530 (1,005.2)	166 (314.4)	5,554 (11,765.8)

by the photographic reconnaissance elements of U.S. Twelfth and Fifteenth Air Forces and by No. 336 Wing for the Royal Air Force. Then, on 5th October, No. 330 Wing and its two Wellington Squadrons, Nos. 142 and 150, were disbanded. These two Squadrons had composed the first night bomber force in North West Africa, doing so in December 1942. Since coming under No. 205 Group R.A.F. in July 1943, they had flown 4,723 operational sorties and dropped 7,187.5 tons of bombs and mines on every type of target in all weathers—no mean achievement within 15 months.

From the break down given in Table II of bomber and fighter-bomber efforts within the battle area in Italy, and north of it and beyond its borders, it will be seen that, though the proportion of the total M.A.A.F. bomber and fighter-bomber effort expended beyond Italy's border was considerably less than in the previous four weeks, that between the amounts expended within and north of the battle area was roughly the same. North of the battle area the air effort remained concentrated upon railway targets, with road and motor transport a poor second. The struggle between the Allied airmen and German repair crews went on unabated with the Germans just keeping pace. The surprising weight of artillery fire which von Senger managed to concentrate in checking the direct American thrust towards Bologna, and the frequency of reports by 8th Army of the intensity of German artillery fire, demonstrate the success of their efforts to keep ammunition and other vital commodities flowing southwards, thereby helping Kesselring to hold the Allies in the Apennines and Romagna. In mid-February 1945 *OB Südwest* would name 'supply, transport and mobility' as the main problems then facing his Army Group, but it was on the need for reinforcement, rather than logistical issues, that he based his case when he sought *OKW's* permission to implement *Herbstnebel* in September 1944.[244] At that time the rail network in northern Italy was too extensive to be totally disrupted by the air effort available. Even the vulnerable Brenner route, though frequently cut, was still operable. With surprising optimism M.A.A.F. issued a directive on 20th October prohibiting attacks on marshalling-yards south of the Po so as not to hamper the advance of the Allied Armies!

Nevertheless, Allied air attacks achieved considerable success in reducing the flow of supplies to the front; also in contributing to the growing shortfall in German export programmes.[245] On several occasions in October *OKW* was informed by Kesselring of cuts in the main line from the Brenner Pass to Verona. Due to similar cuts in the main routes south of Verona the 'terminus' for north-south traffic receded during the month to Bologna, which on 26th October became the terminus for traffic from west to east as well as from north to south. Reports submitted to *OKW* in November 1944 showed that in September the numbers of trucks entering and leaving Italy were down on the August figures by 27% and 35% respectively. There was a further fall in rail traffic both ways in October, when coal shortages and transit restrictions imposed by Switzerland helped to cause a 50% drop in the number of trucks routed through that country to the Reich.

The ding-dong battle between Allied air attack on German rail communications in northern Italy and the German railway repair organisation naturally included the use of the Po crossings. Due to the shrinking potential of the railways this river and its canals had now to carry an increasing volume of industrial traffic, in addition to military supplies; for example the 35,000 tons of coal, ores, foodstuffs and other goods which were thus transported in October represented a 50% rise on September's performance. The numbers of the many vessels on the Po and of its numerous crossing places are unknown, but in being forced to offset the loss of bridges across the river by resorting to every conceivable alternative form of transport the Germans offered more of the types of target which the fighter-bombers could attack—barges, canal locks and other facilities—with either bombing or strafing or both.

A valuable addition to the destruction and damage caused by Allied air attack to enemy rail communications were the attacks by the Italian Partisans.[246] On 29th September they blew up a bridge about two miles south of Padua (*see Map 4*). On 14th October they mined the Verona–Vicenza railway line bringing traffic to a standstill, thus enabling them to blow up a leave train, killing 11 Germans and wounding many more. Then, on 16th October, the Partisans cut the Vicenza–Padua line in nine places with explosives, and on the 20th they blew up bridges on tracks north and northeast of Legnago.

Ways and means of intensifying Allied air action against the enemy's supply lines were constantly sought, and towards the end of October H.Q. M.A.A.F. approved a plan to destroy the power stations and electrical system in the Brenner Pass. It was given the code-name Operation 'Bingo' and will be described in Part III of this Volume Chapter XVI.

We have already described in some detail the direct air support afforded 5th and 8th Armies during the various stages of their offensives. Whereas, *in toto*, direct air support had shown a bias towards 8th Army in the previous period, it was much more evenly balanced during the current period.[247] Surprisingly 8th Army still attracted the greater share although 5th Army were leading the Army Group offensive. The figures show:

	Sorties (bombloads in brackets)	
	5th Army	8th Army
M.A.S.A.F. (Heavy day bombers)	697 (1,135.0)	
M.A.T.A.F. (Medium day bombers)	318 (517.3)	29 (51.7)
D.A.F. (Medium day and light day and night bombers, and fighter-bombers)	1,015 (317.9)	5,120 (2,250.1)
U.S. XXII T.A.C. (light day and night bombers, and fighter bombers)	2,182 (1,120.0)	404 (176.4)
	4,212 (3,090.2)	5,553 (2,478.2)

Compared with the previous four weeks there was in the battle area a noticeable proportionate increase in the weight of bombs dropped on railway targets, roads, motor transports and dumps, as against such operational targets as guns and troops. This change was dictated by the nature of the terrain over which the fighting was taking place.*

During this period several changes took place in the control, direction and means of giving direct air support to the Allied armies, and in the control of army/air support. In Chapter XIII we noted that the tangled story of the Mobile Operations Room Units was sorted out by 25th September. We also described the new areas of responsibility governing air attacks on enemy communications which were laid down in M.A.T.A.F.'s directive of 12th September, to which minor amendments were made on 24th September, and again on 9th October.[248] (One wonders if those responsible really understood the confusion such an excessive issue of instructions was likely to cause in wings and squadrons, and not least to pilots wrestling with much altered maps in the cramped cockpits of aircraft.)

As regards the control of army/air support, the co-location of Advanced Air H.Q. D.A.F. with Main H.Q. 8th Army led to the demise of 2/5 A.A.S.C. on 31st October, and in its place the G(Air) Staff was formed in H.Q. 8th Army with 1 Air Support Signals Unit to provide the specialist air communications previously operated by 2/5 A.A.S.C. The new Air Support Signals Unit (A.S.S.U.) became an integral part of H.Q. 8th Army and was manned entirely by soldiers. The G(Air) Staff was a combined Army/R.A.F. organisation. On the same day No. 7 A.A.S.C. which had

---

* The approximate numbers of sorties flown against and bombloads dropped on targets in Italy, other than ports, during the period dawn 22nd September to dawn 1st November are given in Table III at the end of this chapter. (See also Chapter XIII Table III).

supported No. 2/5 A.A.S.C. with its personnel and tentacles was also disbanded.

A considerable loss in fire-power and bombload resulted when the Cabrank missions controlled by Rover Joe* were reduced on 19th September from six to four aircraft, but this was more than made good on the 27th when Thunderbolt fighter-bombers replaced Spitfire fighter-bombers on this task. The Thunderbolt carried twice the bombload of the Spitfire as well as six Rocket Projectiles.

Another development in army air support techniques was the introduction of an airborne controller. He flew in a light observation aircraft during the period of operations and gave the attacking pilots last minute briefings. A secondary duty was the tactical reconnaissance. The system was known as 'Horsefly', and, though similar in some respects to methods used by D.A.F. to indicate targets, it was not a great success. Maintenance of communication and the briefing of pilots from a moving platform was extremely difficult.

During October M.A.A.F. continued to decline, but its losses were confined mainly to M.A.C.A.F. whose reduction in maritime strength will be described in Part III of this Volume Chapter XVII.

On the German side of the Air coin, shortage of fuel rather than scarcity of aircraft proved to be the limiting factor in Ritter von Pohl's operations.[249] *OKL* decreed in October that half von Pohl's available fuel must be returned to Germany. This resulted in the training and operations of the Italian Republican Air Force's torpedo bombers being stopped and the *Luftwaffe's* reconnaissance effort being reduced by a third. An even more distressing trend from von Pohl's point of view was the syphoning off of surplus *Luftwaffe* manpower to reinforce the German Armies. At the end of August he had 100,000 men including 11,000 Italians. By the end of October 24,000 of his Germans had been transferred to the Army for front line duty in Italy and elsewhere.

German aircraft losses reflect the relative levels of activity and numbers of aircraft available between *OB Südwest's* and *OB Südost's* areas of operations.[250] In the 40 days from dawn 22nd September to dawn 1st November they were as shown in the table on page 453. In addition 12 aircraft, including 4 Ju. 52s, were destroyed on the ground by land forces, presumably Partisans. *Südost* thus lost 111 aircraft including 64 valuable Ju. 52 troop transports.

That the *Luftwaffe* in Italy still retained a sting was confirmed on 19th October, when of 30 Marauders from M.A.T.A.F. attacking a

---

* See Chapter XIII p.236.

	Südwest	Südost		Total
		Ju. 52s	Others	
Missing	2	10	14	26
In the air	2	5	13	20
On the ground	2	44	11	57
Unspecified	1	1	1	3
	7	60	39	106

causeway west of Mantua, two were shot down and one failed to return after an attack by 10–15 Me. 109s.[251] Claims for two Me. 109s shot down and three probably shot down cannot be confirmed from available records.

TABLE II

M.A.A.F. (INCLUDING MALTA BUT EXCLUDING H.Q., R.A.F.,
M.E.) DISTRIBUTION OF BOMBER AND FIGHTER-BOMBER
SORTIES AND BOMBLOADS DAWN 22nd SEPTEMBER
TO DAWN 1st NOVEMBER 1944
(EXCLUDING ANTI-SHIPPING OPERATIONS
AND ATTACKS ON PORTS)

Aircraft	Within the battle area	North of the battle area	Elsewhere than Italy
H.B. (Day)	697 (1,135.0)	1,001 (2,218.5)	5,100 (10,615.9) *
H.B. (Night)	Nil	78 (248.6)	128 (403.6) †
M.B. (Day)	567 (943.1)	2,723 (4,321.8)	102 (108.1)‡
M.B. (Night)	Nil	302 (688.9)	348 (775.2)§
L.B. (Day)	473 (367.6)	125 (101.1)	79 (64.0)
L.B. (Night)	192 (143.7)	248 (198.6)	Nil
F.B. (Day)	7,836 (2,979.0)	2,879 (1,268.5)	248 (65.9)
TOTALS	9,765 (5,568.4)	7,356 (9,046.0)	6,005 (12,032.7)

GRAND TOTAL   23,126 (26,647.1)

* Excludes 68 supply-dropping sorties to France; and 12 sorties flown on special missions and evacuation.
† Excludes 89 supply-dropping sorties (85 sorties to Yugoslavia, one sortie to Poland and three to northern Italy); excludes 84 flare-dropping sorties on bombing missions; excludes 4 mine-laying sorties to the Danube and 4 in Greek waters.
‡ Excludes 117 supply-dropping sorties to Yugoslavia (Wellingtons by day).
§ Excludes 17 mine-laying sorties to the Danube.

APPENDIX I

Principal Commanders
and Staff Officers
in the Mediterranean
and Middle East
May 1944–May 1945

ROYAL NAVY

Commander-in-Chief Mediterranean: Admiral Sir John H. D. Cunningham

Chief of Staff: Rear-Admiral J. G. L. Dundas; Rear-Admiral H. A. Packer (from 25th August, 1944)

Flag Officer Gibraltar and Mediterranean Approaches: Admiral Sir Harold M. Burrough; Rear-Admiral V. A. C. Crutchley (from 14th January, 1945)

Flag Officer Western Mediterranean (appointment created 9th July, 1944): Vice-Admiral G. J. A. Miles

Flag Officer Western Italy (became Flag Officer Northern Area Mediterranean on 25th October, 1944): Rear-Admiral J. A. V. Morse

Flag Officer Tunisia: Admiral Sir Gerald Dickens; Vice-Admiral Sir Herbert Fitzherbert (from 30th April, 1944)

Vice-Admiral Malta and Flag Officer Central Mediterranean: Vice-Admiral Sir Louis H. K. Hamilton; Vice-Admiral Sir Frederick H. G. Dalrymple-Hamilton (from April, 1945)

Flag Officer Taranto, Adriatic and Liaison (Italy): Rear-Admiral C. E. Morgan

Flag Officer Levant and Eastern Mediterranean: Vice-Admiral Sir. H. Bernard Rawlings; Vice-Admiral Sir William G. Tennant (from 30th October, 1944)

Rear-Admiral Commanding 15th Cruiser Squadron: Rear-Admiral J. M. Mansfield

Commodore Commanding 15th Cruiser Squadron: Commodore M. J. Mansergh (from 23rd March, 1945)

Commanding Officer Inshore Squadrons: Rear-Admiral H. H. Bousfield: Captain I. C. T. Wynne (from January (1945)

Captain Coastal Forces Mediterranean: Captain J. S. Stevens

Captain (Minesweepers) Mediterranean: Captain J. W. Boutwood; Captain R. C. V. Ross (from January, 1945)

Rear-Admiral Escort Carriers: Rear-Admiral A. W. La T. Bisset; Rear-Admiral T. Troubridge (from 28th July, 1944)

UNITED STATES

Commander. U.S. Naval Forces Northwest African Waters: Vice-Admiral H. Kent Hewitt, U.S.N.

OPERATION 'DRAGOON'

Commander Naval Task Force: Vice-Admiral H. Kent Hewitt, U.S.N.

Commander Alpha Attack Group: Rear-Admiral F. J. Lowry, U.S.N.

   Fire Support: Rear-Admiral C. F. Bryant, U.S.N.

Commander Delta Attack Group: Rear-Admiral B. J. Rodgers, U.S.N.

   Fire Support: Contre Admiral R. Jaujard, French Navy

Commander Sitka Attack Group (and Fire Support): Rear-Admiral L. A. Davidson, U.S.N.

   Transports and Combat Loaders: Commodore Edgar, U.S.N.

Commander Camel Attack Group: Rear-Admiral D. P. Moon, U.S.N. (died 5th August, 1944); Rear-Admiral S. S. Lewis, U.S.N. (from 5th August, 1944)

   Fire-Support: Rear-Admiral M. L. Deyo, U.S.N.

Commander Carrier Task Force: Rear-Admiral T. Troubridge, R.N.

   Second in Command: Rear-Admiral C. T. Durgin, U.S.N.

THE ARMY

The reader is referred also to Lieutenant-Colonel H. F. Joslen: *Orders of Battle* Volumes I and II, H.M.S.O. 1960)

Allied Force Headquarters

Supreme Allied Commander, Mediterranean Theatre: General Sir Henry Maitland Wilson; Field-Marshal the Honourable Sir Harold Alexander (from 12th December 1944)

Deputy Supreme Allied Commander-in-Chief: Lieutenant-General Jacob L. Devers; Lieutenant-General Joseph T. McNarney (from 22nd October 1944)

Principal Staff Officers

Chief of Staff: Lieutenant-General Sir James Gammell; Lieutenant-General Sir John Harding (from 16th December 1944). Lieutenant-General W. D. Morgan (from 6th March 1945)

Chief Administrative Officers

United States

Commanding General N.A.T.O.U.S.A., later changed to M.T.O.U.S.A. (Mediterranean Theatre of Operations, U.S. Army) Lieutenant-Generals Devers, then McNarney (see above)

Commanding General, Services of Supply M.T.O.U.S.A.: Major-General Thomas B. Larkin

British

Chief Administrative Officer: Lieutenant-General J. G. W. Clark; Lieutenant-General Sir Brian Robertson (from 16th December 1944)

Allied Armies Italy

Commander-in-Chief: General the Honourable Sir Harold Alexander*
(**Alexander's promotion to Field-Marshal was back-dated to the capture of Rome.*)

Principal Staff Officers:
Chief of the General Staff: Lieutenant-General A. F. (from June 1944 Sir John) Harding
Major-General Administration: Major-General Sir Brian Robertson

On 16th December 1944 this headquarters was replaced by:

15th Army Group

Commanding General: Lieutenant-General Mark W. Clark
Chief of Staff: Major-General Alfred M. Gruenther

8th Army

General Officer Commanding: Lieutenant-General Sir Oliver Leese; Lieutenant-General Sir Richard McCreery (from 1st October 1944)

Principal Staff Officers:
Chief of Staff: Major-General G. P. Walsh; Brigadier Sir Henry Floyd (from 18th October 1944)
Administration, D.A. & Q.M.G.: Brigadier E. M. Bastyan; Brigadier G. F. H. Stayner (from 18th October 1944)

5th U.S. Army

Commanding General: Lieutenant-General Mark W. Clark; Lieutenant-General Lucian K. Truscott (from 16th December 1944)

7th U.S. Army
(Operation 'Anvil/Dragoon')

Commanding General: Lieutenant-General Alexander M. Patch
Commander French Army B: General de Lattre de Tassigny

Land Forces Adriatic

Commander Land Forces Adriatic: Brigadier G. M. O. Davy

British Forces in Greece

General Officer Commanding Land Forces Greece becoming *Commander-in-Chief Land Forces and Military Liaison (Greece) 17th December 1944:* Lieutenant-General R. M. Scobie
General Officer Commanding Military Command Athens: Lieutenant-General J. L. I. Hawkesworth (from 17th December 1944)

French Forces in Italy

Commander French Expeditionary Corps: General Alphonse Juin

Polish Forces in Italy

Commander 2nd Polish Corps: General W. Anders
Acting Corps Commander: Major-General Z. Bohusz-Szyszko (March to April 1945)

The Middle East Command

Commander-in-Chief The Middle East Forces: General Sir Bernard Paget

Note: The names of subordinate formation commanders have been mentioned in the text and are not included here.

ROYAL AIR FORCE AND UNITED STATES ARMY AIR FORCE

MEDITERRANEAN ALLIED AIR FORCES

Command Headquarters

Air Commander-in-Chief: *Lieutenant-General Ira C. Eaker, U.S.A.A.F.; *Lieutenant-General John K. Cannon, U.S.A.A.F. (from 24th March, 1945)

(**Also Commanding General Army Air Forces, Mediterranean Theatre of Operations*)

Deputy Air Commander-in-Chief: *Air Marshal Sir John C. Slessor; *Air Marshal Sir A. Guy R. Garrod (from 16th March, 1945)

(**Also Air Officer Commanding-in-Chief Royal Air Force, Mediterranean and Middle East, and, additionally, responsible for Royal Air Force operations in the Middle East beyond the Mediterranean area.*)

Deputy Air Officer Commanding-in-Chief Royal Air Force, Mediterranean and Middle East: Air Marshal Sir John Linnell (Post abolished and 'Chief of Staff' substituted on 1st July, 1944)

Chief of Staff, Royal Air Force, Mediterranean and Middle East: Air Vice-Marshal G. B. A. Baker (from 1st July, 1944)

No. 216 (Ferry and Transport) Group, R.A.F.: Air Commodore Whitney W. Straight

Mediterranean Allied Strategic Air Force

Commanding General: *Lieutenant-General Nathan F. Twining, U.S.A.A.F. (**Also Commanding General of the United States Fifteenth Air Force, the U.S.A.A.F. element of M.A.S.A.F.*)

No. 205 Group, R.A.F.(Under the operational control of M.A.S.A.F. of which it formed the R.A.F. element): Air Commodore J. H. I. Simpson; Brigadier J. T. Durrant, S.A.A.F. (from 3rd August, 1944); Air Commodore A. McKee (from 7th May, 1945)

Mediterranean Allied Coastal Air Force

Air Officer Commanding: Air Vice-Marshal Sir Hugh P. Lloyd; Air Vice-Marshal John Whitford (from 1st November, 1944)

No. 210 Group, R.A.F. (Re-formed under M.A.C.A.F. on 6th July, 1944. Came under A.H.Q. Malta on 20th October, 1944. Disbanded on 25th April, 1945): Air Commodore J. H. Edwardes-Jones: Group Captain D. D. G. Keddie (from 27th October, 1944)

Air Headquarters, Malta (Placed directly under H.Q. M.A.A.F. on 1st February, 1945): Air Vice-Marshal R. M. Foster; Air Vice-Marshal K. B. Lloyd (from 19th October, 1944)

No. 242 Group, R.A.F. (Group disbanded on 14th September, 1944): Air Commodore G. Harcourt-Smith; Group Captain R. W. M. Clarke (from 30th August, 1944)

United States XII Fighter Command (Transferred to M.A.T.A.F. on 20th September, 1944): Brigadier General Edward M. Morris, U.S.A.A.F.; Brigadier General Benjamin W. Chidlaw, U.S.A.A.F. (from 12th September, 1944)

Mediterranean Allied Tactical Air Force

Commanding General: *Major-General John K. Cannon, U.S.A.A.F.; *Major-General Benjamin W. Chidlaw, U.S.A.A.F. (from 5th April, 1945)

(**Also Commanding General of the United States Twelfth Air Force. Major-General Benjamin W. Chidlaw, U.S.A.A.F. became Commanding General on 2nd April, 1945*)

Desert Air Force

Air Officer Commanding: Air Vice-Marshal Harry Broadhurst; Air Vice-Marshal William F. Dickson (from 6th April, 1944); Air Vice-Marshal R. M. Foster (from 3rd December, 1944)

United States XII Support Command (Title changed to 'United States XII Tactical Air Command' on 15th April, 1944. Control of U.S. XII T.A.C. passed to U.S. Ninth Air Force supporting Operation 'Overlord' on 15th September, 1944)

Commanding General: Brigadier General Gordon P. Saville, U.S.A.A.F.; Brigadier General Glenn O. Barcus, U.S.A.A.F. (from 29th January, 1945)

United States 'X' Tactical Air Command (Formed on 20th September, 1944. Replaced the same day by H.Q. U.S. XII Fighter Command on the latter's transfer from M.A.C.A.F. to M.A.T.A.F. Title 'U.S. XII Fighter Command' changed to 'U.S. XXII Tactical Air Command' on 19th October, 1944)

Commanding General: Brigadier General Benjamin W. Chidlaw, U.S.A.A.F.; Brigadier General Thomas C. Darcy, U.S.A.A.F. (from 6th April, 1945)

Mediterranean Allied Photographic Reconnaissance Wing

(*Ceased to function as an Allied formation on 1st October, 1944, when the U.S. 90th Photographic Reconnaissance Wing was withdrawn, leaving No. 336 Wing R.A.F. to undertake the duties previously undertaken by M.A.P.R.W. for the R.A.F.*)

Commanding General: Colonel Karl L. Polifka, U.S.A.A.F.

United States 51st Troop Carrier Wing

Commanding General: Brigadier General Timothy J. Manning

Balkan Air Force
(Formed 1st June, 1944)

Air Officer Commanding: Air Vice-Marshal William A. Elliot; Air Vice-Marshal George H. Mill (from 17th February, 1945)

Air Headquarters, Greece
(Formed as 'Air Headquarters X' on 1st September, 1944. Became Air Headquarters, Greece on 15th October, 1944)

Air Officer Commanding: Air Commodore G. Harcourt-Smith; Air Commodore Geoffrey W. Tuttle (from 12th October, 1944)

HEADQUARTERS, ROYAL AIR FORCE, MIDDLE EAST

Air Officer Commanding-in-Chief: Air Marshal Sir Keith R. Park; Air Marshal Sir Charles E. H. Medhurst (from 8th February, 1945)

Senior Air Staff Officer: Air Vice-Marshal S. E. Toomer; Air Vice-Marshal Sir Brian E. Baker (from 30th April, 1945)

Air Officer-in-Charge Administration: Air Vice-Marshal E. B. C. Betts

No. 203 Group, R.A.F. (Group disbanded on 1st March, 1945, and merged with Air Headquarters, Eastern Mediterranean): Air Vice-Marshal M. L. Taylor

Air Headquarters, Eastern Mediterranean

Air Officer Commanding: Air Vice-Marshal T. A. Langford-Sainsbury; Air Vice-Marshal S. E. Toomer (from 5th May, 1945)

No. 209 Group, R.A.F. (Group disbanded on 15th November, 1944): Group Captain R. C. F. Lister; Wing Commander E. F. Tonge (from 28th July, 1944); Wing Commander J. E. Hibbert (from 9th October, 1944)

No. 210 Group, R.A.F. (Group disbanded in April and re-formed in M.A.C.A.F. on 6th July, 1944): Group Captain E. W. Whitley (until disbandment in April, 1944)

No. 212 Group, R.A.F. (Disbanded on unknown date): Air Commodore Norman S. Allison; Group Captain J. W. A. Hunnard (from 28th July, 1944)
(Re-formed in A.H.Q., Eastern Mediterranean on 15th February, 1945): Group Captain C. S. Riccard (from 8th March, 1945)

No. 219 Group, R.A.F. (Group disbanded on 27th July, 1944): Group Captain The Hon. Maxwell Aitken

Air Headquarters, Egypt
(Re-formed 10th October, 1944)

Air Officer Commanding: *Air Vice-Marshal T. A. Langford-Sainsbury; Air Commodore A. J. Rankin (from 26th March, 1945)
(*Also Air Officer Commanding Air Headquarters, Eastern Mediterranean)

Air Headquarters, Levant

Air Officer Commanding: Air Commodore J. P. Coleman; Air Commodore H. D. McGregor (from 26th November, 1944)

Air Headquarters, Iraq and Persia

Air Officer Commanding: Air Vice-Marshal A. P. Davidson; Air Vice-Marshal R. A. George (from 3rd December, 1944)

Headquarters, British Forces, Aden

Air Officer Commanding: Air Vice-Marshal F. H. Macnamara; Air Vice-Marshal H. T. Lydford (from 12th March, 1945)

Air Headquarters, East Africa

Air Officer Commanding: Air Vice-Marshal H. S. Kerby; Air Vice-Marshal Sir Brian E. Baker (from 17th November, 1944); Brigadier H. G. Wilmott, S.A.A.F. (from 24th April, 1945)

MAINTENANCE

Royal Air Force

No. 206 (Maintenance) Group, R.A.F. (Middle East): Air Commodore P. Slocombe; Air Commodore F. E. Vernon (from 10th June, 1944)

No. 214 (Maintenance) Group, R.A.F. (Italy): Air Commodore G. F. Smylie; Air Commodore P. Slocombe (from 28th December, 1944)

No. 218 (Maintenance) Group, R.A.F. (North West Africa): Air Commodore E. L. Ridley; Group Captain J. F. Young (from 8th January, 1945); Air Commodore H. I. T. Beardsworth (from 14th February, 1945)

APPENDIX 2

Appointments Held by Some German Commanders and Staff Officers May 1944–May 1945

(Some Temporary and Acting Appointments Omitted)

ALTENSTADT, Colonel Schmidt von; Chief of Staff 14th Panzer Corps until June 1944

BEELITZ, Colonel Dietrich: on Kesselring's staff until November 1944, then C.O.S. *AOK 10*

BLASKOWITZ, Colonel-General Johannes von; commander Army Group G in southern France in summer of 1944

DÖNITZ, Grand Admiral Karl; Commander-in-Chief German Navy since January 1943; President of the Reich after Hitler's suicide on 30th April 1945

DOSTLER, General Anton: commander 73rd Corps

FEUERSTEIN, General Valentin: commander 51st Mountain Corps until March 1945

GARTMAYR, Colonel Georg: C.O.S. 51st Mountain Corps from September 1944

GÖRING, Marshal of the Reich Hermann: Commander-in-Chief German Air Force

GRAFFEN, Lieutenant-General Karl von: acting commander 76th Panzer Corps, end of April 1945

HARTMANN, General Otto: acting commander 14th Panzer Corps 17th April–17th May 1944

HAUCK, Lieutenant-General Friedrich-Wilhelm: commander 305th Infantry Division since 1943; acting commander 76th Panzer Corps, November 1944; commander 51st Mountain Corps from March 1945

HAUSER, Major-General Wolf: C.O.S. *AOK 14* until February 1945

HEIDRICH, Lieutenant-General Richard: commander 1st Parachute Division since 1943; commander 1st Parachute Corps from November 1944

HERR, General Traugott: commander 76th Panzer Corps until November 1944; acting commander *AOK 14*, December 1944; commander *AOK 10* from 16th February 1945

HOFER, Franz: Gauleiter of Tyrol-Vorarlberg, and Senior Commissar of Alpine Foreland operational zone, northern Italy

JODL, Colonel-General Alfred: Chief of Operations Branch, *OKW*

KEITEL, Field Marshal Wilhelm: Chief of *OKW*

463

KESSELRING, Field-Marshal Albert: Commander-in-Chief Southwest and Army Group C until March 1945 (absent on sick leave 23rd October 1944–15th January 1945); C.-in-C. West from 10th March 1945, and by 26th April 1945 in control also of operations in Italy and the Balkans, as C.-in-C. South

KLINCKOWSTRÖM, Colonel Karl-Heinrich Graf von: C.O.S. 51st Mountain Corps until August 1944

KRASA, Colonel: C.O.S. 14th Panzer Corps from autumn of 1944

KÜBLER, General Ludwig: commander 97th Corps

LEMELSEN, General Joachim: commander *AOK 14* 7th June–24th October 1944, and again from 17th February 1945; in interim, acting commander *AOK 10*

LÖHR, Colonel-General Alexander: commander Army Group E from August 1943, also C.-in-C. Southeast from 25th March 1945

LÖWISCH, Admiral Werner: German Naval Command Italy from July 1944

MACKENSEN, Colonel-General Eberhard von: commander *AOK 14* until 7th June 1944

POHL, General Maxmilian Ritter von: Commanding General of the German Air Force in central Italy from April 1944

RAINER, Dr Friedrich: Gauleiter of Salzburg and Carinthia, and Senior Commissar of Adriatic Coastland operational zone, northern Italy

RÖTTIGER, General Hans: C.O.S. to C.-in-C. Southwest and Army Group C from 6th June 1944

RUNKEL, Colonel: C.O.S. 76th Panzer Corps until February 1945, then C.O.S. *AOK 14*

SCHLEMM, General Alfred: commander 1st Parachute Corps January–November 1944

SCHLEMMER, General Johann: commander 75th Corps from September 1944

SCHULZ, General Friedrich: commander Army Group G in April 1945, and nominal C.-in-C. Southwest 30th April–2nd May 1945

SCHWEINITZ, Colonel Viktor von: Intelligence Officer HQ Army Group C, and co-signatory of the Instrument of Surrender of the German Armed Forces in Italy, 29th April 1945

SCHWERIN, Lieutenant-General Gerhard Graf von: commander 76th Panzer Corps from December 1944

SENGER UND ETTERLIN, General Fridolin von: commander 14th Panzer Corps

TIPPELSKIRCH, General Kurt von: acting commander *AOK 14*, January 1945

VIETINGHOFF, Colonel-General Heinrich-Gottfried von: commander *AOK 10* until October 1944; acting C.-in-C. Southwest 24th October–15th January 1945; commander Army Group Kurland January–March 1945; C.-in-C. Southwest from 10th March 1945

WEICHS, Field-Marshal Maxmilian Freiherr von: Commander-in-Chief Southeast and Army Group F until March 1945

WENNER, SS Major Eugen; adjutant to General Wolff, and co-signatory of the Instrument of Surrender of the German Armed Forces in Italy, 29th April 1945

WENTZELL, Major-General Friedrich: C.O.S. *AOK 10* until November 1944; C.O.S. Army Group G from March 1945

WESTPHAL, General Siegfried: C.O.S. to C.-in-C. Southwest and Army Group C until 23rd May 1944; C.O.S. to C.-in-C. West from September 1944

WOLFF, General of the Waffen SS Karl: Senior SS and Police Commander in Italy

ZANGEN, General Gustav-Adolf von: commander of Armeegruppe von Zangen in northern Italy until July 1944

ZIEGLER, General Heinz; acting commander *AOK 14* October–November 1944 (wounded)

APPENDIX 3

Operational Code Names Mentioned in Part II of Volume VI

ALLIED

'Anvil'	Allied invasion of southern France, 15th August 1944, re-named 'Dragoon' 1st August 1944
'Bingo'	Air operation to destroy power stations and electrical system in the Brenner Pass, 6th November 1944
'Brassard'	A.F.H.Q. plan to attack Elba, using French troops, launched 17th June 1944
'Diadem'	Allied Spring offensive and advance on Rome, 11th May 1944
'Dracula'	Operation to capture Rangoon, spring 1945
'Dragoon'	Allied invasion of southern France, 15th August 1944, known as 'Anvil' until 1st August 1944
'Ferdinand'	Strategic deception plan for 'Anvil'
'Husky'	Allied invasion of Sicily, 10th July 1943
'Mallory/Mallory Major'	Destruction of the Po bridges by air action, 27th July 1944
'Manna'	British operation to re-establish Greek Government in Athens, 15th October 1944
'Market Garden'	Operation to seize crossings over Maas and Rhine, 17th September 1944
'Noah's Ark'	Plan to harass German troops in the event of a withdrawal from Crete, the Aegean Islands and Greece, summer 1944
'Octagon'	The Second Quebec Conference, September 1944
'Olive'	8th Army's assault on the Gothic Line, 25th August 1944
'Ottrington'	Deception plan for attack on the Gothic Line, initiated July 1944
'Overlord'	Allied invasion of Normandy, 6th June 1944
'Pancake'	Air operation to reduce German defences around Bologna, 12th October 1944
'Pointblank'	Combined Bomber Offensive against Germany from the United Kingdom and Italy

'Rankin'	Outline plans to exploit a German collapse
'Ratweek'	Co-ordinated attack on German communications in Yugoslavia by Balkan Air Force and Y.A.N.L., 1st September 1944
'Sesame'	Air neutralisation of selected strongpoints in the Gothic Line, 9th September 1944
'Sextant'	The Cairo Conference, November–December 1943
'Shingle'	6th U.S. Corps' landing at Anzio, 22nd January 1944
'Strangle'	Air operation to destroy German rail, road and sea communications south of the line Pisa–Rimini, March–May 1944
'Tolstoy'	The Moscow Conference, October 1944
'Ulster'	Deception plan for attack on the Gothic Line, initiated 14th August 1944, replacing 'Ottrington'

GERMAN

Feuerzauber	Operation to demolish bridges over the Arno in Florence (Ponte Vecchio excluded), 3rd August 1944
Herbstnebel	Planning for strategic withdrawal of Army Group C to and beyond the Po, first mooted August 1944

APPENDIX 4

Abbreviations

(Some standard British usages omitted, also abbreviations
of regiments whose full titles appear in the Text and Index)

A.A.	Anti-aircraft
A.A.I.	Allied Armies in Italy
A.A.S.C.	Army Air Support Control
A.C.I.G.S.	Assistant Chief of Imperial General Staff
A.C.G.	Airfield Construction Group
A.F.H.Q.	Allied Force Headquarters
A.F.V.	Armoured Fighting Vehicle
A.G.P.A.	Army Group Polish Artillery
A.G.R.A.	Army Group Royal Artillery
A.G.R.C.A.	Army Group Royal Canadian Artillery
A.G.R.E.	Army Group Royal Engineers
A.H.Q., E.M.	Air Headquarters, Eastern Mediterranean
A.I.	Airborne Interception (radar)
A.L.G.	Advanced Landing Ground
A.M.L.	Allied Military Liaison Headquarters (Balkans)
A.O.C.	Air Officer Commanding
AOK	Army Headquarters
A.O.P.	Air Observation Post
ARK	Modified tank used for bridging
A.R.V.	Armoured Recovery Vehicle
A.S.S.U.	Air Support Signals Unit
A.S.V.	Air to Surface Vessel (radar)
A/Tk	Anti-Tank
AVRE	Assault Vehicle Royal Engineers
B.A.F.	Balkan Air Force
B.G.S.	Brigadier General Staff
C.A.C.	Canadian Armoured Corps
C.A.O.	Chief Administration Officer
C.C.	Combat Command (A or B) (U.S. Army)
C.C.R.A.	Commander, Corps Royal Artillery
C.C.R.E.	Commander, Corps Royal Engineers
C.C.S.	Combined Chiefs of Staff
C.G.S.	Chief of General Staff
C.G.	Commanding General
C.I.G.S.	Chief of Imperial General Staff
C.I.L.	Italian Corps of Liberation
C.L.N.A.I.	Committee of National Liberation for Northern Italy
C.M.F.	Central Mediterranean Forces

C.O.	Commanding Officer
C.O.M.E.C.	Commodore, Escort Carriers
C.O.S.	Chief(s) of Staff
C.R.A.	Commander, Royal Artillery
C.R.E.M.E.	Commander, Royal Electrical and Mechanical Engineers
D.A. and Q.M.G.	Deputy Adjutant and Quarter-Master-General
D.A.F.	Desert Air Force
D.C.I.G.S.	Deputy Chief of Imperial General Staff
DERV	Diesel Engine Road Vehicles (type of fuel)
D.D.	Duplex Drive (amphibious tank)
Do.	Dornier (German aircraft)
D./S.A.C.	Deputy, Supreme Allied Commander
DUKW	Amphibious truck (name derived from factory serial initials)
E-boat	General term for German offensive torpedo craft
E.A.M.	National Liberation Front, in Greece
E.D.E.S.	Greek National Democratic League
E.L.A.S.	Greek People's Army of Liberation
E.P.	Police Branch of *E.A.M.*
F.B.	Fighter-bomber
F.C.P.	Forward Control Post
F.C.U.	Fighter Control Unit
F.D.L.	Forward Defended Locality
F.E.C.	French Expeditionary Corps
F.F.A.F.	Fighting French Air Force
FHW	Foreign Armies West (Intelligence Section at *OKH,* dealing with Europe)
F.O.L.E.M.	Flag Officer Levant and Eastern Mediterranean
F.O.O.	Forward Observation Officer
F.W.	Focke-Wulf (German aircraft)
G.A.F.	German Air Force
G.H.Q.	General Headquarters
G.O.C.	General Officer Commanding
G.R.	General Reconnaissance
G.R.T.	Gross Registered Tonnage
G.T.C.	General Transport Company
H.A.A.	Heavy Anti-Aircraft
H.A.C.	Honourable Artillery Company
H.B.	Heavy bomber
H.D.M.L.	Harbour Defence Motor Launch
He.	Heinkel (German aircraft)
H.E.	High Explosive
How	Howitzer
I.A.C.	Indian Armoured Corps
I.A.F.	Italian Air Force (co-belligerent)
I boat	Infantry landing craft (German)
I.R.A.F.	Italian Republican Air Force
J.A.N.L.	See Y.A.N.L.

J.I.C.	Joint Intelligence Committee
J.P.S.	Joint Planning Staff
Ju.	Junker (German aircraft)
K.K.E.	Communist Party of Greece
KwK	Tank gun (German)
K.T.	War Transport vessel (German)
L.A.A.	Light Anti-Aircraft
L.B.	Light Bomber
L.C.A.	Landing Craft Assault
L.C.I.(L)	Landing Craft Infantry (Large)
L.C.T.	Landing Craft Tank
L.C.T.(R)	Landing Craft Tank (Rocket)
L.F. and M.L.(G)	Land Forces and Military Liaison (Greece)
L.F.A.	Land Forces Adriatic
L.I.	Light Infantry
L. of C.	Lines of Communication
L.R.D.G.	Long Range Desert Group
L.S.I.	Landing Ship Infantry
L.S.T.	Landing Ship Tank
L.V.T.	Landing Vehicle Tracked
M.A.A.F.	Mediterranean Allied Air Forces
M.A.C.A.F.	Mediterranean Allied Coastal Air Force
M.A.P.R.W.	Mediterranean Allied Photographic Reconnaissance Wing
M.A.S.A.F.	Mediterranean Allied Strategic Air Force
M.A.T.A.F.	Mediterranean Allied Tactical Air Force
M-boat	Steam-propelled minesweeper (German)
M.B.	Medium Bomber
M.C.A.	Military Command Athens
Me.	Messerschmitt (German aircraft)
M.E.F,	Middle East Forces
M.F.P.	Naval Ferry Barge (German)
M.G.	Machine Gun
M.G.B.	Motor gunboat
Mk	Mark (of equipment)
M.L.	Motor Launch
MNL	Naval supply lighter (German)
M.O.R.U.	Mobile Operations Room Unit
M.T.	Mechanical Transport
M.T.B.	Motor torpedo-boat
M.V.	Motor Vessel
M/Y	Marshalling-yard
OB	Commander-in-Chief
OKH	High Command of the German Army
OKM	High Command of the German Navy
OKW	High Command of the German Armed Forces
OO	Operation Order
O.P.	Observation Post
ORB	Operations Record Book

Orbat	Order of Battle
O.S.S.	Office of Strategic Services
P.A.I.C.	Persia and Iraq Command
Pak	Anti-tank gun (German)
Pdr	Pounder (artillery shell weight)
PIAT	Projector Infantry Anti-Tank
POL	Petrol, Oil, and Lubricants
P.R.	Photographic Reconnaissance
PT Boat	Patrol Torpedo Boat (U.S. Navy)
Pz AOK	Panzer Army Headquarters
Pzkw	Tank (German)
R-boat	Motor minesweeper (German)
R.A.	Royal Artillery
R.A.A.F.	Royal Australian Air Force
R.A.C.	Royal Armoured Corps
R.A.F., M.E.D.M.E.	Royal Air Force, Mediterranean and Middle East
R.A.M.C.	Royal Army Medical Corps
R.A.O.C.	Royal Army Ordnance Corps
R.A.S.C.	Royal Army Service Corps
R.C.A.	Royal Canadian Artillery
R.C.E.	Royal Canadian Engineers
R.C.H.A.	Royal Canadian Horse Artillery
R.C.T.	Regimental Combat Team (U.S. Army)
RDF	Radio Direction Finding
R.E.	Royal Engineers
R.E.M.E.	Royal Electrical and Mechanical Engineers
R.H.A.	Royal Horse Artillery
R.P.	Rocket Projectile
R.p.g.p.d.	Rounds per gun per day
RSHA	Central Security Department of the Reich
S.A.A.F.	South African Air Force
S.A.C.	Supreme Allied Commander
S.A.E.C.	South African Engineer Corps
S.B.N.O.	Senior British Naval Officer
S.B.S.	Special Boat Squadron (later changed to Service)
S.D.	Special Duty
S.H.A.E.F.	Supreme Headquarters, Allied Expeditionary Force
S. and M.	Sappers and Miners (Indian Forces)
S.O.(M)	Special Operations, Mediterranean
S.O.E.	Special Operations Executive
S.P.	Self-propelled
Strat R.	Strategic reconnaissance
S.S.	Special Service
SS	Lit. protection or guard detachment. Para-military formation of the Nazi Party
TA boat	German torpedo boat (ex-Italian)
T.A.C.	Tactical Air Command

T.A.F.	Tactical Air Force
Tac. R.	Tactical Reconnaissance
UJ vessel	Anti-submarine escort craft (German)
U.S.A.A.F.	United States Army Air Force
U.S.S.T.A.F.	United States Strategic Air Forces
V.C.P.	Visual Control Post
WD	War Diary
W/T	Wireless Telegraphy
Y.A.N.L.	Yugoslav Army of National Liberation

VOLUME VI—PART II

CHAPTER IX

The Pursuit to Lake Trasimeno
(5th June–2nd July 1944)

1   See Part I of this Volume (HMSO 1984) Ch. VI p.312.
2   CAB 121/396 s.73 MEDCOS 125.
3   Ch. VI of this Volume pp.305–6 and Ernest F. Fisher: *Cassino to the Alps*, US Army in World War II, (Washington DC, 1977) p.228.
4   WO 214/33 (File II Part 1) s.29 AFHQ F49066 22.5.44.
5   *Ibid.* s.35 AFHQ 51131 7.6.44.
6   *Ibid.* MA1371 8.6.44.
7   WO 214/15 MA1364 7.6.44.
8   *Ibid.* MA1370 8.6.44. and MA1364 7.6.44. para 10.
9   CAB HIST AL 3000/F/Air/6 (Air Contribution by Gp Capt. Gleave) p.1.
10 ADM/NID Geographical Handbook Series: Italy Vol III Ch. XX and Appx V and Map AMS M592 GF US Army 1:200,000.
11 CAB 106/478 and 479. Fifth Army History Vols V and VI (Lt-Col. Chester G. Starr, Italy). Lt-Col. H. F. Joslen: *Orders of Battle* Vol I (HMSO 1960) Colonel P. Le Goyet: *La Participation Française à la Campagne d'Italie* (Ministère des Armées, Paris 1969) p.514.
12 WO 170/167 (8 Army G Main HQ WD) June 1944 Appx L. Lt-Col. H. F. Joslen: *Orders of Battle* Vol I *op.cit.* Lt-Col. G. W. L. Nicholson: *The Canadians in Italy* Vol II (Ottawa, 1956).
13 CAB EDS 18 Ch. 1 pp.16–17.
14 *Ibid.* Ch. 2 p.3 and Ch. 1 p.16.
15 *Ibid.* Ch. 2 p.3.
16 *Ibid.* p.17.
17 *Ibid.* p.6 and 15.
18 *Ibid.* Ch. 1 p.2.
19 *Ibid.* p.5.
20 *Ibid.* p.17.
21 CAB HIST AL 3000/F/Air/6 p.2.
22 *Ibid.* p.4.
23 *Ibid.* p.4, 9 and 13.
24 CAB HIST AL 3000/F/Air/7 p.13.
25 CAB HIST AL 3000/F/Air/6 p.2.
26 *Ibid.* p.4–5.

27 WO 204/10402 AAI Operation Order 1, 5.5.44.

28 CAB 106/707. Despatch by Field-Marshal Alexander: *The Allied Armies in Italy from 3 September 1943 to 12 December 1944* (The London Gazette 6.6.50). p.2931.

29 CAB 106/479 Fifth Army History Vol. VI Ch. II p.9–13.

30 CAB EDS 17 Ch.3 p.70.

31 WO 216/168 DO correspondence between Lt-Gen. Leese and ACIGS(O).

32 Fisher: *Cassino to the Alps op.cit.* p.237.

33 CAB 106/479 5th Army History Vol. VI pp.20–32 & 41.

34 *Ibid.* p.12 and 31.

35 WO 170/167 (8 Army G Ops Main WD) Narrative 5–9.6.44. and CAB 106/423 (AFHQ: Operations of British, Indian and Dominion Forces in Italy, hereafter referred to as OBIDFI) Ch.1 paras 13–18.

36 CAB 106/422 (OBIDFI) Section E para 27 *et seq.*

37 *Il Corpo Italiano di Liberazione, Aprile-Settembre 1944* (Ministry of Defence, Rome 1950) p.7, 60–2, and Appx 21.

38 CAB 106/644 History of 6 SA Armd Div in Italy, Oct 1942–May 1945, p.18–23.

39 CAB 106/418 (OBIDFI) para 48.

40 CAB 106/423 (OBIDFI) Ch. 1 paras 13–17. WO 170/437 (6 Armd Div WD) nararative 8–9.6.44. WO 170/167 Appx L, 8 Army Orbat of 16.6.44.

41 Hugh Williamson: *The Fourth Division 1939 to 1945.* (London 1951) pp.159–161.

42 WO 170/167 (8 Army G Ops Main WD) Narrative 5–9.6.44. and WO 169/18797 (8 Ind Div G WD) Log 5–9.6.44.

43 R. Kay: *Italy*, Official History of New Zealand in the Second World War, Vol.II (Wellington N.Z., 1967) pp.74–9.

44 *Ibid.* p.83.

45 CAB EDS 18 Ch.2 p.10.

46 D. Pal: *The Campaign in Italy*, Official History of the Indian Armed Forces in the Second World War (Calcutta 1960) pp.256–8 and Lt-Col. G. R. Stevens: *Fourth Indian Division* (Toronto Ontario Canada, 1948) pp.321–3.

47 CAB EDS 18 Ch.2 p.11 and fn (1).

48 WO 170/66 (AAI G Ops WD) AAI I Summary 48 of 8.6.44. and WO 170/203 (8 Army GSI WD) 8 Army I Summaries 739–741 6–10.6.44.

49 WO 214/33 (File II Part 2) s.13 CCS 3116 14.6.44.

50 *Ibid.* s.11 MA 1421 16.6.44.

51 CAB HIST AL/3000/F/36 Gen. Sir Oliver Leese: Unpublished memoirs Chapter 12 p.10.

52 *The Memoirs of Field-Marshal Montgomery* (London 1958) p.165.

53 WO 214/33 (File II Part 2) s.33 HQ AAI 0.2909 0900 hrs 7.6.44.

54 CAB EDS 18 Ch.1 p.4.

55 *Ibid.* pp.19–20.

56 *Ibid.* p.20.

57 *Ibid.* pp.19–22.

58 *Ibid.* p.23.
59 *Ibid.* p.24.
60 *Ibid.* p.25.
61 WO 170/341 (13 Corps G WD) Appx D4 13 Corps OO 24 8.6.44.
62 CAB 106/423 (OBIDFI) Ch.I paras 20–21.
63 CAB EDS 18 Ch.2 pp.16–20.
64 CAB 106/479 Fifth Army History Vol. VI pp.32–6.
65 CAB EDS 16 Ch.5 p.41.
66 CAB EDS 18 Ch.2 p.20.
67 *Ibid.* Ch.1 p.31.
68 CAB 106/479 Fifth Army History Vol. VI p.37.
69 *Ibid.* pp.41–6.
70 CAB HIST AL 3000/F/12. DFB: Study of War Diaries of 26 Armd Bde, and 11 & 38 Inf Bdes 14 June to 1 July 1944.
71 *Ibid.* Study of War Diaries of 26 Armd Bde p.5.
72 CAB 106/423 Ch.I paras 23–25 and CAB 106/644 History of 6 SA Armd Div pp.25–8.
73 WO 170/586 (24 Gds Bde WD) Log 10–13.6.44.
74 CAB EDS 18 Ch.2 p.19.
75 WO 170/167 (8 Army G Ops Main WD) Narrative 14.6.44.
76 CAB EDS 18 Ch.2 p.23.
77 WO 170/499 (78 Div G WD) Log 15.6.44. CAB 106/644 History of 6 SA Armd Div p.29.
78 WO 216/168 DO Correspondence between Lt-Gen. Leese and ACIGS(O) 16.6.44 and WO 170/167 (8 Army G Ops Main WD) 8 Army Op Instr 1425 16.6.44.
79 See, for example, C. Ray: *Algiers to Austria*, History of 78 Division (London 1952) pp.144–5. CAB 106/644 History of 6 SA Armd Div p.30, CAB HIST AL 3000/F/Air/6 p.7.
80 *Algiers to Austria op.cit.* p.144–5, CAB HIST AL 3000/F/12 Study of War Diaries of 11 and 38 Inf Bdes.
81 CAB 106/644 p.31–2.
82 WO 170/341 (13 Corps G WD) 13 Corps I Summary 420 19.6.44.
83 *Ibid.* I Summary 421 21.6.44.
84 CAB HIST AL 3000/F/12 Study of War Diaries of 11 and 38 Inf Bdes (78 Div) p.19.
85 WO 170/341 Appx D10 13 Corps OO 25 21.6.44.
86 CAB 106/423 (OBIDFI) Ch.I paras 26–9.
87 WO 170/305 (10 Corps G WD) and WO 170/437 (6 Armd Div WD) Narrative 9–11.6.44.
88 CAB 106/587 Report on the Operations of 8 Ind Div between Oct 1943–June 1945 Part I Ch.IX pp.10–11.
89 *Ibid.* and WO 170/167 (8 Army G Ops Main WD) Narrative 12–14.6.44.
90 WO 170/305 (10 Corps G WD) 10 Corps Op Instr 40 14.6.44.
91 CAB 106/423 (OBIDFI) Ch.I para 34.
92 CAB 106/587 Report on the Operations of 8 Ind Div Part I Ch.IX pp.11–12.
93 WO 170/305 Appx D5 & 6 and Log for 17.6.44.

94 CAB EDS 18 Ch.2 p.43.

95 WO 170/305 Log for 20.6.44.

96 CAB 44/143 (Major F. Jones: Central Italy April–August 1944) pp.305-7. *Il Corpo Italiano di Liberazione op.cit.* p.79.

97 CAB 44/143 p.449.

98 CAB 106/418 (OBIDFI) p.23.

99 CAB 106/422 (OBIDFI) Section E para 37.

100 CAB 106/435 (OBIDFI) pp.105-8.

101 CAB 106/418 (OBIDFI) p.23.

102 And Fisher: *Cassino to the Alps op.cit.* p.265-6. CAB 106/479 Fifth Army History p.46.

103 WO 214/33 (File II Part 1) s.25. AAI OO 1 p.3; 5.5.44.

104 *Ibid.* s.24 AFHQ F48418 16.5.44.

105 *Ibid.* Pencil note by CGS AAI and WO 214/32 AAI CGS 386, 7.6.44., to AFHQ.

106 WO 214/32 AAI CGS 402, 12.6.44., to AFHQ.

107 *Ibid.* AFHQ F58974 13.6.44.

108 *Ibid.* ADG/321 16.6.44.

109 *Ibid.* AAI/2/6/20/DCGS 20.6.44.

110 CAB EDS 18 Ch.1 p.11.

111 *Ibid.* pp.29-30.

112 *Ibid.* pp.11-12.

113 CAB EDS 18 Ch.2 pp.28-30.

114 *Ibid.* p.45.

115 Harold Macmillian: *Blast of War* (London 1967) p.506.

116 CAB HIST AL 3000/F/Air/6 p.5.

117 *Ibid.* p.6.

118 *Ibid.* pp.6-7.

119 CAB 106/479 Fifth Army History Vol. VI pp.37-8.

120 CAB EDS 18 Ch.2 p.34.

121 CAB 106/479 p.49.

122 Fisher: *Cassino to the Alps, op.cit.* pp.259-60.

123 CAB 106/479 p.54.

124 CAB EDS 18 Ch.2 pp.35-6 and p.48.

125 CAB 106/479 p.53

126 *Ibid.* p.50.

127 CAB EDS 18 Ch.2 p.49.

128 *Ibid.* Ch.1 pp.30-4.

129 *Ibid.* p.2.

130 *Ibid.* Ch.2 p.51

131 *Ibid.* p.49 and CAB 106/479 pp.67-76.

132 CAB EDS 18 Ch.2 p.51.

133 *Ibid.* p.52

134 Fisher: *Cassino to the Alps, op.cit.* pp.265-6.

135 CAB 106/423 (OBIDFI) Ch.II para 4. WO 170/167 (8 Army G Ops Main WD) Appx D Amendment to 8 Army Op Instr 1425 issued on 18.6.44.

136 CAB 106/423 (OBIDFI) Ch.II para 6.

137 *Ibid.* paras. 9-14.

138 CAB 106/644 History of 6 SA Armd Div pp.30-1.

139 WO 170/341 Appx F13 13 Corps I Summary 421 of 21.6.44 and EDS 18 Ch.2 pp.44-5.

140 WO 170/341 Appx D10 13 Corps OO 25 21.6.44. CAB 106/423 (OBIDFI) Ch. II paras 15-35. WO 170/167 Appx L, 8 Army Orbat of 16.6.44.

141 Ray: *Algiers to Austria op.cit.* pp.147-8. WO 170/449 (78 Div G WD) Log 21-22.6.44.

142 WO 170/550 (11 Inf Bde WD) Log 20.6.44.

143 WO 170/606 (38 (Irish) Inf Bde WD) and Log 20-22.6.44. WO 170/1433 (2 LIR WD).

144 CAB 106/644 History of 6 SA Armd Div pp.31-5.

145 WO 170/586 (24 Gds Bd WD) Log 23.6.44.

146 Ray: *Algiers to Austria op.cit.* pp.148-150. CAB EDS 18 Ch.2 p.57.

147 WO 170/606 (38 (Irish) Inf Bde WD) Log 23-24.6.44.

148 WO 170/602 (11 Inf Bde WD) Log 22-25.6.44.

149 WO 170/606 Log 24.6.44.

150 WO 170/602 Log 22-25.6.44.

151 CAB EDS 18 Ch.2 pp.58-9.

152 WO 170/602 Log 25.6.44.

153 Williamson: *The Fourth Division op.cit.* pp.166-8. WO 170/407 (4 Div G WD) Log 24-25.6.44. WO 170/596 (28 Inf Bde WD) Log 24-26.6.44.

154 WO 170/419 (4 Reconnaissance Regt WD) 26-28.6.44.

155 CAB 106/644 History of 6 SA Armd Div. pp.36-7.

156 WO 170/586 (24 Gds Bde WD) Log 24.6.44.

157 Williamson: *The Fourth Division* pp. 167-170 and map p.xxv. WO 170/547 (10 Inf Bde WD) Log 16-30.6.44.

158 WO 170/550 (11 Inf Bde) Log 28.6.44.

159 CAB HIST AL 3000/F/12 Study of War Diaries of 11 and 38 Inf Bdes pp.25-6. Ray: *Algiers to Austria op.cit.* p.55.

160 CAB 106/644 History of 6 SA Armd Div pp.36-7. WO 170/586 (24 Gds Bde WD) Log 28-29.6.44.

161 CAB 106/479 Fifth Army History Vol.VI p.71.

162 Narratives in WO 170/499 (78 Div WD) and WO 170/437 (6 Armd Div WD).

163 CAB EDS 18 Ch.2 pp.63-4.

164 *Ibid.* p.62.

165 WO 170/305 Appx D6 10 Corps OO 41 17.6.44.

166 CAB 106/423 (OBIDFI) Ch.II para 12. WO 170/305 Appx D10 10 Corps OO 42 28.6.44.

167 CAB 106/587 Report on the Operations of 8 Ind Div Part I Ch.IX pp.14-15. CAB EDS 18 Ch.2 p.61.

168 WO 170/305 & 6 (10 Corps G WD) Narratives June and July.

169 WO 170/305 Appx J76 10 Corps Orbat 14 30.6.44.

170 WO 169/18813 (10 Ind Div G WD).

171 CAB 44/143 Major F. Jones: Central Italy April–August 1944 pp.451-4.

172 CAB HIST AL 3000/F/Air/6 p.9.

173 *Ibid*. pp.9–10.
174 *Ibid*. Appendix C.
175 *Ibid*. p.10.

VOLUME VI—PART II

CHAPTER X

The Approach to the Gothic Line
(3rd July to 4th August 1944)

1 Major L. F. Ellis: *Victory in the West* Vol. I (HMSO 1962) pp.272–4.
2 CAB 121/396 s.113 SCAF 53.
3 *Ibid.* s.170 COSMED 139 and WO 214/34 (File 12 Pt 2) s.2 AFHQ FX68641, 5.7.44.
4 WO 214/33 (File 11 Pt 1) s.48 HQ AAI Apprec. No.3, 19.6.44.
5 *Ibid.* Minutes of Conference at Adv HQ AAI, 23.6.44.
6 WO 214/34 (File 12 Pt 1) s.2 CGS Apprec. No.4, 2.7.44, and 5002/CAO 2.7.44.
7 WO 214/33 (File 11 Pt 1) s.48 AAI C422, 25.6.44.
8 CAB HIST AL 3000/F/26 Pt 1 Diary of Major W. M. Cunningham, MA to Field-Marshal Alexander.
9 WO 214/34 *op.cit.* s.2 CGS Apprec. No.4.
10 WO 214/16 AAI MA1528, 21.4.44
11 *Ibid.* WO 62554, 24.7.44.
12 WO 106/3956 Italy Build-up Vol. III s.573 MO4 minute, 4.7.44.
13 *Ibid.* s.606 MO5/BM/1963 with note by MO1 to CIGS.
14 *Ibid.* s.625 WO 61265, 19.7.44; s.643A MO5/BM/1978, 24.7.44; s.687 AFHQ FX83546, 9.4.44.
15 Major L. F. Ellis: *Victory in the West* Vol. II (HMSO 1968) p.84 and pp.106–7.
16 WO 106/3956 s.606 *op.cit.* Note by MO1; s.650 DCIGS/110/15/7, 29.7.44, and WO 170/1426 (11 LF WD) Narr., 5.7.44.
17 WO 214/16 Alexander to CIGS, letter of 18.7.44., and WO 106/3956 s.721 AAI MA1637, 7.9.44.
18 WO 106/3956 s.682 JSM 183, 10.8.44. and CAB 105/146 FAN 387, 10.8.44.
19 WO 106/3956 s.728 MO5/BM/2009/2, 8.9.44.
20 *Ibid.* s.764 WO 79813, 27.4.44. and s.768 WO 80391, 30.9.44.
21 *Ibid.* s.797 AFHQ FX39028, 15.10.44.
22 Lt-Col. G. W. L. Nicholson: *The Canadians in Italy*, 1943–1945 Vol. II (Ottawa 1956) pp.479–80.
23 WO 106/3926 s.627A.
24 CAB EDS 18 Ch.2 pp.66–8. Ch.4 p.46.
25 *Ibid.* Ch.3 pp.14–15.
26 *Ibid.* pp.15–16.

27 *Ibid.* p.9, pp.35–9.

28 *Ibid.* Ch.2, pp.68–9.

29 *Ibid.* Ch.3 p.17.

30 *Ibid.* p.2.

31 *Ibid.* Ch.3 pp.18–23 and Ch.4 Appx 1 pp.8–10.

32 *Ibid.* Ch.3 p.38 and Ch.4 Appx 1 p.13.

33 *Ibid.* Ch.4 Appx 1 pp.8 & 12.

34 *Ibid.* Ch.3 pp.21–3.

35 CAB 106/707 Despatch by Field-Marshal Alexander: *The Allied Armies in Italy from 3rd September 1943 to 12th December 1944* (The London Gazette 6.6.1950) p.2943.

36 WO 214/34 (File 12 Pt 2) 5th Army 3085, 11.7.44.

37 Subsequent references for this section given in CAB HIST AL 3000/F/Air/7 (Air Contribution by Gp Capt. Gleave) pp.1–9 and Appx A–D.

38 WO 214/33 (File 11 Pt 1) s.12 AAI 48/G(Ops), 25.3.44 Appx D p.3.

39 *Ibid.* AAI 61/G(Ops), 19.6.44.

40 WO 204/10416 8th Army M/1338/G(P): The Assault on the Rimini-Pisa (Gothic) Defence Line, 2nd Edition. This appreciation is *undated* but, according to the file's contents sheet, the draft of 25 June 1944 was superseded by a '2nd Edition' of 27 July. The contents sheet of WO 204/10413 also refers to the two drafts: that of 25 June was 'Given to COS 4 July', that of 27 July was 'Given to Army Comd', date unspecified.

41 *Ibid.* Section 7(b).

42 WO 204/1042 AAI Op Instr No.62, 3.7.44.

43 CAB 121/594 s.860 WM(44) 88th Conclusions, Minute 1 Confidential Annex, 7.7.44.

44 WO 214/34 (File 12 Pt 2) 5 Army s.4 AAI MAC/C/470, 19.7.44.

45 Gen. Mark W. Clark: *Calculated Risk* (New York 1950) p.364 and CAB 106/479 Fifth Army History Vol.VI (Lt-Col. Chester G. Starr, Italy) pp.98–9.

46 WO 214/34 (File 12 Pt 1) s.11 AAI 48/G(Ops), 26.7.44.

47 CAB EDS 18 Ch.4 p.3.

48 CAB 106/479 Fifth Army History *op.cit.* Vol. VI pp.77–95.

49 CAB EDS 18 Ch.3 p.26.

50 Ernest F. Fisher: *Cassino to the Alps* United States Army in World War II (Washington DC, 1977) p.281. CAB 106/479 Fifth Army History *op.cit.* Vol. VI pp.81–95.

51 CAB EDS 18 Ch.3 p.26.

52 CAB 106/479 Fifth Army History p.94.

53 CAB EDS 18 Ch.3 p.28.

54 *Ibid.* Ch.2 p.33.

55 *Ibid.* Ch.3 pp.29–30.

56 WO 216/168 *op.cit.* Leese to ACIGS, 25.7.44.

57 CAB EDS 18 Ch.4 p.15.

58 CAB 44/168 Army Narrative by Brig. W. P. Pessell: Principal Administrative Aspects and Operational Maintenance of the Campaign in Italy p.95. CAB 106/426 (AFHQ: Operations of British,

Indian and Dominion Forces in Italy, hereafter referred to as OBIDFI) Section G Ch.IV.

59 WO 170/86 (AAI Q June WD) Appx J28.

60 CAB 106/426 (OBIDFI) Section G Ch.IV para 8.

61 WO 170/408 (4 Div G WD) Information Log, 23 July s.854, 24 July s.943.

62 CAB 106/423 (OBIDFI) pp.33-4 and WO 204/8108 COS/1017/F, Eighth Army Planning Notes No.7, 24.6.44.

63 WO 170/174 (8 Army G Ops Main WD) Appx L Orbat of 6.7.44. amended by CAB 106/587 A report on the operations of 8 Indian Div Pt I Ch IX p.15.

64 WO 170/437 (6 Armd Div G WD) Narr. 4-5.7.44. Hugh Williamson: *The Fourth Division 1939 to 1945* (London 1951) pp.176-9. CAB 106/644 History of 6 SA Armd Div in Italy pp.36-8.

65 CAB 106/423 (OBIDFI) pp.48-52.

66 WO 170/437 (6 Armd Div G WD) Narr. 5-7.7.44.

67 Williamson: *The Fourth Division op.cit.* p.180. WO 170/408 (4 Div G WD) Narr. 6-8.7.44.

68 CAB 106/423 (OBIDFI) p.50-52 and WO 170/437 (6 Armd Div G WD) Narr. 7.6.44.

69 WO 170/306 (10 Corps G WD) Narr. 6.7.44. and Appx J8 O.396.

70 WO 170/437 (6 Armd Div G WD) Narr.

71 WO 170/343 (13 Corps G WD) Appx D1 13 Corps OO.27, 9.7.44. and CAB 106/423 (OBIDFI) pp.52-4.

72 CAB HIST AL 3000/F/Air/6 pp.13-14.

73 CAB 106/423 (OBIDFI) pp.57-50. R. Kay: *Italy* Vol. II Official History of New Zealand in the Second World War (Wellington NZ, 1967) pp.100-110. WO 170/437 (6 Armd Div G WD) Narr. 15-16.7.44.

74 CAB EDS 18 Ch.4 pp.17-18;

75 CAB 106/423 (OBIDFI) p.59.

76 WO 216/168 *op.cit.* Leese to ACIGS, 25.7.44.

77 CAB EDS 18 Ch.4 pp.12-13 & 18.

78 *Ibid.* Ch.3 p.26.

79 CAB 106/423 (OBIDFI) p.54-7. D. Pal: *The Campaign in Italy* Official History of the Indian Armed Forces in the Second World War (Calcutta 1960) pp.283-299.

80 Lt-Col. G. R. Stevens: *Fourth Indian Division* (Toronto Ontario Canada 1948) Appx 1, amended by 8 Army Orbat, 14.7.44. in WO 170/174.

81 CAB 106/424 (OBIDFI) p.55. WO 169/18777 (4 Ind Div G WD) Narr. 7.7.44 and 19.7.44.

82 CAB EDS 18 Ch.4 pp. 14-15.

83 Pal: *The Campaign in Italy op.cit.* pp.287-299. WO 169/18777 (4 Ind Div G WD).

84 WO 170/306 (10 Corps G WD) Narr. 13.7.44.

85 CAB 106/575 MG RE CMF, 9.12.45: Engineers in the Italian Campaign, p.37. Stevens: *Fourth Indian Division op.cit.* p.331.

86 Pal: *The Campaign in Italy op.cit.* pp.270-282.

87   CAB 106/423 (OBIDFI) p.63. WO 170/306 (10 Corps G WD) Appx D6 10 Corps Op Instr 45, 11.7.44.
88   CAB HIST AL 3000/F/Air/6 pp.16A and B.
89   WO 216/168 *op.cit.* Leese to ACIGS, 25.7.44. and WO 204/8227 Report on 2 Pol Corps Operations on the Adriatic Sector p.17.
90   WO 204/8227 and CAB 106/435 (OBIDFI) p.148 *et seq.*
91   CAB EDS 18 Ch.4 p.25.
92   CAB HIST AL 3000/F/Air/6 p.16A.
93   CAB EDS 18 Ch.3 p.27. Ch.4 pp.19-23.
94   WO 170/203 (8 Army GSI WD) 8 Army I Summary 773, 24.7.44. Appx A.
95   CAB HIST AL 3000/F/Air/6 p.16A.
96   *Ibid.* pp.13-16.
97   CAB EDS 18 Ch.3 p.27.
98   *Ibid.* pp.9, 38-9.
99   CAB 106/423 (OBIDFI) pp.79-80.
     WO 170/343/D5 (13 Corps G WD) Appx D5 13 Corps oo 28, 14.7.44.
100 WO 170/437 (6 Armd Div G WD) Narr. 16-17.7.44.
101 CAB 106/644 History of 6 SA Armd Div. p.41-4 WO 170/586 (24 Gds Bde WD) 16.7.44.
102 CAB EDS 18 Ch.4 pp.26-7.
103 CAB 106/423 (OBIDFI) pp.81-2. WO 170/437 (6 Armd Div G WD) Narr. 16-17.7.44.
104 CAB 106/644 History of 6 SA Armd Div pp.41-4.
105 WO 170/343 (13 Corps G WD) Appx F11 13 Corps I Summary 438, 20.7.44.
106 *Ibid.* Appx D9 OO 29, 20.7.44.
107 CAB 106/423 (OBIDFI) pp.85-7. CAB 106/644 History of 6 SA Armd Div pp. 44-9. CAB EDS 18 Ch.4. pp.31-2.
108 Kay: *Italy* Vo.II *op.cit.* pp.120-130.
109 CAB 106/423 (OBIDFI) pp.88-90. CAB 106/687 Report on the Operations of 8 Ind Div between Oct 1943-June 1945 Pt 1 Ch. X pp.6—8. CAB EDS 18 Ch.4 pp.31-2, 40-41.
110 WO 170/437-8 (6 Armd Div G WD) Narr.
111 WO 170/342 (13 Corps G WD) Log p.36.
     CAB EDS 18 Ch.3 p.32.
112 CAB 106/423 (OBIDFI) p.92-3 and Williamson: *The Fourth Division op.cit.* Ch.19 and map p.xxvii; WO 170/408 (4 Div G WD) Log p.434-9 and Appx D6 Div OO 8, 25.7.44. WO 170/437 (6 Armd Div G WD) Narr. CAB EDS 18 Ch.4 p.34, 42.
113 Kay: *Italy* Vol II *op.cit.* pp.137-164.
114 WO 170/342 (13 Corps G WD) Narr. 29.7.44.
     WO 170/343 Appx D14 13 Corps OO 30, 29.7.44.
115 CAB 106/423 (OBIDFI) pp.98-101.
     Kay: *Italy* Vol.II *op.cit.* pp.159-169.
116 CAB EDS 18 Ch.4 pp.33-4.
117 CAB 106/707 *Despatch by Field-Marshal Alexander op.cit.* p.2939. WO 170/343 (13 Corps G WD) Appx D13 Corps Op Instr 11, 28.7.44.
118 CAB HIST AL 3000/F/Air/7 p.23.

119   Kay: *Italy* Vol.II *op.cit.* pp.171–184 and map *facing* p.137. CAB EDS 18 Ch.4 p.35, Ch.6 p.3.

120   CAB 106/644 History of 6 SA Armd Div pp.50–1. CAB 106/423 (OBIDFI) p.101.

121   CAB EDS 18 Ch.6 p.3.

122   *Ibid.* Ch.3 p.35.

123   CAB 106/423 (OBIDFI) pp.63–4. WO 170/306 (10 Corps G WD) Appx J27 Corps signal 0–424, 18.7.44.

124   WO 170/306 (10 Corps G WD) Narr. 21–22.7.44. WO 170/816 (3 Hussars WD) Narr. 21.7.44.

125   WO 170/306 Appx F16 10 Corps I Summary 369, 22.7.44. CAB EDS 18 Ch.4 p.37.

126   WO 169/18777 (4 Ind Div G WD) Narr. 16 & 19.7.44. Stevens: *Fourth Indian Division op.cit.* pp.332–3.

127   WO 170/306 (10 Corps G WD) Appx A131.

128   CAB 106/423 (OBIDFI) pp.67–70. CAB EDS 18 Ch.4 p.38, 41.

129   CAB 106/435 (OBIDFI) pp.90–91, 164, 168–9. WO 204/8227 Report on 2 Pol Corps Operations pp.161–177. CAB 44/143 Army Narrative by Major F. Jones: *Central Italy* pp.449–457.

130   CAB EDS 18 Ch.4 p.39.

131   *Ibid.* Ch.6 p.8.

132   CAB AL 3000/F/Air/6 p.22. AL 3000/F/Air/7 pp 10–11.

133   *Ibid* p.12–27.

134   *Ibid.* pp.20–1.

135   And WO 170/343 Narr. and 13 Corps I Summary 441, 28.7.44.

136   CAB AL 3000/F/Air/7 pp.25–6.

137   AIR AHB Translation VII/147.

138   CAB AL 3000/F/Air/6 p.21.

139   WO 204/8108 8 Army Planning Notes 10, 28.7.44.

140   WO 170/306 (10 Corps G WD) Appx J56–7 Corps Signals O–535 & O–536, 29.7.44, and 170/307 Appx J5–6; J3A 8 Army COS/1031, 2.8.44.

141   CAB 106/479 Fifth Army History Vol. VI *op.cit.* pp. 99–100 and 106/480 Vol. VII p.22. Ernest F. Fisher: *Cassino to the Alps* (US Army, Washington DC, 1977) p.286.

142   CAB EDS 18 Ch.4 Appx 1 pp.14–16.

143   *Ibid.* p.7.

144   *Ibid.* p.12.

145   *Ibid.* Ch.6 p.44.

146   WO 204/10416 M1338/G(P) Assault on the Gothic Line 2nd Ed. 27.7.44. p.5 and Appx D.

147   CAB HIST AL 3000/F/Air/6 pp.22–5.

148   *Ibid.* pp.13–27.

149   *Ibid.* pp.1–27.

150   *Ibid.* pp.7–8.

151   *Ibid.* pp.11–12.

152   AIR AHB 6 Document No.338 (8A-2670 8 *Abteilung*).

153   CAB HIST AL 3000/F/Air/6 p.12.

154   *Ibid.* p.16.

155 *Ibid.* Appx H.
156 See *Mediterranean and Middle East* Vol V (HMSO 1973) p.384.
157 CAB HIST AL 3000/F/Air/6 pp.17–20.
158 *Ibid.* Appx L
159 *Ibid.* Appx M pp.2–3
160 *Ibid.* Appx N.
161 *Ibid.* Appx N
162 *Ibid.* pp.19–20.
163 CAB HIST AL 3000/F/Air/7 Appx E.

VOLUME VI—PART II

CHAPTER XI

The Plan is Changed

1 CAB 106/707 Despatch by Field-Marshal Alexander: *The Allied Armies in Italy from 3rd September 1943 to 12th December 1944* (The London Gazette 6.6.1950) p.2943.

2 WO 216/168 s.36A OL/555, 1.8.44.

3 CAB HIST AL 3000/F/36 Gen. Sir Oliver Leese: Unpublished Memoirs Ch.14 p.1.

4 CAB 106/632 Letter from Gen. Sir Sidney Kirkman, 12.3.48.

5 WO 170/344 (13 Corps G WD) Narrative 3.8.44.

6 CAB 106/587 Report on the Operations of 8 Ind Div between Oct 1943–June 1945 Pt I Ch.X p.7

7 CAB HIST AL 3000/F/18 para 3 Note on discussion with Maj.-Gen. M. W. Prynne, formerly GSO I (Plans) 8 Army.

8 WO 204/8038 8th Army M/1348/G(P), 3.8.44.

9 WO 216/168 s.37A OL/590, 7.8.44.

10 WO 204/10416 8 Army G Plans M/1338/G(P): Assault on the Rimini–Pisa (Gothic) Defence Line.

11 WO 204/90 SAC(44) 81st Meeting, 1.9.44.

12 CAB HIST AL 3000/F/38 Letter from Gen. H. Trettner, 20.10.74.

13 WO 214/34 (File 12 Pt 1) s.11.

14 *Ibid.* s.12.

15 Despatch by Field-Marshal Alexander *op.cit.* p.2943.

16 Ernest F. Fisher: *Cassino to the Alps* United States Army in World War II (Washington DC, 1977) p.305.

17 WO 170/68 (WD AAI G(Ops)) Appx M MA511, 15.8.44.

18 WO 214/34 (File 12 Pt 1) s.11 AAI 48/G(Ops), 6.8.44.

19 IWM/73/7/2 Papers of Maj.-Gen. G. P. Walsh s.46.

20 *Ibid.* s.48

21 Fisher: *Cassino to the Alps, op.cit.*, p.307.

22 CAB HIST AL 3000/F/36 Gen. Sir Oliver Leese: Unpublished memoirs Ch.14 p.3.

23 IWM/73/7/2 Papers of Maj.-Gen. G. P. Walsh s.48.

24 WO 204/6740 Plan 'Ulster', AAI/TAC/C/32, 14.8.44. And WO 204/10417 8 Army G(Plans) Papers M/1345/GP Report on the cover plan for the attack on the Gothic Line, 20.10.44.

25 WO 204/8038 Maj.-Gen. Walsh: Security, 5.8.44.

26 *Ibid.* HQ 8 Army M/1348/G(P) Lt-Col. Prynne: The Attack on the East Coast Sector, 9.8.44.

27   And CAB 106/428 p.16.
28   WO 204/8038. Notes on Army Comd's Conference, 9.8.44.
29   *Ibid.* HQ 8 Army M 225/6 I Production of Overprints, 13.8.44.
30   WO 170/275 (5 Corps G WD) Narrative.
31   CAB 106/429 (AFHQ: Operations of British, Indian and Dominion Forces in Italy, hereafter referred to as OBIDFI) Appx A-1 8 Army Op Instr 1431, 13.8.44.
32   WO 204/8123 8 Army G(SD) Branch History Phase I p.3. And:
33   WO 204/8038 M14196/2 SD1 Concentration Plan, 8.8.44, and Outline Movement Programme, 10.8.44.
34   *Ibid.* Main HQ 8 Army M5/o SD1: Concentration Olive, 13.8.44.
35   WO 204/8129 8 Army CE Branch History p.1 and CAB 106/575 MGRE CMF, 9.12.45: Engineers in the Italian Campaign p.39.
36   WO 204/8123 8 Army G(SD) Branch History p.3. Lt-Col. G. W. L. Nicholson: *The Canadians in Italy 1943–1945* Vol. II (Ottawa 1956) p.497.
37   WO 204/8038 Appx C to Main HQ 8 Army M5/o SD1, Concentration Olive, 13.8.44.
38   WO 204/8132 8 Army AFV Branch History p.2.
39   CAB 106/575 Engineers in the Italian Campaign *op.cit.* pp.38-9.
40   WO 204/8038 Main HQ 8 Army M5/o SD1 *op.cit.* WO 204/8132 8 Army Q Movements Branch History p.2.
41   WO 170/208 (8 Army Movements Rear HQ WD) Narrative 13.8.44 and Appx J: AQMG(M) Progress Report, August 1944.
42   CAB 106/440 (OBIDFI) pp.1-5.
43   *Ibid.* pp.10-11 quoting HQ AAI Admin Instr 55, 26.8.44.
44   CAB 106/428 (OBIDFI) pp.21-22; 106/429 Appx F, 8 Army Admin Instr 34, 24.8.44.
45   WO 170/86 (AAI Q August WD) Appx D4A AAI Admin Instr 53, 15.8.44.
46   CAB 106/438 (OBIDFI) Appx A-1 p.2.
47   AAI Admin Instr 53, 15.8.44. *op.cit.*, and CAB 106/428 (OBIDFI) p.22.
48   WO 170/86 (AAI Q July WD) Appx A26 AAI Admin Instr 40, 19.7.44.
49   CAB 106/428 (OBIDFI) p.22.
50   IWM/73/7/2 Papers of Maj.-Gen. G. P. Walsh s.2 p.14.
51   CAB 106/428 (OBIDFI) pp.24-35 and 106/429 Appx F, 8 Army Admin Instr 34, 24.8.44.
52   CAB HIST AL 3000/F/Air/8 (Air Contribution by Gp Capt. Gleave) pp.37-8.
53   WO 204/10417 8 Army G (Plans) M/1345/G(P), 20.10.44.
54   *Ibid.* pp.39-41.
55   *Ibid.* pp.37-8.
56   *Ibid.* pp.40-1.
57   *Ibid.* Appx L.
58   *Ibid.* p.41.
59   CAB 106/480 Fifth Army History Vol. VII (Lt-Col. Chester G. Starr, Italy) pp.18-19.

60 *Ibid.* pp.21-22 and Annex C, 5 Army Op Instr 32, 17.8.44.
61 WO 170/344 (13 Corps G WD) Appx D8 13 Corps OO 34, 18.8.44.
62 CAB 106/480 Fifth Army History Vol. VII pp.21-2.
63 CAB 106/423 (OBIDFI) pp.101-2. Nicholson: *The Canadians in Italy* Vol II *op.cit.* p.484.
64 WO 170/408 (4 Div G WD) O.647, 4.8.44.
65 R. Kay: *Italy* Vol. II Official History of New Zealand in the Second World War (Wellington NZ, 1967) pp.198-206 & 214-5
66 Hugh Williamson: *The Fourth Division 1939-1945* (London 1951) p.211. CAB 106/423 (OBIDFI) pp.102-3.
67 E. G. Godfrey: *History of the Duke of Cornwall's Light Infantry 1939-45* (Aldershot 1966) p.292.
68 Nicholson: *The Canadians in Italy* Vol.II p.484. WO 170/344 Appx D4 13 Corps oo 32, 8.4.44. WO 170/408 (4 Div WD) Narrative.
69 WO 170/344 (13 Corps G WD) Narrative 10-11.8.44. and Appx F6 Corps I Summary 449, 11.8.44. CAB 106/587 Report on the Operations of 8 Ind Div Pt II p.12.
70 WO 170/344 Appx J6 13 Corps 5544/G, 12.8.44.
71 *Ibid.* Narrative 12-18.8.44.
72 *Ibid.* Appx D8 13 Corps OO 34, 13.8.44. and WO 170/86 (AAI Q WD) AAI Admin Instr 53, 15.8.44.
73 WO 204/10400 AAI OO 3, 16.8.44.
74 CAB 106/480 5th Army History *op.cit.* Annex C 5 Army Op Instr 32, 17.8.44.
75 CAB EDS 18 Ch.5 pp.7-8.
76 *Ibid.* p.8, 33.
77 *Ibid.* p.6.
78 *Ibid.* pp.11-12.
79 *Ibid.* p.16, 19.
80 *Ibid.* pp.17, 20-22.
81 *Ibid.* pp.40 & 45.
82 CAB 106/423 (OBIDFI) pp.72-8. CAB 44/145 Major F. Jones: The Gothic Line 24 August-30 September 1944 pp.151-5. D. Pal: *The Campaign in Italy*. Official History of the Indian Armed Forces in the Second World War (Calcutta 1960) Ch.XVI. Other relevant sources are quoted below.
83 WO 170/307 (10 Corps G WD) J34 Main HQ 10 Corps 54/G, 21.7.44.
84 WO 204/8306 10 Ind Div Narrative of Operations June-Dec 1944 p.11.
85 WO 170/306 (10 Corps G WD) Narrative 29.7.44. and 170/307 Appx D1 Op Instr 47, 2.8.44. WO 169/18777 (4 Ind Div G WD) Op Instr 13, 1.8.44.
86 Pal: *The Campaign in Italy op.cit.* p.355. WO 204/8306 p.11.
87 WO 170/307 (10 Corps G WD) Appx A; WO 169/18777 (4 Ind Div G WD) and WO 169/18814 (10 Ind Div G WD). Relevant narrative and folios.
88 WO 170/307 (10 Corps G WD) J8-9 0598-0600, 3.8.44., and Appx A for 4.8.44. WO 169/18814 (10 Ind Div WD) for 4 & 5.8.44.
89 And CAB EDS 18 Ch.6 p.10.

90 WO 169/18777 (4 Ind Div WD) for 5.8.44.

91 CAB EDS 18 Ch.6 pp.10–11.

92 WO 170/307 Appx A for 6.8.44. WO 169/18777 & 169/18814 for 6.8.44. WO 204/8306 *op.cit.* p.13.

93 CAB HIST AL 3000/F/Air/8 pp.7–8.

94 WO 170/307 (10 Corps G WD) Appx A for 7.8.44. and Narrative 9.8.44.

95 *Ibid.* Appx A42, 8.8.44.

96 *Ibid.* Appx D2 10 Corps Op Instr 48, 9.8.44.

97 CAB EDS 18 Ch.6 pp.12–13.

98 WO 170/307 (10 Corps G WD) Appx A folios 10–25.8.44.

99 WO 204/8227 Report on 2 Pol Corps Operations on the Adriatic Sector paras 52–4. CAB 106/435 (OBIDFI) Ch.4 paras 218–228.

100 CAB 106/435 Ch.4 paras 228–260.

101 CAB HIST AL 3000/F/Air/8 p.9.

102 CAB 106/435 Ch.4 paras 252–4. CAB EDS 18 Ch.6 p.30.

103 WO 204/8227 Report on 2 Pol Corps Operations para 52.

104 *Ibid.* paras 53–4.

105 WO 204/8039 8 Army M/A/8/G, 17.8.44.

106 CAB 106/435 Ch.4 paras 261–281.

107 *Ibid.* paras 289–301.

108 WO 204/8227 Report on 2 Pol Corps Operations para 62.

109 CAB HIST AL 3000/F/Air/8 pp.14–16.

110 CAB 106/480 Fifth Army History Vol.VII *op.cit.* pp.22–5. WO 170/344 (13 Corps G WD) Appx D8 Corps OO 34, 18.8.44.

111 CAB HIST AL 3000/F/Air/8 pp.4–5.

112 *Ibid.* Appx B.

113 *Ibid.* p.6.

114 *Ibid.* pp.7–21.

115 CAB EDS 18 Ch.5 p.37.

116 *Ibid.* pp.39–41.

117 *Ibid.* pp.35–6.

118 *Ibid.* p.45.

119 CAB EDS 19 Ch.2 p.27.

120 CAB EDS 18 Ch.6 p.42.

121 *Ibid.* pp.38–9.

122 *Ibid.* pp.19–22.

123 *Ibid.* p.24

124 *Ibid.* Ch.5 p.38 and Ch.6 p.27.

125 *Ibid.* Ch.6 p.25 & 32.

126 *Ibid.* p.33.

127 CAB HIST AL 3000/F/Air/8 Appx A.

128 *Ibid.* pp.23–24. CAB EDS 18 Air Raid tables for July and August 1944.

129 CAB HIST AL 3000/F/Air/8 Appx E.

130 *Ibid.* pp.25–8.

131 *Ibid.* p.26.

132 *Ibid.* pp.29–30. CAB EDS 18 Ch.3 p.11.

133 CAB HIST AL 3000/F/Air/8 p.31.

134   *Ibid.* and CAB EDS 18 Ch.5 p.27.
135   CAB HIST AL 3000/F/Air/8 pp.34-6.

VOLUME VI—PART II

CHAPTER XII

'Anvil/Dragoon' and Churchill's August Visit to the Mediterranean

1 CAB 121/396 s.24 COSMED 162, 29.7.44.
2 *Ibid.* s.251 COS(44) 260th Mtg (o); s.253 T.1556/4, 4.8.44; COS(W) 229, 5.8.44.
3 *Ibid.* s.261 MEDCOS 169, 6.8.44; s.264 COS to JSM, 7.8.44; and Arthur Bryant *Triumph in the West* (London 1959) p.247.
4 CAB 121/396 s.266B JSM 180, 7.8.44.
5 Winston S. Churchill: *The Second World War* Vol.VI (London 1954) p.61.
6 CAB 121/396 s.273 SCAF 61, 8.8.44. and s.283 COSMED 168, 10.8.44.
7 Churchill: *The Second World War*, *op.cit.* p.79 and CAB 120/138 *passim.*
8 CAB 106/1034 The Seventh United States Army Report of Operations, pp.1-3.
9 *Ibid.* pp.3-4.
10 ADM BR 1736 (36) Battle Summary No.43, p.3.
11 CAB 106/1034 The Seventh United States Army Report pp.7-8. CAB 106/1032 Address by Gen. Jacob L. Devers delivered in Washington DC, 27.5.46., pp.3-5.
12 CAB 106/1034 pp.92-3.
13 CAB 106/1034 pp.14-18 & pp. 51-2.
14 CAB 106/1032 p.5.
15 Captain S. W. Roskill: *The War at Sea* Vol. III Pt II pp.86-92.
16 CAB HIST AL 3000/F/17 FLR: Operation Anvil/Dragoon August-September 1944 and AL 3000/F/Air/10B p.13C & D.
17 *Ibid.* Air p.13, O.
18 WO 204/6740 HQ 'A'F/44/64 23.7.44 paras 12 & 13.
19 *Ibid.* Main 'A'F/44/64 15.8.44 paras 3 & 4.
20 CAB HIST AL 3000/F/Air/10B p.13D.
21 *Ibid.* pp.13E-H.
22 *Ibid.* p.13I.
23 *Ibid.* p.25B.
24 *Ibid.* pp.11, 16-19, 22.
25 *Ibid.* p.26

26 *Ibid.* pp.8, 11, 26.

27 *Ibid.* pp.12 & 13.

28 CAB HIST AL 3000/F/8 FLR: Effect of Anvil/Dragoon on AAI admin. plans, quoting AFHQ Log.P 50/51.

29 CAB 106/1034 The Seventh United States Army Report pp.49–50. CAB 106/1032 Address by Gen. Devers *op.cit.* p.4.

30 Admiral H. Kent Hewitt: 'Planning and Executing Anvil-Dragoon', reprint from *United States Naval Institute Proceedings* Vol. 80 Nos.7–8, July and August 1954 in CAB AL 3000/F/39, p.737, 742.

31 WO 204/10389 7th Army Dragoon Outline Plan.

32 Hewitt: 'Planning Anvil-Dragoon' *op.cit.* p.741.

33 CAB 106/1034 The Seventh United States Army Report pp.55, 59–62, 87 & 95–9.

34 Roskill: *The War at Sea op.cit.* pp.89–91.

35 *Ibid.* p.91n. and ADM BR 1736 (36) Battle Summary No.43.

36 Roskill: *The War at Sea op.cit.* Table 22.

37 Hewitt: 'Executing Operation Anvil-Dragoon' *op.cit.* p.901.

38 CAB 106/1034 The Seventh United States Army Report p.92.

39 Roskill: *The War at Sea op.cit.* p.92.

40 Hewitt: Executing Operation Anvil-Dragoon *op.cit.* p.899.

41 Roskill: *The War at Sea op.cit,* pp 93–6.

42 *Ibid.* and ADM BR 1736 (36) Battle Summary No.43 pp.28–9. And S. E. Morison: *The Invasion of France and Germany* History of US Naval Operations in World War II Vol.XI (London 1957) pp.249–50.

43 CAB EDS 18 Ch.5 pp.9–10 & p.13.

44 *Ibid.* p.13n. (4).

45 *Ibid.* p.5.

46 CAB HIST AL 3000/F/21A. Extract from draft US History of the Army in WW II, 12.8.77.

47 CAB HIST AL 3000/F/Air/10B p.16A.

48 CAB EDS 18 Ch.5 p.13n. 4.

49 *Ibid.* p.9.

50 CAB 106/1032 Address by Gen. Devers *op.cit.* p.1.

51 CAB EDS 18 Ch.5 pp.12–15.

52 *Ibid.* pp.16–19.

53 DEFE3/121 XLs 6753, 6919, 17.8.44.

54 CAB 106/1034 The Seventh United States Army Report p.145–6. CAB HIST AL 3000/F/21 Extract from draft US History of the Army in WW II *op.cit.* IV p.34.

55 ADM BR 1736 (36) Battle Summary No.43 p.26.

56 CAB HIST AL 3000/F/Air/10B p.16.

57 ADM BR 1736 (36) Battle Summary No.43 p.28.

58 CAB 106/1034 The Seventh United States Army Report p.114.

59 CAB HIST AL 3000/F/Air/10 and 10B.

60 CAB 106/1034 The Seventh United States Army Report pp.145–51.

61 *Ibid.* p.126 and ADM BR 1736 (36) Battle Summary No.43 pp.30–6.

62 S. E. Morison: *The Invasion of France and Germany*, Vol. XI *op.cit.* p.241.

63 CAB 106/1034 p.127, 135 & 145.

64 Churchill: *The Second World War* Vol.VI *op.cit.* p.86.
65 CAB 106/1034 The Seventh United States Army Report pp.145-51.
66 *Ibid.* p.173.
67 CAB HIST AL 3000/F/21B EDS: Supplementary Note on 'Dragoon' and CAB 106/1034 The Seventh United States Army Report pp.171-2.
68 CAB 106/1034 pp.174-8.
69 *Ibid.* pp.185-8.
70 *Ibid.* pp.152-69. CAB HIST AL 3000/F/Air/10B 21A.
71 ADM BR 1736 (36) Battle Summary No.43 pp.50-2.
72 CAB 106/1034 pp.189-190, 201-4.
73 CAB HIST AL 3000/F/21B EDS: Supplementary Note on 'Dragoon' p.6.
74 CAB 106/1034 pp.218-20.
75 *The Army Air Forces in World War II* Vol.III US Air Forces Historical Division (University of Chicago, 1951) pp.434-5. CAB HIST AL 3000/F/Air/10B p.21B.
76 CAB HIST AL 3000/F/21B EDS Supplementary Note on 'Dragoon' p.7.
77 CAB 106/1034 p.271 & 286. CAB HIST AL 3000/F/21B p.9
78 CAB 106/1032 Address by Gen. Devers *op.cit.* p.14. CAB HIST AL 3000/F/21B pp.10-11.
79 CAB HIST AL 3000/F/Air/10 p.30, 32 and Appendices M, N, O & P.
80 Dwight D. Eisenhower: *Crusade in Europe* (London 1948), p.322.
81 CAB HIST AL 3000/F/21A Letter from Lt-Gen. Sir Rollo Pain, BDF Washington, 12.8.77.
82 CAB 121/678 s.34c PM to Wilson and Macmillan, 10.6.44: s.61 PM to Pres. Roosevelt T.1342/2, 23.6.44.
83 *Ibid.* s.43 Mr. Broad to FO No.173, 17.6.44; s.45A No.153, 18.6.44.
84 *Ibid.* s.74 FO to Washington No.6188, 8.7.44., s.81 Bari (RM) to Algiers (RM) No.271, 10.7.44. and s.101 Mr. Broad to RM Caserta, 14.7.44.
85 *Ibid.* s.94A PM to Gen. Wilson, 12.7.44 and s.83 Mr. Broad No.273, 10.7.44: telegram by AOC BAF.
86 *Ibid.* s.110B Mr. Macmillan No.15 to FO, 16.7.44. and s.119B 28.7.44 and s.131, 2.8.44.
87 WO 204/85, SAC(44) 74, 9.8.44. covering Minutes of 6th August.
88 CAB 121/678 s.135B MEDCOS 145, 12.8.44. and s.72A No.1477, 5.7.44.
89 WO 204/85 SAC(44) 74, 9.8.44.
90 AIR 23/1666-7 BAF Monthly Supply of Effort—Special Operations.
91 CAB 121/678 s.135B MEDCOS 145, 12.8.44.
92 CAB 120/140 Chain 15, 12.8.44., Chain 27, 13.8.44. CAB 120/138 Memorandum from PM to Marshal Tito, 12.8.44.
93 Also CAB 120/138 Minutes of Conference with Tito, 12.8.44.
94 CAB 120/138 SAC(44) Special (5), 13.8.44. Minutes of Meeting.
95 CAB 120/140 Chain No.38, 14.8.44.
96 *Ibid.* Chain 38 & 39, 14.8.44.
97 CAB 101/126 Miss J. Dawson: Yugoslavia pp.127-8.

98 CAB 121/678 s.311A Brig. Maclean to FO No.45, 15.1.45.
99 CAB 101/126 *op.cit.*
100 WO 214/40 p.189: Memo from PM to Gen. Wilson 23.8.44.
101 Churchill: *The Second World War* Vol.VI (*op.cit.*) pp.94-6. General Mark W. Clark: *Calculated Risk* (New York 1950) p.390
102 CAB 120/138 *passim*.
103 *Ibid.* Paper No. SAC(BR)(44) 1, 19.8.44.
104 *Ibid.* SAC(44) (Special) 6, 20.8.44.
105 WO 204/10392 AFHQ History of Special Operations, Sec X, p.3, and CAB 101/128, Miss J. Dawson: Greece.
106 CAB 106/606 Despatch by Field-Marshal Alexander, p.2 and C. M. Woodhouse: *Apple of Discord* (London 1948). p.72.
107 CAB 121/554 s.641 JP(44) 188, 16.7.44.
108 John Ehrman: *Grand Strategy* Vol.VI (HMSO 1956) pp.57-8.
109 CAB 101/128 *op.cit.* paras 108-113. CAB 121/554 s.319 Mr. Leeper to FO No.215, 5.4.44.
110 Ehrman: *Grand Strategy* Vol. V (HMSO 1956) p.85.
111 CAB 101/128 paras 101-2, 110-113.
112 *Ibid.* paras 114-122.
113 *Ibid.* paras 76-8.
    CAB 121/554 s.641 JP(44) 188, 16.7.44.
114 *Ibid.* s.642 COS(44) 238th Mtg, 17.7.44.
115 CAB 101/128 paras 134-5.
    CAB 121/557 s.25 COS(44) 257th Mtg (O), 3.8.44.
116 CAB 121/557 s.18 COS(44) 640 (O).
117 CAB 101/128 para 139.
118 CAB 121/557 s.33 No.4406 COS to Wilson, 14.8.44.
119 CAB 120/140 Chain 56, 16.8.44.
120 CAB 120/138 SAC(BR) (44) Minutes 1st Meeting, 20.8.44.
121 CAB 120/138 Minutes of Meeting in the British Embassy Rome, 21.8.44.
122 CAB 120/141 Chain 153, 22.8.44.
123 CAB 120/142 Clasp 39, 14.8.44.
124 CAB 121/557 s.33 No.4406 COS to Gen. Wilson.
    CAB 120/140 Chain 57, 16.8.44.
    CAB 120/143 Clasp 235, 26.8.44.
125 CAB 120/138 SAC(BR)(44) 1st Meeting, 20.8.44. and Minutes of Meeting in the British Embassy Rome, 21.8.44.
126 Arthur Bryant: *Triumph in the West* (London 1959) p.223.
127 CAB 120/138 Minutes of Meeting in the British Embassy (Confidential Annex), 21.8.44.,
128 CAB 120/138 SAC(BR)(44) 1st Meeting, 20.8.44.
129 CAB HIST AL 3000/F/Air/9 (Air Contribution by Gp Capt. Gleave) Part I Appx A.
130 *Ibid.* pp.2-5.
131 Roskill: *The War at Sea op.cit.*
132 CAB HIST AL 3000/F/Air/9 p.3.
133 AHB RAF Narrative: The Campaign in Southern France, and Morison: *The Invasion of France and Germany op.cit.*

134 CAB HIST AL 3000/F/Air/9 Appx C and p.4.
135 *Ibid.* Appx E and E1.
136 *Ibid.* pp.9-11.
137 *Ibid.* p.8 and Appx H.
138 *Ibid.* pp.18-21.
139 *Ibid.* pp.6-7 and Appx F and G.
140 *Ibid.* pp.12-14 & 17.
141 AIR 23/1508: A History of the Balkan Air Force, HQ BAF, July 1945, amended by AIR 23/7829: BAF Monthly Record of Sorties.
142 CAB 101/228 Miss D. Butler: Allied Relations with the Yugoslav Army of National Liberation p.70.
143 AIR 23/1508 *op.cit.* p.82.
144 CAB EDS 18 Ch.5 pp.25-6. CAB HIST AL 3000/F/Air/9 pp.15-16.
145 CAB 101/228 Allied Relations with the Yugoslav Army of National Liberation p.43 & 135.
146 AIR 23/7794 s.26A.
147 AIR 23/7829 Study of Operations by squadrons of BAF No.10.
148 *Mediterranean and Middle East* Vol. I and II.
149 *Ibid.* Vols III to V.
150 *Ibid.* Vol. VI.
151 CAB HIST AL 3000/F/Air/11 Sec. x.

VOLUME VI—PART II

CHAPTER XIII

Breaching the Gothic Line

1 CAB 106/429: Operations of British, Indian and Dominion Forces in Italy (hereafter referred to as OBIDFI) Appx A1 8 Army Op Instr No. 1431, 13.8.44.
2 WO 170/177. (8 Army G Ops Main WD) Appx L Orbats for 15 and 29.8.44.
3 CAB 106/377 General Sir Bernard Paget: Middle East Review 1944 p.49.
4 WO 204/8119 8 Army A Branch History p.2 and Appx B.
5 CAB 106/428 (OBIDFI) p.26.
6 WO 204/8038 8 Army Op Instr 1433, 21.8.44. WO 170/275 5 Corps OO 17, 21.8.44
7 R. Kay: *Italy* Vol. II (Wellington NZ, 1967) p.206, 215. WO 170/177 (8 Army G Ops Main WD) Appx L Orbat, 29.8.44.
8 CAB EDS 19 Field Study 1 pp.1–3.
9 *Ibid.* pp.6–7.
10 WO 170/177 (8 Army G Ops Main WD) Appx M. Weekly AFV State 20.8.44. and CAB 106/680 p.686.
11 See Reference 17 below and fn. 4, Chapter XIII p.229.
12 WO 204/7451 s.6A AAI 1707/3/G(SD2), 6.7.44.
13 WO 204/8127 8 Army AFV Branch History p.2 and 21.
14 CAB 121/594 s.905 Chain 115, 18.8.44 and s.907 WO 69997, 21.8.44.
15 CAB HIST AL 3000/F/22 DFB: Some particulars of Br and Gmn Tanks.
16 WO 204/8127 *op.cit.* p.2, 19, 21.
17 CAB EDS 19 FS 1 p.6. WO 170/177 (8 Army G Ops Main WD). Appx N s.5 Artillery Equipment State 26.8.44.
18 CAB 106/440 (OBIDFI) pp.21–2.
19 CAB HIST AL 3000/F/Air/11 (Air Contribution by Gp Capt. Gleave) p.79.
20 *Ibid.* p.10.
21 WO 204/8038 Record of Army Comd's Conference, 9.8.44. IWM 73/7/2 s.61 p.4 GOC 8 Army 26.9.44.
22 WO 216/168 Lt-Gen. Leese to ACIGS, 25.7.44.
23 WO 204/8123 8 Army G(SD) Branch History p.2A.
24 WO 170/275 (5 Corps G WD) Narr. Lt-Col. G. W. L. Nicholson: *The Canadians in Italy* 1943–1945 Vol. II (Ottawa 1956) P.498.
25 WO 169/18798 (8 Ind Div G WD) Appx J5. No copy preserved in 8 Army files.

26   WO 170/275 (5 Corps G WD) Appx Z7 307/2/G, 16.8.44.

27   *Ibid.* Appx Z6 5th Corps Planning Instr 1, 16.8.44.

28   WO 170/398 (1 Armd Div G WD) 12527G, 20.8.44.

29   WO 170/399 (1 Armd Div A/Q WD).

30   CAB HIST AL 3000/G Pt III s.6.

31   CAB 106/428 (OBIDFI) pp.36-7.

32   WO 216/168 Lt-Gen. Leese to ACIGS(O), 12.9.44, and IWM 73/7/2
      s.9 (Papers of Major-Gen. G. P. Walsh) s.9: Outline plan for
      forthcoming ops 9 Sep 44.

33   WO 204/8129 8 Army CE Branch History Phase II. CAB 101/230
      (D. F. Butler: Special Assault Equipment employed in the CMF
      1944-45) pp.2-3, 8. WO 216/168 Lt-Gen. Leese to ACIGS(O), 8.9.44.

34   CAB EDS 19 FS 1 p.2-5.

35   *Ibid.* p.9.

36   CAB EDS 18 Ch.4 pp.43-4.

37   CAB EDS 19 FS 1 p.4.

38   CAB HIST AL/3000/F/Air/11 pp.7-10.

39   *Ibid.* pp.5-6.

40   CAB EDS 18 Ch.5. p.45, Ch.6 p.27, 32.

41   CAB 106/428 (OBIDFI) p.28. Nicholson: *The Canadians in Italy op.cit.*
      pp.505-9. CAB EDS 19 FS 1 p.8.

42   And WO 216/168 Lt-Gen. Leese to ACIGS(O), 8.9.44.

43   WO 170/177 Appx L s.5 8 Army Orbat, 29.8.44.

44   CAB EDS 19 FS 1 p.9.

45   *Ibid.* pp.12-13.

46   CAB EDS 18 Ch.5 p.44.

47   *Ibid.* pp.41-2.

48   CAB EDS 19 FS 1 pp.13-14.

49   CAB 106/435 (OBIDFI) p.206-11 and 106/430 Ch.1 para 4. Nicholson:
      The Canadians in Italy op.cit. pp.512-13.

50   WO 170/275 (5 Corps G WD) Appx 215.

51   CAB 106/428 (OBIDFI) pp.28-9.

52   *Ibid.* and CAB 106/429 Appx A1 8 Army Op Instr 1431. CAB 106/431
      5 Corps oo 17, 21.8.44.

53   CAB EDS 19 FS 1 p.10, 15.

54   CAB HIST AL 3000/F/Air/11 pp.10-22.

55   IWM 73/7/2 (Papers of Major-Gen. G. P. Walsh) s.61 Lt-Gen.
      Leese: Eighth Army Operations . . . August 12th to the Break-Out
      from Rimini into the Po Valley September 21st 1944, p.5. Nicholson:
      The Canadians in Italy op.cit. p.513.

56   CAB HIST AL 3000/F/Air/11 pp.13-18.

57   Nicholson: *The Canadians in Italy* pp.514-18.

58   And CAB EDS 19 FS 1 p.17.

59   CAB 106/430 (OBIDFI) Ch.1 pp.5-7.

60   WO 170/275 Appx Z 5 Corps OO No.17, 24.8.44.

61   D. Pal: *The Campaign in Italy* Official History of the Indian Armed
      Forces in the Second World War (Calcutta 1960) pp.368-73.

62   WO 170/275 (5 Corps G WD) s.38-39, 027 and 034 of 30.8.44 and
      31.8.44. CAB 106/430 (OBIDFI) pp.14-15.

63 CAB 106/312 VC Citations.

64 CAB EDS 19 FS 1 pp.22–3.

65 *Ibid.* p.19.

66 *Ibid.* p.24.

67 CAB HIST AL 3000/F/Air/11 pp.20–1. CAB EDS 19 FS 1 p.21.

68 Nicholson: *The Canadians in Italy op.cit.* pp.519–20.

69 CAB HIST AL 3000/F/25 Letter from Col. H. von Straubenzee; comments p.2.

70 CAB 106/435 (OBIDFI) pp.211–2.

71 Nicholson: *The Canadians in Italy op.cit.* pp.520–22.

72 CAB EDS 19 FS 1 p.25.

73 *Ibid.* pp.28–9.

74 *Ibid.* FS 1 pp.26–8.

75 CAB 106/430 (OBIDFI) pp.15–17.

76 WO 170/481 Appx D2 56 Div OO 3, 4.9.44 and CAB 106/430 (OBIDFI) p.25 *n(2)*

77 CAB HIST AL 3000/F/Air/11 pp.21–2.

78 WO 170/276 Appx D1 5 Corps OO 18, 2.9.44.

79 CAB 106/430 (OBIDFI) p.20. WO 170/459 (46 Div G WD) Narr. 2–1.9.44.

80 WO 170/459 (46 Div G WD) Appx D, Div Op Instr 2, 3.9.44 and Narr. 4.9.44.

81 CAB 106/430 (OBIDFI) p.21. WO 170/201 (8 Army Tac WD) Appx B p.1323 s.8, p.1325 s.16 for 4.9.44.

82 CAB 106/430 (OBIDFI) p.21. CAB EDS 19 FS 1 p.31.

83 WO 170/481 56 Div OO 2, 3.9.44.

84 CAB 106/430 (OBIDFI) p.22. CAB EDS 19 FS 1 p.36.

85 CAB 106/430 (OBIDFI) p.22. WO 170/481 (56 Div G WD) log. s.1405 4.9.44. WO 170/276 (5 Corps G WD) O.175, 5.9.44.

86 CAB HIST AL 3000/F/Air/11 pp.23–5.

87 WO 170/204 (8 Army GSI WD) I Summary 796 and 797.

88 WO 170/276 5 Corps I Summary 366, 4.9.44.

89 CAB EDS 19 FS 1 pp.32–4.

90 *Ibid.* pp.34–5.

91 *Ibid.* pp.37–9.

92 WO 170/276 5 Corps I Summary 366, 0800 hrs 4.9.44.

93 CAB EDS 19 FS 1 p.43.

94 CAB HIST AL 3000/E/2 DFB: New German Equipment in Italy in 1944. L. F. Ellis: *Victory in the West* Vol. I (H.M.S.O. 1962) p.549.

95 WO 204/8038 8 Army M 14202 SD2 31.8.44. WO 170/398 1 Armd Div OO 36, 31.8.44.

96 WO 170/177 (8 Army G Ops Main WD) Appx L Orbat 29.8.44.

97 The History of the 2nd Armoured Brigade from August 1944 until the end of the Campaign in Italy (IWM 516.318) pp.3–4. WO 170/398 (1 Armd Div G WD) Narr. and Sitreps 4.9.44.

98 History of the 2nd Armoured Brigade Appx B.

99 WO 170/525 (2 Armd Bde WD) Narr. 4.9.44 p.3. History of the 2nd Armoured Brigade p.3–4.

100   CAB 106/430 (OBIDFI) p.23. WO 170/820 The Bays WD for 4.9.44. WO 170/823 9th Lancers WD for 4.9.44

101   WO 170/525 (2 Armd Bde WD) Narr. 3-4.9.44. and History of the 2nd Armoured Brigade p.4.

102   WO 170/398 (1 Armd Div G WD) J5 GO 748, 4.9.44. CAB 106/430 (OBIDFI) pp.23-4.

103   WO 170/276 (5 Corps G WD) O.175 5.9.44. WO 170/398 (1 Armd Div WD) J6 GO 759.

104   The History of 2nd Armoured Brigade p.4. WO 170/398 (1 Armd Div WD) Narr. 5.9.44. WO 170/823 (9th Lancers WD) for 5.9.44. CAB 106/430 (OBIDFI) p.24.

105   WO 170/481 Appx D3. Verbal orders by GOC 56 Div, 5.9.44.

106   C. Northcote-Parkinson: *Always a Fusilier* (London 1949) pp.211-13.

107   CAB 106/430 (OBIDFI) pp.24-26.

108   WO 170/481 Appx D2 56 Div OO 3 4.9.44.

109   *Ibid.* Op Log s.1537, 1594, Sitreps for 6 and 7.9.44. CAB 106/430 (OBIDFI) p.28.

110   Nicholson: *The Canadians in Italy op.cit* pp.529-30.

111   CAB EDS 19 FS 1 p.30 & 41.

112   WO 216/168 Lt-Gen. Leese to ACIGS(O), 8.9.44. IWM 73/7/2 *op.cit.* s.61 Leese: Eighth Army Ops. p.8. Nicholson: *The Canadians in Italy op.cit.* p.530.

113   CAB 106/428 (OBIDFI) p.33 para 17.

114   CAB 106/431 (OBIDFI) 5 Corps Op Instr 10, 8.9.44.

115   CAB HIST AL/3000/F/Air/11 pp.24-9.

116   CAB EDS 19 FS 2 pp.19, 32-3.

117   WO 204/10400 AAI Op Instr 3, 16.8.44.

118   Ernest F. Fisher: *Cassino to the Alps* United States Army in World War II (Washington DC, 1977) pp.320-1.

119   CAB 106/480 Fifth Army History Vol VII (Lt-Col. Chester G. Starr, Washington DC) 5 Army Op Instr 34, 4.9.44.

120   WO 170/345 D1 13 Corps OO 36, 5.9.44.

121   CAB EDS 19 FS 1 p.14. CAB 106/480 Fifth Army History pp.31-6.

122   WO 170/344 (13 Corps G WD) Narr. CAB 106/480 Fifth Army History pp.42-4. CAB EDS 19 FS 2 p.5.

123   Clark Diary quoted by Fisher: *Cassino to the Alps op.cit.* p.321.

124   *Ibid.*
      Nicholson: *The Canadians in Italy op.cit.* p.531. WO 214/16 MA 1644 CIGS, 9.9.44.

125   IWM 73/7/2 *op.cit.* s.59 Outline Plan for forthcoming ops, 9.9.44 and s.61 Gen. Leese: Eighth Army Operations pp.8-9.

126   IWM/73/7/2 *op.cit.* s.61 p.8. s.9. Outline Plan of 9.9.44 and Nicholson: *The Canadians in Italy op.cit.* p.530.

127   CAB 106/428 (OBIDFI) p.36, 106/431 Appx B7 5 Corps Op Instr 10, 8.9.44. IWM 73/7/2 s.59 Outline Plan, 9.9.44.

128   IWM/73/7/2 *op.cit.* s.61 Gen. Leese: Eighth Army Operations p.9. CAB 106/428 (OBIDFI) p.35.

129   CAB 106/429 (OBIDFI) Appx I-1. Adv AAI CGS 486, 10.9.44.

130 WO 170/276 (5 Corps G WD) O.234, 0300 hrs 7.9.44. WO 170/481 (56 Div G WD) Op Log s.1569, 7.9.44.

131 *Ibid.* s.1626 and s.1665 8.9.44. CAB EDS 19 FS 1 p.42.

132 CAB 106/431 (OBIDFI) Appx B7 5 Corps Op Instr 10, 8.9.44.

133 CAB 106/430 (OBIDFI) p.26-9. WO 170/481 (56 Div G WD) Op Log s.1655 8.9.44 and s.1737 9.8.44.

134 CAB 106/430 (OBIDFI) p.29-30.

135 WO 170/276 Appx D4 5 Corps OO 19, 9.9.44.

136 WO 170/481 (56 Div G WD) Op Log s.1689 O.335, 9.9.44. WO 170/459 46 Div OO 4 and I Summary 29, 9.9.44. WO 170/634 169 Bde I Summary of 9.9.44.

137 CAB 106/430 (OBIDFI) pp.33-4.

138 Fisher: *Cassino to the Alps op.cit.* p.321-6.

139 CAB 106/437 (OBIDFI) pp.15-17.

140 CAB HIST AL 3000/F/Air/11 p.30-3.

141 WO 170/459 46 Div I Summary 29, 9.9.44.

142 CAB 106/430 (OBIDFI) p.28. CAB EDS 19 FS 1 p.41.

143 CAB HIST AL 3000/F/Air/11 pp.53-60.

144 *Ibid.* pp.61-3. CAB EDS 19 FS 2 p. 4-5.

145 *Ibid.* p.12.

146 WO 204/812/ 8 Army AFV Branch History p.4.

147 CAB EDS 19 Ch.1 pp.36-8.

148 *Ibid.* p.40-42.

149 CAB EDS 19 FS 1 pp.41-2 & 44.

150 *Ibid.* p.45.

151 CAB 106/707 Despatch by Field Marshal Alexander: *The Allied Armies in Italy from 3rd September 1943 to 12th December 1944* (The London Gazette 6.6.1950) p.2947. CAB 106/428 (OBIDFI) p.37.

152 WO 170/276 5 Corps I Summary 376, 14.9.44.

153 CAB 106/430 (OBIDFI) p.36. WO 170/201 (8 Army Tac WD) Appx B p.1378 s.2.

154 Pal: *The Campaign in Italy op.cit.* p.406.

155 CAB EDS 19 FS 1 p.48. WO 170/398 1 Armd Div 1 Summary, 13.9.44.

156 Nicholson: *The Canadians in Italy op.cit.* pp.534-5.

157 History of 2nd Armoured Brigade *op.cit.* p.6. Hugh Williamson: *The Fourth Division 1939-1949* (London 1951) pp.224.

158 WO 170/525 (2 Armd Bde WD) 13.9.44. WO 170/823 (9th Lancers WD) 13.9.44.

159 CAB EDS 19 FS 1 p.49.

160 WO 170/203-4 (8th Army GSI WD) Aug and Sep 1944.

161 CAB EDS 19 FS 1 pp.52-4.

162 *Ibid.* p.65.

163 IWM 73/7/2 *op.cit.* s.61. Leese: Eighth Army Operations p.10.

164 CAB 106/431 Appx B10 5 Corps OO 21, 13.9.44. CAB 106/430 (OBIDFI) pp.37-42.

165 CAB EDS 19 FS 1 p.78. CAB 106/431 Appx B, 5 Corps OO 22, 15.9.44. WO 169/18777 (4 Ind Div G WD) Narr. Lt-Col. G. R. Stevens: *Fourth Indian Division* (Toronto Ontario, Canada 1948) p.534.

166   Nicholson: *The Canadians in Italy op.cit.* p.538–45. Williamson: *The Fourth Division op.cit.* pp.223–7.

167   CAB EDS 19 FS 1 p.55.

168   WO 214/16 MA1665 17.9.44.

169   CAB HIST AL 3000/F/Air/11 pp.35–45.

170   CAB EDS 19 FS 1 p.47, 51.

171   CAB EDS 19 FS 2 pp.6, 10–11.

172   CAB 106/480 Fifth Army History *op.cit.* p.55.

173   CAB EDS 19 FS 2 pp.6–12.

174   CAB 106/480 Fifth Army History pp.57–60, & 86.

175   MOD Whitehall Library History of the First Division Vol II p.36.

176   CAB 106/437 (OBIDFI) pp.21–3. CAB 106/438 Appx D7 13 Corps Op Instr 17, 9.9.44.

177   WO 170/344 Appx J10 13 Corps Orbat, 18.8.44.

178   CAB 106/587 Report on the operations of 8 Ind Div between Oct 1943–June 1945 Part II p.31–4. CAB 106/437 (OBIDFI) pp.22–4.

179   WO 170/438 (6 Armd Div WD) Narr. 13–15.9.44. CAB EDS 19 FS 2 p.14.

180   CAB 106/480 Fifth Army History p.63–7. MOD Whitehall Library History of the First Division Vol II p.36. CAB EDS 19 FS 2 pp.18–19.

181   CAB HIST AL 3000/F/Air/11 pp.64–5.

182   *Ibid.* pp.35–69.

183   CAB EDS 19 FS 2 p.13–19 and p.32.

184   CAB 106/430 (OBIDFI) p.43 para 3.

185   WO 170/276 Appx D8 5 Corps OO 23, 17.9.44.

186   WO 169/18777 Appx M 4 Ind Div Op Instr 15, 17.9.44.

187   CAB EDS 19 FS 1 pp.31–2, 42.

188   Pal: *The Campaign in Italy op.cit.* p.402. C. R. S. Harris: *Allied Military Administration of Italy 1943–45* (HMSO 1957) pp.195–6.

189   Nicholson: *The Canadians in Italy op.cit.* pp.545–9.

190   CAB HIST AL 3000/F/Air/11 pp.43–5.

191   Nicholson: *The Canadians in Italy* p.548–52. WO 204/10415 Reports and Lessons from Operations s.41d p.3.

192   CAB EDS 19 FS 1 pp.67–8.

193   CAB 106/430 (OBIDFI) pp.44–45. WO 170/201 (8 Army Tac WD) Appx B p.1427 s.26, p.1429 s.5. WO 170/481 (56 Div G WD) Op Log s.2379, 2382, 2410. WO 170/629 168 Bde Report. Map: GSGS No.4228 (Revised by 13 Corps Fd Svy Coy RE Feb 1944) 1:25,000.

194   WO 170/536 (7 Armd Bde WD) 19.9.44.

195   WO 170/481 56 Div Op Log s.2432, 2444.

196   WO 170/398 (1 Armd Div G WD) Narr. WO 170/525 Appx D5 2 Armd Bde OO 2A, 19.9.44. WO 170/820 (The Bays WD) Narr.

197   WO 170/201 Appx B p.1434 s.26. WO 170/820 Narr. 1430 hrs 19.9.44.

198   CAB EDS 19 FS 1 p.69, 72, 74.

199   WO 170/481 (56 Div G WD) Op Log s.2478–2485. CAB 106/430 p.47. WO 170/536 (7 Armd Bde WD) Narr. 19–20.9.44.

200   The History of the 2nd Armoured Brigade *op.cit.* pp.8–9. WO 170/525 (2 Armd Bde WD) and 170/820 (The Bays WD) Narr. 20.9.44.

201 WO 170/201 Appx B 8 Army Tac Log. From 5 Corps 0538 hrs 20.9.44. CAB EDS 19 FS 1 p.72. WO 170/398 (1 Armd Div G WD) Narr. WO 170/823 (9th Lancers WD) 20.9.44.

202 CAB 106/430 (OBIDFI) pp.45-7. Pal: *The Campaign in Italy op.cit.* p.400.

203 Nicholson: *The Canadians in Italy op.cit.* pp.550-51.

204 CAB HIST AL 3000/F/Air/11 pp.46-48.

205 Nicholson: *The Canadians in Italy op.cit.* p.552-3. Williamson: *The Fourth Division op.cit.* p.231.

206 Nicholson: *The Canadians in Italy op.cit.* pp.553-7. CAB EDS 19 FS 1 pp.69-70. Williamson: *The Fourth Division op.cit.* p.232.

207 CAB EDS 19 FS 1 pp.72-7.

208 Nicholson: *The Canadians in Italy op.cit.* pp.559-60. CAB 106/430 (OBIDFI) p.48. WO 170/276 5 Corps I Summary, 22.9.44.

209 CAB HIST AL 3000/F/Air/11 pp.47-52. CAB EDS 19 FS 1, p.65, 83.

210 CAB 106/480 Fifth Army History *op.cit.* p.69-73. CAB EDS 19 FS 2 pp.21-3, 26, 33.

211 CAB 106/480 Fifth Army History pp.69-73. CAB 106/437 (OBIDFI) pp.28-30. MOD Whitehall Library History of the First Division Vol. II p.40.

212 CAB 106/433 pp.13-15 and Appx A2 to 10 Corps Op Instr 49, 19.8.44. CAB EDS 19 FS 1 p.65, 76.

213 CAB 106/480 Fifth Army History pp.77-82

214 CAB HIST AL 3000/F/Air/12 p.54.

215 IWM 73/7/2 *op.cit.* s.61. Leese: Eighth Army Operations p.12.

216 CAB 106/723.

217 CAB EDS 19 FS 1 p.61.

218 *Ibid.* Ch.1 p.41.

219 *Ibid.* FS 1 pp.64-5, 71 and 76.

220 *Ibid.* Ch.1 pp.41-4.

221 EDS 19 FS 1 pp.58-9, 81-2.

222 WO 204/8133 Phase II p.6.

223 WO 170/280 (5 Corps A/Q WD) Sep 44. Nicholson: *The Canadians in Italy op.cit.* p.562.

224 CAB 106/428 (OBIDFI) p.37 and 106/429 Appx G. IWM 73/7/2 *op.cit.* s.61. Leese: Eighth Army Operations p.12. For breakdown of tank losses see CAB 106/733.

225 CAB 106/733 (Gen. Leese: Misc Papers) 21.9.44.

226 WO 204/10415 (AFHQ Reports and Lessons from Ops) *Int.al.* s.41 B & D.

227 Cumulative casualties taken from WO 170/280 (5 Corps A/Q WD) and tabulated in CAB HIST AL 3000/F/41.

228 *Ibid.* and CAB EDS 19 FS 1 p.80.

229 WO 216/168 Leese to ACIGS p.3, 8.9.44.

230 CAB EDS 19 FS 1 p.4.

231 CAB HIST AL 3000/F/Air/11.

232 *Ibid.* pp.8-9.

233 *Ibid.* pp.71-6.

234 *Ibid.* pp.77 and Appendices E, F, G, J.
235 *Ibid.* pp.77–8.
236 *Ibid.* p.7, 80–81A.

VOLUME VI—PART II

CHAPTER XIV

Success Beckons in the Mediterranean

1 CAB EDS 18 Ch.5 pp.27–30.
2 CAB EDS 19 Ch.1 pp.21–4.
3 CAB EDS 18 Ch.5 p.31.
4 AIR 23/7806 BJPS(44) 7 Final, 7.8.44.
5 CAB 121/678 s.162 COS (44) 788 (O), 31.8.44. AIR 23/1508 History of the Balkan Air Force (BAF) p.11 & 136. WO 204/85 SAC/44/75, 11.8.44.
6 WO 204/10430 Appx 9 p.30.
7 CAB HIST AL 3000/F/Air/11 p.75 and Appx H, and AIR 22/137 ASO 1382, 7.9.44 *et seq.*
8 AIR 23/1508 History of the BAF pp.137–9.
9 CAB HIST AL 3000/F/Air/11 Appx H.
10 AIR 23/7806 s.56A, 4.9.44. Fitzroy Maclean: *Eastern Approaches* (London 1949) p.48.
11 AIR 22/137 ASO 1386.
12 CAB EDS 19 Ch.1 p.13.
13 *Ibid.* pp.26–7.
14 *Ibid.* pp.11–15.
15 CAB EDS 18 Ch.5 p.30.
16 CAB EDS 19 Ch.1 pp.30–2.
17 *Ibid.* p.18.
18 *Ibid.* p.33.
19 *Ibid.* p.19.
20 *Ibid.* p.30.
21 *Ibid.* Ch.2 pp.20–1.
22 *Ibid.* Ch.1 p.29 *n.*5.
23 CAB EDS 19 Ch.1 p.7.
24 CAB 120/569 serials for 9.8.44–14.9.44.
25 *Ibid.* FAN 409 8.9.44, repeated 14.9.44.
26 *Ibid.* FAN 394, 16.8.44.
27 WO 214/43 AFHQ G3 Report, 17.10.44.
28 WO 204/85 SAC(44) 84, 2.9.44. WO 204/91 SAC(44) 22nd Mtg, 5.9.44. WO 204/5498 MJPS P/209 (Final) Annex C.
29 DEF 2/354 5480/Med. 00388 C-in-C Med Directive to R. Adm. Mansfield, 30.8.44. ADM 199/1045 M 04189/45 Report by R. Adm. Mansfield.
30 AIR 23/1508 History of the BAF pp.24–5. DEF 2/354 MAAF/s.4273 To A.V.M. Elliot, 29.8.44.

31 AIR 24/751 (AHQ Greece ORB) 12.10.44.

32 C. M. Woodhouse: *Apple of Discord* (London 1948) p.203. ADM 199/1045 M 04189/45 Report by R. Adm. Mansfield.

33 WO 204/10392 AFHQ History of Special Operations Section X p.3.

34 DEF 2/354 MJPS P/213 2.9.44 pp.8–9 and MAAF/s.4273 To A.V.M. Elliot, 29.8.44.

35 DEF 2/356 Directive to Lt-Gen. Scobie, 24.9.44.

36 CAB 120/562 Punch JCS 953, 7.12.44.

37 *Ibid.* MJPS P/213 pp.1 & 7.

38 WO 204/91 SAC(44) 22nd Mtg, 5.9.44. WO 204/85 SAC(44) 84, 2.9.44. Final Directive in DEF 2/356 B-1321.

39 WO 204/90 SAC(44) 81st Mtg 31.8.44. WO 214/43 AFHQ G3 Report, 17.10.44. WO 204/10427 History of 2 Indep Para Bde Gp p.25 and Manna OO 1, 4.9.44.

40 CAB 120/150 Cordite 157, 12.9.44.

41 CAB 121/554 s.723. Mr Leeper No.10, 12.9.44 repeated in Cordite 178.

42 *Ibid.* s.724 Mr Warner No.21, 12.9.44 repeated in Cordite 179.

43 CAB 120/152 Gunfire 113, 13.9.44.

44 CAB 120/150 Cordite 175, 13.9.44.

45 *Ibid.* Cordite 263, 15.9.44.

46 *Ibid.* Cordite 267, 15.9.44.

47 CAB 120/153 Gunfire 184 and 202, 16.9.44.

48 CAB 121/529 s.262 C-in-C ME to WO, GO/38729, 6.9.44; s.266 NAF 744, 8.9.44.

49 WO 204/10392 AFHQ History of Special Operations Section X Annex A.

50 DEF 2/354 5850/Med.0038, 20.8.44. WO 204/10429 Land Forces Adriatic (LFA) Report. p.46. AIR 23/1509 History of the BAF p.26.

51 CAB 44/153 History of the Commandos in the Mediterranean p.324.

52 CAB 121/557 s.144a.

53 *Ibid.* s.183 F28750, 22.9.44.

54 AHB Narrative: The RAF in Maritime War Vol. VII Pt II p.88 and Appx 42.

55 NHB m.s.: The Development of British Naval Aviation 1919–1945 Vol. III p.272.

56 CAB EDS 19 Ch.1 p.29.

57 ADM 199/297 M 1027/45 EC No.0675/16 R. Adm. Troubridge: Operations in the Aegean 9–20.9.44.

58 NHB m.s.: The Development of British Naval Aviation *op.cit.* pp.279–80.

59 *Ibid.* p.265, and CAB HIST AL 3000/F/48(b) NHB letter on designation of Force 120 and Force A in the Aegean.

60 ADM 199/1429 (FOLEM WD). ADM 199/297 M 01027/45 FOLEM 1933/00231/20 V. Adm. Rawlings: Report on Aegean Operations 1.9.44–31.10.44 Appx A.

61 *Ibid.* EC No.0675/16 Troubridge report *op.cit.*

62 And NHB m.s.: The Development of British Naval Aviation pp.269–70.

63 ADM 199/297 M 1027/45 FOLEM 1933/00 231/20 Appx C.
64 *Ibid.* Appx A and EC No.0675/16 Troubridge report *op. cit.* and NHB m.s.: The Development of Naval Aviation pp.267-70.
65 ADM 199/805 M 011972/44 HMS *Ulster Queen* Report of Proceedings 26.9.44-4.10.44.
66 *Ibid.* and CAB HIST AL 3000/F/Air/14 Pt II p.18.
67 ADM 199/297 M 01027/45 FOLEM 1933/00231/20 Appx A.
68 ADM 199/1429 (FOLEM WD) p.81.
69 CAB EDS 19 Ch.1 p.30.
70 CAB HIST AL 3000/F/Air/14 Pt II pp.16-17.
71 AHB Narrative: The RAF in Maritime War Vol VII Pt II p.89.
72 CAB HIST AL 3000/F/Air/11 Appx J.
73 CAB HIST AL 3000/F/Air/14 p.17.
74 CAB HIST AL 3000/F/Air/12 Appx 1.
75 CAB EDS 19 Ch.2 pp.21-2 and CAB HIST AL 3000/F/Air/14 pp.19.
76 WO 204/10429 LFA Report pp.46-9.
77 Woodhouse: *Apple of Discord op. cit.* p.27 & 202.
78 WO 204/10429 LFA Report pp.46-50. WO 204/1567 s.39 AFHQ G3 Org memo, 6.1.45.
79 WO 204/10430 Appx 15 BAF to AFHQ BAF/277, 21.9.44. CAB 121/557 s.183 F28750 to COS, 22.9.44.
80 WO 204/10430 Appx 10 Record of Meeting with COS AFHQ 21.9.44. Appx 11 AFHQ Directive 26.9.44.
81 WO 204/10429 LFA Report pp.50-3.
82 WO 204/91 SAC(44) 90th Mtg, 22.9.44. CAB 121/557 s.124 COS 544, 21.9.44, s.183 Gen. Wilson F28750, 22.9.44.
83 WO 204/85 SAC(44) 98, 26.9.44.
84 *Ibid.* and WO 204/90 SAC(44) 93rd Mtg 29.9.44.
85 WO 204/10392 AFIIQ History of Special Operations Section X. EDS 19 Ch.2 pp.22-3.
86 WO 204/91 SAC(44) 92nd Mtg, 26.9.44.
87 WO 204/10429 LFA Rept pp.26-33.
88 *Ibid.* p.104.
89 CAB 101/228 D. F. Butler: Allied Relations with the Yugoslav Army of National Liberation, 1.7.44-8.5.45, p.51.
90 WO 204/10429 LFA Report p.61-6. WO 218/6 (2 SS Bde *Sep* WD) Report on Operation Mercerised, 21.11.44.
91 CAB 99/29 Record of 'Octagon' 1st Plenary Meeting, 13.9.44.
92 WO 214/34 Pt I s.28 AFHQ 31421, 28.9.44.
93 CAB 99/29 CCS 172nd Mtg pp.13-14.
94 *Ibid.* 2nd Plenary Meeting 16.9.44.
95 CAB 121/533 s.3 MEDCOS 181 2.9.44. s.5 & 6, 4.9.44.
96 *Ibid.* s.17, 7.9.44.
97 CAB 99/29 COS (Octagon) 4th Mtg Item 1 8.9.44.
98 *Ibid.* COS (Octagon) 1st Plenary Meeting p.2 13.9.44.
99 CAB 121/533 s.49 FAN 415 13.9.44.
100 CAB EDS Ch.19 FS 2 p.6.
101 CAB 106/480 Fifth Army History Vol VII (Lt-Col. Chester G. Starr, Washington, DC) pp.89-90.

102 *Ibid.* p.97.

103 *Ibid.* p.90 and CAB 106/437 (AFHQ: Operations of British, Indian and Dominion Forces in Italy hereafter referred to as OBIDFI) pp.27-8. MOD Whitehall Library History of the First Division Vol II p.45 21 Sep-3 Oct 1944.

104 CAB 106/480 Fifth Army History pp.91-6.

105 CAB EDS 19 FS 2 pp.26-27.

106 *Ibid.* p.21.

107 *Ibid.* pp.30-2.

108 *Ibid.* pp.35-6.

109 *Ibid.* pp.38-40.

110 CAB 106/480 Fifth Army History pp.93-4.

111 CAB EDS 19 FS 2 pp.36-7.

112 *Ibid.* pp.39-40.

113 CAB 106/480 Fifth Army History pp.93-4.

114 *Ibid.* pp.97-102.

115 CAB 106/437 (OBIDFI) p.28. CAB EDS Ch.19 FS 2 pp.39-40. MOD Whitehall Library History of the First Division Vol II p.40 & pp.46-8.

116 *Ibid.* and WO 170/531 2 Bde WD for 25-26 Sep. WO 170/613 66 Bde WD for 26 Sep.

117 CAB EDS 19 FS 2 p.44.

118 CAB 106/437 (OBIDFI) pp.31-2. CAB 106/438 Appx D – 9 13 Corps Op Instr 19 24.9.44.

119 WO 170/351 (13 Corps A/Q WD) Narr. WO 170/380 (1 Div WD) Narr. 30.9.44.

120 CAB 106/587 A Report on the Operations of 8th Indian Division Part II pp.39-41. CAB 106/437 (OBIDFI) p.33 and WO 170/380 1 Div Op Instr 8 25.9.44.

121 WO 170/478 6 Armd Div WD for 29.9.44. WO 170/610 61 Bde WD for 24-28.9.44.

122 CAB 106/430 Fifth Army History pp.105-8.

123 CAB HIST AL 3000/F/Air/11 p.70 and AL 3000/F/Air/12 pp.54-8.

124 CAB HIST AL 3000/F/Air/11 p.7.

125 CAB EDS 19 FS 2 p.45, 47 & 49.

126 CAB EDS 19 Ch.1 p.49.

127 WO 170/204 Eighth Army Intelligence Summaries 21-30.9.44. CAB 106/428 (OBIDFI) p.41.

128 CAB HIST AL 3000/F/Air/12 pp.14-17.

129 R. Kay: *Italy* Official History of New Zealand in the Second World War (Wellington N.Z., 1967) pp.244-7.

130 Lt-Col. G. W. L. Nicholson: *The Canadians in Italy* 1943-1945 Vol II (Ottawa 1956) pp.366-74.

131 CAB EDS 19 Ch.1 p.50.

132 CAB 106/430 (OBIDFI) pp.55-9.

133 *Ibid.* p.59-60 and WO 170/481 Appx B 56 Div Op Log s.2722 27.9.44. *et seq.*

134 CAB 106/430 (OBIDFI) pp.62-4.

135 CAB HIST AL 3000/F/Air/11 p.52 and AL 3000/F/Air/12 pp.18-25.

136 WO 170/308 Appx D2 10 Corps Op Instr 51, 23.9.44 and D3 Corps
Standing Op Instr 1 24.9.44.

137 *Ibid.* 10 Corps Narr. and CAB 106/433 (OBIDFI) pp.17–19.

138 CAB 106/429 (OBIDFI) Appx B – 5 Main 8th Army COS/1010
25.9.44.

139 *Ibid.* Appx B – 6.

140 WO 214/50 80095 CIGS, and manuscript note initialled HRA.

141 CAB EDS 19 Ch.1 pp.47–9.

142 CAB EDS 19 FS 2 p.44.

143 *Ibid.* Ch.1 p.51.

144 *Ibid.* FS 2 pp.44–6.

145 CAB 106/480 Fifth Army History Vol III pp.94–7.

146 CAB EDS 19 FS 2 pp.44–7.

147 CAB 106/480 Fifth Army History pp.95–6.

148 CAB EDS 19 FS 2 pp.47–8.

149 Ernest F. Fisher: *Cassino to the Alps,* United States Army in World
War II (Washington D.C., 1977) pp.351–2. WO 170/435 Appx D9 13
Corps Op Instr 20, 29.9.44.

150 CAB 106/480 Fifth Army History pp.III.

151 CAB 106/429 (OBIDFI) Appx B6.

152 PREM 3 53/11, 16.5.44. Admiral Lord Louis Mountbatten to PM.
No. 81253, 2.10.44. Lt-Gen. Sir H. Ismay. Major-Gen. S. Woodburn
Kirby: *The War against Japan* Vol IV (HMSO 1965) pp.113–8.

153 WO 214/16 Manuscript letter from CIGS, 22.7.44.

154 CAB HIST AL 3000/F/18 Notes by Major-Gen. M. W. Prynne.

VOLUME VI—PART II

CHAPTER XV

Frustration in Italy: October 1944

1   CAB EDS 19 Ch.2 p.11–19.

2   *Ibid.* p.25.

3   In addition to the divisional histories and reports regularly quoted in these references, description of fighting conditions may be found *inter alia* in: D. S. Daniell: *The Royal Hampshire Regiment* Vol. III (Aldershot 1955); Major E. G. Godfrey: *History of the Duke of Cornwall's Light Infantry* (Aldershot 1966); L. Melling: *With the Eighth in Italy* (Manchester 1955). And for 5 Army sector: WO 170/4404 1 Gds Bde Report, 17.2.45; Hertfordshire Field Gazette: Italian Campaign Aug 1944–Jan 1945 in the MOD Whitehall Library.

4   CAB 106/428 (AFHQ: Operations of British, Indian and Dominion Forces in Italy, hereafter referred to as OBIDFI) p.43–4.

5   CAB 106/686 CE 15 Army Gp: 8 Army Engineer Operations 9 Apr–2 May p.1. CAB 106/575 p.56.

6   CAB 106/428 p.43–4 modified by Lt-Col. G. W. L. Nicholson: *The Canadians in Italy* 1943–1945 Vol II (Ottawa 1956) p.647.

7   CAB EDS 19 Ch.3 p.14.

8   CAB 106/428 p.43–6.

9   CAB 106/686 *op.cit.* p.1–2.

10 WO 170/204 8 Army I Summary 819.

11 WO 204/8129 8 Army CE Branch History p.3.

12 CAB 106/438 (OBIDFI) Appx A1 p.4 and A5 p.14–15.

13 Ernest F. Fisher: *Cassino to the Alps* United States Army in World War II (Washington DC, 1977) p.411 & 414. CAB 106/480B Fifth Army History (Lt-Col. Chester G. Starr, Washington DC) 5 Army Orbat 16.10.44. CAB 106/549 DST AFHQ: History of RASC Services in Italy p.236–7.

14 WO 204/10408 s.37. AAI 4B/V&R: Animal returns 3.11.44.

15 CAB 106/438 Appx 2 p.9 & 12.

16 CAB 106/480 Fifth Army History p.112.

17 CAB 106/437 (OBIDFI) p.27–28.

18 CAB 106/428 p.46 para 10.

19 CAB HIST AL 3000/F/1 DFB: The Reinforcement Problem in the CMF March 1944–April 1945, p.5.

20 WO 214/34 (File 12 Pt 1) s.25 Adv HQ AAI to WO, MA1670 22.9.44.

21 CAB HIST AL 3000/F/1 p.7–8.

22 CAB 106/440 (OBIDFI) p.28.

23 CAB HIST AL 3000/F/1 p.10. WO 214/52 s.12.
24 CAB 66/59 WP(44) 705, 4.12.44. MOD Library MEF General Orders: No.646, 16.6.44; No.1259, 17.11.44.
25 *Ibid.* No.1143/44 and 497/45.
26 *Ibid.* No.1284, 24.11.44.
27 WO 170/83 (AAI A WD) Narr. 12.11.44 & J4 CAO/1100, 12.11.44.
28 WO 204/6701 s.6A Gen. Wilson to AG War Office, ADC/561 25.7.44.
29 WO 204/6701 s.12, Lt-Col. J. Sparrow: Notes of Tour of Italy, 17.7.44, and WO 110/Gen/6371 s.61A.
30 For example, see Report to 4 Ind Div of 25.2.44 para 11 in WO 204/6701 s.5B.
31 CAB 106/453 (OBIDFI) Monograph No.5.
32 WO 214/62 Pt III Gen. Sir Ronald Adam, 27.6.44.
33 Comd. 6548, 22.9.44. WO 204/6714 s.14 8 Army R 19201A, 22.10.44.
34 *Ibid.* s.15 AAI 5063/15/A (PS), 30.10.44.
35 *Parliamentary Debates* (Hansard) Fifth Series Vol. 406 House of Commons Column 1343.
36 WO 204/6701 s.56A p.2.
37 WO 110/Gen/6371 s.61A. p.7.
38 WO 204/8119 8 Army A Branch History Annex C to A(PS) Notes.
39 WO 110/Gen/6371 s.61A p.7.
40 WO 204/6714 s.14 8 Army R 19201 Lt-Gen. McCreery, 22.10.44, Annex A.
41 WO 214/34 (File 12 Pt 2) Fifth Army s.13, No. 8839 6.10.44.
42 *Ibid.* No.8937 9.10.44.
43 *Ibid.* No.6367 19.10.44.
44 *Ibid.* MA1723 15.10.44
45 *Ibid.* S-62508 16.10.44.
46 John Ehrman: *Grand Strategy* (HMSO 1956) Vol VI p.25.
47 CAB 106/440 Appx N DCIGS letter of 14.10.44.
48 WO 204/8133 8 Army RA Branch History, Phase V p.1. Phase VI p.14 and Phase VIII.
49 CAB 106/480 Fifth Army History p.149.
50 WO 214/34 (File 12 Pt 1) s.25 AAI DO/C/549, 21.9.44.
51 *I Gruppi di Combattimento* (Ministero della Difesa Rome, 1951) p.14. WO 214/53 Pt 2 MA1733, 17.10.44.
52 WO 214/54 AFHQ L Sec Rept 26.9.44 and MA1521, 19.10.44. WO 204/10377 SAC(44) 112, 23.10.44.
53 WO 214/34 (File 12 Pt 1) s.24. FX 46713 AFHQ to AAI, 1.11.44.
54 *Ibid.* s.29 Conference Notes for 2.10.44.
55 WO 204/91 SAC(44) 95th Mtg, 3.10.44 and SAC(44) 97th Mtg, 7.10.44.
56 CAB 121/533 s.75 COS(44) 912 (O), 22.10.44, covering minutes of Meeting of 8.10.44.
57 CAB 121/533 s.61 MEDCOS 201, 9.10.44.
58 CAB 120/163 Drastic No.129, 17.10.44.
59 CAB 121/533 s.72 Drastic No.145, 17.10.44.
60 CAB 120/163 Drastic No.185, 21.10.44.
61 WO 214/34 (File 12 Pt 1) s.29 CGS/429, 10.10.44.

62   WO 204/10377 SAC(44) 112 Notes on the Meeting with PM and CIGS on 21 Oct, dated 23.10.44.

63   CAB 121/533 s.81 MEDCOS 205, 24.10.44.

64   CAB 101/227 D. F. Butler: Allied Forces and the Italian Resistance, p.11D & Annex 3.

65   *Ibid.* and: WO 204/91 SAC(44) 103rd Mtg, SAC(44) 104th Mtg, SAC(44) 105th Mtg. WO 204/52 SAC(44) 107th Mtg.

66   CAB 101/227 p.11D.

67   WO 204/92 SAC(44) 107th Mtg.

68   WO 214/34 (File 12 Pt 1) s.30. CGS/451, 23.10.44.

69   WO 204/91 SAC(44) 98th Mtg, 10.10.44.

70   WO 170/204 8 Army I Summaries: 818, 2.10.44. 820, 7.10.44. 832, 28.10.44. 834, 2.11.44.

71   CAB 106/480 Fifth Army History p.111-2 and Fisher: *Cassino to the Alps op.cit.* p.363-7.

72   CAB EDS 19 Ch.3 p.3-4.

73   CAB 106/480 p.143-5.

74   CAB EDS 19 Ch.3. p.3.

75   CAB 106/480 p.114. CAB EDS 19 Ch.3 p.3-9.

76   CAB 106/427 (OBIDFI) p.13 para 32. CAB 106/337 p.36-7.

77   CAB 106/438 Appx B3 and C. Ray: *Algiers to Austria,* History of 78 Division (London, 1952) p.155-7.

78   *Algiers to Austria* p.61.

79   CAB 106/480 Fifth Army History p.123. Fisher: *Cassino to the Alps op.cit.* p.365.

80   CAB EDS 19 Ch.3 p.8, 12.

81   *Ibid.* Ch.2 p.30.

82   CAB 106/480 Fifth Army History p.131.

83   *Ibid.* and p.144. Ray: *Algiers to Austria* p.163.

84   CAB 106/480 p.131-7.

85   CAB 106/432 (OBIDFI) p.40-41. Ray: *Algiers to Austria* p.164-7.

86   CAB 106/480 p.216 and (for *note*) p.122, 130, 139.

87   Fisher: *Cassino to the Alps,* p.375.

88   CAB HIST AL 3000/F/Air/12 p.53-70.

89   CAB 106/480 Fifth Army History p.140-2. CAB 106/644 History of 6 SA Armoured Div p.64-7.

90   CAB 106/480 p.170-3.

91   CAB 106/438 Appx. D12 13 Corps OO 21, 5.10.44. D. Pal: *The Campaign in Italy,* Official History of the Indian Armed Forces in the Second World War (Calcutta 1960) p.513-18. WO 170/438 6 Armd Div WD.

92   CAB 106/587. Report on the Operations of 8th Indian Division between Oct 1943-June 1945 Pt II p.45-6.

93   CAB 106/438 Appx A2 p.14. WO 170/4404 (Bde Feb 45 WD) Operations of 1 Gds Bde in the N. Apennines p.8.

94   CAB 106/575 MG RE CMF: Engineers in the Italian Campaign, 9.12.45, p.44-5. MOD Whitehall Library: History of the 1st Division Pt II p.119.

95   CAB HIST AL 3000/F/26.

96 MOD Whitehall Library History of the 1st Division p.56–64, 73, 113.

97 And CAB 106/312 VC Citations 8.10.44.

98 And CAB 106/437 p.41.

99 CAB 106/587 Report on the Operations of 8 Ind Div *op.cit.* p.48–9. Pal: *The Campaign in Italy op.cit.* p.518–9.

100 WO 170/438 (6 Armd Div WD) Narr.

101 CAB 106/428 (OBIDFI) p.54–6. CAB 106/435 p.221.

102 CAB 106/435 p.220 *n.*1–3 & p.221 quoting McCreery to Anders, 7.10.44. WO 170/309 (10 Corps G WD) Narr. 8.10.44.

103 CAB 106/429 Appx A-4 8 Army COS/1031.

104 CAB 106/435 p.221.

105 CAB 106/428 p.55.

106 CAB EDS 19 Ch.3 p.16–8.

107 *Ibid.* p.19 quoting 29 PG Div History p.418.

108 *Ibid.* p.20–1.

109 CAB 106/428 pp.55. CAB 106/430 p.68.

110 Nicholson: *The Canadians in Italy op.cit.* p.576, 583–4.

111 Pal: *Campaign in Italy* p.470, 478–82. CAB 106/430 p.72–3.

112 Pal: *Campaign in Italy* p.482–3. CAB 106/430 p.72–3.

113 *Ibid.* Appx B29 5 Corps Op Instr 14, 11.10.44. Hugh Williamson: *The Fourth Division* (London 1954) p.236.

114 CAB HIST AL 3000/F/Air/12 p.26–33.

115 WO 170/4370 56 Div History Pt III D, p.10–13.

116 CAB 106/430 p.74–6. Pal: *Campaign in Italy* p.484.

117 WO 170/309 (10 Corps G WD) Narr. 12–14.10.44. CAB 106/435 p.224–5.

118 WO 214/16 MA1728.

119 Nicholson: *The Canadians in Italy op.cit.* p.577–9.

120 CAB EDS 19 Ch.3 p.36.

121 Nicholson: *The Canadians in Italy,* p.583–4.

122 CAB HIST AL 3000/F/Air/12 p.26–46.

123 Pal: *Campaign in Italy* p.487–8.

124 CAB EDS 19 Ch.3 p.38.

125 CAB 106/431 Appx B24 5 Corps O.14 14.10.44.

126 CAB 106/430 p.77–8.

127 WO 170/460 (46 Div WD). CAB EDS 19 Ch.3 p.60.

128 Nicholson: *The Canadians in Italy* p.579–80.

129 CAB EDS 19 Ch.3 p.40.

130 *Ibid.* p.32, 38–42.

131 *Ibid.* Ch.2 p.32.

132 *Ibid.* Ch.3 p.33, 41–2.

133 CAB 106/430 p.78–9. CAB 106/431 Appx B-26 5 Corps o.87.

134 WO 170/460 (46 Div WD) Narr. 19–20.10.44. Williamson: *The Fourth Division op.cit.* p.238–9.

135 CAB 106/430 p.79–80.

136 *Ibid.* and WO 204/8306 10 Ind Div Narrative of Operations p.22.

137 CAB 106/430 p.79–80. Williamson: *The Fourth Division* p.238–9. WO 170/409 (4 Div WD) Narr. 20.10.44.

138 CAB 106/575 Engineers in the Italian Campaign. *op.cit.* p.41. WO 170/409 (4 Div WD) Log 21–24.10.44.

139 CAB 106/428 (OBIDFI) p.59.

140 CAB HIST AL 3000/F/Air/12 p.38–47.

141 *Ibid.* and WO 170/409 (4 Div WD) Narr. 20.10.44.

142 CAB 106/480 Fifth Army History *op.cit.* p.149-50.

143 *Ibid.* and Fisher: *Cassino to the Alps op.cit.* p.379.

144 WO 170/499 (78 Div WD) Narr. 15–16.10.44 and Appx D – 20.

145 *Cassino to the Alps* p.379–381. CAB 106/480 p.150–3.

146 CAB EDS 19 Ch.3 p.27–30.

147 *Cassino to the Alps* p.381. CAB 106/480 p.150–7.

148 CAB EDS 19 Ch.3 p.27–29, 50.

149 CAB EDS 19 Ch.3 p.13.

150 *Ibid.* p.44.

151 *Ibid.* p.28, 31-2.

152 *Ibid.* p.44.

153 CAB 106/480 p.157–9. *Cassino to the Alps* p.382–3.

154 CAB 106/480 p.159–62. *Cassino to the Alps* p.385–8.

155 CAB EDS 19 Ch.3 p.66–8.

156 *Ibid.* p.55.

157 *Ibid.* p.66–8. CAB 106/480 p.162–4 and *Cassino to the Alps* p.385–8.

158 WO 214/34 (File 12 Part 1) s.30 CGS/451, 23.10.44.

159 CAB 106/480 p.163 and Appx A.

160 CAB 106/480 p.66–7.

161 CAB 106/438 (OBIDFI) Appx D14 13 Corps OO 37, 16.10.44.

162 CAB 106/437 p.46.

163 CAB EDS 19 Ch.3 p.52.

164 CAB 106/432 p.46–7. Ray: *Algiers to Austria op.cit.* p.170–2.

165 CAB 106/437 p.47–9. Pal: *The Campaign in Italy op.cit.* p.525–7.

166 CAB 106/438 Appx D15 13 Corps Op Instr 23, 22.10.44.

167 Ray: *Algiers to Austria* p.173–5.

168 CAB 106/437 p.49–51.

169 CAB HIST AL 3000/F/Air/12 p.70–5.

170 CAB EDS 19 Ch.3 p.50.

171 *Ibid.* p.57.

172 *Ibid.* p.67.

173 *Ibid.* Appx 1.

174 *Ibid.* p.58.

175 *Ibid.* Ch.4 p.40.

176 *Ibid.* Ch.2 p.36–41.

177 *Ibid.* Ch.4 p.50.

178 *Ibid.* Ch.2 p.39 *n*.4.

179 *Ibid.* Ch.4 p.50-1

180 *Ibid.* Ch.2 p.36.

181 *Ibid.* p.46-9.

182 CAB 106/429 (OBIDFI) Appx B7 COS/1005 Lt-Gen. McCreery to Lt-Gen. Harding, 24.10.44.

183 CAB 106/428 p.63–4.

184 CAB 106/430 p.85.

185 CAB 106/435 p.224-36 and 106/436 Appx 37 Corps Admin Instr 8, 18.10.44; Appx 38 Corps Op Instr, 14.10.44.

186 CAB 106/435 p.246, 248, 250. CAB 106/436 Appx 39 Corps Op Instr, 24.10.44.

187 CAB 106/428 p.69.

188 CAB 106/435 p.242-3.

189 Nicholson: *The Canadians in Italy op.cit.* p.585-93.

190 CAB 106/428 p.67. Pal: *Campaign in Italy op.cit.* p.497-9.

191 CAB EDS 19 Ch.3 p.63-4.

192 *Ibid.* p.74.

193 *Ibid.* Ch.2 p.36.

194 *Ibid.* Ch.3 p.74.

195 CAB 106/428 p.67. 106/430 p.86.

196 CAB 106/435 p.250.

197 CAB 106/430 p.86-7 and WO 170/204 8 Army I Summary 831, 25.10.44. Williamson: *The Fourth Division op.cit.* p.242-50.

198 WO 170/409 (4 Div WD) Narrative and Log for 26.10.44. Major-Gen. Sir Hereward Wake: *Swift and Bold* Story of the KRRC in WWII (Aldershot 1949) p.209-12.

199 CAB EDS 19 Ch.3 p.75.

200 CAB 106/430 p.88.

201 CAB 106/435 p.248-51.

202 CAB EDS 19 Ch.3 p.76.

203 CAB HIST AL 3000/F/Air/12 p.47-50, 245.

204 CAB 121/558 s.1 & 12, FX35652 7.10.44, FX39084 16.10.44.

205 CAB 106/377 Gen. Sir Bernard Paget: Middle East Review 1944 p.4-6.

206 CAB 120/566 Mr Macmillan No.399, 25.9.44.

207 WO 204/91 SAC(44) 96th Mtg 5.10.44 and 97th Mtg 7.10.44.

208 CAB 120/566 MEDCOS 202, 9.10.44.

209 CAB 121/529 s.294 GO/49278, 8.10.44 received 9.10.44. AIR 24/112 (BAF ORB) Appx E320 Daily Summary No.105, 10.10.44.

210 ADM 199/1045 M 04189/45 p.2. DEF 2/356 Orders of R. Adm. 15 CS No. 0321/14, 15.9.44. MAN 1 p.2.

211 WO 204/10429 Land Forces Adriatic (LFA) Report p.57. WO 204/10430 Appx 19 Bucket Force E75, 6.10.44; Appx 21 BAF WE/119, 8.10.44.

212 WO 170/4009A HQ Adriatic Bde WD.

213 WO 204/10430 Appx 22 BAF/336, 9.10.44.

214 WO 204/10429 p.58.

215 WO 204/8805 AFHQ FX37402, 12.10.44.

216 WO 204/10429 p.58-9. WO 204/10427 History of 2 Indep Para Bde Gp p.25.

217 DEF 2/355 51 TC Wing USAAF Tac Air Plan 'Manna' 6.9.44 and Amendments up to 28.9.44.

218 CAB 44/153 History of the Commandos in the Mediterranean p.333-5. AIR 24/112 (BAF ORB) Appx E261, BAF 385 16.10.44. CAB HIST AL 3000/F/48 NHB comments of 29.5.1984.

219 ADM 199/1045 M 04189/45, 15 CS Report by R. Adm. Mansfield.

220   DEF 2/356 FOLEM 00170/25/19, 23.9.44. GON XB Ships Distribution List. And ADM 199/1429 (FOLEM WD) p.108–112.
221   CAB HIST AL 3000/F/48 NHB comments of 29.5.1984.
222   ADM 199/297 FOLEM 1933/00231/20 of 2.11.44.
223   ADM 199/1045 M 04189/45 Report by R. Adm. Mansfield. AIR 24/107 (BAF ORB) 12/13.10.44
224   ADM 199/1045 M 04189/45 *op.cit.*
225   MOD Whitehall Library: 23rd Armoured Brigade Operations in Greece p.2. DEF 2/355 Force 140 OO 1 Appx C, 10.10.44. WO 170/581 23 Armd Bde Adm Instr 3, 10.10.44.
226   (fn) *Ibid.*
227   ADM 199/1045 M.04189/45 *op.cit.* p.14 *et seq.* and Encl. 7, SO 5 M/S Flotilla Report.
228   WO 204/10377 SAC(44) 107, 17.10.44, Annex to PC(44) 29th Mtg.
229   DEF 2/356 AFHQ FX41590, 20.10.44.
230   WO 170/250 Appx D2 3 Corps Op Instr 4, 20.10.44.
231   WO 204/10427 History of 2 Para Bde p.26.
232   WO 170/250 Appx D3 3 Corps Directive 8, 10.10.44.
233   MOD Whitehall Library: 23rd Armoured Brigade Operations p.3–6. WO 204/10427 p.26.
234   ADM 199/1045 M 04574/5 Encl 1 & 9. CAB HIST AL 3000/F/46 Note by A. McLeod re 2 Levant Schooner Flotilla, 17.9.82.
235   WO 204/10429 L.F.A. Report p.59.
236   ADM 199/1045 M 04189/4513 Encl 2. ADM 199/1429 (FOLEM WD). ADM 199/297 FOLEM 1933/00231/20 Appx A. NHB m.s.: The Development of British Naval Aviation 1919–1945 Vol. III p.275–9.
237   ADM 199/1045 M 04189/4513 FOLEM 587/00231/9/10 Encl 2. ADM 199/1429 (FOLEM WD) P.151–2.
238   CAB 121/558 s.70B Mr Leeper No.96, 31.10.44.
239   WO 170/250 (3 Corps WD) Narr. 25–29.10.44. CAB 121/558 s.239.
240   CAB 121/558 s.28. Mr Leeper No.12, 22.10.44. Miscellaneous cables 26–31.10.44 and WO 204/91 SAC(44) 101st Mtg 19.10.44.
241   CAB HIST AL 3000/F/Air/12 p.1–2.
242   *Ibid.* p.81–83.
243   *Ibid.* p.1.
244   CAB EDS 20 Ch.2 p.7.
245   CAB HIST AL 3000/F/Air/12 p.78–80.
246   *Ibid.* Appx D.
247   *Ibid.* Appx C.
248   *Ibid.* p.10–11.
249   *Ibid.* p.85–7.
250   *Ibid.* p.5.
251   *Ibid.* p.85.

INDEX

In this Index, as in that for Part I, subjects are entered wherever possible in their alphabetical places, in preference to large composite headings. Inter-Service and Theatre commands are indexed by title. Army Commands and Forces are grouped by branch, formation and unit under their respective nationalities, Naval and Air units under Royal Navy, Royal Air Force and other national equivalents; for the German Air Force, see under Luftwaffe. For code-named operations, see Appendix 3 and individual entries, also Naval, Army and Air sub-heads. German Defence Lines are in their alphabetical places, also localities and features of whatever country and ships of whatever nationality. Supplies and services are indexed by name.

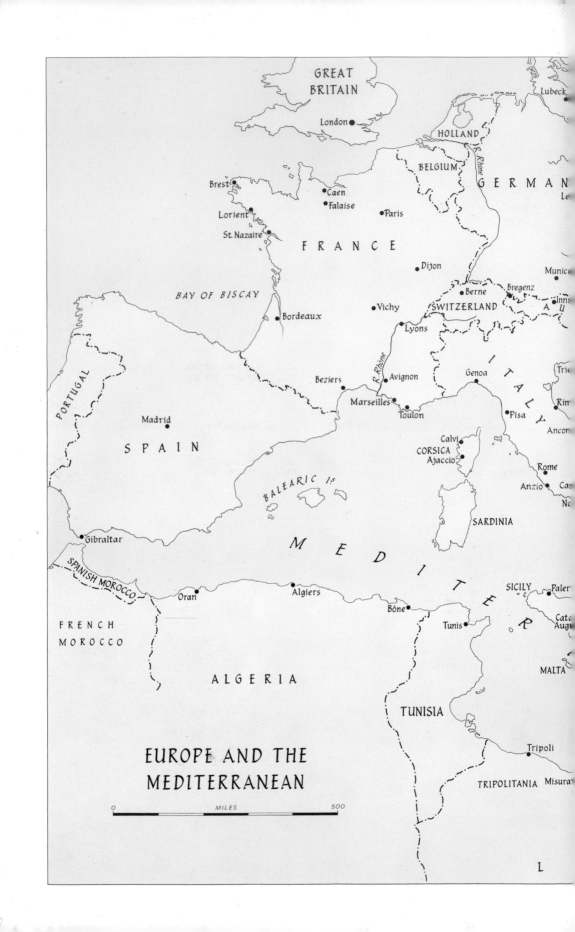

EUROPE AND THE MEDITERRANEAN